Studies in Early Modern English

Topics in English Linguistics 13

Editor

Herman Wekker

Mouton de Gruyter
Berlin · New York

Studies in
Early Modern English

Edited by

Dieter Kastovsky

Mouton de Gruyter
Berlin · New York 1994

Mouton de Gruyter (formerly Mouton, The Hague)
is a Division of Walter de Gruyter & Co., Berlin.

∞ Printed on acid-free paper which falls within the guidelines
of the ANSI to ensure permanence and durability.

Library of Congress Cataloging-in-Publication Data

Studies in early modern English / edited by Dieter Kastovsky.
       p.   cm. − (Topics in English linguistics ; 13)
    Includes bibliographical references and indexes.
    ISBN 3-11-014127-2 (cloth : acid-free) :
    1. English language − Early modern, 1500−1700 −
Grammar.
    I. Kastovsky, Dieter, 1940−   . II. Series.
    PE821.S78   1994
    425′.0903 − dc20   94-17971
                                          CIP

Die Deutsche Bibliothek − Cataloging-in-Publication Data

Studies in early modern English / ed. by Dieter Kastovsky. −
Berlin ; New York : Mouton de Gruyter, 1994
    (Topics in English linguistics ; 13)
    ISBN 3-11-014127-2
NE: Kastovsky, Dieter [Hrsg.]; GT

Contents

Introduction[1]

Dieter Kastovsky

Early Modern English as a separate period in the history of English is a
relatively recent addition to the original tripartite division into Old
English, Middle English and Modern English (cf. Penzl, this volume:
261). It started out merely as a subdivision of Modern English, cf.
Zachrisson's (1913) distinction between early and late Modern English,
or Luick's (1921 – 1940: §§ 470, 556) "frühneuenglische" and "spät-neuenglische Periode" (note the lower case initial of "early" and "früh"!). This
still is its status in the classical handbooks and introductions to the
history of English. But more recently it has been elevated to the position
of a separate linguistic period, cf., e. g., the capital initials in Görlach's
Einführung ins Frühneuenglische (1978) and *Introduction to Early Modern
English* (1991), and the fact that the forthcoming *Cambridge History of
the English Language* devotes a separate volume to this period. That this
development is justified is very convincingly argued for by Herbert Penzl
in his contribution to this volume, where he also points out parallels with
the development of the periodisation of German. Nevertheless, compared
to Old and Middle English, Early Modern English is still an underre-
searched area, so that Görlach's (1988) epithet "Cinderella of historical
English linguistics", which he had intended to refer merely to the study
of regional variation in Early Modern English, might well be applied to
the period as a whole. This does not mean, of course, that there are no
areas within this period which would have attracted the special attention
of anglicists. Thus, the Great Vowel Shift (cf. the Stockwell – Minkova/
Lass controversy in Bauer – Kastovsky 1988 for a summary of the extended discussion of this topic), the rise of the obligatory *do*-periphrasis
and the word-order change to SVO (cf. the contributions in Kastovsky
1991), to mention just a few, have received extensive coverage over the
years. They are, therefore, not dealt with in this volume, because its
editor had, in his invitation to EMEC (Early Modern English Conference,
Tulln, Austria, July 7 – 11, 1991), specifically asked that the participants
should stay away from these belaboured topics, and they did. Which
brings me to the genesis of this volume.

The Institut für Anglistik und Amerikanistik of the University of
Vienna is one of the oldest of its kind in central Europe, and scholars

like Zupitza, Schipper, Kellner, Luick, Wild, Koziol, Pinsker, who taught at this department, have provided lasting contributions to English historical linguistics. Anniversaries connected with two of them, Luick and Kellner, had already prompted the organisation of conferences on historical English linguistics in 1985 and 1988 with corresponding publications (cf. Kastovsky—Bauer 1988 and Kastovsky 1991), but the department itself had not yet provided such an opportunity. Now it just so happened that in 1991 the Institut für Anglistik und Amerikanistik could celebrate its 100th "administrative" birthday, i. e., its existence as a separate administrative entity. It had been founded in 1872 as part of a Seminar für französische und englische Sprache, with Julius Zupitza als Extraordinary Professor for North-Germanic Languages (but of course mainly teaching English philology), and in 1891 it was split up into two fully independent departments, after the two divisions had already led a relatively separate scholarly existence for some time. This centenary thus provided an ideal reason (and, moreover, an excellent fund-raising opportunity) for a conference in 1991, which would, moreover, be in keeping with the triannual rhythm that I had intended for such conferences. What remained was to decide on a topic. In connection with my work on a project funded by the Austrian Fonds zur Förderung der wissenschaftlichen Forschung (cf. fn. 1) I had become increasingly aware of the relatively unsystematic treatment of Early Modern English in the existing literature, although this period is crucial in many ways for the development of Modern English. This is not only true of phonology (cf. the Great Vowel Shift and the establishment of a new system of morphophonemic alternations in the non-native vocabulary, type *sane ~ sanity, divine ~ divinity*), but also with respect to syntax (establishment of AUX, do-support, and SVO), or word-formation and the lexicon in general (integration of a tremendous number of Latinate loans and non-native word-formation patterns), to name only a few areas.[2] This underrated period thus seemed to constitute a genuine gap in the treatment of the history of English, and therefore well worth having a conference devoted to it. This feeling was corroborated by participants of the Kellner Festival, with whom I discussed potential topics for another conference. Thus EMEC was born, and I am grateful to the editor of this series, Herman Wekker, and to Mouton de Gruyter, for allowing me to keep the baby alive in the form of this publication. Of the 30 papers presented at the conference, 27 are included in this volume. Three further papers by Manfred Markus, Jacek Fisiak, and Helena Raumolin-Brunberg—Terttu Nevalainen have been added, although they were not presented in Tulln. Manfred Markus and Jacek Fisiak had to withdraw from the conference at very short notice, having already prepared their papers. And the paper by Raumolin-Brunberg — Nevalainen, which had been presented at the Inaugural Conference of the European Society for the Study of English (ESSE) in Norwich, September 1991, in my section "History of English", so nicely summarises some of the major trends and issues discussed at the conference that I decided to ask the authors to submit it, when publication of the linguistic papers of the ESSE conference did not prove feasible.

As mentioned above, I had asked prospective participants not to take up the old-established Early Modern English hits, but otherwise there were no restrictions as to topics. Nevertheless, quite a few of the contributions cluster around relatively specific areas such as pronouns, the structure of the Verb Phrase, or the lexicon, which gives the volume a certain homogeneity, although not to such an extent that it would have been justifiable to divide it into topical sections, which, moreover, would have been very uneven quantitatively. I therefore decided to arrange the contributions in alphabetical order, as I had done in *Historical English syntax* basically for the same reason. In view of this decision, it might be useful to point out some of the areas that have been dealt with in more than one paper.

The greatest number of papers are devoted to syntax in the widest sense, ranging from word order changes to the structure of the Verb Phrase and the use of pronouns.

Leiv-Egil Breivik — Toril Swan's "Initial adverbials and word order in English with special reference to the Early Modern English period" deals with the shift from Old English (not completely consistent) verb second order to Modern English SVO. They argue that this shift had been far from complete in Early Modern English, where we still find many instances of Adv V S, whose stylistic and sociolinguistic causes have yet to be determined. Matti Rissanen's "The position of *not* in Early Modern English questions" investigates the varying order of *not* and a personal pronoun subject (occurrence before or after the pronoun) in interrogative clauses. He links the increase of the order V/AUX + *not* + personal pronoun to the development of negative cliticisation (cf. forms such as *can't, shan't, won't*), which he assumes to have taken place earlier than hitherto thought, and to the rise of obligatory *do*-periphrasis, since weakened *not* would cliticise more easily with periphrastic *do* than with a full verb.

Quite a few papers discuss the internal structure of VP and the AUX constituent. Approaches range from Government and Binding to variationist frameworks. In his "Infl in Early Modern English and the status of *to*", Stephen Nagle investigates the split infinitive construction, which appeared in Middle English, but disappeared from late Middle and Early Modern English, reappearing in the late eighteenth century. The loss occurs at the same time when preverbal and pre-auxiliary elements were becoming more common, which indicates that in Early Modern English *to* had not yet reached Infl/T status, which it is accorded today. Three papers deal with modal and periphrastic modal auxiliaries. Dieter Stein in his corpus-based "The expression of deontic and epistemic modality and the subjunctive" shows that the distribution of the surface representations of modality (modal verb vs. subjunctive) was governed by various factors: a semantics-based preference for modal verbs (which are semantically more specific) was matched by a morphological parameter, viz. the tendency to omit an inflectional ending, which was possible in the subjunctive, and which seems to account for the increase of subjunctive forms during the period in question. This development parallels the extension of the *do*-periphrasis, which was also used as a device for avoiding verbal inflectional endings of a certain type. Susan Wright deals with "The mystery of the modal progressive", i. e., forms of the type *I'm warning you*, which seem to suggest some kind of subjective involvement of the subject akin to modality. She argues that there was a general gradual "subjectivisation" of VP constituents in Early Modern English, by which modals developed epistemic meanings, *do* shifted from a "superfluous" constituent to one denoting emphasis, and the basically aspectual progressive developed a modal, non-aspectual "subjective" use. Andrei Danchev and Merja Kytö describe "The construction *be going to* + infinitive in Early Modern English" on the basis of extensive material from the *Helsinki Corpus* and other sources, suggesting that this "andative" construction with future time reference was grammaticalised earlier than assumed so far, and that the grammaticalisation might have been influenced by the French construction *aller* + Inf. in connection with translations from French, at the same time filling a gap in the emerging aspectual system. Another aspect of the Verb Phrase is the elaboration of the passive construction, dealt with in Lilo Moessner's "Early Modern English passive constructions" within the framework of "serial relationship" as developed by Jan Svartvik, and focusing on various syntactic features characterising the passive constructions, such as absence of an overt subject or agent, or the type of passive auxiliary (*be, become, come, rest, get, have*) and the need to find a form for an unambiguously dynamic passive, which came to be *get*.

Another area figuring prominently among the contributions to Early Modern English syntax are pronouns. Jonathan Hope in "The use of *thou* and *you* in Early Modern spoken English: Evidence from depositions in the Durham ecclesiastical court recordings" not only widens the traditional data base by including this kind of material, but also challenges the view that the literary usage of *you* and *thou* as evidenced in contemporary drama is a mirror of real contemporary spoken usage. In the court records investigated, *thou* is already (viz. around 1560) decidedly marked, while *you* is the neutral or default form. Thus *thou* has to be specifically motivated socially or pragmatically (e. g., by the expression of anger); while *you* does not need any such motivation. Thus, written and genuine spoken usage were definitely different. Helena Raumolin-Brunberg's paper "The development of the compound pronouns in *-body* and *-one* in Early Modern English" focuses on the grammaticalisation of the compound pronoun forms, i. e., their shift from a normal N + N compound to a grammaticalised pronoun form. It turns out that the grammaticalisation of the *one*-pronouns is tied up with the rise of one as prop word, and that the whole process of grammaticalisation is linked to the demise of the indefinite pronoun *man*. Finally, Gunnel Tottie's "*Any* as an indefinite determiner in non-assertive clauses: Evidence from Present-day and Early Modern English", based on an extensive corpus analysis (*LOB* and *Helsinki Corpus*), investigates the use of unstressed *any* with singular count nouns as a kind of indefinite article. She demonstrates that *any* originated as a stressed unlimited quantifier in law texts, then was used extensively in private correspondence reflecting emotionality and involvement, from where it was transferred to the spoken language as an unstressed article.

A considerable number of the contributions deal with lexicological aspects — not surprisingly in view of the tremendous changes in this area during the Early Modern English period. Covering the borderline between syntax and semantics, Terttu Nevalainen investigates "Aspects of adverbial change in Early Modern English" in a study of focusing adverbials. Her analysis, based on the *Helsinki Corpus*, discusses two related changes, the generalisation of *-ly* as adverbial suffix and functional-semantic shifts within the adverbials, e. g., towards sentence adverb, disjunct or focusing subjunct. Hans Peters' paper "Degree adverbs in Early Modern English" is devoted to a corpus-based study of boosters, whose number and diversity considerably increased in the Early Modern English period, thus corroborating Nevalainen's findings about the changes in this area. Edgar Schneider's contribution "*You that be not able to consyder thys order of thinges:* Variability and change in the semantics and syntax of a mental verb in Early Modern English" investigates the polysemy of the verb *consider* and its syntactic behaviour, especially the interdependence of its semantic structure and its role structure. Another contribution discussing the interface of syntax and semantics is Risto Hiltunen's "On phrasal verbs in Early Modern English: Notes on lexis and style", which deals with the occurrence of phrasal verbs in Early Modern English and Modern English. On the basis of the *Helsinki Corpus* material he shows that there are more parallels with Modern English than with Middle English. Thus, structurally, the Modern English usage has already been reached, but the frequency of the particles still differs. Also, there seem to be differences according to text type, but on the whole the construction is native and there is a tendency to employ phrasal verbs when the action denoted by the combination is in the foreground.

Besides these semantic-syntactic investigations there are also some strictly semantic papers, e. g., Arthur Mettinger's "Lexical semantics and the Early Modern English lexicon: The case of antonymy", a corpus study of antonyms based on Shakespeare's comedies, demonstrating how the classical structural-semantic framework can be used for diachronic investigations. In this connection it is interesting to note that the type *important — unimportant* is not instanced in the material investigated, i. e., all *un*-formations of this type seem to have originated at a later date. Another study in the lexical field framework is Andreas Fischer's "*Sumer is icumen in:* The seasons of the year in Middle English and Early Modern English", investigating the replacement of *len(c)ten* and *hærfest* by *spring* and *autumn/fall*, which seems to have been prompted by a climate-induced dominance of *summer* and *winter*, and which in turn made the other two seasonal terms vulnerable and susceptible to change. Christiane Dalton-Puffer's contribution "Are Shakespeare's agent nouns different from Chaucer's? — On the dynamics of a derivational sub-system" investigates shifts in the morphosemantics of concrete noun derivation from Middle English to Early Modern English, showing that while the instrumental suffix *-el(s)* is lost, the realisation of the Agent and/or Attributive categories are considerably enriched. Clausdirk Pollner in his "The ugly sister — Scots words in Early Modern English dictionaries" takes up another neglected area, viz. the relationship between the emerging Southern English standard and Scots, as reflected in the dictionaries of the period, pointing out that the dictionary makers did not indicate Scots usage because this former national language lost its status precisely at the time when dictionary making got into full swing. Finally, Mats Rydén's "William Turner and the English plant names" not only portrays a fascinating all-round scholar of this period — clergyman, scientist, herbalist —, but also his contribution to the development of botanical terminology.

The discouragement to revisit the Great Vowel Shift did not mean, of course, that there were no papers on Early Modern English phonology. After all, there are many other aspects that still need to be covered. One intriguing phenomenon is the behaviour of post-vocalic *r*, which sparked off two papers, viz. Angelika Lutz's "Vocalisation of "postvocalic *r*": An Early Modern English sound change?" and Michael Windross's "Loss of postvocalic *r*: Were the orthoepists really tone-deaf?". Lutz argues that the vocalisation of post-vocalic /r/ should not be treated in connection with vocalic changes, as is usually done in the traditional accounts, but as a genuine consonantal change. As a consequence, the consonantal system appears to have been by no means as stable as is generally claimed. Moreover, this change fits into a more general tendency towards weakening and vocalisation of certain consonants, which has been going on since pre-Old English. Windross, on the other hand, is more concerned with the phonetic aspects of /r/-loss, arguing on the basis of orthoepist evidence that postvocalic /r/ had not yet been lost in the standard pronunciation of the eighteenth century. He attributes the origin of /r/ loss to sociolinguistic factors: this feature had been characteristic of vulgar/London accent, but with the rise of a new middle class gradually became part of the standard, i. e., involved the change of a prestige norm rather than a simple sound change. Orthoepists are also discussed in Veronika Kniezsa's paper "Orthoepists and reformers", which investigates the spelling reforms and the competing orthographic principles of the period and argues that eventually spelling pronunciation and custom prevailed. Manfred Markus takes a look at the development of the prosodic system in his paper "From stress-timing to syllable-timing: Changes in the prosodic system of Late Middle English and Early Modern English". He argues that Old English had been neither stress- nor syllable-timed, while Middle English was syllable-timed on account of French influence (loans, poetic tradition), but towards the end of the Middle English period and during Early Modern English an alternating rhythm, especially favoured in poetry (cf. Chaucer) acts as the nucleus for an emerging stress-timed rhythm. Jacek Fisiak in "The place-name evidence for the distribution of Early Modern English dialect features: The voicing of initial /f/" demonstrates that place-name evidence is inconclusive because of problems with its evaluation, but that it is very likely that initial voicing was much more wide-spread in Early Modern English than it is today.

Two contributions venture into the realm of text linguistics. Udo Fries in his "Text deixis in Early Modern English" uses the resources of the *Helsinki Corpus* to determine the form and frequency of text-deictic constructions in various text types. And Laura Wright's "Early Modern London business English" provides a glimpse at a widely unknown text type, viz. accounts, showing how the account-keeping conventions changed from the Middle English Latin-English macaronic style to a purely English form.

It is of course difficult to judge how far these papers reflect the state of the art — the Early Modern English volume of the *Cambridge History of the English Language* will certainly provide a more balanced survey in this respect. Nevertheless, certain tendencies are obvious, the most significant perhaps being the dominance of corpus-based studies within a variationist framework. This is true not only of syntactic, but also of morphosemantic and lexical studies. Most of these studies are directly or indirectly based on the *Helsinki Corpus*, which is at last generally accessible and will certainly be one of the major tools for historical research in the future. Another tendency, already noted in Kastovsky (1991: 7), is the absence of theoretical debates, and the concentration on empirical data. This may of course have been due to the selection of the participants, and may thus be coincidental, but I think it does reflect a more general reorientation of historical linguistics towards a more data- and less theory-minded type of research.

If the conference was a success (and I hope it was), then this is due primarily to the help that I received when I was organising it and for which I am deeply grateful. First and foremost my thanks go to the Bundesminister für Wissenschaft und Forschung, Herrn Dr. Erhard Busek, and the then Landeshauptmann of Niederösterreich, Herrn Hofrat Mag. Siegfried Ludwig, both for accepting the patronage of the conference and for subsidising it substantially. I also gratefully acknowledge the assistance of the British Council, who again helped with travel and other (fluid) grants. Furthermore, I owe a debt of gratitude to the Mayor and the Town Councillor for Cultural Affairs of Tulln for the hospitality extended to the conference in the form of a wonderful open air dinner reception (and, perhaps?, for the weather that they provided: some liked it hot, but some had second thoughts). A special word of thanks goes to the staff of the Hotel Rossmühle, our venue, who did everything possible to make our stay comfortable and our weight increase. Last, but by no means least, I would like to thank the conference secretary, Frau Christine Klein (for those who don't know: she is the one who really does all the organising and tells me what to do when I forget things) for the various run of the mill and not so run of the mill miracles that she performed; and a word of thanks also goes to Angelika Hirsch (M. A.), who helped with the editing of the manuscript, and to Gunther Kaltenböck (M.A.), Hans Platzer (M.A.) and Corinna Weiss (M. A.), who helped with the proof-reading and the indices; the remaining errors have to be debited to the editor.

I don't want to conclude this introduction, however, without thanking the conference participants — for coming, for providing stimulating papers, for being convivial but still disciplined, and generally for enjoying themselves and making this conference possible. What would conferences be without them?

Notes

1. The Early Modern English Conference, whose papers form the bulk of this volume, was organised in connection with a project supported by the Austrian Fonds zur Förderung der wissenschaftlichen Forschung (Project-No. P6454), viz. the revision of Karl Brunner, *Die englische Sprache. Ihre geschichtliche Entwicklung* (Tübingen 1960—1962).
2. Cf. also the paper by Raumolin-Brunberg—Nevalainen below, who show that certain important changes finally resulting in the Modern English state of affairs coincide and culminate between 1580 and 1660.

References

Brunner, Karl
  1960—62 *Die englische Sprache. Ihre geschichtliche Entwicklung.* 2 vols. Tübingen: Niemeyer.
Görlach, Manfred
  1978 *Einführung ins Frühneuenglische.* Heidelberg: Quelle and Meyer.
  1988 "The study of early Modern English variation — the Cinderella of English historical linguistics", in: Jacek Fisiak (ed.), *Historical dialectology: Regional and social.* Berlin: Mouton de Gruyter, 211—118.
  1991 *Introduction to Early Modern English.* Cambridge: Cambridge University Press.
Helsinki Corpus
  1991 *The Helsinki Corpus of English Texts (diachronic part).* Norwegian Computing Centre for the Humanities and the Oxford Text Archive.

Kastovsky, Dieter (ed.)
1991   *Historical English syntax.* [Topics in English Linguistics 2.] Berlin: Mouton
          de Gruyter.
Kastovsky, Dieter — Gero Bauer (eds.)
1988   *Luick revisited. Papers read at the Luick Symposium at Schloß Liechtenstein.*
          1. 5. — 18. 9. 1985. Tübingen: Narr.
Luick, Karl
1921 — 40 *Historische Grammatik der englischen Sprache.* Leipzig: Tauchnitz.
Zachrisson, R. E.
1913   *Pronunciation of English vowels. 1400 — 1700.* Göteborg: Wettergren and Ker-
          ber.

Initial adverbials and word order in English with special reference to the Early Modern English period

Leiv Egil Breivik — Toril Swan

1. Introduction

It is well known that Present-day English is a verb-medial, or SVO, language. In his pioneering article on the development of English word order, Fries (1940) claims that in the actor-action-goal construction the modern word order seems to form a clear pattern in the fourteenth century, and that it seems to be fully established by the middle of the fifteenth century. Thus, according to Fries, the position before the verb has become the territory of the subject in declarative actor — action — goal sentences in Early Modern English. Instead of examples (1) — (4) we find (5), "where distinctive features of word order operate without taxemes of selection" (1940: 200).

(1)   *Se mann þone beran sloh.*

(2)   *Þone beran se mann sloh.*

(3)   *Þone beran sloh se mann.*

(4)   *Sloh se mann þone beran.*

(5)   *The man struck the bear.*

Fries cites quantitative data in support of his claim concerning the development of English word order patterns. Our paper addresses a problem which is not explicitly dealt with by Fries, viz. the relative order of subject and finite verb after initial adverbials. We shall examine sentences containing the following types of adverbial: (a) sentence adverbials like *unfortunately*, as in example (6), and (b) non-sentence adverbials like *yesterday, if we can meet at 5, on the table* and *in Oslo*, as in examples (7) — (10):

(6)   Unfortunately *the man struck the bear.*

(7)   Yesterday *we met the Norwegian ambassador.*

(8)   If we can meet at 5 *we'll have time for dinner.*

(9)   On the table *lay a book about architecture.*

(10)   In Oslo *there was a demonstration against the American pres-
           ident.*

Our class of non-sentence adverbials is coextensive with the class of
adjuncts as defined by Quirk *et al.* (1985). As appears from examples
(7)—(10), the adverbials in question can be realised by adverbs, clauses
or prepositional phrases; we shall be concerned with time, place and
manner adverbials, as well as clauses of condition, concession, reason
etc. In our discussion of non-sentence adverbials, we shall also take
account of existential sentences, that is, sentences containing existential/
locative *be* or an intransitive verb which has included in it the meaning
'be in existence' or 'come into existence'. Existential sentences are exemplified in (9)—(10) above.

Sentence adverbials are subjective speaker comments and situation-
independent. As further examples of this type, we could mention *probably,
sadly, unquestionably* and *wisely*. By contrast, non-sentence adverbials are
situation-dependent. Furthermore, there is a close bond between verb
and adverbial in this category, which is not the case with sentence
adverbials. In Present-day English, subject-verb (SV) is the only possible
pattern after initial sentence adverbials, while the other category may be
followed by inversion as well as non-inversion, though the former pattern
is very rare indeed (Green 1980, Stockwell 1984).

Our paper presents the results from a joint project, which so far makes
use of data taken from Breivik (1990), Swan (1988) as well as from Swan
(forthcoming) and Breivik—Swan (forthcoming). The two former works,
however, do not deal specifically with the problems taken up in the
present paper. We are currently involved in a large-scale diachronic study
which will include adverbials of the types referred to above as well as
other categories.

In order to account for the situation in Early Modern English, it is
necessary to go all the way back to Old English and see how the various
sentence elements were serialised. We shall trace the relevant patterns
from Old English up to Present-day English, paying special attention to
Early Modern English. By using this procedure, we propose to place the
Early English data in a wider typological perspective. The exposition is
organised as follows. §2 outlines some of the major tendencies of Old
English word order. This section will serve as a starting-point for our

discussion of word order patterns in sentences containing adverbials in initial position. §3 seeks to establish to what extent sentence adverbials influence subject-verb order, while §4 examines sentences (including existential sentences) containing non-sentence adverbials from the same point of view. We shall restrict our attention to declarative sentences. §5 summarises the main results of our investigation.

2. On Old English word order

The study of Old English syntax has received considerable attention since the end of the nineteenth century. One of the most controversial issues has been whether the Modern English device to indicate syntactic relationships by means of word order is established and functioning in the Old English period. A number of scholars have described Old English as a language in which syntactic relationships depend on inflections alone or at least to a very high degree. Fries is a typical exponent of this viewpoint. He argues that "In Old English practically all the grammatical relationships to which the language gives attention ... can be expressed by inflections ..." (1940: 207−208) and that "the order of the words ... has no bearing whatever upon the grammatical relationships involved" (1940: 199). However, several detailed analyses of Old and Middle English texts have shown that word order is established as a grammatical device before the loss of inflections. The traditional view was abandoned in studies such as Carlton (1970), Gardner (1971) and Shannon (1964).

More recently, linguists have discussed Old English from the point of view of word order as a typological parameter. It is widely assumed that Old English has some sort of verb-second constraint, i.e., the constraint whereby the finite verb must be the second constituent in a declarative main clause. Thus Stockwell (1977, 1984) claims that Old English prose is characterised by a V2 rule that is not fully grammaticised. By adopting van Kemenade's (1987) analysis of Old English personal pronouns as syntactic clitics, Stockwell−Minkova (1991) are able to dispose of certain apparent exceptions to the V2 rule. They write:

> ... one of the many desirable consequences of the analysis is that main clauses with two or three personal pronouns in front of the verb, which previously looked like horrendous counter-examples to the claim of second position for the finite verb, are no longer problematic. In such sequences, a clitic (*ne* and personal pronouns) in the absolutely first position (which is the topic slot) counts in calculating verb-second; other clitics (except ...

after an operator) are attached to the left periphery of INFL (the finite verb) and do not count as separate constituents. (1991: 387 — 388)

Among other linguists who have claimed that Old English is a V2 language we may mention Haiman (1974), Hock (1985, 1986), Pintzuk — Kroch (1985), Vennemann (1974, 1984), von Seefranz-Montag (1984) and Weerman (1989). We agree with Stockwell — Minkova that "verb-second is much more than a mere tendency" (1991: 388). In Breivik (1990: 194) it is concluded that "although declarative main clauses may exhibit both verb-third and verb-first order, the verb-second constraint is so well established that Old English can be classified as a verb-second language ..." (cf. also Breivik 1991). The data presented in the subsequent sections further reinforce the view that Old English is far from being a consistent verb-second language.

It is beyond the scope of the present paper to go into the question of the underlying word order of Old English, which has recently become a matter of considerable debate. We note, however, that Lightfoot (1977) and especially van Kemenade (1987) argue persuasively that, from a theoretical point of view, Old English is an SOV language; that is, a sentence S in Old English rewrites as an NP and a VP, and in the latter the verb is base-generated in final position. Within van Kemenade's framework, the rule of verb-second obliterates the underlying order in root clauses.

3. Sentence adverbials

In earlier types of English, up to and including the Early Modern English period, the class of sentence adverbials was very rudimentary and not as semantically diversified as in Present-day English. However, one subset has been fairly common from Old English onwards, namely those that emphasise the truth (termed truth intensifiers in Swan 1988), and thus are precursors of true epistemic adverbials in Present-day English like *unquestionably, undoubtedly* and *certainly*. Examples from Old English include *soðlice, gewislice* and *witodlice*. In Old English this class occurs quite frequently in initial position, functioning as "propositional setting". Other types of Old English sentence adverbials (or better, embryo sentence adverbials), are those called epitheticals, such as *rihtlice,* and evaluatives, such as *wundorlice* (cf. Swan 1988: chapter 2). In accordance with what we have said already, it is their behaviour as initial adverbials that is of interest here and will be traced up to the Early Modern English period.

It is commonly assumed that Old English adverbials trigger inversion. Thus Haiman (1974: 63) states: "After sentence-initial demonstrative adverbs, subject-verb inversion in Old English was an almost unshakable rule ..." A similar observation is made by Andrew (1940: 1). However, our data demonstrate that Old English sentence adverbials are not as a rule accompanied by inversion; indeed, their frequent occurrence in adverbial-subject-verb (ASV) patterns is partly what establishes them as a separate category of adverbials. In Swan (1988) it was found that initial sentence adverbials are followed by VS order at a rate of 21,6 percent; that is, four out of five of these sentences are non-inverted. Consider the Old English examples in (11)−(19), which all have an initial sentence adverbial and SV order, while (20)−(26) exemplify VS order:

SV

(11)   *Witodlice se winterlica mona gæð norðor þonne*
        'Truly the winterly moon goes more northwards than' (Anglo Saxon manual 9)

(12)   *Witodlice gemetegung is eallra mægena modor*
        'Truly moderation is the mother of all virtues' (Ælfric I 20)

(13)   *Soðlice ðæs monan gear hæfð seofon ⁊ twentig daga*
        'Truly the moon's year has seven and twenty days' (Anglo Saxon manual 7)

(14)   *Soðlice fram Gode he is send*
        'Truly he is sent from God' (Blickling 247)

(15)   *Suiðe ryhtlice hit wæs awriten*
        'Very rightly it was written' (Cura Pastoralis 157)

(16)   *Swiðe rihtlice ⁊ swiðe gesceadwislice þu hæfst me ofercumen ⁊ gefangen*
        'Very rightly and wisely you have overcome and captured me (Boethius 83)

(17)   *& earmlice hi Godes cyrican hyndan & bærndon*
        'pitiably they God's churches laid waste and burned' (Anglo Saxon Chronicle 39)

(18)   *Suiðe ryhte ða sacerdas sint gehaten sacerds*
        'Very properly priests are called sacerds' (Cura Pastoralis 139)

(19)   *Suiðe medomlice Iacobus se apostol his stirde ða he cuæð*
'Very justly James the apostle this forbade when he said' (Cura
Pastoralis 33)

VS
(20)   *Witodlice on þisre endebyrdnesse geondscrið se circul his ryne*
'Assuredly in this order runs the cycle its course' (Byrhtferth
46)

(21)   *Witodlice on his timan hæfdon men mycel geswinc*
'Assuredly in his time had men much oppression' (Anglo
Saxon Chronicle 220)

(22)   *Soþlice unc gecyþeþ ure Drihten Hælend Crist his mægen*
'Truly to us will manifest our Lord Saviour Christ his power'
(Blickling 159)

(23)   *Soðlice on þam heofenlicum eðele nis nan niht gehæfd*
'Truly in the heavenly country not-is no night had' (Anglo
Saxon manual 5)

(24)   *Suiðe ryhte wæs ðæm sacerde forboden*
'Very rightly was the priest forbidden' (Cura Pastoralis 139)

(25)   *Ða soðlice geendode þe gebeorscipe*
'Then verily ended the entertainment' (Apollonius 28)

(26)   *Þus earmlice wæs þone abbotrice gifen betwix Cristesmesse ⁊
Candelmesse at Lundene*
'Thus despicably was the abbacy bestowed between Christmas
and Candlemas in London' (Anglo Saxon Chronicle 258)

Since they occur frequently in ASV structures, sentence adverbials would
seem to override the V2 constraint. According to Robert Stockwell
(personal communication), the data in (11)−(19) can be accounted for
under the analysis of Old English word order proposed in Stock-
well−Minkova (1994). Stockwell−Minkova posit the basic structure in
(27).

Within this framework, a V2 clause has V-to-INFL raising, and the
COMP is filled either by raising a lower topic node or by a lexical
complementiser. Light adverbials (which originate under the AP node)
may float to the left of INFL (Chomsky-adjoined to S). This, then, would
account for the structure of sentences like (11)−(19), and these sentences
would only apparently be counter-examples to the V2 constraint.[1]

(27)

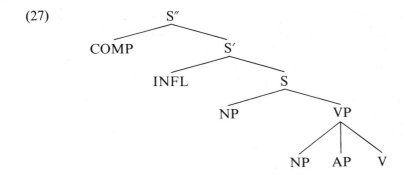

However that may be, the Old English data in (11)−(19) are inconsistent with those of other V2 languages. Thus in Old Norse, whose V2 status is beyond question (cf. Christoffersen 1980 and Faarlund 1990: 110), initial sentence adverbials are invariably followed by VS order (as are all other types of initial adverbials). The corresponding Old Norse adverbials are very similar to (and indeed cognates of) Old English sentence adverbials, yet they behave exactly like other adverbials; that is, the order is invariably AVS (cf. Christoffersen 1994). In Modern Norwegian, too, sentence adverbials usually cause inversion of subject and verb; only in a very few, highly marked, cases can certain types of sentence adverbials be followed by SV order (cf. Swan 1991). The typical word order is exemplified by (28).

(28)   *Tydeligvis elsket hun ham.*
        'Obviously loved she him'

If it is the case that a true V2 language requires VS order following all adverbials, then Old English is not a true V2 language. However, such subjective speaker comments or sentence adverbials may be interpreted differently by the two languages. In this connection it may be relevant to note that in many of the Old English sentences with sentence adverbial and inversion there are other topicalised, or fronted, constituents. Thus inversion occurs frequently in sentences like (23), since these have an initial topicalised element immediately following the sentence adverbial.[2] Note, however, (14), which does not have inversion.

Middle English sentence adverbials are not greatly different from those of the Old English period; that is, the largest and most important class is still the truth intensifier class (to which are added new adverbs such as *certes, certeynly, verraily* etc. from French). However, the sentence adverbials increasingly establish themselves in initial position in the Middle English period, while the rate of inversion drops sharply (Middle English 9.9 percent vs. Old English 21.6 percent). Middle English sentence adverbials are exemplified in (29)—(39). It should be noted that the true sentence adverbials (i. e., at this time only the truth intensifiers) occur in inverted sentences only at half the rate of the other, less sentence adverbial-like type. These latter adverbials are undoubtedly seen as topicalised in initial position and therefore more regularly trigger inversion. According to Jacobsson (1951: 88), in Middle English inversion is still the common order following initial adverbials. In Middle English as well, then, adverbial categories differ with respect to syntactic environment; sentence adverbials occur more and more rarely in VS structures, while non-sentence adverbials apparently still induce inversion in a majority of cases. This, of course, would tend to support the idea that sentence adverbials (or rather, English sentence adverbials) are perceived as clause-external in initial position.

SV

(29)   *and doubtles þei were founde gilty* (Capgrave 127)

(30)   *Certes þai war men and wymen as we er* (Rolle 81)

(31)   *Now sicurly þese ben foule begyled* (Sermons 276)

(32)   *Dredeles som men haue so gret delectacion in þer synne* (Sermons 275)

(33)   *And certeynly, the ful purpos of the persones toforn nempned was to haue* (Book of London English 24)

(34)   *Forsoth it hath be oftyn told me þat in Berwik I schuld be* (Capgrave 222)

VS

(35)   *And certes rightfully ne mowe ye take no vengeance* (Melibee 178)

(36)   *Fullȝewiss is clene saule Cristes riche* (Vices and virtues 121)

(37)   *And skillefulliche may loue be likened to a fote* (Sermons 77)

(38)   *Verrayly es he my salvacion* (Rolle 16)

(39)   *Vor-zoþe ariȝt acorsed ssel by þer uram reuþe* (Ayenbite 189)

We now come to the Early Modern English period. The sentence adverbial class as we know it today has still not been developed fully; that is, it lacks a true class of evaluative (or truth-presupposing) sentence adverbials such as *unfortunately* and *sadly*, a category which is extremely large and productive in Present-day English. However, the category of truth-intensifying adverbs has become very diversified, including true epistemic adverbials as well as other semantic subsets. This category can now truly be called a modal adverb category. In addition, the evaluative (truth-presupposing) adverbs are clearly beginning to make their appearance in the course of the Early Modern English period, as are the speech act adverbials (cf. Hanson 1987, Swan 1988: 412 and Swan 1991, Traugott 1989). Interestingly, other types of adverbials also start to develop in this period (cf. Nevalainen, this volume). It would appear that speakers have acquired a new need to codify in one word sentence-modifying speaker comments such as *it is natural that* > *naturally*. This new system involves several changes, such as the expansion of the syntactic scope and the pragmatic reorientation of manner and degree adverbs. Thus they become speaker-oriented as well as change orientation from the concrete situation to the discourse. These changes are usually concurrent with word order changes, in particular the increasing initial placement of the new sentence adverbials as well as predominant SV order.

As a class the sentence adverbials occur initially at increasingly higher rates in Early Modern English. The inversion proportion, relative to that of Old English, has decreased, though not dramatically, given the long time span between the two periods. Examples of the most commonly used pattern are given in (40) — (47); the more marked pattern is illustrated in (48) — (54). Table 1 sums up the relevant percentages. In this connection we may mention that it was shown in Swan (1988) that VS is a possible pattern after initial sentence adverbials even in the period 1700 — 1900. However, in that period this is clearly becoming a highly marked pattern, used for stylistic effect. Thus it is extensively used by, for instance, Carlyle in the nineteenth century.

To sum up, historically, English sentence adverbials have always tended to occur with SV order, unlike other types of adverbials, and unlike those of Modern Norwegian and Old Norse. Nevertheless, the VS order is quite productive even as late as Early Modern English. In other words, in the sentences under discussion the present-day pattern is far from fully established.

SV

(40)   *And truly the twelve Miles home agen, was so tedious a Journey.* (Behn 19)

(41)   *Doubtlesse a wise man must needes take great pleasure* (R. Lever 14)

(42)   *For vndoubtedly he that hath the couetousnes of Iudas in his hert, he wyll playe* (T. Lever 74)

(43)   *belyke they did this because they had forgotten.* (Verstegan 30)

(44)   *Then needes it must be that* (Queen Elizabeth's Boethius 66)

(45)   *Peraduenture ye wyll saye* (T. Lever 43)

(46)   *So wisely he brake of the Cardinals vnpleasante talke, so that* (Ro:Ba 43)

(47)   *for fitly it runneth with the/Currant of our noble nature* (Ro:Ba 9)

VS

(48)   *Verely not without cause are they called Angles.* (Verstegan 141)

(49)   *then surely doost thou prouoke God to powre doun vengeaunce vpon the.* (T. Lever 56)

(50)   *then doubtlesse would the names still remain vnto them euen from one posteritie vnto another* (Verstegan 23)

(51)   *Rightly dost thou think* (Queen Elizabeth's Boethius 85)

(52)   *And craftilie goe they about to cast out all the Cleargie* (Ro:Ba 90)

(53)   *not vnfitly then may old England haue had at the first in the ancient Teutonic language that domination.* (Verstegan 124)

(54)   *Yet nedes wold the king haue his owne will* (Ro:Ba 187)

Table 1. Proportion of inversion in sentences with initial sentence-adverbial

Old English	Early Modern English
21.6%	7.6%

4. Non-sentence adverbials

Examples of non-sentence adverbials are given in (55)–(58). Sentences of the type *þa ... þa* and *þonne ... þonne* have been included as well (cf. Mitchell [1985: 296, 971] on the subordinate status of clauses such as [58]), while sentences such as (59) with initial *ne* are excluded (including these latter would have increased the inversion proportion).

(55)   Gif þu þisne cræft healst, *þu bist þe sylf un-hal.*
        'If you keep back this instrument you will be diseased yourself'
        (Ælfric I 134)

(56)   Æfter þisum *het se heard-heorta dema*
        'After this the hard-hearted judge commanded' (Ælfric I 110)

(57)   Orsorhlice *ic forseo þine þeow-racan.*
        'Without care I despise your threatenings' (Ælfric I 176)

(58)   Ðonne heo up arist, *þonne wyrcð heo dæg.*
        'When it arises, then it causes day' (Byrhtferth 122)

(59)   Ne *wæs þæt holinga*
        'Not was that without reason' (Bede 148)

Sentences with initial non-sentence adverbials have a strong tendency to be XVS; this differentiates them from sentences with initial sentence adverbials which, as we have seen, gravitate towards XSV order. However, it is important to bear in mind that even with initial non-sentence adverbials, there is no obligatory inversion like that of true V2 languages such as Modern Norwegian. Our corpus yields a rate of inversion which corresponds fairly closely to the results of other studies such as Bean (1983), Jacobsson (1951) and Kohonen (1978). Thus the overall rate of inversion in Old English declarative sentences with initial non-sentence adverbials is 68.3 percent. If we exclude those sentences whose initial adverbial is a subclause, the percentage is slightly lower (67.6 percent). As we shall see, this differentiates Old English from Early Modern English, and it suggests that initial subclauses in Old English tend to be accompanied by inversion:[3]

SV
(60)   7 *gif hyt byð todæled hyt mæg cuman to þære annysse*
        'if it is divided it may come to unity' (Byrhtferth 118)

(61)   *And gif ge þonne git nellað eow wendan to me . ic sende eow swurd to and eow sleað eowre fynd.*
'And if you even then will not turn to me, I will send you the sword to and your enemies shall slay you' (Ælfric I 294)

(62)   *Þa ðis gecweden wæs, Drihten him æteowde his onsyne on fægeres cildes heowe, & him to cwæð*
'When this was said, the Lord appeared unto him his face like that of a fair child, and said to him' (Blickling 235)

(63)   *Ða Godes Ælmihtiges mycelnys ealle þing wundorlice gesceapen hæfde, ealle þing he gesette on gemete*
'When the greatness of Almighty God had wonderfully created all things, all things He ordained in measure' (Byrhtferth 8)

VS

(64)   *Gyf Eastron beoð on kl. Aprilis, þonne beoð Gangdagas on N. Mai*
'If Easter is on April 1st, then will be Rogationtide on May 7th' (Byrhtferth 168)

(65)   *gif mon hine on fyr deþ, þonne fleoþ þær neddran onweg.*
'If one puts it into the fire fly adders from it' (Bede 26)

(66)   *& mid þy þe he þis gecweden hæfde, þa ascean samninga mycel leoht on hire huse*
'And when he had said this, then shone suddenly a great light upon her house' (Blickling 145)

(67)   *Sona þæs þe he nealehte to þæm herige, þa sceat he mid þy spere*
'As soon as he approached the sanctuary then cast he his spear' (Bede 138)

(68)   *Gif he þonne is unmilde ⁊ oferhygdig, þonne is þæt cuð þæt he nis of Gode*
'If however he is not meek but proud, then is it clear that he is not of God' (Bede 100)

Note that in many of the sentences with VS order, the main clause starts with *þa* or *þonne*; this is (mutatis mutandis) often the case in Old Norse and Modern Norwegian as well. Thus Old Norse has *þá*, while in Modern Norwegian main clauses following many types of adverbial subclauses may have an optional *så* ('then', 'so') preceding the verb.

(69)   a. *En er han fell, þá hlióp svá mikit bloð or sárum hans.*
         'And when he fell, then ran so much blood from wounds his'
         (Old Norse)

         b. *Hvis du sier det, (så) skriker jeg.*
         'If you say that, (so) scream I' (Modern Norwegian)

In Old English one type of initial subclause is, however, so frequently followed by inversion as to constitute an obligatory pattern, viz. the correlative *þa ... þa* (or *þonne ... þonne*). According to Denison (1987: 146), these "notoriously show the most consistent order distinction between (X)SXV for the subordinate member and X'VS for the main clause". Additionally, Mitchell (1985: 296) suggests that "With *þa* and *þonne*, however, the pattern Conj. S (...) V, adv. VS is well established in the prose of all periods ..." Examples are given below.

SV
(70)   *Ða he þa hæfde þone hired gesibbodne þe he þær to ferde, & þær dagas wel manige wæs, þa he þa eft mynte mid his discipulum to his mynstre feran.*
         'When he had reconciled the household to which he had gone, then he purposed with his disciples to go back to his monastery' (Blickling 225)

VS
(71)   *Ða se dema þas word gehyrde, ða wæs he mid mycclum wylme 7 yrre onstyred.*
         'When the judge heard those words then was he with great wrath and fury stirred' (Bede 36)

(72)   *Þonne we us gebiddað mid byle-witum mode, þonne sprece we soðlice to gode sylfum swa*
         'When we pray with simplemindedness, then speak we verily to God himself thus' (Ælfric I 286)

Other correlative pairs are possible as well, e.g., *nu ... nu*; these, too, generally have inversion in the second member:

(73)   *Nu we habbað sceortlice amearcod þæra hiwa gefeg, þe boceras gymað, nu þincð hyt us gedafenlic þæt*
         'Now that we have briefly depicted the way to make the symbols to which grammarians give their attention, now it seems to us fitting that (Byrhtferth 188)

There is another type of sentence where XVS predominates, viz. that with initial *þa* (or, slightly less so, *þonne, þær,* etc.).

(74)   *Ða feng Neron to rice æfter Claudie þam casere.*
'Then Nero came to power after Claudius the emperor' (Bede 30)

(75)   *Þa com færlice mycel wynd*
'Then came suddenly a great wind' (Ælfric I 70)

(76)   *Þa scinon þa ban swa beorhte swa steorran.*
'Then shone the bones as brightly as stars' (Ælfric I 254)

However, as shown by (77), *þa* may also be followed by SV. This is especially common if *þa* is preceded by exclamatory discourse markers such as *hwæt*. If *þa* is preceded by *hwæt* (or similar elements), it might be seen as within the scope of *hwæt* (which functions much like a sentence adverbial) and therefore exempt from the V2 rule. Examples (78) — (79) have SV, while (80) has inversion.

(77)   *& þa æt nehstan he let his lichoman on rode mid næglum gefæstnian*
'and then at last he permitted his body to be fastened with nails to the cross' (Blickling 85)

(78)   *Hwæt þa florus ferde fægen him to-geanes*
'Lo, then Florus went joyfully to meet them' (Ælfric I 156)

(79)   *Efne ða se bisceop eode to his huse.*
'Lo, then the bishop went to his house' (Ælfric I 476)

(80)   *Hwæt ða færlice com fæger godes engel*
'Lo, then suddenly came a fair angel of God' (Ælfric I 136)

In her discussion of word order in the *Anglo Saxon Chronicle*, Schmidt (1980: 85) points out that there is less inversion after *þa* + adverbial than after *þa* alone. It will be seen that in (77) *þa* is followed by the adverbial *æt nehstan*.

Sentences containing other initial non-sentence adverbials than those discussed above do not show any marked preference with respect to the relative order of subject and verb. In Kohonen's material from Late Old English and Early Middle English "there was a tendency for the SV order to occur with light, short pronoun subjects, while long, nominal or clausal subjects were more often postponed. ... There was a similar correlation between the givenness of the subject and its position: new subjects tended to be postponed, while given subjects could stay in the XSV syntax" (1978: 172 – 173). As examples (81) – (91) show, it is not always possible to account for word order differences in our corpus in terms of such pragmatic principles as end-weight and end-focus. Nor does style appear to play a decisive role. Note that two or even more initial adverbials may be followed by VS, as illustrated by (80) and (91). These latter examples should be compared with (77) and (83), which have SV order. By contrast, the V2 language Modern Norwegian normally allows only one constituent before the finite verb (cf. Faarlund [1981: 48] and Johansson – Lysvåg [1987: 262]).

SV
(81)   *Nu we wyllað eft fullum mode her gecyðan*
        'Now we will fully declare at this point' (Byrhtferth 154)

(82)   *& on þæm dæge heofon biþ befealden swa swa boc*
        'and on that day heaven shall be rolled up like a book'
        (Blickling 91)

(83)   *On þone wodnes dæg wide geond eorðan sacerdas bletsiað swa swa*
        'On the Wednesday throughout the whole world the priests bless even as' (Ælfric 262)

(84)   *On synne he bið geeacnod & on his modor sare hi bið acenned.*
        'In sin he is conceived and in his mother's pain he is brought forth' (Blickling 59)

(85)   *þus hi dweledon mid heora leas-sagulan*
        'Thus they erred with their lying speech' (Ælfric I 510)

VS
(86)   *Nu wylle we heom her amearkien gewiss ymbe his ryne*
        'Now will we note down for them all that is definite concerning its course' (Byrhtferth 160)

(87)   *On þæm dage gewiteþ heofon & eorþe, & sæ*
        'On that day shall pass away heaven and earth and sea'
        (Blickling 91)

(88)   *On þyssum dæge astag þæt heofonlice goldhord on þysne ymbhwyrft fram þæm heahsetle ure gescyppendes.*

'On this day descended the heavenly treasure into this world
from the throne of our creator' (Blickling 11)

(89)   *On Egiptum beoð hira breost gehnescod*
'In Egypt are their breasts softened' (Cura Pastoralis 405)

(90)   *Ðus cydde se cempa*
'Thus related the soldier' (Ælfric I 66)

(91)   *Ac færlice ymbe ðreo niht sende se casere his bydelas*
'But suddenly in about three days sent the emperor his heralds'
(Ælfric I 490)

Though it is difficult to discern any factors which particularly induce
verb-medial order, it is clear that some styles or genres are especially apt
to use *þa* as a device to bring forward the narrative, almost formulaically;
these have high percentages of V2.[4] This is true of Ælfric and of Bede,
which also have the highest rates of inversion in our material (79 and
72.5 percent, respectively). The lowest proportion was found in Byrhtferth
(56.2 percent); V2 sentences in this latter work often have initial clauses
(often *if*-clauses). The romance *Apollonius* has many initial *þa* (and V2),
but also a great many initial clauses followed by SV. Clearly, inversion
is optional also in a main clause preceded by a subordinate clause.

We thus see that initial non-sentence adverbials present a rather heterogeneous picture with respect to verb-second positioning in main
clauses. Even though such adverbials (including subclauses) frequently
induce inversion, there seems to be an optionality wholly unknown in
true V2 languages. A scrutiny of our examples will reveal that it is often
difficult to discern any regularity in the choice.

We have not yet investigated in detail the non-sentence adverbials in
our Middle English corpus, but as the examples in (92)—(106) show,
both V2 and verb-medial are possible following initial adverbials of all
types. In Jacobsson (1951: 88, 97), it is suggested that introductory
members of all types are frequently accompanied by inversion in Middle
English, specifically *then* (< *þonne/þanne*), *here, now,* etc. (cf. also Świeczkowski 1962: 43). Note, however, that when *then* is combined with a
sentence adverbial, the V2 constraint may be overruled, as in (94), which
has two sentence adverbials.

SV
(92)   *Thanne Melibee took hem up fro the ground* (Melibee 187)

(93)   *And than on foote they drew there swerdis and dud ful actually.*
(Morte Darthur 165)

(94)   *Thanne certes withoute doute alle the thingen shollen be doon* (Boece 383)

(95)   *In this manere it folweth thanne that* (Boece 363)

(96)   *For in the same yere the forsaid Nichol, with-outen nede, ayein the pees made dyuerse enarmynges bi day* (Book of London English 34)

(97)   *Also, atte Goldsmithes halle, when al the peple was assembled, the mair, John Norhampton, reherced as euel as he koude of the eleccion on the day to-forn* (Book of London English 28)

(98)   *Also is ordeined þat, if any brother or soster dyeþ & haue nouȝt of his owen for to be buried, he schal be honestliche buried at þe costages of þe brothered.* (Book of London English 42)

(99)   *and wyth a ranke swerde he was mervylously wounded.* (Morte Darthur 223)

VS

(100)   *Thenne was the kyng wonderly wroth.* (Morte Darthur 7)

(101)   *Đanne wunest ðu sikerliche on gode.* (Vices and virtues 39)

(102)   *In this wise mai nede be conforted by richesses* (Boece 344)

(103)   *In þis same yer was a Gret differens & distaunce Off sugar by-twyxt John de la Towr, Catalanys, and* (Book of London English 200)

(104)   *[Also, a]tte thilk parlement, was pursuwed a patent to the mair for to chastise vsurers* (Book of London English 26)

(105)   *Also is ordeined þat, if any brother or soster dieþ honeste deþ out of London þe mountance of twelue myle & he haue nouȝt of wher-of to be buried of his owen, þan schul þe wardeynes of þe brotherede wenden þyder & burie hym on the comune costages of þe broþered.* (Book of London English 42)

(106)   *And with this swerd shal I sleen envie.* (Astrolabe 546)

We turn now to the period which is our main concern, the Early Modern English period. According to Görlach (1991: 107), "SVO had become the normal word order in affirmative statements by 1500; a few types of deviant structure had, however, not been fully adapted to the dominant pattern ..." Görlach goes on to suggest that the frequency of V2 varies with author and text type, but that inversion becomes rare in the seventeenth century. In our material from Early Modern English, non-sentence adverbials in initial position are still accompanied by VS order relatively frequently, though concededly at much lower rates than in the Old English period. The percentages of Old English and Early Modern English are shown in Table 2.

Table 2. Proportion of inversion in sentences with initial non-sentence adverbials

	Old English	Early Modern English
All sentences	68.3%	26.5%
Initial subclauses not included	67.5%	39.5%

Evidently, Early Modern English has still not become completely verb-medial. However, some changes have undoubtedly occurred. The relative frequency of sentences with initial adverbial has apparently decreased since the Old English period. This is consistent with Kohonen (1978: 174), who assumes that the proportion of topicalisation will decrease as SVO increases. V2 languages seem to have very high proportions of topicalised elements. Thus Faarlund (1981) states that 40 percent of spoken language sentences in Norwegian do not have an initial subject. As far as Early Modern English is concerned, one quite obvious change is that of the word order in a main clause following an initial subclause; in Early Modern English these are almost invariably SV. Following Dahlstedt (1901), Jacobsson (1951: 119) suggests that since heavy initial elements prefer SV, subclauses naturally do not trigger V2. Furthermore, our Early Modern English material has a much higher proportion of initial subclauses than our Old English material; in Old English the subclauses constitute 22.5 percent of all the initial adverbials (the majority of these are accompanied by VS in the main clause); the corresponding Early Modern English figure is 39.7 percent, and only a small proportion are accompanied by inversion in the main clause.

Unlike the Old English period, there is great variation between the different works as to inversion proportion, some late seventeenth century writers (e. g., Behn) having no inversion at all. There are even some early ones with low percentages. Thus in Ro:Ba only 12.6 percent of the relevant sentences have VS order. The highest proportion is found in T. Lever's *Sermons* (38.5 percent; without subclauses 48 percent).

As mentioned above, the decrease of V2 in sentences with initial adverbials is particularly obvious in sentences introduced by subclauses.

Although such clauses may be followed by the verb, main clauses with SV by far dominate (as Table 2 implies); cf. (107)−(113). It will be noted that in (114)−(118) the main clause is preceded by *yet* and *then*; this is generally the case in correlative structures with *as ... so, albeit ... yet, if ... yet/then*. Occasionally, the SV main clauses will have such initial correlative adverbs as well, as in (112)−(113). If it is the case that heavy initial elements tend to counteract V2, then this might be expected (Jacobsson 1951: 118). However, it should be pointed out that in V2 languages, initial subclauses trigger V2 just like any other initial element, and that in this respect neither Old English nor, of course, Early Modern English is a true V2 language.

SV

(107)   *Had Orestes been Judge, he would not have acquitted that Lystrian rabble of madnesse* (Pseudodoxia 18)

(108)   *And yf any man should think that those partes of Germanie were not then peopled, hee is deceaued* (Verstegan 39)

(109)   *If either wyf or mayd were found in dishonestie, her clothes were cut of round about her* (Verstegan 58)

(110)   *When Lancelot perceaued it, he prouided himselfe for the like purpose.* (Chinon 17)

(111)   *And after he had be long tyme in oryson/ he fylle a slepe.* (Caxton 74)

(112)   *Albeit he delighted in all kinde of melodie, yet he seemed not of nature to be apte and meete to sing himselfe.* (Harpsfield 141)

(113)   *And whan I herde saye of the companye/ that sayde for to please me/ loo there is a wel bodyed woman/ which is wel worthy to be bilouyd of somme knyght/ Thenne al my herte reioysed in me/* (Caxton 46)

VS

(114)   *Although the matter they take in hand seemeth commonlie on appearaunce rude and homely, yet doo they indeede vtter in the same plesaunt and profitable delight.* (W. Webbe 52)

(115)   *If he be good, then am I naught to hate him.* (Ro:Ba 54)

(116)   *If hee were slain, then was hee caryed away & honorably buried;*
(Verstegan 65)

(117)   *and albeit there residence were somtyme changed, yet continued
it longest in Palestine.* (Verstegan 7)

(118)   *And also when her fader and moder were a bedde . thenne must
she goo ete somme good morse ‖ . or somme good mete* (Caxton
18)

Though there are no truly obligatory V2 structures in our Early Modern
English corpus, *then/thenne* very frequently retains this pattern, as shown
by (127) — (132). Occasionally there are sequences of a "dramatic" use of
then, for example in T. Lever's *Sermons* and Ro:Ba; cf. (131) — (132). In
some works, notably Caxton, there are quite frequent occurrences of *then*
with SV order as well; cf. (119) — (126). In Harpsfield the very few *then*
+ SV that are found usually have long constructions between subject
and verb, as in (125) — (126). The main difference, however, between Old
English *þa* and Early Modern English *then* is that the former is used
initially a great deal, while the latter is often found following the verb/
auxiliary (or the subject), as in (124).

SV
(119)   *Thenne he cam to her* (Caxton 47)

(120)   *Thenne I shall speke and saye to them thus* (Caxton 13)

(121)   *Thenne this hooly man declared to her hou she shold* (Caxton
47)

(122)   *And thenne I shalle retourne ageyne to the tale* (Caxton 69)

(123)   *Then they aduised him* (Verstegan)

(124)   *An apparent reason must then be sought* (Verstegan 108)

(125)   *Then the Lord of Wilshire, for hatred of his religion preferrer
of his sute, with much reioysing saide vnto the Lordes;* (Harpsfield 153)

(126)   *Then Sir Thomas More, as his accustomed maner was (as we
haue declared) when he had any matter of weight in hande,
went to Churche and was confessed* (Harpsfield 166)

VS

(127)   *then doubtlesse would the names still remain vnto them* (Verstegan 23)

(128)   *Thenne cam these coynted and Ioly doughters in to the hoost* (Caxton 85)

(129)   *Then goeth he on, & telleth* (Verstegan 83)

(130)   *Then ... are you happely come into these Confines* (Chinon 14)

(131)   *Then wyll not God by workyng of miracles declare mercy, but Then shall God doo wonderfull miracles in Englande* (T. Lever 58)

(132)   *Then shall heresies be preached; then shall ... then shall ... then shall hoares and theeues, beggers and baudes, increase without number.* (Ro:Ba 91)

Other time adverbials do not trigger V2 as frequently as *then*, but V2 is possible and indeed does not seem highly marked stylistically. Thus Caxton begins most of his chapters with various versions of sentences such as (133) and (136), and certainly these introductory formulas are in free variation.

SV

(133)   *Now I shalle telle yow vpon this matere of a good lady whiche* (Caxton 53)

(134)   *After the death of Alexander they sayled towards Africa.* (Verstegan 29)

(135)   *And oftymes he ros fro his wyf/and wente to his concubynes/* (Caxton 32)

VS

(136)   *Now wylle I telle yow thexample of an euylle/cruel/ an dyuerse quene/* (Caxton 96)

(137)   *By this tyme was Chinon come to the place where we first left Michander* (Chinon 59)

(138)   *Some few ages after came the poet Geffrey Chaucer* (Verstegan 203)

As is well known, Early Modern English allows non-inversion, whereas Present-day English requires inversion after the negative frequency adverbial; cf. (139)—(142). Jacobsson (1951: 43) observes that "the presence of a nominal subject helps to preserve the straight order ...", but as (140) shows, even pronominal subjects may occur in SV structures. According to Görlach (1991: 108), inversion after negative adverbials becomes obligatory in the seventeenth century.

SV

(139)   *but neuer none that euer refused the mercye of God hath escaped the vengeaunce of God* (T. Lever 22)

(140)   *And neuer he tooke cause in hand that he did not seriouslie and aduisedly examine the Iustice and equitie thereof.* (Ro:Ba 30)

VS

(141)   *neuer did nature before compose of so rude a Chaos comely a creature:* (Chinon 7)

(142)   *Neuer was there anie man that sought releife and help at his handes that went not from him cheerfull.* (Ro:Ba 53)

Place adverbials, both prepositional phrases and adverbs, may be followed by SV or VS; cf. (143)—(150). As in Old English, there are relatively few initial place adverbials apart from short adverbs like *here* and *there*. This is of course the case in Present-day English as well; place adverbials are generally seen as relatively marked in initial position, compared to for instance time adverbials (cf. e. g., Nordeng 1986, Quirk *et al.* 1985). On the other hand, many of the remaining V2 patterns of Present-day English have initial place adverbials (cf. Breivik 1990 and Swan 1989).

SV

(143)   *heere I found you and heere I leaue you* (Lyly 44)

(144)   *and yet herein we should not want experiment and great authority.* (Pseudodoxia 99)

(145)   *There I staide 3 yeeres attendant on my maister* (E. Webbe 18)

(146)   *On his head hee wore a Crown of Gold* (Verstegan 74)

VS

(147)   *Heere mayst thou see that which I sigh to see* (Lyly 38)

(148)   *And heer by this occasion am I now brought to speak of* (Verstegan 165)

(149)   *There were we beaten three times a weeke with a horse tayle*
          (E. Webbe 18)

(150)   *On his brest was carued a bear* (Verstegan 79)

If the place adverbial is followed by a verb of movement like *walk, come*
and *go*, the clause frequently has VS order. Such constructions are
particularly common in Chinon; the adverbial seems to have some sort
of connective function, or to provide the setting:

(151)   *Next him steps Triamore* (Chinon 31)

(152)   *And thyther cam many knyghtes/squyers ladyes and damoysels*
          of the Countre (Caxton 48)

Manner adverbials (including *thus*) are only rarely fronted; if they are,
however, they frequently trigger inversion. Examples are given in
(153) − (164):

SV
(153)   *And so firmely he was rooted and fixed in it that he continued*
          very resolute (Ro:Ba 148)

(154)   *& thus the knyght saued hym self* (Caxton 43)

(155)   *Thus he prechyd vnto the lady.* (Caxton 38)

(156)   *So in lyke manner ... such of these Normannes as came to plant*
          themselues in England did there grow to the name of Englishmen
          (Verstegan 185)

VS
(157)   *Vehemently hast thou invayde against the Senates Iniustice.*
          (Queen Elizabeth's Boethius 15)

(158)   *The more willingly this doo we because his bookes be rare.*
          (Harpsfield 100)

(159)   *And thus displeasantly departed they.* (Harpsfield 160)

(160)   *Thus encreased the Saxons their bounds* (Verstegan 83)

(161)   *And thus lost she the loue and thonoure of her husbond* (Caxton
          32)

(162)   *So in lyke manner do the lower Germans or Netherlanders,*
          vulgarly call the present french toung wals (Verstegan 153)

(163)   *In lyke manner are wee stil termed by the name of Sasons*
          (Verstegan 1)

(164)   *And in lyke sorte might Tuisco deserue the name of a God*
          (Verstegan 11)

There seems to be a tendency for manner *thus* to trigger inversion more
often than does the conjunct *thus* (to the extent it is possible to distinguish
them). Examples (165)—(166) both contain the conjunct:

(165)   *Thus they commonly affect no man any further then hee deserts*
          his reason (Pseudodoxia 17)

(166)   *And thus by one meanes or other may they haue bin somuch*
          worne away and diminished, that (Verstegan 186)

So far existential sentences have not been given explicit attention. Existential sentences containing a non-sentence adverbial in initial position
are exemplified in (9) *On the table lay a book about architecture*, and (10)
In Oslo there was a demonstration against the American president. Breivik
(1990) examined the longitudinal development of such sentences in an
extensive corpus drawn from Old English, Middle English and Early
Modern English. In Old English about 70 percent of all existential
sentences have V2 order with a non-sentence adverbial in initial position,
as in (167)—(168):

(167)   *On ðam ylcan dæge com sum bisceop helenus gehaten*
          'On that same day came a bishop who was called Helenus'
          (Ælfric I 28)

(168)   *Nu synd ðreo heah-mægnu . ðe menn sceolan habban.*
          'Now are three chief virtues which men must have' (Ælfric I
          352)

In Middle English and Early Modern English, *there* is increasingly inserted in preverbal position, parallelling the gradual fixation of the SVO
order. Existential sentences like (167)—(168) are presentative constructions. The increasing use of *there* can thus be taken as a compromise in
the conflict between the pragmatic structure and the fixation of the SVO
syntax: the logical subject, the communicative core, is allowed to remain
in post-verbal position in accordance with the principles of end-focus and
end-weight, while the initial subject slot is filled by the formal subject
there. The stabilisation of the pattern "dummy subject + verb" is strik-

ingly illustrated by the following examples from *The Nativity of Christ* (quoted from Kaiser 1961: 15 – 16):

(169)   *And þa wæs færinga ȝeworden mid þam engle mycelnes heo-fonlices werodes god heriendra and þus cweþendra* (Old English, West Saxon Translation)

(170)   *And sudenli þer was maad with þe aungel a multitude of heuenli knyȝthod, heriynge God and seiynge* (Middle English, Wyclif-Purvey)

(171)   *And streight waye ther was with the angell a multitude of hevenly sowdiers, laudynge God and sayinge* (Early Modern English, Tyndale)

The data presented in Breivik (1990) show that by the middle of the sixteenth century, English has gone a long way towards generalising the SV order in existential sentences. However, we are still witnessing an ongoing change; the present-day order has not yet become fixed, as shown by the following examples:

(172)   *And in alle the world is no gretter treson/ than for to deceyue gentyll wymmen* (Caxton 12)

(173)   *Now on a nyght/ ther cam to her a Vysyon* (Caxton 21)

(174)   *In that tyme was ther a Baron a good man a right good knyght* (Caxton 83)

Clearly, in Early Modern English, V2 has decreased a great deal in sentences introduced by a non-sentence adverbial. Subclauses generally do not trigger inversion, nor does *then* to the extent it did in Old and Middle English. Yet V2 still operates in one fifth of all clauses with initial non-sentence adverbials (almost 40 percent if we exclude initial sub-clauses). As our examples show, Early Modern English has remarkable freedom as to the selection of V2 after initial adverbials.

As far as style/genre is concerned, it is at this point too early to say anything definite. Chinon, a romantic dramatic tale, and T. Lever's *Sermons* have high proportions of inversion, which might suggest that this type of word order is characteristic of the rhetorical style. However, the percentage of VS in the scientific or academic treatise of Verstegan is not very much lower. It would seem that a sentence such as *On the pavement sat a sad little cat* is not marked to the same extent as it is in Present-day English.

5. Conclusion

We began this paper by referring to Fries's claim that in the actor-action-goal construction the modern word order seems to be fully established by the middle of the fifteenth century. However, from the foregoing pages, it is clear that the situation is still generally unsettled in Early Modern English sentences containing an adverbial in initial position.

What, then, does our investigation tell us about the typological status of Early Modern English? As pointed out in section 2, the present paper is not concerned with changes in underlying structure. However, on the basis of data cited by Hiltunen (1983), van Kemenade (1987) and others, it is reasonable to assume that the change in underlying word order from SOV to SVO must have been completed by 1200. Van Kemenade argues that the loss of the V2 constraint must be dated later, around 1400. She writes (1987: 180):

> V2 as in OE became more limited in scope in the course of the late ME period. While V2 in late OE occurred with all kinds of first constituents – subject, object, PP, adverbial – and was accompanied by 'subject-verb inversion' when the first constituent was not the subject, in the course of ME V2 became limited to cases where the first constituent was a wh-element. Later on, negative constituents were again included in the class of elements triggering V2, giving rise to the Modern English situation ...

Our data show that van Kemenade is on the wrong track here: it is clearly not true that V2 becomes limited to cases where the first constituent is a *wh*-element in the course of the Middle English period. Or, to put it differently, Early Modern English is in a state of flux with respect to V2 and verb-medial. In our material from this period, 26.5 percent of the clauses introduced by a non-sentence adverbial have inversion of subject and verb (39.5 percent if we do not take account of subclauses). In this connection we would like to cite some of Jacobsson's (1951) findings. He demonstrates that even as late as 1600 inversion is quite common after many adverbials, especially non-negative connective ones (e. g. *now, here,* and *then*). His figures are: 44 percent for the period 1370–1500, 34 percent for 1500–1600 and 7 percent for 1600–1712. Recall here that even Present-day English has V2 patterns like (9), *On the table lay a book about architecture.* Today such patterns are limited to sentences containing an initial locative adverbial; they represent a specialisation of a once general rule.

As far as constructions with an initial sentence adverbial are concerned, our data are rather confusing with regard to the V2 constraint. In Old

English, only 21.6 percent of such sentences exhibit inversion, as against 68.3 percent of their non-sentence adverbial counterparts. However, what we can conclude beyond doubt is that Early Modern English sentences with an initial sentence adverbial are far from having reached the present-day stage, where the initial adverbial does not trigger subject-verb inversion. In our Early Modern English material, 7.6 percent of the relevant sentences are still inverted and the proportion has not changed greatly since the Middle English period.

Given that inversion is used as frequently as it is in Early Modern English, a large-scale investigation of the stylistic and/or social aspects of its use is one of the research tasks we have ahead of us. To what extent is the use of inversion marked? In what types of texts does it occur most often? These are questions which we will try to answer in Breivik—Swan (forthcoming).

Notes

1. As we saw in section 2, Stockwell—Minkova also assume a rule of clitic positioning of subject and object pronouns. Thus the following example (from Stockwell—Minkova 1991: 388) is claimed to have V2 order: *ich hi ne lufige* 'I him not love'.
2. Curiously enough, in Early Modern English (in contradistinction to Old English and Middle English, sentence adverbials which are preceded by a topicalised element are less frequently accompanied by inversion than those sentence adverbials that are sentence-initial; that is, the pattern *X + Sentence adverbial + Verb + Subject* is more likely in Old English and Middle English than the pattern *Sentence adverbial + Verb + Subject*, whereas in Early Modern English it is the other way round. However, in all periods the pattern *Sentence adverbial + X + Verb + Subject* is more frequent than the pattern *Sentence adverbial + Verb + Subject + X* (where X may be an NP or adverbial).
3. In this connection we may note the following statement by Stockwell—Minkova (1991: 385):

    Campbell (1964: 192), in criticising Bacquet (1962), argues (correctly, we believe) that a sentence like

    (30) *æftere þæm þe Romeburg getimbred wæs iiii hunde wintrum ond xxvi, feng Alexander to Mæcedonia rice, Orosius*, ed. Sweet, 122

    is not an instance of verb-first in the main clause, but rather an inversion "which is part of the general tendency to invert subject and verb in principal clauses if the subject has not the first place, so that the verb remains in the second place".
4. Enkvist (1972) hypothesises that one of the functions of the Old English adverb *þā* is to mark actions and sequences of actions:

    The question suggested in the title of the present paper has arisen from an originally casual, but increasing suspicion that passages describing vigorous physical action in Old English tend to be marked by a frequent use of adverbial þā, 'then'. If so, the frequent occurrence of adverbial þā can be regarded as a feature which contributes to their texture and flavour. It becomes a style marker for passages of action. (1972: 90)

Primary texts

The texts examined are listed below. Within each period, the texts are arranged in the alphabetical order of the abbreviations used for them.

Old English

Anglo Saxon Chronicle = *Two of the Saxon chronicles parallel*
    1892   Vol. I. Edited by Charles Plummer — John Earle. Oxford: Oxford University Press.
Anglo Saxon manual = "Anglo Saxon manual" in: *Popular treatises on science.*
    1941   Edited by Thomas Wright. London.
Ælfric I = *Ælfric's Lives of saints*
    1881   Vol. I.i. Edited by Walter W. Skeat. London (EETS): Oxford University Press.
    1885   Vol. I.ii. Edited by Walter W. Skeat. London (EETS): Oxford University Press.
    [1966]   [Reprinted as one volume. London.]
Apollonius = *The Old English Apollonius of Tyre*
    1958   Edited by Peter Goolden. Oxford: Oxford University Press.
Bede = *The Old English version of Bede's* Ecclesiastical history of the English people.
    1890   Vol. I.i. Edited by Thomas Miller. London (EETS): Oxford University Press.
    1891   Vol. I.ii. Edited by Thomas Miller. London (EETS): Oxford University Press.
Blickling = *The Blickling homilies*
    1874   Vol. I. Edited by Richard Morris. London (EETS): Oxford University Press.
    1876   Vol. II. Edited by Richard Morris. London (EETS): Oxford University Press.
    1880   Vol. III. Edited by Richard Morris. London (EETS): Oxford University Press.
    [1967]   [Reprinted as one volume.]
Boethius = *King Alfred's Old English version of Boethius* De consolatione philosophiae
    1899   Edited by William J. Sedgefield. Oxford: Clarendon Press.
Byrhtferth = *Byrhtferth's manual*
    1929   Edited by S. J. Crawford. London (EETS): Oxford University Press.
Cura Pastoralis = *King Alfred's version of Gregory's* Pastoral care
    1871   Edited by Henry Sweet. London (EETS): Oxford University Press.

Middle English

Astrolabe = "A treatise on the astrolabe" in: *The complete works of Geoffrey Chaucer*
    1974   2nd ed. Edited by F. N. Robinson. London: Oxford University Press.
Ayenbite = *Dan Michael's Ayenbite of Inwyt*
    1866   Edited by Richard Morris. London: Oxford University Press.

Boece = "Boece" in: *The works of Geoffrey Chaucer*
　　1974　　　2nd ed. Edited by F. N. Robinson. London: Oxford University Press.
Book of London English = *A book of London English 1384—1425*
　　1931　　　Edited by R. W. Chambers—Marjorie Daunt. Oxford: Clarendon Press.
Capgrave = *John Capgrave's Abbreuiacion of Cronicles*
　　1983　　　Edited by P. J. Lucas. Oxford (EETS): Oxford University Press.
Melibee = "The prologue and tale of Melibee" in: *The works of Geoffrey Chaucer*
　　1974　　　2nd ed. Edited by F. N. Robinson. London: Oxford University Press.
Morte Darthur = *The works of Sir Thomas Malory*
　　1967　　　2nd ed. Edited by Eugéne Vinaver. Oxford: Oxford University Press.
Rolle = *The English writings of Richard Rolle, hermit of Hampole*
　　1931　　　Edited by Hope Emily Allen. Oxford: Clarendon Press.
Sermons = *Middle English sermons*
　　1940　　　Edited by Woodburn O. Ross. London: Oxford University Press.
Vices and virtues = *Vices and virtues*
　　1888　　　Edited by Ferdinand Holthausen. London (EETS): Oxford University Press.

Early Modern English

Behn = "The history of the nun" [by Aphra Behn] in: *Restoration prose fiction 1666—1700*
　　1970　　　Edited by Charles Mish. Lincoln, Nebraska.
Caxton = *The book of the knight of the tower*
　　1971　　　Edited by M. Y. Offord. London (EETS): Oxford University Press.
Chinon = *The famous historie of Chinon of England by Christopher Middleton*
　　1925　　　Edited by W. E. Mead. London.
E. Webbe = *His trauailes* [by E. Webbe]
　　1868　　　Edited by Edward Arber. London.
Harpsfield = *Harpsfield's Life of More*
　　1932　　　Edited by Elsie V. Hitchcock. London.
Lyly = *Eupues. The anatomy of wit* [by John Lyly]
　　1868　　　Edited by Edward Arber. London.
Pseudodoxia = *Sir Thomas Browne's Pseudodoxia epidemica*
　　1981　　　Edited by Robin Robbins. Oxford: Clarendon Press.
Queen Elizabeth's Boethius = *Queen Elizabeth's Englishings of Boethius*. De Consolatione Philosophiae
　　1899　　　Edited by Caroline Pemberton. London (EETS): Oxford University Press.
R. Lever = *The arte of reason, rightly termed witchcraft* [by Ralph Lever]
　　1573　　　Reprinted 1972 (English Linguistics 1500—1800). Menston.
Ro:Ba = *The life of Syr Thomas More* [by Ro:Ba]
　　1950　　　Edited by Elsie V. Hitchcock—P. E. Hallett. London.
T. Lever = *Sermons* [by T. Lever]
　　1870　　　Edited by Edward Arber. London.
Verstegan = *A restitution of decayed intelligence* [by Richard Verstegan]
　　1605　　　Reproduced 1979. Amsterdam.

W. Webbe = *A discourse of English poetrie* [by W. Webbe]
1870   Edited by Edward Arber. London.

References

Andrew, Samuel Ogden
  1940   *Syntax and style in Old English.* Cambridge: Cambridge University Press.
Bacquet, Paul
  1962   *La structure de la phrase verbale à l'époque Alfrédienne.* Paris: Faculté des Lettres.
Bean, Marian C.
  1983   *The development of word order patterns in Old English.* London: Croom Helm.
Breivik, Leiv Egil
  1990   *Existential* there: *A synchronic and diachronic study.* Oslo: Novus.
  1991   "On the typological status of Old English", in: Dieter Kastovsky (ed.), 31 – 50.
Breivik, Leiv Egil — Toril Swan
  forthcoming "Word order changes in English in a typological perspective".
Campbell, Alistair
  1964   "Review of Paul Bacquet 1962", *Review of English Studies* 15: 190 – 193.
Carlton, C. R.
  1970   *Descriptive syntax of the Old English charters.* The Hague: Mouton.
Christoffersen, Marit
  1980   "Marked and unmarked word order in Old Norse", in: Elizabeth Traugott (ed.), *Papers from the 4th International Conference on Historical Linguistics.* Amsterdam: Benjamins, 115 – 123.
  1994   "Initial adverbials in Old Norse", in: Toril Swan — Endre Mørck — Olaf M. Jansen Westvik (eds.), 75 – 89.
Dahlstedt, August
  1901   Rhythm and word-order in Anglo-Saxon and Semi-Saxon with special reference to their development in Modern English. [Doctoral dissertation, Lund.]
Denison, David
  1987   "On word order in Old English", in: G. H. V. Bunt — E. S. Kooper — J. L. Mackenzie — D. R. M. Wilkinson (eds.), *One hundred years of English studies in Dutch universities.* Amsterdam: Rodopi, 139 – 155.
Enkvist, Nils Erik
  1972   "Old English adverbial *þā* — an action marker?", *Neuphilologische Mitteilungen* 73: 90 – 96.
Faarlund, Jan Terje
  1981   "Obligatory fronting in a verb-initial language: An attempt at pragmatic syntax", *Papers from the 7th Regional Meeting of the Chicago Linguistic Society*, 45 – 58.
  1990   *Syntactic change: Toward a theory of historical syntax.* Berlin: Mouton de Gruyter.
Faarlund, Jan Terje (ed.)
  1985   *Germanic linguistics: Papers from a symposium at the University of Chicago April 24, 1985.* Bloomington: IULC.

Fisiak, Jacek (ed.)
1984   *Historical syntax*. Berlin: Mouton.
Fries, Charles C.
1940   "On the development of the structural use of word-order in Modern English",
            Language 16: 199–208.
Gardner, Faith F.
1971   *An analysis of syntactic patterns of Old English*. The Hague: Mouton.
Görlach, Manfred
1991   *Introduction to Early Modern English*. Cambridge: Cambridge University
            Press.
Green, Georgia
1980   "Some wherefores of English inversions", *Language* 56: 582–601.
Haiman, John
1974   *Targets and syntactic change*. The Hague: Mouton.
Hanson, Kristin
1987   "On subjectivity and the history of epistemic expressions in English", *Papers
            from the 23rd Regional Meeting of the Chicago Linguistic Society*, Part I,
            133–147.
Hiltunen, Risto
1983   *The decline of the prefixes and the beginnings of the English phrasal verb*.
            Turku: Turun Yliopisto.
Hock, Hans Henrich
1985   "Pronoun fronting and the notion 'verb-second' position in Beowulf", in: Jan
            Terje Faarlund (ed.), 70–86.
1986   *Principles of historical linguistics*. Berlin: Mouton de Gruyter.
Jacobsson, Bengt
1951   *Inversion in English with special reference to the Early Modern English period*.
            Uppsala: Almqvist and Wiksell.
Johansson, Stig–Per Lysvåg
1987   *Understanding English grammar*, Part II. Oslo: Universitetsforlaget.
Kaiser, Rolf (ed.)
1958   *Medieval English. An Old English and Middle English anthology*. (3rd. rev.
[1961]   and greatly enlarged edition). Berlin: Rolf Kaiser.
Kohonen, Viljo
1978   *On the development of English word order in religious prose around 1000 and
            1200 A. D.: A quantitative study of word order in context*. Åbo: Research
            Institute of the Åbo Akademi Foundation.
Lightfoot, David
1977   "Syntactic change and the autonomy thesis", *Journal of Linguistics* 13:
            191–216.
Mitchell, Bruce
1985   *Old English syntax*, Vol. II. Oxford: Clarendon.
Nevalainen, Terttu
this volume "Aspects of adverbial change in Early Modern English".
Nordeng, Vivi
1986   A pragmatic analysis of temporal and locative adverbials. [Unpublished
            M. A. thesis, University of Tromsø.]

Pintzuk, Susan — Anthony S. Kroch
1985   "Reconciling an exceptional feature of Old English clause structure", in: Jan
            Terje Faarlund (ed.), 87 — 111.
Quirk, Randolph — Sidney Greenbaum — Geoffrey Leech — Jan Svartvik
1985   *A comprehensive grammar of the English language.* London: Longman.
Schmidt, Deborah Ann
1980   A history of inversion in English. [Unpublished Ph. D. dissertation, Ohio
            State University.]
Shannon, Ann
1964   *A descriptive syntax of the Parker manuscript of the Anglo Saxon Chronicle
            from 734 — 891.* The Hague: Mouton.
Stockwell, Robert P.
1977   "Motivations for exbraciation in Old English", in: Charles N. Li (ed.),
            Mechanisms of syntactic change. Austin: University of Texas Press, 291 — 314.
1984   "On the history of the verb-second rule in English", in: Jacek Fisiak (ed.),
            575 — 592.
Stockwell, Robert P. — Donka Minkova
1991   "Subordination and word order change in the history of English", in: Dieter
            Kastovsky (ed.), 367 — 408.
1994   "Kuhn's laws and Old English verse", in: Toril Swan — Endre Mørck — Olaf
            M. Jansen Westvik (eds.), 213 — 231
Swan, Toril
1988   *Sentence adverbials in English: A synchronic and diachronic investigation.* Oslo:
            Novus.
1989   "A note on initial adverbials and word order in Norwegian and English", in:
            Leiv Egil Breivik — Stig Johansson — Arnoldus Hille (eds.), *Essays on English
            language in Honour of Bertil Sundby.* Oslo: Novus, 331 — 334.
1991   "Adverbial shifts: Evidence from Norwegian and English", in: Dieter Kas-
            tovsky (ed.), 409 — 438.
forthcoming "Early Modern English adverbials".
Swan, Toril — Endre Mørck — Olaf M. Jansen Westvik (eds.)
1994   *Language change and language structure: Older Germanic languages in a
            comparative perspective.* Berlin: Mouton de Gruyter.
Świeczkowski, Walerian
1962   *Word order patterning in Middle English.* The Hague: Mouton.
Traugott, Elizabeth Closs
1989   "On the rise of epistemic meanings in English: An example of subjectification
            in semantic change", *Language* 65: 31 — 55.
van Kemenade, Ans
1987   *Syntactic case and morphological case in the history of English.* Dordrecht:
            Foris.
Vennemann, Theo
1974   "Topics, subjects, and word order: From SXV to SVX via TVX", in: John
            M. Anderson — Charles Jones (eds.), *Historical linguistics. Proceedings of the
            First International Conference on Historical Linguistics.* Vol. I, Amsterdam:
            North-Holland, 339 — 376.
1984   "Verb-second, verb late, and the brace construction: Comments on some
            papers", in: Jacek Fisiak (ed.), 627 — 636.

von Seefranz-Montag, Ariane
   1984   " 'Subjectless' constructions and syntactic change", in: Jacek Fisiak (ed.),
            521 – 553.
Weerman, Fred
   1989   *The V2 conspiracy: A synchronic and a diachronic analysis of verbal positions
            in Germanic languages.* Dordrecht: Foris.

Are Shakespeare's agent nouns different from Chaucer's? — On the dynamics of a derivational sub-system

Christiane Dalton-Puffer

1. The present paper provides a longitudinal study of an area of word-formation: the formation of agent nouns. In doing this, a fairly extended timespan is taken into account, of which Early Modern English is only one part. After a note on the data and a definition of what I understand by agent nouns, the first main part of the paper will establish an inventory of the morphological forms available for agent noun formation from Early Middle English through to Early Modern English. After that I shall present a semantically-based descriptive model applying it to the data of this study. In doing this, I hope to show that the diachronic development of a suffix or a word-formation pattern should not be regarded in isolation. Rather, morphological forms and semantic functions are interlocked in word-formation systems and changes take place as realignments within these systems.

2.1. The temporal angle towards Early Modern English in this paper is somewhat unusual in that the period in question is approached "clockwise", that is from an earlier period (i.e., Middle English), rather than "anti-clockwise", which would take Modern English as point of reference and comparison. The reason for this is quite simply that in a separate study on Middle English derivation I thought I could detect the beginning of certain developments and was thus interested in obtaining a diagnostic whether these suspicions could be verified on the basis of Early Modern English data.

2.2. The data on which the following discussion is based all stem from full-text corpora rather than dictionaries or handbooks. Everything I say about Middle English is based on material collected from the diachronic part of the *Helsinki Corpus of English Texts*, henceforth referred to as HC. The HC was compiled along the principles of the variationist approach towards language change and it therefore contains excerpts from texts by different authors, in different styles and belonging to different text-types. Inasmuch as this is at all possible for a corpus-language like Middle English, the HC can thus be said to be representative. The Early Modern English corpus I have used for this study is very different: it simply consists of Shakespeare's comedies.[1] That is to say, the Early Modern material is not a collection of many short excerpts but of a limited number of full texts. Moreover, there is a much more limited number of text-types and styles. The only parameter which I have successfully tried to keep stable is corpus size — but we shall not concentrate on quantitative aspects as such. It is thus clear that any claims or generalisations I make in the course of my discussion have validity primarily for the corpora in question — especially in the case of the Early Modern period.[2]

2.3. The discussion in this paper is limited to one area of lexical derivation, i. e., derived concrete nouns. The reason for this is very practical: derived concrete nouns constitute a derivational subsystem which is fairly easy to delimit. The ambitious aim behind it is that I hope this will contribute to a claim about the behaviour of derivational systems in general. On a less ambitious level this article is simply a longitudinal study of English agent nouns from ca. 1150 — 1600 in three quasi-synchronic cross-sections.

Before we can delve into the matter, we need to come up with a definition of what we are going to discuss. I have already used both the term "concrete noun" and the term "agent noun" to refer to the objects of my study. Agent nouns, in fact, are the most frequent derived concrete nouns. Typically, they are deverbal derivatives expressing a meaning vaguely paraphrasable as 'agent executing action expressed in verb'. As they are such frequent items, "agent nouns" will serve as a quick reference term. However, we must be quite clear about the fact that the term is not sufficiently comprehensive. Instruments and bearers of qualities are inextricably mixed among agent nouns proper. In order to be really accurate one ought to call them "derived concrete nouns".

3. Let us now turn our attention to the observable linguistic objects, the suffixes deriving agent nouns, and find out what forms were available at the different periods under scrutiny here. In order to do this, a process of stocktaking was necessary which consisted of two stages: first, a list of possible forms was put together from handbooks (e. g., Marchand 1969, Kastovsky 1992), the *Middle English Dictionary*, and also from intuition. Then, the items on the first "stock-list" were searched for in the corpora with the help of the Oxford Concordance Programme. It is thus logically possible, though highly unlikely that some alternatives were never discovered.

Table 1 lists the forms which are attested, adopting a standardised spelling. The actual occurrences of the forms, of course, show a great number of spelling variants.

Table 1. English agent noun suffixes at different periods

Early ME (1150 – 1250)	Late ME (1350 – 1420	Shakespeare (c. 1600)	examples
ERE	*ER*	*ER*	*bearer, potter*
ESTER	*STER*	*STER*	*whitster, gamester*
(EL(S)			*birel, hidels*
ENDE			*scepend*
ILD			*beggild*
LING	*LING*	*LING*	*youngling*
	MAN	*MAN*	*workman*
	ARD	*ARD*	*dullard*
	(ANT)	*ANT*	*attendant*
	(ARY)	*ARY*	*adversary*
(ESSE)	*(ESS)*	*ESS*	*huntress*
	(EREL)		*pykerel*
		IAN	*musician*
		IST	*Brownist*
		ITE	*convertite*
	OUR	*?OUR*	*inheritor*

In interpreting Table 1 we have to remind ourselves that at the moment we are merely concerned with morphological forms. We can thus say that some forms have been there all the time (and still are), such as *ER, LING, STER*. Some forms disappeared *(ENDE)* and others emerged from somewhere. In Late Middle English and even more so in Early Modern English we have many new suffixal forms originating from French and Latin. These have been separated from the native forms in the layout of Table 1. If a form is given in brackets, this indicates that there is only a marginal number of types and tokens in the corpus material.

If a form can be found in all three columns, or indeed in Present-day English, this does not automatically mean that nothing has changed since the twelfth century. Since at the moment we are exclusively concerned with morphological forms we cannot say anything definite. Before we can attempt to do that, we need to correlate our present findings with our findings from a semantic investigation. As indicated in the introduction, my main hypothesis would be that the precise quality of those links between morphological form and morphological meaning is the most diachronically dynamic aspect of derivation.

4.0. We have by now invoked the semantics of derivation several times and it is this aspect that we now turn to explicitly. In comparison with other areas of derivational semantics, we are in the lucky position that a substantial amount of work on the semantics of derived concrete nouns is already available.[3] Instead of giving a review of the literature on the topic, Table 2 a lists the notions which have recurred and/or figured prominently in this discussion.

Table 2.

a.	b.
Agent occasional	Agent
Agent habitual/professional	Instrument
Instrument	Location
Place	
Source	Female
Female	Attributive
Male	Diminutive
Pejorative	Pejorative
Diminutive	
Augmentative	

The above notions come under different guises. Sometimes they are called semantic functions, which is usually the case if the focus of interest is morphological form. If the focus of interest is semantic content, these notions tend to have the status of derivational categories, where a category happens to be realised by the morphological form(s) x, y and/or z. It will soon become obvious that I adhere to the second approach even though the inner chronology of this article seems to contradict this. One of the basic tenets of the following discussion is thus the existence of abstract meanings which are typically expressed by a certain kind of formal exponent which we call derivational suffixes.

The remainder of this article will be dedicated to the discussion of the above list of semantic notions. The end-product of this discussion will be column b in Table 2, which is descriptively adequate to the material from the corpora studied here. A first glance at column a in Table 2 makes it clear that while being heterogeneous, it is by no means unstructured. The discussion will follow the structure of this list interweaving theoretical aspects with an application to the corpus material.

4.1. The first group of items which clearly belong together are the first four, Agent, Instrument, Place and Source. The question of occasional versus habitual or professional agents will be excluded, on the grounds that the distinction seems to work on a less basic semantic level than the one between Agents, Instruments and Places/Sources itself. As a rule, agent nouns are given the "occasional" reading, e. g., *bringer (of news)* in (1) below, unless there is evidence to the contrary either from lexical-isation or from our knowledge of the world.

(1)   a. Mod. E. *bringer (of news)* vs. *collector* vs. *baker*
        b. E. Mod. E. *shooter*
           "— Well then, I am the shooter. — And who is your deer?"
           (LLL IV.1)

Collector thus gets the reading 'habitual', while *baker* gets the reading 'professional'. In a very general sense, both these factors, lexicalisation and knowledge of the world, contribute to the context of such a derivative. There is, of course, also the immediate syntactic context, the importance of which becomes evident from the Shakespearean example (1 b). Here we lack a certain amount of shared knowledge of the world and thus have to fall back on the immediate linguistic context in order to be able to interpret a formation correctly.[4]

But even once we have decided to ignore the habituality question, things are not as clear as the remaining neat labels would suggest. On the surface the difference between Agents and Instruments is quite ob-vious: Agents are typically persons or at least animate, and Instruments are typically things and inanimate. However, there are also impersonal (inanimate) agents and one can also conceive of animate instruments (if one does not have any ideological objections). In any case, the borderline between the categories Agent and Instrument is a fuzzy one. It has been claimed that there is a hierarchical ordering among these functions:

(2)   Agent > Instrument > (Location, Source) (Dressler 1986: 526)

According to this, the most probable or default reading for any derived concrete noun is thus "animate agent" as there exists a unidirectional implicational relationship between the first two items. It reads "Every instrument implies an agent" but does not apply vice versa. The relationship with the locative readings seems to be more tenuous and it has been argued that it is a matter of lexicalisation rather than anything else (Panagl 1987: 136). The most powerful argument justifying the close link between Agent, Instrument and Place is, however, not semantic but morphological: the three categories are very often expressed by an identical formal exponent. In English the main common exponent is *ER*, but there are also others, as we shall see.[5] The matter, however, is not just that three entirely distinct categories happen to have a formally identical exponent. With a specific derivative it is often impossible to decide what derivational category it represents. Many derivatives allow, actually or potentially, all three readings and often only the context can provide disambiguation between an agent noun, an instrumental noun, or a locative noun. Take the word *tooth-drawer* (LLL V.2) from the Shakespeare corpus. As the derivative *drawer* is the head of a nominal compound, we already have a small amount of context in the shape of the determinant *tooth*, but in this case this is not enough for disambiguation. From a present-day point of view a *tooth-drawer* is most likely a "box-shaped receptacle, fitting into a space in a cabinet or a table, so that it can be drawn out horizontally, used to store a person's set of dentures".[6] That is to say, as speakers of late twentieth century English we would prefer the last reading in the hierarchy represented in (2), which suggests that nowadays *drawer* is lexicalised. By virtue of the implicational relationship which holds in (2), our first choice for *tooth-drawer* ought to be 'somebody who pulls out teeth' or, with a bit of extralinguistic information thrown in, 'somebody who professionally pulls out other people's teeth'. It could, however, also denote some implement such a person would use to perform his or her task. Such an instrumental reading is clearly asked for in example (3 a):

(3)   a. *I will go on the slightest errand now to the Antipodes that you can devise to send me on. I will fetch you* a tooth-picker *now from the furthest inch of Asia ... fetch you a hair off the Great Cham's beard; ...* (ADO II.1)

        b. *B: Saint George's half-cheek in a brooch.*
           D: Ay, and in a brooch of lead.
           B: Ay, and worn in the cap of a tooth-drawer.
           (LLL V.2)

On reading (3 b) we realise that for *tooth-drawer* the default reading is the correct one.

We can thus sum up that several factors contribute equally towards our interpretation of such deverbal derivatives: the implicational rule given in (2), the immediate linguistic context, our knowledge of the world, and our knowledge of lexical meanings (lexicalisations).

The question which remains to be solved is how to grasp this relatedness on a deeper grammatical level. Among the speculations about the nature of this essential "sameness" one can make out several different kinds with a basic divide running between approaches based on case and approaches based on cognitive concepts.

In Beard's (1981) deep-case account the partial semantic identity of Agent, Instrument, and Place consists in the fact that Agent and Instrument represent the means by which an action is carried out, no matter whether they are animate or inanimate. In other words, Agent and Instrument are specifications of the same deep case node. It should be mentioned that these deep cases operate on a completely abstract level and Beard claims that their historical origin lies in Indo-European primary cases, that is to say in those original functions marked by prepositionless cases in Latin, Greek and Sanskrit.[7] What is missing at the moment is the connection with place. But since place "and even the old ablative of source" (Beard 1981: 201) were also primary case relations of the Proto-Indo-European language, their connection with Agent and Instrument can be established. In short, there seems to be "a deep and fundamental relation between lexical derivation and the case system of IE languages" (Beard 1981: 203).

An alternative to Beard's claims about Indo-European languages is offered by the claims made by the adherents of the cognitivist approach(es) which would by definition be universal.[8]

Zbierska (1991: 30−31), for example, makes a difference between cognitive concepts which are primary (e.g., PERSON, ACTION, THING, ENTITY, PLACE ...) and cognitive concepts which are secondary or relational. The latter consist of a combination of two or more primary concepts. AGENT would thus be a relational category combining ACTION and PERSON. The derived locative nouns create some problems here: we could relate them directly to the primary concept of PLACE, but then it is difficult to see why these nouns should be hierarchically inferior to agent nouns, which are matched with a secondary concept. The situation might be salvaged by establishing a separate secondary concept LOCATION which would be defined as a combination of ACTION and PLACE. But without giving a full grounding of one's cognitive theory and the status of the concepts involved, the whole operation is in danger of turning into a game of shifting around empty labels.

The conclusion I draw from this short discussion is simple, if unsatisfactory. For the time being, I will leave undecided the question about the nature and theoretical status of my category labels, noticing with relief that there is a remarkable overlap between theories of dramatically different backgrounds. In the following I shall simply use the terms Agent, Instrument and Location as they are needed in the description of my data and simply take their underlying connectedness for granted.

The illustrations in (4)−(6) display how the existing forms link up with the functions we have just discussed. In an ideal world there would be just bi-unique relationships, but it is easy to see that things are not as simple as that. (6 a) shows the suffix *ER* in all three functions much as we know it from Modern English. At an earlier stage another form, *ELS*, had these three functions. Early Middle English (4 a) shows the reflexes of this situation, even though the form *ELS* was not productive any more at the time. Interestingly, the number of instrumental and location nouns formed by *ELS* was rather high in relation to *ELS* agent nouns, so that it is difficult to see them as mere by-products of a default agent-noun reading. This means that if English ever had a specialised instrumental noun suffix, *ELS* was it. Looking at (4 a) through (6 a), it looks decidedly as if *ER* was taking over functions from *ELS* in this respect. But *ER* was also taking over from *ENDE*. While in the earliest period, (4 a), the great bulk of agent nouns proper were taken care of by both *ENDE* and *ER*, *ENDE* disappears from the scene completely some time before 1250.

MAN, which has always occurred as the second element in compounds, shows signs of gaining suffixoid status in the Shakespeare material. Maybe it is not quite justified to leave out the brackets yet, but the possible collocations of *MAN* have clearly undergone a dramatic expansion.

Regarding the forms borrowed from French/Latin, one can observe that they show a strong tendency to specialise. Or put differently, they tend to stick to the specialised meanings of the words in which they happened to enter the English language. Their type numbers are very low.

4.2. Let us now turn to the discussion of the next "group" of derivational categories in Table 2, column a, Male and Female. It is obvious that these two notions cannot be regarded as operating on the same level as Agent and Instrument, since they cannot be realised independently of them, but only if the condition "animate agent" is fulfilled. Beard regards them as "involving subcategorisation features" very similar to Plural and Singular, thus practically equating them with "declensional features" (1981: 180). I would not agree with this position, as it seems counter-intuitive to claim some gender-related inflectional element for a language like Middle English, where grammatical gender had already been given up. But if we think of inflection and derivation in terms of a scale rather than two discrete sets of rules, we could certainly say that the categories Female and Male occupy a place much nearer the inflection end of the scale than the derivational categories which are based on cases.

In an ideally bi-unique derivational system we would imagine the existence of a neutral agent suffix to which a specialized sex-marking affix can be attached if need be. As such systems exist only rarely — if at all —, we can alternatively expect a male agent suffix and a female agent suffix both of which attach to verbs. This seems indeed to have been the case at some time in Old English and/or before, e. g., *bæcere* vs. *bæcestre*, where derivatives in *ER* would denote male agents and derivatives in *ESTRE* female agents. Also the suffix *ILD* was specialised in

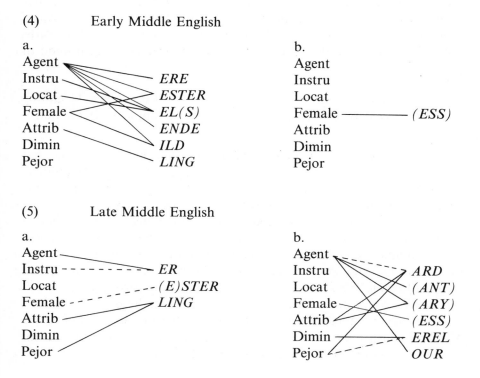

(4)   Early Middle English

a.
Agent
Instru
Locat   ERE
Female   ESTER
Attrib   EL(S)
Dimin   ENDE
Pejor   ILD
        LING

b.
Agent
Instru
Locat
Female ————— (ESS)
Attrib
Dimin
Pejor

(5)   Late Middle English

a.
Agent
Instru - - - - - - - - ER
Locat   - - - (E)STER
Female - - -   LING
Attrib
Dimin
Pejor

b.
Agent
Instru   ARD
Locat   (ANT)
Female   (ARY)
Attrib   (ESS)
Dimin   EREL
Pejor   OUR

(6)   Early Modern English

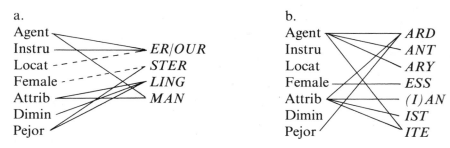

creating [+ female] nouns from verbs. This situation has left its traces in
(4 a). For whatever reasons, the system was already fairly untidy in Early
Middle English with the so-called generic reading of the former [+ male]
suffix spreading and formations in *ESTRE* allowing for [+ male] interpretations. *ILD*, on the other hand, had only very low type and token
figures. It is thus clear that the French *ESSE* with its specialisation must
have been welcome to clarify the situation, which is witnessed by the
increase in type numbers and the existence of formations with a native
base (e. g., *huntress*). Note, however, that in *ESSE* the function Agent
itself is absent. Consequently, the suffix cannot directly attach to verbs
but only to nouns which already contain the element of agenthood or
personhood, cf.

(7)   *huntress, traitress*   explicit agent-marking
           princess, giantess   implicit personhood

4.3. Looking back on our first list of notions in Table 2, we notice that
a last group of three remains to be discussed: Pejorative, Diminutive,
Augmentative. It has been suggested that they be subsumed under the
heading of gradational derivations (Beard 1981), as they share the idea
that the referent is somehow compared to an implicit norm either in
terms of size or (moral) value. In general, these gradations can be applied
to both animate and inanimate referents and often the formal exponents
for Pejorative and Augmentative are morphologically related (if not
identical), while the formal exponents of the Diminutive are often, but
not always, connected with emotionally positive readings.

   In trying to exploit this function-complex for the description of the
Middle English material I met a certain problem: there simply did not
seem to be anything which needed, or indeed, could be described in these

terms. That is to say there were no diminutives or pejoratives to be found in the texts. On the other hand, there remained a number of formations for which no label had as yet been found. Here I am referring to items like *youngling, foundling* etc., whose context makes it quite clear that they simply topicalise some attribute of the subject without any implied evaluations or "gradations". The attribute in question is denoted by the adjective or participle, which serves as the derivational base. Occasionally a pejorative or diminutive reading is possible, which suggests a partial overlap with gradational derivations after all.

In spite of what I said above about playing around with empty labels, I would like to go back to the cognitivists' idea of primary cognitive concepts briefly introduced above. Among those concepts we find PERSON and PROPERTY. If we take the liberty of postulating another relational category linking these two, we can come up with an umbrella term for our cases *youngling, foundling*, etc. and take care of their tendency to develop pejorative or diminutive (or augmentative) readings at the same time. I would like to call this relational category Attributive (cf. Szymanek 1988: 179). Pejorative, Diminutive and Augmentative would be special sub-cases of it. The three are connected by the fact that they do not only topicalise an attribute of the referent, they also relate to the speaker and his/her judgement of the referent: they are expressive categories.

Equipped with these general considerations let us now look at the diagrams (4)−(6) again. The first thing we notice is that the subcategory Augmentative is missing from the list. We do not need it for the description of our English material.

It is difficult to believe that Early Middle English was totally devoid of expressive word-formation, but this is the picture the data give and consequently this is what is represented in (4 a). In Late Middle English (5 a, b) the expressive categories link up with quite a number of forms: *LING* has developed a pejorative reading. *EREL*, which has been borrowed from French, is diminutive/pejorative but only of limited currency. It is above all *ARD* which comes alive as a pejorative suffix in its own right. This is underlined by the fact that we also find formations with native bases (*drunkard, niggard, dullard*). What may have contributed to its popularity is the wide currency and high frequency of such items as *bastard* and *coward*. They are not derivatives themselves but share a pejorative semantic element together with an identifiable phonological string. In the Shakespeare Corpus *ARD* is still going fairly strong, having given rise to another native-based derivative, namely *sluggard. EREL*, on the other hand, does not seem to have caught on. It can be found only in names of fish (e. g., *pickerel*). The other non-native suffixes or suffixoids provide only marginal numbers of types and tokens: *IST Brownist, papist, (I)AN Athenian, musician, ITE convertite*. Among the Germanic suffixes, *STER* has lost entirely its connection with Female (except in lexicalisations such as *spinster*) and turned pejorative in all new formations (*lewdster*). *LING* seems to be developing diminutive readings (*eanling*) in addition to the pejorative ones (*lifeling, changeling*) we already noticed in Middle English. At the same time *MAN* shows signs of taking over from *LING* for non-expressive attributive formations.

5. The data-base of this study is probably too small for definite conclusions, but some clear tendencies suggest themselves nevertheless. There are several obvious, if not dramatic, shifts in the morphosemantics of concrete noun derivation from Middle English to Early Modern English. English loses the last traces of a specialised instrumental suffix *EL(S)* while the realisation of the Agent and/or Attributive categories are enriched considerably, not least through loans from French and Latin.

In short, there seems to exist a limited number of basic semantic functions a subset of which are realised derivationally in a specific language. The formal morphological representatives for these derivational categories may represent one or more categories just as a derivational category may have one or more formal representations. In this manner multiple options can arise, as is for instance the case with Pejorative in Middle English, and it is through a change in the preferability of certain options that derivational systems change.[9]

Notes

1. The corpus was compiled from the *Oxford Electronic Shakespeare*.
2. I hope to replicate the data study with material from the Early Modern part of the Helsinki Corpus in the near future when I have access to that part of the corpus.
3. For example, Dressler (1986), Panagl (1987), Booij (1986), Beard (1981), Szymanek (1988), Zbierska (1991).
4. I am aware that my claim about placing the occasional/habitual/professional distinction on a different level than the Agent-Instrument-Place one is not absolutely watertight. After all, context turns out to be of crucial importance also for the Agent-Instrument-Place distinction.
5. As it stands so far, the argument is still shaky, however. After all, what we have here might be three separate derivational patterns whose formal exponent is identical through

sheer coincidence. Though we should start to wonder, if we find that this "coincidence" repeats itself in many languages. See Plank (1981: 48–49).

6. My adaptation of the OED definition of *drawer*.

7. In his 1981 book Beard maps the main lexical derivations of Indo-European languages (derivational categories in my terminology) onto Indo-European primary cases (1981: 205).

8. It may seem unfair to say this without offering a more detailed discussion of the basics of cognitive linguistics, but in working with them I cannot help being reminded of the good old-fashioned case-labels of traditional grammar. Admittedly, cognitive concepts make for very neat analyses (cf. Szymanek 1988, Zbierska 1991).

9. The idea of multiple options is of course inspired by Aitchison's (1991) concept of "multiple births" and its role in language change.

References

Adamson, Sylvia *et al.* (eds.)
1990   *Papers from the 5th International Conference on English Historical Linguistics.* (Current Issues in Linguistic Theory 65). Amsterdam: Benjamins.

Aitchison, Jean
1991   "Tadpoles, cuckoos and multiple births: language contact and models of change". Paper read at the *Conference on Language Contact and Linguistic Change*, Rydzyna (Poland), June 1991.

Beard, Robert
1981   *The Indo-European lexicon. A full synchronic theory.* Amsterdam: North Holland.

Best, Karl
1905   Die persönlichen Konkreta des Altenglischen nach ihren Suffixen geordnet. [Ph. D. dissertation, University of Straßburg.]

Booij, Geert E.
1986   "Form and meaning in morphology: the case of Dutch 'agent nouns'", *Linguistics* 24: 503–517.

Dressler, Wolfgang U.
1986   "Explanation in natural morphology, illustrated with comparative and agent-noun formation", *Linguistics* 24: 519–548.

Dressler, Wolfgang U. – Willi Mayerthaler – Oswald Panagl – Wolfgang U. Wurzel
1987   *Leitmotifs in natural morphology.* (Studies in Language Companion Series 10.) Amsterdam: Benjamins.

Güte, Johannes
1908   Die produktiven Suffixe der persönlichen Konkreta im Mittenglischen. [Ph. D. dissertation, University of Straßburg.]

Ihalainen, Ossi – Merja Kytö – Matti Rissanen
1987   "The Helsinki Corpus of English Texts: Diachronic and dialectal. Report on work in progress", in: Willem Meijs (ed.), 21–32.

Kärre, Karl
1915   *Nomina agentis in Old English.* Uppsala: Akademiska Bokhandeln.

Kastovsky, Dieter
1992   "Semantics and vocabulary". Chapter V, in: Richard M. Hogg (ed.), *The Cambridge History of the English language* Vol. 1. *The beginnings to 1066.* Cambridge: Cambridge University Press, 290—408.
Kurath, Hans, *et al.*, (eds.)
1956   *Middle English dictionary.* Ann Arbor: University of Michigan Press.
Kytö, Merja
1991   *Manual to the diachronic part of the Helsinki Corpus of English Texts. Coding conventions and lists of source texts.* Helsinki: University Press.
Kytö, Merja — Matti Rissanen
1988   "The Helsinki Corpus of English Texts: Classifying and coding the diachronic part", in: Ossi Ihalainen *et al.* (eds.), 169—179.
Marchand, Hans
1969   *Categories and types of present-day English word-formation.* (2nd edition.) München: Beck.
Markus, Manfred
1990   *Mittelenglisches Studienbuch.* Tübingen: Francke.
Marle, Jaap van
1986   "The domain hypothesis: the study of rival morphological processes", *Linguistics* 24: 601—627.
Mejis, Willem (ed.)
1987   *Corpus linguistics and beyond. Proceedings of the 17th International Conference of English Language Research on Computerized Corpora.* Amsterdam: Rodopi.
OCP.   *Oxford Concordance Programme. 1988. Micro-Computer version.* Oxford: Oxford University Press.
Panagl, Oswald
1987   "Productivity and diachronic change in morphology", in: Wolfgang U. Dressler *et al.* (eds.), 127—151.
Plank, Frans
1981   *Morphologische (Ir-) Regularitäten. Aspekte der Wortstrukturtheorie.* (Studien zur deutschen Grammatik 13). Tübingen: Narr.
Schlesinger, I. M.
1989   "Instruments as agents: On the nature of semantic relations", *Journal of Linguistics* 25: 189—211.
Shakespeare, William
1990   *Oxford Electronic Shakespeare.* Oxford: Oxford Electronic Publishing.
Szymanek, Bogdan
1988   *Categories and categorization in morphology.* Lublin: Katolickiego Uniwersytetu Lubelskiego.
Zbierska, Anna
1991   Semantic aspects of derivational affixation in the AB language. [Ph. D. dissertation, University of Poznań.]

The construction *be going to* + *infinitive* in Early Modern English

Andrei Danchev — Merja Kytö

1. Introductory notes

The development of the *be going to* + *infinitive* construction with future time reference in Early Modern English, otherwise called the andative (Ultan 1972 [1978]) or the *go*-future (Fleischman 1982), seems to be a somewhat neglected area of research. Whereas the present-day meanings and functions of this construction have received a fair amount of attention so far (cf., e. g., Wekker 1976, Fleischman 1982, Danchev — Kytö forthcoming and the references therein), the main work concerning its historical development still seems to be Mossé (1938), to which later investigators such as Scheffer (1975), Wekker (1976) and a few other more recent authors do not appear to have added anything very substantial.

This is why it might be worthwhile to (1) take a new look at the familiar old data and assumptions, (2) try to unearth some new data and (3) perhaps offer some new interpretations.

The present paper is meant to be part of a larger project, aimed at the comprehensive synchronic and diachronic contrastive analysis of the andative futures in English (with *go*) and French (with *aller*). Another part of our work, where more attention has been given to the contrastive angle (Danchev — Kytö forthcoming) was presented at the Workshop on the Origin and Development of Verbal Periphrases organised within the programme of the Tenth International Conference on Historical Linguistics held in Amsterdam in August 1991.

2. Analytic procedure

Following the practice of most authors who have investigated the *go*-futures of English, French and other languages, we have used semantic features. For this purpose we drew up a list of all the meanings that have been attributed to such forms by various researchers and subsumed them under a set of basic categories with respective subcategories. This produces something like a set of semantic distinctive features, against which the meanings of the examples drawn from various sources can be checked.

Such a procedure has its obvious advantages, its chief asset being that it facilitates the comparison with the findings of other authors who have worked on the *go*-futures of English and other languages. On the other hand, it also has some obvious shortcomings. Thus, for example, one will have to take into account the varying interpretations of different authors of the same classificatory labels, as well as the general criticisms usually levelled against this kind of semantic description.

The following set of both more generalised categories and more specific subcategories (for details, cf. Danchev—Kytö forthcoming) has been adopted for the time being:

MOVEMENT: SPATIAL DISPLACEMENT.
TEMPORALITY (FUTURITY): NEAR FUTURE, DISTANT FUTURE, FUTURE IN THE PAST.
MODALITY: INTENTION.
ASPECTUALITY: DURATION, PRESENT RELEVANCE, INCHOATIVITY.
EXPRESSIVITY: COLLOQUIALISM, EMPHASIS.

3. Data survey

In the data survey to follow we shall concentrate more on the earlier examples, up to the middle of the seventeenth century, and less so on the later ones. The computer corpora we have checked systematically include the Middle and Early Modern English sections of the *Helsinki Corpus* (basic and supplementary parts, cf. Kytö 1991: 1—2), the *Shakespeare Corpus* and the *Elizabethan and Jacobean Drama Corpus* (henceforth *Drama Corpus*), totalling in all to some 2,900,000 words.[1] For discussion, we shall also draw examples freely from basic reference works. Owing to the relatively small number of examples found in the corpora excerpted, our approach will be qualitative rather than quantitative.

3.1. The earliest examples

Beginning with the survey itself it must be admitted that it is not quite clear which to consider as the first attested instance.

Mossé (1938: § 290) adduces the somewhat dubious early example:

(1)   *Philip* (...) Was going too þe *ouer Greece*
           (*King Alisaunder*, line 901, early fourteenth century)

assuming that *þe* may stand for OE *þeon* 'thrive'. Other authors (e. g.,
Mustanoja 1960: 592−593, Pérez 1990: 56), however, have viewed it with
understandable scepticism. The fact that no other examples have been
attested between the first half (or even quarter) of the fourteenth century,
whereas this text is believed to have been written in Middle English (cf.
Baugh 1948: 182), and the next instance about a century later (see [2]
below), suggests that the example in *King Alisaunder* may not have been
a *go*-future. Had it been one, it would be somewhat strange that the next
instance should not have occurred earlier.

What should be regarded as the next example is also somewhat unclear.
Most authors accept the one given in the *Oxford English Dictionary* dated
1482 (see [3 a] below), but our search through the Middle English section
of the *Helsinki Corpus* yielded an example worth quoting, because it does
not seem to have been taken into account so far, namely:

(2)   *And thanne come Englissh folk to the seid Merchauntȝ of the*
           Maryknyght and bad theym beware whom they had lefte yn
           their Ship sayng that yt was likely be taken And there vppon
           the seid persones of the ship of Hull goyng to do *the said wrong*
           | yaf to oon henry wales Gentilman duellyng abowte the coste
           of Develyn x marcȝ to lette and arreste the seid Maister and
           Merchauntȝ wan they come downe toward their Ship cleped
           Maryknyght
                                    (*Chancery English* 1438: 174)

where the semantic features of MOVEMENT, INTENTION and NEAR
FUTURE seem to co-exist in a hierarchy that is difficult to determine.
Thus, we face here a problem that is familiar to all investigators of the
periphrastic future forms.

The example most authors regard as the first is

(3)   a. *Therfore while thys onhappy sowle by the vyctoryse pompys of*
              her enmyes was goyng to be broughte *into helle for the synne*
              and onleful lustys of her body. Loe sondenly anon came done
              an hye fro heuyn a gret lyght
                                    (*The Revelation to the Monk of Evesham* 1482: 43)

The Latin version (dated ca. 1196), commonly given as the source text,
runs as follows:

(3)   b. *Dum itaque quasi triumphalibus hostium pompis infelix ob carnis*
            illecebras agitur *in gehennam, lux repente de sublimi celorum*
            cardine copiosa emicuit

                                    (*Visio Monachi de Eynsham* 1169: 260).

As regards (3 a), it is a noteworthy fact that one of the first examples
(according to many authors *the* first) is in the past tense and in the
passive voice. It may also be noted that the translation is functionally
adequate, because the Latin verbal form *agitur* is in the passive voice and
its semantic structure contains the element of MOVEMENT, whereas the
past tense in the English text (the Latin verb is in the historical present)[2]
might be due to structural factors such as the sequence of tenses. Be that
as it may, with one of the very first examples we encounter the problem
of the relation between the original text and its translation. Was the
specific form of the translation influenced in any way by the phrasing of
the original, or did the translator use a form that was already available
in the spoken language of that time? As regards the hierarchy of the
semantic features, worth noting is Hopper — Traugott's (1993: 83) comment that in this example "the destination of the journey (hell) is an
adjunct not of *goyng to* but of *broughte*, the directionality of *going* is also
demoted, and the inference of *imminent future* (emphasis added) resulting
from the purposes of the judges of the dead is promoted". Although
Hopper — Traugott do not mention the INTENTION feature, the very
fact that prominence is given to the NEAR FUTURE component is
certainly relevant, because it suggests the possibility of early grammaticalisation, in any case earlier than has usually been assumed with respect
to this construction. We will return to this issue later on in our paper.

    Whereas in example (3 a) the text was translated from Latin, more
interest will conceivably go to translations from French, because that is
where any possible influence could have come through. Thus, for instance,
one of the early examples (mentioned by Mossé (1938: § 290), but without
the French text), namely

(4)   a. *'sir,' quod Gerames, 'we be frenchmen, pylgrymes, &* are goyng
            to offre *at ye holy sepulcre*

                                    (*Huon of Burdeux* 1534: 191)

was translated from the French

        b. *Sire ce dist gerasmes nous sommes francois qui* venons de
            aourer *le sainct sepulchre*

                                    (*Huon de Burdeux* 1513: xlviii recto)

There can hardly be any doubt that in both examples the verbal forms *goyng* and *venons* are used in their literal meaning of MOVEMENT, although one could also argue for underlying INTENTION. The crucial problem here, however, is to decide whether the use of *going* in the translation is in any way connected with the presence of *venons* in the French original, that is, whether the use of a verb of motion in the original text determined the use of a verb of motion (albeit not the exact equivalent) in the translation.

This is obviously a difficult question to answer, but it is a highly relevant one, because it reminds us of the very important circumstance that a large number of various texts were translated from French into English during the Later Middle English and Early Modern English periods. A number of authors (e. g., Workman 1940, Prins 1948, Orr 1962) have studied the effects of translations from French on the lexical and grammatical structure of English and have adduced numerous examples of such influence, in many cases amounting to straightforward calquing.[3] We too have checked on a selection of such English and French texts although our yield has not been very encouraging so far (for details cf. Danchev — Kyto forthcoming). Nevertheless, we still think that further investigation might produce some relevant results, that is, data that might fill the rather widely spaced chronological gaps between the early examples available to us now. We also hope that it might throw some light on the possible channels of penetration of such forms into English.

Another relatively early example, also quoted by Mossé (1938: §292), is:

(5)   *when you* are going to lay *a tax upon the people*
                                (Burton, *Parl. Diary* 1567: 12.1)

which seems to have only the features of INTENTION and FUTURITY, the literal sense being implied, but not made as explicit as in other examples of that period.

In the *Helsinki Corpus* we found:

(6)   *The alewyf and hir husband having long drunk owt the gayn of ther bruying indented twyxt them selvs that nether shold have a stope* [tankard] *of the best withowt money; the man being drie was content to lay down a gally halfpeny for watring his throt and began* [pledged] *to his wyf but swapt* [drank] *al of. I pledge you, sir, quoth she, and* going to fil *more.*
                                (Madox, *Diary* 1582: 88 — 89)

If we assume this to be an elliptic (with the auxiliary *am* form left out) *going to* construction, then we can say again that there are the three features of MOVEMENT, INTENTION and NEAR FUTURE in a mutually dependent configuration of implied relations, the assignment of first position hinging on the pragmatic interpretation of the specific situation.

3.2. Later examples

Let us take a look at some presumably new examples from sixteenth century drama (not including Shakespeare) thrown up by the *Drama Corpus*:

(7)   *How now, Michael, whither* are you going?
       Michael: My master hath new supped,
       and I am going to prepare *his chamber.*
                    (*Drama Corpus, Arden of Feversham* 1592)

In addition to its evidently literal meaning of MOVEMENT, example (7) also carries EXPRESSIVITY and confirms the frequent dependence of future time reference in the *going to* + *infinitive* construction on the broader context. Whereas in the question addressed to Michael, *going* is part of the progressive form, used more or less in the manner it could be used in today, the second instance of *going* in Michael's answer is combined with the infinitive of *prepare* and beside its literal meaning it also has an obvious future time reference. What is worth noting in this case is the emphatic repetition of *going* in Michael's answer, *going* thus also emerging as a text-cohesion element, i.e., as a *texteme*, which contributes to the stronger link between the different parts of the dialogue. The obvious inference to be drawn from this and other similar examples is that in a number of cases the development of the *go*-future in English (and other languages too) ought to be tackled from a text-linguistic point of view. This reminds us of Nehls' (1988: 302) words that "text types, types of speech acts and the pragmatic context, have, however, also to be taken into account when choosing the correct expression of future time in English".

The literal meaning (MOVEMENT) is again prominent in the next example, excerpted from the same source:

(8)   *But now I* am going to see *what flood it is,*
          for with the tide my master will away;
                    (*Drama Corpus, Arden of Feversham* 1592)

Depending on how we bracket examples of this type (and this would hold true of Modern English as well) we could give priority either to the features of MOVEMENT or of INTENTION, the combination of both resulting in FUTURITY.

A similar situation obtains in a third example in the same play:

(9)   *and as she followed me, I spurned her down the stairs,*
         and broke her neck, and cut her tapster's throat,
         and now I am going to fling *them in the Thames.*
                        (*Drama Corpus, Arden of Feversham* 1592)

As has been noted by various authors, the sense of MOVEMENT is also foremost in a number of examples in the works of Shakespeare, e. g.,

(10)   *... there is a messenger*
         That stays to bear my letters to my friends,
         And I am going to deliver *them.*
                        (*The Two Gentlemen of Verona* 1590 − 1591: III.1.54)

(11)   *The Duke himself will be tomorrow at court,*
         and they [the Germans] *are going to meet* him.
                        (*The Merry Wives of Windsor* 1597 − 1598: IV.3.3)

(12)   *How will you do to content this substitute,*
         and to save your brother?
         Isabella: I am *now* going to resolve *him.*
                        (*Measure for Measure* 1603: III.1.191)

(13)   *Escalus: I* am going to visit *the prisoner.*
                        (*Measure for Measure* 1603: III.1.515)

According to Nehls (1988: 305), example (13) means "I'm going *in order* to visit the prisoner", and a similar interpretation can undoubtedly be placed on most of the other examples mentioned here, including the next one:

(14)   *Pisanio: I* was going, *sir,*
         To give him welcome.

                        (*Cymbeline* 1610: I.6.56B)

There can be little doubt indeed about the prominence of the literal meaning of MOVEMENT in these examples. On the other hand, the meaning of INTENTION is clearly discernible too, and its combination with the end of the MOVEMENT actually implies future time reference.

It may also be claimed that Shakespeare did not always distinguish consistently between the simple present and present progressive judging by such examples as:

(15)   *Orlando: Then but forbear your food a little while*
         Whiles, like a doe, I go to find *my fawn*
         And give it food.
                                        (*As You Like It* 1599 — 1600: 2.7.128)

(16)   *Messala: Seek him, Titinius, whilst I* go to meet
         The noble Brutus
                                        (*Julius Caesar* 1599: 5.3.72)

which throw into relief the fact that the meaning of NEAR FUTURE can also be conveyed by the serialisation, as it were, of *find* and *give*.

The alternation of consecutive verbs with *going to* can be seen in

(17)   *Allwit: I'le* goe bid *Gossips presently my selfe*
         …
         Allwit: I am going to bid *Gossips for your W^ps child Sir*
                 (Middleton, *A chaste maid* 1630 [staged 1611 — 1613]: 19)

where *goe bid* and *going to bid* seem to function as mutually reinforcing synonyms. Given the fact that consecutive verbs "refer to two actions in discourse, one of which is *temporally subsequent* [emphasis ours] to the other" (Disterheft 1986: 293), it follows that they would often have future time reference. Examples of this type undoubtedly deserve close attention.

Worth noting is the following example, where in addition to (3 a) we have another early instance of the *going to* construction in the passive voice:

(18)   *He is fumbling with his purse-strings, as a Schoole-boy with his*
         points, when hee is going to be Whipt
                                        (Earle, *Microcosmography* 1628: 71)

also quoted by Mossé (1938: § 291) and Scheffer (1975: 271). This example, too, displays early grammaticalisation with NEAR FUTURE prominent here.

Ambiguous interpretation seems applicable to

(19)   *I thinke it is not comly to deliver privatly Notes withowt any*
         name to it to the Elders, for than whan we are goinge to pray

or to administer *the Sacrament, a note may be delivered in privat.*
(*Helsinki Corpus* [supplementary part, American English],
Keayne, *Notes* 1640),

although the INTENTION and FUTURITY features seem to prevail here.

Of particular interest is

(20)   *About to, or* going to, *is the signe of the Participle of the* future *[emphasis ours] ...: as, my father when he was about [to] die, gave me this counsell. I am [about] or* going [to] read.
(Poole 1646: 26; square brackets in the source text),

because this is an instance showing how a native speaker of that time (the author of *The English Accidence*, 1646) defined the meaning of the *going to* construction. Quite explicitly he indicates synonymy with *to be about to*, that is, NEAR FUTURE plus INTENTION.

The same interpretation can undoubtedly also be applied to

(21)   *Blanch Bodorthe doth testifie vppon Oath, that soone after this threatninge Speech, as she* was going to Bedd, *and had put on her Wastcote made of red shag Cotten, and as she was* going to hang *it vp on a pin, she held it vp betweene her Hands, and then she saw a Light*
(*Helsinki Corpus* [supplementary part, American English],
Witchcraft Annals 1649/1650: 225)

Chronologically, the next example worth considering in the *Helsinki Corpus* is:

(22)   *so they did not know whether he might not have stepped aside for debt, since at that time all people were calling in their money, (...). The council sat upon it, and* were going to order *a search of all the houses about the town; but were diverted from it, by many stories that were brought them by the duke of Norfolk:*
(Burnet, *Burnet's history of my own time* a1703: 1, II, 163–164)

The interesting thing to note here is the foregrounding of INTENTION with MOVEMENT and FUTURE IN THE PAST in second position; substitution with *will* seems impossible here. Although the clustering of semantic features is again as close as in most of the remaining examples, their ordering is clearly different. The absence of the literal meaning here (along with the above examples [19], [20] and [21]) again suggests that grammaticalisation may have set in before the middle of the seventeenth century (as claimed by Mossé [1938: §292] and various authors after him). Besides, the early development of the future-in-the-past form with its specific meaning of unfulfilled intention (cf. also example [3 a]) also indicates early paradigmatic extension, which is often regarded as another characteristic feature of grammaticalisation processes (cf. §4).

4. Discussion

The survey of the data, some of which were adduced in the foregoing section, has thrown into relief several basic issues such as the mechanism of the change whereby such originally lexical collocations were gradually grammaticalised, the time of that grammaticalisation and the causation of the whole development.

4.1. The grammaticalisation process

Concerning the grammaticalisation issue (considered at more length in Danchev — Kytö forthcoming), one might start by recalling that even the so-called ordinary future (with *shall/will*) of Modern English is regarded by numerous twentieth century authors as not yet being fully grammaticalised. Concerning the *be going to + infinitive* construction this has been noted explicitly by Hopper — Traugott (1993: 3), according to whom "the various stages of grammaticalization of *be going (to …)* coexist in Modern English."[4] We will therefore proceed from the premise that grammaticalisation ought to be regarded as a scalar, rather than as a binary phenomenon. That is, we will speak of degrees of grammaticalisation instead of binary oppositions in terms of ± GRAMMATICALISATION and this is why the features we have employed have not been prefixed by either pluses or minuses. This is where, by the way, the notion of "lexico-grammatical" category, particularly popular in recent Soviet linguistics, could be used profitably.

If we are to apply now the set of criteria for the grammaticalisation of verbal periphrases as formulated by various authors, we would get the following picture in respect of the early instances of the *go*-future in Early Modern English.

The first criterion involves the ratio between the literal and more abstract meanings of that construction. In the preceding section we saw that both seem to coexist from the very beginning (cf. [3 a]), the former prevailing though during the sixteenth century. The question arises, of course, whether the purely quantitative parameters should be taken as being the decisive ones, or whether it would not be more expedient to operate with the convenient above-mentioned blanket notion of a lexico-grammatical category. In such a case we could sidestep the tricky problem of having to fix a cut-off point of grammaticalisation (like Mossé, who indicates the mid-seventeenth century), which would appear to be a rather artificial endeavour. The difficulties of deciding whether "reanalysis" (e. g., in terms of Lightfoot 1979) is sudden or gradual are well-known. It would seem better to speak of the varying proportions of the two components — the grammatical and lexical — of this construction.

A second criterion is provided by the possible combinations of *going to* with various verbs. Although the number of early examples is rather limited, of course, from the very beginning there did not seem to be any constraints on the type of verbs that could be included in the *be going to* + *infinitive* construction. Thus, for instance, in the examples up to the seventeenth century we have verbs such as *administer, bid, bring, deliver, do, fling, give, hang, lay, meet, offer, pray, prepare, read, resolve, see, visit, whip* and others. As can easily be seen, the most varied verbs occur in this list and the variety keeps increasing throughout the second half of the seventeenth century and later, when even *go* and *come* begin to appear in this position.

The paradigmatic expansion of the respective language units offers a third criterion. It can be established at once that the present-day paradigm of the *be going to* + *infinitive* construction — present and past tense forms both in the active and passive voice — again emerged from the very beginning (it may be recalled that one of the very first examples [3 a] is in the past tense and in the passive voice). We thus confirm once more that the transition from lexical collocation towards grammatical structure in this case cannot be identified with any distinct qualitative differences during the period under consideration, but is rather a matter of changes in quantitative proportions.

As a whole, from a cross-linguistic point of view, there is nothing very remarkable about this grammaticalisation process. In fact, the gradual transition of verbs of motion, mainly *go*, towards auxiliaries of future time reference has been observed in a number of languages, e. g., in Western Romance (French, Spanish, Catalan, Portuguese), some of the

Germanic languages and dialects (above all English, but also Southern Dutch — cf. the references and data in Rooij 1985/1986), Hebrew, some Arabic dialects, a number of African languages, and elsewhere (cf. Givón 1973, Ultan 1972 [1978], Bybee *et al.* 1991). In terms of the language change typology applied in some previous work (Danchev 1989, 1991) this can therefore be considered as a fairly general (or near-universal) development.

On the other hand, as far as the notion of grammaticalisation itself is concerned, it is common knowledge that ever since its introduction by Meillet in 1912, it has been the object of frequent discussion and controversy. It has figured prominently in the works of numerous leading linguists such as Jespersen, Guxman (and a number of well-known Soviet linguists), Lightfoot, and in recent years it has attracted the attention of various cognitively oriented authors. Explanations in terms of cognitively motivated metaphorical processes have indeed been applied to a variety of grammaticalisation types, especially to the *go*-futures. As pointed out by Traugott (1988: 407), metaphorisation has traditionally been recognised primarily in lexical change, but recently many arguments have been put forward that semantic change in the course of grammaticalisation is also strongly motivated by metaphoric processes. Further on she remarks that "examples of spatio-temporal metaphors in the process of grammaticalization are widely known, and include the use of *go* for future ..." (1988: 408). More specifically this kind of explanation for the emergence of *go*-futures has been developed by Sweetser (1988: 391), who writes that "the semantic domain of time appears to be metaphorically structured in terms of motion along a linear path." In their recent work, however, Hopper—Traugott (1993: 84) claim that "The metaphor account, whereby a trajectory through space is mapped onto a trajectory in time, does not give adequate insight into why the progressive and most especially *to* are involved in the English expression *be going to.*"

Worth recalling at this point are the words of Kuryłowicz (1965: 61) "... the expression of the future is permanently renewed by forms referring to the moment of speaking", which "owing to their still perceived bond with the concrete speech situation are more expressive than the old ones." Kuryłowicz thus emerges as an eminent forerunner of all those present-day authors who speak of the PRESENT ORIENTATION (Wekker 1976: 126), CURRENT ORIENTATION (Palmer 1979: 121), or PRESENT RELEVANCE (Fleischman 1982, 1983) aspectual meanings of the *go*-futures. Another point to note in those insightful statements by Kuryłowicz is his reference to the expressive nature of such forms, which helps to explain their emergence and spread.

4.2. The actuation of change and the contact hypothesis

What has remained unclear, however, is the actuation (in terms of Weinreich *et al.* 1968) of the change. Why did it develop in English and not, say, in Standard German or Swedish, and why did it appear in English at that particular time, i. e., in Late Middle and Early Modern English and not earlier or later?

Given the fact that a very similarly constructed andative future time verbal periphrasis emerged in French somewhat earlier than in English and developed along practically parallel lines (for more details cf. Danchev — Kytö forthcoming), it is rather odd that the authors who have investigated this issue so far should have ignored this rather intriguing aspect. Could the rise of the *go*-future in English be due to transfer from French? This hypothesis gains additional support from the fact that French influence has been invoked for the existence of *go*-futures in Southern Dutch (for details cf. Rooij 1985/1986: 96 — 123, 5 — 23) and some Western German dialects (cf. Bruch 1953: 142 — 143), that is, in other French — Germanic contact areas. In view of such an overall pattern the language/dialect contact hypothesis cannot be dismissed lightly. In any case, it should be quite clear by now that the problem of the rise and spread of the *go*-future in English ought no longer to be studied in isolation, that is, within the framework of English only. Curiously, if the external influence hypothesis is taken seriously, this could actually mean foreign origin twice over, provided, of course, that one accepts the possibility of foreign influence in the appearance of the progressive tenses in English (e. g., from Celtic, Latin or French, as has been suggested by various authors — for details and references cf. Scheffer 1975: chapters XVIII and XIX).

The contact hypothesis also receives some indirect support from the lack of references (so far) to any specific dialectal developments concerning the *going to* form. On the contrary, judging by the examples in the supplementary part of the *Helsinki Corpus* it seems that *go*-futures began to appear in rather far-flung varieties of English, including Scottish and American English, within a relatively short time span.

Pursuing the contact theme further (for more details, cf. however, Danchev — Kytö forthcoming), the next question to be raised is a usual one in such cases. Assuming for the time being that the contact hypothesis is the right one, we will have to probe into the so-called "wants" and "needs" theory (cf. Vachek 1962 and for some comments Danchev 1988). Did English borrow this construction from French, because the language needed it and was it "in harmony" (as Vachek puts it in his above-mentioned paper) with the internal trends of development, or was it "imposed" on English, as happens sometimes when the contact is intense and prestige factors are involved (cf. Danchev 1990; on the distinction between "borrowing" and "imposition" cf. Guy 1990 and also van der Wurff 1991)? It may be recalled (cf. § 3) that quite a few lexical collocations and specific grammatical patterns were demonstrably calqued from French into English.

In this particular case we tend to credit the first assumption, namely that the availability through language contact of the andative construction for the expression of future time filled a need for further aspectual nuancing (cf. also the views of Kuryłowicz, mentioned above). It may be claimed indeed that after the decay of the Proto-Germanic aspectual system (presumably similar to the Slavic one), based mainly on morphological markers (prefixes), aspectual meanings began to be expressed by a variety of other means — new verbal paradigms of a mainly periphrastic nature, lexically and syntactically, i. e., through a variety of contextual means. Despite some recent advances (cf., e. g., Brinton 1988 and the references therein), English historical aspectology is still a greatly under-researched area. Even so, however, there can be no doubt that such specific aspectual meanings as DURATION, PRESENT RELEVANCE and INCHOATIVITY have played an important role in the nascence and further spread of the *go*-future in English (and other languages too). The development of the *be going to + infinitive* was evidently also facilitated by the existence of progressive *-ing* forms already fossilising into a grammatical paradigm.[5] This undoubtedly provided an important structural pattern.

5. Concluding remarks

The following points could be made to conclude this paper. First of all, despite recent advances and insights, the grammaticalisation issue still remains elusive. However, the evidence available so far and the criteria applied to its analysis suggest that the *be going to + infinitive* construction with future time reference developed somewhat earlier than has traditionally been believed, i. e., earlier than the middle of the seventeenth century. As regards its possible causation, a combination of internal and external factors seem to have been at work, the exact proportions of which are difficult to determine. There seems to be no doubt, however, that a more broadly based cross-language approach and a language change typology in terms of general (or near universal) group and idiosyncratic changes offer a more productive overall framework. Finally, the search for new evidence ought to continue.

Notes

1. The examples were retrieved using the Word Cruncher and OCP programs. The source texts and dates of composition are given for the examples cited only. The examples taken from Shakespeare's works follow the modernised spelling of the electronic version; the examples from the *Drama Corpus* are given in modern upper and lower case (the electronic version is typed in upper case throughout); the examples taken from the *Helsinki Corpus* follow the spelling conventions of the source texts.
2. For competent help in analysing correctly the Latin text we are indebted to Dr. A. Nikolova, Associate Professor at the Department of Classical Philology at the University of Sofia.
3. A number of examples have been quoted in our paper devoted to the contrast and possible contact between the *go*-futures in English and French (cf. Danchev — Kytö forthcoming).
4. According to Hopper — Traugott (1993: 3) the grammaticalisation of *be going (to)* originated in the fifteenth century of perhaps even earlier. This assumption sounds attractive, despite the fact that it does not seem to be backed up by any new evidence in their book.
5. Worth noting are the attempts to establish a connection between Old English *beon/ wesan gangende* and the later development of the *be going to* + *infinitive* construction in Early Modern English (for more details cf. Pérez 1990).

Primary texts

Burnet, Gilbert =
    1897 — 1900 Osmund Airy (ed.), *Burnet's history of my own time*. Part I. *The reign of Charles the Second*. Volumes I — II. Oxford: Clarendon Press.
Chancery English =
    1984   John H. Fisher — Malcolm Richardson — Jane L. Fisher (eds.), *An anthology of chancery English*. Knoxville: The University of Tennessee Press.
Drama Corpus =
    1980   Louis Ule — T. Howard Hill (comps.), *Elizabethan and Jacobean Drama Corpus*. Oxford: Oxford Text Archive.
Helsinki Corpus =
    1991   *The Helsinki Corpus of English Texts (diachronic part)*. Norwegian Computing Centre for the Humanities — Oxford Text Archive.
Huon de Burdeux =
    1513   *Les prouesses et faitz merveilleux du noble Huon de bordeaulx per de france, duc de guyenne*. Paris: Michel Le Noir.

Huon of Burdeux =
1882   S. L. Lee (ed.), *The boke of Duke Huon of Burdeux done into English by Sir John Bourchier, Lord Berners, and printed by Wynkyn de Worde about 1534 A. D.* (Early English Text Society, E. S. XL, XLI.) London: The Early English Text Society.
Keayne, Robert =
1639 — 46   *Notes of sermons by John Cotton and proceedings of the First Church of Boston.* MSS at the Massachusetts Historical Society.
Madox, Richard =
1976   Elizabeth Story Donno (ed.), *An Elizabethan in 1582: the diary of Richard Madox, fellow of all souls.* London: Hakluyt Society.
Middleton, Thomas
1969   *A chaste maid in cheapside, 1630.* (Facsimile). Menston: The Scolar Press Limited.
The Revelation to the Monk of Evesham =
1869   Edward Arber (ed.), *The Revelation to the Monk of Evesham. 1196. Carefully edited from the unique copy, now in the British Museum, of the edition printed by William de Machilinia about 1482.* (English Reprints 18.) London: Edward Arber.
Shakespeare Corpus =
1989   Stanley Wells — Gary Taylor (eds.), *William Shakespeare. The complete works. Electronic edition for the IMB PC.* Oxford: Oxford University Press.
Visio Monachi de Eynsham =
1903   Herbertus Thurston (ed.), *Visio Monachi de Eynsham.* (Excerptum ex Analectis Bollandianis XXII.) Bruxelles: Typis Polleunis et Ceuterick.
Witchcraft Annals =
1467   Samuel G. Drake (ed.), *Annals of witchcraft in New England, and elsewhere*
[1967]   *in the United States, from their first settlement.* (Woodward's Historical Series VIII.) New York: Benjamin Blom.

References

Alston, R. C. (ed.)
1969   *English linguistics 1500 — 1800.* (A Collection of Facsimile Reprints 5.) Menston: The Scolar Press Limited.
Axmaker, Shelley — Annie Jaisser — Helen Singmaster (eds.)
1988   *Proceedings of the Fourteenth Annual Meeting of the Berkeley Linguistics Society. General Session and Parasession of Grammaticalization.* Berkeley: Berkeley Linguistics Society.
Bahner, Werner — Joachim Schildt — Dieter Viehweger (eds.)
1991   *Proceedings of the Fourteenth International Congress of Linguists, Berlin/GDR, August 10 — August 15, 1987.* Berlin: Akademie-Verlag.
Baugh, Albert C. (ed.)
1948   *A literary history of England.* London: Routledge and Kegan Paul.
Brinton, Laurel J.
1988   *The development of English aspectual systems.* (Cambridge Studies in Linguistics 49.) Cambridge: Cambridge University Press.

Bruch, Robert
1953   *Grundlegung einer Geschichte des Luxemburgischen.* Luxemburg: P. Linden.
Bybee, Joan L. — William Pagliuca — Revere D. Perkins
1991   "Back to the future", in: Elizabeth Closs Traugott — Bernd Heine (eds.),
          17—58.
Danchev, Andrei
1988   "Language contact and language change", *Folia Linguistica* 22: 37—53.
1989   "Language change typology and adjectival comparison in contact situations",
          Folia Linguistica Historica 9: 161—174.
1990   "A note on simplification and/or complication in language contact", in:
          Lyubima Yordanova (ed.), 47—58.
1991   "Some aspects of a language change typology", in: Bahner *et al.* (eds.), 1340—
          1342.
Danchev, Andrei — Merja Kytö
forthcoming "The *go*-futures in English and French viewed as an areal feature", *Paper
          presented at the Workshop on Verbal Periphrases at the Tenth International
          Conference on Historical Linguistics, 12—18 August, Amsterdam, 1991.*
Disterheft, Dorothy
1986   "Consecutives and serials in Indo-European", in: Dieter Kastovsky —
          Aleksander Szwedek (eds.), 293—300.
Fleischman, Suzanne
1982   *The future in thought and language. Diachronic evidence from Romance.* (Cam-
          bridge Studies in Linguistics 36.) Cambridge: Cambridge University Press.
1983   "From pragmatics to grammar", *Lingua* 60: 183—213.
Givón, Talmy
1973   "The time-axis phenomenon", *Language* 49: 890—925.
Greenberg, Joseph H. (ed.)
1978   *Universals of human language.* Volume 3. Stanford: Stanford University Press.
Guy, Gregory R.
1990   "The sociolinguistic types of language change", *Diachronica* 7: 47—67.
Hopper, Paul J. — Elizabeth Closs Traugott
1993   *Grammaticalization.* Cambridge: Cambridge University Press.
Kastovsky, Dieter — Aleksander Szwedek (eds.)
1986   *Linguistics across historical and geographical boundaries,* Volume 1. Ber-
          lin — New York — Amsterdam: Mouton de Gruyter.
Kuryłowicz, Jerzy
1965   "The evolution of grammatical categories", *Diogenes* 51: 55—71.
Kytö, Merja
1991   *Manual to the diachronic part of the Helsinki Corpus of English texts: Coding
          conventions and lists of source texts.* [2nd edition, 1993.] Helsinki: Department
          of English, University of Helsinki. Cf. *Helsinki Corpus,* above.
Lehmann, Winfred P. — Yakov Malkiel (eds.)
1968   *Directions for historical linguistics: a symposium.* Austin — London: University
          of Texas Press.
Lightfoot, David W.
1979   *Principles of diachronic syntax.* (Cambridge Studies in Linguistics 23.) Cam-
          bridge: Cambridge University Press.

Mossé, Fernand
1938   *Histoire de la forme périphrastique* être + participe présent *en Germanique*. Paris: Klincksieck.
Mustanoja, Tauno F.
1960   *A Middle English syntax*. I. (Mémoires de la Société Néophilologique de Helsinki 23.) Helsinki: Société Néophilologique.
Nehls, Dietrich
1988   "Modality and the expression of future time in English", *International Review of Applied Linguistics* 26: 295—307.
The Oxford English dictionary
1888—1933 Edited by James A. H. Murray, Henry Bradley, W. A. Craigie and C. T.
[1989]   Onions. Oxford: Clarendon Press [Reprinted 1970] [Second edition 1989].
Orr, John
1962   *Old French and Modern English idiom*. Oxford: Blackwell.
Palmer, Frank R.
1979   *Modality and the English modals*. London—New York: Longman.
Pérez, Aveline
1990   "Time in motion. Grammaticalisation of the *be going to* construction in English", *La Trobe University Working Papers in Linguistics* 3: 49—64.
Poole, Joshua
1646   *The English accidence*, in: R. C. Alston (ed.), 1969.
Prins, Anton Adriaan
1948   "French phrases in English", *Neophilologus* 32: 28—39, 73—82.
Rooij, J. de
1985—86 "De toekomst in het Nederlands I, II. Over het uitdrukken van de toekomende tijd in standaardtaal en dialect", *Taal en Tongual* 37/38: 96—123, 5—32.
Scheffer, Johannes
1975   *The progressive in English*. (North-Holland Linguistic Series 15.) Amsterdam: North-Holland.
Sweetser, Eve E.
1988   "Grammaticalization and semantic bleaching", in: Shelley Axmaker—Annie Jaisser—Helen Singmaster (eds.), 389—405.
Traugott, Elizabeth Closs
1988   "Pragmatic strengthening and grammaticalizaton", in: Shelley Axmaker—Annie Jaisser—Helen Singmaster (eds.), 406—416.
Traugott, Elizabeth Closs—Bernd Heine (eds.)
1991   *Approaches to grammaticalisation*. Volume II: *Focus on types of grammatical markers*. (Typological Studies in Language 19.) Amsterdam—Philadelphia: Benjamins.
Ultan, Russel
1972   "The nature of future tenses", *Working Papers on Language Universals* 8:
[1978]   55—100.
         [Reprinted in: Joseph H. Greenberg (ed.), 83—123].
Vachek, Josef
1962   "On the interplay of external and internal factors in the development of language", *Lingua* 11: 433—448.

van der Wurff, Wim
  1991   Language contact and syntactic change: Some formal linguistic diagnostics,
             [Paper presented at the International Conference on Language Contact and
             Linguistic Change, Rydzyna, 4—8 June, 1991.]
Weinreich, Uriel — William Labov — Marvin I. Herzog
  1968   "Empirical foundations for a theory of language change", in: Winfred
             P. Lehman — Yakov Malkiel (eds.), 95—195.
Wekker, H. Chr.
  1976   *The expression of future time in contemporary British English.* (North-Holland
             Linguistic Series 28.) Amsterdam: North-Holland.
Workman, Samuel K.
  1940   *Fifteenth century translation as an influence on English prose.* (Princeton
             Studies in English 18.) Princeton: Princeton University Press.
Yordanova, Lyubima (ed.)
  1990   *Problems of sociolinguistics* 1. Sofia: Bulgarian Academy of Sciences.

"Sumer is icumen in": the seasons of the year in Middle English and Early Modern English

Andreas Fischer

1. "Ðæt gewrixle ðara feower tyda ðæt is lencten and sumer and herfest and winter": This passage from the Alfredian translation of Augustine's *Soliloquies*[1] together with a number of others demonstrates that Old English had four terms for the seasons of the year. All of these were still current in the early Middle English period, as evidenced, for example, in the early thirteenth century *Orrmulum* (ll. 11252−55):[2] "Illc an ȝer himm sellf iss all / O fowwre daless dæledd, / O sumerr & onn herrfessttid, / O winnterr & o lenntenn." The following centuries, however, saw a great deal of lexical change, beginning with the term(s) for the first season of the year. The traditional *len(c)ten*, for example, is still found in "Lenten ys come wiþ loue to toune", one of the early fourteenth century Harley lyrics, but another word, *sumer*, appears in the early thirteenth century lyric that has given this paper its title ("Sumer is icumen in") and in the late thirteenth century *The Thrush and the Nightingale*: "Somer is comen wiþ loue to toune."[3] It is clear from the context that all three poems celebrate the beginning of spring rather than summer.[4] This replacement of *len(c)ten* by *sumer* is no isolated event, but forms part of a much larger process which is the subject of this paper. Put briefly, it may be said that the "balanced" system of four Old English season words underwent considerable disturbance in the Middle English and especially the Early Modern English period, of which the extension of the meaning of *sumer* in "Sumer is icumen in" and "Sumer is comen wiþ loue to toune" is an early indicator. This disturbance went hand in hand with a process of restructuring, which eventually resulted in the Modern English system (Figure 1). In the following section, the mechanism of this process will be outlined, while section 3. constitutes an attempt to explain its ultimate causes.

2. In order to understand the situation in all its complexity it is necessary to begin with an overview of all season-words in use from Old English to Modern English.[5] As a first observation we may note that throughout the history of English there are hardly any lexical variants for 'summer'

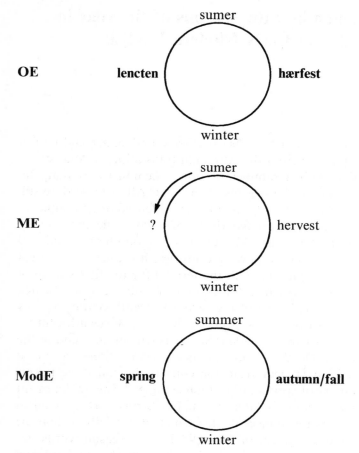

Figure 1

and 'winter', whereas there are a great many terms for 'autumn' and above all 'spring'. In the following the few attested synonyms of *summer* and *winter* will therefore be disregarded, and the focus will be on the terms for 'spring' and 'autumn'.

Already in Old English the terms *lencten* and *hærfest* were polysemous, the former meaning 'time for fasting, Quadragesima' in addition to 'first season of the year',[6] the latter 'season for reaping and gathering, harvest' in addition to 'third season of the year'. This polysemy, which is metonymic in nature, might in principle have remained stable, but the available evidence shows that both words lost their seasonal meaning some time after the Old English period and have survived only with their non-seasonal ones. Middle English *lent(en)*, the successor of Old English *lencten*, lost its seasonal meaning in the course of the fourteenth and fifteenth centuries, but as the two instances of *sumer* 'spring' quoted at the beginning show, the process may well have begun somewhat earlier.[7] The same eventually happened to *hærfest/harvest*, but its seasonal meaning did not disappear before the end of the eighteenth century.[8] Figures 2 and 3 illustrate this development in the form of semasiological diagrams.[9]

The evidence also shows that the gradual loss of the seasonal meanings of *lent(en)* and *harvest* was accompanied by a complementary development, i.e. by the emergence of new words for the seasons. It would be somewhat of an exaggeration to say that the disappearance of *lent(en)* 'spring' and, later, *harvest* 'autumn' opened up a lexical gap,[10] since there never was a time when speakers of English had no word to express the concepts 'first (or third) season of the year'. What actually happened may rather be seen as changes designed to prevent or counteract the opening up of such a lexical gap. One solution to the problem caused by the imminent disappearance of *lenten* 'spring' was the extension of the meaning of *sumer*, which is documented in the lyrics quoted at the beginning.[11] This was probably not an ideal solution from either a systematic or a functional point of view, since it destroyed the balance of the inherited season-words by making the meaning of one term (*sumer*) wider and thus potentially ambiguous. Another solution was the introduction of new terms, which is documented for both the first and third season. The onomasiological Figures 4 and 5 show all terms for 'spring' and 'autumn' in the order in which they are first attested in writing, and they further indicate the period of time during which they were (or still are) current.[12]

A comparison of Figures 4 and 5 shows that the new 'spring'-words are generally earlier than the new 'autumn'-words, which probably reflects the earlier disappearance of *lenten* meaning 'spring'.[13]

From a lexicological point of view the attested replacements fall into several groups. The earliest of these (Figure 6) comprises borrowings from either Latin and/or French, namely *ver(e)*,[14] *prime-temps* and *autumn*, all of them first documented in the fourteenth century, i.e. the period of greatest lexical intake from French, as shown by Jespersen and Baugh.[15]

A second group (found only among the 'spring'-terms) contains metonymic expressions which highlight one aspect of the season in question (*springing-time, seed-time*). *Springing-time* as a metonymic term in turn

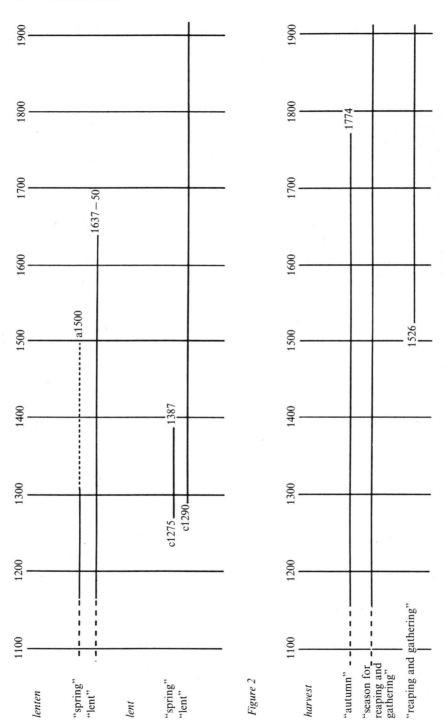

Figure 2

Figure 3

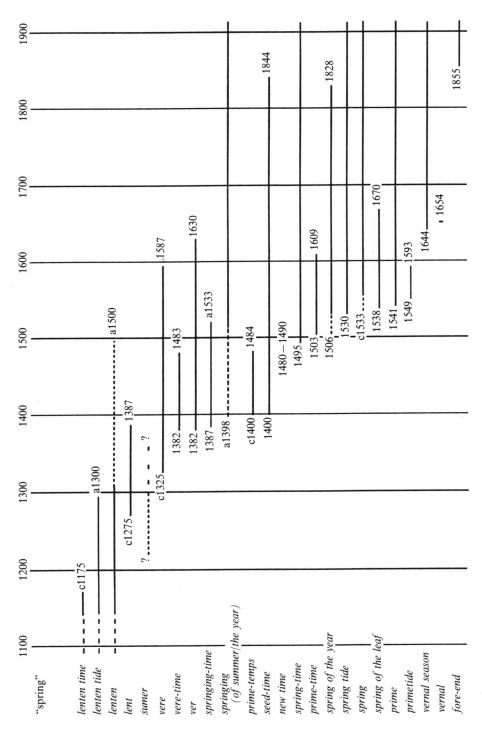

Figure 4[16]

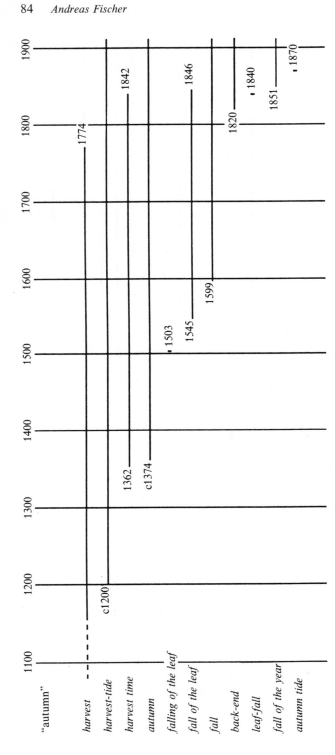

Figure 5

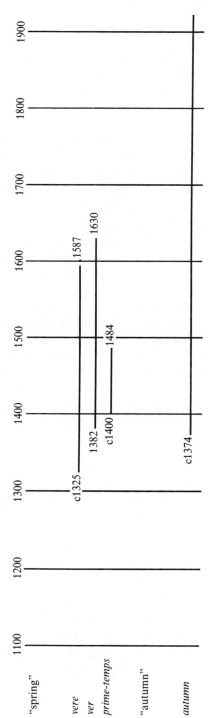

Figure 6

provides a link to a third group of words (*springing, spring, falling, fall*), which are both metonymic and metaphoric, as combinations like *spring of the leaf* (metonymic) and *spring of the year* (metaphoric) show. Like the borrowings from Latin and French, these metonymic-cum-metaphoric terms appear together, namely at the end of the fourteenth century (*springing*) and at the very end of the fifteenth and during the sixteenth centuries (Figure 7).

I should like to suggest here that it is the 'double motivation' through metonymy and metaphor, together with their semantic parallelism,[17] which may have contributed to the eventual establishment of the terms *spring* and *fall* at the expense of others. The chronology documented in Figure 7 further suggests that *fall(ing)* was coined on the analogy of *spring(ing)*, and that the presence of both *autumn* and *fall* in the vocabulary of English from the sixteenth century onwards may have hastened the demise of *harvest* 'autumn' in the eighteenth. This would indicate that while *spring* ultimately owes its existence to a drag-chain mechanism, the disappearance of *harvest* may be due to a push-chain.[18]

The evidence presented so far thus shows that the loss of two inherited season-words in English was made up for — therapeutically or preventively — by a whole series of possible replacements. These replacements coexisted with each other for considerable periods of time, but since our material so far only consists of types, that is lexemes collected from dictionaries, we know little about their status and their actual use. I have just suggested a possible reason for the eventual establishment of *spring* and *fall*, but the details of their coexistence (and competition) with the other available terms remain unclear. It is equally unclear why from all the available synonyms *spring* and *autumn* would eventually emerge as the Standard English terms, and *spring* and *fall* as the General American ones.[19] In order to find answers to these questions we would like to know more about the actual use of these words, that is, to paraphrase Fishman (1965), "who used what word to whom and when?" Following a suggestion made in Fischer (1989 a) I consulted the two available computer corpora, namely the *Helsinki Corpus of Historical English*[20] and the *Innsbruck Corpus of Middle English and Early Modern English Letters,*[21] plus the complete works of Chaucer[22] and Shakespeare.[23] The Helsinki Corpus, which comprises about 1,5 million running words, is divided into eleven periods, namely four Old English ones (O1 — O4), four Middle English ones (M1 — M4) and three Early Modern English ones (E1 — E3). The much smaller Innsbruck Corpus, comprising 48 personal letters amounting to 167,427 running words, covers the period from 1386 to

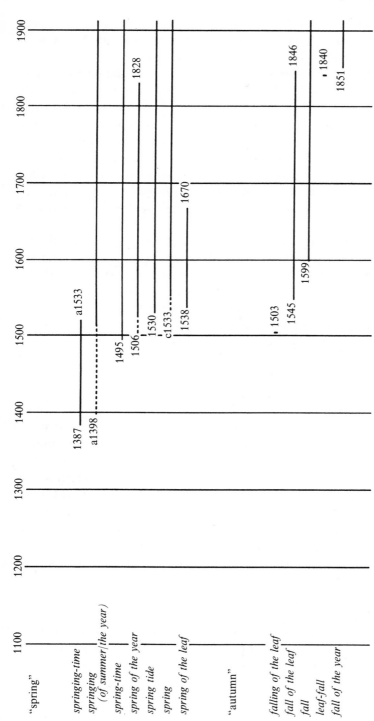

Figure 7

1688, i. e. roughly three centuries.[24] Chaucer's complete works comprise 428,915 running words,[25] Shakespeare's about twice that number, namely 884,647.[26] While such a quantitative approach may, in principle, yield interesting insights,[27] my search for season-words (i. e. the terms listed in Figures 4 and 5) proved disappointing. The two diachronic corpora with their period subsections, in particular, turned out to be too small to be useful for this particular purpose: most lexemes are represented by such few tokens that generalisations are hardly possible, and quite a few of the lexemes documented in the dictionaries are not represented at all. The two concordances turned out to be marginally more rewarding, but since each of them is the record of only one idiolect and a 'poetic' one at that, one hesitates to make any generalisations without corroborating evidence.

A look at some of the 'spring' words as used by Chaucer and Shakespeare may nevertheless show what results the method can yield. Chaucer uses *lent* four times in its religious sense, but he apparently avoids the traditional, perhaps obsolescent *lent(en)* 'spring'. His only words for 'spring' are *ver* (found once, in *Troilus and Criseyde*, I. 157), and *prime temps* (used three times in his translation of the *Roman de la Rose*, always spelled as two words). The dictionary evidence shows that both *ver(e)* and *primetemps* are new words in the fourteenth century, but the paucity of examples unfortunately makes it almost impossible to determine what status they had in Chaucer's language. Some two hundred years later, Shakespeare's normal words are clearly *spring* and *spring-time* (with together nearly forty examples), while all the other terms found in his works are so rare that they have to be seen as marked or foregrounded. This is especially true of *ver*, a word which according to the *OED* disappeared from the vocabulary of English after 1630. Shakespeare uses it three times in just two of his plays, i. e. in *Love's Labour's Lost* (c1595) and in *The Two Noble Kinsmen* (c1613). In the former play *Ver* and *Hiems* are the names of the allegorical characters that sing a song at the end (V.ii.891 − 93): "This side is Hiems, Winter; this Ver, the Spring; the one maintained by the owl, th' other by the cuckoo. Ver, begin." In *The Two Noble Kinsmen* the word is used in a similarly allegorical context, namely in the boy's song at the beginning of the play (I.i.7 − 8): "Primrose, first-born child of Ver, / Merry spring-time's harbinger." The examples from Shakespeare thus suggest that *ver*, once an 'ordinary', unmarked term, had become rare and semantically restricted before disappearing completely. This also confirms the information given in the *OED* (s. v. *ver* b) that the transferred, "more or less personified" meaning of the word survived longer than its primary one.

An example like the one just given shows that a close study of quantitative evidence may, indeed, reveal a great deal about the mechanisms of lexical and semantic change. The season-words, however, are not (yet) documented sufficiently, and most questions concerning their coexistence and competition must, for the moment at least, remain open.

3. The tacit assumption so far has been that the (linguistic) division of the year into four seasons represents a natural one. However, while sequences like the year or the 24-hour day are recurring natural periods, their beginning as well as their division into, for example, calendar months or hours is not. Cruse, who calls such temporal sequences helical chains (to distinguish them from cyclical ones),[28] comments (1986: 191):

> None of the segmentation found in helical chains seems to be wholly unmotivated, although the repeat period may be: the day, the lunar month and the year are 'natural' periods, but the week and the twelve-year cycle of Chinese year names are arbitrary. Many cases show a combination of naturalness and arbitrariness: the day is a natural period related to the rotation of the earth about its axis, but the location of the point where one day passes into the next is arbitrarily imposed.

In the case of the seasons naturalness and arbitrariness interact in various ways. While the annual cycle is characteristic of the earth as a whole (caused by its revolution around the sun), the incidence of seasons as natural phenomena varies from region to region. In the low latitudes between the tropics (that is, roughly, the equatorial belt) there are hardly any seasonal differences,[29] whereas the middle latitudes are characterised by a definite seasonal rhythm, or cycle, of temperature conditions. These temperature conditions do not change abruptly (and are subject to a great deal of fluctuation), but astronomical facts (that is, the two equinoxes on 21 March and 23 September and the two solstices on 21 June and 23 December) provide a means of segmenting this cycle into four seasons. This somewhat abstract astronomical division is paralleled by the observable and directly experienced vegetational cycle of growth/planting, maturation, decay/harvesting and rest.[30] This vegetational cycle would be of central importance in agrarian cultures of the middle latitudes, and thus most European languages have a four-word system for the seasons of the year. While in the middle latitudes the four seasons are of about equal length (astronomically, at least), "[i]n polar latitudes, the year essentially has only two seasons: a short summer and a long winter; this division is based primarily on sunlight, as there is continuous darkness all winter and continuous daylight or twilight all summer" (*Encyclopædia Britannica, Micropædia* s. v. *seasons*).

From these natural facts it follows that central and southern Europe are characterised by four distinctly felt seasons, while further north spring and autumn are shorter, distinctly transitional and thus peripheral by comparison with summer and, above all, winter. One would not be surprised to find these natural facts mirrored somehow in the languages of Europe.[31] On the basis of comparative evidence provided by the Germanic languages, supplemented by a passage from Tacitus' *Germania*, it is generally assumed that the Germanic peoples originally only distinguished between winter and summer, and that they acquired the concepts of the other two seasons later (first spring, then autumn).[32] By the time of the earliest written records the Germanic languages had acquired four-season systems, but there were, and are, remnants of the older two-season one. The Old English word *missere* 'half-year', for example, testifies to a thinking in half-years rather than quarterly seasons, as does the counting of years by winters.[33] And König (1978: 191) reports that "[i]n Teilen Schwedens haben die Mundarten bis heute noch kein Wort zur Bezeichnung der zwischen Sommer und Winter gelegenen Jahreszeiten."

It is another reflection of the original two-season system of Germanic that the terms for summer and winter are exceptionally stable in all Germanic languages,[34] whereas those for spring and autumn are unstable geographically and chronologically. The geographical instability may be seen in the many heteronyms for spring and autumn in the modern dialects of German and English, as illustrated, for example, by the maps in König (1978: 190 – 191) for German, or in Orton – Wright (1974: 188, Map 121) and Upton – Sanderson – Widdowson (1987: 35, Map 18) for English.[35]

The chronological or historical instability, on the other hand, is the phenomenon presented in detail at the beginning of this paper. Seen from this point of view, then, the mechanisms of semantic shift and lexical replacement observed in the English words for 'spring' and 'autumn' are not coincidental, but are a direct consequence of the nature of the system of season-terms in Germanic: the two prototypical Germanic season-terms were *winter* and *summer*, and this prototypicality persisted even after the two-season system was extended to a four-season one, manifesting itself in the diachronic and diatopic instability of the terms for spring and autumn. What this explanation does not account for, of course, are the chronology and the details of the changes observed. Why, for example, did *lent(en)* 'spring' fall into disuse in the late Middle English period, and why did *spring* become its eventual replacement? At present I have no answer to the first question, but as suggested above, the eventual victory of *spring* and the (subsequent) replacement of *harvest* by *fall* may be due to the dual (that is metonymic as well as metaphoric) motivation of *spring* and *fall* and their semantic parallelism.

Notes

1. Quoted from *BT* s. v. *hærfest*.
2. Quoted from *MED* s. v. *lent(en)* 1.
3. All three lyrics are printed in Brown (1932: 145 f. (No. 81), 13 (No. 6) and 101 – 107 (No. 52)).
4. Note, for example, the near-identity of "Lenten ys come wiþ loue to toune" (No. 81) and "Somer is comen wiþ loue to toune" (No. 52).
5. This overview is based on my own research, but owes a great deal to Enkvist's (1957) monograph and to material from the *Glasgow Historical Thesaurus of English* project. *The Glasgow Historical Thesaurus of English*, when completed, will present the total vocabulary of English in a manner resembling Roget's *Thesaurus*. I should like to thank Dr. Christian Kay for supplying me with photocopies of the relevant slips and for allowing me to use them.
6. Enkvist (1957: 197) points out that *lencten*, which is a common West Germanic word, acquired its special religious meaning 'Quadragesima' only in Old English. According to him the resulting ambiguity of *lencten* "explains the reluctance of many Middle English poets to use it in their descriptions of spring".
7. According to the *OED lenten* and *lent* 'spring' are last attested before 1310 and 1387, respectively, but the *MED* attests *lenten* 'spring' until before 1500.
8. The *OED* last attests it in 1774.
9. The following conventions are used in Figures 2 – 7:
   – words are listed from top to bottom in the order of their first attestation
   – broken lines (until about 1150) indicate that the words in question are already found in Old English
   – solid lines indicate the "life-span" of words according to the *OED*
   – dotted lines indicate ante- or postdatings taken from other sources; the details are given in footnotes.
10. I used this term in Fischer (1989 a: 74 – 79, esp. 76).
11. The *OED*, interestingly, does not document this meaning of *summer* at all. The *MED* (s. v. *somer* 1.) simply notes that summer is "variously dated, sometimes including part of spring". Enkvist (1957: 88 – 91) gives further examples and points out the earliest discussions of the problem known to him, by Goyle (1933) and Moore (1948), both published in *Notes and Queries*.
12. The dates of first and — sometimes — last attestation are taken from the *OED*, but are supplemented by evidence from the *MED* and other sources. If the last quotation in the *OED* is from the second half of the nineteenth century, no final date is indicated.

13. It is less evident why the potential replacements of *lenten* should be so much more numerous than those of *hervest*. The token-frequency of the 'autumn'-words is also considerably lower than that of the 'spring'-words.
14. The *OED* lists *ver* and *vere* as two separate lexemes.
15. See Baugh–Cable (1978: 177–178/§ 133).
16. Some notes concerning Figure 4:
    — *lenten:* last attested before 1310 in the *OED*, postdating according to the *MED*
    — *summer:* the available sources allow no precise dating
    — *springing:* first attested in 1513 in the *OED*, antedating according to the *MED*
    — *new time:* listed in neither the *OED* nor the *MED*, attestations (two quotations from Caxton) from Enkvist (1957: 198 and 209)
    — *spring of the year:* first attested in 1530 in the *OED*, antedating according to Enkvist (1957: 199 and 209)
    — *spring:* first attested a1547 in the *OED*, antedating according to Enkvist (1957: 199 and 210).
17. A similar semantic parallelism is exhibited by *fore-end* and *back-end* in the nineteenth century; see Figures 4 and 5 above.
18. On the notion of drag-chains and push-chains in lexicology, see especially Samuels (1972: 64–87/Ch. 5).
19. Useful general discussions of the problem of interdialectal lexical variation (or heteronymy) are to be found in Algeo (1989) and Görlach (1990). In rural English dialects both *autumn* and *fall* are common, and *autumn* is also current in American folk speech, but the history of the two terms in the two varieties between the seventeenth and twentieth centuries remains to be investigated.
20. I should like to thank Prof. Rissanen and Merja Kytö for allowing me to make use of material from the corpus and for their help in general. The actual excerpting was done by Minna Palander-Collin.
21. Information on the Innsbruck Corpus is to be found in Markus (1988) and Rainer (1989). I should like to thank Prof. Markus for allowing me to use material from the corpus. The actual excerpting was done by Peter-Martin Meier.
22. I used the concordances by Tatlock–Kennedy (1927) and Oizumi (1991), the latter being based on the *Riverside Chaucer* (Benson 1987).
23. I used the concordance by Spevack (1968–1980), which is based on the *Riverside Shakespeare* (Evans 1974).
24. See Rainer (1989: 30–38).
25. See Vol. 10 of Oizumi's *Concordance* (1991: 3).
26. See Vol. 4 of Spevack's *Concordance* (1969: 1).
27. See Fischer (1989 a) and (1989 b).
28. Cyclical configurations are typical of conceptual systems that are closed (that is, not extendable), but can be subdivided in a variety of ways. This subdivision may be universal, as has been claimed for the colour terms, or it may vary from culture to culture or from language to language.
29. "Seasonal differences [in the low latitudes] are caused by the distribution of the rainfall: winter becomes synonymous with the dry period, and summer with the wet period, in all regions except those very close to the equator where there is no seasonal variation at all." (Collier's *Encyclopedia* s. v. *seasons*).
30. Astronomy, of course, provides only one of several (ultimately arbitrary) methods of fixing the beginnings of the four seasons. Other ways of dividing the year in the

Germanic world are mentioned in Hoops (1911−1919) s. v. *Jahrteilung* and *Zeitmessung*.

31. It is beyond the scope of this paper to compare the season-terms in all European languages or, indeed, in the languages of the world. Such a comparison would be highly desirable, however.

32. See Hoops (1911−1919) s. v. *Zeitmessung*, and König (1978: 191): "Die Germanen unterschieden nur zwischen Winter und Sommer; auch einen Begriff für das Jahr hatten sie ursprünglich wahrscheinlich nicht. Die Zeit wurde vor allem nach Wintern berechnet. Diese beiden Begriffe sind im Germ. auch synonymenlos geblieben: Sie gelten auch heute noch in allen germ. Sprachen und Mundarten.
[...] Tacitus scheint uns ein Zwischenstadium um Christi Geburt zu überliefern, indem er berichtet, dass die Germanen keinen Herbst kennen."

33. In poetic language, too, years are counted as winters or summers, but not, as far as I can see, as springs or autumns. See, for example, Shakespeare's "Five summers have I spent in farthest Greece" (*Comedy of Errors* 1.1.132) or "What is six winters? they are quickly gone" (*Richard II* 1.3.260). The possibility, in German, to count a girl's age in 'springs' (*Lenze*) may be the exception that proves the rule.

34. See note 32.

35. See also *EDD*, for example s. v. *back-end, fall* and *fore-end*.
German dialects show a great deal of heteronymy for spring and autumn, English ones mainly for autumn. This is surprising in view of the fact that historically the English terms for 'spring' show greater heteronymy than those for 'autumn'.

References

Algeo, John
1989   "British-American lexical differences: a typology of interdialectal variation", in: Ofelia García−Richard Otheguy (eds.), *English across cultures, cultures across English: A reader in cross-cultural communication*. (Contributions to the Sociology of Language 53.) Berlin, New York: Mouton de Gruyter, 219−241.

Baugh, Albert C.−Thomas Cable
1978   *A history of the English language*. (3rd edition) Englewood Cliffs, New Jersey: Prentice-Hall.

Benson, Larry D. (ed.)
1987   *The Riverside Chaucer*. (3rd edition, based on *The Works of Geoffrey Chaucer*, ed. F. N. Robinson.) Boston: Houghton Mifflin.
[1988]   [Reprinted Oxford: Oxford University Press.]

Bosworth, Joseph−T. Northcote Toller (= BT)
1889   *An Anglo-Saxon dictionary*. Oxford: Oxford University Press.
1921   *An Anglo-Saxon dictionary. Supplement,* edited by T. Northcote Toller. Oxford: Oxford University Press.
1972   *An Anglo-Saxon dictionary. Addenda and corrigenda,* edited by Alistair Campbell. Oxford: Oxford University Press.

Brown, Carleton (ed.)
1932   *English lyrics of the XIIIth century*. Oxford: Clarendon Press.

Collier's *Encyclopedia*
1970   24 vols. [No indication of place.] Crowell-Collier Educational Corporation.
Cruse, David Allan
1986   *Lexical semantics.* (Cambridge Textbooks in Linguistics.) Cambridge: Cambridge University Press.
The *[New] Encyclopædia Britannica*
1974   15th ed. 20 vols. Chicago: Encyclopædia Britannica.
English Dialect Dictionary (= *EDD*)
1898–1905 Ed. Joseph Wright. 6 vols. London: Henry Frowde.
Enkvist, Nils Erik
1957   *The seasons of the year: Chapters on a motif from Beowulf to the Shepherd's Calendar.* (Societas Scientiarum Fennica, Commentationes Humanarum Litterarum XXII,4.) Helsingfors.
Evans, G. Blakemore (textual ed.)
1974   *The Riverside Shakespeare.* Boston: Houghton Mifflin.
Fischer, Andreas
1989 a   "Aspects of historical lexicology", in: Udo Fries–Martin Heusser (eds.), *Meaning and beyond: Ernst Leisi zum 70. Geburtstag.* Tübingen: Narr, 71–91.
1989 b   "Lexical change in late Old English: From *æ* to *lagu*", in: Andreas Fischer (ed.), *The history and the dialects of English: Festschrift for Eduard Kolb.* (Anglistische Forschungen 203.) Heidelberg: Winter, 103–114.
Fishman, Joshua A.
1965   "Who speaks what language to whom and when?" *Linguistique* 2: 67–88.
Görlach, Manfred
1990   "Heteronymy in international English", *English World-Wide* 11: 239–274.
Hoops, Johannes (general ed.)
1911–1919 *Reallexikon der Germanischen Altertumskunde.* 4 vols. Strassburg: Trübner.
König, Werner
1978   *dtv-Atlas zur deutschen Sprache.* (dtv 3025.) München: Deutscher Taschenbuch-Verlag.
Markus, Manfred
1988   "Middle English and Early Modern English letters as the basis of a linguistic corpus", in: Manfred Markus (ed.), *Historical English: On the occasion of Karl Brunner's 100th birthday.* (Innsbrucker Beiträge zur Kulturwissenschaft, Anglistische Reihe 1.) Innsbruck, 167–185.
Middle English Dictionary (= *MED*)
1952 ff.   Ed. Hans Kurath–Sherman M. Kuhn. Ann Arbor: The University of Michigan Press.
Oizumi, Akio (ed.)
1991   *A complete concordance to the works of Geoffrey Chaucer.* 10 vols. Hildesheim: Olms-Weidmann.
Orton, Harold–Nathalia Wright
1974   *A word geography of England.* London and New York: Seminar Press.
The Oxford English Dictionary (= *OED*)
1989   (2nd edition) J. A. Simpson–E. S. C. Weiner (eds.) 20 vols. Oxford: Clarendon Press.

Rainer, Eva Maria
   1989   *Das Perfekt im Spätmittel- und Frühneuenglischen: eine Frequenz und Funk-*
               tionsanalyse anhand von Brieftexten. (Innsbrucker Beiträge zur Kulturwissen-
               schaft, Anglistische Reihe 2.) Innsbruck.
Samuels, Michael Louis
   1972   *Linguistic evolution with special reference to English.* (Cambridge Studies in
               Linguistics 5.) Cambridge: Cambridge University Press.
Spevack, Marvin
   1968—1980 *A complete and systematic concordance to the works of Shakespeare.* 9 vols.
               Hildesheim: Georg Olms.
Tatlock, John S. P.—Arthur G. Kennedy
   1927   *A concordance to the complete works of Geoffrey Chaucer and to the Romaunt*
               of the Rose. Washington: The Carnegie Institution of Washington.
   [1963]   [Reprinted Gloucester, Mass.: Peter Smith.]
Upton, Clive—Stewart Sanderson—John Widdowson
   1987   *Word maps: A dialect atlas of England.* London: Croom Helm.

The place-name evidence for the distribution of Early Modern English dialect features: the voicing of initial /f-/

Jacek Fisiak

1.1. With the publication of *A linguistic atlas of late Medieval English*[1] (McIntosh *et al.* 1986) regional variation in Late Middle English has been well documented. Three surveys of Modern English dialects (Ellis [1889], Wright [1905] and Orton *et al.* [1962 – 1971]) provide ample evidence for the geographical variation of Modern English from the mid-nineteenth century to the second half of the present centennial. The period in between, however, has been very much neglected in this respect. Görlach (1988) calls it "the Cinderella of historical English linguistics". Indeed very little has been published on the subject thus far. The few comprehensive treatments of Early Modern English dialects available to date focus on the phonology of South Western English (Matthews 1939, Wakelin 1982, 1988). In addition there are a few works, likewise scarce, treating a single regional dialect, a dialect of a writer, or a group of writers (cf. Fisiak 1987). As both Görlach (1988: 211) and Wakelin (1988: 609) rightly point out, it is strange and not fully comprehensible why the sixteenth and the seventeenth centuries, the formative period of Modern English, have attracted so little attention of linguists with respect to the regional variation of the language, which is after all "at the heart of so many peculiar features of existing varieties of the modern world language, features which are still incompletely understood because their historical sources have not been properly investigated" (Görlach 1988: 226). This is also true, at least about some aspects, of Standard English, although unlike regional variation, it has been studied more extensively and is well-documented (see especially Dobson 1968).

1.2. One reason for the neglect of regional variation in Early Modern English is the evidence, i. e. its nature and quantity (when compared with Middle English there is much less relevant written evidence as a result of the spread of standardisation). This, however, has been compensated by local informal writings, statements of orthoepists and early grammarians, dialect imitations in literature (this type of evidence has to be handled with extreme caution), place-names recorded at the time, as well as contemporary dialect surveys and place-name studies.

The Early Modern English place-name evidence seems to be unfortunately most neglected. We hope to demonstrate below that it can provide a substantial amount of information concerning the distribution of dialectal features in Early Modern English.[2]

2.1. In what follows we will discuss the distribution of one of the most persistent dialect features, i. e. the voicing of initial /f-/ in place-names. There is plenty of evidence both onomastic and non-onomastic to study its expansion and retraction from late Old English until today (see Fisiak 1985, 1991, in preparation; Kristensson 1986). Place-names demonstrate that the voicing of /f-/ formed a relatively stable isogloss from the thirteenth to the seventeenth century (see Maps 1 to 4). The feature has been widely used by Early Modern English writers as one of the most typical and conventional signs of rusticity. For example, it appears in Shakespeare in Edgar's alleged dialect in *King Lear* (1608) when he addresses Oswald the Steward (IV.6).

> *"without* vurther *'casion*
> *'twould not ha' bin zo long 'tis by a* vortnight
> *let poor* volk *pass".*

Ben Jonson employs it in *The tale of the tub* (1596 − 1597) where, e. g., *vellow* is used instead of *fellow*. The play is "set in 'Finnsbury Hundred' (i. e., in North London) thus making it clear that this type of dialect was still being spoken much further east, even at the end of the 16th century, than it was later" (Wakelin 1982: 9). As will be seen below this is corroborated by the place-name evidence. In 1553 the author of *Respublica* uses *volke, vele* and *vorth*. In *Gammer Gurton's Needle* (mid-sixteenth century) we find forms like *vilthy, vest, vathers*, etc.

Alexander Gil in his *Logonomia Anglica* (1619) characterised the voicing of initial /f-/ as a feature of southern, eastern and western dialects which roughly corresponds to the distribution of relevant place-names in Map 4, although there is no information in *Logonomia* as regards its northern boundary.

2.2. In the fifteenth century the northern boundary of the occurrence of the voicing of /f-/ in the onomastic material runs from the east along the northern border of Essex, Hertfordshire, across the northern tip of Buck

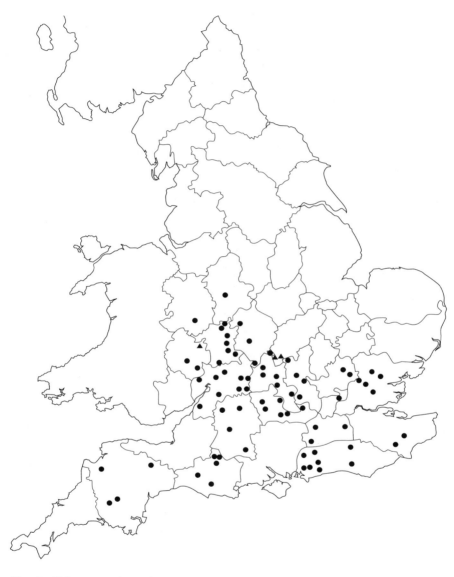

Map 1   13th century (names)
● <v– >
▲ <v– > (earlier forms)

Map 2   15th century (names)
● /v−/
▲ /v−/ approximate (Sundby 1963)

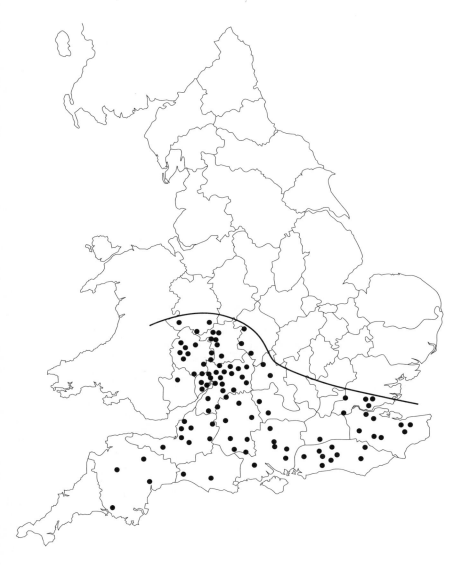

Map 3   Late Middle English (1350–1500)
McIntosh/Samuels (from Fisiak 1985)
● /v–/

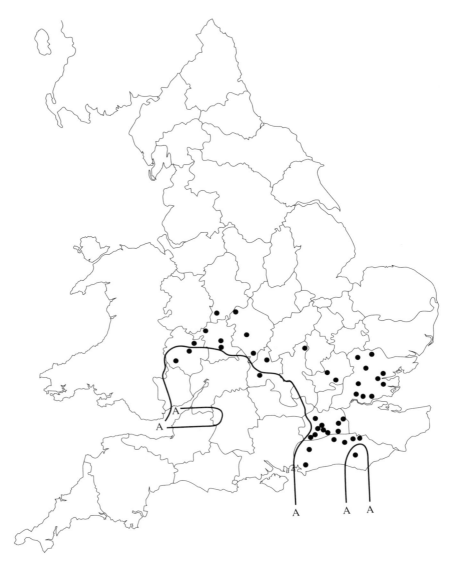

Map 4   1500−1650 (names)
- /v−/
A − SED (ORTON *et al.*)

Map 5
● Modern English /v−/ (names)
(Weber, M. 1970)

inghamshire and Northamptonshire, along the northern border of Warwickshire and across south-western Staffordshire (cf. Map 2).[3] On the basis of the textual evidence McIntosh and Samuels have established the isogloss slightly more to the south (cf. Map 3). The distribution of voiced forms in place-names in Early Modern English (1500—1650) is almost identical with that in the fifteenth century (cf. Map 4)[4] except that no forms could be found in Kent and Middlesex.

2.3. The following place-names with the voiced initial /f-/ have been recorded in Early Modern English (see Map 4):

ESSEX: *Venokes* 1542 (PHOENIX in Fairstead, EPNS XII,[5] 286), *Vanners* 1485—1509 (FANNER'S FM in Grat Totham, EPNS XII, 311), *alias Vochers croft* 1508 (J. FOUCHER from Great Warley, EPNS XII, 135), *Vambriege* 1541 (FAMBRIDGE, EPNS XII, 135), *Vulvan shott* 1605 (THE FULFEN in Saffron Walden, EPNS XII, 538), *Fyvelde* 1545 (FYFIELD, EPNS XII, 56—57), Hovells (Simon de Holeuolde 1326) 1604 (HOVEL'S FM in Great Coggeshall, EPNS XII, 366), *Bulvand* 1547 (BULPHAN ['bulvən], EPNS XII, 144), *Grenevylles* 1530 (GREENFIELDS FM in Stambourne, EPNS XII, 457), Vange 1480[6] (VANGE, EPNS XII, 174—175).

HERTFORDSHIRE: *Barven* 1556 (BARVIN PARK in Northaw, EPNS XV, 114), *Bamvylewod* 1487 (BAMVILLE in Wheathampstead, EPNS XV, 56[7]).

BUCKINGHAMSHIRE: *Veny Stratford* 1493 (FENNY STRATFORD, EPNS II, 26).

OXFORDSHIRE: *Veron Hill, Vyrynhille* 1551—1552 (FERNHILL COPSE in Upton and Signet, EPNS XXIV, 331), *Verne Hille* (FERNHILL FM in Wardington, EPNS XXIV, 427).

WARWICKSHIRE: *Veny* 1594, 1601 (FENNY COMPTON, EPNS XIII, 269), *Vernehill* 1550 (FERNHILL in Warwick St. Mary, EPNS XIII, 264), *Sutton in Colvyle, Sutton Coluell* 1503, 1504 (SUTTON COLDFIELD, EPNS XIII, 49).

STAFFORDSHIRE: *le Valowe fild* 1501 (in Bradley, EPNS XL, 140).

WORCESTERSHIRE: *Vernalls* 1613 (FERNHALLS FM in Rock, EPNS IV, 71), *the Verdroe* 1649 (FOREDRAUGHT LANE in Himbleton, EPNS IV, 136), *Edvin Loche* (EDVIN LOACH, EPNS IV, 49).

HEREFORDSHIRE: *Valde* 1545 (THE VAULD, Bannister,[8] 196), *Venn(e)* 1545, 1567 (VENN, Bannister, 197), *Vouchurch* 1538 (VOWCHURCH, Bannister, 197).

SURREY: *Vanhurst* 1684 (in Bramley, EPNS XI, 229), *Fann al Vann* 1635 (VANN FM in Hambledon, EPNS XI, 203), *Vann* 1619 (VANN HO in Ockley, EPNS XI, 278), *Vulvans* 1575 (VOLVENS in Abinger, EPNS XI, 264), *William Vallor* 1664 (VOLLERS POND in Witley, EPNS XI, 218), *Voxole* 1515 (FOXHOLES WOOD in Albury, EPNS XI, 222), *Vastspechebrigge* 1506, 1523 (FASTBRIDGE ['vɑ:stbridʒ] in Alford, EPNS XI, 222), *Veckelesholes Water* 1574 (FICKLESHOLE FM in Chelsham, EPNS XI, 314), *Vellond* 1528 (FELLAND COPSE in Horley, EPNS XI, 296), *Velley greene* 1605, 1684 (FELLOW GREEN in Chobham, EPNS XI, 115), *J. Vytel* 1544 or *Vytler* 1547 (FIDLER'S GROVE in Belchingley, EPNS XI, 310).

SUSSEX: *Verd(e)ley* 1542, 1611, 1637 (VERDLEY in Easebourne, EPNS VI, 20), *Verrege* 1565 (VERRIDGE WOOD in Frant, EPNS VII, 376), *Le Verth Wood* 1524 or *Le Vert* 1551 (VERT WOOD in Laughton, EPNS VII, 403), *Venytrowe* 1531 (VINNETROW FM in North Mundham, EPNS VI, 75), *Vexemeade* 1567 (VOX END in Horsted Keynes, EPNS VII, 337), *Venn Lands* 1649 (FENLAND in Worth, EPNS VII, 283), *Vyveashendowne* 1543 (FIVE ASH DOWN, EPNS VII, 392).

2.4. The evidence presented above is, however, uneven and requires closer examination. The conventions governing the rendering of pronunciation variants in spelling are not entirely clear. This is particulary true when it comes to non-standard local features. Socially stigmatised phonetic forms could often have been concealed behind spellings conforming with the standard. We witness it today and there is no reason why the same situation could not have existed a few centuries earlier. A cursory investigation of Forster (1981) reveals that a number of place-names spelled with ⟨f-⟩ or ⟨ph-⟩ are locally pronouned /v-/ in certain areas of England, as in the following instances:

FAIRBOARD COPPICE (WILT[9])	/'vɛərbərt/ EPNS XVI, 170
FAIRFIELDS (IW)	/'vɛərvildz/ PNIW, 286
FAIRLEE (IW)	/'vɛərli/ PNIW, 241
FALSTONE POND (WILT)	/'vɔlstən/ EPNS XVI, 345
FARFORD (D)	/'værid/ EPNS VIII, 73
FASTBRIDGE FM. (SR)	/'vɑ:stbridʒ/ EPNS XI, 222[10]
FAUNSTONE (D)	/'vænstoun/ EPNS III, LXIX
FERNEY BOTTOM (IW)	/'vɛəni/ Forster 1981, 92
FERNHILL FM. (IW)	/'və:rnil/ PNIW, 174
FINGEST (BK)	/'vindʒəst/[11] EPNS II, 176

FISHBOURNE (IW)	/'viʃbərn/ PNIW, 43
FIVE ACRES (IW)	/'vaiv/ Foster 1981, 93
FOLLATON (D)	/'vɔlətən/ Mawer 1924, 285
FORD (IW)	/'vɔ:rd/ PNIW, 286
FORE DOWN (IW)	/'vɔ:r/ PNIW, 220
FORELAND (IW)	/'vɔ:rlən(d)/ PNIW, 285
FROGHILL (IW)	/'vrɔgil/ PNIW, 286
FROSTHILLS (IW)	/'vrɔstilz/ PNIW, 286
FULFORD (IW)	/'vulvərd/ PNIW, II
FULLHOLDING (IW)	/'vulhoudn/ PNIW, 285
FURSEY BUTT (IW)	/'vʌzi/ PNIW, 286
FURZYHURST (IW)	/'vʌzihʌst/ PNIW, 187
BULPHAN (ESS)	/'bulvən/ EPNS XII, 144

2.5. Now turning to the evaluation of the Early Modern English evidence presented earlier in the paper we have to ask the fundamental question whether each ⟨f-⟩ spelling represents /f-/ and ⟨v-⟩ always renders /v-/. As has been noticed above, in Present-day English this is not always the case. Moving back into history one can likewise posit that the assumption "one wrote as one spoke" ("Man schrieb wie man sprach", cf. Stanley (1988) for a critique of this stance) is inaccurate and the existence of a perfect graphemic-phonemic one-to-one match should not be expected and is not at all corroborated by modern evidence. How then should we interpret the spelling ⟨f⟩ in *Blosefyld*, 1584 if the earlier (*Blosmeville* 1424) and the Present-day English forms (*Newton Blossomville*) contain /v-/? In this case there is only one logical solution, i. e., to recognise the fact that in some instances ⟨f-⟩ represented /v-/, as in several place-names today. ⟨f⟩ in *Blosefyld* can be accepted as a reverse spelling, a phenomenon not infrequent still in Early Modern English.

The place-name evidence adduced above is in the main unambiguous. Whenever ⟨v-⟩ appears in Early Modern English and contemporary English or is pronounced as /v-/ today, even if spelled as ⟨f⟩ or ⟨ph⟩, the voiced fricative can safely be posited for the earlier period. The consistent occurrence of ⟨v-⟩ in the sixteenth and the seventeenth centuries can be interpreted as the sign of voicing, even if Modern English has ⟨f-⟩, particularly if ⟨v-⟩ appeared also in the fourteenth and the fifteenth centuries (cf. earlier spelling conventions in *LALME* and Lass 1993). The devoicing of the initial /v-/ between Early and Present-day English can be observed in a number of a place-names under the growing influence of Standard English. The same development can be observed in the local spoken dialects (cf. Map 3 and Map 4, Line A). More difficult to interpret are the names which exhibit the ⟨f⟩ ~ ⟨v⟩ alternation in Early Modern English, represented by /f/ in Present-day English pronunciation and preceded in the fourteenth and the fifteenth centuries by ⟨f⟩-forms. One could argue equally well for both /f-/ and /v-/ in *Fulven* ~ *Vulven* 1605 Ess, *Voxhole* 1515 ~ *Foxhole* 1541 Sr, *Fekilskild* 1568 ~ *Veckelsholes* 1574 Sr, etc. Fortunately, there are only seven such debatable place-names from Sussex, Surrey and Essex altogether. If we remove them from our evidence, the northern boundary of the distribution of the voiced /v-/ will remain intact. Following, however, the variationists' approach (Chen, Labov, Toon), we might accept the ⟨f⟩ ~ ⟨v⟩ spellings as reflecting items which were voiced variably and not categorically.

3. In conclusion it is possible to say, based on place-name evidence, that the voicing of the initial /f-/ > /v-/ had almost the same distribution in Early Modern English as in the thirteenth and the fifteenth centuries (cf. Maps 1, 2 and 4). There is no way to reconstruct it for the Early Modern English period in non-onomastic material at the moment. This will have to await a detailed investigation of private local records, letters, diaries and other informal writings. The comparison of the fifteenth century textual evidence (see Map 3) and Orton's *Survey of English dialects* (see Line A in Map 4) shows, however, that a drastic change occurred some time between late Middle English and now. For all we know, it did not happen between 1500 – 1700. The comparison of the voicing in place-names in Early Modern English and now seems to corroborate this. /v-/ still appears in place-names in Essex, Hertfordshire, Buckinghamshire, Worcestershire, Warwickshire, Herefordshire, Northampton, Surrey and Sussex.[12] Voitl argues convincingly that "the decisive step in the process of the ousting of initial fricative voicing through London and standard speech influences, and its recession to its relic extent as we find it in dialect maps today, only occurred with the onset of industrialisation, and the first wave of urbanisation in the early nineteenth century" (Voitl 1988: 580). Place-names which are always more conservative, can still be found in Present-day English with the initial voicing outside the relic areas referred to by Voitl (i. e., line A in Map 4).

Notes

1. Henceforth abbreviated as *LALME.*
2. Although Wakelin and others recognise the value of the place-name evidence, to our knowledge no systematic study of it has been presented thus far.

3. Wakelin (1982: 9) has established the western part of the isogloss further to the south ignoring Staffordshire and Warwickshire.
4. Since the focus of the paper is on the northerly boundary of the distribution of the voiced forms, no information has been mapped for the South-East and South-West England in Map 2 and the South-West England in Map 4.
5. EPNS 12 = *English Place-Name Society Survey*, vol. 12 (ESSEX).
6. Since /v-/ appears earlier and later, one can safely assume that the initial consonant was also voiced in Early Modern English. Its absence from written records is purely accidental.
7. See note 6 above.
8. See Bannister, A. T. in *References*.
9. Wilt = Wiltshire, IW = Isle of Wight, D = Devon, Sr = Surrey, Bk = Buckingham, Ess = Essex.
10. *Vastspechebrigge* 1506, 1523.
11. /'findʒəst/ also occurs.
12. Cf. Map 5 and the list of place names on pages 105 and 106.

References

Armstrong, A. M., *et al.*
  1952   *The place-names of Cumberland.* Vol. III. (EPNS XXII). Cambridge: Cambridge University Press.
Bannister, A. T.
  1916   *The place-names of Hertfordshire.* Cambridge: Cambridge University Press.
Dobson, Eric J.
  1968   *English pronunciation 1500 — 1700.* Oxford: Clarendon Press.
Ellis, Alexander J.
  1889   *On early English pronunciation.* Vol. V. London: Philological Society.
Fisiak, Jacek
  1985   "The voicing of initial fricatives in Middle English", *SAP* 17: 3 — 16 (+ 7 maps).
  1987   *A bibliography of writings for the history of English.* Berlin: Mouton de Gruyter.
  1991   "A note on the voicing of initial /f-/ in English in the 15th century: onomastic evidence", in: Arthur van Essen — Ned Burkart (eds.), *Homage to William R. Lee.* Berlin: Mouton de Gruyter, 233 — 237.
  in preparation "A note on the voicing of initial fricatives in Early Middle English: Place-names."
Fisiak, Jacek (ed.)
  1988   *Historical dialectology: social and regional.* Berlin: Mouton de Gruyter.
Forster, John
  1981   *A pronouncing dictionary of Engl. place names: including standard local and archaic variants.* London, Boston, Henley: Routledge & Kegan Paul.
Gelling, Margaret
  1953 — 54 *The place-names of Oxfordshire.* (EPNS XXII — XXIV). Cambridge: Cambridge University Press.

Görlach, Manfred
1988   "The study of early Modern English variation — the Cinderella of English historical linguistics", in: Jacek Fisiak (ed.), 1988: 211—228.
Gover, J. E. B. *et al.*
1931—32   *The place-names of Devon.* (EPNS VIII—IX). Cambridge: Cambridge University Press.
1934   *The place-names of Surrey.* (EPNS XI). Cambridge: Cambridge University Press.
1936   *The place-names of Warwickshire.* (EPNS XIII). Cambridge: Cambridge University Press.
1938   *The place-names of Hertfordshire.* (EPNS XV). Cambridge: Cambridge University Press.
1939   *The place-names of Wiltshire.* (EPNS XVI). Cambridge: Cambridge University Press.
Kökeritz, Helge
1940   *The place-names of the Isle of Wight.* (PNIW). Uppsala: Almqvist & Wiksell.
Kristensson, Gillis
1986   "On voicing of initial fricatives in ME", *SAP* 19: 3—10.
Lass, Roger
1993   "Old English fricative voicing unvisited", *SAP* 25—27: 3—45.
Matthews, William
1939   "South Western dialect in the early modern period", *Neophilologus* 24: 193—209.
Mawer, A.
1924   "English place-names and their pronunciation", *Discovery* 5: 284—299.
Mawer, A.—F. M. Stenton
1925   *The place-names of Buckinghamshire.* (EPNS II). Cambridge: Cambridge University Press.
1929—30   *The place-names of Sussex.* (EPNS VI—VII). Cambridge: Cambridge University Press.
Mawer, A. *et al.*
1927   *The place-names of Worcestershire.* (EPNS IV). Cambridge: Cambridge University Press.
McIntosh, Angus *et al.*
1986   *A linguistic atlas of late Medieval English.* 4 vols. Aberdeen: Aberdeen University Press.
Oakden, J. P.
1984   *The place-names of Staffordshire.* (EPNS LV). Cambridge: Cambridge University Press.
Orton, Harold *et al.*
1962—71   *Survey of English dialects.* 4 vols. Leeds: Arnold.
Reaney, Percy H.
1935   *The place-names of Essex.* (EPNS XII). Cambridge: Cambridge University Press.
Stanley, Eric G.
1988   "Karl Luick's 'Man schrieb wie man sprach' and English historical philology", in: Dieter Kastovsky—Gero Bauer (eds.), *Luick revisited.* Tübingen: Narr, 311—334.

Sundby, Bertil
   1963   *Studies in the Middle English dialect material of Worcester records.* (Norwegian
              Studies in English 10.) Bergen, Oslo: Norwegian University Press.
Voitl, Herbert
   1988   "The history of voicing of initial fricatives in Southern England: A case of
              conflict between regional and social dialect", in: Jacek Fisiak (ed.), 565—600.
Wakelin, Martyn
   1982   "Evidence for spoken regional English in the sixteenth century", *Revista
              Canaría de Estudios Ingleses* 5: 1—25.
   1988   "The phonology of South-Western English 1500—1700", in: Jacek Fisiak
              (ed.), 609—644.
Weber, Michael
   1970   Die südenglische Anlauterweichung der stimmlosen Spiranten [f, s, θ, ʃ] in
              den englischen Orts- und Personennamen. [Unpublished MS, University of
              Erlangen.]
Wright, Joseph
   1905   *The English dialect grammar.* Oxford: Clarendon Press.

Text deixis in Early Modern English

Udo Fries

1. Introduction

This is a first survey of text deictic construction in Early Modern English based on a preliminary version of the *Diachronic Part of the Helsinki Corpus of Texts.*[1] A general discussion of text deixis can be found in Fries (in press). Here I repeat some of the basic notions which are necessary for an understanding of this paper.

In text deixis, an encoder differentiates a domain within the course of a text as closer or more distant. "The point of orientation represents the momentary situation of the encoder in the course of a text" (Rauh 1983: 42).

What we have got to distinguish is 1) the here and now, 2) the before, 3) the after. Within these three spheres we may look for text-deictic expressions of varying degrees of complexity. Table 1 is adapted from Kurzon (1985: 192) and gives a summary of the most common types of text deixis.

Table 1. Text-deictic constructions

(1)	Adverbials	*here, now, above, below*
	Prepositional phrases	
	(a) with *this*	*in this section*
	(b) with *above/below* etc.	*in the above figures*
	Noun phrases (as subjects or objects)	
	(a) with *this*	*this section*
	(b) with *above/below* etc.	*the above figure*
(2)	dependent clauses	
	(a) relative	*in the first sense mentioned above, as has been suggested above*
	(b) others	*Before going further*
	main clauses	
	(followed by subordinated clauses)	*The illustrations in the following/above passages will show how ...*
	independent clauses	*Values for this function are presented in Figure 1/above.*

We must distinguish between central words — adverbials, prepositional phrases, the demonstrative *this* — (as shown in Table 1[1]) and their occurrence in a particular context (shown in Table 1[2]). As a rule, it is not the central words alone that are text-deictic, i.e. the adverb, the prepositional phrase, or the noun phrase, but only their occurrence within a specific structure, a sentence or a clause, that gives the whole structure its text-deictic function (cf. Kurzon 1985: 190). The central parts are, however, as we will see presently, of great importance for locating these constructions in texts.

There are obvious and well-known difficulties attached to the work with corpora, which I need not reiterate here; let me, quite on the contrary, point to one of the advantages of this particular corpus: its classification of the entire material into text-prototypes and text types, with a uniform system from Old English to Early Modern English.

2.   Text deixis in Early Modern English
2.1. *Here* and *now*

The most obvious candidates for text deixis in Early Modern English are the adverbs *here* and *now*. Just as in Present-day English the vast majority of these adverbs, however, do not function text-deictically, and it is the human investigator, not the computer, who has to distinguish between those which do and those which do not.

Contrary to expectations, *here* has not been a major item of text deixis in the history of English. For Old English, of the 660 instances of the adverb *hēr* in the *Helsinki Corpus*, only 7 occur together with a present tense form of *secgan*, 5 of which are text-deictically relevant. For the Middle English part of the corpus, it is only 5 instances, of which two are clearly instances of text-deixis.

Now, on the other hand, is more interesting. All sentences in which *now* occurs text-deictically have either *we* or *I* as their subjects, which gives us a clue of how to find text-deictic *now* in the corpus: we take a look at all combinations of *now* + the first person pronouns *I* or *we*, and in a second step eliminate all constructions which do not refer to the areas of speaking, writing, or listening. For Old English this procedure yielded 45 text-deictic examples of *nū* + *Ic/wē*. There are fewer Middle English *now* + *I/we* examples. The best-known may be the one from the prologue to the *Canterbury Tales*:

(1)   *Now haue I toold you soothly, in a clause,*
             Th'estaat, th'array, the nombre and eek the cause

ME3 NI FICT CTPROL *EMS: 24

In the Early Modern English (EModE) part of the corpus, such an attempt of finding text deictic candidates of text deixis yields 30 instances of *now + I/we*. As in the earlier periods of the language, the author tells the reader what he/she (= the author) is going to say or do now, which also includes what he is going to say or do next.

(2)   *your Grace to accepte graciously and favorably the thinge which*
             now I write both for the ardent love which I bere unto your
             Grace, ...

EB1 XX CORO TUNSTAL HIGH PR: 2

This is a useful means of structuring a text, establishing a contrast between something that was mentioned before and something that is going to come later on, as in (3):

(3)   *I haue spoken of Briberie and Simonie, and now I must speake*
             of their sister Vsurie.

EB2 IR SERM SMITH PROF: Heading
             Now I proceed in my letter, it is Moonday, past 6

EB3 XX CORP HOXINDE PROF: 293

Instead of the simple present (*now I write, now I must speake, now I proceed*), forms with *will* or *shall* are frequent.

(4)   *Now will I procede seriously and in a due forme to speke more*
             particulerly of these thre vertues.

EB1 IS/EX EDUC ELYO HIGH PR: 148
             Wherefore I will now attempt to make a generall and faithfull
             perambulation of learning, ...

EB2 EX EDUC BACON HIGH: 22
             This hath been a very wet day here at London.
             I shall now say no more then that no man can have a more real
             heart toward any then hath to Thee and Thine

EB3 XX CORP HOXINDE PROF: 293

Besides reference to the point of writing and to future activities, there is an old tradition of employing *now* in constructions referring to the immediate past, as in Chaucer's example in (1). The author/speaker tells the reader/listener what he has heard before, summing up a passage at the time of speaking. Again this is a means of structuring a text. The only example in the Early Modern English corpus is (5):

(5)   *Notwithstanding, seeing now I haue toulde you of it, I will take
            my gelding and get me home.*

EB2 NI FICT DELONEY OTHER: 84

The *Helsinki Corpus* distinguishes between three periods of Early Modern English: I (1500−1570), II (1570−1640), and III (1640−1710). The construction is found more frequently in periods I and II, less frequently in period III. The results are summarised in Table 2.

Table 2. Occurrence of *now + I/we*

Period I:	12
Period II:	13
Period III:	6

The decrease of examples in period III may be due to a different set of text types included in that period. This will have to be investigated more closely.

There are 16 different verbs employed in these constructions with *now*: they are *speak* (used 6 times), *say* and *proceed* (occurring 3 times each), *ask, write, think, add, attempt, tell* (twice each), and *endeavour, begin, confess, treat, set down, intend* and *receive* (once each). These verbs should be followed up in eighteenth and nineteenth century English. The verbs are listed in table 3.

Table 3. Individual verbs used with *now + I/we*

Period	I	II	III	Total	Period	I	II	III	Total
speak	2	4	—	6	endeavour	1	—	—	1
say	2	—	1	3	begin	1	—	—	1
proceed	1	1	1	3	confess	—	1	—	1
ask	2	—	—	2	treat	—	1	—	1
write	2	—	—	2	set down	—	1	—	1
think	1	1	—	2	intend	—	—	1	1
add	—	—	2	2	receive	—	—	1	1
attempt	—	2	—	2					
tell	—	2	—	2					

Shall, will and *would* are employed 16 times, the simple present 11 times, various auxiliaries twice, and the present perfect twice, one of which is example (5) above (cf. Table 4).

Table 4. Use of tenses in constructions of *now* + *I/we*

Period	I	II	III	Total
Shall/will/would	7	6	3	16
Present tense	5	4	2	11
Auxiliaries	–	2	–	2
Present perfect	–	1	1	2

The *now* + *I/we*-construction is mainly found in expository and instructive text prototypes (Table 5).

Table 5. Occurrences of *now* + *I/we* in prototypical text categories

Prototypical text category		Period			Total
		I	II	III	
IS/EX	Instruction secular/expository	4	3	–	7
EX	expository	3	3	2	8
IR	instruction religious	2	1	–	3
AR	argumentative	2	3	–	5
NI	narration imaginative	–	1	–	1
NN	narration non-imaginative	–	–	1	1
XX	text type X	1	2	3	6

With regard to text types, it is educational treatises, science ('other': not medicine), and proceedings/trials, which are most important, followed by sermons and correspondence (Table 6).

Table 6. Occurrences of *now* + *I/we* in individual text types

Text type		Period			Total
		I	II	III	
IS/EX	Educational treatise	4	3	–	7
EX	Science, 'other'	3	1	2	6
EX	Science, medicine	–	2	–	2
IR	Sermon	2	1	–	3
AR	Proceeding, trial	2	3	–	5
NI	Fiction	–	1	–	1
NN	Diary	–	–	1	1
XX	Correspondence, not private	1	–	–	1
XX	Correspondence, private	–	–	3	3
XX	Philosophy	–	2	–	2

On the whole, the figures obtained through the *Helsinki Corpus* for the construction *now* + *I/we* is not very high and should be supplemented by a more careful study of the text types yielding the best score in the *Helsinki Corpus*.

2.2. Reference to preceding sections
2.2.1. *before*

In Old English, the adverbs most commonly used for reference to earlier passages in a text are *ǣr*, *beforan*, and *bufan*. Of these *ǣr* is the one most frequently used in Old English, followed by *beforan*, and *bufan*. The *Helsinki Corpus* lists 137 instances of Old English *before*, 30 odd of which are text-deictical. In the Early Modern English part of the corpus *before* occurs altogether 840 times. Less than 10% of which, i. e. 81 instances, are text-deictic.

All of them occur together with a verb of saying or − in one instance − hearing. Table 7 gives a list of all the verbs involved in the Early Modern English corpus:

Table 7. Verbs occurring in text-deictic constructions with *before*.

allege	make report	rehearse
describe	mention	say
direct	name	show
express	note	speak
give	observe	specify
hear	propound	tell

A majority of instances occurs in impersonal constructions (66%): *as is seid before, before expressed, before specyfyed, mentioned before*, etc. Words which occur in both impersonal and personal constructions are *describe, give, rehearse, say, show, speak,* and *tell. Say* is the most common one, with 18 instances, 8 in impersonal constructions (*as is seid before*), and 10 in personal ones (*as I [have] seid before*). Among the impersonal constructions, *mentioned before* is the most frequently used item.

With regard to prototypical text categories these impersonal constructions occur chiefly in non-imaginative narration and expository texts, followed by secular instruction and statutory texts (Table 8).
Individual expressions cluster in the same texts:

as (is) before **directed** occurs only in secular instruction text type "other" handbooks, and in one text: T. Langford, Plain and Full Instructions to Raise All Sorts of Fruit-Trees that Prosper in England, 1699.

the matter/those remedies before **rehearsed** occurs only in expository texts, text type science, medicine, and in one text: William Clowes, Treatise for the Artificiall Cure of Struma, 1602.

as before is **showed** occurs once in imaginative narration, but clusters in non-imaginative narration, three times in the text type history, again

Table 8. Occurrences of *before* in impersonal constructions in prototypical text categories

Prototypical text category		Period			Total
		I	II	III	
IS/EX	Instruction secular/ expository	1	–	–	1
EX	expository	2	11	–	13
IR	instruction religious	–	2	–	2
IS	instruction secular	4	2	3	9
AR	argumentative	1	1	–	2
NI	narration imaginative	1	–	–	1
NN	narration non-imaginative	4	6	5	15
STA	statutory	3	–	5	8
XX	text type X	–	–	1	1

in just one text: Robert Fabyan, THE NEW CHRONICLES OF ENGLAND AND FRANCE, 1516.

before **expressed** occurs in periods 1 and 2 in the statutory text category, text type law, THE STATUTES OF THE REALM, PRINTED BY COMMAND OF HIS MAJESTY KING GEORGE THE THIRD IN PURSUANCE OF AN ADDRESS OF THE HOUSE OF COMMONS OF GREAT BRITAIN, VOLS. 3 AND 4. The same texts use the phrase *before* **mentioned**, which is one of the more frequent expressions used in periods 2 and 3, vols. 4 and 7, respectively.

before **named** clusters in period 1 in secular instruction, text type "other" handbooks, text William Turner, A NEWE BOKE OF THE NATURES AND PROPERTIES OF ALL WINES, 1568, and has another instance in period 2, of the same categories, in Gervase Markham, CONTREY CONTENTMENTS, 1615. In period 2 it clusters (4 instances in only a few lines) in the expository text category, text type science, medicine, text: William Clowes, TREATISE FOR THE ARTIFICIALL CURE OF STRUMA, 1602, which, thus, occurs for the second time, after *the remedies before rehearsed* (above).

said **before** occurs in period 2 in the expository category, in two text types, science, "other", and science, medicine, Blundeville, A BRIEFE DESCRIPTION OF THE TABLES OF THE THREE SPECIALL RIGHT LINES BELONGING TO A CIRCLE, CALLED SIGNES, LINES TANGENT, AND LINES SECANT, 1597, and the Struma text mentioned before. In period 3 it clusters in non-imaginative narration, text type history, John Milton, The History of Britain, THAT PART ESPECIALLY NOW CALL'D ENGLAND, 1670.

Among the personal constructions, *as I (have) seid before* is the most frequent one (10 instances), followed by *I tolde (you) before* (4 instances), *as before I have shewyd*, and *as before I described him* (2 each). The others (1 instance each) are: *I rehersed before, I alledged unto you, I have before*

made report, I have before given, I have spoken before, and *I before noted*.
   Personal constructions with the second person pronoun *you* — i. e.
reference to the reader also occur — albeit very seldom only: *as ye have hard before, as you are before tolde*.
   With regard to prototypical text categories these personal constructions occur chiefly in expository texts, followed by non-imaginative narration and secular instruction (Table 9).

Table 9. Occurrences of *before* in personal constructions in prototypical text categories

Prototypical text category		Period			Total
		I	II	III	
IS/EX	Instruction secular/ expository	1	—	—	1
EX	expository	3	6	—	9
IR	instruction religious	2	—	—	2
IS	instruction secular	1	1	3	5
AR	argumentative	—	1	1	2
NI	narration imaginative	2	1	—	3
NN	narration non-imaginative	3	1	2	6
STA	statutory	—	1	—	1
XX	text type X	1	1	—	2

Comparing the results with Table 8 we can see that the same prototypical text categories are in the lead, though in a reverse order: expository texts and non-imaginative narration. Secular instruction is third in both types, while statutory texts clearly prefer the impersonal construction.
   If we take all the text-deictic *before*-constructions together we get the figures shown in Table 10.

Table 10. Occurrences of text-deictic *before* in prototypical text categories

Prototypical text category		Period			Total
		I	II	III	
IS/EX	Instruction secular/ expository	2	—	—	2
EX	expository	5	17	—	22
IR	instruction religious	2	2	—	4
IS	instruction secular	5	3	6	14
AR	argumentative	1	2	1	4
NI	narration imaginative	3	1	—	4
NN	narration non-imaginative	7	7	7	21
STA	statutory	3	1	5	9
XX	text type X	1	1	1	3

Individual expressions do not cluster to the same extent as we found with the impersonal constructions: the only instance is *as I (have) seid before* in expository texts, text type science, "other": Blundeville, and the same in secular instruction, text type educational treatise: John Locke: DIRECTIONS CONCERNING EDUCATION. The text by Blundeville we encountered before with the impersonal *said before*-construction. The personal/impersonal dichotomy, therefore, does not seem to be relevant for this particular text.

An exact reference to the place referred to in the text is relatively rare: this is the whole list:

(6)   *that was spoken of in the laste Chapter before*
                                    (EB1 EX SCIM VICARY PROF: 29)
            as before in the ende of the Story of the seconde Ryharde is shewyd
                                    (EB1 NN HIST FABYAN PROF: Heading)
            as ys before expressed in and by the said Statute made in the Fyfte and Sixt yeres of Kinge Edwarde ...
                                    (EB2 STA LAW STAT4 X: 5)

2.2.2. afore and fore

So far we have discussed *before* in isolation, but *before* is just one of the text deictic elements referring to earlier text passages. In the Middle English part of the corpus there are, e. g., many text-deictic instances of *afore* and *fore*, usually before a past participle as a reduced relative clause. Often they form compounds with a verb of speaking. This usage is carried over into Early Modern English, but *afore* as a word of its own gradually disappears from the language: in the first part of the corpus there are still 36 instances of *afore*, in the second 8, and in the third just one. Of the 36 instances in the first part, one third (i. e. 12) are text-deictic, of the 8 in the second part, 4 are text-deictic; the single instance of the third period is not text-deictically used. This gives us 16 instances altogether, of which *afore seid* (both with and without *to be*) is the most common one.

(7)   *as is afore seid*   (EB1 STA LAW STAT3 X: 2)
            accronding to the wordes of the Theoreme afore saide.
                                    (EB1 EX SCIO RECORD PROF: 20)

Other combinations with *afore* include *as I haue told you afore, afore rehersed, specified, declared, I have spoken afore, afore remembred* and *mencioned*. This means that two verbs must be added to the list in Table 7: *declare* and *remember*.

It does not come as a surprise that non-imaginative narration figures again prominently in the constructions with *afore*; as a new feature we find the largest number of instances of *afore* in statutory texts (cf. Table 11, period I and total), both *afore said* and *afore rehearsed* are typical for the Statutes of the Realm (vol. III).

Table 11. Occurrences of text-deictic *afore* in prototypical text categories

Prototypical text category		Period			Total
		I	II	III	
EX	expository	1	–	–	1
NN	narration non-imaginative	4	–	–	4
STA	statutory	7	1	–	8
XX	text type X	–	3	–	3

While we see a decrease during the Early Modern English period of instances of *afore* as a separate word, we find an increase of *afore* as the first part of the compound participle verbs: *aforesaid, aforenamed,* and *aforerehearsed. Aforesaid* occurs in all three periods, *aforenamed* in the first and second, *aforerehearsed* in the first only. There is an increase from 37 examples in the first, via 74 examples in the second, to 77 examples in the third period. *Aforesaid* competes with the shorter *foresaid*, which has a long history in English. *Aforesaid* is, beyond all doubt, typical for the statutory text category (Table 12).

Table 12. Occurrences of *afore*-compounds in prototypical text categories

Prototypical text category		Period			Total
		I	II	III	
EX	expository	4	1	–	5
AR	argumentative	3	1	–	4
NN	narration non-imaginative	5	6	4	15
STA	statutory	25	61	72	158
XX	text type X	–	5	1	6

Table 13 shows us that *aforesaid* may be used predicatively − (example in [8]), with ellipsis of *to be* in the phrase *as aforesaid*, cf. (9), postpositively, following a noun, in particular *auctoritee*, cf. (10), but also many others, cf. (11), and attributively, preceding a noun, cf. (12). With the exception of the last category (12), all these constructions occur in the statutory texts. The attributive construction occurs mainly in the expository and non-imaginative narrative text categories, and text type X text category.

Table 13. Occurrences of *afore*-compounds

	I	Period II	III	Total
as/than is aforesaid	8	10	2	20
as aforesaide	–	16	26	42
auctoritee aforeseide	8	14	30	52
NP + *aforesaide*	15	24	19	58
aforesaide + NP	3	9	–	12

(8) *persons as shall pass over the see or bide uppon the see in the Kynges service as is aforeseid*

EB1 STA LAW STAT3 X: 2

(9) *Sale shall be used in all Poyntes and Circumstaunces as aforesaide,*

EB2 STA LAW STAT4 X: 1

(10) *Also it be enacted by auctoritie aforeseid*

EB1 STA LAW STAT3 X: 1

(11) *whereby the seid power comons of the craftes aforsaid*

EB1 STA LAW STAT3 X: 5

experience and knowlege in any of the diseases sores and maladies aforesaide

EB1 STA LAW STAT3 X: 10

Englishe shipps lying in Kingrode and Hungrode, being portes or havens of the Citie or Towne of Bristoll aforesaide

EB1 STA LAW STAT3 X: 10

and shall trulie declare to the Toltaker or other Officer aforesaide

EB2 STA LAW STAT4 X: Heading

(12) *And the aforesayde spirite or breath taketh a further digestion, and there it is made animal;*

EB1 EX SCIM VICARY PROF: 30

I being at dinner with those aforesaid Gentlemen,

EB2 NN TRAV JOTAYLO OTHER: 4

> *And also that every such aforesaid Scholer, being a Graduate,*
> *shall wear abroad in that University, going out of his College,*
> *a gown and a hoode of clothe*
>
> EB2 XX CORO WCECIL PROF HI: 2

As we can see from (12), it is science, medicine (Thomas Vicary, THE ANATOMIE OF THE BODIE OF MAN, 1548), travelogues (John Taylor, THE PENNYLES PILGRIMAGE, 1630) and non-private correspondence (William Cecil, Letters — from the collection of ORIGINAL LETTERS; ILLUSTRATIVE OF ENGLISH HISTORY), which show the attributive construction.

The variant *foresaid* occurs 39 times, and only in attributive function, 13 times in the first period, 25 times in the second, and just once in the third period. There are an additional 9 instances of *forenamed*, 3 of which occur in the first, and 6 in the second period.

Aforesaid and *foresaid*, thus, compete with one another only in attributive function, with *foresaid* clearly the more common form (Table 14).

Table 14. Occurrences of *aforesaid* and *foresaid* in attributive function

	Period			Total
	I	II	III	
aforesaide + NP	3	9	—	12
foresaide + NP	13	25	1	39

Table 15. Occurrences of text-deictic *aforesaid* and *foresaid* in prototypical text categories

Prototypical text category		*aforesaid*	*foresaid*
EX	expository	3	9
AR	argumentative	1	1
NN	narration non-imaginative	4	12
STA	statutory	—	4
XX	text type X	4	13

Foresaid, according to Table 15, is typical for text type X, non-imaginative and expository text categories. In period I it is particularly frequent in history: Robert Fabyan, THE NEW CHRONICLES OF ENGLAND AND FRANCE, 1516, (cf. 13), in period two in science, "other". Blundeville, once again (cf. 14).

(13)   *And in this yere the kynge at the Request of the duke of*
        Orleyaunce sent ouer the foresayd duke his sone to ayde

        EB1 NN HIST FABYAN PROF: 31

(14)   *of which fiue Zones, the foresaid foure circles are the true bounds*

EB2 EX SCIO BLUNDEV PROF: 17

The use of *aforesaid* and *foresaid* precludes a reference to a more detailed place in the text, as it occurs occasionally with *before*, as shown in (6) above.

2.2.3. above

In the Old English part of the corpus there are only 11 examples with *bufan*, most of them in combination with the past tense of *cweðan*, but also with other verbs such as *dōn*, *sprecan*, and *gemynegian*. In Middle English the verbs are *schewen*, *saien*, and *speken*. The majority of the Middle English examples are instances in which *above* occurs before a past participle. Spellings as one word, *above* + participle indicate the development to a compound as in *aforesaid*, above.

(15)   *þe manere and fourme aboue expressid*

ME3 STA DOC LPROCL **EMS: 100

            of oure chirche abouesaid

ME3 XX CORO HENRY%C EMS: 95

Surprisingly, there are very few Early Modern English examples of *above* in text-deictic function: 14 instances with decreasing frequency in the three periods, plus another 8 compounds: *abovesaid* and *abovementioned* (Table 16).

Table 16. Occurrences of text-deictic *above*

	Period			Total
	I	II	III	
above	7	5	2	14
above-compound	2	3	3	8

The *above*-examples occur in a wide range of prototypical text categories (Table 17).

Table 17. Occurrences of text-deictic *above* in prototypical text categories

Prototypical text category		Period			Total
		I	II	III	
EX	expository	–	3	1	4
IS	instruction secular	1	–	–	1
NI	narration imaginative	1	–	–	1
NN	narration non-imaginative	2	1	1	4
STA	statutory	2	1	–	3
XX	text type X	1	–	–	1

The 3 examples of the expository text category of period II are, once again, from the Blundeville text:

(16)   *because it is not enough to know the signification of the things*
            aboue specified to use the foresaid Tables when neede is
                                        EB2 EX SCIO BLUNDEV PROF: 3

Of the 8 *above*-compounds, there are 5 instances of *abovesaid* (those in periods I and II), all of them in the statutory law-texts (example in 17), and 3 of *abovementioned*, all in one expository, science-"other" text: Robert Boyle, ELECTRICITY AND MAGNETISM, 1675-6. (Cf. 18) (Table 18).

Table 18. Occurrences of text-deictic *above*-compounds in prototypical text categories

Prototypical text category		Period			Total
		I	II	III	
EX	expository	—	—	3	3
STA	statutory	2	3	—	5

(17)   *within theire severall Precinctes and Jurisdictions abovesaide,*
                                        EB2 STA LAW STAT4 X: 13

(18)   *the feather would be disposed to apply it self again to the*
            abovementioned Bodies.
                                        EB3 EX SCIO BOYLE HIGH: 33

2.2.4. The said

A text-deictic analysis would not be complete without an analysis of the use of *the said* as encountered in the first example in (11) above and those in (19).

(19)   *Moreouer, the said Erle hath, as is said, discovered al the whole*
            matter to the Chancellor
                                        EB1 AR TRI THROCKM X: 9
            the bedells or other Officers therunto appoynted within the said
            University
                                        EB2 XX CORO WCECIL PROF HI: 3
            then for this saide Offence to be punsihed as a Vagabond
                                        EB2 STAT LAW STAT4 X: 13

In the Early Modern English corpus we find 2015 instances of *said* in 9 different spellings, 675 or 33% of which are used text-deictically (Table 19).

Table 19. Spelling variants of *said*

Form	no. of occurrences	text-deictic	%text-deictic
said	985	292	30%
saide	276	217	79%
sayd	296	43	15%
sayde	275	31	11%
sayed	63		
sayid	1		
saied	3		
seyd	35	17	49%
seid	81	75	93%
Total	2015	675	33%

More than 80% of the instances spelled *saide* and *seid* are instances of text deixis, a considerable number also of the *seyd* and *said* variety, relatively few, however, of the *sayd* and *sayde* variety. Differences in spelling often occur within the same text.

A text-deictic *said* follows the definite article, a possessive or a demonstrative pronoun (*my, his, her, our, your, their,* and *this*), or a relative *which*. The combination with the definite article is the most frequent one: 623 against 52 others (Table 20).

Table 20. Occurrences of *the said* and other combinations

Definite Article	Others	Possessive	Demonstrative	Relative	Genitive
623	52	40	2	7	3

Of these 623 instances with the definite article 311 occur in period I, 180 in period II, and 132 in period III: once again, there is a decline in examples (Table 21).

Table 21. Occurrences of *the said* in prototypical text categories

Prototypical text category		I	Period II	III	Total
IS/EX	Instruction secular/ expository	4	–	3	7
EX	expository	5	33	–	38
IS	instruction secular	3	–	–	3
AR	argumentative	25	1	–	26
NN	narration non-imaginative	64	24	–	88
STA	statutory	173	106	125	407
XX	text type X	37	16	4	57

Clearly the statutory text category is in the lead. There are many instances among non-imaginative narration, expository and argumentative texts in the first or second periods. In the third period, the number in the statutory texts is still very high, whereas outside this category the construction loses quickly in importance.

The said very often occurs in combination with *above-* or *beforesaid.*

2.3. Reference to following sections

A study of the expressions belonging here must be left to a later investigation. Among others, there is the longer form *herinafter*, with the full set of instances given in (20) − all in the statutory text category −

(20)   *hereinafter mentioned*   E3 STA LAW STAT7 VIII, 454: Heading
         herein after mentioned   E3 STA LAW STAT7 VIII, 456: Heading
         herein after mentioned   E3 STA LAW STAT7 VIII, 459: Heading
         as herein after foloweth E3 STA LAW STAT VII, 97: Heading

and the shorter form *hereafter*, in 6 different spellings, spread more evenly among the text categories, but clearly typical for the expository text category (Table 22).

Table 22. Occurrences of text-deictic *hereafter* in prototypical text categories

Prototypical text category		Period			Total
		I	II	III	
IS/EX	Instruction secular/ expository	1	−		1
EX	expository	4	11	−	15
IS	instruction secular	−	−	1	1
NN	narration non-imaginative	1	2		3
STA	statutory	−	2	1	3

Eight out of the 11 instances among the expository texts in period 2 are, once again, from Blundeville: examples in (21):

(21)   *whereof we shall speake hereafter more at large when we come to treate of the Longitude and the Latitude of the earth*
                        E2 EX SCIO BLUNDEV 154R: Heading
         you shal better understand hereafter, when wee come to shew the vses of the globe
                        E2 EX SCIO BLUNDEV 154V: Heading
         whereof we shall speake hereafter when we come to treat of the earth.
                        E2 EX SCIO BLUNDEV 157R: Heading

2.4. References to chapters, etc.

References to a written text may also be interpreted as text-deictical if they refer to the very text in which they occur and do not point to another text. In the Early Modern English corpus there are the few references to other sections of the text together with *above* mentioned in (8). Apart from these I can adduce three examples with the noun *chapter*, which as far as I can see are the only ones.

(22)   *speake of the latitude and longitude of the earth in the 8. chapter.*
                                    EB2 EX SCIO BLUNDEV PROF: 11
         whereof we haue already spoken in the 11. Chapter.
                                    EB2 EX SCIO BLUNDEV PROF: 12
         I will expresse my minde in the two next chapters
                                    EB3 IS EDUC HOOLE PROF: 28

3. Outlook

The preliminary version of the *Helsinki Corpus of Texts* yields an impressive number of instances of text deixis. For a full appreciation the final version will have to be consulted. In any case, it is reassuring that a diachronic corpus of the type of the *Helsinki Corpus* can be useful for the solution of textlinguistic problems. As a proper textlinguistic analysis, however, we will eventually have to go back to the texts themselves and one may well want to start with a complete analysis of those texts of which sections are included the *Helsinki Corpus*. The Corpus cannot tell us anything about the position and the density of occurrence of text deixis in any one text, without which we cannot establish the importance of these constructions for the development of the various genres. We have, thus, still a far way to go before we arrive at a complete history of text deixis in English.

Note

1. There are only a few changes in the final version of the Helsinki corpus, which is now generally available (cf. Kytö 1991).

References

Fries, Udo
  in press   "Towards a description of text deixis in Old English", in: Klaus Grinda – C.-
              D. Wetzel (eds.) *Festschrift für Hans Schabram.*
Kurzon, Dennis
  1985   "Signposts for the reader: A corpus study of text deixis", *Text* 5: 187 – 200.
Kytö, Merja
  1991   *Manual to the diachronic part of the Helsinki Corpus of English Texts.* Helsinki:
              Department of English, University of Helsinki.
Rauh, Gisa
  1983   "Aspects of deixis", in: Gisa Rauh (ed.), 9 – 60.
Rauh, Gisa (ed.)
  1983   *Essays on deixis.* (Tübinger Beiträge zur Linguistik 188.) Tübingen: Narr.

On phrasal verbs in Early Modern English: notes on lexis and style

Risto Hiltunen

1. Introduction

In the Preface to his *Historical syntax of the English language*, F. Th. Visser points out that in the course of his study he will give numerous examples of trends in diction that were — often vehemently — reprobated by the schoolmasters but which later developed into universally recognized idioms in standard speech (Visser 1963: vi). The phrasal verb is a case in point; it is now part and parcel of the English language, but its importance has not always been adequately recognised.

The present-day constructions made up of a verb and particle are variously described in grammatical treatises. Quirk *et al.* (1985: 1150), among others, make the familiar distinction between phrasal, prepositional and phrasal-prepositional verbs, based on various syntactic and other characteristics of the verb-particle constructions. This paper will be concerned with what they call phrasal verbs, i. e. combinations of verbs and adverbial particles, in the period from 1500 to 1700.[1] The following particles, which also occur as spatial adverbs (and some of them occasionally as prepositions), will be included: *away, back, down, forth, off, out* and *up*. Thus, the examples to be discussed represent only a sample of possible collocations. The above particles may, however, be regarded as typical in the sense that they belong to the most productive elements forming phrasal verbs in contemporary English.

More specifically, the paper will discuss: (a) the occurrence of phrasal verbs in Early Modern English (EModE) compared with Present-day English (PDE), and (b) the variation in the use of collocations of verbs and particles in the Early Modern period. Both of these will be viewed primarily from the point of view of lexis and style. In addition, it will be relevant to consider briefly (c) the relevant descriptions of the construction by the grammarians of the period as background for (a) and (b).

2. The descriptions by the early grammarians

The attitude of the sixteenth and seventeenth century grammarians to-wards the verb-particle construction can be characterised as confused. The confusion is due to the fact that in Latin grammar, which generally provided the model for the description of English, there was no need to deal with such multi-word formations as phrasal verbs. The negative attitude towards them is in part a consequence of this particular dissim-ilarity between the two languages.

Another reason for the confusion lies in the word-class approach of the grammars. The sections on "Syntax", where they exist at all, usually consist of only desultory prescriptive statements. The syntax has to be inferred from what is said or implied in the description of the various parts of speech. As for the verb-particle construction, syntactic comments are scarce, especially in the sixteenth and seventeenth centuries. There is some development towards recognising the phrasal verb in the course of the eighteenth century, when grammarians begin to state their observa-tions about the position of the particle in relation to the verb in various syntactic contexts.[2]

In describing the non-verb member of the construction, the grammar-ians make use of three categories: adverb, preposition and particle. Most grammars call it either adverb or preposition. Of these, the former is more straightforward, for its function is less ambiguous and the class contains fewer items. It is in the category preposition where most of the relevant words are to be found. This is also a more problematic class because of the possibility of prepositions becoming adverbs in certain contexts. The designation particle, which becomes more common only in the eighteenth century, is introduced as a common denominator for all indeclinables. It does not significantly affect the actual description of the construction.

In spite of the emphasis on the part-of-speech approach, an awareness of the unity between the elements in the verb-particle constructions emerges gradually. The process starts indirectly, with phrasal verbs being used to translate Latin prefixed verbs. Thus, in Walker's *A treatise of English particles* (1655), the following examples appear under *About: To bring a thing about*, 'Efficere, Effectum dare, &c'; *To go about from place to place*, 'Circumvenire'; with the comment, "(About) is sometimes part of the signification of the foregoing Verb" (Walker 1655: 3). The difference between English and Latin on this point is too striking to pass unnoticed.

A comment from *The English grammar* by Guy Miège, published in 1688, will serve as a further example:

> Whereas in [Latin] Verb Compounds the Preposition goes first, and makes but one Word with the Verb, the English has another way besides using Prepositions, viz. after the Verb, and distinct from it. As, *to look upon*, for to view; *to look for*, to seek; *to put out*, for, to extinguish; *to go after*, for, to follow. (Miège 1668: 81)

Thus, the Latin model can be said to have had both a retarding and a stimulating effect on the grammatical analysis of the phrasal verb. In the course of the eighteenth century there are already several grammarians who try to deal with the construction in its own right (Hiltunen 1983b: 384 – 5).

The relationship between the grammars and the material to be examined below is difficult to ascertain. We do not know to what extent the rules and recommendations of the grammarians were actually familiar to writers in individual cases, but considering the quantity of prescriptive material produced in the period, they may have been well known, at least among the better educated.

3.   The usage in Early Modern English

3.1. The data

To find out how phrasal verbs were used in Early Modern English, samples of data were retrieved from the *Helsinki Corpus of English Texts*.[3] Altogether eight different text types represented in the Corpus, covering the period 1500 to 1710, were examined. In the following, the categories will be treated as if they represented real types, but it has to be remembered that classifying texts by types can be problematic in individual cases. Conclusions about possible interdependences between text types and particular linguistic characteristics on the basis of an overall categorisation will therefore have to be regarded as tentative.

3.2. The usage before and after Early Modern English

Before discussing the present material in more detail, it will be relevant to consider briefly the Early Modern English verb-particle construction in relation to the earlier and later stages of its development. The parallel with contemporary English is naturally more complete than with either Old or Middle English. There are two major differences between the early and present stages in this respect; one has to do with the structure, the other with meaning. In Old English, the position of the particle was more variable, and several patterns existed side by side (see Hiltunen 1983 c). By Early Modern English, however, the positional variation had been regularised in favour of postposition (cf. Görlach 1991: 106—7). Semantically, on the other hand, the early collocations are mostly concrete, with only incipient metaphorical developments in certain contexts. In today's English, on the other hand, much of the distinctiveness of the phrasal verb lies in the semantic versatility of many of the combinations. In Early Modern English, metaphorical combinations seem to have been fewer on the basis of the present material, for most of the groups are semantically concrete. To what extent this indicates that semantic specialisation came late in individual groups, and to what extent it is due to the nature of the material, are questions that have to be left aside for now.[4]

Table 1. The verb-particle construction in EModE and PDE

	EModE (*HC*)	PDE (*LOB*)
away		
take	57	22
go	38	34 (2)
put	18	4
cast	14	—
run	13	17
...		
get	2	48 (1)
turn	2	28 (3)
back		
come	9	117 (1)
go	7	92 (2)
bring	5	23
get	1	49 (3)
look	1	43
forth		
come	24	—
bring	22	—
set	22	3
put	14	—
send	14	—
down		
come	55	29
set	39	2
go	38	71 (2)

Table 1. Continued

	EModE (*HC*)	PDE (*LOB*)
sit	32	93 (1)
lay	27	29
send	15	4
pull	6	6
look	5	52 (3)
off		
cut	43	24 (3)
take	10	26 (2)
carry	7	7
go	2	36 (1)
out		
find	44	112
fall	27	—
go	26	148 (2)
cry	18	12
come	13	110
...		
set	9	114
carry	8	168 (1)
get	6	104
take	6	42
point	2	118 (3)
turn	1	75
up		
bring	34	50
take	33	102 (1)
go	32	—
come	25	97 (2)
lift	22	6
set	16	69
raise	14	—
...		
make	9	93 (3)

In terms of structure, there were no examples in the present data where the syntactic arrangement would not be acceptable in contemporary English. As regards the variation in the position of the object in transitive constructions (types *he took off his hat* and *he took his hat off*), the pattern Verb + Particle + Object is the predominant one if the object is nominal. Among the total of 851 examples, there were only some 30 cases where a nominal object or (in 6 instances) an adverb intervened between the verb and the particle. The pronoun object regularly takes this position, however.

Before leaving these comparisons, let us consider the frequency of particular verbs with the particles mentioned above. The material for Present-day English comes from the frequency analysis of word combinations in the *London — Oslo/Bergen Corpus* by Johansson — Hofland (1989: 370 — 376). In the light of the (conflated) figures, the two periods appear remarkably similar in this respect, although there are also some obvious differences. Table 1 gives the distribution of the most frequent combinations in the Early Modern English section of the *Helsinki Corpus* (*HC*) and in the *London — Oslo/Bergen Corpus* (*LOB*), representing contemporary written British English. It is the relative order of frequency within both corpora that is interesting. Where the order in *LOB* is different from that in *HC*, this is indicated in brackets after the *LOB* figures.

Table 1 shows that most of the verbs are the same in both sets and that in some cases even the relative order of frequency is similar (cf. *back* and *up*). As the corpora are not of equal size (the EModE section of *HC* is only about half the size of *LOB*), it is not possible to compare these frequencies directly. Also, the corpora consist of different text types, respectively.[5] Nevertheless, the figures suggest that the most common collocations tend to be made up of the same lexical items in both periods. Some of the differences may indicate more general tendencies, as in the case of *forth*, while others may reflect stylistic preferences or differences in the subject matter in the individual text samples (e. g. *set down* is very frequent in *HC*, but *LOB* has only two examples).

Among the interesting differences in Table 1, we may further note that *to get away* is the most frequent of the combinations with *away* in *LOB*, but in *HC* there are only two examples. Similarly, *to look back* is fairly common in *LOB*, but occurs only once in *HC*. On the other hand, combinations with *forth* are frequent in *HC*, but only three examples occur in *LOB*. Among the combinations with *down, sit down* is the most frequent in *HC*, and *come down* in *LOB*. Fluctuations of this kind probably depend more on the subject matter of the text than the productivity of the combinations in either period (with the possible exception of *forth*). In the groups with *out*, it is interesting to note that there are, on the whole, more very frequent combinations in *LOB* (with over a hundred instances). Of the three most common, *carry out, go out* and *point out*, two (*carry out* and *point out*) are matched, however, by less than ten examples in *HC*. Thus, among the above particles, *out* would seem to be the one that has extended its domain most since Early Modern English.

3.3. The distribution of the examples

The present data contain 851 examples from the following eight text types in *HC*: statutes, official letters, sermons, trials, private letters, handbooks, fiction, and the Bible.[6] Stylistically, most of the texts can be characterised as either formal or semi-formal, although some (especially private letters, trials and fiction) also contain passages of a more informal flavour. There are some differences between the texts in the various categories as measured in the number of words, and this has to be kept in mind if the absolute frequencies are compared with each other.[7] The average length per category (excluding trials, private and official correspondence) is ca. 34,000 words. The data representing trials and private correspondence are longer (43,960 and 41,680 words, respectively), while the material for official letters in *HC* is only about a half of the length of the other texts (17,830 words). The texts from the Bible consist of three samples: two from Tyndale's translations and one from the Authorised Version (32,830 words altogether).

The distribution of the token examples is given in Table 2, and that of the types in Table 3. The diachronic aspect cannot be discussed here and, consequently, no reference will be made to the three sub-periods of Early Modern English distinguished in *HC*.[8]

Besides the factors already mentioned, there are certain text-specific features that influence the frequencies in Table 2, e. g. one and the same combination may be repeated several times in succession. Usually this is due to the subject matter of the text, as in the case of *lift up* in the Bible and *cut off* in the handbooks on gardening. Nevertheless, Table 2 suggests that the particles fall into three groups in terms of their rate of occurrence: (1) *back, off, forth,* all with frequencies less than a hundred; (2) *down, away,* with frequencies over a hundred; and (3) *out, up,* predictably the most comprehensive group, with over two hundred examples, respectively. The frequencies of these particles are fairly consistent throughout the categories, e. g. combinations with *away* are approximately equally common throughout, those with *back* equally rare. The most distinctive particle is *out*, for its frequencies show most variation from one category to another.

Table 2. The distribution of tokens

	CorO	Stat	Serm	CorP	Tri	Bible	Fict	Handb	Total (No.	and %)
back	—	—	3	3	8	3	2	2	21	2.4
off	1	—	4	5	3	1	3	40	57	6.7
forth	4	5	6	6	5	19	15	24	84	9.9
down	2	4	14	29	13	22	26	15	125	14.7
away	4	18	10	11	20	17	29	18	127	14.9
out	9	13	22	19	27	30	44	45	209	24.6
up	5	21	24	25	26	54	34	39	228	26.8
Total	25	61	83	98	102	146	153	183	851	
%	2.9	7.2	9.7	11.5	12.0	17.2	18.0	21.5		100.0

(Abbreviations: CorO = official correspondence, Stat = statutes, Serm = sermons, CorP = private correspondence, Tri = trials, Fict = fiction, Handb = handbooks)

Table 3. The distribution of types

	CorO	Stat	Serm	CorP	Tri	Bible	Fict	Handb	Total No.	and %)
back	—	—	2	2	4	3	2	2	15	3.2
off	1	—	3	5	2	1	3	11	26	5.5
forth	1	4	5	5	4	7	8	9	43	9.2
away	4	4	5	9	6	8	12	9	57	12.2
down	2	4	10	12	8	10	15	12	73	15.5
out	8	8	15	12	17	18	23	26	127	27.1
up	3	9	16	15	14	16	23	32	128	27.3
Total	19	29	56	60	55	63	86	101	469	
%	4.1	6.2	12.0	12.8	11.7	13.4	18.3	21.5		100.0

As far as the text types are concerned, it is interesting to note that the groups are most frequent in the Bible, fiction and handbooks. There are reasons why this should be so, but first a word about the other text types.

It is not surprising that the statutes (and official letters) should have a low incidence of verb-particle groups (7.2% and 2.9%, respectively). In fact, these figures are higher than might be expected for this kind of prose. The low frequency may indicate a preference for Latin-based verbs in the official documents generally (although this is not shown by the present data). What is clear, on the other hand, is that these particular texts make use of only a limited set of verbs in the collocations (cf. Table 3).

The next group consists of sermons, private letters, and trials. Here the rate of occurrence is somewhat higher (from 9.7% to 12%), but not as high as might be expected for texts that are basically very interactive in character. The three categories are similar also in that the various particles tend to occur with approximately the same number of verb types (56, 55, and 60, respectively). The selection of verbs is wider than in the statutes (and official correspondence), but more restricted than in the Bible (63), fiction (86), and the handbooks (101).

The sermons are characterised by the biblical idiom and many of the combinations found in this text type also occur in the Bible, e. g. *bring forth* (fruit), *take away* (faith, hope), *lift up* (eyes), *pass away, fall down, throw down*, and *give up* (faith, hope).

The sample from private letters ought to come closest to representing informal language among the texts studied here, and it does indeed have combinations that are not used elsewhere and that give a casual impression, e. g. *put away* (folk), 'dismiss', *get away*, 'travel', *fling away* (money), 'waste'; *pull down* (houses), *set down* (in writing), *get down*, 'come back'; *spoil off, get off, leave* (it) *up* (to them), *keep* (him) *up*. This qualitative difference is noteworthy in view of the fact that quantitatively the private letters do not have as many examples as might have been expected.

In the trial texts the combinations are concrete expressions of the type *take away* (life/money), *run away, go away*, etc. But there are also instances of more specialised combinations, e. g. *seek out* 'to try', *give out* 'to make known', *look back* (to) 'to remember', and *track out* 'trace'.

The remaining categories, the Bible, fiction, and handbooks, are very different from each other and yet they have the highest frequencies of both tokens and types. The results for the Bible readily confirm the preference of both Tyndale and the translators of the Authorised Version for the native idiom. Although the Bible is a highly prestigious text, the two versions make extensive use of the phrasal verb. This is, no doubt, a deliberate choice on the part of the translators to make the text more readily accessible to readers. The possible influence of the Bible on the currency of phrasal verbs as equivalents for the Latin-based verbs may have been considerable. Tyndale's original contribution is important here and it was fully recognised by the translators of the Authorised Version, who kept most of Tyndale's combinations and even extended the usage further.

In the samples from fiction, representing imaginative writing, the usage is similar to that in the handbooks in that the majority of the combinations are semantically concrete. However, the function of the groups tends to be different. While in the instructive texts the focus is usually on the action denoted by the combination (e. g. *cut off, take away*, usually expressed through the second person singular), in the texts from fiction, especially in the narrative sections, the phrasal verbs serve as a means of backgrounding (X *sits down, runs away, goes forth, stands up*, etc). Another notable characteristic in the fictional texts is the frequency of the pattern Particle + Verb + Subject (i. e. the type *out comes Jack*), not found in the other categories.

The combinations in the handbooks are characterised by concreteness. Groups such as *put forth, shoot forth, cut away, cast away, cut down, lay down, take off, cut off, pluck off, put up, grow up, grow out* and *keep out* are some of the examples found in Langford's *Plain and Full Instructions to Raise All Sorts of Fruit-Trees that Prosper in England* (1699). However, considering that such books may have been widely read and that it is often the everyday and commonplace images that serve as the basis of metaphor, there is but a step from the concrete to the abstract in combinations such as those above. In fact, many of them occur with abstract objects in the religious texts of the data, the sermons and the Bible.

Computing the type/token ratio on the basis of Tables 2 and 3 for the different text types gives the following results shown in Table 4.

Table 4. The type/token ratio in the text types

Sermons	0.6747
Private letters	0.6122
Fiction	0.5621
Handbooks	0.5519
Trials	0.5392
Statutes	0.4754
Bible	0.4315

The sermons and private letters have the highest value for the ratio, while the statutes and the Bible have the lowest, indicating that their phrasal verbs are repeated more often than is the case in the other texts.[9] The data from fiction, trials and handbooks occupy an intermediate position on this scale. The differences indicate a stylistic continuum, for the texts with a relatively higher type/token ratio make use of a more varied vocabulary. A similar conclusion may be drawn from the frequency of the *hapax legomena* (single-occurrence items). The more *hapax legomena* a text has, the more varied its vocabulary. Here, too, the private letters and the sermons have the highest proportion (47% and 45% of all tokens, respectively), with handbooks and fiction next (both 38%), followed by trials (31%), statutes (28%) and the Bible (24%). It is interesting to note that the sermons and the Bible occupy the highest and the lowest position on this scale, respectively.

4. Concluding remarks

In the above experiment with data from the *Helsinki Corpus of English Texts*, the phrasal verbs of the Early Modern period were approached quantitatively and qualitatively from the angle of text types. The analysis indicated that the usage may in some respects be related to this variable, although there are, no doubt, also other factors that play a role in the variation, e. g. the preferences of individual writers in the choice of lexis and the possibility of variation of styles in the samples representing particular text types. Without pursuing them any further, however, I conclude the paper by once again drawing attention to the common denominator for the various motives of using phrasal verbs in Early Modern English, as well as other times, viz. the fact that the construction is a native, homely idiom. By virtue of this characteristic it can be employed for a variety of purposes besides that of conveying overt informality. Relevant examples in the present material include the use for various didactic and instructive purposes, whether religious or secular. A feature connected with such functions is the tendency to employ phrasal verbs when the action denoted by the combination is itself in the fore-ground. An indication of this is their frequent co-occurrence with the imperative mood, which can be seen in most of the texts. In the statutes, however, this is less evident, but the fact that phrasal verbs occur at all in legal writing is yet another sign of the construction belonging to the very core resources of the English language.

Notes

1. In an earlier study of the phrasal verb (Hiltunen 1983 a) I was concerned with Old and Early Middle English developments.
2. For further discussion of the phrasal verb in the early grammars, see Hiltunen (1983 b).
3. I would like to thank Dr. Merja Kytö for generous help with the *Helsinki Corpus* in situ.
4. Generally speaking, the fact that the majority of instances are semantically concrete is in line with the fact that (a) phrasal verbs, being more characteristic of colloquial language, are less frequently employed in the written texts, and (b) the metaphorical combinations tend to be even more marked as colloquial and therefore avoided in the written language.

5. For the description of the *London — Oslo/Bergen Corpus (LOB)*, see Johansson (1978: 3).
6. For bibliographical information about the texts in the *Helsinki Corpus*, see Kytö (1991: 16 — 17; 133 — 163).
7. For information about the length of the individual text samples, see the reference in note 6 above.
8. The subperiods for EModE in the *Helsinki Corpus* are: (1) 1500 — 1570; (2) 1570 — 1640; (3) 1640 — 1710. For some data on the diachronic development of the phrasal verb during the EModE period, see Spasov (1966: 19 — 24).
9. The texts representing official letters are excluded from Table 4 because of their relatively smaller sample size.

References

Görlach, Manfred
  1991   *Introduction to Early Modern English*. Cambridge: Cambridge University Press.
Hiltunen, Risto
  1983 a   *The decline of the prefixes and the beginnings of the English phrasal verb.* (Annales Universitatis Turkuensis, Series B., Vol. 160.) Turku.
  1983 b   "The phrasal verb in English grammar books before 1800", *Neuphilologische Mitteilungen* 84: 376 — 386.
  1983 c   "Syntactic variation in the early history of the English phrasal verb", in: Sven Jacobson (ed.), *Papers from the second Scandinavian symposium on syntactic variation.* (Stockholm Studies in English LVII.) Stockholm: Almqvist & Wiksell, 95 — 108.
Johansson, Stig
  1978   *Manual of information to accompany the Lancaster-Oslo/Bergen corpus on British English*. Oslo: Department of English.
Johansson, Stig — Knut Hofland
  1989   *Frequency analysis of English vocabulary and grammar. Vol. 2: Tag combinations and word combinations*. Oxford: Clarendon Press.
Kytö, Merja
  1991   *Manual to the diachronic part of the Helsinki Corpus of English Texts: Coding conventions and list of source texts*. Helsinki: Department of English.
Miège, Guy
  1688   *The English grammar*. London.
Quirk, Randolph — Sidney Greenbaum — Geoffrey Leech — Jan Svartvik
  1985   *A comprehensive grammar of the English language*. London: Longman.
Spasov, Dimiter
  1966   *English phrasal verbs*. Sofia: Naouka i Izkoustvo.
Visser, Frans Theodor
  1963   *An historical syntax of the English language*. Part 1: *Syntactic units with one verb*. Leiden: Brill.
Walker, William
  1655   *A treatise of English particles*. London.
  [1970]   [Reprinted. Menston: The Scholar Press.]

The use of *thou* and *you* in Early Modern spoken English: evidence from depositions in the Durham ecclesiastical court records[*]

Jonathan Hope

1. Introduction

The theoretical base for any study of the use of *thou* and *you* in Early Modern English is Brown and Gilman's (1960) power and solidarity analysis of TV pronoun systems in European languages.[1] Translated into an Early Modern English context, the notions of power and solidarity provide an explicative (even arguably a predictive) model for the pronoun usages encountered in dramatic texts: characters "+ power" (monarchs, the rich, men, parents, masters and mistresses) can be expected to give *thou* and receive *you* when interacting with those "− power" (subjects, the poor, women, children, servants). Theoretically under this model we expect characters of equal power, or social class, to exchange reciprocal *you* if they are upper class, and *thou* if they are lower.

Beyond these socially conditioned uses, there are, in the English context, emotionally expressive ones which can produce rapidly modulating forms addressed to the same person. Such usages are often found in Shakespeare (see McIntosh 1963, Mulholland 1967, Barber 1981, Wales 1983). Up until Lass (forthcoming) such usages have traditionally been characterised as taking their pragmatic force as the result of being "deviations" from the power and solidarity predicted "norms" (e. g., if *you* is expected on a social basis, *thou* can express anger or insult).

The major difficulty in analysing Early Modern English pronoun usage, and testing the suitability of the power and solidarity model, is our lack of "real" evidence. Before Lass (forthcoming) almost all of the published work has been on drama, and Shakespearean drama at that. Brown and Gilman, recently broadening their attention to politeness strategies as a whole, and focussing historically on the Early Modern period, use as evidence data collected from Shakespeare's "four major tragedies" (1989, quotation from their title). They explicitly justify their use of literary data, stating that this is inevitable "because there is nothing else" (Brown—Gilman 1989: 170), and claiming that Shakespeare's usage of *thou* and *you* in his plays surely "mirrored general usage" (1989: 179). There are a great number of assumptions being made here, which it would take a different paper to explore fully, but the basic implications would seem to be:

1. The best, indeed only, evidence for Early Modern English speech patterns is in the drama.

2. Dramatic usage of linguistic features will mirror the "real" usage of those features in "real" Early Modern spoken English.

This paper challenges both of these notions by presenting exchanges employing *thou* and *you* pronouns as they are recorded in depositions made to the Durham ecclesiastical court in the north-east of England in the 1560s. Not only do these depositions provide us with an alternative source of evidence to the drama, but they challenge the notion that literary *thou* and *you* usage, as attested in the drama, is a mirror of contemporary spoken usage. The evidence presented here suggests that our current accounts of *thou* and *you* usage need to be significantly adjusted, both in terms of chronology, and in the details of the semantic-pragmatic aspects of *thou* and *you* usage (see Wakelin [1982] for further sources of evidence for spoken sixteenth century English).

2. The Durham Depositions

The Durham Depositions are the records of the ecclesiastical court of Durham. They are held at Durham University, and selections from the cases were published in the nineteenth century (Surtees Society 1845). This paper draws solely on the published selections from the records, although the transcriptions in the quoted examples have been checked against the originals.

The use of depositions as evidence is frequent within historical studies (see Ingram 1987 and Sharpe 1980, and also Rushton 1982, 1983, 1985, 1985—1986, 1986, 1989, for work on the Durham Depositions themselves). Depositions are the rough equivalent of modern police statements — they were dictated by witnesses and litigants to court clerks, and were written down at the time. The full texts of the depositions could be taken to represent a form of written Early Modern English which, in Helsinki variationist terms, is closer to the spoken language than other written forms (see Kytö—Rissanen 1983). This is not to ignore problems raised by clerk's conventions, legal phrasing, and so on, which certainly do occur, but which can be monitored by the researcher.

The evidence used in this paper, however, represents a further movement towards the oral: the figures and quotations given here are drawn solely from actual conversations recounted within the depositions. That is, these are not transcripts of court room exchanges, but accounts of conversations which occurred in everyday life, repeated by witnesses for the benefit of the court. Again, this is not to ignore problems of witness reliability: this is certainly a factor. Because of the nature of most of the cases before the court ("defamation" — equivalent to slander), however, we can expect close attention to have been paid to the actual words used at the time of the offence — that is, the direct speech (reported within depositions) which this paper takes as its evidence. It is striking to note, following this point, that in those cases where there are multiple accounts of the same conversation, the accounts almost always preserve identical pronoun forms (in the published selection, examples of this can be found in cases number 64, 110, 145, 292, 297, 331, 342).

3. Qualitative evidence

I will now consider the evidence from direct speech in the depositions: first qualitatively, by quoting some notable exchanges which illustrate the flavour of the records, and give some indications of how *thou* and *you* were actually used by real Early Modern English speakers and then by means of a quantitative analysis of the pronoun forms found in the depositions. Passages in double quotation marks are direct speech, passages in single marks are quotations from the narrative of the depositions.

The first example illustrates the familiar asymmetric usages of the pronoun forms to encode differences in social status. This exchange concerns sheep stealing, and is between two relatively high class men, Masters Antony and Ratcliff, and the relatively lower class Roger Donn.

(1)   Case no 61, from the deposition of "Christofer Egleston, of Hunstonworth, yoman, aged 40 years" (Surtees Society 1845, 62 – 64):

Mr. Antony: "Dyd not *thou* promess me that *thou* wold tell me and the parson of Hunstonworth who sold George Whitfeld sheep?"

Roger Donn: "I need not unless I woll"

Mr. Ratcliff: "*Thou* breaks promess"
Roger Donn: "*You* will know yt soon enowgh, for *your* man, Nicoll Dixson, stole them, that ther stands, upon Thursday bifore Christenmas then last past"

'Donn said that he [Ratcliff] shuld never be able to prove hym a theif ...'

Roger Donn: "For although *ye* be a gent., and I a poore man, my honestye shalbe as good as *yours*"
Mr. Ratcliff: "What saith *thou*? liknes *thou thy* honestye to myn?"

The asymmetry is particularly pointed in this exchange, given Donn's explicit attempt to set himself on an equal social plane with Ratcliff — "my honestye shall be as good as yours" even though "ye be a gent" — and Ratcliff's hammering home of the distinction in his repetitive pronouns: "What saith *thou*? liknes *thou thy* honestye to myn?". This exchange provides us with a strong confirmation of Brown and Gilman's power semantic functioning at the social-pragmatic level to encode differences in social status. Similar asymmetric usages from masters to servants, and from parents to children can also be found in the records.

Beyond the power semantic, however, as is well known, lie usages of the pronoun forms which are not socially pragmatic, but which appear to encode emotional attitudes, and which may shift between utterances to the same individual. Much has been made of such shifting, or modulation, in Shakespeare, and Lass (forthcoming) studies such micro-pragmatic usages in letters.

None of the exchanges in the depositions show the kind of multiple shifting relatively common in Shakespeare, and analysed by Lass, but there are examples of obviously micro-pragmatically motivated shifts, sometimes implying subtle manipulation of the forms by speakers.

My second example illustrates an emotive usage of *thou* common in the records — the shift from *you* into *thou* to encode anger:

(2)   Case. 139: Deposition of "Agnes Wheitley ... of Segefield, aged 33 years" (Surtees Society 1845, 104):

Bullman's wife [to Styllynge]: "Noughtie pak"
Styllynge [to Bullman's wife]: "What nowtynes know *you* by me? I am neyther goossteler nor steg [gander] steiler, I would *you* knew ytt"

> Bullman's wife   [to Styllynge]: "What, noughty hoore, caull *thou* me goose steiler?"
>
> Styllynge   [to Bullman's wife]: "Nay, mayry, I know *thee* for no such, but I thank *you* for *your* good reporte, whills *you* and I talk further"

Here, Bullman insults Styllynge ("Noughtie pak"), who replies with a neutral *you*, but none the less manages to imply that she thinks that Bullman is a goosestealer. This enrages Bullman, who replies with an insult strong enough to be actionable under law at the time ("noughty hoore"), and an insulting *thou* form ("call thou me goose steiler?"). Styllynge immediately matches this *thou* of anger with one of her own, but just as quickly shifts back into a *you* which strikes me as an effective ploy: it is potentially mollifying, apparently offering the hand of friendship, but at the same time retains for Styllynge the high moral ground of restraint, and implies a superiority in keeping with the formal tone she adopts. Clever manipulation of the micro-pragmatic implications of the forms allows Styllynge to have her argumentative cake and eat it here, and I suspect that Bullman's wife was left with the uneasy impression that she had been bested in some way, but unable to say exactly how.

The final quotation confirms the implication of the above exchange that speakers were aware of the connotations of the forms, and could consciously manipulate them to their own advantage. This comes from a case which records multiple accounts of a quarrel between John Rosse and Ralph Ogle. The two families to which the men belong have fallen out over the ownership of some goods seized from some "Egypcions". When Rosse and Ogle meet by chance in a local churchyard, there is an exchange of words which allegedly ends with Ralph Ogle drawing his dagger on John Rosse. Ogle denies the allegation.

The first two accounts of the quarrel are relatively similar, and certainly agree on the pronoun forms used (Surtees Society 1845: 258–263):

(3)   a.   John Rosse: "Father, come away: what doo *you* stand their, and they brabling with *you*?"
           Ralph Ogle [to John Rosse]: "What saith *you*, slave?"
           John Rosse [to Ralph Ogle]: "Howe be [by] *your* selfe?" [ie. modern "You and whose army?"]

and the second version:

      b.   John Rosse: "Father, what doo *ye*, sitting here and se them brag *you* as they do?"

> Ralph Ogle [to John Rosse]: "What saith *you*, slave?"
> John Rosse [to Ralph Ogle]: "S^r, what by *yourself*?"

In the third account however, that of John Rosse himself, we find an alteration in the pronoun Ogle is alleged to have used to Rosse:

> c.   John Rosse: "Come away, for ther words and brawling ys
>   known well enough"
>   Ralph Ogle: "What, slave, what is that *thou* saith?"
>   John Rosse: "What, man, by *your* self?"

What had been *you* in the other accounts is now *thou*. Now this could be a case of bad memory, or poor copying by the clerk, but it could also be significant that the defendant's pronoun should be changed in the complainant's deposition. The effect of the change is to make Ogle appear more rude, angry and hot-headed, more likely to have drawn his dagger. What we have here, possibly, is John Rosse's attempt to doctor the evidence, to show Ogle in as bad a light as possible.

So far then, evidence from the records has confirmed our expectations of socially-pragmatic usages encoding differentials of status, and has supported non-social, what Lass calls micro-pragmatic usages, encoding anger. Furthermore, we have seen evidence for conscious manipulation of the forms by speakers. This does not result in the frequent shifts in form found in Shakespearean drama, or the letters Lass studies, but I am tempted to group these usages together as examples of the high degree of subtlety attainable on the micro-pragmatic plane of meaning.

4. Quantitative evidence

So much for the anecdotal evidence. I will now move on to consider the quantitative evidence from the records, which presents something of a challenge to our previous accounts of the forms in Early Modern English. I want to make two particular points here: one is about Lass's proposed macro- and micro-pragmatic levels for the pronouns, and the basis on which we interpret the forms when we encounter them in literary texts; the other has to do with our historical accounts of the shift from *thou* to *you* as the neutral pronoun of everyday speech.

The quantitative results are presented in two forms. In Table 1, I give figures for whole conversations; in Table 2, I give figures for the total numbers of individual instances of each pronoun. The figures for conversations support my first point, the absolute figures support my second.

In Table 1, conversations are further divided into "address", where only one of the participants uses a pronoun form, and "exchange", where they both do. The usefulness of such a division is that it illustrates the effect of face to face interaction on the use of the forms, as can be seen from the graphic Figure 1.

Table 1. Conversations by pronoun(s) used (raw figures, N = 89)

conversation type:	address	exchange
pronoun type		
thou	29	8
you	28	13
thou and *you*	1	10

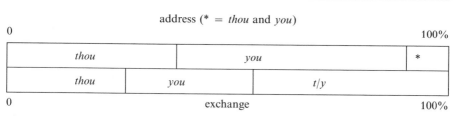

Figure 1. Relative proportions of pronoun forms used in address and exchange

This confirms that mixing the forms, that is, non-socially (micro) pragmatic usage, is strongly linked to interaction. Only one address out of 58 shows a shift in pronoun forms.

Clearly this imbalance, with 32 percent of exchanges shifting against only 2 percent of addresses, may partly be due to the fact that addresses, usually shorter than exchanges, simply give less opportunity for shifting. It also indicates, however, the way in which micro-pragmatic factors come more into play as a conversation develops. Presumably conversations tend to begin with socially pragmatic usages, and move on into non-socially pragmatic usages once a context has been established.

This may seem an obvious and relatively trivial point, but in the past, such modulating usages have been analysed from the point of view of a norm-deviant model. Such a model demanded the identification of a "normal" form for any exchange on the basis of the social relationship of the speakers, a form which by definition held good for the whole of the exchange. In other words, only one of the forms became available for carrying emotive meaning. Work on pronoun forms in Shakespeare's

As You Like It on this basis has been done by McIntosh (1963) and Mulholland (1967). Switching from this to a macro/micro, or social/non-social system, frees both forms as potential carriers of meaning, and allows much more powerful, and satisfactory, analyses of usage.

The remaining point I want to make at first appears to be a simple matter of chronology, concerning the point at which *thou* becomes the marked form in English. In fact it has deeper implications. The standard histories are not agreed on the point at which *thou* becomes marked, although most place it sometime between 1500 and 1600.[2] In his study of Shakespeare's usage however, Barber (1981) states that it is not really possible to talk of *thou* and *you* in Shakespeare in terms of marked and unmarked, and my own study of Marlowe's usages would tend to confirm this as true for Marlowe as well. So as late as the 1590s in drama, it is possible to find writers who do not seem to have "marked" one of the forms over the other.

The situation is very different in the court records however. Here *thou* is unquestionably the marked form — and this is in only 1560. There is no doubt that for these speakers, *you* is the default, or neutral form, and *thou*, when it is used, is almost always motivated in some obvious way.

This can be seen from Table 2, where *thou* and *you* are seen to be present in roughly equal numbers. The significance of this is that the nature of the conversations recorded in depositions (arguments, insults, and accusations) ought to favour *thou* use very strongly.

Table 2. Second person singular pronoun forms — individual occurrences of each form (N = 377)

pronoun type:	*thou*	*you*
total	185	192

The markedness of *thou* in the court records is further shown by the fact that when exchanges do shift, it is from *you* into *thou* (nine times) rather than from *thou* into *you* (twice). The strong implication of this is that Shakespeare's dramatic usage, if it bears any relation to "real" Early Modern usage at all, preserves modes of usage which have long disappeared from everyday speech. My own feeling is that *thou* and *you* lead separate lives in the written and spoken mediums, and that *thou*, and the micro-pragmatic plane of meaning, are much more evident in writing (either drama or letters) than they ever were in speech. Written Early

Modern English usage of the forms is often highly complex, and requires historical explication, but we would be wrong to do it from a standpoint which mapped written usage onto some "reconstructed" spoken language.

Notes

* Work on this paper was carried out while the author was Earl Grey Memorial Research Fellow in the Department of Speech at the University of Newcastle upon Tyne. I am grateful to the staff of the Department of Palaeography and Diplomatic at the University of Durham for assistance and access to the records. It is a pleasure to be able to thank Lisa Jardine (London University) and Keith Wrightson (Cambridge University) for introducing me to the material, Dieter Kastovsky for inviting me to EMEC, and my fellow conferees for a stimulating response to the paper which has prompted several important revisions.

1. Barber (1981) and Wales (1983) — which adapts Brown and Gilman's system to the Early Modern English context — remain the major studies focussed on the Early Modern period. Byrne (1936) and Finkenstaedt (1963) provide book-length, descriptive surveys of usage in Shakespeare and English generally. I am grateful to Edgar Schneider for bringing Finkenstaedt to my attention at EMEC.

2. For example: Strang (1974: 149), Barber (1976: 210) and Görlach (1978 [1991]: 85) all have *you* as unmarked by 1600, while Baugh and Cable (1978: 242) and Leith (1983: 108) have *thou* as marked "by the sixteenth century" and "from about 1500" respectively.

References

Barber, Charles
1976   *Early Modern English*. London: Deutsch.
1981   "*Thou* and *you* in Shakespeare's *Richard III*", *Leeds Studies in English*, New Series, 12: 273—280.
[1987]   [Reprinted in: Vivien Salmon—Edwina Burness (eds.), *A reader in the language of Shakespearean drama*. Amsterdam: Benjamins, 1—14.]
Baugh, Albert—Thomas Cable
1978   *A history of the English language*. London—New York: Routledge & Kegan Paul.
Brown, Roger—Albert Gilman
1960   "The pronouns of power and solidarity", in: Thomas Sebeok (ed.), *Style in language*. New York—London.
1989   "Politeness theory and Shakespeare's four major tragedies", *Language in Society* 18: 159—212.
Byrne, Geraldine
1936   *Shakespeare's use of the pronoun of address, its significance in characterisation and motivation*. Washington, D. C.: Catholic University of America Press.
Finkenstaedt, Thomas
1963   You *and* thou: *Studien zur Anrede im Englischen*. Berlin: De Gruyter.

Görlach, Manfred
1991   *Introduction to Early Modern English*. Cambridge: Cambridge University Press.
Ingram, Martin
1987   *Church courts, sex and marriage in England, 1570—1640*. Cambridge: Cambridge University Press.
Kytö, Merja — Matti Rissanen
1983   "The syntactic study of early American English: The variationist at the mercy of his corpus?", *Neuphilologische Mitteilungen* 84: 470—490.
Lass, Roger
forthcoming "Morphology.", in: Roger Lass (ed.), *The Cambridge history of the English language*. Vol. 3. *1476—1776*. Cambridge: Cambridge University Press.
Leith, Dick
1983   *A social history of English*. London: Routledge & Kegan Paul.
McIntosh, Angus
1963   "*As you like it:* A grammatical clue to character", *Review of English Literature* 4: 68—81.
Mulholland, Jean
1967   "*Thou* and *you* in Shakespeare: A study in the second person pronoun", *English Studies* 48: 34—43.
Rushton, Peter
1982   "Women, witchcraft and slander in Early Modern England: Cases from the church courts of Durham, 1560—1675", *Northern History* 18: 116—132.
1983   "Purification or social control? Ideologies of reproduction and the churching of women after childbirth", in: E. Gamarnikow (ed.), *The public and the private*. London: Heinemann, 118—131.
1985   "The broken marriage in Early Modern England: Matrimonial cases from the Durham church courts, 1560—1630", *Archaeologica Aeliana* fifth series, 13: 188—196.
1985—86 "The testament of gifts: Marriage tokens and disputed contracts in North-East England, 1560—1630", *Folklife* 24: 25—31.
1986   "Property, power and family networks: The problem of disputed marriage in Early Modern England", *Journal of Family History* 11/3: 205—219.
1989   "The church courts in North-East England in the sixteenth and seventeenth centuries: An historical gossip column?", *Sunderland History* 5 (volume XXXII of the papers of the Sunderland Antiquarian Society).
Sharpe, James A.
1980   "Defamation and sexual slander in Early Modern England: The church courts at York", *Borthwick Papers* 58, Borthwick Institute: University of York.
Strang, Barbara M. H.
1974   *A history of English*. London: Methuen.
Surtees Society
1845   *Depositions and other ecclesiastical proceedings from the courts of Durham extending from 1311 to the reign of Elizabeth*. Ed. J. Raine. (Publications of the Surtees Society, vol. 21.) London — Edinburgh.

Wakelin, Martyn
  1982   "Evidence for spoken regional English in the sixteenth century", *Revista Canaria de Estudios Ingleses* 5: 1—25.
Wales, Katherine
  1983   "*Thou* and *you* in Early Modern English: Brown and Gilman revisited", *Studia Linguistica* 37/2: 107—125.

Orthoepists and reformers

Veronika Kniezsa

1. After the Norman Conquest had destroyed the West Saxon scribal traditions, and scriptorial decentralisation became the order of the time in the Middle English period, orthography became a feature of regional traditions. A great variety of notational conventions had developed, partly due to the dialectal differences in pronunciation and phonological developments, partly as a result of trying to find adequate notations for the speech sounds. One of the major innovations of the Middle English scribes was the realisation of the necessity to mark vowel quantity. A number of varieties developed, partly based on phonological/phonetic developments, e. g., the doubling of consonant graphs when the vowel of the stressed syllable was short (e. g. *written*), or the employment of mute *-e* on the model of words where Middle English Open Syllable Lengthening (MEOSL) operated (e. g. *name* and *wife*). In other instances doubling of vowel graphs was used, a means already employed in Medieval Latin texts (e. g. *green, boot*), and the Old English digraph ⟨ea⟩ (e. g., *read*) was reintroduced together with the new ⟨oa⟩ as its velar counterpart (e. g., *boat*). There were no rules, however, as to the use of the various markings. Digraphs were used to mark those English consonants which were not part of the Latin sound system, and for whose notation consequently no special graphemes were available: these were adopted mostly from the Anglo-Norman orthographical system: ⟨ch⟩ for /tʃ/, ⟨th⟩ for /ð/ and /θ/, ⟨ṡh⟩ for /ʃ/, ⟨gh⟩ for /ç/ and /x/, and the Old English sequence /hw/ was spelled ⟨wh⟩, even though in the southern dialects it lost the /h/ element and became homophonous with /w/.

2. It was the introduction of the printing press that made it necessary to find a national orthographic system. However, at the end of the fifteenth century, the time was not yet ripe for such a task, and the orthographic idiosyncrasies of authors and printers became the characteristic feature of printed books, cf. the reference on the 9 variants of the word 'coney' in Greene's *A Notable Discovery of Cosnage* 1591: *cony, conny, conye, conie, connie, coni, cuny, cunny, cunnie* (Baugh 1973: 252), and these inconsistencies have remained one of the stumbling blocks for Present-day English. The disadvantages of the early attempts to fix spelling became even more apparent after the great phonological changes, when to the great variety of possible notations the total discrepancy between the actual sounds and the accepted "potestas" of the graphemes was added.

Since the sixteenth century we have witnessed a number of attempts to remedy the state of English orthography, and also their failure. Although well known, these attempts at reform have not yet been examined from the point of view of orthography, but only as to how they could be used to describe contemporary pronunciation (e. g. Ekwall, Dobson); even when considered in the context of the history of spelling, they were treated rather cursorily (e. g. Zachrisson, Baugh — Cable).

There were some reformers who, despite developing new orthographies and using them in their writings, did not elaborate on them (e. g. Cheke, Lanham). Others provided descriptions of their principles in addition to texts as examples (e. g. Hart). And there were those who gave detailed theoretical descriptions of their systems, but did not use them in their own writings (e. g. Smith).

In this paper I will discuss ten authors, some of whom published works aimed at reforming English spelling, some who described English grammar in general, others English phonology in particular, while still others wanted to help people to learn the right pronunciation or spelling of the language, whether native speakers or foreign learners of English. The discussion will consider the texts in chronological order of publication, thus trying to trace the development of the ideas on English orthography.

The texts in order of publication are:

John Hart: *The Opening of the Unreasonable Writing of our Inglish Toung* 1551
Anon.: *An ABC for Chyldren* a1558
Thomas Smith: *De Recta et Emendata Linguae Graecae Pronutiatione* 1568
Thomas Smith: *De Recta et Emendata Linguae Anglicae Scriptione, Dialogus* 1568
John Hart: *An Orthographie* 1569
John Hart: *A Methode* 1570
Richard Mulcaster: *The First Part of Elementarie* 1582
Alexander Hume: *Orthographie and Congruitie of the Britain Tongue* c1618
Alexander Gill: *Logonomia Anglica* 1619

Ben Jonson: *The English Grammar* 1640
Richard Hodges: *The English Primrose* 1644
John Wallis: *Grammatica Linguae Anglicanae* 1653
Cristopher Cooper: *The English Teacher* 1687

3. The earliest well-known spelling reformer was Sir Thomas Smith. He arrived at the idea of reform through his studies of ancient Greek, when he and John Cheke propagated a reconstructed pronunciation as opposed to the contemporary one based on Modern Greek pronunciation. Smith argues in *Lingua Graecæ* that it is confusing to have the same pronunciation, e. g. [i], for a variety of spellings such as ⟨e⟩, ⟨i⟩, ⟨ei⟩, ⟨ai⟩ and ⟨oi⟩, and states that his students found it easier to pronounce five different vowels instead of just one. Besides, if there were individual letters, these were probably meant to be used to mark different sounds. The principle was then reformulated in *Linguae Anglicae*, stating that just as the ancients had invented an individual grapheme for the notation of each separate sound, so the same should be introduced for English spelling. He propagated the "one sound — one single grapheme" principle of marking, opposing the custom of digraphs, which he accepted only in the case of diphthongs, where each of the graphemes had the task of marking a sounding element. Thus he was prepared to use digraphs to mark vowel diphthongs, but did not notice the binary character of the affricates, and decided to create or reintroduce old graphemes to mark them: from Old English he adopted ⟨c⟩ for /tʃ/ and ⟨ʒ⟩ (Old English "yogh") for /dʒ/. The other digraphs with ⟨h⟩ were also replaced by single letters: he again went back to Old English for the barred Latin d ⟨ð⟩("eth"), both in its capital and lower case forms, for the voiced interdental fricative /ð/, and ⟨þ⟩ for the voiceless one together with the Greek graphemes for the same sound, viz. ⟨θ⟩, and an inverted ⟨z⟩ as symbol for /ð/ (Figure 1).

Δ ẟ Δ Đ	*thou, there, bathe*
Ʋ ∇ ꝼ	*will, five, strive*
Ɉ ʒ	*George, lodge, just*
⩽ ⩽	*fish, shrill*
Τ Θ θ þ	*thin, thaw, pith*

Figure 1. Thomas Smith's special consonant graphemes

Smith wanted to mark vowel length by means of diacritics. He suggested three: ⟨¨⟩, ⟨^⟩, ⟨-⟩: e. g. 'mane' ⟨män, mân, ma-n⟩; in the text, however, he preferred to use the diaeresis *ä, ë, ï, ö, ü*, a new symbol, italic ⟨*ü*⟩ for /ju:/, and double diacritics in ⟨ë̈⟩ for Middle English/Early Modern English close /e:/.

He could not dissociate himself from the written forms when he discussed the use of ⟨i⟩ and ⟨u⟩. Since these symbols had double notational use in Latin, and in initial position represented a consonant, Smith was of the opinion that treating /j/, /v/ and initial /w/ as consonants was a gross mistake. He described "you", "vine" and "water" as diphthongs, and, in his treatment, "wine" and "vine" became both homographs and homophones ⟨vïn⟩. Since Smith wrote his book in Latin and restricted his thesis to the description of his basic principles by means of monosyllabic examples, we cannot form a complete picture of his system, determining whether he was aiming at a *phonetic* spelling; i. e. a very close representation of pronunciation, or a *phonemic* one, with the various morphemic elements attached to the base form and disregarding subsequent changes (e. g. '*wife — wives*').

4. John Hart, in *The Opening of the Unreasonable Writing of our Inglish Toung* (1551), describes his misgivings towards objections to a reform of English spelling. Opponents argued that a phonetic notation would destroy the difference between homophones, thus causing misunderstandings. Hart correctly remarks that in speech there are no means to make any formal difference between such words; the context itself seems to be sufficient for the hearer to decide which of the words fits the sentence heard, and he will not confuse, e. g., *bear* (noun) with *bear* (verb). A further objection was that an orthography following pronunciation would obscure the etymology of the words, and it would be impossible to tell from which language the word had been borrowed. But the strongest argument against spelling reform seems to be that of custom. This provokes Hart's analysis of the shortcomings of English spelling. He also rejects the suggestion that if changes are at all necessary, they should be introduced "by litell and litell (and with long continewance)" (Danielsson 1955: 119). One can hear similar arguments nowadays in defence of English orthography.

Hart expounds his system both in theory and practice in *An Orthographie*; in the second half of the treatise he uses his own spelling forms. Hart, too, worked along the "one sound — one simple symbol" lines. He also used diacritics to mark vowel length (a dot below the vowel grapheme), and diaeresis on the second vowel in the case of hiatus. In marking the vowels, he propagated spelling following pronunciation, i. e. he departs from traditional notations, remarking that only ⟨a⟩ is correctly used, while all the other graphemes are, in his opinion, grossly abused. Thus, he uses ⟨i⟩ for Early Modern English /i:/ < Middle English /e:/, which is ⟨ee⟩ in Middle English and Present-day English notation and ⟨ë⟩ in Smith's system. In this way Hart uses only the five traditional vowel graphemes ⟨a, e, i, o, u⟩ in contrast to Smith's seven, where two graphemes were due to the modification of the traditional letters.

huer-uiß hį in-dµ-ë d̃ us

Figure 2. John Hart's notation of vowel length and hiatus

Where Smith tried to represent consonants unknown in Latin by graphemes used for similar notations in the Middle Ages or antiquity, Hart invented his own graphemes for /θ, ð, tʃ, ʃ/; it is only in the case of /dʒ/ that he goes back to Old English "yogh" ⟨ʒ⟩. He explains that one of his guiding motives in forming his special graphemes was the ease of writing them.

    ꝸ   ꝫ   ꝺ   ꝳ   ꝷ

*Sh*eares; A *I*erkin; *The* Sunne; A *Ch*aine; A *Th*imble

Figure 3. John Hart's special consonant graphemes.

In *A Method*, Hart gives advice to teachers on how to teach reading with the help of his notational system. This is where he states that his spelling represents London English "where the generall flowerr of all English countrie speaches". With the help of these texts we can analyse his system, as it covers considerably more ground than a mere table of examples could. It becomes apparent that what Hart offers is again a fairly narrow phonetic notation. Hart belongs to the group of grammarians who deny the existence of English /w/, which he describes as a vowel and thus equates with /u/, resulting in some curious forms in his transcription when a word begins with a prevocalic /w/, cf. ⟨urd, uld⟩ for *word, would*, etc.

5. Not all sixteenth-century spelling reformers were as radical as Smith and Hart. Richard Mulcaster (1582) is of the opinion that "our English tung hath matter enough in hir own writing. which maie direct her own

right, if it be reduced to certain precept, and rule of Art, tho it haue not
as yet bene thoroughlie perceaued". Mulcaster is strictly against any kind
of spelling reform, claiming that writing according to pronunciation is
not necessary and custom is the most important principle. The only
concession he was willing to make was in instances of superfluous letters,
misrepresented letters, and in some cases he even omitted letters. Actually,
in these questions he agreed with all other reformers, Smith and Hart
included, who severely condemned the custom of abusing letters. The
kind of amendments suggested by Mulcaster were those which have been
implemented in the formation of present-day spelling; e. g., *putte* > *put*,
musicke > *music*, etc.

On account of his strict adherence to custom, Mulcaster had a sounder
basis in the employment of ⟨y⟩ and ⟨w⟩, the two graphemes which had
been rejected entirely by Smith and Hart. But he also adopted the
ambiguous employment of ⟨u, v⟩ and ⟨i, j⟩, advocating the custom valid
until well into the eighteenth century, which used both ⟨u⟩ and ⟨v⟩ for
both the vowel /u/ and the consonant /v/, only depending on the position
of the sound. Thus, initially it was ⟨v⟩, medially it was ⟨u⟩, either vowel
or consonant.

6. Since this notation was fairly confused for such a long time, it is
interesting to quote Alexander Hume's (ca. 1617) description explaining
that there are six different sounds which would therefore need six different
notational forms. In his suggestions he follows custom, but in the case
of ⟨i, j⟩ and ⟨u, v⟩ his description suggests the present patterns, viz. that
the vowels /i/ and /u/ should be represented by ⟨i⟩ and ⟨u⟩, the English
semivowels /j/ and /w/ by ⟨y⟩ and ⟨w⟩, while "Latin i" (i. e. initial /dʒ/
in borrowings) and /v/ should be represented by ⟨j⟩ and ⟨v⟩.

With respect to other questions Hume seems to be of two minds. On
the one hand he states that Scottish writing truly represents the sound;
on the other hand he suggests the adoption of traditional English notational forms which follow the "one word − one pattern" principle in the
case of homonyms, i. e. *hall, hail, hale* to which Scottish *hal* = English
whole can be added.

7. Alexander Gill blames the chaos of spelling on the printers. He
acknowledges Smith's and Hart's attempts to remedy the shortcomings
of English orthography and remarks that in his attacks on Smith and
Hart Mulcaster "wasted a great deal of time and good writing, concluding
that everything should be decided by the tirant Custom". He himself is

"in agreement with M. Fabius: in morals in agreement of good men, and in language the practice of the learned, is the determining rule" (Danielsson 1972: II.86). He explains that he considers four points to be of great service to spelling: 1) derivation: even in the case of difference in pronunciation the derivatives should follow the spelling of the primitives, and the primitives should follow the derivatives: e. g., ⟨personz⟩ because of ⟨personal⟩ etc. and not ⟨parsonz⟩; 2) difference: this principle overrules his phonetic principle, because he agrees that homonyms should be spelled differently, e. g. ⟨I⟩ 'ego', ⟨ei⟩ 'oculus', ⟨ëi⟩ 'ita'; 3) accepted custom: he allows such traditional forms as ⟨qu⟩ for /kw/, since he prefers "to dissolve custom by degrees rather than cut it off abruptly" (Danielsson 1976: II.88); and 4) dialect: here he allows spelling alternatives. Since these do not belong to the norm, "in moderation, poets are permitted to use metaplasm". He also devised a complete phonetic alphabet, using diacritics to mark vowel length (a macron above the graphemes), varieties of types, e. g. Italic type, Greek characters; there is some confusion in their use, however: sometimes it is the short vowel which is marked by one type, (e. g. italic *a* = *a* short, italic *a* + macron = *a* long; 'eta' = *e* short, italic *e* = *e* long; the two *o* sounds are marked with "omikron" and "omega", which runs counter to the other vowels). He gives special vowel quantities to ⟨v⟩ = /u/ long and ⟨j⟩ narrow, i. e. /ai/ (Figure 4).

Figure 4. Alexander Gill's special graphemes to mark vowel quantity

Gill invented special symbols for special English consonants, but he also preserved some digraphs from traditional writing (Figure 5).

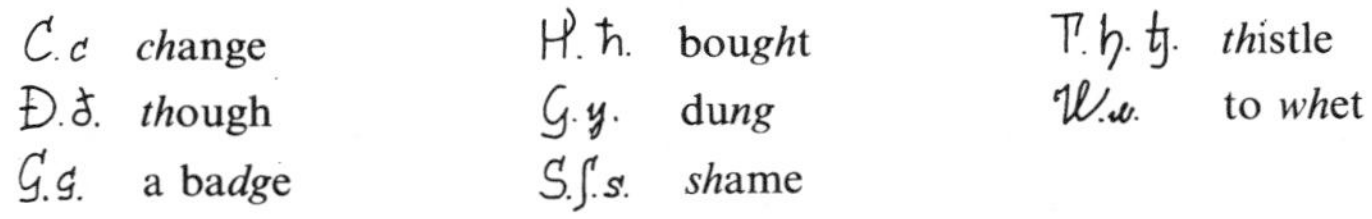

Figure 5. Alexander Gill's special consonant graphemes

In the second edition Gill explains that he excluded the use of double consonants (e. g. as in *fatter, better, robbing*) from his system, because his conviction was that "those double consonants are an error which is not to be permitted in spelling". From his samples (a couple of short sentences in the first edition in 1619, and the text of five Psalms in the second edition in 1621) we can conclude that he devised a rather narrow phonetic notational system, which could be attacked on the ground that it overlooked, among other things, the morphemic principle, i. e. the same morpheme will appear in different forms, e. g. 3rd Pers. Sg. Pres. Ind. i. e., *livz* — *siks* (Danielsson 1976: I.19).

8. The other group of authors whose work is worth discussing are the phoneticians and grammarians of the time. Their main aim was to describe the language. However, in their discussions of phonology, on account of the traditional confusion between phonemes and graphemes, both being referred to as "letters", they could not help making remarks concerning various problems of English orthography.

9. Ben Jonson intended his *English Grammar* for strangers who "live in communion and commerce with us". He made few remarks on orthography, joining the group which accepted ⟨i, j⟩ consonant-initially, ⟨u⟩ both as a vowel and a consonant as vantage, and ⟨w⟩ "though it have the seate of a *Consonant* with us, the power is alwayes *Vowellish*, even where it leades the *Vowell* in any Syllable: [...] *ou-ine*. Y is also meere Vowellish ... and hath only the power of i." He complains about the ambiguous use of ⟨c⟩ saying that "our Fore-fathers might very well have spar'd [it] in our tongue", calls ⟨k⟩ a necessary symbol, similarly on ⟨q⟩ "with her waiting-woman" ⟨u⟩. When discussing /h/, he also treats the digraphs with ⟨h⟩ as their second element. ⟨gh⟩ is again discussed as a "piece of ill writing with us. Only, the writer was at leisure, to adde a superfluous Letter, as there are too many in our *Pseudographie*." He regrets the loss of the Old English graphemes ⟨ð⟩ and ⟨þ⟩ for the interdental fricatives instead of ⟨th⟩. When treating "diphthongs", he actually means digraphs, and instead of using ⟨oa, ee⟩ he suggests the use of the mute -*e*. In the introductory enumeration of the letters he remarks that capital letters are used at the beginning of a sentence, of nouns and as Roman numerals.

10. John Wallis is considered to be the first true phonetician of the English language. He treats /w/ as a consonant, ⟨y⟩ as /j/ and as vowel /i/; ⟨y⟩ is preferred at the end of words, ⟨i⟩ in the middle. ⟨v⟩ is a consonant.

When treating the vowels, he accepts doubled graphemes and digraphs to mark long vowels. He gives an historical explanation for mute -*e*, and also of the logic of its use in English spelling, in three instances: 1) it ensures that the quantity of the preceding vowel remains the same; 2) it indicates the softer pronunciation of ⟨c, g, th⟩; 3) it helps to distinguish /v/ from /u/. In all other instances he is against its use, as, e. g., in the type *candle*. He also does not object to the consonant digraphs with ⟨h⟩.

11. Though it belongs to the sixteenth century, the anonymous *An ABC for Chyldren* is mentioned here together with two other books, viz. Hodges' *Primrose* and Cooper's *English Teacher*, because it has the same aim. They are pronouncing books, which means that they accepted the orthography as they found it, and tried to help the learners to make a connection between sound and form. Thus the attitude of these authors toward English orthography is that of acceptance. They are aware of the difficulties of English spelling and they want to offer guiding rules for the learner on how to overcome these.

12. Richard Hodges' method is to group English words according to certain principles; what he actually provides is a kind of phonotactics. As he explains in his preface, the reason why children cannot learn to read properly lies in the fact that the English language is "uncertain, and perplext, and intricate" in its expression; therefore he tries "to shew how the same may be remedied, *without infringing of custom*" (my italics). He claims that his method has the advantage that students will not only be able to read and pronounce the words properly, but also "they shall bee able to give a reason for what they do". It is noteworthy that Hodges calls attention to the fact that there are graphemes in the make-up of the orthographic pattern of a great number of words which do not have any function in representing speech sounds, simply with the aim to ensure the right pronunciation of these words, e. g. *wrought*. On the whole, he quotes a great number of "difficult words", i. e. long, learned words such as *supererogatorious*, where the pronunciation is enabled by breaking up the words into syllables. What is important for my particular interest is that he simply marks the "taskless" graphemes at the composition junctures in obscured compounds, where the elements are still clearly represented in the written form, e. g. *hus-wives, cup-boards, shep-herds*, without commenting on the correctness or incorrectness of the forms, as we shall observe from the remarks of later orthoepists.

13. The other orthoepist on my list, Christopher Cooper, is somewhat more critical with regard to English orthography. He is of the opinion that the English alphabet is 1) defective, "for there are no Characters distinct enough to express *a* in *hot, ng, dh*"; 2) superfluous, "for two simple sounds are exprest by one character"; and finally 3) incongruous, "for the Character expresses many sounds, *a* three, *o* four, *ou* and *oi* three" (Sundby 1953: 19).

Of the authors discussed, only two remarked on varieties of pronunciation. Gill made frequent references to the pronunciation of the Mopsae, the pronunciation of his pupils' parents at St. Pauls School, and also denounced certain pronunciations, which, judging from his remarks, were rather advanced in the simplification of consonant clusters. He claims he prefers the pronunciation *lundun* instead of *lunun*, or *lüun* as suggested by some. Cooper gives a longish list of examples in Chapter IX, "Of Barbarous Speaking": "He, that would write more exactly, must avoid a Barbarous Pronunciation; and consider for facility, or thorow mistake, many words are not sounded after the best dialect." Among these words are some examples where Cooper's correction favours spelling pronunciation: *ex-tree = axle-tree, gim me = give me; hankecher = handkerchief; Vitles = victuals; wumme, wuth me = with me*. Hodges still teaches [vitls] as the proper pronunciation of *victuals*, but according to the evidence of eighteenth century pronouncing dictionaries, Cooper represented the new way of pronouncing the word; apparently in the forty years between the publication of Hodges' and Cooper's books spelling pronunciation was gaining ground (according to Ellis, Jones still quoted [vitels] in 1701). This is also the form suggested in eighteenth century pronouncing dictionaries (e. g., Buchanan 1760, Sheridan 1780), as it in fact still is in Daniel Jones' Pronouncing dictionaries. *Handkerchief* is taught as [hænd.kətshər] by Jones (1701), but as [hæq.kertshif] by Sheridan (1780), which means that in Cooper's list of "do nots" we have an early example of the change towards the dominance of writing over the spoken language. As the two examples show, in some of the cases, especially in obscured compounds, spelling pronunciation won over natural sound changes (e. g. *handkertchief*).

Cooper also realises that there are a variety of spelling forms in use and decides to seek the best of them. In Chapter XX he gives a list of such words. He remarks that "Latin derivatives for the most part, are written as their primitives, but some words follow both the Latin form or the French one", e. g. the prefix *in-* or *en-*. In a list of words he quotes French spelling forms and others, where the origin of the variant spelling is not at all certain, e. g. *ba-let and Fr. ba-lad (where Cooper prefers the first form). In this list he marks the French forms with a dagger and the ones he prefers with an asterisk. Thus he prefers *Bedlam* to *Bethlehem*; *butcher* to *boucher*; *divel* to *devil*; *divide, virtue* to *devide, vertue*, etc. In the case of French words he prefers the form nearest to the original, e. g. *verdigreece* instead of *vertgrease* (which might represent a touch of folk etymology, and should therefore be rejected). His preferences, however, sometimes seem to rely on personal habit rather than any kind of principle, e. g. he prefers *frois* to *phrase*, *Porridge* to *Pottage*, and *Yelk* to *Yolk* (*yellow*). In these examples some of Cooper's preferences correspond to present-day forms, others go in the opposite direction.

14. The reformers tried to invent their notational system based on the model of the antique languages, Greek and Latin, claiming that the "letters" were originally devised to represent the speech sounds, and the way they were used in English was a blatant mishandling of them; therefore they propagated a "one sound — one grapheme" type of spelling, adding diacritics to indicate vowel properties (length and hiatus), but rejecting the employment of digraphs. Thus the strongest argument against their systems was the invention of unfamiliar graphemes to mark consonants absent in Latin (Smith, Hart).

All known attempts at spelling reform from the sixteenth to the twentieth century failed, mostly because of the view that spelling should express the etymology of the word as well as differentiate homonyms, and, moreover, there should not be any change in the notational conventions because "use" had already confirmed them. The more successful attempts were those which introduced the least changes in the accustomed orthographic form and aimed only at standardising orthography by the acceptance of just one spelling form of one special word without attempting to construct a system (Mulcaster). These scholars set down the rules for present-day orthography.

While the reformers tried to organise English spelling on a more or less revolutionary scale, orthoepists were against such changes. In general they were not interested in the spelling of words at all, or at best they were the ones who tried to systematise the existing notational forms. In more extreme cases they even condemned pronunciations which did not closely adhere to the written form.

Thus, in the struggle to make English spelling a system, "custom" won hands down, because as Cooper remarks, Smith, Hart, Wade, Bullokar, Gill and Butler "successively pursued the same design, which was nothing to our business in hand; for that was wholy to reform, and bring a new; but not to teach the present way of writing, which through the prevalency of Custom, and want of publick Authority, and learned men to back it, fell to the ground" (Sundby 1953: 5).

Primary Sources

Sundby, Bertil (ed.)
  1953   Christopher Cooper, 1687. *The English teacher.* (Lund Studies in English 22.)
              Lund: Gleerup.
Danielsson, Bror (ed.)
  1955, 1963 *John Hart's works,* 2 vols. [1551: "The opening of the unreasonable writing
              of our inglish toung"; 1569: "An Orthographie"; 1570: "A methode of com-
              fortable beginning for all vnlearned".] (Stockholm Studies in English 5, 11.)
              Stockholm: Almqvist & Wiksell.
  1978–1983   Sir Thomas Smith, Vol. 1. *Literary and linguistic works* (1542, 1549, 1568).
              Vol. 2. *De Recta et Emendata Linguae Graecae Pronuntiatione* (1549). Vol. 3.
              De Recta et Emendata Linguae Anglicae Scriptione, Dialogus (1568). (Stock-
              holm Studies in English 50, 56.) Stockholm: Almqvist & Wiksell.
Danielsson, Bror – Arvid Gabrielson (eds.)
  1972   Gill, Alexander, 1619. *Logonomia Anglica.* (Stockholm Studies in English 26,
              27.) Stockholm: Almqvist & Wiksell.
Flügel, E. (ed.)
  1891   "An Abc for chyldren 1551–1558", *Anglia* 13: 461–467.
Herford, C. H. – Percy Simpson – Evelyn Simpson (eds.)
  1947   *Ben Jonson.* Vol. 8. *The poems. The prose works.* (1640–1641 "English Gram-
              mar"). Oxford: Clarendon Press.
Kauter, Heinrich (ed.)
  1930   Richard Hodges, 1644. *The English primrose.* (Germanische Bibliothek. Abs.
              2. Bd. 8.) Heidelberg: Winter.
Kemp, J. A. (ed.)
  1972   John Wallis: *Grammar of the English language.* With a translation and com-
              mentary by J. A. Kemp. London: Longman.
Wheatly, Henry B. (ed.)
  1865   Alexander Hume: c. 1617 *Of the orthographie and congruitie of the Briton
              tongue.* (EETS). London: Oxford University Press.

References

Baugh, Albert C. – Thomas Cable
  1978   *A history of the English language.* Englewood Cliffs, N. J.: Prentice-Hall.
Bourcier, Georges
  1978   *L'orthographie de l'anglais.* Paris: Presses Universitaires de France.

Craigie, Alexander
    1928   *English spelling, its rules and reason.* London: Harrap.
    1942   *Some anomalies of spelling.* (S. P. E. Tract No. 59.) Oxford: Clarendon Press.
Grosse, Eginhard
    1937   *Die neuenglische ea-Schreibung.* Leipzig: Mayer & Müller.
Jespersen, Otto
    1909—1949 *A Modern English grammar on historical principles.* 7 vols. London: Allen
              and Unwin.
Kniezsa, Veronika
    1989a   "Attitudes toward written English", in: Lehel Vadon (ed.), *Studies in English
              and American culture.* Eger: Tanárképzô Fôiskola Sokszorosító Üzeme,
              225—233.
    1989b   "Accents and digraphs in the Peterborough Chronicle", *Studia Anglica Pos-
              naniensia* 21: 15—23.
    1992   "The due order and reason: histories of the history of English spelling". *Folia
              Linguistica Historica* 12: 209—218.
    forthcoming "English spelling: attitudes and principles", *Studies in English and American*
              Budapest: ELTE Department of English Language and Literature.
Marcus, Hans
    1917   *Die Schreibung ou in frühmittelenglischen Handschriften.* Berlin: Mayer &
              Müller.
Osselton, N. E.
    1984   "Informal spelling systems in early Modern English: 1500—1800", in: Nor-
              man F. Blake—Charles Jones (eds.), *English historical linguistics: Studies in
              development.* (CECTAL Conference Papers Series No. 3.) Sheffield: University
              Printing Unit, 123—137.
Reinhold, C. A.
    1934   *Neuenglisch ou (ow) und seine Geschichte.* (Palaestra 189.) Leipzig: Mayer &
              Müller.
Schlemilch, Willy
    1914   *Beiträge zur Sprache und Orthographie spätaltengl. Sprachdenkmäler der Über-
              gangszeit (1000—1150).* Halle/Saale: Max Niemeyer.
Scragg, D. G.
    1974   *A history of English spelling.* Manchester: Manchester University Press.
Sommer, Immanuel
    1937   *Die frühneuenglische Orthographie und Lautlehre in Lord Bacons englischen
              Werken.* Heidelberg: Winter.
Umpfenbach, Heinz
    1935   *Die oa-Schreibung im Englischen.* (Palaestra 201.) Leipzig: Mayer & Müller.
Vachek, Josef
    1973   *Written language.* The Hague: Mouton.
    1976   *Selected writings in English and general linguistics.* Prague: Akademia.
Vallins, G. H.
    1965   *Spelling.* (With a chapter on American Spelling by J. W. Clark. Revised by
              D. G. Scragg). London: Deutsch.
van der Gaaf, Willem
    1919   "Notes on English orthography (ie and ea)", *Neophilologus* 5: 133—159;
              333—348.

Weiss, Helmut
    1937   *Die ie (ee)-Schreibung im Englischen und ihre Geschichte.* [Ph. D. dissertation
            Berlin]. Bottrop: Wilhelm Postberg.
Wijk, Axel
    1959   *Regularised English.* Stockholm: Almqvist & Wiksell.
    1966   *Rules of pronunciation for the English language.* Oxford: Oxford University
            Press.
Wokatsch, Werner
    1932   *Unhistorisches ea in angelsächsischen und frühmittelenglischen Handschriften.*
            [Ph. D. dissertation Berlin.] Berlin: Mayer & Müller.
Zwerina, Helmut
    1930   *Neuenglisch o gesprochen wie u.* [Ph. D. dissertation Berlin]. Leipzig: Mayer
            & Müller.

Vocalisation of "post-vocalic *r*" — an Early Modern English sound change?

Angelika Lutz

The most far-reaching change of the system of long vowels after the Great Vowel Shift was caused by a development termed "*r*-Wirkungen" by Luick and others. The final results of this change may be summarised as follows:[1]

(1) a. Short vowels + /r/ developed into long monophthongs:
     V̆ + r > V̄, namely Standard English /ɑ:/, /ɜ:/, /ɔ:/;
     cf. Modern Standard English *hard, star* (< ME *sterre*); *bird, turn, herd; corn.*

   b. Most long vowels + /r/ developed into centring diphthongs, some of which have since been monophthongised:
     V̄ + r > Vv, namely Standard English /ɪə/, /ɛə/, /(j)ʊə ~ (j)ɔ: /, /ɔə ~ ɔ:/;
     cf. Modern Standard English *steer, fear; bare, hair, bear; cure, poor; lore.*

This change resulted in a considerable extension of the system of complex vowel phonemes: the centring diphthongs /ɪə/, /ɛə/, /ʊə/ (and /ɔə/) and the central long monophthong /ɜ:/ derive exclusively from vocalisation of "post-vocalic *r*" and its fusion with the preceding vowel, the long back monophthongs /ɑ:/ and /ɔ:/ partly so (cf. Gimson 1989: 82 – 83, 92 – 146). The South-Eastern varieties of English including Standard English had almost reached this stage by the end of the Early Modern English period (cf. Horn – Lehnert 1954: 913 – 921); in this sense the classification of the change in the handbooks as basically an Early Modern English development may be considered correct.

The handbooks have described this sound change in great detail, but their treatment of the change is biased. By this I mean the classification of phonological changes as vocalic or consonantal developments mainly from the point of view of whether the speech sound resulting from the change was a vowel or a consonant and not depending on whether the speech sound affected by the change was a vowel or a consonant. Thus, most of the information on the vocalisation of "post-vocalic *r*" in the handbooks of Luick, Brunner, Horn – Lehnert, and Dobson is to be found in the sections on the changes of the accented vowels, whereas the subsequent sections on consonantal changes in these handbooks usually contain only a few additional remarks.[2] It is certainly legitimate and worthwhile to describe a sound change from the viewpoint of its result – the more so in this particular case, since most of the written evidence for the gradual vocalisation of [r], including the writings of the early phoneticians, reflects the effects of the change on the pronunciation of the preceding vowels. However, this bias on the vocalic results has obscured the understanding not only of this particular sound change but also its relation to similar changes in the earlier and later history of English.

Moreover, this bias has resulted in what I consider a more general misjudgement of the phonological development of English as one which is characterised by a great number of vocalic changes but by a remarkable stability of the consonants throughout its history and prehistory. Statements of this kind can be found both in traditional studies and in structuralist treatments. Thus, Brunner states: "Der Vokalismus des Englischen ist durch weitgehende Verschiebungen gekennzeichnet" (1960: 229) … "Anders als die Vokale zeigen die englischen Konsonanten ein starkes Beharrungsvermögen. In vielem ist der englische Konsonantismus noch heute altertümlicher als der anderer germanischer Sprachen" (1960: 360).[3] Similarly, Plotkin (1972: 88) speaks of "a 'quiet' consonantism diachronically" with reference to English.

The aim of my paper is to show that this overall view of the history of English sounds is based on the classification of changes such as the vocalisation of "post-vocalic *r*" and its fusion with the preceding vowel as mainly vocalic developments, and that this biased view of such changes is incorrect in the sense that it has obscured the understanding of general lines of development which have determined the history of English from pre-Old English to Modern English. Developments of this kind, which have hitherto been viewed as an incoherent sequence of diverse changes of accented vowels, will turn out to be successive stages of one coherent and directed consonantal development.

This coherence and directedness of consonantal changes becomes apparent when sufficient attention is paid a) to the basic phonetic characteristics of consonants; b) to their behaviour under different phonotactic conditions. Both factors may be defined with reference to the phonological concept of consonantal strength. For one, this concept allows us to classify consonants as inherently stronger or weaker on a scale of consonantal strength depending on their basic phonetic characteristics, with the voiceless plosives at one end of the scale, the open vowels at the opposite end:[4]

(2)   Scale of inherent consonantal strength

consonantal strength

←————————————————

vl plosives	vd plosives	vd fricatives	nasals	laterals	*r*-sounds	*w*	*j*	closed	open
	vl fricatives							vowels	vowels

Liquids and semivowels, on account of their vowel-like character, are inherently weak consonants, with the lateral /l/ being the strongest of this group, followed by /r/, the velar semivowel /w/, and the palatal semivowel /j/. For the liquids and semivowels of Modern English, the place on the scale of consonantal strength may be directly correlated with the (independently established) phonetic criterion of formant structure, which is least vowel-like for /l/ and most vowel-like for /j/.[5]

In addition to the inherent strength of a consonant it is necessary to consider its grade of positional strength, which depends on its syllable, phrase, and accent position.[6]

(3)   Positional strength gradation

a. syllable position		b. phrase position		c. accent position	
[C]	[c]	[C]	[c]	[C]	[c]
ˇhead	coda	initial/final	medial	+accent	−accent

Positional strength gradation, such as between head and coda allophones of a speech sound, affects inherently strong and inherently weak consonants alike.[7]

(4)   Inherent and positional strength

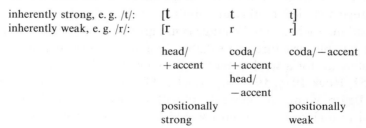

inherently strong, e. g. /t/:	[t	t	t]
inherently weak, e. g. /r/:	[r	r	ɾ]
	head/	coda/	coda/−accent
	+accent	+accent	
		head/	
		−accent	
	positionally		positionally
	strong		weak

Thus, both inherent strength and positional strength contribute to the specific value of consonantal strength of a consonant in actual speech, together with a third constitutive factor — pragmatic strength, which is determined by stylistic parameters such as speed of utterance.[8]

For the present purpose of explaining vocalisation of "post-vocalic *r*" and its relation to similar changes in the history of English it will turn out to be sufficient to refer only to the inherent and positional strength of the consonants concerned. It will be shown that this sound change and its temporal relation to similar changes in the history of English was determined by the inherent and positional strength of the consonants that were affected by the change.[9]

So far, I have used the term 'vocalisation of "post-vocalic *r*"' to describe the conditions for this sound change and for the resulting distributional restrictions of /r/, in accordance with most studies of Modern English and its history; yet, at the same time, by using double inverted commas, I have tried to indicate that the conditions should be characterised in a different way. They should be stated with reference to syllable position (cf. Kahn 1980: 22−23, 106−120, 155−159):

(5)   Conditions for the distribution of /r/ in Standard English

head: +, coda: −
a. in words: *hearing, hearer* /'hɪə.rɪng, 'hɪə.rə/ vs. *hear, hears, hearsay* /hɪə(z), 'hɪə.seɪ/;
b. in phrases (linking *r*): *near us* /'nɪə.rʌs/ vs. *near me* /'nɪə.mi:/.[10]

The traditional description with reference to adjacent vowels (as, e. g., in Wells 1982: 222−227, Gimson 1989: 99, 302−304) is at the same time less precise and more complicated, since it requires further specification for intervocalic [r] both in word- and in phrase-internal position.

A description with reference to syllable position[11] is not only simpler but also provides the basis for an adequate explanation of the sound change that led to this distribution, namely weakening of /r/ in coda position. Such a sound change is in agreement with universal preferences for syllable structure and syllable structure change, particularly with the preference for a weak coda (Vennemann 1988: 21−27; see also Martinet 1952, Hock 1976, 1991, and Locke 1983: 113−115, 164−166).

Before going into more detail with regard to the positional conditions and to dialectal variation, I would like to point out some distributional parallels of /r/ with other consonants in Modern English and with their historical development. In Modern Standard British English four consonants are restricted to syllable head position, namely /j/, /w/, /h/, and /r/. Three of the four consonants, /j/, /w/, /r/, may be described as inherently very weak on account of their vowel-like character. The fourth — Modern English /h/ — is usually characterised as a "fortis, voiceless, glottal fricative" (e. g. in Gimson 1989: 192); but the description of /h/ proposed by Pike (1943: 71) as a fricative resulting from "*cavity friction*, that is, voiceless resonance of a chamber as a whole caused by air going through it as through an open tube" is much more to the point, since it explains why /h/ differs from the other fricatives by exhibiting rather weak friction noise[12] and, consequently, by not possessing a lenis counterpart.

In Old English all four consonants occurred both in the head and the coda of accented syllables, but in the course of the history of English one consonant after the other became restricted to the head position, and this gradual phonotactic restriction correlates with the consonants' values of inherent strength: the development began with the palatal semivowel in Old English and very early Middle English,[13] it was followed by the stronger, velar semivowel in late Old English and early Middle English,[14] then by /h/ in Middle English and Early Modern English,[15] and then by /r/ — the weaker of the two liquids, in very late Middle English and Early Modern English; and in certain varieties of English, especially in Cockney, this development has progressed even further to include /l/, the stronger of the two liquids (cf. Wells 1982: 258 — 259, 313 — 317).

In each case the consonant underwent progressive weakening, i. e. vocalisation,[16] and gradually fused with the preceding vowel. The end-result from a phonemic point of view was a complex vowel, namely either a long monophthong or a diphthong.[17] The end-result from a phonotactic point of view was the restriction of the consonant to the syllable head position. Thus, the Early Modern English sound change described as "*r*-Wirkungen" on accented vowels turns out to be but one stage in a phonotactically determined and directed consonantal development, namely that of progressive weakening of consonants in coda position, which spans the entire history of English and which, in the case of the inherently weak consonants, has resulted in their phonotactic restriction to the stronger syllable head position.

These are the outlines of my argument. The following section will be devoted to a sketch of certain features of this development and of its dialectal diversity, which is intended to show that all these changes are indeed only successive stages of one single, phonotactically determined consonantal development. I will concentrate this very selective description on three of the five consonants, starting with the history of /r/ and then pointing out parallels in the developments of /l/ and /h/.

Modern Standard English belongs to those varieties of English which have total vocalisation of /r/ in accented (and in unaccented[18]) syllable codas but only partial vocalisation of /r/ in unaccented syllable heads. From this it may be concluded that the positional strength grade of /r/ in unaccented syllable heads is somewhat higher than that of /r/ in accented syllable codas. At least in some cases, this difference of positional strength of the consonant corresponds with a less centralised quality of the accented vowel:

(6)   Conditions for total and partial vocalisation of /r/ in Standard English

accented coda: total; unaccented head: partial
Standard English *fear* [fɪə] vs. *fearing* ['fɪ°.ɹɪŋ]

In other, more conservative varieties of British English, weakening of /r/ in accented codas reached the final stage of total vocalisation much later or has not quite reached it so far. E. g., in parts of Yorkshire and Lincolnshire, coda /r/ is totally vocalised only in word-medial but not in word-final position (Wells 1982: 367−370). For even more conservative varieties such as Scottish English, the development may be termed an incipient change: In Lowland Scots "single tap" and weak fricative variants in accented codas, as opposed to the strongly trilled /r/ of syllable heads, have been observed since the beginning of the twentieth century.[19] Northern Scottish dialects still have trilled /r/ even in coda position (Wells 1982: 411).

The dialectal variation in the strength grade of /r/ in accented coda position corresponds with the grade of deviation of the vowel preceding /r/ from that before other, inherently stronger consonants. In non-rhotic dialects of English all vowels before original /r/ differ markedly from their Middle English equivalents before other consonants, whereas in weakly rhotic varieties this difference is less pronounced and in strongly rhotic ones hardly noticeable.[20]

The dialectal pattern observed in the modern dialects − with Cockney being the most progressive variety and Northern Scots the most conservative − holds for the entire Modern English period since the fifteenth century:[21] The earliest occasional ⟨r⟩-less spellings for etymological /r/

in accented syllable coda position occur in South-East Midland private letters of the fifteenth century, where they are first recorded after the short open vowel and earlier before covered /r/ than word-finally, namely in spellings such as *haad* 'hard'. The same documents also record lowering of short /e/ to /a/ before /r/ and another consonant, which happened early enough to be reflected in the English orthography (e. g. in *hart* < ME *herte*). And ever since, it has been the London dialect, especially that of lower styles, which has taken the lead in the successive stages of this development as well as in the subsequent changes of the vowels deriving from it; the Northern and Scottish dialects on the other hand have remained especially conservative since the fifteenth century.

However, the very earliest instances of the lowering of /e/ to /a/ before coda /r/ are recorded from Northern manuscripts of the fourteenth century. These early Northern spellings reflect a much more general progressiveness of the Northern dialects throughout the Old and Middle English periods.[22]

For the following sections, which deal with /l/ and /h/, the same distributional and dialectal characteristics have to be kept in mind as have been observed in the development of /r/ in accented syllable codas, namely:
1. earlier and more far-reaching changes
   a) in pre-consonantal position than in syllable- and word-final position,
   b) after short vowels than after long vowels,
   c) after open vowels than after closer vowels; and
2. a general phonological progressiveness of the Northern dialects in Old and Middle English, but of the South-East Midland dialects (and London in particular) from very late Middle English onwards.

The lateral liquid of Modern Standard English is characterised by a marked allophonic differentiation between clear [l] (as in *lip*) and dark [ɫ] (as in *pill*). The rules for the distribution of the two allophones is in most cases stated with reference to adjacent vowels.[23] A description with reference to syllable position, as offered, e. g., by Ohala (1974: 256−258), Hawkins (1984: 267) and Lass (1987: 100), is not only simpler but, at the same time, carries explanatory force: dark, more vowel-like [ɫ] can be explained as the result of coda weakening, i. e. as an instance of partial vocalisation in a weak syllable position.

(7)   Conditions for the distribution of /l/-allophones in Standard English

> head: clear [l]; cf. *let, blow, valley, feeling; feel upset, fall off;*
> [let, blǝʊ, væl̥i, fiː.lɪŋ; fiː.lʌp.set, fɔː.lɒf]
> coda: dark [ɫ]; cf. *feel, milk, shelter; feel free, fall down*
> [fiːɫ, mɪɫk, ʃeɫ.tǝ; fiːɫ.friː, fɔːɫ.dɑʊn]

Thus it exactly parallels the description of the conditions for the total vocalisation of the inherently weaker, central liquid /r/ in the same phonotactic position given above in (6), or for its partial vocalisation in more conservative varieties of English. Under the same phonotactic conditions modern Cockney exhibits total vocalisation of /l/ to a velar vowel and fusion with the preceding vowel to form a complex vowel:

(8)   Conditions for the distribution of /l/ in Cockney

> head: +; cf. *fooling* ['fʊu.lɪŋ];
> coda: −; cf. *fall, milk, shelf* [fʊu, mɪʊk, ʃeʊf].

According to Wells (1982: 258 − 259, 321 − 322) this Cockney development is very recent and not yet completed. It was first described by Jones (1909: § 298) as a feature of "London dialectal speech", but has since been seeping into adjacent dialects. Wells (1982: 259) therefore assumes that "It seems likely that it will become entirely standard in English over the course of the next century."[24]

The polar opposite of Cockney with its largely vocalised /l/ in syllable coda position are varieties of Modern British English with very slight allophonic differentiation between head and coda /l/ and, correspondingly, with very little difference between vowels preceding coda /l/ and other, stronger consonants, such as Scottish English and some Northern English varieties.[25] Thus, the vocalisation of /l/ in accented syllable codas may be characterised as an ongoing change even for the progressive dialects of English.

However, under special additional conditions concerning both the preceding vowel and the following consonant, coda /l/ reached the final stage of total vocalisation to a velar vowel much earlier, namely in early Middle English and in Early Modern English. The early Middle English development affected /l/ between a front open vowel and the fortis affricate /tʃ/:

(9)   OE *ǣlc* > EME *ę̄uch* > ME *ę̄ch* > ModE *each*.[26]

The Early Modern English development occurred between half-open or open back vowels and labial or velar consonants:

(10)   a. ModE *calf* /kɑ:f/ < ME *calf* < OE *calf/cealf*;
            ModE *psalm* /sɑ:m/ < ME *psalm* < OE *(p)salm/sealm*;
        b. ModE *yolk* /jəʊk/ < ME *yolk* < OE *geoloc*.[27]

The early Middle English development is first recorded in Northern manuscripts, the Early Modern English change manifested itself first in fifteenth century South-East Midland texts. Thus, the restricted developments of coda /l/ exhibit the same dialectal pattern as has been described above for the general vocalisation of coda /r/ in Middle English and Early Modern English.

The complete restriction of Modern Standard English /h/ to the syllable head position of accented syllables dates back to the fifteenth to early seventeenth centuries.[28] Old English /h/, whose primary source is the Germanic velar fricative, is generally believed to have had an allophonic distinction between [h] in heads and [x] in codas. For the coda allophone, prevelar and postvelar assimilatory variants depending on the preceding vowel must be assumed at least for late Old English.[29] Throughout the Old English period, the letter ⟨h⟩ was used for both head and coda variants of /h/. But in the course of Middle English, a clear spelling distinction between ⟨h⟩ for heads and ⟨gh⟩ for codas was established; this testifies to the growing allophonic differentiation due to progressive weakening of coda /h/, which had by then developed into palatal and postvelar allophones respectively. Their gradual vocalisation resulted in the development of a palatal or velar glide between the vowel and the weakened fricative. These Middle English weakening processes occurred early enough to be reflected in the orthography of Modern Standard English:

(11)   a. ModE *eight* /eɪt/ < ME *eighte* ['aɪç.tə] < OE *eahta*;
        b. ModE *bought* /bɔ:t/ < ME *boughte* ['boʊχ.tə] < OE *bohte*.

Only in very late Middle English do we get clear indications for total vocalisation of the fricative, namely in the form of both phonetic spellings such as late Middle English *niit* for Standard English *night* and reverse spellings such as Standard English (< late Middle English) *delight* < Old French *delite*. This final stage of the development was reached too late in the emerging standard language to have had a lasting effect on Modern English orthography.[30]

Again, it is the dialectal pattern of the development that I would like to draw attention to, especially that of the Early Modern English period: The very earliest instances of phonetic and reverse spelling of the type *niit/delight* are from early fifteenth century London texts. In the Southumbrian dialects in general, the complex vowels resulting from vocalisation of /h/ developed early enough to be included in the Great Vowel Shift: These dialects do not distinguish between words with original, Old English /i:/ (as in ModE *time*) and those with /i:/ deriving from Middle English /i/ + /h/ (as in ModE *night*), whereas some Northern English dialects do. In some Northern English varieties and in the Southern Scottish dialects coda /h/ was preserved even until the early twentieth century, and the Northern Scottish varieties preserve it until today.[31] The handbooks describe the entire development and its dialectal differentiation with precision and in great detail, but they do it with the same bias towards the vocalic results of the change as in the case of the vocalisation of coda /r/, whereas its phonotactic cause — weakening of the consonant in a relatively weak phonotactic position — does not receive sufficient attention.[32]

At the beginning of this paper I stated that such a biased description "is incorrect in the sense that it has obscured the understanding of the general lines of development which determined the history of English from pre-Old English to Modern English". This statement may have appeared somewhat full-mouthed, at least with reference to the changes of /h/, /r/ and /l/ sketched above, which extend from Middle English to Present-day English. Therefore, before concluding, I would like to point out some parallels between these Middle English and Modern English weakening processes and certain pre-Old English developments that are connected with the same three consonants and, in addition, with /w/, namely "breaking" and "retraction" of palatal vowels.

Campbell (1959: § 139) describes breaking and retraction as changes of accented vowels "due to the influence of consonants on the front vowels" — namely that of "(1) *l, r, χ* , when they are followed by a consonant, (2) single *χ*, and (3) single *u.*" That breaking and retraction are indeed only different grades of one development, namely partial and total backing of front vowels, and that the changes caused by following /w/ are of the same character as those caused by /l/, /r/, and /h/, was first made clear by Luick (1914—1940: §§ 133—159).[33]

Again, the handbook descriptions of the change are detailed and precise, but biased towards the vocalic results, whereas the phonetic characteristics of the consonants that cause breaking and retraction and the phonotactic conditions under which they do so have received insufficient attention so far.[34] In particular, this bias towards the vocalic results has obscured the understanding of the parallels between pre-Old English breaking and retraction on one hand and the weakening processes described above on the other.

The handbooks assume that the phonetic feature which is common to all four consonants and which causes breaking or retraction of palatal vowels is velarity, namely inherent velarity in the case of /w/ and /h/, and positional velarity in the case of the liquids.[35] Yet this can only be partly true, since the velar fortis plosive does not have such a velarising effect on front vowels.

For the following sketch of the basic conditions for breaking/retraction and of its dialectal differentiation, I refer to a small selection of examples given in (12), whose arrangement is principally determined by the inherent strength of the consonants as stated above in (2) and as established for the total vocalisation of /l/, /r/, and /h/ in accented syllable codas. Parallel forms with retraction instead of breaking are separated by dashes, parallel or related forms without breaking or retraction are added in brackets:

(12) a. OE (WS) *healdan* 'hold'/Angl. *haldan*; *seolh* 'seal'; Angl. *seolf* 'self' [WS *self*];

  b. OE (WS) *earm* 'arm'/North. *arm*; *steorra* 'star'; *hierde* 'shepherd';

  c. OE (WS) *eahta* 'eight'; *feoh* 'cattle'; *Piohtas* 'Picts'; *lēoht* 'light' [Angl. *lēht*; LWS *līht*]; *sēon* < **seohan* 'see' [Angl. *sēan* < **sehan*];

  d. OE (WS) (G. D. Sg. *clawe* 'claw' [N. Sg. *clēa* < **clau*]; *hweowol* 'wheel'; *ðriowa* 'three times'; *trēow* < **treu̯u̯ō* 'tree'.

In my view (cf. Lutz 1991: III.B.3), the conditions for breaking and retraction can be stated with reference to five factors, the first three of which concern the consonants, the remaining two the preceding accented vowel. These factors are:
1. inherent strength;
2. phonotactic position;
3. velarity of the consonant;
4. degree of aperture of the preceding vowel;
5. quantity of the vowel.
Four of these five factors determined the progression of total vocalisation of the four consonants since the Old English period.[36] The following description of the conditions for breaking/retraction of palatal vowels before /l/, /r/, /h/, and /w/ exhibits remarkable parallels to the conditions for total vocalisation of the same consonants from Old English onwards.

/l/ causes breaking only if in coda position and covered by another consonant, and it affects only the short, open vowel; the mid vowel is only broken if /l/ is followed by /h/, which causes breaking by itself. In Anglian the velarising effect of coda /l/ is more pronounced than in West Saxon: It exhibits retraction (i. e. total velarisation) of the open vowel, and breaking of the mid vowel also when followed by /f/. Thus, in the case of /l/, which is the inherently strongest of the four consonants, breaking is essentially restricted to that position in which later, in Early Modern English, total vocalisation of both /l/ and /r/ occurred earliest.

Before /r/, breaking is less restricted than before /l/; /r/, if in coda position and followed by another consonant, affects all three short front vowels. In Northumbrian, the open vowel is totally velarised. Thus, in the case of /r/, the same restriction to the coda position applies as in the case of the lateral, stronger liquid, but the velarising effect of coda /r/ is more pronounced on account of its lesser inherent strength.

Breaking before /h/ is least restricted. It affects both short and long vowels, and it is not only caused by /h/ in covered codas but also in uncovered codas and in unaccented syllable heads, both on account of its inherent velarity and its inherent weakness; the latter becomes apparent in intervocalic position in total vocalisation (i. e. in "contraction"[37]) very soon afterwards. Most effects of breaking on palatal vowels before coda /h/ are later on suspended by "smoothing" before all velars − in Anglian already in pre-Old English, in West Saxon only in late Old English.[38] Thus, both the especially large extent of breaking before /h/ and its abandonment by way of smoothing (or, partly, by contraction) testify to the inherent weakness of /h/.

Breaking or retraction before /w/ is most frequent if the velar semi-vowel stands in unaccented syllable head position; i. e., it is caused primarily by the stronger positional variant. By contrast, /w/ in coda position after the short open vowel is totally vocalised before it can cause breaking or retraction, and the resulting diphthong joins in the development of Gmc. *au* to OE *ēa*. Thus, in the case of the inherently weakest of the four consonants, breaking can only be observed in those vowels after which total vocalisation of all four consonants sets in particularly late; after the short open vowel (the only position in which coda /l/ normally causes breaking if followed by an other consonant), coda /w/ is already totally vocalised.

In short, pre-Old English breaking and retraction were caused by four inherently weak consonants in basically the same phonotactic positions in which the very same consonants suffered total vocalisation later on.

Moreover, breaking and retraction exhibit the same dialectal distribution as the above-mentioned changes of /l/, /r/, /h/, and /w/[39] that occurred in Middle English: the Northern varieties (Anglian in general and Northumbrian in particular) were affected earlier than those farther south.

From these distributional and dialectal parallels I conclude that pre-Old English breaking should not primarily be viewed as a combinatory vowel change but as the earliest stage of a phonotactically determined weakening process affecting inherently weak consonants in certain weak phonotactic positions. In the case of the liquids, this weakening process was restricted to preconsonantal coda positions of accented syllables. For the liquids in that position we have to assume weakened, partially vocalised, velar allophones. These had a velarising effect on preceding short palatal vowels.[40] Thus, pre-Old English breaking and retraction can be viewed as the first stage of a progressive, directed development which has shaped the entire history of English sounds.

Within this ongoing process spanning a millennium and a half, Early Modern English saw the final stage of weakening of /r/ in accented syllable codas in the more progressive dialects.[41] It is only in this sense that vocalisation of /r/ in coda position may be termed an Early Modern English development.

Notes

1. For details of this change cf. Luick (1914−1940: §§ 505−511, 549−553, 559−560, 562, 564−570, 804), Horn−Lehnert (1954: 440−506, 904−931), Brunner (1960: 332−344, 390), and Dobson (1968: II, §§ 42−49, 198−218, 401 c, 427).
2. E. g., in Luick's treatment of the change, only two paragraphs out of 29 are devoted to the consonant, in Dobson's two out of 31, in Brunner's one out of 14; Horn−Lehnert's description is an exception, with 28 pages in the second volume (which is devoted to the changes of the consonants) compared to 67 in the first volume (where the effects on the vowels are dealt with). The standard accounts of the Modern English dialect situation (esp. Wells 1982 and the dialect atlases of Orton−Sanderson−Widdowson 1978 and Kolb *et al.* 1979) exhibit a similarly strong imbalance.
3. 'English vocalism is characterised by large-scale shifts.' ... 'Contrary to the vowels the English consonants exhibit a powerful stability. In many respects the English consonantal system is more conservative than that of other Germanic languages.'
4. See Lutz (1988: 222−223) and Murray (1988: ch. 2) for such scales and for references.
5. See Lehiste (1964) for Present-day American English. For strong consonants such as the plosives, different phonetic criteria, e. g. the fortis : lenis contrast, may be adduced; cf. Kohler (1984). The actual phonetic characteristics of a consonant are in part language-specific (and, indeed, also dialect-specific). Naturally, this is also true for the actual value of inherent strength of a consonant in a given language or dialect; e. g.,

in the case of the central liquid /r/ we need to assume different values of inherent strength for the frictionless continuant [ɹ] of Modern Standard English than for the strongly trilled [r] of Scottish English or Italian. Nevertheless, we may assume the scale of consonantal strength to be universally valid in the sense that in languages with both a central and a lateral liquid, /r/ tends to be weaker than /l/ or, with even greater confidence, that in languages with a fortis : lenis contrast in plosives the lenis plosives of a given language are weaker than their fortis counterparts.

6. See Lutz (1988: 223–224) for a first systematic account of positional strength gradation and its importance for explaining sound change; for a more detailed account and for references to the literature on the phonetic correlates of strength gradation cf. Lutz (1991: "Einleitung" and IV.1). Naturally, the phonetic correlates of positional strength gradation are different for different (types of) speech sounds.

7. See Coker–Umeda (1975) and Umeda–Coker (1975) for a phonetic comparison of head and coda variants of all consonants of Present-day American English.

8. See Lutz (1991: "Einleitung") for a more detailed description of this extended concept of consonantal strength and for references to the literature on some of its phonetic correlates.

9. For an extensive and detailed treatment of phonotactically determined change in the history of English see Lutz (1991).

10. The same rule applies in the case of "intrusive *r*" as in *law and order* /'lɔː.r ənd .../ or in *vanilla ice-cream* /və'nɪlə.'raɪs .../ by way of *rule inversion* (Vennemann 1972: 216); in this case it was at first restricted to the non-standard varieties of London, but since the late nineteenth century has become increasingly common in Standard English as well; see Wells (1982: 222–227) and Gimson (1989: 99, 302–304). The use of full-stops to mark syllable boundaries is here restricted to aspects of syllabification under discussion.

11. The accent position of /r/ may be ignored for the moment, since it is of no importance for the present argument; but I will return to this question later on.

12. Cf. Luick (1932: § 63): "... ein ganz gelindes Reibegeräusch, das bedeutend schwächer ist als das der eigentlichen Reibelaute." ['... a very light friction noise, which is considerably weaker than that of the ordinary fricatives.'] For a differentiating treatment of the fricatives in the history of English see Lutz (1988) and esp. Lutz (1991: chs. I, II) (with more detailed reference to the literature on phonetic correlates).

13. For details see Luick (1914–1940: §§ 252, 257, 372–373, 399–401, 626, 633, 642–643, 710), Campbell (1959: §§ 120, 266–269, 271, 402), Kuhn (1970: 44–46).

14. Cf. Luick (1914–1940: §§ 100, 134, 257, 399–400, 402, 633, 641, 711), and Jordan–Crook (1974: §§ 104–110).

15. Cf. Luick (1914–1940: §§ 400–403, 768–769), Horn–Lehnert (1954: 849–863), and Jordan–Crook (1974: §§ 96–100, 196–198, 294–295). So far, no independent phonetic correlate for the inherent strength of /h/ in Modern English relative to the semivowels and the liquids can be adduced. But see below for the same relative order of development — /w/, /h/, /r/, /l/ in the case of pre-Old English breaking.

16. Progressive vocalisation was the normal development in the history of English; the rarer case of weakening by assimilatory fusion with the following consonant (as in dial. *hoss* 'horse') or of replacement of the weakened consonant by a similar but inherently stronger consonant (as in ModE *draft* < ME *draught*) is ignored here; cf. Lutz (1991: ch. 3).

17. For the rise of new vowel phonemes as a consequence of the vocalisation of /j/, /w/, and /h/ in the history of English cf. the references in notes 13.–15. above. For new complex vowel phonemes in present-day Cockney as a consequence of the vocalisation of /l/ see Wells (1982: 258, 315–317).

18. In the coda of unaccented syllables, as in *heater* ['hi:.tə], the stage of total vocalisation of /r/ was reached considerably earlier; cf. Horn–Lehnert (1954: 917).

19. See Romaine (1978) and Wells (1982: 410–411). For young speakers of Lowland Scots Romaine even notes instances of [r]-lessness.

20. This is clearly shown by the maps in Orton–Sanderson–Widdowson (1978: Ph 11–12, 19–21, 30–31, 47–49, 58–59, 68, 83–84, 101–102, 112, 146, 155–157, 169, 193), and in Kolb *et al.* (1979: 280–323).

21. Cf. Luick (1914–1940: § 550), Wyld (1936: 298–301), Horn–Lehnert (1954: 448–454, 667, 915–921), and Dobson (1968: II, §427).

22. In the handbooks this general progressiveness of the Northern dialects during the earlier periods of the history of English is noted repeatedly.

23. E. g. in Horn–Lehnert (1954: 887–888), Brunner (1960: 396), Wells (1982: 258), and Gimson (1989: 201–206).

24. Note that in unaccented syllable codas total vocalisation of /l/ is also gaining ground in Present-day Standard English, e. g. in *careful, table* (Gimson 1989: 205); cf. note 18 above for total vocalisation of /r/ in unaccented codas in Early Modern English, which preceded the development of /r/ in accented syllable codas.

25. See Wells (1982: 307, 370–371, 390, 411–412, 431, 446), and the dialect maps for accented vowels preceding /l/ in Orton–Sanderson–Widdowson (1978: Ph 8–10, 16–18, 28, 41–43, 55–56, 82, 100, 132–135, 144, 165, 186) and in Kolb *et al.* (1979: 246–279).

26. Cf. Luick (1914–1940: § 707), Lutz (1991: 168).

27. For details see Luick (1914–1940: §§ 502–504, 521, 707, 770–771), Horn–Lehnert (1954: 506–518, 564–568, 887–904), Dobson (1968: II, §§ 60, 88, 146, 169, 174, 219, 425), and Lutz (1991: 168–171). Before alveolar consonants /l/ was only partially vocalised, but the effect on the preceding vowel was similarly far-reaching (cf. ModE *salt, bold*).

28. Luick (1914–1940: §§ 403, 407–408, 513, 542, 768.3 b), Horn–Lehnert (1954: 849–862), Brunner (1960: 259–260), and Jordan – Crook (1974: 121–129). Unlike the liquids and semivowels, whose low degree of inherent strength derives from their vowel-like character as inherently voiced consonants, /h/ derives it from weakly developed consonantal characteristics such as weak friction noise. This explains why /h/ in unaccented heads (i. e. mostly in intervocalic position) was vocalised at a very early date (cf. Campbell 1959: §§ 234–239, Lutz 1991: 23–25 for contraction in pre-Old English), whereas vocalisation of the semivowels and the liquids in this position clearly postdates their vocalisation in unaccented codas.

29. Cf. Luick (1914–1940: § 636), Campbell (1959: § 50.3), Brunner (1960: 373), Kuhn (1970: 31–35), Lutz (1991: 21–22).

30. Cf. Jespersen (1909: 285), Horn–Lehnert (1954: 851–852).

31. Cf. Horn–Lehnert (1954: 849–862), Orton–Sanderson–Widdowson (1978: Ph 103–108, 116), and Wells (1982: 358–359, 408).

32. Yet, a mere shift of emphasis to the consonants affected by the change is not by itself sufficient, as is shown by a series of studies on "peripheral phonemes" of English (among them /h/, /j/, and /r/) published by Josef Vachek in the 1960s and republished

in a larger context roughly a decade later (Vachek 1976: section C). Vachek tried to explain the distributional restriction of some consonants, which developed in the course of the history of English, with reference to the idea of functional load (cf. King 1967 for the rather doubtful explanatory value of this concept). Such attempts, which ignore the phonetic characteristics of the consonants concerned and their allophonic differentiation due to syllable and accent position, are unable to explain, e. g., why these consonants became restricted to the "pre-vocalic" position or why /h/ was affected earlier than /r/.

33. Sievers distinguished between "Brechungen" before /l/, /r/, and /h/ and "Vokalentwicklungen vor *w*", and this distinction has been maintained in the later editions revised by Brunner; see Sievers — Brunner (1965: §§ 83 — 89).

34. This is especially true for the treatment in Campbell (1959: §§ 139 — 156), with its arrangement according to the quality and quantity of the original vowel, not — as in the descriptions of Luick and Sievers — Brunner — according to the consonants that caused breaking or retraction.

35. Cf. Luick (1914 — 1940: § 143), Lass (1977, 1983) for /r/; for a critique of this view see Howell (1991).

36. For details of the development of /w/ cf. Luick (1914 — 1940: §§ 100, 134, 257, 399 — 402, 633, 641, 711), Jordan — Crook (1974: §§ 104 — 110), Lutz (1991: 155 — 157).

37. Cf. Luick (1914 — 1940: §§ 245 — 248), Campbell (1959: §§ 234 — 239), Sievers — Brunner (1965: §§ 127 — 134), Lutz (1991: 23 — 25).

38. This monophthongisation of all centralising diphthongs (including those originating from breaking before /h/) is due to progressive allophonic differentiation of all velar consonants (including coda /h/) into prevelar allophones after front vowels and post-velar allophones after back vowels; cf. Luick (1914 — 1940: §§ 235 — 241, 269 — 280), Campbell (1959: §§ 222 — 233, 304 — 314), Sievers — Brunner (1965: §§ 119 — 123), Lutz (1991: 175).

39. Cf. Luick (1914 — 1940: §§ 399 — 400, 402, 633, 711), Jordan — Crook (1974: §§ 104 — 110), Lutz (1991: 155 — 157).

40. Cf. Howell (1991), who independently arrives at the conclusion that Old English breaking should be viewed as a weakening process that affected weak consonants in weak positions, though he fails to note that the different extent of the process is determined by the difference of inherent strength of the consonants involved.

41. The final result — total vocalisation and, consequently, total restriction to the stronger head position — has only been reached in the cases of the inherently very weak consonants, namely /j/ and /w/, in most varieties also in the case of /h/. In the case of /r/ this is true for progressive varieties; in the case of /l/ only the most progressive varieties are reaching this stage. Various clear indications of coda weakening are, however, also found in the history of the inherently stronger consonants; cf. Lutz (1991: III.B.4).

References

Brunner, Karl
    1960   *Die englische Sprache: Ihre geschichtliche Entwicklung*, Vol. I: *Allgemeines/Lautgeschichte*. (2nd edition.) Tübingen: Niemeyer.

Campbell, Alistair
1959   *Old English grammar*. Oxford: Clarendon Press.
Coker, C. H. — N. Umeda
1975   "The importance of spectral detail in initial-final contrasts of voiced stops",
            Journal of Phonetics 3: 63 — 68.
Dobson, Eric J.
1968   *English pronunciation 1500 — 1700*. 2 vols. (2nd edition.) Oxford: Oxford
            University Press.
Gimson, A. C.
1989   *An introduction to the pronunciation of English*. (4th edition, rev. by Susan
            Ramsaran.) London: Edward Arnold.
Hawkins, Peter
1984   *Introducing phonology*. London: Hutchinson.
Hock, Hans Henrich
1976   "Final weakening and related phenomena", in: Frances Ingemann (ed.), *1975
            Mid-America linguistics conference papers*. Lawrence, Kansas: Department of
            Linguistics, 219 — 259.
1991   *Principles of historical linguistics*. (2nd edition.) Berlin: Mouton de Gruyter.
Horn, Wilhelm — Martin Lehnert
1954   *Laut und Leben. Englische Lautgeschichte der neueren Zeit (1400 — 1950)*.
            2 vols. Berlin: Deutscher Verlag der Wissenschaften.
Howell, Robert B.
1991   *Old English breaking and its Germanic analogues*. (Linguistische Arbeiten
            253.) Tübingen: Niemeyer.
Jespersen, Otto
1909   *A Modern English grammar on historical principles*. Part I: *Sounds and spelling*.
            Copenhagen: Munksgaard.
Jones, Daniel
1909   *The pronunciation of English*. (1st edition.) Cambridge: Cambridge University
            Press.
Jordan, Richard
1974   *Handbook of Middle English grammar: Phonology*. (Translated and revised
            by Eugen Joseph Crook.) (Janua Linguarum, Series Practica 218.) The Hague:
            Mouton.
Kahn, Daniel
1980   *Syllable-based generalizations in English phonology*. New York: Academic
            Press.
King, Robert D.
1967   "Functional load and sound change", *Language* 43: 831 — 852.
Kohler, Klaus
1984   "Phonetic explanation in phonology: The feature fortis : lenis", *Phonetica* 41:
            150 — 174.
Kolb, Eduard — Beat Glauser — Willy Elmer — Renate Stamm
1979   *Atlas of English sounds*. Bern: Francke.
Kuhn, Sherman M.
1970   "On the consonantal phonemes of Old English", in: James L. Rosier (ed.),
            *Philological essays: Studies in Old and Middle English language and literature
            in honour of Herbert Dean Meritt*. The Hague: Mouton, 16 — 49.

Lass, Roger
1977   "On the phonetic specification of Old English /r/", *Studia Anglica Posnaniensia* 9: 1—16.
1983   "Velar /r/ and the history of English", in: Michael Davenport—Erik Hansen—Hans Frede Nielsen (eds.), *Current topics in English historical linguistics*, 67—94.
1987   *The shape of English: Structure and history.* London: Dent.
Lehiste, Ilse
1964   *Acoustical characteristics of selected English consonants.* The Hague: Mouton.
Locke, John L.
1983   *Phonological acquisition and change.* New York: Academic Press.
Luick, Karl
1914—40 *Historische Grammatik der englischen Sprache.* 2 vols. Leipzig—Stuttgart: Tauchnitz.
1932   *Deutsche Lautlehre mit besonderer Berücksichtigung der Sprechweise Wiens und der österreichischen Alpenländer.* (3rd edition; 1st edition 1904.) Leipzig: Deuticke.
Lutz, Angelika
1988   "On the historical phonotactics of English", in: Dieter Kastovsky—Gero Bauer (eds.), *Luick revisited. Papers read at the Luick-Symposium at Schloß Liechtenstein, 15.—18. 9. 1985.* Tübingen: Narr, 221—239.
1991   *Phonotaktisch gesteuerte Konsonantenveränderungen in der Geschichte des Englischen.* (Linguistische Arbeiten 272.) [Habilitationsschrift, University of Munich, 1989.] Tübingen: Niemeyer.
Martinet, André
1952   "Langages à syllabes ouvertes: le cas du slave commun", *Zeitschrift für Phonetik und allgemeine Sprachwissenschaft* 6: 145—163.
Murray, Robert W.
1988   *Phonological strength and Early Germanic syllable structure.* (Studies in Theoretical Linguistics 6.) München: Fink.
Ohala, John J.
1974   "Phonetic explanation in phonology", in: Anthony Bruck—Robert A. Fox—Michael W. La Galy (eds.), *Papers from the parasession on natural phonology, April 18, 1974.* (Chicago Linguistic Society.) Chicago, 251—274.
Orton, Harold—Stewart Sanderson—John Widdowson
1978   *The linguistic atlas of England.* London: Croom Helm.
Pike, Kenneth L.
1943   *Phonetics. A critical analysis of phonetic theory and a technic for the practical description of sounds.* Ann Arbor: University of Michigan Press.
Plotkin, V. Y.
1972   *The dynamics of the English phonological system.* (Janua Linguarum, Series Practica 155.) The Hague: Mouton.
Romaine, Suzanne
1978   "Postvocalic /r/ in Scottish English: Sound change in progress?", in: Peter Trudgill (ed.), *Sociolinguistic patterns in British English.* London: Edward Arnold, 144—157.
Sievers, Eduard—Karl Brunner
1965   *Altenglische Grammatik.* (3rd edition.) Tübingen: Niemeyer.

Umeda, N. – C. H. Coker
1975 "Subphonemic details in American English", in: G. Fant – M. A. A. Tatham (eds.), *Auditory analysis and perception of speech.* New York: Academic Press, 153–176.

Vachek, Josef
1976 *Selected writings in English and general linguistics.* (Janua Linguarum, Series Maior 92.) The Hague: Mouton.

Vennemann, Theo
1972 "Rule inversion", *Lingua* 29: 209–242.
1988 *Preference laws for syllable structure and the explanation of sound change. With special reference to German, Germanic, Italian, and Latin.* Berlin: Mouton de Gruyter.

Wells, J. C.
1982 *Accents of English.* 3 vols. Cambridge: Cambridge University Press.

Wyld, Henry Cecil
1936 *A history of Modern Colloquial English.* (3rd edition.) Oxford: Blackwell.

From stress-timing to syllable-timing: changes in the prosodic system of Late Middle English and Early Modern English

Manfred Markus

1. Introduction

At the International Conference on Language Contact and Linguistic Change at Rydzyna (near Poznań) on 5 – 8 June, 1991, one of the papers, presented by Gasiorowski, dealt with the intricate question of how word stress changed in Middle English due to the impact of Anglo-Norman loan words. Present-day English word stress was basically explained as an outcome of the Middle English collision of the Old English stem-initial stress with the principle of alternating stress. While, according to Gasiorowski, the "indigenous" stress rule of Old English mainly worked from left to right, the Middle English and Modern English stress rule is diametrically opposite (a "mirror image"), revealing the principle of stress distribution within a word from right to left. In its history English has thus been under the impact of two different stress patterns, the Germanic and the Romance one. Though the hypothesis comes close to the assessment suggested by Hogg and McCully in various recent contributions (Hogg – McCully 1986, McCully – Hogg 1990), I find many of the questions raised by Gasiorowski unsolved and had the impression at Rydzyna that there was still a great deal of disagreement and uncertainty amongst the audience, particularly as to the main principles of word stress in Old English, Middle English and Modern English.

In this paper it is assumed that Middle English is basically a syllable-timed language, and Modern English a stress-timed language. Having dealt with Old English, which I take to be neither syllable-timed nor stress-timed, elsewhere (Markus 1992), I shall focus here on the change in Early Modern English from the one to the other of these principles of word stress, focussing on both the reasons for and the consequences of this change.

Methodologically, historical studies of prosodic features like word stress confront us with particular problems — we do not have direct evidence of how the language was used orally. Two methodological conclusions can be drawn from these restrictions:

1) Of the previous studies that are at all available and relevant to the topic, we should take into account as many as possible, no matter whether they are fairly old (as, for example, Langenfelt 1933) or very new (as, for example, Lutz 1991 and the paper by Gasiorowski 1991 mentioned above); moreover, no matter whether they are traditionally descriptive (as Fudge 1984) or can be seen as strongly conditioned by a certain academic school, temporarily or presently thriving, as, for example, Halle — Keyser 1971 (Transformational-Generative Grammar) and Hogg — McCully 1986 (metrical phonology).

2) Prosodic features raise complex linguistic problems that have been seen and, in fact, have to be seen from different angles. Pitch, phonotactics, syllable theory (Vennemann 1986), metrical phonology (Giegerich 1980, 1985; Goldsmith 1990), phonetology (in the sense of Bailey — Maroldt 1988) and speech rhythm (Adams 1979) are all closely connected with each other and with word stress, so that methodological purism and a strict separation of the different prosodic questions seem out of place.

2. Word stress in Middle English

After the inundation of English by Romance words (Halle — Keyser 1971: 97), the basic Old English rule of stressing words on their first stem syllable was strongly restricted in its relevance in favour of the Old French rule, which, scanning words from right to left, put the stress on the last or — in the case of obscure final -*e* — on the last but one ("penultimate") syllable. This "final" stress rule is, by the way, generally in line with the original stress in Vulgar Latin.[1]

Middle English speakers must have been irritated by the two different, even contradictory stress rules. In any case, they did not simply abide by the Romance stress rule, but steered a course of compromise: there was an obvious tendency to move the main stress in short words forward to the left; in long words there was a tendency to cut them into disyllabic feet and to attribute secondary stress to the first syllable of every foot except the one with the main stress. In short loanwords we thus partly find the French final stress, as in *avís, defét, relés*, but also a considerable number of stressed prefixes, like in *éngin, prófit, récord*.[2] Gasiorowski (1991: 4) rightly argued that these exceptional loanwords with stressed prefixes are mainly to be found among nouns and that this is in line with the familiar model of Old English: nominal prefixes, unlike the verbal ones, usually carry stress in Old English.[3]

More interesting and important than this survival of an Old English principle of word stress is the emergence of a new one, based on the entirely changed role of the syllable, the foot and rhythm. Long words tended to be rhythmically partitioned in Middle English, so that there were regular changes of stressed ("ictus") and unstressed ("recess") syllables. Obviously, there was a growing sense of a disyllabic foot, and, as a result, of an alternating rhythm. First evidence of this new norm can be provided from Present-day English, with its many well-known rules of syllable reduction,[4] and also from Middle English verse: in the late twelfth century, end-rhyme and an iambic/trochaic metrical rhythm began to substitute the traditional alliterative long line (cf. Diller 1978: 69 – 74).[5]

But of course neither the conditioning of syllables by word stress in Present-day English nor the dominant role of alternating rhythm in Middle English verse can simply be extrapolated into Middle English (everyday) prose. The trend to an alternating speech rhythm did not affect the prosodic system of Middle English yet, but can only be traced to the fact that long words tended to be structured by disyllabic feet, due to the primary and secondary stresses marking the foot-initial syllables. All in all, Middle English was not stress-timed yet (in the sense of an approximately equal temporal distance between one ictus and the next), but syllable-timed.[6] This means that the syllable was the dominant prosodic parameter, for its part interacting with and partly affecting phonemes, morphemes and word stress.

2.1. Phonemes

That Middle English phonemes often changed within the framework of the syllable becomes obvious from those various rules of traditional Middle English grammar that refer to the syllable structure. First and foremost we have to think of the so-called MEOSL rule (Middle English open syllable lengthening),[7] which, as is well-known, is, among other things, based on the number of syllables in a word and on the openness of the (stressed) syllable concerned.[8] Trisyllabic words were not affected by it, but had rather undergone shortening since the end of the Old English period (Pinsker 1974: § 33,2; 50,2). Shortening of a syllable nucleus was also caused by a succeeding nasal (a weak consonant) plus a plosive (Pinsker 1974: § 50,3), thus giving rise to short pronunciation in *dumb, lamb, long,* etc. Qualitative changes of stem vowels in Middle English were likewise caused by succeeding weak consonants, above all *r*. The opening of short *e* to (short) *a* before *r* (as in *ferre* > *farre*, cf. (Pinsker 1974: § 51,1) is just one example of this seemingly "spontaneous" change.

With the consonants it is even more obvious that the reason for change during Middle English was mainly a phonotactic one. Initial and final position in a syllable, in combination with certain consonant combinations, caused various changes (elimination, voicing; cf. Pinsker 1974: § 83 — 85). Clusters with the "weak" consonants, i. e. with nasals, liquids and half-vowels, were reduced on a large scale (Pinsker 1974: § 86 — 89). Lutz (1991) has studied these and other changes based on certain structural preferences within the syllables in detail,[9] summarising (Lutz 1991: 280) that consonants in stressed syllable codas were generally weakened throughout the history of English and that weak consonants were gradually restricted to syllable onsets. She has also given detailed evidence for the fact that the weight of the original syllable is usually kept unreduced in that the loss of a weak consonant in the coda is compensated for by a growth of weight (often lengthening) in the syllable nucleus, i. e. of the vowel. I would only like to add that phonotactically conditioned rules, while not limited to Middle English, have never played as striking a role in the history of English phonology as in that very period, when French syllable-timing, verse poetry and the growth of polyphonic music give common evidence for a new sense of sound.[10]

Even more typical of this new sense of sound are the many "misspellings" in sources of the fourteenth and fifteenth centuries, later rejected by the humanist schoolmen and thus put aside on a half-forgotten shelf of language history. Langenfelt (1933: 66) has listed some of these misspellings, which are interpretable as phonetic spellings and give further evidence of the real pronunciation in the late Middle English period. Here are a few examples referring to the loss of [r] and [l]:

pale (= Fr. *parler*)
ame ('soul') confused with *arme* ('weapon')
woship (= *worship*)
cops (= *corps*)
ʒhely (= *yearly*)
capenter (= *carpenter*)
mussel (= *morcel*)
akoded (= *accorded*)
cadenall (= *cardinal*)
wod not (= *would not*)

fookes (= *folks*)
samon (= *salmon*)
shan (= *shall not*)[11]

2.2. Morphemes

One of the phonotactic rules in Middle English seems to have been that syllables were not supposed to begin with a vowel.[12] Accordingly, vocalic prefixes like *a-* or *e-* (in French loanwords), as other word-initial vowels, were sometimes misinterpreted to be part of the preceding morpheme (or word). In many other cases morphemes fell victim to the normal syllable structure and were dropped. Aphaeresis, i. e. the loss of a syllable nucleus, is, though mentioned by Langenfelt (1933: 68 ff.) in the same breath as agglutination, widely limited to the late fifteenth century and Early Modern English.[13] But agglutination or deglutination, which both only rearrange the juncture between two syllables without actually eliminating any syllable, seem to have been quite common in Middle English prose. Here are a few examples (Langenfelt 1933: 66; Koziol 1937: 683 – 688):

ittis, tys (for *it is*); *a tained* (for *attained*); *a pereth* (*appeareth*); *a nekename* (for *an ekename*); *the ton* (for *thet on/that one*); *the tother* (for *thet other*); *my nuncle* (for *mine uncle*); *my nowlde* (*myn owlde*) etc.; lexicalised: *pigges-nye* (for *pigges-ye*); *newt* (< ME *an ewte* 'Eidechse'); *nugget* (< *an ingot* 'Barren'); *an adder* (for *a nadder*); *an apron* (*a naperon*).

The examples aptly show that some speakers or scribes of late Middle English did not care about keeping traditional morphemes or words intact, but in their pronunciation and spelling followed the inherent rules of an ideal syllable structure.

2.3. Word stress

The way a word was stressed was highly variable by Chaucer's time. In verse, many a word could be stressed according to metrical context (e. g. *cómfort — comfórt*[14]); and Germanic suffixes, for example *-ness(e)*, were stressed in alignment with the rhyming French suffix *-esse* for the sake of rhyme (cf. Fries 1985: 31). Moreover, function words, if metrically in an ictus position, were, exceptionally, stressed, contrarily content words would have lost their stress in a recess position. Of course metrical language is not representative of the word stress in everyday language. But there is some cumulative evidence in favour of a variable word stress in Middle English. Apart from verse, we know for sure that the French word stress in loanwords moved from the final syllable forward to a syllable that at first must have carried a secondary stress (as mentioned above), so that there must have been variants at some stage — like *rebèllióun* and *rebéllióun*. We also know that the weakening (and eventual loss) of "unstressed" syllables was a matter of degree, depending on variables such as the Romance or Germanic origin of the word concerned, the suffix vs. prefix role, the phonotactic position of the syllable nucleus,[15] the number of syllables in a word[16] and, finally, dialect attribution, the north generally being more advanced in the weakening of unstressed syllables.[17] The phonotactic effects of word stress had also been complemented by those of sentence stress — as can be seen, for example, from the voicing of spirants in some of the (usually unstressed) function words (*the, this, these, that, those, his* etc., *is, was, with* and *as*[18]).

In sum, we have quite a number of interlinked factors concerning phonotactics, morphology and stress attribution and there is a great deal of variability and flexibility in what analysts would prefer to be constant during the Middle English period. But in Middle English, as a substratum of French for a few hundred years, hardly anything was stable; neither words, including their stress and their meaning, nor morphemes, nor the single phonemes. The main principle, which the English had imported from the French and which counted for a while, was that speech could be timed in syllables and that syllables were metrically fixed. The syllables were the most general frame of reference for the various changes, but they themselves remained intact until the fifteenth century. Chaucer's metrically motivated dropping or insertion of syllables was limited to verse and restricted to the special cases all known from classical metrics, such as elision of schwa and synicesis (for example in *mariage*).[19]

3. Early Modern English — a stress-timed language

In Early Modern English, and probably the latter half of the fifteenth century, too, rhythmical alternation of stress became the new dominant prosodic principle of English. It very much affected the structure of the syllables, which, from the fifteenth century, were under the impact of the norm of isochrony and rhythmical alternation.[20] English had started to be a stress-timed language.

A pre-condition of this new norm was that towards the end of Middle English word-stress was widely fixed in the many words previously borrowed from French. While Chaucer's English still reveals some flexibility in this respect, Peter Levins' *Manipulus vocabulorum* (1570), a rhyming dictionary with stress markings and thus a main source for the study of word stress in Early Modern English, includes no stress doublets.[21]

As a result of this definite distribution of stress there was less chance of adapting stress to rhythm — as had still been possible in Chaucer's verse, for example in

Whán that Áprill with his shóures sóote
The dróughte of Márch has pérced tó the róote,
And báthed évery véyne in swých licóur,
Of whích vertú engéndred ís the flóur ...

Here the norm of alternating rhythm was relatively easy to follow. But 200 years later, by Levins' and Shakespeare's time, words like *Aprill* and *vertu* were definitely stressed on the first syllable only.[22] On this ground alone it was by degrees more difficult for a prosodist, let alone an everyday speaker, to find the proper words fitting into the pattern of the alternating rhythm.

The Chaucer lines remind us of the fact that there were other reasons for the increasing difficulties people in the Renaissance had in speaking rhythmically. Not only word stress, but also metrical conventions and syntax had in Chaucer's time been flexible enough for an author/speaker to find an alternating rhythm. As to meter, there had always been, as is well-known, the possibility for an author to drop or to keep unstressed schwa in open and partly in covered syllables, as in the case of Chaucer's *shoure, soote, droughte, perced, roote, bathed, every, veyne*. As to syntax, many structures allowing prosodic flexibility were (as yet) ungrammaticalised and thus stylistically optional:[23] personal or demonstrative pronouns before proper names (*this Nicolas*), the use of *gan* before infinitives, the two types of comparison of the adjectives (*-er* vs. *more*, etc.), the availability of different tense forms with a fairly equivalent meaning[24] — to mention only the main examples.

By Shakespeare's time most of these syntactic options had been semantically functionalised, and the schwa of suffixes and many prefixes and infixes had simply disappeared in the pronunciation. But the sense of the alternating rhythm, naturally, had not disappeared. Since this is a psychological assumption, there is no possibility of proving it, but we have plenty of cumulative evidence. As in a crime story we have a motive, a consequence of the "deed", and several clues.

The motive is that language users would have become accustomed to the smoothly alternating rhythm of the time of Chaucer and, judging from poetry of the time, seem to have liked stressed syllables to change regularly with unstressed ones. This norm of poetry was also enhanced by the English school pronunciation of Latin and Greek words, where the accent was commonly placed on alternating syllables.[25]

The consequence of this preference is that, as it became more difficult for speakers to stick to the alternating rhythm (due to the sound changes described above), the reduction of almost all unstressed syllables, particularly of function words, was introduced as an option.[26] Since the many "rules" of reduction or, in the extreme case, elimination, are well-known from Present-day English,[27] they need not be discussed here in detail. The point to emphasise, however, is that quantitative reduction — qualitative reduction is of less interest here — allows all unstressed syllables (unstressed in the word or in the sentence) to adapt to the span of time available for the recess. It is therefore that, apart from the function words, the unstressed syllables of content words are also eligible for optional reduction; as a result, isochrony not only operates in verse but also in prose. We may assume that Early Modern English was not very different in this respect from Present-day English, the more so since the principle of the stress-timed rhythm has had repercussions in grammar, too: the present rules of the comparison of adjectives and adverbs are fully in line with the validity of isochrony[28] and therefore depend on the number of syllables and the position of stress in the words concerned.[29]

The clues indicating the dominant role of a stress-timed rhythm during (and since) the Early Modern English period are threefold: circumstantial evidence, spelling evidence and stress evidence.

Circumstantial evidence is provided by the fact that in English verse disyllabic feet, i. e. those meters that by classical terminology are commonly referred to as iamb, trochee and spondee, were and always have been absolutely predominant. Of course there has been some experimenting with other meters, but the classical genres, the sonnet, blank verse, the rhymed couplet, clearly favoured the meter with an alternating rhythm, which thus seems most natural in a stress-timed language.[30]

There seems to have been an experimental phase of some weight towards the end of the Middle English period and in the sixteenth century. It may well be argued that when the Middle English flexibility of both stress and syllable number was petering out, some writers gave up rhythmical alternation altogether. This would have been the proper reaction of the culturally conservative provincials, who contributed to the Alliterative Revival, and also of the Humanist schoolmen of the sixteenth century, who would have turned a deaf ear to the isochronic language of the people and would have re-introduced dactyls and other Latin rhythms. A temporary tendency towards ternary verse in the fifteenth/sixteenth centuries is exactly what has been stated by Diller (1978: 83—87) in his history of English metrics.

But the prosodic mainstream was marked by rhythmical alternation. And the most conclusive evidence comes from the field of spelling and stress distribution. First spelling. From the fifteenth century a large number of more or less phonetic spellings have come down to us which, refuted by the humanists of the sixteenth century, have not survived. But some less knowledgeable writers of the fifteenth century did not shy away from reducing the number of syllables by elision, both in the spelling and the pronunciation. As a result, we have a great many disyllabic words that were originally tri- or tetrasyllabic. The following list of such shortened words has been selected from Langenfelt (1933: 59—63). They all come from fifteenth century manuscripts :

Alson (Alison)	*hostry (hostelry)*
Amrel (a(d)miral)	*lybraly (liberally)*
bachler (bachelor)	*Marget (Margaret)*
basnites (bassinets)	*nunrye (nunnery)*
benste (benedicite)	*onresnably (unreasonably)*
brybre (bribery)	*particlerly (particularly)*
cardnale/carnal (cardinal)	*perlously (perilously)*
chansler (chansellor)	*repracion (reparation)*
considring (considering)	*restew (residue)*
cristiante (Christianity)	*robrye (robbery)*
cytsyn (citizen)	*sectory (secretary)*
curioste (curiosity)	*sengler (singular)*
easly (easily)	*solister (solicitor)*
emprore (emperor)	*sprytuel (spiritual)*
flatryng (flattering)	*tempraly (temporally)*
	vylney (villany)
	watring (watering)[31]

Part of the motivation behind these variants may be the wish to make them shorter and easier; most of them are in fact based on "hard words".[32] But in many of the cases (like *vylney* or *watring*, the last two) the main strategy seems to have been the reduction of two or more recess syllables to one, so that an alternating rhythm ensued.[33]

Finally, stress distribution. I will again follow Levins' *Manipulus Vo-cabulorum* (cf. above) as referred to by Halle — Keyser (1971) and Dobson (1968: 19 — 30; 447 — 449), but also use Danielsson's (1948) long list of loan-words up to 1700, which are marked for accent. A discussion of all criteria of stress distribution in Early Modern English would fall outside the scope of this paper. One interesting aspect is the prevalence of the alternating rhythm in the word stress of Early Modern English borrow-ings. Since disyllabic words were necessarily stressed on one of the two syllables (no matter which), I will focus on polysyllabic words.

Halle — Keyser (1971: 109 — 123) have handled these words by applying the Romance Stress Rule (the accent tends towards the end of a word) and the Stress Retraction Rule (the accent moves towards the beginning of a word). In order to explain the stress variants and apparent inconsis-tencies in Levins' word-list, they mainly take refuge in the distinction of the vowel features [tense] and [lax]. But there seems to be a great deal of *petitio principii* in this.[34] I would rather argue here in terms of word formation:[35] in the first group of words we are dealing with derivations, exhibiting the stress pattern of the words they are derived from; in the second group we do not have Early Modern English derivations at all (*antique* was hardly generally accepted in English by Levins' time[36]), so the word accent was not urged by analogy, but could move "freely" from the final syllable (Romance Stress Rule) to the last but two syllable or "antepenult" (Stress Retraction Rule).

This shift of word accent by two syllables to the left, starting from the originally stressed syllable further right, seems to be the leading principle of Early Modern English word accent. It implies that longer words have one main (or "tonic") stress and one or more secondary stresses.[37] What happened when classical words were Englished and conformed to English speech habits is that the tonic and a secondary accent changed places. Thus, from French *acàdemíe* (with a secondary and a primary accent) English produced *acádemỳ* (with the primary accent first and the second-ary accent on the final syllable). This process was clearly seen even in the eighteenth century, and Danielsson (1948: 26 ff.) has quoted some of the earliest grammarians as giving evidence of this shift of accent, which he calls the "countertonic principle". He has also rightly observed (1948: 30) that the principle was valid until around 1660, but that from the Restoration on, Romance word accent became fashionable again. And there is still another factor whose relevance for stress seems to have increased from the Restoration onwards: the type of the French or Latin suffix. Along these lines, Fudge (1984: 40 ff.) could convincingly structure his description of the rules of present-day word stress in line with suffixes.

From today's point of view the picture is accordingly complex. But in Early Modern English, it seems to me, word accent functioned in a fairly simple way: the alternating rhythm was the main principle of word stress in Early Modern English. Saying this we must take into account that syllables could be weakened as needed, and this is exactly what happened in the examples described above. On this basis we can rightly assume that in oral speech surplus syllables were either smoothed away, as in *bárbarity* (Halle−Keyser 1971: 114), which would then have been pronounced /'bɑ:rbrətɪ/, or at least reduced quantitatively, i. e. shortened, as in *húmidity* (Halle−Keyser 1971: 114).[38]

Word accent today is very much a question of dialectal variation[39] and obviously was so in Shakespeare's time. This is why Halle−Keyser (1971: 116), taking Shakespeare's implicit stress rules into account, could find differences between him and his contemporary Levins as to the accent in words ending on *-ity* and *-ory*: *ínventory* (Levins) vs. *invéntory* (Shakespeare), etc. Danielsson's (1948) long list shows that there is hardly a polysyllabic loan-word which, in the course of time from the sixteenth to the eighteenth century, does not show variation of accent. The variations are sometimes very revealing. The verb *to temporise*, for example, is given the stress pattern − − ' − for 1665 (Danielsson 1948: 38), initial stress ' − − − for 1700 (and after), and double stress ' − − ' − for the verse by Shakespeare and two of his contemporaries. It can be assumed that the word had a secondary stress on its first syllable even in the everyday language of 1665. It is not surprising that Christopher Cooper, only 20 years later (1685), made a point of many words having two accents and of indicating them both.[40]

4. Summary and outlook

In sum, there is no proof, but plenty of evidence that polysyllabic loan-words in Early Modern English were forced into the alternating rhythm known from Middle English poetry. Given that the reasons for the position of the tonic accent were partly historical (depending on the age of a word), partly phonotactic (heavy vs. light syllables[41]), partly rooted in word-formation, the chaos of "rules" was reacted to by the persisting simple principle of the alternate rhythm. A loan-word with an original Romance stress soon developed a secondary and ternary stress, thus being structured in terms of feet. Within these, stressed syllables were strengthened (long vowels for example by the Great Vowel Shift), and unstressed syllables were reduced, or entirely smoothed away; in some cases (like *curtsy* < *courtesy*) the process even reached spelling.

These English speech habits up to around 1660 were understandably disliked by the schoolmasters and purists of the Restoration and the eighteenth century. Words ending in *-ise* were again marked for accent on the last syllable; thus, we have *advértise* and *ádvertise* for 1582 and 1570 respectively, but *advertíse* for 1665 (see Danielsson's list 1948: 239 f.). Obviously the motivation of such (and many other) changes of word stress is etymological, in the present case a reminder of the Romance origin of the suffix *-ise* (from French *-iser*, Lat. *-isare*). In spite of this etymological "restoration",[42] English prosody has remained under the influence of the isochronic principle of late Middle English and Early Modern English ever since. Today the principle has, as is well-known, not only affected the integration of loan-words, but the prosodic structure of the language as a whole.

In Middle English up to Chaucer's time, on the other hand, the main principle of stress distribution and the reason for a great many sound changes was the inviolability of the syllable. Rhythm, metrical feet and the smoothing away of supernumerary syllables or the insertion of missing ones — all these were restricted to the stylised language of verse.

It seems evident, then, that after the Norman invasion English changed from a syllable-timed language — a language allowing time for the pronunciation of all the syllables in a word to be fully articulated and a language with a fairly variable word stress — to a stress-timed language, which makes rhythmical stress the highest feature in the prosodic hierarchy, thus reducing the syllable to a variable and a contributor to the ever-valid isochrony.

Seen in this light, the Great Vowel Shift can be interpreted as a very natural outcome of the new role of isochrony[43] and rhythm: the loss of recess syllables in late Middle English caused the ictus syllables to be complementarily strengthened, either by raising or by diphthongisation.[44] Be that as it may, rhythmicity still seems to be a dominant feature of Present-day English. I have often heard pop-musicians argue that English is a better medium for their hits than other common European languages. In view of the role of isochrony and stress-timed rhythm since Early Modern English, we can now agree: English *is* the better language.

Notes

1. Plurisyllabic words had the accent on the penultimate syllable if the vowel was long (e. g. in *colóres*) and in a few special cases of the vowels or consonants involved (cf. Bodmer n. d.: 303 f.; Rheinfelder 1976: 16). Due to the loss of suffixes in French, original penults came to be in final position.

2. I trust the evidence of the — not absolutely reliable — later stress in these words: the Great Vowel Shift affected the (long and stressed) stem vowels of the first three words, not the short and unstressed ones of the second group. In addition, spelling variants of the 15th century (like *avise, deffait, relese*) are revealing as to the feature [+ -length].

3. For the reason for this and further details concerning this rule cf. Markus (1992). The reason why we have different stress patterns in the two groups of words may stem from the different dates of borrowing; the words with prefix stress were — according to the *MED* and the *OED* — borrowed in the 13th century, those with stem stress in the 14th.

4. Cf. Arnold—Hansen (1979: 192—203); Gimson (1989: 266—269).

5. For a detailed description of this change cf. Puhlmann (1971). The change may have been triggered off by the example of Anglo-Norman verse, cf. Pyle (1930).

6. This role of syllable-timing can be taken as part and parcel of the lexical influence of Anglo-Norman: word stress and syllabification are just as influential in a situation of language contact as are the words themselves. Weinreich (1966) does not say anything about this point (cf. 26—28; 47—62); but cf. 26 f. about the attempts of bilingual speakers "to reproduce the borrowed morpheme with its original sounds."

7. Cf. Pinsker (1974: 39), Markus (1987: 280 f., 1987—1988).

8. In view of these criteria a mere reference to the "Verstärkung des Druckakzents" (Lutz 1991: 284) seems insufficient.

9. One of her main points is the dropping of the /h/, for which she has distinguished eight steps — from pre- and early Old English to Present-day English. The role of the syllable in Middle English is confirmed by Lutz' result: only those steps of change that are conditioned by the structure of the stressed syllable (and not by other factors such as stress in the sentence) are to be associated with the Middle English (or a later) period.

10. See Markus (1992).

11. More examples are given in Markus (1992).

12. See Langenfelt (1933: 66).

13. The examples listed by Langenfelt (1933: 68—70), second-hand and stemming from Slettengren (1912), are in fact all taken from prose of that time or — if earlier — from verse. The point of aphaeresis has been topicalised by, for example, John Hart (1551), cf. Danielsson (1955, I: 153).

14. For further examples of stress doublets cf. Halle—Keyser (1971: 103).

15. Covered nuclei survived longer than the vowels of open unstressed syllables.

16. Trisyllabic words more easily lost unstressed syllables than disyllabic ones.

17. For a more detailed discussion of all these conditioning factors cf. Markus (1990: 69).

18. See Pinsker (1974: § 83, 2/3).

19. See Fries (1985: 41—45). Apart from elision (syncope/apocope) and synicesis (with synaeresis as a subtype), we are also talking about hiatus ($\neq$ synicesis), diaeresis ($\neq$ synaeresis) and epenthesis.

20. About the basic role of alternation of stress in Modern English, see Chomsky—Halle (1968: 77—79, 86 f., 95 f., 157 f.).

21. The same holds true for Butler (1634). The difference between Chaucer's stress-diversity and Levins' uniformity of stress has been pointed out by Halle—Keyser (1971: 109 f.), but their interpretation of the "quite generally accepted view" (110) somewhat deviates from mine in the following.

22. Levins (1570 [1867]: 124, 27 and 95, 10) does not mark the accent in these special cases, but cf. Butler (1634: 54) about *virtu*. *April* was affected by the Great Vowel Shift and therefore must have been stressed on the first syllable.

23. See Markus (1990: 73), and the long list of the various examples in Fries (1985: 41—51).

24. Visser (1963—73, II: 713, 717) has rightly pointed out the role of metrics in the choice of tense and the expanded form in Middle English, but he has overgeneralised the validity of the alternating rhythm. In alliterative poetry alternating rhythm is hardly relevant; cf. my criticism of Visser's position as to tense and the expanded form in the Gawain works in Markus (1971: 19).

25. This classical background has been discussed at length in Danielsson (1948: 39—54). The author convincingly refers to both the popularity of medieval rhythmical verse in Latin hymnody (445) and the accentual Cursus tradition in medieval Latin prose (47).

26. There are a few exceptions; cf. Liberman—Prince (1977: 283—286).

27. Cf. n. 4.

28. For a detailed discussion of the role of rhythm and foot in the rules of comparison (from both a diachronic and a synchronic point of view) see Markus (1988).

29. Of the many phonological studies that, in one way or another, have closely argued in favour of an alternating rhythm in Present-day English, I would like to select Martin (1972) and Liberman—Prince (1977). Cf. also Baldwin (1990).

30. In German verse, in contrast, dactyls, anapests and other three (or more) syllabled feet are far more common than in English; cf. von Wilpert (1959: 95). On the whole question of verse feet in Present-day English cf. Bonheim (1990: 322—336).

31. A shorter version of this list has been presented in Markus (1990: 275 f.).

32. For "hard words" as a language barrier for the lower classes, cf. Berndt (1986).

33. Many of the examples of aphaeresis quoted in context by Langenfelt (1933: 68—70); cf. n. 13 above) would also fit here — such as *greabyll* ('agreeable'), *mendement* ('amendment') etc.

34. Thus it is not at all clear why the suffix *-ity* should end with a tense vowel in *príncipality, prósperity, húmidity, bárbarity* etc., but with a lax vowel in *antíquity, fratérnity, dextérity* and *infírmity*.

35. Halle—Keyser (1971: 115) consider this possibility, but prematurely reject it.

36. According to the *OED*, *antique* was first used in the 16th century, *antiquity* in the 14th.

37. In this survival of a secondary stress Dobson (1968: 445) has seen the most important difference between the Early Modern English system of accentuation and that of Present-day English.

38. Since the ending *-y* (coming from French *-é*) has secondary stress, the second and third syllables must be in the recess.

39. The suffix *-ise* of verbs is stressed in many English varieties (e. g. *to realise*); in Ireland I recently heard *committee* stressed on the last syllable. Also cf. the many examples of US English vs. British English.

40. I have taken this hint from Halle—Keyser (1971: 122), who quote Cooper literally and give word examples.

41. This distinction is much older than the similar opposition of the Chomsky—Hallean features [tense] and [lax] would have us believe. Even Jespersen (1926: 14.71) argued in terms of this concept.

42. Dobson (1968: 447), however, has argued that the influence of etymologically related words on each other is not much in evidence before 1700, compared with the 18th century.
43. Here I am coming close to Chomsky—Halle (1968: 77—79, 254—259), though they avoid the phonetic term "isochrony".
44. A merely phonotactic explanation of the Great Vowel Shift does not seem to be feasible, which is perhaps why Lutz (1991: 285) does not offer any, but only refers to the Great Vowel Shift in a short comment.

References

Adams, Corinne
    1979   *English speech rhythm and the foreign learner.* The Hague: Mouton.
Arnold, Roland—Klaus Hansen
    1979   *Englische Phonetik.* (3. Auflage.) München: Hueber.
Bailey, Charles-James N.—Karl Maroldt
    1988   *Grundzüge der englischen Phonetologie: Allgemeine Systematik.* (2nd edition.) (Arbeitspapiere zur Linguistik/Working Papers in Linguistics.) Berlin: Institut für Linguistik der Technischen Universität Berlin.
Baldwin, J. R.
    1990   "Some notes on rhythm in English", in: Susan Ramsaran (ed.), *Studies in the pronunciation of English. A commemorative volume in honour of A. C. Gimson.* London: Routledge, 58—63.
Berndt, Rolf
    1986   "Reflections on the development of social varieties of English in the Late(r) Middle English and Early Modern English period", *ZAA* 34: 235—249.
Bodmer, Frederick
    n. d.   *Die Sprachen der Welt. Geschichte — Grammatik — Wortschatz in vergleichender Darstellung.* Köln—Berlin: Kiepenheuer & Witsch.
Bonheim, Helmut
    1990   *Literary systematics.* Woodbridge: Boydell & Brewer.
Butler, Charles
    1633   *The English grammar.* Oxford.
Chomsky, Noam—Morris Halle
    1968   *The sound pattern of English.* New York: Harper & Row.
Danielsson, Bror
    1948   *Studies on the accentuation of polysyllabic Latin, Greek, and Romance loanwords in English with special reference to those ending in* -able, -ate, -ator, -ible, -ic, -ical, *and* -ize. Stockholm: Almqvist & Wiksell.
    1955   *John Hart's works on English orthography and pronunciation [1551, 1569, 1570].* 2 parts. Stockholm: Almqvist & Wiksell.
Diller, Hans Jürgen
    1978   *Metrik und Verslehre.* (Studienreihe Englisch.) Düsseldorf—Tübingen: Bagel/ Francke.
Dobson, Eric J.
    1968   *English pronunciation 1500—1700.* 2 vols. (2nd edition.) Oxford: Clarendon Press.

Fries, Udo
1985   *Einführung in die Sprache Chaucers. Phonologie, Metrik und Morphologie.* Tübingen: Niemeyer.
Fudge, Eric
1984   *English word-stress.* London: Allen & Unwin.
Gasiorowski, Piotr
1991   Through the looking-glass: Stress rules in collision. Paper delivered at the International Conference on Language Contact and Linguistic Change, Rydzyna, Poland, June 5—8, 1991. MS.
Giegerich, Heinz J.
1980   "On stress-timing in English phonology", *Lingua* 51: 187—221.
1985   *Metrical phonology and phonological structure; German and English.* Cambridge: Cambridge University Press.
Gimson, Allan C.
1989   *An introduction to the pronunciation of English.* (4th edition, revised by Susan Ramsaran.) London: Arnold.
Goldsmith, John A.
1990   *Autosegmental and metrical phonology.* Oxford: Blackwell.
Halle, Morris—Samuel Jay Keyser
1971   *English stress: Its form, its growth, and its role in verse.* London: Harper & Row.
Hayes, Bruce
1984   "The phonology of rhythm in English", *Linguistic Inquiry* 15: 33—74.
Hogg, Richard M.—C. B. McCully
1987   *Metrical phonology. A coursebook.* Cambridge: Cambridge University Press.
Jespersen, Otto
1926   *Lehrbuch der Phonetik.* (4. Auflage.) Leipzig: Teubner.
[1904]
Koziol, Herbert
1937   *Handbuch der englischen Wortbildungslehre.* Heidelberg: Winter.
Langenfeldt, Gösta
1933   *Select studies in colloquial English of the late Middle Ages.* Lund: Ohlsson.
Levins, Peter
1570   *Manipulus vocabulorum.* Edited by Henry B. Wheatley. (EETS). Oxford: Oxford University Press.
[1867]
Libermann, Mark—Alan Prince
1977   "On stress and linguistic rhythm", *Linguistic Inquiry* 8: 249—336.
Lutz, Angelika
1991   *Phonotaktisch gesteuerte Konsonantenveränderungen in der Geschichte des Englischen.* Tübingen: Niemeyer.
Markus, Manfred
1971   *Moderne Erzählperspektive in den Werken des Gawain-Autors.* (Regensburger Arbeiten zur Anglistik und Amerikanistik 3.) Nürnberg—Regensburg: Carl.
1987   "Länge und Silbe im historischen English", *Archiv für das Studium der neueren Sprachen und Literaturen* 224: 270—285.
1987—88   "Noch einmal: zur me. Vokaldehnung in offener Silbe", *Klagenfurter Beiträge zur Sprachwissenschaft* 13/14: 384—410.

1988   "Zur Distribution von synthetischer und analytischer Steigerung im historischen Englisch", *Arbeiten aus Anglistik und Amerikanistik* 13: 105—121.
1990   *Mittelenglisches Studienbuch.* (UTB. Große Reihe.) Tübingen: Francke.
1992   "From sense to sound: The role of the morpheme in OE word stress and its substitution by syllable-timing in early ME", *Anglistentag 1991 Düsseldorf. Vorträge.* Tübingen: Niemeyer, 327—340.

Martin, J.
1972   "Rhythmic (hierarchical) versus serial structure in speech and other behavior", *Psychological Review* 79: 487—509.

McCully, C. B.—Richard M. Hogg
1990   "An account of Old English stress", *Journal of Linguistics* 26: 315—339.

MED =
1956 ff.   Hans Kurath—Sherman M. Kuhn (eds.), *Middle English dictionary.* Ann Arbor, Michigan: University of Michigan Press.

OED =
1989   J. A. Simpson—E. S. C. Weiner (eds.), *The Oxford English dictionary.* 20 vols. 2nd ed. Oxford: Clarendon Press.

Pinsker, Hans Ernst
1974   *Historische englische Grammatik.* (4. Auflage.) München: Hueber.

Puhlmann, H.
1971   *Die Entwicklung vom reintonischen zum syllabischtonischen Metrum in der mittelenglischen Verserzählung.* Nürnberg: Carl.

Pyle, F.
1930   "The place of Anglo-Norman in the history of English versification", *Hermathena* 44: 22—42.

Rheinfelder, Hans
1976   *Altfranzösische Grammatik.* Erster Teil: *Lautlehre.* (5. Auflage.) München: Hueber.

Slettengren, Emrik
1912   Contributions to the study of aphaeretic words in English. [Ph. D. dissertation, University of Lund.]

Vennemann, Theo
1986   *Neuere Entwicklungen in der Phonologie.* Berlin: Mouton de Gruyter.

Visser, Frans Theodor
1963—1973 *An historical syntax of the English language.* 3 vols. Leiden: Brill.

Weinreich, Uriel
1966   *Languages in contact. Findings and problems.* (4th printing.) The Hague:
[1953]   Mouton.

Wilpert, Gero von
1959   *Sachwörterbuch der Literatur* (2. Auflage.) Stuttgart: Kröner.

Lexical semantics and the Early Modern English lexicon: the case of antonymy

Arthur Mettinger

1. Oppositeness of meaning, usually loosely referred to as "antonymy", has been a current topic in structuralist lexical semantics during the past thirty years. As far as antonymy in the English vocabulary is concerned, major contributions to the study of this type of semantic relation have been made by Lyons (1963, 1977), Lehrer (1974, 1985), Lehrer – Lehrer (1982), Kastovsky (1982), Cruse (1986), to name just a few. Mettinger (1988, 1994) is the first corpus-based study of oppositeness of meaning in Present-day English and will thus form the point of departure for a few remarks on a corpus-based study of semantic opposition in Early Modern English.

Though the analysis of linguistic data will be given considerable space in this paper, its main issue is a more general one and concerns both the goals and the methodology of lexical semantics: does the subject-matter of semantics consist in an autonomous linguistic structure of semantic relationships between words, which can be established and explained by an autonomous methodology, or should the study of natural language semantics be incorporated into cognitive science at large and the language-immanent approach be given up? (cf. Geeraerts 1992: 259, 266) The former position characterises structural semantics, the latter is the one taken by cognitive semanticists.

In the following, I will outline the theoretical basis, the descriptive apparatus, the goals and results of a structuralist description of oppositeness of meaning, for reasons of space restricting myself to adjectival opposites as contained in a Present-day English corpus and an Early Modern English one. The more general issue will be taken up later.

2.1. The analysis of adjectival opposites in Present-day English as undertaken in Mettinger (1988, 1994) is based on a collection of more than 350 contextualised pairs of opposites gathered from 43 (predominantly British) novels published between 1922 and 1984. One of the major goals of the investigation of these *parole*-data was to arrive at a coherent description of properties characterising the semantic relationship between the members of a pair of opposites with regard to *langue*. The meaning-relations obtaining between the adjectival opposites discussed in the following can be regarded as stable and context-independent, thus allowing a semantic analysis within a structuralist framework. Such an analysis assumes that the meaning of a linguistic sign is determined by its position in the linguistic structures in which it takes part and that it is the semantic structure of the language that demarcates the meanings of individual words with regard to each other (cf. Weisgerber 1927: 178 – 183; Geeraerts 1992: 259).

2.2. These basic tenets have led to the adoption of semantic field-theory for the description of semantic opposition, which regards a given pair of opposites as constituting a semantic microfield characterised, on the one hand, by a hierarchical relation with regard to an archisememe, and, on the other, by a non-hierarchical semantic relation obtaining between the members of the pair.

It is very important to keep the notions "archisememe" and "semantic dimension" strictly apart, as they perform different tasks: the archisememe acts as "basis of comparison" and thus accounts for the similarities in the elements opposed to each other; the semantic dimension, on the other hand, states with regard to which property/quality the meanings of the lexical items of a pair of opposites are opposed to each other, cf.: "La dimension, ce n'est pas non plus ce qui est commun aux termes d'une opposition (la 'base de comparaison'): c'est ce qui est commun aux **différences** entre ces termes, c'est-à-dire à leurs traits distinctifs" (Coseriu 1975: 36).

The specification of the meanings of two lexemes A and B with regard to a semantic dimension is performed by means of semantic features. For adjectival opposites such as *big* and *small*, variable relational features (let us call them x and y) have been assumed that exhibit the following characteristics:

a) they are relational with regard to the semantic dimension involved;
b) they are relational with regard to each other, i. e. it is the x to y ratio that determines the type of oppositeness obtaining between the meanings of lexeme A (*big*) and lexeme B (*small*);
c) they are variable, i. e. they can represent any value along a semantic dimension, unless either of them must meet certain conditions with regard to the range of its value.

2.3. As far as the semantic dimensions constituted by adjectival opposites are concerned, a closer look at the behaviour of the opposites with regard to gradability can serve as the basis for establishing scalar and non-scalar (digital) ones.

The term "gradability" is used to denote syntactically observable phenomena such as the insertability of gradable adjectives into syntactic frames of the *more/less ... than*-type, their occurrence in superlative or equative constructions, in exclamatory sentences, and in combination with intensifiers; the term "scalarity" refers to the semantic properties that are mirrored by the syntactic behaviour of the respective lexical items, i. e. scalarity is not directly observable but must be inferred.

Ungradable opposites constitute digital dimensions; thus, *male* and *female* would constitute the digital dimension SEX — the semantic features have absolute values and exhaust the dimension completely, and one feature can be represented as the negation of the other.

When scalar semantic dimensions are involved, a distinction must be made between "type of scale" and "kind of scale":

"Type of scale" refers to the distinction between uni-directionally open scales, i. e. scales that have a zero- or starting-point and extend infinitely into one direction, and bi-directionally open scales, i. e. scales characterised by a turning point T (which is not to be understood as a zero-value but rather as a pivot) from which the scale extends infinitely in opposite directions.

"Kind of scale" refers to the distinction between degree scales and quality scales: along degree scales, the features express various degrees or different amounts of the properties denoted by the dimension; along quality scales, on the other hand, one feature expresses an evaluatively "positive" specification of a dimension rather than a degree, the other feature expresses the appropriate evaluatively "negative" counterpart (cf. *good—bad* along the dimension QUALITY).

Degree scales exist on their own, whereas quality scales, as a consequence of their scalarity, are also inherently degree scales.

2.4. Characterising opposites in terms of archisememes, semantic dimensions, and semantic features means applying a strictly autonomous methodology:

Firstly, relations between linguistic signs are described on the level of content, as the result of abstractions from actual occurrences; the focus on content allows the treatment of morphologically related pairs of opposites (*true—untrue, wise—unwise, important—unimportant*, etc.) along the same semantic lines as morphologically unrelated ones (*true—false, wise—foolish*, etc.).

Secondly, both dimensions and features are established on intra-linguistic, functional grounds, result from immediate oppositions between the meanings of linguistic signs and do not claim any psychological validity; the labels that have been given to semantic dimensions and features in the course of the linguistic analysis are metalinguistic in nature.

Thirdly, the result of such a strictly autonomous analysis consists in a typology of oppositeness of meaning in English which forms a basic frame of reference for categorising adjectival opposites, too. Moreover, the same frame of reference can be taken as the point of departure for the investigation of adjectival opposites in other periods, for example Early Modern English.

2.5. In the following, I will present the five major types of oppositeness of meaning characteristic of adjectival opposites in Present-day English and check whether adjectival opposites in Early Modern English exhibit identical semantic properties. The material investigated is twelve comedies by William Shakespeare written between 1590 and 1605 as compiled in the *Oxford Electronic Shakespeare* (1990): *Two Gentlemen of Verona* (TGV), *The Taming of the Shrew* (Shr), *The Comedy of Errors* (Err), *Love's Labour's Lost* (LLL), *A Midsummer Night's Dream* (MND), *The Merchant of Venice* (MV), *Merry Wives of Windsor* (Wiv), *Much Ado About Nothing* (Ado), *As You Like It* (AYL), *Twelfth Night* (TN), *Measure for Measure* (MM), *All's Well that Ends Well* (AWW).

Such a procedure is, I think, perfectly in accordance with the structuralist claim that "because semantic change has to be redefined as change in semantic structures, synchronic semantics methodologically precedes diachronic semantics: the synchronic structures have to be studied before their changes can be considered" (Geeraerts 1992: 259).

3. On the basis of the Present-day English situation we can single out the following types of adjectival opposites:

3.1. Scalar opposites
3.1.1. The S1-type

Pairs like *strong — weak, old — young, fast — slow*, etc. in Present-day English constitute scalar semantic dimensions. Both members are gradable, but whereas the x-value (characterising *strong, old, fast* ...) moves towards infinity in the case of intensification, the y-value (characterising *weak, young, slow* ...) moves towards zero without, however, ever equalling zero. This is why we cannot, for example, say **completely slow* when we mean 'stationary' (Cruse 1986: 206). This type of oppositeness of meaning is thus characterised by a scalar semantic dimension of the type 'uni-directionally open scale with non-attainable zero-value' and the feature-relation $x > y > 0$. Adjectival opposites belonging to the S1-type in Present-day English show no basically different semantic properties in the Shakespeare-corpus, cf.:

(1)   *Not yet old enough for a man, nor young enough for a boy.*
         (TN)

(2)   *I am not fat enough to become the function well: nor lean*
         enough to be thought a good student: ... (TN)

Both in the Present-day and in the Early Modern English corpus the S1-type consists of primary, i. e. underived lexical items only.

3.1.2. The S1 → 0-type

In Present-day English pairs like *important — unimportant, produc-tive — unproductive, selfish — unselfish, curious — incurious* etc. operate over uni-directionally open degree-scales, too. As with the *fast — slow*-type, i. e. the S1-type, the value of the feature denoting a lesser degree of the scaled property moves towards zero, when intensified; in contradistinction to the former type it may, however, even reach the zero-value of the dimension involved, which explains why the corpus contains cases like *completely unimportant, utterly incurious, totally unproductive, completely un-selfish*. This type of oppositeness of meaning is represented primarily by pairs with one prefixed member.

The investigation of the Shakespeare-corpus with regard to adjectival opposites of this type results in the surprising observation that the corpus does not contain any S1 → 0-type adjectival pairs. There are two instances of *important*, cf.:

(3)   *Who I made lord of me and all I had*
         At your important letters — this ill day
         A most outrageous fit of madness took him, (Err)

(4)   *The fault will be in the music, cousin, if you be not wooed in*
         good time: if the prince be too important, tell him there is
         measure in everything, and so dance out the answer. (Ado)

In both instances *important* means 'urgent, pressing' and does not seem to have an opposite. According to the *OED*, *important* in today's sense is first attested in 1586, its opposite *unimportant* only in 1750. The majority of the adjectival opposites that belong to the S1 → 0-type in Present-day English are post-Shakespearean coinages: *incurious* (1613), *unintelligible* (1616), *unsubstantial* (1617), *productive* (1612) — *unproductive* (1756), *selfish* (1640) — *unselfish* (1698).

Though the data-base strongly suggests a systematic gap in the oppositional system of Shakespeare's English it would be premature to uphold this claim without analysing a more extended corpus.

3.1.3. The S2-type

Pairs like *good—bad, happy—sad, happy—unhappy, wise—foolish* operate over bi-directionally open quality scales in Present-day English, where the semantic dimension is measured in terms of POSITIVE/NEGATIVE evaluation rather than just in terms of MORE/LESS. Whenever one member of the pair of adjectival opposites contains a prefix, the prefixed member covers the evaluatively negative part of the scale.

The same type of oppositeness of meaning can be singled out in the Shakespeare-corpus:

(5)   a. *Happy the parents of so fair a child,*
           Happier the man whom favourable stars
           Allot thee for his lovely bed-fellow! (Shr)
        b. *But by my coming I have made you happy.*
           [Silvia] *By thy approach thou mak'st me most unhappy.* (TGV)
        c. *How now, are you sadder than you were before?* (TGV)

(6)   a. *Lord, how wise you are!* (LLL)
        b. *Thou art as wise as thou art beautiful.* (MND)
        c. *The wisest aunt telling the saddest tale ...* (MND)
        d. *Where is the foolish knave I sent before?*
           [Grumio] *Here, sir, as foolish as I was before.* (Shr)

(7)   a. *An old Italian fox is not so kind, my boy.* (Shr)
        b. *A kinder gentleman treads not the earth.* (MV)
        c. *The dearest friend to me, the kindest man,*
           The best-conditioned and unwearied spirit ... (MV)
        d. *Blow, blow, thou winter wind,*
           Thou art not so unkind
           As man's ingratitude. (AYL)

Further instances of this type are *civil—uncivil, worthy—unworthy,* and probably also *virtuous—unvirtuous,* the latter once again illustrating one of the major problems of a corpus-based approach: though the corpus contains ample evidence for the gradability of *virtuous*, there is only one instance of *unvirtuous*, cf.:

(8)   *... If they can*
         find in their hearts the poor, unvirtuous, fat knight
         shall be any further afflicted, ... (Wiv)

As this instance is inconclusive with regard to gradability, it is impossible to say with certainty that the pair belongs to the S2-group. Still, I would suggest that as long as there is no evidence to the contrary, we may claim group-membership on the basis of the semantic properties of one member of the pair and on the basis of the pair's status in Present-day English.

3.1.4. The S1/0-type

This sub-group of oppositeness of meaning in Present-day English, made up of pairs like *clean — dirty, certain — uncertain, safe — dangerous, sane — mad*, etc., is characterised by the fact that the semantic dimensions constituting them must be regarded as 'uni-directionally open scales with obligatory zero-value', i. e. one feature represents the zero-value of the scale involved. So *clean* would be analysed as 0-DIRTINESS, which explains why *clean* collocates with *perfectly/completely/totally* and also with *almost* (the latter indicating approximation towards a zero-digit). The semantic feature characterising *dirty*, then, represents any value other than zero, which explains why *a bit dirty, slightly dirty, very dirty*, etc., is possible. If morphologically related pairs are involved, it is the unprefixed member (e. g. *certain*) that denotes the digit, whereas the prefixed member (e. g. *uncertain*) covers the rest of the scale.

In the Shakespeare-corpus the evidence is conclusive for *safe — dangerous*, cf.:

(9)   a. *... answer me*
            In what safe place you have bestowed my money, ... (Err)
         b. *Thus ornament is but the guile'd shore*
            To a most dangerous sea, ... (MV)

as well as for *quiet — disquiet*:

(10)   a. *Be quiet and depart. Thou shalt not have him.* (Err)
         b. *I pray you, husband, be not so disquiet.*
            The meat was well, if you were so contented. (Shr)

Possible candidates are *certain — uncertain*, cf.:

(11)   a. *... I would do the*
            man what honour I can, but of this I am not certain. (AWW)

     b. [Paroles] *Right; as 'twere a man assured of a, —*
       [Lafeu] *Uncertain life and sure death.* (AWW)

and *sure — unsure,* cf.:

(12)   a. *I am sure you know him well enough.* (Ado)
       b. *Present mirth hath present laughter.*
         What's to come is still unsure. (TN)

One of the most interesting cases is *clean — unclean* and *clean — dirty.* The Present-day English corpus has *clean — dirty* as the default pair along the dimension DIRTINESS and *unclean* operating along the dimension MORAL/RELIGIOUS IMPURITY (cf. *unclean meat*). The data in the Shakespeare-corpus suggest that the dimension DIRTINESS was lexicalised in terms of *clean — unclean,* cf.:

(13)   a. *In any case let Thisbe have clean linen,* ... (MND)
       b. *... to put good meat into an unclean dish.* (AYL)
       c. *... a musk-cat that has fallen into the unclean fish-pond of her*
         displeasure ... (AWW)

In some instances *unclean* might, however, be interpreted in terms of MORAL IMPURITY, cf.:

(14)   a. *Then let them all encircle him about,*
         And, fairy-like, to pinch the unclean knight,
         And ask him why, ... (Wiv)
       b. *... for where an unclean mind*
         carries virtuous qualities, there commendations go ... (AWW)
       c. *a sweet virtue in a maid with clean hands.* (TGV)
       d. *... And thus I cured him, also this*
         way will I take upon me to wash your liver as clean
         as a sound sheep's heart, ... (AYL)

Dirty as contained in the Shakespeare-corpus can in no way be regarded as an opposite of *clean*; rather, *dirty* seems to be a derivative of *dirt* n. 'the wet mud or mire of the ground, consisting of earth and waste matter mingled with water' (*OED*), cf.:

(15)   a. *Tell her my love, more noble than the world,*
         Prizes not quantity of dirty lands. (TN)
       b. *And here the maiden, sleeping sound*
         On the dank and dirty ground. (MND)

3.2. Non-scalar opposites

This type of oppositeness of meaning is characterised by the non-scalarity of the semantic dimension, which is inferred from the non-gradability of both members of a pair of adjectival opposites, cf.:

(16)   *I will forget that Julia is alive,*
         Rememb'ring that my love to her is dead, ... (TGV)

Whereas pairs like *right−wrong*, *true−false*, and *true−untrue* can be considered as non-scalar in the Present-day English corpus, this is not necessarily the case in the Shakespeare-corpus. In fact, whenever either of the three pairs operates on a dimension that might be labelled AGREE-MENT WITH FACTS/ASSUMED STATE OF AFFAIRS, they are non-scalar, cf.:

(17)   a. *You say not right, old man.* (Ado)
         b. *... I have*
            deceived you both, I have directed you to wrong places. (Wiv)

(18)   a. *O Tranio, till I found it to be true*
            I never thought it possible or likely. (Shr)
         b. *If it appear not plain and prove untrue,*
            deadly divorce step between me and you. (AWW)

(19)   [Sir John] *... Is this true, Pistol?*
         [Evans] *No, it is false, if it is a pickpurse.* (Wiv)

The pair *true−untrue* occurs as a non-scalar pair only; *true* and *false*, on the contrary, move into the S2-type whenever they constitute a bi-directionally open quality scale LOYALTY, cf.:

(20)   a. *As true as truest horse that yet would never tire:*
            I'll meet thee, Pyramus, at Ninny's tomb. (MND)
         b. *... We to ourselves prove false*
            By being once false forever to be true
            To those that make us both, fair ladies, you. (LLL)
         c. [Katherine] *Go, get thee gone, thou false, deluding slave, ...*
            (Shr)

4. The above analyses have, I hope, shown that the structuralist methodology is capable of characterising important semantic aspects of adjectival opposites. The corpus-based investigation of antonymy performed so far has been able to describe relations between the meanings of individual lexical items without, however, having led to a degree of knowledge that allows statements about how the entire lexicon of a language at a given point of time is structured in terms of various types of oppositeness. A considerable enlargement of the corpora and the development of more sophisticated methods of analysis will certainly make such a goal attainable.

Recent years have, however, brought about a tendency in lexical semantics to shift the focus of attention from the intralinguistic description of lexical relations to the description of linguistic phenomena as manifestations of human cognition in general (cf. Geeraerts 1992). As far as oppositeness of meaning is concerned, this shift of interest raises questions such as: What is the cognitive basis of oppositeness of meaning? Why do we find various sub-types? Which cognitive principles govern the semantic structuring of the vocabulary? In what way have cognitive contrast phenomena been lexicalised at different stages in the development of a language? These questions are of a different nature than the ones structuralist semantics has been answering up to now. Still, this does not mean that structuralist semantics is superfluous — on the contrary, structuralist methodology is an excellent means to investigate and to describe systemic properties of languages. In fact, I would argue, the results of structuralist analyses must serve as one of the bases for further investigations within a cognitive semantics framework — work that will occupy semanticists for decades to come.

References

Abbott, Edwin Abbott
    1966   *A Shakespearian grammar. An attempt to illustrate some of the differences between Elizabethan and Modern English.* (3rd edition.) New York: Dover.
Brook, George Leslie
    1976   *The language of Shakespeare.* London: Deutsch.
Chaffin, Roger
    1992   "The concept of a semantic relation", in: Adrienne Lehrer—Eva Feder Kittay (eds.), 253—288.
Coseriu, Eugenio
    1975   "Vers une typologie des champs lexicaux", *Cahiers de lexicologie* 27: 30—51.
Cruse, David Alan
    1986   *Lexical semantics.* (Cambridge Textbooks in Linguistics.) Cambridge: Cambridge University Press.
Franz, Wilhelm
    1939   *Die Sprache Shakespeares in Vers und Prosa unter Berücksichtigung des Amerikanischen entwicklungsgeschichtlich dargestellt. Shakespeare-Grammatik.* (4th edition.) Halle/Saale: Niemeyer.

Geeraerts, Dirk
1992   "The return of hermeneutics to lexical semantics", in: Martin Pütz (ed.),
            257–282.
Kastovsky, Dieter
1982   *Wortbildung und Semantik.* (Studienreihe Englisch 14.) Düssel-
            dorf–Bern–München: Bagel und Francke.
Lehrer, Adrienne
1974   *Semantic fields and lexical structure.* (North-Holland Linguistic Series 11.)
            Amsterdam–London: North-Holland.
1985   "Markedness and antonymy", *Journal of Linguistics* 21/2: 397–429.
Lehrer, Adrienne–Eva Feder Kittay (eds.)
1992   *Frames, fields, and contrasts. New essays in semantic and lexical organization.*
            Hillsdale, New Jersey: Lawrence Erlbaum.
Lehrer, Adrienne–Keith Lehrer
1982   "Antonymy", *Linguistics and Philosophy* 5: 483–501.
Lyons, John
1963   *Structural semantics.* Oxford: Blackwell.
1977   *Semantics.* 2 vols. Cambridge: Cambridge University Press.
Mettinger, Arthur
1988   Aspects of semantic opposition in English. A corpus-based study of binary
            meaning-relations. [Unpublished Ph. D. dissertation, University of Vienna.]
1994   *Aspects of semantic opposition in English.* (Oxford Studies in Lexicography
            and Lexicology.) Oxford: Clarendon Press.
Pütz, Martin (ed.)
1992   *Thirty years of linguistic evolution. Studies in honour of René Dirven on the
            occasion of his 60th birthday.* Amsterdam–Philadelphia: Benjamins.
Shakespeare, William
1990   *Oxford electronic Shakespeare.* Oxford: Oxford Electronic Publishing.
Weisgerber, Leo
1927   "Die Bedeutungslehre – ein Irrweg der Sprachwissenschaft?", *Germanisch-
            Romanische Monatsschrift* 15: 161–183.

Early Modern English passive constructions

Lilo Moessner

1. Introduction: Descriptive models

1.1. The primitive transformational model

Like many others, the standard grammars of Present-day English by
Quirk *et al.* introduce passive constructions with reference to corresponding active constructions.[1] This is not necessarily a tribute to transformational grammar, because Chomsky was by no means the first who
considered the transformational approach most appropriate for this purpose. But although even traditional grammarians like Jespersen[2] and
Poutsma used the same method, it is mainly with Chomsky and his
followers that we associate rules like

$$NP_1 - Aux - V - NP_2 \rightarrow NP_2 - Aux + be + en - V - by - NP_1.$$

The shortcomings of this rule have repeatedly been pointed out. Among
them are the unnaturalness of some passive constructions which are
derivable by this rule (e. g. *English and French can be read by Harry*
derived from *Harry can read English and French*); the non-existence of
the alleged synonymy of base and transform (e. g. *Some girls were kissed
by only five of our officers* as a transform of *Only five of our officers
kissed some girls*; the passive construction implies that each girl was kissed
by all five officers, some even by more, whereas the base implies much
less kissing: only five officers are involved, and it is not even certain that
each of them kissed all the girls available); and also the fact that some
passive constructions cannot be derived by this rule at all (e. g. the passive
construction *That the conference should take place in July was decided by
the organisation committee* is in line with the passive transformation rule,
the probably more frequent passive construction *It was decided by the
organisation committee that the conference should take place in July* is
not). Obviously, a more complex model is needed for the adequate
description of English passive constructions.

1.2. Svartvik's model of serial relationship

Svartvik's model of serial relationship seems appropriate here. Its basic idea is that some passive constructions are more passive than others, and that their degree of passiveness is measurable and can be mapped on a passive scale. Svartvik himself applied it in a corpus-based study of Present-day English passive constructions, and he proceeded along the following lines: He established a set of syntactic features, and he checked each potential passive construction of his corpus against it. It turned out that some syntactic features tend to co-occur, and on the basis of these feature clusters he defined six passive types. They are interrelated by virtue of the fact that there is an overlap of syntactic features between them. This is what he calls "serial relationship". His first three types share the feature of a straightforward active-passive correspondence, and they constitute the core of Present-day English passive constructions.

In the following I shall apply Svartvik's model to the description of Early Modern English passive constructions, considering syntactic features of the subject, the agent, and the verbal constituent in turn, here concentrating on passive constructions with the auxiliary *have*.

2.   Syntactic features of Early Modern English passive constructions
2.1. The subject

The realisation of the subject function by a substantival syntagm or a pronoun need not be mentioned, because it is a feature of all English passive constructions, and it is not specific for any single period. More interesting are cases which are usually called "impersonal passives", e. g.

(1)   *but it was supposed, and so it is written by Lopez, that he perished on the seas* [WR 29]

(2)   *it was inhibited that they should dispute anye further* [SE 144]

(3)   *it hath been held for infallible that whatsoever ship or boat shall fall therein can never disembark again* [WR 62]

(4)   *It was also told me ere I departed England that Villiers the Admiral, was in preparation for the planting of the Amazons* [WR 40]

These constructions are covered by van der Gaaf's definition of one type of impersonal construction, a type which is characterised by so-called "quasi-impersonal verbs" which "have *it* for their grammatical, provisional subject, while the real, logical subject is expressed in the form of a clause." (van der Gaaf 1904: 2). In Early Modern English, *it* commutes with the elements *this* and *there*, e. g.

(5)   *this was appointed that they should not come within the command or keepe of anye harbour in Spaine* [SE 156]

(6)   *there was found among prophecies in Peru (...), in their chiefest temples, amongst divers others which foreshowed the loss of the said empire, that from Inglatierra those Ingas should be again in time to come restored, and delivered from the servitude of the said conquerors* [WR 148]

The initial position of *it, this,* and *there* invites the argument that these are automatic and consequently non-functional elements which are conditioned by the post-verbal position of the *that*-clauses. This hypothesis is clearly refuted by my data, which include constructions with a *that*-clause in post-verbal position, but without any "grammatical subject", e. g.

(7)   *to the message might bee added here that my Lord Lieutenant sent a warrant to raise monies in Yorkeshire* [SEJ 29]

(8)   *they were two days aboard, and would be unknown that they could speak any word of Spanish* [WR 189] '... they desired it to be unknown that they could speak any word of Spanish'

Of all grammatical subjects, *it* is the element with the highest frequency. That it commutes with zero can also be demonstrated with the following pair of examples:

(9)   *it had been refferd to certain Iesuites what was to bee done* [SE 145] (subject: *it* + *wh*-clause)

(10)   *What had been begunn yesterday was whollye continued too day* [SE 159] (subject: *wh*-clause)

Apart from a *that*-clause, the logical subject which accompanies the grammatical subject *it* can also be a clause without an introductory conjunction, or an infinitive construction, e. g.

(11)   *it was concluded I should go downe with him the day following* [SE 69] (subject: *it* + clause)

(12)   *it shall be found a weak policy in me either to betray myself or my country* [WR 104 f.] (subject: *it* + infinitive construction)

The form of the logical subject depends on the syntactic features of the verbs involved. If they govern a *that*-clause in active constructions, the logical subject is also in the form of a *that*-clause, if they govern an infinitive construction in the active, the passive subject is also an infinitive construction, etc.

The grammatical subject *there* can also be combined with a logical subject, which is realised by a substantival syntagm. The general rule is then that the grammatical subject is in initial position, and the logical subject is preceded by the passive auxiliary and followed by the past participle, e. g.

(13)   *ther was a rumour divulged, of certaine conditions proposed by the pope to the King* [SE 135]
(14)   *ther was a new union made* [SE 67]
(15)   *ther was a shipp sett on fire and burnt to ashes in the river Thames* [SE 167]

Only in a few cases does the logical subject follow the verbal constituent, e. g.

(16)   *there were not left above 120 soldiers* [WR 46]
(17)   *there was sent me a basket of delicate white manchet* [WR 164]

Chronologically, *there* is the successor of *it* in this pattern, e. g.

(18)   *For it nere   neuere clad   ne naked*
         for it not-were never   clothed nor naked
         In a þede samened   two [HK 2889 f.]
         in a place brought-together two [persons]
         'never did in any country under any circumstances two persons meet'

This function of *it* must have survived until the fifteenth century, since Carstensen quotes examples from the Paston Letters, e. g.

(19)   *that it be provided ... a reward* (Carstensen 1959: 201)
(20)   *it may be pondered ... the grete lossez and damages* (Carstensen 1959: 201)

Apart from the combinations *this/there + that*-clause, none of the subject realisations quoted so far are completely unacceptable in Present-day English. In histories of English, it is usually pointed out that the subject developed from an optional to a compulsory clause constituent; Early Modern English is regarded as the transition period. After describing

Early Modern English syntagms with a subject and a predicate as "the commonest type of sentence" (Barber 1976: 196), Barber (1976: 284 f.) admits that under certain circumstances the subject may be lacking.

One pattern where a zero subject is rather frequent is illustrated by the following examples:

(21)   *as shall be declared hereafter* [WR 27]
(22)   *as had been formerlye saied* [SE 155]

Such references to earlier or later parts of the same text can have the same form in Present-day English, and they have an exact equivalent in German, e. g. *wie noch auszuführen sein wird, wie bereits gesagt wurde,* etc.

I mention this parallelism with German, because the most intriguing case of a zero subject which I found in my data also reminds me of a German construction. An adverbial complement in initial position is followed by a passive predicate, e. g.

(23)   *Monday was prettilye well studied* [SE 129]
(24)   *Wednesday was moderatelye studied* [SE 137]
(25)   *Friday alsoe was moderatelye well studied* [SE 141]

The examples are all of the same type; the adverbial complement is realised by one of the days of the week, the verbal constituent contains the past participle of *to study*. A comparison with equivalent German constructions like *heute abend wird getanzt, manchmal wird geraucht* makes me assume that it is the intransitive verb *to study* which is used in this construction and not the homophonous transitive verb. Further research is needed to answer the question whether other English verbs occur in this construction.

2.2. The agent

The term agent will be used for that constituent in a passive construction which realises the subject function in a corresponding active construction. Svartvik distinguishes *by*-agents, i. e. agents which are grammatically determined, and quasi-agents, i. e. agents which are lexically determined.[3] This distinction is not adequate for Early Modern English for two reasons. With the exception of the verb *to know* which governs a *to*- or *unto*-agent, my data do not allow predictions as to which preposition will be used with a given verb, i. e. lexical determination scarcely exists; on the other hand, grammatically determined agents are not only introduced by the preposition *by*, e. g.

(26)   *so much of the world as is known to the Spanish nation* [WR 24]
(27)   *he is well known to Monsieur Mucheron's son* [WR 108]
(28)   *our desire of gold, or our purpose of invasion, is not known unto those of the empire* [WR 119]
(29)   *It was also attempted by Diego de Ordaz* [WR 28]
(30)   *it is written by Lopez, ..., and of other writers diversely conceived and reported* [WR 29]
(31)   *he was followed with 700 horse* [WR 39]
(32)   *of some it is believed, of others not* [WR 42]
(33)   *they were spoiled of their women* [WR 117]
(34)   *hee was borne a prince and was therfore admired of all* [SE 133]
(35)   *the soldiers were grieved with travels and consumed with famine* [WR 34]
(36)   *the King was exceedinglye offended with it* [SE 106]
(37)   *his nose had been eaten away with whoring* [SE 141]
(38)   *I was comforted with my fathers returne* [SE 161]

As examples (30)−(38) show, the prepositions *of* and *with* were freely used as introductory elements of the agent in Early Modern English.

Although all agents in my prose database are realised by a prepositional syntagm, I should mention that − probably depending on the text type − we must be prepared to find other realisation possibilities, too, e. g.

(39)   *I am appointed him to murder you* [WT I.2.412]

Visser, who mentions this example, does not offer an analysis of his own, but simply reports: "This is, however, usually taken as standing for: 'I am appointed to be him (the person) who is to murder you'" (Visser 1973: § 1988). This reading cannot be definitely excluded, it would be parallel to Present-day English constructions like *John was elected president*. There are, however, some elements in the context which support the analysis of *him* as a passive agent. The relevant context is:

(40)   Camillo:
         Sir, I will tell you;
         Since I am charg'd in honour, and by him
         That I think honourable. Therefore mark my counsel,
         Which must be ev'n as swiftly followed as

I mean to utter it, or both yourself and me
Cry lost, and so goodnight.
Polixenes:
On, good Camillo.
Camillo:
I am appointed him to murder you.
Polixenes:
By whom, Camillo?
Camillo:
By the King.

When Camillo first alludes to his mission to kill Polixenes, the passive agent is *by him*, a prepositional syntagm; the referent of *him* is ⟨King Leontes⟩. This referent is, however, not made explicit. Then he announces in plain terms what is going to happen. Polixenes' incredulous question and the following answer make not only the referent of *him* explicit, but also its syntactic function as passive agent.

Not only the realisation of the Early Modern English agent, but also its position, is more variable than in Present-day English, e. g.

(41)   *Another Spaniard was brought aboard me by Captain Preston* [WR 37 f.]

(42)   *he was sent by his father into the island of Trinidad* [WR 50]

(43)   *he was by Berreo prevented in the journey of Guiana itself* [WR 53]

(44)   *which was by him and his companies very resolutely performed* [WR 37]

(45)   *hee was by him stoutly and wisely answered* [SE 55]

(46)   *which is also by others called Marañon* [WR 28]

Whereas (41) illustrates the end position of the agent, which has become generalised after the Early Modern English period, the agent of (42) precedes the prepositional object, and in the last four examples the passive agent is inserted between the passive auxiliary and the past participle. As a result, the verbal part is realised as a discontinuous constituent.

2.3. The verbal constituent

The verbal constituent, which I prefer to call the passive syntagm, consists of two immediate constituents, a passive auxiliary and a past participle. The neutral auxiliary is *be*; besides, other lexically marked auxiliaries (e. g. *become, come, rest, stand*) are used, cf.

(47)   *this empire of Guiana is become ... adorned with so many great cities* [WR 23]

(48)   *those Ingas ... come restored, and delivered from the servitude of the said conquerors* [WR 148]

(49)   *the Howse rested satisfied* [SEJ 107]

(50)   *he might bee sequestred and stand committed for two or three daies* [SEJ 29]

The passive syntagm can be expanded by a modal auxiliary, or by a form of *to have* for the expression of the periphrastic past tenses, or by a combination of both, e. g.

(51)   *it may be sailed with an ordinary wind in six weeks* [WR 141]

(52)   *the graves have not been opened* [WR 142]

(53)   *the poor English merchant would have been ruined* [WR 157]

The following examples illustrate paradigmatically some of the more complex expansions:

(54)   *little amendment was to bee hoped for* [SE 55]

(55)   *the King was likely to have been drowned* [SE 58]

(56)   *his arrivall in England which will shortelye come to bee remembred* [SE 155]

(57)   *Cranfeild ... began to bee questioned* [SE 189]

3. Passive constructions with the auxiliary *have*

In Svartvik's classification, the minor passive types are characterised by the fact that instead of the neutral auxiliary *be* the verbal constituent can contain a lexically marked auxiliary. Such a passive type occurs quite frequently in my data, e. g.

(58)   *Berreo ... had so many of his people poisoned with the tawny water of the marshes* [WR 109]

(59)   *Wee had ill newes spread abroad by the papists* [SE 180]

(60)   *I was informed of one of the Caziqui of the valley of Amariocapana which had buried with him, a little before our arrival, a chair of gold most curiously wrought* [WR 137 f.]

(61)   *one of the kings phisitians offred to have the usher kelled privatelye* [SE 93]

(62)   *allsoe through Gods mercye I had my tooth pulled out* [SE 72]

The common feature of these constructions is the passive auxiliary *have*. When we compare them to corresponding passive constructions with the neutral auxiliary *be*, we notice a structural and a connotational difference. The subject of the *have*-passives has either no equivalent in the corresponding *be*-passives, or it realises an expansion in one of the substantival syntagms, cf.

(58′)   *so many of Berreo's people were poisoned with the tawny water of the marshes*

(59′)   *ill newes was spread abroad by the papists*

(60′)   *a chair of gold was buried with one of the Caziqui*

(61′)   *the usher was kelled privatelye*

(62′)   *my tooth was pulled out*

The occurrence of an additional nominal constituent correlates with an additional meaning component. The semantic relation between the subject of the *have*-passives and the action denoted by the verb varies. The subject can be viewed as the direct initiator of the action, but not as its agent. The subject of (62) did certainly not pull out his/her own tooth, but it may be assumed that this person asked somebody to do it. How far the king's physicians in (61) were actually involved in the killing of the usher is not quite clear, but they had definitely an interest in the murder. The native of (60) may have expressed his wish of a special kind of burial during his life-time, but the action must have been ordered by someone else. The attribute *ill* in (59) indicates that the subject has to be interpreted as adversely affected by the spreading of the news. The intended meaning of (58) becomes only clear from the context. The poisoning of many of his people was disadvantageous for Berreo, because it thwarted his plans to explore Guiana.

When discussing Early Modern English constructions, we usually do so in a diachronic context. Two questions seem therefore appropriate; one concerns the origin, the other the subsequent development of the *have*-passive. I shall deal with its origins first.

The examples quoted so far are from seventeenth century texts, and in these they are fairly numerous. In lesser numbers they can be found in sixteenth century texts, e. g.

(63)   *Some three halfe penyworth of Latine here also had he throwen at his face* [TN 247]

(64)   *This great Lord, ..., thought no scorne ... to haue his great veluet breeches larded with the droppinges of this daintie liquor* [TN 210]

(65)   *In his owne person, which hee woulde not haue reproched, hee*
         meant to take more liberty of behauior [TN 253]

Visser records earlier examples, e. g.

(66)   *of oðer   hand-wimmen twa*
         by other women   two
         he had iiij   sones giten him [CM 3900 f. MS Fairfax]
         he had four   sons   born to-him
         'he had four sons born to him by two other women'

But it is important to mention that all his Middle English examples have
one feature in common. The *have*-passive occurs only in what Svartvik
calls the ditransitive clause type, i. e. the passive constructions correspond
to active constructions with a direct and an indirect object. The earliest
examples without an indirect object date from the sixteenth century. I
am going to offer an explanation of these perhaps puzzling facts.

The first occurrences of the *have*-passive in ditransitive clauses coincide
with the first occurrences of the so-called indirect passive, i. e. the passive
type in which the subject corresponds to the indirect object of an active
construction. Early examples of both constructions date from the fourteenth century. Visser's Old English examples have been refuted by Bruce
Mitchell and Jacqueline Russom, his Early Middle English ones in my
book *Early Middle English syntax* (Moessner 1989). The indirect passive
has the advantage that it allows the foregrounding of the person-denoting
object, e. g. *he was given a present*. This may be one of the reasons why
it developed at all. This advantage is counterbalanced by the danger of
a wrong analysis. When confronted with an expression like *he was given
a present*, the reader/listener tends to analyse the subject as the goal of
the action denoted by the verb, and it is only fairly late that he recognises
that this analysis is not correct; the subject is not the goal, but the
beneficiary. The danger of a wrong start is probably one of the reasons
of the unpopularity of the indirect passive construction, and this unpopularity accounts for the parallel development of the *have*-passive in
ditransitive clauses.

This argument can, of course, not be used as an explanation for the
have-passive in mono- or complex transitive clauses. In my opinion, two
factors are relevant here. One is the fact that *have*-passives are unambiguously dynamic, the other is their special connotation.

The English *be*-passive is very often ambiguous. It can express an
action, then it is called a "dynamic" or a "kinetic" passive; or it can

express a state or result, then it is called a "static" or "stative" passive. Curme (1931: 445 f.) illustrated the ambiguity of the construction from the sentence *The door was shut at six when I went by, but I don't know when it was shut.* The first occurrence of *was shut* denotes a state, the second an activity. Curme considered the generalisation of *be* a "great misfortune for our language".

In Old English two auxiliaries were used in passive constructions, *beon/ wesan* on the one and *weorþan* on the other hand. Old English evidence of *weorþan*-passives and a comparison with the German cognate of *weorþan*, i. e. *werden*, and its use in passive constructions, which are unambiguous in German, support the hypothesis of a dichotomy stative : dynamic in Old English passive constructions. It must be admitted, however, that the distribution of the two Old English auxiliaries is not quite so straightforward as one would wish. The context of the following example makes it very probable that an activity is described, not its result:

(67)   *Hræþe   wearð   on yðum   mid   eofer-spreotum*
         quickly   was   on waves   with   boar-spears
         heoro-hocyhtum   hearde   benearwod [BWF 1437 f.]
         sharp-barbed   fiercely   harried
         'quickly it was fiercely harried in the waves with sharp-barbed boar-spears'

This is the passage where Beowulf kills one of the sea-monsters, which is then dragged ashore. Other *weorþan* examples are more ambiguous, and we must admit a considerable overlap between the two auxiliaries. Despite a number of borderline cases, we note a general tendency for *weorþan* to be used mainly in dynamic passive constructions.

The situation changed at the end of the Middle English period, when *weorþan* was lost. If the first examples of the dynamic *have*-passive dated from the fourteenth century, we could explain them as a new realisation of an old construction type. The dynamic passive which was formerly realised by the *weorþan* construction would now be realised by the *have*-construction. Apart from the fact that this would leave the additional meaning component of the *have*-passive unexplained, a time gap remains. The first occurrences of the *have*-passive in monotransitive and complex transitive clauses date from the sixteenth century. This time gap is bridged by *have*-passives in ditransitive clauses. Probably due to the presence of objects, they — like indirect passives — are always analysed as dynamic passives. Furthermore, there is coreference between their subjects and their indirect objects. This is why the semantic case "beneficiary", which is usually associated with the indirect object also became associated with the subject in these *have*-passives. This feature of *have*-passives in ditransitive clauses, namely that the subject benefits from the action denoted by the verb or at least is viewed as an interested party, contributed to the extension of the *have*-passive to mono- and complex transitive clauses.

But the existence of the *have*-passive in ditransitive clauses neither explains the date of the appearance of *have*-passive in the other clause types, nor the causative relation between the subject and the verb which we find in some *have*-passives. This can be accounted for by the influence of another passive construction, which is illustrated by the following example from the seventeenth century:

(68)   *I gott them* [= the new propositions] *sett downe in writing*
        [SE 124]

Although this is the earliest example in my own data collection, this passive type with the auxiliary *get* must be older, cf.

(69)   *it shulde be good for the kynge of Englande to geatte alied to him the duke Aulbert* (16th century; quot. Visser 1973: § 2115)

Both examples illustrate a strong causative relation between the subject and the action denoted by the verb. The *get*-passive must be interpreted as a competitor of the *have*-passive, because the two types share several characteristic features. They are exclusively dynamic, and they express a particular involvement of the subject in the action. It is therefore not surprising that the causative connotation of the *get*-passive should have been extended to the *have*-passive. As this could happen only after the *get*-passive was well established, we cannot expect *have*-passives in mono-transitive and complex transitive clauses before the sixteenth century.

After offering a hypothesis which accounts for the emergence of the *have*-passive, I am going to suggest an explanation for the fact that it never developed into one of the major passive types with a high frequency.

Here again it is appropriate to distinguish between *have*-passives in ditransitive clauses on the one, and *have*-passives in other clause types on the other hand. A characteristic feature of *have*-passives in ditransitive clauses is that the entity which is denoted by the subject is expressed twice. This is unusual for the syntactic patterns of Present-day English, especially for those used in the written medium. This accounts at least for the low frequency of the construction in corpora based on Present-day English written texts. Further studies are needed before we can make reliable statements about the frequency of the construction in the oral medium.

The reason for the low frequency of the *have*-passive in mono- and complex transitive clauses has to be sought elsewhere. As pointed out before, the *get*-passive and the *have*-passive have more or less the same grammatical and connotative meaning, and when two rivals fight for the same ground, and both survive, each can win only a partial victory. But the co-existence of the *have*-passive and the *get*-passive accounts only partly for their low frequency. Another factor seems relevant, too. From the sixteenth century onward, the neutral passive with the auxiliary *be*, too, developed a device for the unambiguous expression of a process. The first step consisted in the form '*be* + present participle', cf.

(70)   *whyles a commodye of Plautus is playinge* (More, Utopia; quot. *MEG* IV.208)

The next stage was reached at the end of the eighteenth century, when the combination of the progressive aspect and passive voice became possible, cf.

(71)   *A fellow whose uttermost upper grinder is being torn out by the roots by a mutton-fisted barber* (1795; quot. Visser 1973: § 2158)

Whether the last step in the development of the English verb phrase, the combination of a modal, a perfective, a progressive, and a passive auxiliary in front of a verb, has already been accomplished or not is a matter of dispute. The authors of *A grammar of contemporary English* describe this structural pattern as "uncommon but grammatical"; it is illustrated by the example

(72)   *They might have been being examined* (Quirk *et al.* 1972: § 3.13)

We need not go into details here. In our context it is only relevant to note that the *have*-passive with its special connotation has a rival in the *get*-passive, and as an exclusively dynamic passive it has an additional rival in the neutral *be*-passive when this is marked as dynamic by the auxiliary of the progressive aspect. The existence of competing constructions is perhaps also the reason why the *have*-passive has largely gone unnoticed so far, and has not received the attention it deserves.

Notes

1. "In the verb phrase, the difference between the two voice categories is that the passive adds a form of the auxiliary *be* and the past participle ... of the main verb.

At the clause level, passivisation involves rearrangement of two clause elements and one addition. (a) The active subject becomes the passive agent, (b) the active object becomes the passive subject, and (c) the preposition *by* is introduced before the agent." (Quirk *et al.* 1972: § 12.2).

2. "What was the object ... in the active sentence is made into the subject, and what was the subject in the active sentence is expressed ... by means of a prepositional group, in English with *by*." (Jespersen 1924: 164).

3. "The preposition introducing grammatically determined agents is *by*, and they will therefore usually be referred to as '*by*-agents'. Lexically determined agents are introduced by a variety of prepositions and will be referred to as 'quasi-agents'. Unlike *by* in *by*-agents, these prepositions are not voice-conditioned, but are selected by collocation with particular verbs." (Svartvik 1966: 102).

Sources

The examples were collected from the following sources; they are quoted in the form indicated in square brackets. Numbers refer to lines in poetic texts, act, scene and line in the Shakespeare text, otherwise to pages.

Alexander, Peter (ed.)
    1951   *William Shakespeare. The complete works.* London and Glasgow: Collins. [WT]
Bourchier, Elisabeth (ed.)
    no date   *The diary of Sir Simonds d'Ewes 1622–24.* Paris: Didier. [SE]
Holthausen, Ferdinand (ed.)
    1928   *Havelok.* (3rd edition). Heidelberg: Winter. [HK]
McKerrow, Ronald Brunlees (ed.)
    1966   *The works of Thomas Nashe.* Oxford: Blackwell. [TN]
Morris, Richard (ed.)
    1874   *Cursor Mundi or þe Cours of þe Werlde. A Northumbrian poem of the 14th century (4 Versions).* Part I. (EETS.OS 57.) London: Trübner. [CM]
Notestein, Wallace (ed.)
    1923   *The journal of Sir Simonds d'Ewes: From the beginnings of the Long Parliament to the opening of the trial of the Earl of Strafford.* New Haven: Yale University Press. [SEJ]
Raleigh, Sir Walter
    1887   *The discovery of Guiana and the journal of the second voyage thereto.* London– Paris–New York–Melbourne: Cassell & Company. [WR]
Schaubert, Else von (ed.)
    1963   *Beowulf.* (18th edition). Paderborn: Schöningh. [BWF]

References

Barber, Charles
    1976   *Early Modern English.* London: André Deutsch.

Carstensen, Broder
1959 *Studien zur Syntax des Nomens, Pronomens und der Negation in den 'Paston Letters'*. Bochum: Pöppinghaus.
Chomsky, Noam
1957 *Syntactic structures*. The Hague: Mouton.
Curme, George O.
1931 *A grammar of the English language*. Vol. 3: *Syntax*. Boston: Heath & Company.
Jespersen, Otto
1909–49 *A modern English grammar on historical principles*. 7 vols. London–Copenhagen: Allen & Unwin–Ejnar Munksgaard.
1924 *The philosophy of grammar*. London: Allan & Unwin.
Mitchell, Bruce
1979 "F. Th. Visser 'An historical syntax of the English language': Some caveats concerning Old English", *English Studies* 60: 537–542.
Moessner, Lilo
1989 *Early Middle English syntax*. Tübingen: Niemeyer.
Quirk, Randolph – Sidney Greenbaum – Geoffrey Leech – Jan Svartvik
1972 *A grammar of contemporary English*. London: Longman.
1985 *A comprehensive grammar of the English language*. London: Longman.
Russom, Jacqueline H.
1982 "An examination of the evidence for OE indirect passives", *Linguistic Inquiry* 13: 677–680.
Svartvik, Jan
1966 *On voice in the English verb*. The Hague: Mouton.
van der Gaaf, Wilhelm
1904 *The transition from the impersonal to the personal construction in Middle English*. Heidelberg: Winter.
1924 "The conversion of the indirect personal object into the subject of a passive construction", *English Studies* 11: 1–11.
Visser, Frans Theodor
1963–73 *An historical syntax of the English language*. 3 vols. Leiden: Brill.

Infl in Early Modern English and the Status of *to*

Stephen J. Nagle

1. Introduction

The phrase-structure category Infl, formerly called AUX in Chomskyan grammar, is held to be a package of tense, agreement and modality features that appear variously in languages as affixes or lexical items. English has tended increasingly toward the lexical scheme over the last thousand years, most notably with the grammaticalisation by Early Modern English of many preterit-present verbs as auxiliaries which differ morphologically and syntactically from verbs (Lightfoot 1974, 1979). A central difference between Middle English and Early Modern English is that in the former Infl contained affixes which attached to verbs in a derivation, while in the latter Infl may be realised lexically by items such as the modal auxiliaries.

Chomsky's (1986) proposal that Infl is the head of the sentence in English, rendering former S as IP (Infl Phrase), coupled with a similar extension of the complementiser category Comp to have a phrasal projection CP, yields an isomorphic view of phrase structure with each category having an XP-X'-X structure:

(1)

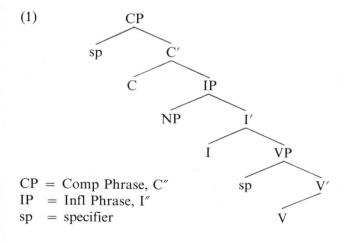

CP = Comp Phrase, C"
IP = Infl Phrase, I"
sp = specifier

In addition to containing the English modal auxiliaries, Infl is also assumed to be the D-structure home of *to* in *to*-infinitives (e. g., Chomsky 1986). Thus, a sentence such as *He wants to go* would be rendered as bi-clausal with the subject of the lower clause infinitive rendered as the empty PRO as in (2):

(2)   *He wants ...* (CP)

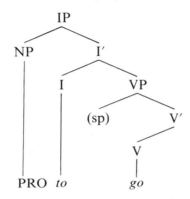

Recent work by Pollock (1989), Roberts (1993) and others has split IP into two phrasal categories TP (Tense Phrase) and AgrP (Agreement Phrase). Though their approach to phrase structure differs on some other matters, the English modals are generated under T for both Pollock and Roberts, who also proposes that *to* is the head of TP, in a phrase structure schema we will see in section 2.3.

We will begin with the more usual version (1) as our model of post-Middle English phrase structure and assume that one basic difference between Middle English and Early Modern English is that in Middle English Infl contained only bound morphemes (to which verbs attached to undergo inversion), whereas in English since that time it has contained the modals. Regarding the history of *to* as an Infl item, we will look at the diachrony of the so-called "split infinitive" construction, in which the *to* + verb sequence allows an intervening adverb.

2.1. Changes in INFL in Early Modern English

Lightfoot's outline (1974, 1979) of the development of the English modals from verbs to auxiliaries has been revised and criticised on many points, including its chronology of events both in deep and surface grammar (cf., e. g., Nagle 1989, van Kemenade 1989). However, the central notion that the modals are categorially distinct from verbs — an idea that evolved in the 1960s in Chomsky's work — and at least a weak version of Lightfoot's reanalysis hypothesis continue to endure in the generative tradition today maintained in the Government-Binding theory.

Lightfoot argued that several independent changes in the modals in Middle English combined to force the reanalysis of the modals in Early Modern English as d-structure auxiliaries:

a) the demise of the non-modal preterit-present verbs;
b) the failure of the modals to develop a following *to*-infinitive;
c) the increasing opacity of the present/past tense relationship between pairs such as *can/could* and *may/might*; and
d) the modals' loss of direct object complementation.

The reanalysis in turn yielded several additional Early Modern English surface changes including:

e) the modals' loss of participles and gerunds; their failure to co-occur;
f) the rise of quasi-modal verbal substitutes (e. g., *have to*);
g) and the revision of question (inversion) and negation rules to apply to auxiliaries and no longer verbs, perhaps giving rise to obligatory *do*.

Roberts (1985, 1993) proposes that the primarily Middle English loss of agreement morphology helped trigger the Early Modern English reanalysis which led to these changes.

2.2. Agreement and infinitive morphology in Early Modern English

In Early Modern English, remnants of earlier English verb morphology remained, notably in the second and third persons of the present tense (*-est, -eth/-s*), though the general loss of second-person familiar reference fairly quickly leveled the former. Third-person *-s* in current English is a rather curious and elusive survivor. Late Middle English infinitive morphology (*-n, -e*) remained moribundly very early in Early Modern English, giving way to *to*, though they were not mutually exclusive alternatives in Middle English, since both "bare" and *to* infinitives might have the infinitive morpheme.

Regarding the *to*- versus the bare infinitive, with or without final infinitive morphology, Fischer (1990) has outlined semantic and syntactic contexts for the use of one or the other. It would be convenient if we were to find infinitive morphology only with the bare infinitive — that is, *to*- and the final morpheme being in complementary distribution — since in theory only one can serve as Infl, being a head; but it is likely

that in the transition period the final morpheme was increasingly devoid
of transparent syntactic purpose and appeared to be part of the verb, not
a separate morpheme.

2.3. *To* as part of the reanalysis package

Roberts (1993) proposes that *to* was reanalysed similarly to the modals
in Early Modern English and like them is generated under T in (3) (NegP
is Negative Phrase, a phrasal representation of negation proposed in
Pollock (1989), and *for* in *for ... to* clauses is a complementiser):

(3)

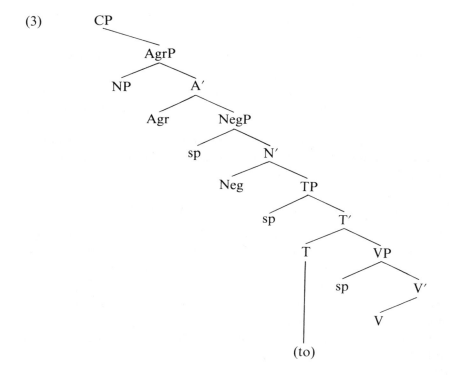

The loss of earlier infinitive morphology, in its final stages in Early
Modern English, made it possible for speakers to reanalyse *to* as its
functional equivalent (Roberts 1993: 259—262). Semantic factors aside,
this may be one reason that the modals, also Infl items, generally do not
allow a contiguous *to*-infinitive after Middle English. There are some
instances of a modal followed by *to* + V in Middle English (cf. Nagle

1989), but after the syntactic restructuring in Early Modern English, this is no longer a possibility.

3. Changes in surface *to*-structures since Old English

Lightfoot (1979) has claimed that the *to*-infinitive was a nominal construction in early English and was reanalysed as VP in Middle English. Lightfoot (1979: 189—194) points to the many nominal properties of the Old and Middle English infinitive, whether "bare" or with *to*, the latter of which in Old English usually required the dative morpheme *-enne* (i. e. *to singenne* vs. *singan*). In early Middle English *for to* appeared for the first time as an infinitive marker in sentences such as (4) a and b, presented in modern form by Lightfoot; *for to* was also sometimes written as one word as in (4) c, cited by Roberts (1993) from Visser:

(4)   a. *(I) for to go is necessary.*
        b. *It is good for to go.*
        c. *That wol not auntre forto winne* (Visser 1963—1973: § 1194, cited in Roberts 1993: 260)

We will leave open the question of whether *for* is a preposition in these examples or whether *for to* might be a compound complementiser similar to *for* in current English (which is evident from its optionality in many contexts, as in *I want (for) John to go*) or, finally, whether *to* might be itself a complementiser, since the alternatives do not appear to bear critically on our analysis below.

A critical grammatical change took place in late Middle English with the advent of the *for* + N + *to* + V construction. Lightfoot (1979: 187—188) gives examples of several current English types and their dates of first attestation, the earliest three types being from 1380, 1385 and 1391 respectively:

(5)   a. *This left room for the controversy to go on.*
        b. *It is necessary for/to a man (for) to go.*
        c. *I'm afraid for them to see it.*

The emergence of this construction and the subsequent demise of the old *for to* infinitives signal some sort of reanalysis, for Lightfoot the shift from NP to VP. Roberts (1993) reinterprets Lightfoot's position in light of more recent views on phrase structure to support his claim that *to* was reanalysed as T (or, for our purposes, Infl) in Early Modern English[1].

4. The split infinitive

The split infinitive, once the schoolmaster's whipping boy, is now quite common; and attempts to avoid the construction by putting the offending adverbial before *to* yield awkward-feeling results:

(6)   a. *He wanted to quickly put an end to the controversy.*
       b. ?*He wanted quickly to put an end to the controversy.*

The construction first came under attack in the mid-nineteenth century, but it actually dates to Middle English (cf. Visser 1963 – 1973: §997). According to Visser, it disappeared in late Middle English and Early Modern English to resurface only in the late eighteenth century. Intervening direct object nominals, remnants of SOV word order, disappeared for good in late Middle English. The following are Visser's citations of the last instances of infinitives "split" by intervening adverbs of place or time, adverbs of manner and degree, *not*, and elements of more than one word:

(7)   a. *þe oon is redi forto soon move þe oþir.* c1454 Pecock *Folewer* 112, 10
       b. *To quite rid himselfe out of thraldome.* 1606 G. Woodcocke *Hist. Ivstine* IV, 23 [OED]
       c. *would ye not be as hasty to not belieue it?* 1533 St. Thomas More, *Wks.* 1125, A 1
       d. *forto iustli and vertuoseli do a dede* ... c1454 Pecock *Foweler* 155, 9

Viewing the bulk of Visser's citations, (7) a and (7) b are rather isolated and probably archaic instances of their type, thus suggesting that late Middle English was the period of rapid decline of the split infinitive. In contrast with the wealth of comments by prescriptivists once the construction reappeared in writing in the late eighteenth century, there is no record of its being proscribed earlier. Thus, it is very likely that the construction's demise is a genuine grammatical development and not the result of tampering with the written language.

4.1. *To* + V as VP in Early Modern English

The split *to*-infinitive lost its intervening elements around 1500, just at the time when pre-verbal and pre-auxiliary adverbials were becoming much more common. This resulting situation held for 200 – 300 years,

which we would not expect to be the case if *to* were already an Infl item
(T). Assuming that the specifier position in VP is available for adverbs,
we would expect pre-verbal *to* (whether a Comp or Infl item) to allow
intervening adverbials, and to show no change in its interaction with
adverbs as one or the other. Yet clearly a prohibition existed in Early
Modern English.

Returning now to Lightfoot's original position that the *to*-infinitive
was reanalysed as VP, we apparently find an intermediate stage in the
development of this construction since Middle English. If *to* were to have
been reanalysed in late Middle English as a specifier within VP (or as an
adjunct to it as some theorists propose for adverbs), there would presumably be no position available to adverbs, thus ruling out the formerly
grammatical split infinitive, until a later reanalysis of *to* as Infl occurred.
The change would yield the following phrase structure in Early Modern
English, prior to a subsequent reanalysis of *to* as Infl − that is:

(8)

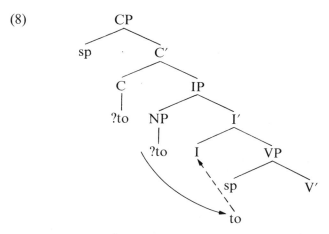

Two things may have spurred the later reanalysis of *to* from a specifier
to an Infl item: the reanalysis of the modals, as Infl (T) became available
to free morphemes (cf. Roberts' discussions); and the awkward situation
of the verbal specifier position being available to adverbs in all but *to*
contexts.

5. Conclusion

The reanalysis of the *to*-infinitive appears to have been in two stages: a)
a shift to VP with *to* as pre-verbal specifier or Adjunct in late Middle

English or Early Modern English signaled by the rise of *for* + N + *to* + V structures; and b) a further reanalysis of *to* as a functional head (I or T) later in Modern English. The demise of the split infinitive in late Middle English and then its rapid ascent testify to the two developments. These two changes over several hundred years were, of course, tied in with other systemic changes, notably the reanalysis of the modals; and the broad picture indicates a gradual evolution of the grammatical system. Just as the modals may not have been categorially reanalysed at a stroke but rather to some degree gradually and individually, so the development of *to* as a head of a functional category (IP or TP) itself proceeded incrementally.

Note

1. Roberts uses superscript° to indicate heads of phrases, as in T°. Here, we will use simply the upper case letter for the same purpose, as in T.

References

Anderson, John M. – Charles Jones (eds.)
    1974   *Historical linguistics. Proceedings of the First International Conference on Historical Linguistics.* Amsterdam: North Holland.
Chomsky, Noam
    1986   *Barriers.* Cambridge, Mass.: M. I. T. Press.
Fischer, Olga
    1990   Factors conditioning infinitive marking in late Middle English. [Paper presented at the Sixth International Conference on English Historical Liniguistics, University of Helsinki, Finland, May 1990.]
Kemenade, Ans van
    1989   The diffusion and implementation of the category "modal" in Middle English. [Paper presented the Ninth International Conference on Historical Linguistics, Rutgers University, New Brunswick, NJ, USA, August 1989.]
Lightfoot, David W.
    1974   "The diachronic analysis of English modals", in John M. Anderson – Charles Jones (eds.), 219 – 249.
    1979   *Principles of diachronic syntax.* Cambridge: Cambridge University Press.
Nagle, Stephen J.
    1989   *Inferential change and syntactic modality in English.* (Bamberger Beiträge zur Englischen Sprachwissenschaft 23.) Frankfurt am Main: Lang.

Pollock, Jean-Ives
1989   "Verb movement, universal grammar, and the structure of IP", *Linguistic Inquiry* 20: 365–424.
Roberts, Ian G.
1985   "Agreement parameters and the development of the English modal auxiliaries", *Natural Language and Linguistic Theory* 3: 21–58.
1993   *Verbs and diachronic syntax: A comparative history of English and French.* Dordrecht: Kluwer.
Visser, Frans Theodor
1963–73   *An historical syntax of the English language.* Leiden: Brill.

Aspects of adverbial change in Early Modern English

Terttu Nevalainen

1. Introduction

Compared with the number of works on Shakespeare's language, there are only a handful of monographs whose titles include the period specification Early Modern English. Barber (1976) and Görlach (1991) are notable exceptions. As there is to date no comprehensive treatment of Shakespeare's adverb usage, we should not expect to find a monograph entitled *Early Modern English adverbs*, either. Much neglected though the field of adverbial studies has been in the history of the English language, new prospects are opening up. Extensive new findings are presented in Swan (1988) and (1991) on sentence adverbs from Old to Late Modern English, and Peters (1993) on intensifiers from Middle English to the present day. In Nevalainen (1991), I concentrate on focusing adverbials in Modern English (1500 – 1900). The topic of this article is two related aspects of adverbial change in the Early Modern English period between 1500 and 1700, namely morphological regularisation of adverb formation and functional-semantic shifts within the category of Early Modern English adverbs.

Swan (1991: 434) suggests that it may be the predominance of the *-ly* suffix that has facilitated the rapid increase in the sentence adverb class that is so typical of Present-day English. My evidence partly supports her argument, showing that the *-ly* suffix was not so widespread in Early Modern English as it is today. This is not to say that there would have been some clear morphological limitations on semantic-functional shifts within the adverbial category at large. Overall, my findings provide evidence for two on-going processes in Early Modern English. First, morphological regularisation was progressing at the expense of zero derivation, but was by no means fully implemented. Secondly, the various processes of adverbialisation were active throughout the period. This means that in certain categories functional-semantic shifts continued to occur irrespective of the form of the adverb.[1]

This paper offers a survey of these processes. I begin by discussing morphological regularisation (section 2). My principal concern here is the Early Modern English development of adverbs that have a dual morphology, i. e. both *-ly* and zero forms, in Present-day English. The question is whether the pattern was still productive at the time. The form of Early Modern English intensifiers is also briefly discussed. Section 3.1 summarises Early Modern English contributions to the sentence adverb category. I finish with a more detailed discussion of the kinds of semantic development that altered the composition of the Early Modern English focusing adverb class (3.2).

2. Morphological regularisation

The issue of morphological regularisation of English adverbs towards the end of the Early Modern English period is one of the commonplaces in textbooks on the history of English. The generalisation of the adverbial suffix *-ly* is usually attributed to the effects of standardisation. Fisher *et al.* (1984: 49) point out that adverbs were already regularly marked by the *-ly* suffix in the Chancery documents in the fifteenth century. The acceptance of the Chancery Standard was not, however, explicit outside the Chancery itself. At the beginning of the Early Modern English period, it was the printers and educators who began to assume dominant roles in the transmission of the written standard (see Nevalainen — Raumolin-Brunberg 1989: 83 — 88). The growing feeling for grammatical "correctness" that Knorrek (1938: 104) and Strang (1970: 139), for instance, refer to is well documented in Robert Lowth's *Short Introduction to English Grammar*. Bishop Lowth writes in 1762:

> Adjectives are sometimes employed as adverbs: improperly, and not agreeably to the genius of the English language. As, '*indifferent* honest, *excellent* well: Shakespear, Hamlet, '*extreme* elaborate:' Dryden, Essay on Dram. Poet. '*marvellous* graceful:' Clarendon, Life, p. 18. (Lowth 1762/1775: 93)

Prescriptive grammar is not the only source of *-ly* forms. Such pleonastic forms as *oftenly* and *soonly* can be found as early as the late fifteenth and early sixteenth centuries, and must be attributed to analogy. Incidentally, Dr. Johnson includes *soonly* in his 1755 *Dictionary*, although he provides his illustrative example with this comment:

> This word I remember in no other place; but if *soon* be, as it seems once to have been, an adjective, *soonly* is proper. (Johnson 1775, s. v. *soonly*)

2.1. Intensifiers

Early Modern English adverb categories vary in their morphological development. As Lowth's examples above illustrate, it was the highly variable class of intensifiers that particularly attracted grammarians' attention. A number of intensifiers were regularised towards the beginning of the Late Modern period, and the suffix -*ly* was being increasingly appended to such short forms as *devilish, dreadful, exceeding, extraordinary*, and *terrible* (Strang 1970: 139). To see whether any watershed period could be detected in the usage of the time, I turned to the Early Modern English section of the *Helsinki Corpus*.[2] The adverbs with two forms that I checked make up a random set of ten amplifiers, adverbs that scale upwards from an assumed norm (see Quirk *et al.* 1985: 590 − 597). They were: *cruel* vs. *cruelly, exceeding* vs. *exceedingly, excellent* vs. *excellently, extraordinary* vs. *extraordinarily, full* vs. *fully, might* vs. *mightily, pure* vs. *purely, singular* vs. *singularly, terrible* vs. *terribly*, and *whole* vs. *wholly*.

The results of my search were negative in the sense that in most cases both the short and the long form could be found in the Corpus data. In other words, long forms did occur well before the introduction of normative grammars in the eighteenth century, and even before the discussions of correctness in the latter half of the seventeenth. Some items, such as *exceedingly, purely, singularly* and *terribly*, already appeared in sixteenth century texts. They are also similarly attested in the *OED*.

In the chase of intensifiers, some of the factors that covary with the choice of the form are syntactic. Even today, the -*ly* adverbs tend to occur with verbal and participial heads, and the short, zero forms with adverb and adjective heads (Ungerer 1988: 261 − 263). Consider the illustrations with *exceeding(ly)* in (1)−(3), below, which date from the latter half of the seventeenth century. That we are only talking about a syntactic tendency here is shown by *perfectly round* in example (1). The suffixed form was also acceptable in adjectival contexts.

(1)   *One experiment, which does very much illustrate my present Explication, and is in it self* exceeding *pretty, I must not pass by: And that is a way of making small Globules or Balls of Lead, or Tin, as small almost as these of Iron or Steel, and that* exceeding *easily and quickly, by turning the filings or chips of those Metals also into* perfectly *round Globules.* (EModE3, Hooke 13.5, 47)

(2)   *I returned home: The whole Nation now* exceedingly *alarm'd
            by the French fleete braving our Coast even to the very Thames
            mouth.* (EModE3, Evelyn 927)

(3)   *But to alay much of this the French fleete having* exceedingly
            *beaten the Dutch fleete, & ours not daring to interpose, ride at
            present in our Chanell* ... (EModE3, Evelyn 928)

This kind of common pattern of syntactic conditioning nonetheless partly
accounts for the generalisation of such short intensifiers as *very* and
pretty, for instance, which never take a verbal head (see Bäcklund 1973:
158 – 159, 266 – 267).

2.2. Adverbs based on elementary adjectives

The adverbial suffix -*ly* is not, however, generalised with all verb-modifiers
in Present-day English either. The exceptional class consists of adverbs
that are derived from what Ungerer in his *Syntax der englischen Adverbialen* (1988: 31) calls elementary adjectives. Following Dixon (1977: 31),
he defines this class of basic adjectives in terms of the semantic types of
DIMENSION, PHYSICAL PROPERTY, SPEED, and VALUE. They
are lexemes that denote dimensions or other observable physical properties, such as length, breadth, height, depth, weight, brightness, texture
and temperature. The category also includes adjectives that denote basic
values, such as *good, cheap*, and *right*. Generally speaking, these basic
adjectives are used by the speaker for the purposes of relatively objective
expression. They may be contrasted with the more subjective category of
adjectives that relate to what Dixon (1977) calls HUMAN PROPEN-
SITY, items such as *sad, odd* or *crazy*.

The lexical properties of Ungerer's elementary adjectives include the
following (see Ungerer 1988: 31 – 32):

1)   They are objectively gradable.
2)   They are organised in terms of antonymic pairs (*high* vs. *low,
            thick* vs. *thin, rough* vs. *smooth*, etc.).
3)   Pairs of dimension and measure adjectives also have an un-
            marked term that is used with measure expressions (e. g. *75
            years old, two meters deep, five feet tall*; Quirk *et al.* 1985:
            470).

From the point of view of adverb formation, elementary adjectives share
the property that they regularly display a suffixless form in Present-day

English. In many cases this fact may be related to their close association with subject and object complementation (see below). Adverbs derived from elementary adjectives usually also have a suffixed form, but it tends to be either functionally or distributionally differentiated from the short one. The Present-day English situation is further discussed in Ungerer (1988: 231–247), and Opdahl (1989, 1990).

The items that only have the short, suffixless form include *much, little, big, small, tall, long, straight, far, early, fast, still, good* and *ill*. Some of them clearly have heavy collocational restrictions (e. g. *big: talk big*), or only appear in certain varieties of English. Others are of the widest possible currency as core adverbs in the language (*much, little, far*, etc.). These items show that there is not necessarily any stigma attached to well-established zero forms in Present-day English.

What is more interesting, however, are the items that give rise to two adverb forms. My question is whether the pattern of zero formation was still current in Early Modern English. More specifically, is the Present-day English category a Middle English relic, as it were, or were new items added to it in Early Modern English? If the first alternative were true, we might assume that the short forms could in fact be remnants of the older pattern of adverb formation by means of the suffix *-e*. On the other hand, if the dual pattern was productive in Early Modern English, we would have clear counterevidence concerning any strong version of the process of morphological regularisation of adverb formation in Early Modern English.

The list of elementary adjectives that I used to study the issue is based on Ungerer's account of the Present-day English class (1988: 232–236). It includes the 62 items listed in Table 1. I checked each adverb pair against the evidence provided by the *OED* and *MED*. The columns marked *pre-EModE* and *EModE* show the approximate periods in which the forms were first recorded. The indentation further singles out the adverbs that were introduced in Early Modern English.

In order to find out more about their distributions, I checked the dual form pairs in the Early Modern English section of the *Helsinki Corpus*. The systematic corpus data showed one interesting area of overlap between the adjectival and adverbial uses of these items, namely compound adjectives consisting of an adverb and a past participle. Unlike syntactic constructions which consist of an intensifier and a past participle, these compounds frequently display the zero form. The contrast in use is clear in the two examples from Celia Fiennes's *Journeys* in examples (4) and

Table 1. Adverbs derived from elementary adjectives

Adverb	pre-EModE	EModE	Adverb	pre-EModE	EModE
great	+		− closely		+
greatly	+		late	+	
large	+		lately	+	
largely	+		− tight		+
fine	+		− tightly		+
finely	+		loose	+	
short	+		loosely	+	
shortly	+		thick	+	
wide	+		thickly	+	
− widely		+	thin	+	
broad	+		thinly	+	
− broadly		+	heavy	+	
narrow	+		heavily	+	
narrowly	+		light	+	
high	+		lightly	+	
highly	+		− rough		+
low	+		roughly	+	
lowly	+		smooth	+	
deep	+		smoothly	+	
deeply	+		sharp	+	
− shallow		+	sharply	+	
− shallowly		+	− blunt		+
even	+		bluntly	+	
evenly	+		hard	+	
flat	+		hardly	+	
flatly	+		firm	+	
plain	+		firmly	+	
plainly	+		soft	+	
steep	+		softly	+	
− steeply		+	hot	+	
direct	+		hotly	+	
directly	+		cold	+	
(a)wry	+		coldly	+	
− wryly		+	warm	+	
near	+		− warmly		+
− nearly		+	cool	+	
clear	+		− coolly		+
clearly	+		bright	+	
close	+		brightly	+	

Table 1. Continued

Adverb	pre-EModE	EModE	Adverb	pre-EModE	EModE
— dark		+	— dirtily		+
darkly	+		dear	+	
sweet	+		dearly	+	
sweetly	+		— cheap		+
sour	+		— cheaply		+
— sourly		+	rich	+	
bitter	+		richly	+	
bitterly	+		(poor)		
loud	+		poorly	+	
loudly	+		— bad		+
— quiet		+	badly	+	
quietly	+		fair	+	
quick	+		fairly	+	
quickly	+		foul	+	
slow	+		foully	+	
slowly	+		right	+	
strong	+		rightly	+	
strongly	+		wrong	+	
— weak		+	wrongly	+	
weakly	+		true	+	
clean	+		truly	+	
cleanly	+		false	+	
— dirty		post-EModE	falsely	+	

(5). The short form often persists in Present-day English with adverbial compounds, such as *deep-seated, firm-set, new-laid, true-born, rough-hewn, soft-spoken*, and *wide-spread* (see Quirk *et al.* 1985: 1577).

(4) … *and there is still a very fine Church, all carv'd in stone hollow work one tire /tier/ above another to the tower that ascends not very high but* finely *carve'd also*; (EModE3, Fiennes 145)

(5) … *in those chambers where were loose looking-glasses, which were with* fine *carv'd head and frames some of them naturall wood others gilt, but they were the largest looking-glasses I ever saw;* (EModE3, Fiennes 154)

As we can see from Table 1, most of the adverb pairs do go back to pre-Early Modern English times. This is not very surprising because these adjectives are mostly native, and represent some of the basic notions expressed by adjectival means in English. At the same time, there are altogether 23 new adverb forms of this kind that were introduced to the language after the Middle English period. They divide almost evenly between the suffixed -*ly* forms and the zero formations.

The 13 -*ly* forms are, in the order that I have listed them in Table 1: *widely, broadly, shallowly, steeply, wryly, nearly, closely, tightly, warmly, coolly, sourly, dirtily*, and *cheaply*. Two illustrations of these forms are given in examples (6) and (7). The ten zero formations consist of the following: *shallow, tight, rough, blunt, dark, quiet, weak, dirty, cheap*, and *bad*. The form *slow* could perhaps also have been included here, because it is not positively established as an adverb until the latter half of the 15th century according to the *MED*. Illustrations of *rough* and *slow* are given in examples (8) and (9).

(6)   *On the south side of this area is the bisshop's palace dichid* brodely *and waterid about by the water of S. Andres streame let into it.* (EModE1, Leland I, 146)

(7)   *... and so I have turned her off: besides her loosing my linnen and washing* dirtily *she hath also grosly abused me, and one or two others*; (EModE3, Strype 181)

(8)   *At nyght we sorted out men and I being the 4 person of necessytie must be a larbord man. We cam back agayn to the Cows because the tyde sets* rugh *at Yermowth.* (EModE2, Madox 129)

(9)   *... you place your Churn in a paile of cold water as deep as your Creame riseth in the Churne; and in the churning thereof let your stroakes goe* slow*, and be sure that your churne be cold when you put in your creame*: (EModE2, Markham, 112)

Rough in (8) shows the close connection between some of the short adverbs and, in this case, the subject complement. We may compare it with *Roughly* in (10), and further with such instances as *The sun shines bright/brightly*, which go back to Middle English.

(10)   *When the wynde contrary to our hope began to blow* rughly *at the sowth we retyred back agayn and cam to the Cows but the vyceadmiral rode yt owt at Yermowth.* (EModE2, Madox 134)

Some of the items in Table 1 need a separate comment. According to the dictionary sources, the adjective *poor* does not appear to have developed a short adverb form. The distributions of *dark* and *weak* are limited, since the *OED* gives them only in participial compounds. Also, according to the sources used in Ungerer (1988), *dark* and *weak* do not appear in adverbial use in Present-day English. The form *cheap* is first dated to the beginning of the sixteenth century by the *OED* both in its adjectival and adverbial functions. It goes back to the Middle English adverbial phrase *good chepe* which in turn was modelled on the French *à bon marché*.

Finally, *dirty* is the only short adverb in this category to acquire the function after the Early Modern English period. It differs from most of the others in that it is used as a booster, as in *dirty big*, for instance. Here we no longer have any direct semantic link between the adverb and the concrete elementary adjective, which is usually preserved in earlier instances. Unlike the case of *dirty*, it is much more common for the adverbs to be polysemous. Thus figurative senses readily occur with some of the new short adverbs in Early Modern English. We have, for instance, *blunt-spoken* and *speak rough*.

In this context it is interesting to note that the semantic difference between subjective and objective reference has been found to regulate the morphological variation of the long and short adverbial forms in Middle English. This is the result that Donner (1991) reached in his comprehensive study based on the *Middle English Dictionary*. Although he does not as a rule distinguish the groups on the basis of their source adjectives, he often illustrates the semantic differentiation of the short and long forms using items derived from elementary adjectives. He states, for instance:

> To indicate the range of contrasts by some illustrative pairings, *foul* may refer to how pigs root, *foully* to how men sin; *bright* to how the moon shines, *brightly* to how anchoresses should see and understand God's runes; *heavy* to how prisoners are fettered with iron, *heavily* to how men are burdened with God's commands; *high* to how a sword is raised, *highly* to how ladies are attired; (Donner 1991: 4)

In the light of the present evidence, it appears that this type of semantic distinction is no longer systematically observed in Early Modern English. As we have seen, the new short adverbs based on elementary adjectives have quite a few exceptions and limitations in their use. On the basis of these cases, it would be easy to dismiss the pattern as non-productive. The problem is, however, that we also have items such as *tight*, and *cheap*, which establish themselves in Early Modern English. Besides, the comparative and superlative forms of such Late Middle English items as *slow* continue in wider use than their positive forms until the present day.

Instances like this extend the process of change over a long period of time. They also show how imperfectly such broad tendencies as morphological regularisation are in fact implemented.

I feel inclined to agree with Ungerer (1988: 247) that the zero pattern is still current in Present-day English, but does not give rise to analogical formations based on non-elementary adjectives. This makes the Early Modern English era a transitional period. During that time, the category of adverbs based on elementary adjectives was still being augmented, but the core of its membership was inherited from Middle English. Because of their central position in pre-Early Modern English adverbial syntax and semantics, we may assume that short adverbs based on elementary adjectives had served as a model for other zero formations. It remains to be seen how productively this model operated in Early Modern English (see Nevalainen forthcoming).

3. Semantic-functional shifts

One of the semantic aspects of adverbs derived from elementary adjectives is that they often have a number of different senses. Some of them are so far removed from their source adjectives that the connection is barely recognisable. Besides minimisers such as *hardly*, they include the focusing adverb *even* in contexts like *Even Mary likes Mozart*, and *right* in *right away* and *right now*.

Semantic change, of course, forms one of the principal ways of diversifying the adverbial means of expression throughout the history of English. From the viewpoint of the adverbial function, most interesting changes are those that result in functional differentiation. Peters (this volume) shows that intensifiers are indeed a case in point here. But functional-semantic shifts are not limited to intensifiers in Early Modern English. In the remaining part of this survey, I shall focus on these processes of change in adverbial categories that Quirk *et al.* (1985) call disjuncts and focusing subjuncts. As the above examples of *hardly, even*, and *right* indicate, semantic-functional shifts are not limited to either of the two morphological classes of adverbs. Both short and long adverbs undergo these changes. As Swan (1991: 434) has pointed out, it is mostly the *-ly* adverbs that are involved in the sentence adverbial category of disjuncts. By contrast, the most important additions to the focusing adverbial category consist of suffixless adverbs.

3.1. Sentence adverbs

It has been shown by Swan (1988) that the English sentence adverbial category has become remarkably diversified in the course of time. Sentence adverbs are derived from word-modifiers, mainly from manner adverbs and intensifiers. The syntactic shift from a word-modifier to a sentence-modifier usually also involves a semantic change towards a more subjective, abstract meaning (cf. the difference between *they did it naturally* and *naturally, they did it*). Swan (1988: 7 – 73) distinguishes four categories within the class of sentence adverbs:

1) evaluative adverbs (*naturally, luckily, oddly*)
2) modal adverbs (*probably, evidently, surely*)
3) subject disjuncts (*cleverly, foolishly, justly*)
4) speech act adverbs (*frankly, seriously, precisely*).

The results of Swan's empirical study from Old to Present-day English indicate that the class has grown steadily. English has, in other words, developed a tendency to adverbialise speaker comments. The modal type of sentence modifier is quantitatively predominant in all periods including Old English. In the Early Modern English period the class is greatly diversified, and includes both high- and low-probability adverbs (e. g., *probably, necessarily, undoubtedly* vs. *possibly, perhaps*; Swan 1988: 366 – 387). Hanson (1987: 138) uses the *OED* illustrations to show the gradual development of modal adverbs such as *probably*. The first attested sense of *probably* is related to a manner adverbial function, 'in a way that approves itself to one's reason for acceptance or belief'. In the course of the Early Modern English period it also acquires the modern epistemic sense 'qualifying the truth of the assertion as a whole'. The two are illustrated by (11) and (12), respectively.

(11)   *You wrote so* probably *that hyt put me in a feare of daungerys to come.* (*OED*, Starkey, *Let.* 1535)

(12)   *A source, from whence those waters of bitterness … have …* probably *flowed.* (*OED*, Clarendon, *Hist. Reb.* 1647)

Swan (1988: 526) concludes that the evaluative type, by contrast, has only become extremely productive in this century. In Early Modern English it consists of very few items, including *happily, fortunately*, and often more ambiguously, *naturally*. The instance in (13) from *The Famous Historie of Chinon of England* by Christopher Middleton is one of the first of this kind in Swan's Early Modern English corpus.

(13)   vnhappily *falling uppon his Masters leg, so brused it* ... (Swan
            1988: 393)

These findings again make Early Modern English a transition period in
terms of adverbial change. They show that important developments
continue in Late Modern English (1700 – 1900), and some of them only
gather momentum in the twentieth century.

3.2. Focusing adverbs

Similar observations can be made about the category of focusing adverbs.
In terms of subclasses and adverb items, the category is much smaller
than the category of disjuncts. It consists of three semantic types, which
all share certain syntactic properties.[3] As the name implies, a focusing
adverb focuses on a clause element, and suggests alternative values for
it. The main semantic types of focusing adverbs and their typical representatives in Present-day English are the following:

1) exclusives (*only, merely, just*)
2) additives (*also, too, even*)
3) particularisers (*exactly, particularly, just*).

To simplify matters, we may say that exclusives exclude all focus alternatives except the current one (*only Mary* 'no one other than Mary'),
while additives add a new focus value to a previous one (*me, too* 'me and
somebody other than me'), and particularisers identify or specify the
focus value under discussion. Exclusives differ from the rest in that they
affect the truth conditions of the sentences in which they occur (see
Nevalainen 1991: 31 – 88).

The focusing adverb category goes back to pre-Early Modern English
times, but some important changes took place in Early Modern English.
In the case of additives, *eke* lost its long-standing status as a common
core item on a par with *also*, while *even*, one of the central items in
Present-day English, developed its additive sense. No similar semantic
change has, to my knowledge, taken place with *eben* and *även*, its German
and Swedish cognates. *Even* derives from the corresponding adjective
which originally meant 'flat', 'smooth', and 'equal'. In Middle English
the polysemous adverb had a variety of senses ranging from 'evenly' and
'smoothly' to 'equally' and 'exactly'. In both Middle English and Early
Modern English, the 'exactly' meaning of *even* also appeared in contexts
where the identity of two objects or persons was emphatically asserted,
as in (14):

(14)   Val. *But tell me, dost thou know my lady Silvia?*
            Speed. *She that you gaze on so, as she sits at supper.*
            Val. *Hast thou observ'd that?* Even *she I mean.*
            (Shakespeare, *The Two Gentlemen of Verona*, II, i, 37 – 39)

Towards the end of the sixteenth century, *even* developed its additive
sense common today, which implicates that the element focused on by
even is more than might be expected. Thus the *OED* instance of *In Warre,
even the Conqueror is commonly a loser* may be glossed as 'so certainly
everyone else is' (*OED*, 1641, J. Jackson *True Evang. T.* III.209). This
sense development appears to go back to the well-established sense
'exactly' being used in contexts where the coincidence was unexpected
and remarkable (see König 1989: 328). This kind of pragmatic strengthening of meaning is based on contextual inferencing, and involves a
notion of scale, in this case one of likelihood or informativeness. We can
present the Early Modern English change as follows:

PARTICULARISER → SCALAR ADDITIVE

We may trace the sense shifts of *just* in order to obtain a better idea of
the rise of subjective meanings of this kind. The highly polysemous adverb
just came to Late Middle English from French, and goes back to the
Latin adjective *just(us)* and adverb *juste* (< *jūs* 'law'). It is related to the
adjective *just*, which had a number of related senses, such as 'fair',
'righteous', 'correct', 'legitimate', 'well-founded', as well as 'fitting', 'precise', and 'exact'. In her discussion of the semantic change, Traugott
(1990: 504) points out that the development of the word in both French
and English crucially depends on the change of the basic adjectival senses
'righteous' and 'legitimate' to 'fitting' and 'exact', 'precise'. This shift
would appear to be based on the inference that whatever is 'just' is done
in precisely the right way. Metaphoric abstraction hence motivates the
adjective 'exact' ('no more and no less than') and the derived adverb *just*
'in exact degree', which appeared in English around 1400. Example (15),
taken from the diary of Dr. John Dee, presents an Early Modern English
instance of the particulariser *just* (Nevalainen 1991: 153).

(15)   *Jan. 9th, Francys christened afternone. Francys went with her
            nurse to Barne Elms. Mr. Edward Maynard borne in the morn-
            ing betwene 2 and 3 after mydnight.* (Dee 1592, 39)

            *Jan. 7th, I receyved letters from Lord Lasky from his capitay-
            nate in Livonia, and I wrote answer agayn. Jan. 10th, this day*

> *death seased on him. This day at none dyed Edward Maynard*
> just *on yere old.* (Dee 1593, 43)

Unlike *even*, however, *just* does not become an additive in Early Modern English. It relaxes one of its meaning components and establishes itself as an exclusive focusing adverb synonymous with *merely* and *only* 'no more than' towards the end of the seventeenth century. The change again appears to be inferential. *Just* in the sense 'exactly x' is being employed in contexts where x is not presented or regarded as of great importance. Around this time, *just* also often collocates with other exclusives, which may add a metonymic element to the change (Nevalainen 1991: 151–154):

(16)   *... Books of Physick: which the ill state of health he has fallen into, made more necessary to himself: and which qualifi'd him for an odd adventure, which I shall* but just *mention.* (HC, EModE3, Burnet 27)

The focusing adverb system thus also presents functional-semantic shifts from particulariser to exclusive:

PARTICULARISER → SCALAR EXCLUSIVE

The use of the exclusive *just* gained ground in the late Modern English period, and *just* has reached the position of a quantitative prototype in present-day colloquial language. Both *even* and *just* have thus gained central positions in their respective focusing adverbial categories in Present-day English. While the semantic changes giving rise to these developments go back to Early Modern English, their spread takes place in the Late Modern period.

4. Conclusion

In conclusion, all my evidence for adverbial change, for both morphological regularisation and semantic change, points to the transitional status of the Early Modern English period. Adverbial usage clearly distinguishes Early Modern English from Present-day English, but not so much in absolute terms, or presence and absence of certain categories and processes, as in terms of gradual and distributional differences.

The suffix *-ly* had not fully replaced the zero morpheme in Early Modern English as the standard derivation. Although most dual forms based on elementary adjectives, for example, go back to Middle English, suffixless adverbs of this category also continued to be formed in Early Modern English. Similarly, dual forms are not uncommon in the category of intensifiers even at the end of the period. As the intensifier category shows, the Early Modern English adverbial resources are also augmented by functional-semantic shifts. They diversify the membership of various sentence adverbial categories, such as modal adverbs, and change the composition of the main focusing adverbial ones. All these changes imply a drift towards a more subjective expression by adverbial means in the Early Modern English lexicon.

Notes

1. There were, of course, other adverbial suffixes in Early Modern English besides -*ly*. In his *Pamphlet for Grammar* (1586: 40), William Bullokar also mentions -*wise*, on a par with -*ly* and zero: "Qualities end in *ly, wise*, or are adiectiues, compounded with *a*, or vsed aduerbially: al generally answering to *how?*" Because of this fluctuation, and syntactic-semantic shifts within the category, I prefer to relate adverb formation to derivation rather than to inflection.
2. For the texts included in the *Helsinki Corpus* (*HC*), see the Manual (Kytö 1991). The principles of compilation of the Early Modern English section are discussed in Neva-lainen — Raumolin-Brunberg (1993); see also Nevalainen — Raumolin-Brunberg (1989).
3. Some accounts only distinguish two main types, restrictive and additive, and include exclusives and particularisers in the former as its subcategories (Nevalainen 1991: 54 — 58).

References

Bäcklund, Ulf
    1973   *The collocation of adverbs of degree in English.* (Studia Anglistica Upsaliensia 13.) Uppsala: University of Uppsala.
Barber, Charles
    1976   *Early Modern English.* London: Deutsch.
Bullokar, William
    1586   *Pamphlet for grammar.* London. [Reprinted in: *The works of William Bullokar*,
    [1980]   Vol. 2, *Pamphlet for grammar* (Leeds Texts and Monographs, N. S. 1.) (Fac-simile edition.)] Leeds: The University of Leeds, School for English.
Dixon, R. M. W.
    1977   "Where have all the adjectives gone?" *Studies in Language* 1: 19 — 80.
Donner, Morton
    1991   "Adverb form in Middle English", *English Studies* 72: 1 — 11.

Fisher, John H. — Malcolm Richardson — Jane L. Fisher
1984   *An anthology of Chancery English.* Knoxville: The University of Tennessee Press.
Görlach, Manfred
1991   *Introduction to Early Modern English.* Cambridge: Cambridge University Press.
Hanson, Kristin
1987   "On subjectivity and the history of epistemic expressions in English", in: Barbara Need — Eric Schiller — Anna Bosch (eds.), *Papers from the 23rd Annual Meeting of the Chicago Linguistic Society.* Chicago: Chicago Linguistic Society, 133 — 147.
Johnson, Samuel
1755   *A dictionary of the English language.* London. [Reprinted London: Times
[1983]   Books.]
Knorrek, Marianne
1938   *Der Einfluss des Rationalismus auf die englische Sprache. Beiträge zur Entwicklungsgeschichte der englischen Syntax im 17. und 18. Jahrhundert.* Breslau: Plischke.
König Ekkehard
1989   "On the historical development of focus particles", in: Harald Weydt (ed.), *Sprechen mit Partikeln.* Berlin — New York: de Gruyter, 318 — 328.
Kytö, Merja (comp.)
1991   *Manual to the Diachronic Part of the Helsinki Corpus of English Texts, coding conventions and lists of source texts.* Helsinki: Department of English, University of Helsinki.
Lowth, Robert
1762   *A short introduction to English grammar.* London. [A facsimile reprint of the
[1979]   1775 edition. Delmar, New York: Scholars' Facsimiles & Reprints.]
Nevalainen, Terttu
1991   *BUT, ONLY, JUST: Focusing adverbial change in Modern English 1500 — 1900.* (Mémoires de la Société Néophilologique de Helsinki LI.) Helsinki: Société Néophilologique.
forthcoming Adverbial derivation in Late Middle and Early Modern English.
Nevalainen, Terttu — Helena Raumolin-Brunberg
1989   "A corpus of Early Modern Standard English in a socio-historical perspective", *Neuphilologische Mitteilungen* 90: 67 — 110.
1993   "Early Modern English", in: Matti Rissanen — Merja Kytö — Minna Palander-Collin (eds.), *Early English in the computer age: Explorations through the Helsinki Corpus.* Berlin: Mouton de Gruyter 53 — 73.
Opdahl, Lise
1989   "'Did you purchase it direct or directly?' On *direct* and *directly* as verb modifiers in British and American English", in: Leiv Egil Breivik — Arnoldus Hille — Stig Johansson (eds.), *Essays on English language in honour of Bertil Sundby.* Oslo: Novus, 245 — 257.
1990   "*Close* or *closely* as verb modifier? In search of explanatory parameters", in: Graham Caie — Kirsten Haastrup — Arnt Lykke Jakobsen — Jørgen Erik Nielsen — Jørgen Sevaldsen — Henrik Specht — Arne Zettersten (eds.), *Proceedings from the Fourth Nordic Conference for English Studies.* Vol. 1. Copenhagen: Department of English, University of Copenhagen, 201 — 212.

Peters, Hans
1993   *Die englischen Gradadverbien der Kategorie* booster. (Tübinger Beiträge zur Linguistik 380.) Tübingen: Narr.
Quirk, Randolph — Sidney Greenbaum — Geoffrey Leech — Jan Svartvik
1985   *A comprehensive grammar of the English language*. London: Longman.
Strang, Barbara M. H.
1970   *A history of English*. London: Methuen.
Swan, Toril
1988   *Sentence adverbials in English: A synchronic and diachronic investigation.* Tromsø: University of Tromsø.
1991   "Adverbial shifts: evidence from Norwegian and English", in: Dieter Kastovsky (ed.), *Historical English syntax*. (Topics in English Linguistics 2.) Berlin — New York: Mouton de Gruyter, 409 — 438.
Traugott, Elizabeth Closs
1990   "From less to more situated in language: The unidirectionality of semantic change", in: Sylvia Adamson — Vivien Law — Nigel Vincent — Susan Wright (eds.), *Papers from the 5th International Conference on English Historical Linguistics* (Current Issues in Linguistic Theory 65.) Amsterdam — Philadelphia: Benjamins, 497 — 517.
Ungerer, Friedrich
1988   *Syntax der englischen Adverbialen* (Linguistische Arbeiten 215.) Tübingen: Niemeyer.

Periodization in language history: Early Modern English and the other periods

Herbert Penzl

1. Periodizations

It is doubtful whether a merely annalistic description without any division into significant periods of a language can ever constitute adequate historiography, if complete data are available. A relative break in the chronological continuity of otherwise clearly linked language data is a case where at least distinct periods will have to be recognized. The alternative would be the assumption of separate, even if closely related languages. A "period" is by definition a part of a language continuum; it should be a "natural" stage within the documentable history of a language. Its historical reality is not simply assured by scholarly tradition or practice, but only by definitely established, describable initial and terminal boundaries and by criteria applicable to the corpus of the entire period in question.

The criteria and the divisions themselves can only be purely language-specific, but it is not surprising when we find similar or parallel features of periodization in cognate languages. The topic of our Tulln conference was the Early Modern English period. The original version of this paper as read in Tulln stressed particularly the similarities and differences between Early Modern English and *Frühneuhochdeutsch* ('Early Modern German'). In the case of the historiography of (High) German, scholarly practice on the whole changed from the traditional threefold divisions Old High German (*Althochdeutsch*, Penzl 1986), Middle High German (*Mittelhochdeutsch*, Penzl 1989), Modern German (*Neuhochdeutsch*) to a fourfold division including Early Modern German (*Frühneuhochdeutsch*, Penzl 1984). Many handbooks dealing with the history of English have not abandoned the traditional division into Old English, Middle English, Modern English, but the special attention given to the early part of the modern period (*early* [lower case!] Modern English), 1500 (or 1450) — 1700, is on the increase. The implied or explicitly labelled subdivision of the modern period starts with the study by Zachrisson (1913) and Karl Luick's (1921 — 1940) differentiation between the "frühneuenglische Periode" (Luick 1921–1940: §470) and the "spät-neuenglische Periode" (Luick 1921–1940: §556). Baugh (1978) mentions a "renaissance" period from 1500 to 1650. *Frühneuenglisch* is the title of a book by Görlach (1978), to which I shall return below. I have characterized, in separate chapters, the language of such texts as the Paston Letters, John Hart's books, Shakespeare's plays, the Verney Memoirs as "frühneuenglisch" (Penzl 1994).

To evaluate the significance of recognizing Early Modern English as a special fourth period between Middle English and Modern English, it is necessary also to review the methods of periodization applied in the traditional threefold division. These methods are determined by the task of the historiographer, who is expected to provide an account of the internal history of a language (Luick's *historische Grammatik*): the development and changes in phonology, morphology, syntax, and the lexicon, but within the frame of the external history of the language, which involves the history of its speakers and their response to changing political, cultural, religious contact conditions. Periodizations have always been based on the facts of both internal and external language history.

2. The prehistory of English

The handbooks, whether published in the U.S.A. or in Europe, do not adequately include the textless "prehistory" of English in their accounts. There is no handbook in the field of English that can compare in comprehensiveness and quality with the one describing in 2251 pages the history of German (Werner Besch *et al.* 1984), yet even there we only find a token account of the prehistory, which seems completely inadequate. The difficulty of combining internal and external history for the periods preceding the "historical" era must seem too formidable a handicap for the historiographers. The concept of an *Ursprache* (proto-language) includes that of an *Urheimat* (ancestral home of the speakers), a joint area of settlement in the case of Germanic, from which migrations and thus new contacts caused dialectal splitting up into the attested Old Germanic dialects like Old English, Old High German, Old Saxon, Old Norse, Gothic, and others. Alleged sub-proto-languages (*Zwischenursprachen*) like "Urdeutsch", Anglo-Frisian, Gotho-Nordic, even West Germanic, had to be abandoned as (in the structuralist sense) merely scholarly hocus-pocus (Penzl 1972: §15.1 b), because the known external history and chronology of migrations and settlements cannot support this type of explanation of the complex network of shared internal isoglosses. I am convinced, however, that extant monuments like the Horn of Gallehus of 350 A. D. and many other short inscriptions justify the assumption of a Nordic-Westgermanic proto-language, which Elmer H. Antonsen (1975) has called Northwest Germanic, and which certainly included Old English among its daughters. I call it Nordic-Westgermanic and "Runengermanisch" (Penzl 1994) because of the type of script involved, since I do not want to exclude Old High German, which I find represented, e. g., in the fibula of Freilaubersheim of 550 A. D. (Penzl 1986: § 7).

3. Old English / Middle English

It is a typological characteristic of Germanic that the vowels in the fully stressed stem-syllables, the lexives, show nondistinctive, allophonic variation under the assimilative influence of following more weakly stressed formatives or flexives, the two other types of morphemes. We find *i*-umlaut, i. e. the fronting variation of velar vowels in all Germanic languages except Gothic, thus must assume it to be a feature of our attested Nordic-Westgermanic proto-language (see 2 above). The differences in the chronology of the phonemicization of umlaut allophones between Old English and Old High German fit Otto Höfler's *Entfaltungstheorie* (Penzl 1972: § 9.4). In both languages the evidence clearly establishes loss or change of *i*-sounds ([i] [i:] [j]) in "Nebensilben" as responsible for the phonemic status of the rounded palatal vowels of the stem syllables. In both languages coalescence of /o/, /a/, /e/ in a schwa-sound written ⟨e⟩ in weakly-stressed endings characterizes the development towards the end of the oldest period: also the *i*-sounds were affected and either changed or were lost. English scholars like Alexander Ellis and Henry Sweet in the nineteenth century recognized the similarity of the changes in Old English and Old High German. Ellis translated umlaut as "transmutation", which became simply "mutation" (*the* sound-change?) in the use of Henry Sweet. Was this done to hide the German origin of the concept? In his book *A history of English sounds from the earliest period* Henry Sweet writes in the preface (1888: VII): "Things have changed in the last fifteen years. The adoption of German methods is no longer a bar to recognition and success ..."

The change of the Old High German endings really revolutionized the morphology, thus no German handbook failed to consider this schwa-change as the boundary between Old High German and Middle High German (Penzl 1989). The date given dates from about 1075, also 1100. We find, e. g., the Old High German forms *geba* (nominative, accusative, genitive), *gebu* (dative). *gebā* (nom, acc. plural) replaced by uniform *gebe*. Old English, on the other hand, already shows early syncretism: *giefu* (nom.), *giefe* (acc., gen., dat. singular, Anglian nom., acc. plural).

A highly important fact of external history, the victory of the French-speaking Norman invaders in the Battle of Hastings (1066) with the resulting administrative and sociological supremacy of French over English for centuries, has, since the days of Alexander Ellis and Henry Sweet, been generally recognized as the boundary marker between Old English and Middle English. This seems particularly attractive if we assume the early fifteenth century, the date of the principal manuscripts of Chaucer, to be the end of the Middle English period: it coincides with the complete disappearance of French as England's upper-class language. From the point of view of the internal history of English it has been pointed out that French had its only decisive influence on part of the vocabulary. New syntactical patterns such as participial and other constructions have mostly been attributed to the renewed influence of Latin. The French origin of features of the phonology (dialectal reintroduction of lost umlaut-vowels?) and morphology (spread of *-s* as the plural ending?) remain doubtful. The variation of the verbal endings *-es* (third person sing./plural) and *-eth* shows Scandinavian influence. When we consider the internal history, it is not surprising to find at least one eminent scholar, Kemp Malone (1930), who advocated an earlier boundary for Middle English, similar to the one generally accepted for Middle High German as discussed above, basing his assumption on his collection of many cases of vowel confusions in the inflectional endings in manuscripts from the late ninth or tenth centuries. Most of them may very well indicate the spoken language of the scribes, but they indicate no systematic substitutions as are found, for example, in a text like *Merigarto* (Penzl 1989: § 195 ff.), where we find it difficult to decide whether the language of the text is late Old High German or early Middle High German.

The Middle English period is characterized by its regional written dialects, i. e. by what I called *Schriftdialekte* in Early Modern German (Penzl 1984). Moore, Leech and Whitehall (1935) established the five Middle English dialectal varieties in their geographic distribution: Kentish, Southern (in the Southwest), East Midland, West Midland, Northern. The end of the Middle English period and the beginning of our

Early Modern English period shows the disappearance of all these dialectal written and literary varieties with the exception of the dialect of Edinburgh in Scotland through their replacement by the dialect of London, the capital.

4. Early Modern English

Paradoxically, the end of the Middle English written dialects and the emergence of a uniform standard system of orthography coincides with the Early Modern English beginning of major spoken dialects even within the still fluid London standard. The so-called "Great English Vowel Shift" with its controversial *singular*, attacked by Robert P. Stockwell and Donka Minkova, and defended by Roger Lass (cf. Kastovsky–Bauer 1988: 355–394; 395–410; 411–433), involved all the Middle English long vowels and diphthongs. The uncontested linkage between the Early Modern English raising of Middle English /e:/ and /o:/ and the Early Modern English diphthongization of Middle English /i:/ and /u:/ led to a vigorous controversy regarding the relative chronology of the two processes: Karl Luick favoured raising as the event triggering diphthongization. The last change among the vowel shifts seems to have been the merger of the reflexes of Middle English /e:/ and more open Middle English /ɛ:/ into Modern English [i:]. For the sound-values of assumed intermediate stages within the vowel shifts, the evidence of occasional spellings and of rhymes by poets has proven quite inadequate, unlike the transcriptions and descriptions by spelling reformers and grammarians. They clearly reveal varieties within the London standard as well; thus in 1619 Alexander Gill (cf. Danielsson–Gabrielson 1972) attacked the descriptions in the books of John Hart in 1551, 1569, 1570 (Danielsson 1955) regarding the speech of London society ladies known as "Mopsae". Their vowels are described as being far ahead of the "great" shift of their time. Until the time of Jonathan Swift there is no reference to the language of the London theatre (the "Bühnenaussprache" to use the term of Theodor Siebs) as having any influence in spreading a certain variety of London pronunciation. But it has become practically routine in handbooks to publish transcribed passages from Shakespeare's plays in their entirety to show his pronunciation of verse lines. The great differences between the assumed sound values in transcriptions by Ellis (1871), Viëtor (1906), Franz (1939), Kökeritz (1953), Marckwardt (1958), Lass (1989), and myself (Penzl 1994; chapter 11) show the great difficulty of establishing specific phonetic values of the past without relevant graphic data in the text.

The papers in this volume clearly show in my opinion that the handbooks are correct in pointing out that not only vowel-values between 1450 (1500) and 1700, but also other criteria have to be considered for this period. For example, in Early Modern English we find negative and interrogative sentences without *do* as auxiliary, maintaining the Middle English *-es/-eth* and the *thou/you* variations, and still rarely including any "expanded" form of the verb with an aspect distinction. The end of the period cannot be related to any event of external history. The spread of English into the New World, which began in the seventeenth century, created new dialects there but had no internal effect on London's standard language; neither did the loss of Scotland's written norm. But by 1700 also the short vowels, e. g., those written ⟨a⟩ (*at*), ⟨u⟩ (*but, put*) had reached their modern values, and the grammatical norms were firmly established.

Görlach (1978) described the features of Early Modern English texts in detail. His initial date for Early Modern English is 1500. He feels that the dividing lines between periods should preferably be placed where internal changes and external events ("mit offensichtlicher Auswirkung auf die Sprache") coincide. As examples of the latter, relevant for establishing the beginning of Early Modern English, he mentions: "Beginn des Buchdrucks (1476); Ende der Rosenkriege (1471); Beginn des Humanismus (Oxford Reformers 1485−1510); Trennung der engl. Staatskirche von Rom (1534); Entdeckung Amerikas (1492)."

5. Concluding remarks

A major advantage of specific and maximal periodization is the fact that it by no means handicaps the description of the transition to adjacent periods, but on the contrary forces the historiographers to consider internal change as well as internal cohesion and the impact of external historical events. The question may be raised whether in the linguistic analysis of the Early Modern English period the optimal state of the art has been reached or whether there are still significant gaps. After Dobson's (1968) comprehensive study it is not likely that any important orthoepic source could have been overlooked, but the descriptions hardly ever mention the Early Modern English rural spoken dialects. No evidence indicates that the established London standard threatened their existence

during the Early Modern English period. Additional scholarly work on
the Early Modern English period will have to pay attention to England's
rural dialects between 1450 and 1700; they will have to be reconstructed
from the records of modern dialectal field-work. Thus the urban "di-
glossia" of spoken standard and old dialect will find an adequate description.

References

Antonsen, Elmer H.
    1975   *A concise grammar of the older Runic inscriptions.* Tübingen: Niemeyer.
Baugh, Albert C.
    1963   *A history of the English language.* (2nd edition; 3rd edition 1978.) New York:
        Appleton-Century-Crofts, Inc.
Besch, Werner, *et al.* (eds.)
    1984   *Sprachgeschichte. Ein Handbuch zur Geschichte der deutschen Sprache und
        ihrer Erforschung.* Berlin: de Gruyter.
Danielsson, Bror
    1955   *John Hart's works on English orthography and pronunciation.* Stockholm:
        Almqvist & Wiksell.
Danielsson, Bror − Arvid Gabrielson
    1972   *Alexander Gill's Logonomia Anglica (1619).* Stockholm: Almqvist & Wiksell.
Dobson, Eric J.
    1968   *English pronunciation 1500−1700.* Oxford: Oxford University Press.
Görlach, Manfred
    1978   *Einführung ins Frühneuenglische.* Heidelberg: Quelle & Meyer.
Kastovsky, Dieter − Gero Bauer (eds.)
    1988   *Luick revisited. Papers read at the Luick-Symposium at Schloß Liechtenstein
        15.−18. 9. 1985.* Tübingen: Narr.
Luick, Karl
    1921−40   *Historische Grammatik der englischen Sprache.* Leipzig: Tauchnitz.
Malone, Kemp
    1930   "When did Middle English begin?", in: *Curme Volume of Linguistic Studies.*
        (Language Monographs. Linguistic Society of America, 7), 110−117.
Moore, Samuel − Sanford B. Meech − Harold Whitehall
    1935   "Middle English dialect characteristics and dialect boundaries", in: *Essays
        and Studies in English and Comparative Literature* 13. Ann Arbor, Michigan:
        University of Michigan.
Penzl, Herbert
    1972   *Methoden der germanischen Linguistik.* Tübingen: Niemeyer.
    1984   *Frühneuhochdeutsch.* (Langs Germanistische Lehrbuchsammlung 9.) Bern:
        Lang.
    1986   *Althochdeutsch. Eine Einführung in Dialekte und Vorgeschichte.* (Langs Ger-
        manistische Lehrbuchsammlung 7.) Bern: Lang.

1989   *Mittelhochdeutsch. Eine Einführung in die Dialekte.* (Langs Germanistische
            Lehrbuchsammlung 8.) Bern: Lang.
1994   *Englisch: eine Sprachgeschichte nach Texten von 350 n. Chr. bis 1992.* Bern:
            Lang.
Zachrisson, R. E.
  1913   *Pronunciation of English vowels. 1400 – 1700.* Göteborg: Wettergren & Kerber.

Degree adverbs in Early Modern English

Hans Peters

1. Introduction

This paper will be concerned with some aspects of the history of degree adverbs in Early Modern English, namely,
a) the semantic domains that provide degree adverbs;
b) the incidence and distribution of degree adverbs in letters.
As both the most rapid rate of change and the most interesting semantic developments occur in those categories termed "maximisers" and "boosters" by Quirk *et al.* (1985),[1] discussion will be restricted to these, with special reference to the ever-fluctuating booster class, thereby neglecting all down-toning intensifying adverbs. The data used come from Early Modern English letters written between 1424 and 1739. Before the material is presented, some general considerations on degree adverbs, particularly boosters, and semantic change appear to be appropriate.[2]

Boosters, like degree adverbs of other categories, develop by means of scale transfer from adverbs performing other types of modification:
a) local/dimensional adverbs (*highly, extremely*);
b) quantitative adverbs (*much, vastly*);
c) qualitative adverbs (*terribly, violently*);
d) emphasisers (*really*);
e) taboo/swear words (*damned*, etc.).
Scale transfer is a special case of metaphorical meaning change: a concrete meaning develops into a more abstract one on the basis of a semantic component in the concrete meaning which facilitates at first the occasional use and later the transition of an adverb with full lexical meaning into the class of degree adverbs. The case of the originally quantitative adverbs *maximally, much, little* and *minimally* may serve as illustration of the process of scale transfer: initially, they all marked a certain position on a quantitative scale, each one referring to a perceived given quantity. In due course, these quantitative adverbs were transferred to a comparable slot on a scale of degree intensification. From the point of view of lexical semantics, a lexeme involved in scale transfer first becomes a polysemic lexeme, i. e. a lexeme containing more than one lexical unit, as the

"original" meaning is still firmly linked to the linguistic form. The "degree meaning" as the new second lexical unit is, at first, optional. However, it may (and in many cases has) come to be the only possible meaning of an adverb, which in the event develops into a monosemic lexeme once again. This process is, as a rule, accompanied by a gradually increasing loss of collocational restrictions. *Terribly*, for example, was initially confined to collocations of the type *terribly threatening*; the type *terribly good*, certainly perfectly "normal" today, would not have been possible for the earlier meaning 'evoking terror'.[3]

To disambiguate between the two lexical units, it is often necessary to consider not only the linguistic, but also the extralinguistic context. The importance of the latter stands in correlation with the degree to which an adverb's original collocational restrictions are preserved. If a given adverb occurs within its original collocational sphere, it is in principle only the situational context which allows a decision between the possible interpretations either as, e. g., adverb of manner or as degree adverb.[4] The process of change is complete with the emergence of a monosemic lexeme with only degree-modifying function, which is (nearly) free from collocational restrictions, and does not depend on situational context for disambiguation; a showcase example for such a process is, of course, *very*.

The sketched process of change, as it is a metaphorical one, should also be considered from the cognitive point of view. The newer, the more unusual and the more "original" a degree adverb is, the more inventiveness or cognitive effort the speaker invests into his utterance. The novel use by the speaker necessitates a complementary process of inference on the hearer's side, which must take account of the extralinguistic context in order to rule out the "literal" interpretation of the speaker's utterance; in addition, he has to find out the basis for the speaker's metaphorical use. So, the hearer's cognitive performance in recognising and correctly interpreting the speaker's communicative intention must also be valued more highly. With well-established degree adverbs, the cognitive process will be less complex for both participants; the minimum is reached with "pure" degree adverbs (like *very*). This suggests the existence of a scale of cognitive performance, which correlates with the complexity of those factors which are influential in the correct interpretation of a lexeme in communication. If the right interpretation is possible on the basis of linguistic cotext, the associated cognitive performance is on a lower level than in cases where disambiguation depends on the (extralinguistic) context. Expressed in terms of usage, this means that boosters which are still only occasionally used as such are cognitively more demanding than degree adverbs of long standing.

Turning to the question of usage, it is a well-known fact that among degree adverbs, it is the booster class which has the highest degree of fluctuation, more than all other categories. This can be associated with the communicative function of different types of degree adverbs: maximisers must serve the communicative intention of expressing that a state, quality, etc. is present to the maximum degree; minimisers, conversely, are expected to warrant a minimal degree. Boosters, however, only have to express a "very high"/more than average degree on the intensity scale, which is something rather more diffuse than what is expressed by either maximisers or minimisers, for instance.

This may be part of the reason why adverbs referring to emotions tend to be employed as boosters; in contrast to adverbs like *completely*, no means of objective verification is given, nor is this necessary in the communicative context (as it is with maximisers).

One reason for the ever-continuing change regarding boosters can be seen in a "taste for hyperbolic expression" in language: speakers desire to be "original", to demonstrate their verbal skills, and to capture the attention of their audience. In addition, boosters frequently function as symbols of group identification. The knowledge and use of a particular booster often signals in-group membership. When the use of that booster spreads to other groups in the speech community, the word loses its function of group identification, and the linguistic "trend-setters" will then normally put a new group-symbol into circulation. Such shibboleths thus tend to change rapidly; they are subject to fashion.

2.   Boosters in Early Modern English
2.1. Aims of description and data base

The growth of the booster class during Early Modern English, and also the rate of change in the repertoire, are paralleled neither in earlier nor in later periods of English. What is striking about the new items is that they have their sources mainly in qualitative adverbs, whereas most earlier boosters had developed from local, dimensional or quantitative adverbs. Of particular importance are adverbs which originally referred to emotions: these require a cognitive performance of a different type than dimensional or quantitative adverbs, as the starting point is more abstract. On the part of the speaker, introducing a new intensifier necessitates greater inventiveness and originality or, in other words, a cognitive act of a different quality than that involved in using *highly* as an intensifier, for instance. The receiver will have to make the right inferences, i. e. to appreciate the speaker's originality.

Originality can be expected not only in text types written by professionals depending on creating a "captive audience", but will be aimed at by speakers in ordinary situations as a means of focussing parts of their utterance, demonstrating their speaking skills, and generally appearing interesting and original.

According to the *OED*, first records for boosters occur mainly in:
a) dramatic dialogue; amongst the authors we find Shakespeare, Heywood, Chettle, Middleton, Jonson, Marston, Nashe, Rowley, Fletcher, Wycherley;
b) political and religious polemics; boosters here are useful in propagandistic language;
c) for more learned words (hard word boosters): handbooks, instructive prose;
d) travel literature, where boosters are employed in the depiction of the new and sensational;
e) from the early eighteenth century: magazines and newspapers (*Tatler, Spectator*).

In comparison, letters hardly figure as sources.

New boosters are particularly rife in the period between 1590 and 1610:

ample (1607 Shaks. *Timon*), *capitally* (1606 Warner *Alb. Engl.*), *damnable* (1611 Shaks. *Wint. T.*), *damnably* (1596 Shaks. *I Hen.* IV), *detestable* (1610 *Histriom.*), *exquisitely* (1603 Florio *Montaigne* tr.), *extreme* (1593 H. Smith *God's Arrowe*), *grievous* (1596 Shaks. *Hen. IV*), *grossly* (1594 Hooker *Eccl. Pol.*), *horribly* (1599 Shaks. *Much Ado*), *intolerable* (1592 Chettle *Kindehart's dreame*), *pocky* (1601 Deacon & Walker), *rarely* (1606 Shaks. *Ant. & Cl.*), *spaciously* (1608 Middleton *Mad World*), *strenuously* (1601 Jonson *Poetaster*), *superpassing* (1608 J. Day *Law Trickes*), *surpassing* (1598 Marston *Pygmal.*), *terribly* (1604 E. Grimstone), *tyrannically* (1602 Marston *Antonio's Rev.*), *uncountably* (1599 Nashe *Lenten Stuffe*), *unutterably* (1605 Marston *Dutch C.*), *vehemently* (1594 Nashe *The unfortunate Traveller*), *villainous* (1610 Shaks. *Temp.*), *violently* (1601 Sir W. Cornwallis *Disc. Seneca*)

Another peak occurs between 1650 and 1660, when almost exclusively words of a foreign etymology are introduced.

Thus, Early Modern English is the first period documenting the changes in fashion which the English language experiences in this respect, both in terms of the number of new items and in the rapidly growing diversity of lexical sources. This situation is without doubt due to the emergence of more colloquial styles in Early Modern English written sources. In this respect, letters must certainly be ranked among the most important (and interesting) text types, although we would be mistaken to regard them as pure colloquial language.[5] Letters are largely regarded as more useful in detecting changes than (more standardised or elaborate) literary sources. Accordingly, much use has been made of letters in investigations of Early Modern English grammar: e.g., in studies of relative pronouns.[6] Obviously, colloquial language is also a typical domain of degree adverbs, where they occur more frequently and in greater diversity. My interest in studying Early Modern English letters with reference to degree adverbs is therefore:

1. Which degree adverbs appear in the various letter collections, in comparison to other text types? This implies the question: which type of etymological provenance is represented most usually? A further aspect to be considered is standardisation; this may be assumed to surface in the use of *full* and *right* in the earlier part of the corpus, and − obviously − *very* in the later letters. Also, the relationship between suffixed and zero-marked adverbs must be considered.
2. How "modern" are Early Modern English letters in this respect, i.e. what relation is there between the first records of boosters according to *OED* and usage in the letters?
3. Do letters themselves provide first records for boosters?
4. Can we recognise gender and/or age-related variation in the usage of boosters?

The *Cely Letters* can largely be addressed as specimens of fifteenth century business correspondence,[7] with little narrative included.

A somewhat different category is represented by the *Shillingford Letters*, which are either reports on legal negotiations or instructions for proceeding in these: so, no colloquial style is likely to be documented. While the remaining fifteenth century sources (*Paston* and *Stonor Letters*) contain material of an equally prosaic type, they also include personal messages and sometimes even exciting narrative, as in Margaret Paston's account of the raid on Hellesdon House, or Richard Betson's love letters in the *Stonor Letters*.

The later collections included here are:
1. The *Wentworth Papers* (1597 – 1628);
2. the *Basire Correspondence* (between 1634 and 1675);
3. the *Wentworth Papers* (1705 – 39).

Thus the writers generally are members of the "upper classes" or even the aristocracy, such as the Earls of Strafford. At the same time, these collections are likely to highlight gender-related differences in language use (if there are any), as both men and women figure prominently among the writers.

Textual contents range from political matters (the earlier *Wentworth Papers*) to Church business (*Basire Correspondence*) and downright personal correspondence, especially between close and fond relatives or husband and wife.

It must be supposed that text content will have some bearing on the frequency and the inventory of boosters. Supposedly, "new" boosters will appear in contexts where a stronger personal and emotional involvement of the speaker/writer is in evidence. On the other hand, strictly business-like letters can be expected to display few and only well-established boosters, often appearing only in formulaic expressions like introductory or valedictory greetings.

But even in narrative passages, differences between the early and the late corpus are bound to appear. The writers in the latter may be said to be more literate, both in terms of formal education and receptively (i. e., concerning their acquaintance with written texts), than the former. This must have enabled them to write with greater fluency and freedom of expression, while the earlier letters often follow patterns (almost timidly), proving that letter-writing was not yet a familiar and well-developed form of expression for these authors. The influence of instructive handbooks on letter-writing becomes clearly visible here.

2.2. The fifteenth century corpus
2.2.1. The Paston Letters

The most frequent boosters in the *Paston Letters* are *right*[8], *wel*[9] and *full*[10], in that order. In this respect, the *Paston Letters* continue the Middle English situation, where all three adverbs play an important role. The Pastons may even be considered conservative in their continued use of *gretely* (26 cases, mainly with finite verbs and participles) and especially *sore* (52 cases, almost exclusively verbs and participles). On the other hand, the younger generation documents *very* as a booster (14 cases; only with adjectives), which remains completely unattested for older family members. A closer analysis shows that the oldest Paston generation employs only five boosters, namely *right, wel, sore* (only Agnes Paston), *hertily* and *interly* (the last one being on the borderline between maximiser and booster). They appear almost exclusively in the formulaic components of letters;[11] their function may thus be said to be merely the reinforcement of the function of these components (polite address, etc.). This is a function which may be regarded as standardised throughout Early Modern English letters (and, for that matter, letters in general).

The second generation letters display a larger inventory of boosters, and now they also occur in the main body of letters. The enlarged inventory includes the recent Latinate words *excessive* and *fervently* (only one case each, however), with comparable new arrivals coming from lexical items with a longer history in the English language. Even the third generation does not employ particularly fanciful new boosters; new items include *mervailously, perfectly, specially*, and, above all, *very*.

Within the second generation, Margaret Paston's inventory contains thirteen intensifiers (yielding 107 tokens).[12] In comparison, her husband John uses only ten (32),[13] mainly in the formulaic elements. However, Margaret Paston's inventory bears hardly any traces of inventiveness or originality, with *right* being the most frequent item. Nor are the "standard" boosters ousted from their position in those of Margaret's letters dealing with the dramatic and violent events she becomes involved in during the feud between the Pastons and their Norfolk opponents.

2.2.2. *The* Stonor Letters

In comparison to the *Paston Letters*, the data gleaned from the *Stonor Letters* show hardly any difference in the use of boosters; the rise of *very* in the last quarter of the fifteenth century is shown in its relatively high frequency (nine cases) in the letters of Thomas Betson, a young Londoner who marries into the Stonor family, and who belongs to the same age group as the youngest Paston. Again, it is a female writer (Elizabeth Stonor) who commands the largest inventory, although remaining rather traditional.[14] However, both her inventory and her use of it nearly coincide with what can be observed in Thomas Betson's writings.[15] Possibly, this may hint at a generalisation according to which a gender-based differentiation within one generation may develop into an age-based differentiation if the next generation is included in the analysis. Not surprisingly, it is those letters with a pronouncedly emotional content which provide a noticeable clustering of boosters, namely Thomas Betson's love letters to his future wife Katheryne Ryche; one of these alone (dated 1 June, 1476) has four instances of *very*. In contrast, Betson uses only *right, hertely* and *resonably* (as a compromiser), all well-established and formal, in a letter to William Stonor (Kingsford No. 207).

2.2.3. *The* Cely Letters

This part of the corpus reveals no striking differences to the picture presented so far, neither concerning the inventory nor the frequency and usage of boosters. More proof can be found for the tendency of the older generation to restrict boosters to formulaic elements, while younger writers employ them elsewhere as well. As the bulk of the *Cely Letters* is of a sober, businesslike character, the overall incidence of degree adverbs is relatively low. The only exception is found in a letter by the younger Richard Cely, where the nonbusiness passages refer to the forthcoming family reunion at Christmas, and to news about dogs and horses. In this letter, *right* appears six times (once in the opening formula), *well* twice, and *sore*. *Very* is once again used only by the younger Cely generation (William (six times) and the younger Richard (twice)).

2.2.4. *The* Shillingford Letters

These rather formal documents display a booster inventory which contains the same central units as that of the early Paston, Stonor, and Cely

Table 1. The *Shillingford Letters*

	adj.	adv.	pres. part.	past part.	verb	quantifier
alle	6					
full	3	4		1		1
fully	1			3	4	
hertely					1	
most	4	1				
much	2					
right	53	45				14
sore						1
strongly					1	
truly				1	1	
verily			3		5	
well		2		3	15	

writers, namely *right* (112 cases), *well* (20) and *full* (nine). In their distribution over the components of letters and in their collocations, *right* and *well* show the same characteristics as in the other collections. Other intensifiers used by Shillingford are:

a) emphasisers: truly (*two cases*), *verily* (eight);
b) boosters: *full* (nine), *hertely* (one), *most* (four), *myche* (two), *sore, strongly* (one each);
c) maximisers: *all(e)* (six), *fully* (eight).

Very is still absent.

2.2.5. Conclusions

Summing up, it may be said that the fifteenth century letters give evidence for only a restricted set of boosters and degree adverbs in general, although some innovative tendencies are exemplified by younger writers. This result can be explained by the matter-of-fact character of most letters; the writers usually report on events rather than giving space to their own thoughts, feelings and opinions. In addition, the older writers were arguably less well accustomed to expressing themselves in writing, and, as a consequence, adopted a terse and formal style even outside the formulaic elements. In the latter, the relatively frequent use of degree adverbs was determined by prefabricated patterns for such components. However, the prominent role of "old" boosters like *ful, wel, right* may also be associated with the observation that the authors are, with few exceptions, people without an elaborate formal education, which might have made them familiar with some of the Latin and Greek words which find their way into English around this time and enter the booster class (e. g., *abominable, excellently, horrible, ineffably, terrible*). Thus, the booster inventory of the fifteenth century letters appears traditional from the point of view of historical lexicology in that Middle English boosters continue in use, but it is arguably close to common colloquial language as well: words bearing a learned character are not included.

2.3. The seventeenth century corpus

2.3.1. *The* Wentworth Papers *(1614 – 29)*

From the *Wentworth Papers (1614 – 29),* the letters of Sir Thomas Wentworth, Earl Strafford (1593 – 1641) were selected. These texts are mainly of a semi-official nature, dealing with political matters; but there are also letters of a rather more private character.

Concerning boosters, a thoroughgoing change in the inventory becomes apparent in relation to the fifteenth century. *Full* has disappeared completely; *right* survives, but is largely confined to formulae and fixed collocations (*glad, sorry, hartely, well*) which are also documented in the fifteenth century corpus, and which are certainly a frequently recurring element of letters. *Very* is now by far the most frequent booster; its dominant status is further documented by its inclusion in those stereotypical formulaic elements which previously were the domain of *right*. The added boosters include: *exceeding(ly)*, *infinitely*, *marvellous*, *wonderful(ly)*, *wondrous*, *deeply*. Of these, *exceeding(ly)* has the highest frequency, followed by *deeply*.

None of Wentworth's boosters can be said to be brand-new items, considering their *OED* datings (*exceeding(ly)* 1535, *wondrous* 1535—41, *infinitely* 1584, *marvellous, deeply, wonderful(ly)* going back to Middle English). Thus, Wentworth's style can hardly be termed innovative or progressive. Notable concentrations of degree adverbs occur in a letter meant to dissuade the addressee from wrongfully accusing and divorcing his wife (29 July 1617; ten adverbs) and in other letters including advice in family affairs. [16]

Table 2. The *Wentworth Papers (1614—29)*

	adj.	adv.	pres. part.	past part.	verb	quantifier
deeply	1		1	3	2	
exceeding	3	1				
exceedingly				2	1	2
hartely	1	1			1	
harty	1					
infinitely	1					
marvelous	1					
passing	4					
sore				1		
right	19	3				
rightly	1					
strangly	1			1		
very	77	19				12
well	4			7	8	
wonderfull	1					
wonderfully				1	1	
wondrous		1				

2.3.2. *The* Basire Correspondence (1634—75)

This collection contains letters written by the Reverend Dr. Isaac Basire, his wife and various of his colleagues. Isaac Basire de Préaumont was born in 1607 at Rouen, France, and died in 1676 at Durham. In 1629, he came to England and began a career in the Anglican Church. In 1636, he married Frances Corbett, a Shropshire gentlewoman; in the same year he was presented to the parish of Egglescliff in Durham. As a keen royalist, he had to leave England in 1649, not returning until 1661 and then becoming Archdeacon of Northumberland. Although English was not Basire's native tongue, his letters do not reveal any conspicuous deficits in linguistic proficiency. However, it cannot be expected that Basire ever grew very familiar with colloquial English, let alone its more fashionable trends; his letters are virtually free from colloquialisms. This situation is reflected by his booster inventory, as will be shown.[17] Mrs. Basire's letters, on the other hand, may be regarded as excellent specimens of colloquial speech; this becomes apparent in her spelling and syntax as well. Frances Basire, née Corbett, came from a Shropshire family; after her marriage she lived at Egglescliff, throughout her husband's long absence. All her letters were written during this separation.

The Doctor's inventory contains only well-established degree adverbs, with the exception of *extraordinarily* (5 August 1635: *He loves and respects Sir Andrew of your name so extraordinarily*, Darnell 1831: 17). If intensive use is indeed documented here, this would antedate the first acceptable record of the *OED* by 86 years. It has to be noticed, though, that the adjectival adverb *extraordinary* is first recorded in 1632, so it cannot be entirely ruled out that the *-ly*-adverb acquired intensive function around the same time. For similar pairs, the earliest records in the *OED* form no uniform pattern as to the order in which suffixless and suffixed boosters appear.

Table 3. Dr. Basire's letters

	adj.	adv.	pres. part.	past part.	verb	quantifier
abundantly					1	
earnestly					1	
excellently		1				
extraordinarily					1	
far	1					
heartily	1				2	
highly					1	
much	3					
utterly					1	
verily	1					
very	12	3				2
wholly[18]					1	
wonderfully					1	

Mrs. Basire's letters, although allowing many insights into the collo-quial English of the time, offer hardly any extraordinary degree adverbs, nor boosters, in particular; standardised *very* is most frequent, and only *exceeding* and *extremely* (once each) represent the contemporarily doc-umented multitude of new, Latinate intensifiers. In total, twelve degree adverbs appear in Mrs. Basire's letters (47 cases). The contents of her writings are generally of a private, often emotional character; so it comes as no surprise that degree adverbs are by no means a rare feature in Mrs. Basire's style; up to fifteen occur in a medium-length letter. Nor is there a particularly high incidence in formulaic elements, which are not very elaborate throughout. Thus, my conclusion would be that Mrs. Basire's letters mirror a colloquial style which freely used degree adverbs, but not of a fanciful or imaginative type; only the well-established degree adverbs belong to her repertoire. Possibly this may be explained by her Shropshire origins and her relatively secluded life as a village parson's wife. Nor would her husband's fourteen years' absence have had any positive effects on her social life in terms of contact with fashionable circles using "progressive" language.

Table 4. Mrs. Basire's letters

	adj.	adv.	pres. part.	past part.	verb	quantifier
ernestlye					1	
exceding	1					
extremly					1	
hartily					2	
holy					1	
most		4				
much	1				1	
so	1					1
somthing	1					
to(o)	1	1				
very	13	10				6
well	1					

2.4. The early eighteenth century: The *Wentworth Papers* (1705—39)

The remaining part of my corpus consists of the letters of the Wentworth family, written between 1705 and 1739. They are all addressed to Thomas Wentworth, the third Earl of Strafford (created in 1711), formerly Lord Raby, who served as ambassador in Berlin (1703—1711) and The Hague

(1711 — 1714), where he was active in the negotiations resulting in the Peace Treaty of Utrecht. After the downfall of the Tory government in 1714 he was recalled and spent the remainder of his life away from the political stage. His three most important correspondents are his mother Isabella (died 1733; 77 letters), who had been lady-in-waiting to Queen Beatrix, and whose language Wyld (1936: 164) regards as an excellent example of contemporary colloquial speech; his brother Peter (died 1739; 203 letters), who also held court offices; and last, but not least, his wife, Lady Anne Strafford (43); there are also letters from his children Lucy (6) and William (14).

As documents for colloquial English, Isabella's letters must indeed rank highest, on the same criteria as those of Frances Basire. Their contents range from society gossip over suggestions for potential marriages to news about her pet dogs and monkeys. Isabella employs 26 degree adverbs (273 cases). Among these, *very* is by far the most frequent item (181). Next in number are *infinite* and *most*. The surprisingly high frequencies of *infinite* and *most* must immediately be qualified, though, because the words invariably occur in Isabella's concluding formula *your most infenit affectionat mother*. The seven instances of *hartely* also appear in relatively fixed collocations (with the verbs *thank, pray, wish*; adjectives: *sorry, welcome*). Among the remaining boosters, quite a number had achieved this function only recently, according to the *OED*: *terribly* (1604), *desperet* (1653), *real* (1658), *vastly* (1664), *particularly* (1676), *vast* (1687), *violent* (1709); some cases even precede the *OED*'s first records: *positively* (1777; collocation *possetivly sure* in a letter of July, 1709), *pretty* (1775; Lady Isabella uses the collocations *prety well* (23 February 1706) and *prety senceble* (27 February 1706), both of which do not represent clear evidence for a booster). As can be seen from Table 5, the assumption that degree adverbs are a prominent feature of colloquial language is again borne out in Lady Isabella's writings.

The numerous letters by Peter Wentworth contain 35 degree adverbs (437 cases, of which *very* claims 324). Thus, he has the largest repertoire of all investigated writers, adhering at the same time to the standard in his frequent use of *very*. Some other boosters may be ranked amongst his favourites, namely *pretty* (15, though this adverb, then as now, may be either a booster or a compromiser, in which case it exerts a downtoning effect), *mightily* (thirteen), *mighty* (seven); he never uses *vast* or *vastly*, though (each used once by his mother). His one instance of *damn'd* as a booster antedates the *OED*'s first record by some 40 years: *that you have been damn'd uneasie to have one sent that ...* (11 January 1712). To sum up, Peter's letters exemplify a colloquial style of a somewhat higher level than Isabella's (also syntactically), but both Wentworths may be said to show an equal predilection for using degree adverbs.

Table 5. Isabella Wentworth's letters

	adj.	adv.	pres. part.	past part.	verb	quantifier
bitter	1					
dearly					3	
desperet		1				
excessif	2					
exssteem	2					
exstreemly	3	1			2	
hardly					1	
hartely	2				6	
highly	2				1	
infenit	21					
mightely					2	
much	1	1			3	
myghty	3					
most	19					
partecularly	1					
possetively	1					
prety	2					
quite	2					
real	1					
sadly					1	
sartainly	1					
so						1
terribly					1	
vast	1					1
vastly	1					
vyolent	1					
very	149	16				16
wunderfull	3					

The 43 letters by Lady Strafford display seventeen intensifiers (134 cases, 88 for *very*). So, she has an inventory which is noticeably smaller than those of her relatives, and which is also of a comparatively conservative character, with (by that time) well-established *extremely* coming second after standard *very*.

Her children, Lucy and William, provide few letters. Lucy uses eight degree adverbs (23; thirteen *very*). *Vastly* occurs three times; it also figures prominently in her brother's letters (seven out of 42 cases, second only to *very*, which has 28; his total repertoire also numbers eight). Here, it seems clear that *vastly* represents contemporary fashion in boosters, with Peter Wentworth's *mighti(ly)* on its way out with the younger generation (only once used by William).

Table 6. Peter Wentworth's letters

	adj.	adv.	pres. part.	past part	verb	quantifier
absolutely	2	1				
all	1					
certainly	1					
damn'd	1					
desparately	1					
exstreame	1					
fain	1					
flatly				1		
fully				2		
hardly	2				1	1
heartily				1	3	
highly					3	
intire		1				
intirely[19]	1	3			1	
might(i)ly				13		
mighty	4	3				
most	2					
much	2			4		
perfectly		2				
perticular	1					
plainly	2				1	
pretty	9	4				2
purely[20]		1				
quite	1	2	1			
really	1	1			1	
sincerely					1	
soundly					1	
strangely					1	
totally		1		1		
truely[21]				1		
very	195	91	10	2		26
well				7	2	
whole				1		
wholly		2				

Table 7. Lady Strafford's letters

	adj.	adv.	pres. part.	past part.	verb	quantifier
exstremly	3	1	1	1	5	
hardly		1			3	
hartely					1	
infinetly		1				
intirely	2				1	
might(i)ly				5	3	
mighty	2					
most	1					
much	1	1		1		
perfectly	4				1	
quite	1					
truly					1	
very	60	21	1	2	9	
wholly				1		

2.5. Suffixed and suffixless boosters

In Early Modern English, we often find both suffixed and unsuffixed forms of degree adverbs/boosters side by side. The picture presented by the *OED* quotations suggests that zero-marked forms occur with adjectives, while suffixed adverbs modify verbs. I would like to offer a short survey of the evidence that can be found for the use of the two types in the seventeenth and eighteenth century letters analysed here. For each form, the collocations will be stated, with the exception of such adverbs (e. g., *right, very*) which are particularly frequent, where only the word classes will be given.

The earlier *Wentworth Papers* have:
exceeding (*advantageous, glad, rich; cheerfully*);
exceedingly (twice *much + desire; strained, importuned*);
marvelous (*painful & daungerous*);
sore (*bruised*);
right (adjectives and adverbs)
rightly (once, *affectionate*);
wonderfull (*desirous*)
wonderfully (VP *approve your course*; participial construction *bent upon living apart*);
wondrous (well pleased).

Mrs. Basire only uses exceding (once, with *glad*).

Isabella Wentworth has her stereotypical *infinite* (*affectionate*), but also many others:
bitter (*cold*);
desperet (*in love*);
extreme (twice with *kind*);
extremely (*afflicted, good, kind; about, extoll, want*);
excessive (twice with *cold*);
mighty (*engaging, willing, fond*);
mightily (*flatter*);
real (*merry*);
vast (*rich*);
vastly (*rich*);
violent (*ill*);
wonderful (*pretty, good, rich*).

Peter Wentworth's letters contain:
damn'd (*uneasy*);
entire (*of that mind*);
entirely (with adverbs, adjectives and verbs);
extreme (*careful*; no *extremely* in Peter's letters);
mighty (*angry, fond, fine*);
mightily (only with participles);
particular (*civil*);
whole (*confounded*);
wholly (*upon them; from*);

Lady Strafford uses *mighty* (*witty, good*) and *mightily* (with participles and verbs).

In the three later collections treated here, suffixless boosters do not occur with particular frequency, but they make their presence felt in the inventories. The material indicates that in the later Wentworth corpus, there does not seem to be a strict division of labour between the two adverbial variants, as the -*ly*-forms now occur with adjectives as well. Also it becomes apparent that Isabella Wentworth has the highest number of suffixless intensifiers, which may lead to the hypothesis that such adverbs were still a characteristic of contemporary colloquial style. This last remark, however, can only be of a very tentative nature, as the description and definition of "colloquial Early Modern English" still awaits detailed investigation.

3. Conclusions

I hope to have shown that the investigated letter corpora do indeed document changes in booster usage. However, the evidence suggests that letters are definitely not spearheading fashionable trends in creating and accepting boosters. On the whole, the fifteenth century collections represent a conservative position regarding intensifying adverbs; innovation becomes visible only with the youngest generation of writers. This is indicated by the beginning rise of *very*, while Latinate boosters are not yet incorporated. Gender-related differences may become apparent in both a larger repertoire and higher incidence. The content type also has an easily identifiable influence on these factors. Formulaic elements as a rule contain "standard" degree adverbs, i. e. those which have the highest incidence throughout; this may, very tentatively, be interpreted as a feature connecting the fifteenth century letters with an emerging written standard.

The later collections are most clearly related to the standard by the omnipresent use of *very*. Formulaic components continue to make regular use of degree adverbs. New boosters are incorporated by the more accomplished letter writers in the later *Wentworth Papers*, while the earlier Wentworth corpus and the *Basire Correspondence* transmit a more conservative picture for various reasons which have been mentioned. For the whole corpus, it is true that letters of a private and/or emotional content provide the highest incidence of degree adverbs in general, and boosters in particular; this was to be expected.

In some cases, especially in the later *Wentworth Papers*, we succeeded in finding earlier booster records than given by the *OED*; this does not, however, establish private letters as an unfairly neglected source of first records, as in the majority of the attested adverbs the first recorded uses are earlier, and occur in other types of sources.

Notes

1. Cf. Quirk *et al.* (1985: 589—590) for a classification of degree intensifiers; the terms "booster", "maximiser", "compromiser", "minimiser", intensifier" and "down-toner" will be used here as defined there.
2. For a fuller discussion, cf. Peters (1993: 52—59, 355—370).
3. This is not to imply that *terribly* is a monosemic lexeme in Present-day English.
4. A number of linguistic tests disregarding situational context have been suggested, which may not be discussed in detail here; for a full discussion, see Peters (1993: 21—51).

5. Qualifications must be made by taking into account the influence of patterns for letter-writing, the purpose of the letter, the writer's social position and educational background, the position of the addressee, among other factors.
6. For a survey of recent literature on this topic, see Peters (1992).
7. Cf. Hanham (1975: xxi—xxv).
8. 180 cases, exclusively with adjectives and adverbs; one third of the cases are found in formulas of address of the type *right worshipful, right reverend.*
9. About 60 cases, in collocations with adjectives, participles, verbs of knowing and understanding (*knowe, understande, wite*); frequently in greetings of the type *I grete you wel.*
10. 29 cases, only with adjectives and adverbs.
11. E. g., *I grete yow hartely well; my most entierly beloude mother.*
12. These are: *fervently, full, fully, gretely, hertily, interly, passyng, right, sore, straungely, verily, well, wode.*
13. *Evill, excessiue, full, fully, gretely, hertily, right, well.*
14. Her inventory contains: *full, gretely, hartely, sore, resonably, right, truly, veraly, ver(a)y, well;* cf. William Stonor: *right, sore, verily,* and Thomas Stonor: *fully, gretely, hertely, sore, well.*
15. Thomas Betson uses: *full* (7), *gretely, hartely* (8), *resonable, right* (23), *truly, very* (9), *well.*
16. Letter to Lord Clifford (19 September 1620), advising against the addressee's intended break with his father; four boosters (five cases); but cf. also a letter to Richard Marris (4 November 1626), which contains directions concerning the management of Wentworth's estate; yet, Wentworth uses six boosters in this letter.
17. The closeness of Basire's language to the standard of his day is also indicated by his use of relative pronouns (cf. Peters 1992).
18. Also as an emphasiser (sentence adverb).
19. Also as a sentence adverb.
20. Once as a sentence adverb.
21. Four times as a sentence adverb.

References

Bäcklund, Ulf
   1973   *The collocations of adverbs of degree in English.* (Acta Universitatis Upsaliensis, Studia Anglistica Upsaliensia 13.) Uppsala: Almqvist & Wiksell.
Bailey, Richard W. (ed.)
   1978   *Early Modern English. Additions and antedatings to the record of English vocabulary 1457—1700.* Hildesheim: Olms.
Bolinger, Dwight
   1972   *Degree words.* The Hague: Mouton.
Cartwright, James J. (ed.)
   1883   *The Wentworth Papers 1705—1739. Selected from the private and family correspondence of Thomas Wentworth, Lord Raby, created in 1711 Earl of Strafford, of Stainborough, Co. York. With a memoir and notes.* London: Wyman & Sons.

Cooper, J. P. (ed.)
1973   *Wentworth Papers 1597—1628.* (Camden Fourth Series, vol. 12.) London: Camden Society.

Darnell, W. N. (ed.)
1831   *The correspondence of Isaac Basire, D. D., Archdeacon of Northumberland and prebendary of Durham in the reigns of Charles I. and Charles II. with a memoir of his life.* London: John Murray.

Davis, Norman (ed.)
1971—76   *Paston Letters and Papers of the fifteenth century.* Vols. 1—2. Oxford: Oxford University Press.

Greenbaum, Sidney
1970   *Verb-intensifier collocations in English.* The Hague: Mouton.

Hanham, Alison (ed.)
1975   *The Cely Letters 1472—88.* (EETS 273.) Oxford: Oxford University Press.

Kingsford, Charles L. (ed.)
1919   *The Stonor Letters and Papers 1290—1483.* Vols. 1—2. (Camden Third Series XXIX, XXX.) London: Camden Society.

Kühner, Gertrud
1934   *Die Intensiv-Adverbien des Frühneuenglischen.* [Ph. D. dissertation, Heidelberg University.]

Lipka, Leonhard
1990   *An outline of English lexicology. Lexical structure, word semantics, and word formation.* Tübingen: Niemeyer.

Peters, Hans
1992   "Zur Entwicklung der englischen Relativpronomina: typologische und soziolinguistische Aspekte", *NOWELE* 20: 89—141.
1993   *Die englischen Gradadverbien der Kategorie booster.* (Tübinger Beiträge zur Linguistik 380.) Tübingen: Narr.

Quirk, Randolph—Sidney Greenbaum—Geoffrey Leech—Jan Svartvik
1985   *A comprehensive grammar of the English language.* London: Longman.

Searle, John R.—Daniel Vanderveken
1985   *Foundations of illocutionary logic.* Cambridge: Cambridge University Press.

Sperber, Dan—Deirdre Wilson
1986   *Relevance. Communication and cognition.* Oxford: Blackwell.

Sweetser, Eve
1990   *From etymology to pragmatics. Metaphorical and cultural aspects of semantic structure.* Cambridge: Cambridge University Press.

Traugott, Elizabeth Closs
1990   "From less to more situated in language: the unidirectionality of semantic change", in: Sylvia Adamson—Vivien Law—Nigel Vincent—Susan Wright (eds.), *Papers from the 5th International Conference on English Historical Linguistics, Cambridge, 6—9 April 1987.* Amsterdam/Philadelphia: John Benjamins, 497—517.

Vermeire, Antoine
1979   *Intensifying adverbs. A syntactic, semantic and lexical study of fifteen degree intensifiers, based on an analysis of two computer corpuses of Modern English.* Vols. 1—2. [Unpublished Ph. D. thesis, Lancaster.]

Wyld, Henry C.
1936   *A history of colloquial English.* (3rd edition.) Oxford: Blackwell.

The ugly sister — Scots words in Early Modern English dictionaries

Clausdirk Pollner

1. In his useful survey entitled *The languages of Britain,* Glanville Price (1984: 170) refers to English in the British Isles as a killer language. He says this:

> If there are still parts of the United Kingdom, in Wales, Scotland and the Channel Islands, where sizeable communities speak languages that were there before English, sometimes as their first language, nowhere in these islands is English not in everyday use and understood by all or virtually all. It is English that has now totally replaced Irish as a first language in Northern Ireland. And it is English that constitutes such a major threat to Welsh and Scottish Gaelic, and to French in the Channel Islands, that their long-term future must be considered to be very greatly at risk.

Price is talking here mainly about Gaelic varieties in Britain that were replaced by English; he could easily have added Scots (and indeed later devotes a separate chapter to this variety) as one of those languages not only threatened but almost extinguished by English — at least as the literary language that it used to be.

Scots represents a separate development of a northern standard language from Northumbrian English sources, and between 1375, when John Barbour's *Bruce* appeared, and the end of the sixteenth century it developed fully into a national language: "The King (or Queen) of Scotland's Scots" as opposed to "The King (or Queen) of England's English". For a comparatively brief period there is an unprecedented flowering of a national body of literature not only written in Scotland but in Scots as well: see for instance the impressive first volume of the recently published *History of Scottish literature* (Jack 1988). This covers the period during which an Edinburgh and Fife based variant of Middle Scots was used for all sorts of literary purposes: epics, poetry, drama (albeit only one), songs, essays, letters, official announcements and town council minutes, courtly and parliamentary texts etc.

Scots, in other words, was the fully employed and accepted medium in the Kingdom of Scotland for both spoken and written discourse.[1]

Between the end of the 16th century and the beginning of the 18th century, Scotland is confronted by three events — religious, social and political — that pose threats to its national language and eventually extinguish it, at least as a written medium used for serious purposes: the Reformation with its *English* translation of the Bible, the Union of Crowns with King James VI leaving his Edinburgh court for London and changing his own speech and writing from Scots to southern English and finally the Union of Parliaments, which left Scotland without its own legislative body. Murison (1979: 9) sums this up admirably when he says:

> Scots became more and more restricted in use and scope, having lost spiritual status at the Reformation, social status at the Union of the Crowns, and political status with the Parliamentary Union.

It has to be pointed out that some Anglicisms or Southernisms in written Scots occurred quite early in the history of Scottish literature — even in Early Middle Scots, when the Makars composed some ot the most distinguished literary texts in Scots, we find scattered examples of southern English spellings, probably under the influence of writers such as Gower and Chaucer. But these were certainly the exception rather than the rule. The major onslaught of southern English on written Scots happened in the 17th and 18th centuries.[2]

2. At the end of the 1752 edition of his *Political discourses* the Scottish philosopher David Hume published, somewhat incongruously, a list of Scotticisms together with their southern English equivalents. Later editions of the work discontinue the list. It was republished eight years later in the *Scots Magazine* (1760: 686 — 687) and then added to and partially altered in another issue of the *Scots Magazine* (1764: 187 — 189) by a correspondent who calls himself "Philologus" and who may have been the Scottish writer and philologist James Elphinston (Rohlfing 1984: 8).

Hume's list of Scotticisms consists of just over one hundred items altogether; his list offers no particular order, neither alphabetic nor systematic. For the purpose of this paper, I have ordered his material into four systematic groups:[3]

(1) Different lexical items in Scots and English:
    ex.: Sc. *tender*   Engl. *sickly*
          Sc. *annualrent*   Engl. *interest*
(2) Different morphological forms/different word formation:
    ex.: Sc. *pled*   Engl. *pleaded*
          Sc. *bankier*   Engl. *banker*
(3) Different prepositional use:
    ex.: Sc. *on a sudden*   Engl. *of a sudden*

(4) Different idiomatic phrases/different order of items:

ex.:   Sc. *butter and bread*   Engl. *bread and butter*.

If all of Hume's words and phrases were indeed genuine Scotticisms, then it must be worthwhile looking at some early English dictionaries — particularly some of those that explicitly include varieties other than southern standard English — to find out how these items were treated. "Philologus" in the *Scots Magazine* (1764: 187) makes the following remark:

> ... it seems proper, because possible, to improve some of the criticisms [i. e. of the original list of 1760] which are far from wanting merit; and to warn our countrymen equally against fancying all Scoticisms [sic] to be here contained, or all there contained to be Scoticisms [sic].

This scepticism concerning the source and use of Hume's items is confirmed when one consults a selection of dictionaries of the time; although it must be pointed out that most Early Modern English dictionary compilers seem to have had their difficulties with Scots words — they either leave them out altogether or they point out their locality wrongly or vaguely or words are entered in the dictionaries without being marked as Scotticisms.

3. Cawdrey (1604) is the first English — English dictionary; according to the title page, this compilation consists of "hard usuall English words" — i. e. those loanwords that were fully integrated into the English language. Cawdrey has only three items of Hume's list: *discretion, depose* and *deduct*, even though Middle Scots was full of Latinisms and French-based words. The three words are neither marked as Scots nor given Hume's definition.

Bullokar (1616) lists six of Hume's words, but only two of them are given the Scots meaning: *defunct* and *debitor*; neither is marked Scottish.

Coles (1676) is more relevant to our present question because his is the first dictionary to include dialect material in a general word-list:

> Here is a large addition of many words and phrases that belong to our English Dialects in the several Counties, and where the particular Shire is not exprest, the distinction ... is more general into North and South-Country words. (preface; n. p.)

Coles has the abbreviation *Sc* in his list of areas of origin or usage and he mentions seven words from our corpus: *incarcerate, discretion, park, anent, wright, defunct, condescend*. Of these, only one is marked *Sc: anent*. Only three of the other six are given with Hume's meaning: *incarcerate, park, defunct.* On the other hand, Coles does have quite an extensive list of marked Scotticisms that goes beyond Hume's selection, including a number of place names and encyclopedic entries: e. g. *Angus* 'part of North Scotland'; *Berthinsec* 'a Scotch law which only whips men for stealing so much as they can carry (in a sack)'; *Cambel* 'a famous castle of Argile in Scotland'; *cro/croy* 'which the judge (if he ministers not justice) is to pay the nearest of kin to a slain man'; *ennoy* 'annoy'; *fraine* 'to ask'; *girthol* 'a sanctuary'; *kerk/kirk* 'a church'; *law* 'a hill'; *Merch* 'part of South Scotland'; *Niddesdale* 'part of South Scotland'; *pedler* 'a Scotch or wandering merchant'; *tyte* 'quite' etc.

Incidentally, Coles seems to lose interest in things Scottish − both lexical and encyclopedic − half way through his compilation: he has quite a number of Scottish entries, both marked and unmarked, under letters B, C, K, L, M and hardly any under N, O, P, R, T, U and W. Another point that strikes readers of this dictionary is the fact that a number of Scottish and northern entries can be found categorised under *o* for "old word" or *Sa* for "(Anglo) Saxon". This happens in the not infrequent cases where Scots has kept ancient Germanic items that southern English has dropped in the course of time: *barn/bern/bearn* 'Sa. child'; *byg/bigg* 'o. build'; *ken* 'Sa. to see or know ...'; *lither* 'o. lazy, sluggish'; *mickle* 'Sa. much'; *raa* 'o. a roe'; *sowter/sutor* 'o. a shoemaker'; *viage* 'o. for voyage' etc. This is a problem that faced other Early Modern English dictionary makers as well: local and etymological sources cannot always be clearly defined. Scots and northern English were originally the same thing − Northumbrian dialect − and some Germanic word stock was and is used both in Scotland and south of the border. To mark entries as "old" or "Saxon" is helpfully vague and quite a clever way of getting round this particular problem.

Ray (1691) is the first dictionary to be entirely devoted to words not from southeast Midland English. Ray has two main sections: "North Country Words" and "South and East Country Words". The relevant − first − section has surprisingly few items marked as Scotticisms: *anent*; *bleit/blate* 'bashful', with a proverb added in order to indicate the proper use of the word: "A toom purse makes a bleit merchant" ('An empty purse makes a shamefac'd merchant'); *to bourd* 'to jest'; *to breid/brade of* 'to be like in condition'; *to greit* 'to weep'; a *lown/loon* 'a lout', "The Scots say, a fausse, i. e. a false loon". The only two words of Hume's list in Ray's dictionary are *anent* and *wright* 'carpenter', the latter being attributed to Yorkshire, however. On the other hand, Ray admits quite a number of Scottish words that are either not attributed to Scotland or are given for some northern English county: *bannock* 'oat cake'; *fudder* 'load'; *garre* 'make'; *gate* 'way'; *grow* 'be troubled'; *ingle* 'fire'; *kale* 'cabbage'; *ken* 'know'; *kenspecked* 'marked'; *kye* 'kine/cows'; *kyrk* 'church'; *mickle* 'much'; *midding* 'dunghill'; *murk* 'dark'; *sackless* 'innocent'; *sark* 'skirt'; *sike* 'such'; *skatloe* [probably a misprint for] *skathe* 'loss, harm'; *to tent* 'to tend, look to'; *thole* 'endure'; *till* 'to'; *toom* 'empty'; *war* 'worse'; *yane* 'one'.

This is by far the longest list in the dictionaries considered so far; but Ray is obviously rather hesitant in marking an entry as Scots. He prefers to list — like Coles — words that are used both north and south of the border. Incidentally, he indicates a particular Scottish pronunciation which can still be observed: the vocalisation of medial [l], e. g. in *fausse* 'false' or *aud* 'old'.[4]

Bailey (1721) is the earliest of the more important eighteenth century dictionaries. He lists 22 of Hume's words, but only one is marked Scottish: *anent*. (This is, by the way, exactly what Coles does.) Of the other 21 words only the following are defined in Hume's way: *conform, to maltreat, to incarcerate, park, to learn, to effectuate, defunct, to evite*. Bailey follows some of Skinner's (1671) rather doubtful etymologies. One such example is *to fuddle*:

> *To Fuddle*, (from the word *Puddle*, q. d. to drown himself in a Puddle of Liquors; or from *Full*, by an interposition of the letter *d*; and hence the Scots use the word *Full* for one that is drunk) to bib or drink till one be tipsey or drunken.
> (quoted from Starnes and Noyes (1946: 253))

This is, of course, the kind of muddle that gives the Early Modern English etymologists a bad name.

Samuel Johnson's famous remark that "the noblest prospect that a Scotchman ever sees, is the high road that leads him to London" is to a certain extent reflected in his dictionary (1755).[5] Neither his *Plan of a dictionary* (1747) nor the actual *Preface* (1755) have much to say about dialectal variation, let alone Scottish English.

Of Hume's list and with Hume's definition Johnson has the following items: *conform, advert, incarcerate, tender, park, denude, anent, answer* 'to protest', *learn* 'to teach', *effectuate, defunct, want, bygone, yesternight, depone, crave, stomach* 'appetite'. Of all these only two entries are marked Scottish: *anent* and *bygone*. In one case, he calls Hume's Scotticism "a corruption", namely *alongst* — "a corruption, it seems, of along".

One of Johnson's amanuenses for the fourth edition of the dictionary was a Scot, William Macbean, who suggested a number of Scottish additions to the original word-stock. Johnson rejected most of them, however (Reddick 1990: 99; 218).

Another dictionary maker who was not exactly enamoured of things Scottish or Irish was William Kenrick, whose introduction to his *New dictionary of the English language* (1773) was published separately under the title *A rhetorical grammar of the English language* (1784). Two brief quotations show very clearly the negative attitude of an English lexico-grapher towards his Scottish colleagues:

> There seems indeed a most ridiculous absurdity in the pretensions of a native of Aberdeen or Tipperary, to teach the natives of London to speak and to read. (1784: I)

> Various have been nevertheless the modest attempts of the Scots and the Irish, to establish a Standard English pronunciation. That they should not have succeeded is no wonder. Men cannot teach others what they do not themselves know. (1784: II)

Kenrick is particularly critical of the Scottish orthoepist James Buchanan; a Scotsman cannot possibly — *pace* Kenrick — publish a book on how to pronounce English properly, and if he does, he is doomed to failure.

Walker (1791) has *conform, to advert, to incarcerate, out of hand, park, to denude, anent, to learn* ('to teach' is one of the definitions given), *defunct, to want, bygone, yesternight, to depone, to crave* of Hume's list and with Hume's "Scottish" definitions. In the case of *to learn* 'to teach' Walker adds "improperly used in this sense".

This is a pronunciation dictionary and we do not, as a rule, find localities or counties indicated, and Walker's preface material is mainly about the sounds of English. He remarks about the Scots that they "pronounce almost all their accented vowels long" (1791: XI), which vaguely but correctly refers to the difference in vowel-quantity between English and Scots. Walker then goes on to tell his Scottish readers how this can be corrected — so that a Scotsman does not sound Scottish any longer. He calls Irish and Scottish accentuation of both words and sentences "wrong" and goes on to say:

> ... though the people of London [i. e. the uneducated] are erroneous in the pronunciation of many words, the inhabitants of every other place are erroneous of many more. (1791: XIII)

4. Considering the fact that educated Scottish and Irish speakers of the seventeenth and eighteenth centuries were under considerable linguistic pressure — the negative attitude towards their accents and words can clearly be seen from some of my quotations — it is surprising that there was not a full "didactic" dictionary of Scotticisms enabling people to rid themselves more thoroughly of offensive Scottish words. Knowing which words to avoid must have been quite difficult, because not even the existing dictionaries bothered to list more than a small group of items, as my selection has shown. The problem of what Aitken (1979: 106 – 107) refers to as overt ("marked") vs. covert ("unmarked") Scotticisms no doubt existed in the Early Modern English period, when anglicisation was rampant. Speakers from Scotland no doubt used words and expressions that they did not realise were characteristically Scottish items. Even Hume's list is not very helpful; as the sceptical Philologus in 1764 implied, not all of his items were real Scotticisms: at least *maltreat, advert to, incarcerate, learn* 'teach', *effectuate, defunct* and *bygone* were used in England as well and not just in Scotland and immediately south of the border.

The lack of a full "teaching" dictionary may well have been one of the reasons why so many Scottish vocabulary items have survived the Early Modern English anglicisation tendencies and are still with us today.

Southern English dictionary makers obviously felt it was quite unnecessary to itemise Scottish words in any systematic way, because this former national language lost its status precisely at the time when dictionary making got into full swing. Scots had become an ugly sister and was best ignored.

Notes

1. A selection of publications outlining this growth of a northern standard language: Aitken (1992), Murison (1977, 1979), Pollner (1990), Price (1984), Templeton (1973).
2. In including the eighteenth century in this paper I do not follow the textbooks by Barber (1976) and Görlach (1978), where the Early Modern English period is delimited from 1500 to 1700, but rather Pyles – Algeo (1993) with its chapter "The Modern English Period to 1800", which is followed by "Recent British and American English". This seems to me to be particularly sensible in the context of lexicography, where the eighteenth century is of major relevance – and yet the dictionaries compiled during that century can certainly not be called Modern English dictionaries.
3. A selection of items from Hume's list, ordered systematically:

(1)			(2)		
Sc.	maltreat	(E. abuse)	Sc.	proven	(E. proved)
	advert to	(attend to)		improven	(improved)
	incarcerate	(imprison)		pled	(pleaded)
	tender	(sickly)		drunk, run	(drank, ran)
	discretion	(civility)		alongst	(along)

(1)		(2)	
park	(inclosure)	effectuate	(effect)
mind it	(remember it)	evite	(avoid)
denuded	(divested)	dubiety	(doubtfulness)
anent	(with regard to)	heritable	(hereditary)
allenarly	(soleley)	superplus	(surplus)
learn	(teach)	forfaulture	(forfeiture)
wright	(carpenter)	debitor	(debtor)
defunct	(deceased)	exeemed	(exempted)
difficulted	(puzzled)	amissing	(missing)
rebuted	(discouraged)	depone	(depose)
prejudge	(hurt)	deduce	(deduct)
common soldiers	(private men)	vacance	(vacation)
bygone	(past)	notour	(notorious)
chimney	(grate)	bankier	(banker)
annualrent	(interest)	alwise	(always)
condescend	(specify)	etc.	
discharge	(forbid)		
extinguish	(cancel)		
a compliment	(a present)		
misgive	(fail)		
to crave	(to dun)		
etc.			

(3)	(4)
Sc. tear to pieces (E. tear in pieces) in the long run (at long run) notwithstanding of that (notwithstanding that) with child to a man (with child by a man) to enquire at a man (to enquire of a man) to be angry at a man (to be angry with a man) to send an errand (to send of [off?] an errand) to furnish goods to him (to furnish him with goods) to open up (to open) come in to the fire (come near the fire) to take off a new coat (to make up a new suit) cut out his hair (cut off his hair) on a sudden (of a sudden) lookt over the window (lookt out at the window)	Sc. friends and acquaintances (E. friends and acquaintance) butter and bread (bread and butter) pepper and vinegar (vinegar and pepper) paper, pen, and ink (pen, ink, and paper) as ever I saw (as I ever saw) a pretty enough girl (a pretty girl enough) to get a stomach (to get an appetite) etc.

The present paper is based on items from columns (1) and (2), for the obvious reason that items from columns (3) and (4) — prepositional use and idiomatic expressions — cannot usually be found in Early Modern English dictionaries.

4. Ray has one particular entry — *to knack* — that has nothing to do with Scots but a lot with people's attitude to southern English, highlighting the comparative contempt other varieties were treated with: *to knack* according to Ray means "to speak finely. And it is used of such as do speak in the Southern dialect". To speak southern English was to speak finely; to use northern English was not.

5. Johnson's famous "high road" dictum is not the only example of "Johnsonisms on Scotland"; here are some more:

   a) Much may be made of a Scotchman, if he be caught young.

   b) Seeing Scotland, Madam, is only seeing a worse England.

   c) Boswell: I do indeed come from Scotland, but I cannot help it.

   Johnson: That, Sir, I find, is what a very great many of your countrymen cannot help.

(*The Oxford Book of Quotations* [3rd edition 1979, revised 1985]

References

a. Dictionaries and word lists

Anon.
1760   (David Hume) "Scotticicms", *Scots Magazine* 22: 686—687.
Anon.
1764   ("Philologus") "The table of Scoticisms [sic] corrected and enlarged", *Scots Magazine* 26: 187—189.
Bailey, Nathan
1721   *A universal etymological dictionary*. London. [reprinted Anglistica & Americana 52. 1969.]
Bullokar, John
1616   *An English expositor*. London. [reprinted Anglistica & Americana 72. 1971.]
Cawdrey, Robert
1604   *A table alphabeticall*. London. [reprinted The English Experience 226. 1970.]
Coles, Elisha
1676   *An English dictionary*. London. [reprinted Anglistica & Americana 76. 1973.]
Johnson, Samuel
1747   *The plan of a dictionary*. London. [reprinted Scolar Press 1970.]
1755   *A dictionary of the English language*. (2 vols.) London. [reprinted Anglistica & Americana 1. 1968.]
Kenrick, William
1784   *A rhetorical grammar of the English language*. London. [reprinted English Linguistics 1500—1800 332. 1972.]
Ray, John
1674   *A collection of English words*. London. [reprinted English Linguistics 1500—
[1691]   1800 145. 1969.]
Skinner, Stephen
1671   *Etymologicon Linguae Anglicanae*. London.

Walker, John
1971   *A critical pronouncing dictionary.* London. [reprinted English Lingistics 1500 –
          1800 117. 1968.]

b. Monographs and articles

Aitken, Adam J.
1979   "Scottish speech: A historical view, with special reference to the standard
          English of Scotland", in: Adam J. Aitken – Tom McArthur (eds.), 85 – 118.
1992   "Scots", in: Tom McArthur (ed.), 893 – 899.
Aitken, Adam J. (ed.)
1973   *Lowland Scots.* Aberdeen: Association of Scottish Literary Studies.
Aitken, Adam J. – McArthur, Tom (eds.)
1979   *Languages of Scotland.* Edinburgh: Chambers.
Anon
1757   "Review of Buchanan's Linguae Britannicae Vera Pronuntiatio", *Monthly
          Review* 17: 82 – 83.
Barber, Charles
1976   *Early Modern English.* London: André Deutsch.
Görlach, Manfred
1978   *Einführung ins Frühneuenglische.* (UTB 820) Heidelberg: Quelle und Meyer.
Jack, Ronald D. S. (ed.)
1988   *The history of Scottish literature.* Vol. 1: *Origins to 1660.* Aberdeen: Aberdeen
          University Press.
Long, Percy W.
1909   "English dictionaries before Webster", *Bibliographical Society of America* 4:
          25 – 43.
Mathews, Mitford M.
1933   *A survey of English dictionaries.* New York: Russell and Russell.
[1966]
McArthur, Tom (ed.)
1992   *The Oxford companion to the English language.* Oxford: Oxford University
          Press.
Murison, David
1977   *The guid Scots tongue.* Edinburgh: Blackwood.
1979   "The historical background", in: Adam J. Aitken – Tom McArthur (eds.),
          2 – 13.
Pollner, Clausdirk
1990   "From riches to rags. – From rags to riches?", in: Peter Zenziger (ed.),
          51 – 69.
Price, Glanville
1984   *The languages of Britain.* London: Edward Arnold.
Pyles, Thomas – Algeo, John
1971   *The origins and development of the English language.* (4th ed.) New York:
[1993]   Harcourt Brace Jovanovich.
Reddick, Allen
1990   *The making of Johnson's dictionary 1746 – 1771.* Cambridge: Cambridge Uni-
          versity Press.

Rohlfing, Helmut
   1984   *Die Werke James Elphinstons (1721—1819) als Quelle der englischen Lautge-
               schichte.* (Anglistische Forschungen 172). Heidelberg: Winter.
Starnes, De Witt T.
   1937   "English dictionaries of the 17th century", *Studies in English,* University of
               Texas 1937: 15—51.
Starnes, De Witt T.—Noyes, Gertrude E.
   1946   *The English dictionary from Cawdrey to Johnson 1604—1755.* Chapel Hill:
               University of North Carolina Press.
Templeton, Janet
   1973   "Scots — an outline history", in: Adam J. Aitken (ed.), 4—19.
Wiener, Leo
   1896   "English lexiography", *Modern Language Notes* 11: 352—366.
Zenzinger, Peter (ed.)
   1990   *Scotland — literature, culture, politics.* (Anglistik & Englischunterricht 38/
               39.) Heidelberg: Winter.

The development of the compound pronouns in *-body* and *-one* in Early Modern English*

Helena Raumolin-Brunberg

1. Introduction

The purpose of this paper is to present an overall view of how the indefinite pronouns with personal reference ending in *-body* and *-one* became established in the English language during the Early Modern English period (1500 – 1700). General works on Early Modern English, such as Barber (1976) and Görlach (1978), pay very little attention to indefinite pronouns, and in fact, this study will show that Görlach's assertion (1978: 98) of an obligatory *-one, -body* or *-thing* in the singular phrases with *some, any, no* and *every* from the sixteenth century onwards is too categorical.

Where we in Present-day English use compound pronouns like *anybody* or *someone*, Middle English writers usually chose simple pronouns like *any* and *some* or compound forms with *man*. My study of noun phrases in early sixteenth-century English shows that the indefinite compound pronouns with personal reference were not yet in general use at the beginning of the Early Modern period (Raumolin-Brunberg 1991: 147). According to the *Oxford English Dictionary*, the introduction of the compound pronouns *everyone, somebody, nobody, anyone* and *anybody* took place during the Middle English period (*OED*, s. v. *every* 10.c., 1225, s. v. *somebody* 1., 1303, s. v. *nobody* 1., 1338, s. v. *any* 8., 1449, s. v. *anybody* 1., 1490).[1] The first quotations with *everybody* and *someone* date back to somewhat later days, 1530 and 1545, respectively (*OED*, s. v. *everybody* 1., s. v. *some* III.10.). I have not found an entry for *no one* in the *OED*.

2. The data

This study is based on material retrieved from the Early Modern English section of the *Helsinki Corpus of English Texts* (Kytö [comp.] 1993; Rissanen — Kytö — Palander-Collin [eds.], 1993). The Early Modern English section of the *Helsinki Corpus* (550,000 running words) is temporally divided into three subsections covering the periods 1500−1570 (E1), 1570−1640 (E2) and 1640−1710 (E3). Past synchrony is sought by concentration on text material from the beginning of the sixteenth century, the turn of the century and the end of the seventeenth century. All three subsections contain samples of the same 16 genres, viz. law, handbooks, science, educational treatises, philosophy, sermons, trial proceedings, history, travelogue, diaries, biography, fiction, comedies, private and official letters, the Bible (E1 and E2; for a general presentation of the material, see Nevalainen−Raumolin-Brunberg 1989 and 1993).

Table 1. Indefinite pronouns with personal reference
Compound pronouns and their equivalents

Assertive 'someone'	Nonassertive 'anyone'	Negative 'no one'	Universal 'everyone'
Some	*Any*	*None*	*Every/each*
Some man	*Any man*	*No man*	*Every/each man*
Some body	*Any body*	*No body*	*Every body*
Some one	*Any one*		*Every one*

Table 1 shows the four paradigms under study. The classification has been adopted from Quirk *et al.* (1985: 377). As the aim is to trace the development of forms equivalent to Present-day English indefinite compound pronouns, only items in the singular with a general personal reference have been included in the study. The forms at issue are basically used to pick up one indefinite referent from a set or a group of people, the size of which can vary from three to all people in the world.[2] The sets or groups can be implicit or they can be expressed by modifiers, or given explicitly in the context. Since the purpose of this study is not to go in depth into the complex semantic properties of the different indefinite pronouns, only very general characterisations are given in the following descriptions.

The paradigms include the compounds in *-body* and *-one*, whose development is here under scrutiny. They also comprise the alternatives, the forms with *man* and the simple pronouns *some, any, none* and *every/ each*. It is worth noticing that the negative paradigm does not contain the form *no one*, because it does not occur in the corpus. The spelling is standardised in the table. It is also noteworthy that it is only in the last subperiod of the Early Modern English section (1640−1710) that we occasionally find the compound forms written as one word.

2.1. The assertive paradigm

The forms of the assertive set are connected with positive statements. The sentences where they appear assert the truth of a proposition (Quirk *et al.* 1985: 83, 383). Examples (1)–(4) show the uses of the items in the assertive paradigm.

(1)   *"Al thes are come (sayde he,) to see yow suffer deathe; there ys* some *here that ys come as farre as Lyengkecon [...], but I truste ther commynge shal be yn vayne.*
                        (E1: Mowntayne, *The Autobiography*, 203)

(2)   *In which mater somtyme they seeme to haue dispensation, for that* som mans *nature is so headstrong & rash, that neede of necessities cause may make him fall into a mischeefe, ...*
                        (E2: Elizabeth I, *Boethius*, 95)

(3)   *I have spoken with Sir Tho: Peyton twice and find him in such passions as I have no manner of hopes of his assistance; hee doth mee twice as much hurt as good;* some bodie *hath incensed Him very much against mee, ...*
                        (E3: Henry Oxinden, *Letters*, 273)

(4)   *But let us grant, that it is possible that* some one *may be able to distinguish betwixt the Good and the Bad; ...*
                        (E3: Preston, *Boethius*, 195)

2.2. The nonassertive paradigm

While the assertive forms are connected with expressions asserting the truth of a proposition, the nonassertive forms are not. They usually occur in negative statements, questions, conditional clauses etc. (Quirk *et al.* 1985: 83–84, 389–391). The grammatical context is not, however, decisive, but just as items of the *some* series can appear in negative, interrogative and conditional clauses, if the basic meaning is assertive, so can forms with *any* be found in affirmative clauses in the meaning 'any, no matter which' (Sahlin's Any III [1979: 110–131]). The four items in the nonassertive paradigm are exemplified in (5)–(8).

(5)   *Marry, sayes the man, Ile help you to him straight; for, I tell you,* not any *in the court durst but haue sought him, which this man did, and it was told him.*
                        (E2: Armin, *A Nest of Ninnies*, 43)

(6)   *Yf* eny man *eate of this breed, he shall live forever.*
                                    (E1: *The New Testament*, Tyndale, VI)

(7)   *I do assure you, my Lord, for my own part, I did abhor those*
           that were in that horrid Plot and Conspiracy against the King's
           Life; I know my Duty to my King better, and have always
           exercised it, I defy any body *in the world that ever knew the*
           contrary, to come and give Testimony.
                            (E3: The Trial of Lady Alice Lisle, 122, C2)

(8)   *A wise man will not wrangle with* any one, *much less with his*
           dearest relative; and if it be accounted undecent to Embrace in
           publick, it is extremely shameful to Brawle in publick; ...
                        (E3: Jeremy Taylor, *The Marriage Ring*, 24)

2.3. The negative paradigm

As mentioned above, the negative paradigm has only three members,
since the fourth, *no one*, does not occur in the Early Modern English
section of the *Helsinki Corpus*. It must have been introduced into the
language during the Early Modern period, because Shakespeare has it (5
instances in Spevack [1969 – 74 s. v. *one*]), but the nonoccurrence in the
Helsinki Corpus testifies to an infrequent use.[3] Examples from the corpus
are given as (9) – (11).

(9)   *Dyd not Moses geve you a lawe, and yet* none *of you kepeth*
           the lawe?
                                    (E1: *The New Testament*, Tyndale, VII)

(10)   *... the acc^t of God Almighty's wonderfull preservation of you in*
           the late most dreadfull storm, wch no man *liveing can remember*
           the like.
                                (E3: Richard Haddock, Letters, 45)

(11)   *L. C. J. Was there any body else besides them two in the Court?*
           Dunne. There was no body *but Hicks and Nethorp and I and*
           Mr. Carpenter.
                            (E3: The Trial of Lady Alice Lisle, 114, C2)

2.4. The universal paradigm

The universal paradigm consists of items with distributive meaning. The
compound pronouns have the determiner *every* as their first morpheme,
and, contrary to Present-day English, *every* can also be used as an

independent pronoun. Since, however, the Present-day English distinctions between *each* and *every* had not fully developed yet (Kahlas-Tarkka 1993), I also included forms with *each* in the corpus. The independent pronoun *each* and the phrase *each man* were found as alternative forms in the corpus. *Each* does not occur in the expressions with -*body* as a variant form. Examples of the universal paradigm are found as (12)−(15).

(12)   *And thes Orders, together with all other good Orders heretofore taken for exercises of Learning within the aforesaid University, I require you and* every *of you duely to observe and precisely to kepe according to your Oath and duties, ...*
         (E2: Robert Cecil, Letters, 321)

(13)   *Wherfore when* ech man *hath his own misery, it must needes be, that by tryple misfortune, they be vexed, whom thou dost see haue a will do doo the worst."*
         (E2: Elizabeth I, *Boethius*, 85)

(14)   *... when they finde it was only a kindnesse to them and a care to make them capable to deserve the favour of their parents and the esteeme of* everybody *else.*
         (E3: Locke, *Directions Concerning Education*, 55)

(15)   *And this is the will of him that sent me, that* every one *which seeth the Sonne, and beleeueth on him, may haue euerlasting life: ...*
         (E2: *The New Testament*, Authorised Version, VI)

In the compilation of the corpus for this study I encountered several problems connected with blurred categories and fuzzy borderlines. Very often it was difficult to be sure whether the simple pronouns *some, any* and *none* had singular or plural reference. There were several ambiguous cases where neither the context nor the verb form revealed the number. I included in the corpus cases where a Present-day English reading with the corresponding singular compound pronoun sounded natural.

The forms with *man* created another problem. In the use under examination the meaning of *man* had to be connected with its old meaning 'person', and not with the sense 'adult male person, male human being' that also existed (*OED*, s.v. *man* I.1, II.4, for further discussion, see sections 4 and 7, below). It goes without saying that the instances where *man* referred to a male human being as opposed to a woman or a human being as opposed to God were not to be included in the data. Early

Modern England represented a socially hierarchical society where the male sex played the most important role in public life (see e. g. Houlbrooke 1984: 96 – 126). Hence it is natural that the texts included in the *Helsinki Corpus* very often discuss events and actions in mens' life. We cannot be sure whether the general statements with indefinite pronouns were meant to refer to human beings in general or the male population only.

The use of synonyms was employed as one criterion for choice. If the same text, apart from forms in -*man*, contained synonymous noun phrases headed by *person*, or corresponding simple pronouns, or compound forms in -*body* and -*one*, the *man* items were included. There were other instances where very general contextual information was necessary to make the decision. Example (16) represents a case in point. In order to find out that the reference of *any man* can be extended to embrace women, it is necessary to know that the oath in question, the Oath of Succession, which Sir Thomas More refused to swear, was also sworn by women like More's daughter Margaret Roper (Marius 1984: 465).[4] Yet another method was used for the occurrences in the Bible: they were compared with a new English Bible translation, *The revised English Bible* from 1989, and cases where an Early Modern English phrase with *man* corresponded to a Present-day English indefinite pronoun were included.

(16)   *How be it (as helpe me God), as touchinge the whole othe, I
         never withdrewe* any man *from it, nor neuer aduised any to
         refuse it,...*

                              (E1: Sir Thomas More, Letters, 507)

A further problem was the borderline between the pronominal *one* as the head morpheme in the compounds with *one* and the numeral *one*. Clear numeral cases, such as contrasts with larger numbers were excluded.

Table 2. Number of occurrences

	Assertive 'someone'	Nonassertive 'anyone'	Negative 'no one'	Universal 'everyone'	Total
E1 (1500 – 1570)	11	77	83	58	229
E2 (1570 – 1640)	12	79	61	50	202
E3 (1640 – 1710)	9	73	39	31	152
Total	32	229	183	139	583

Table 2 shows the number of occurrences. The reason for the fewer instances in the third subperiod is the absence of Bible extracts, which account for a very large number of occurrences in the first two subsections, 55 each. The Bible is not represented in E3, because no new standard translation was made during this time.

3. Syntactic and semantic differences within the paradigms

A substantial syntactic difference can be discerned between the types of items: only the simple pronouns and the compounds in -*one* can appear as heads of partitive *of*-phrases (examples [9], [12] and [17]). *Every* is only found with *of*-phrases.

(17)   *Philip answered him, Two hundred peny-worth of bread is not sufficient for them, that* euery one *of them may take a litle.*
        (E2: *The New Testament*, Authorised Version, VI)

(18)   *There was* none *so poore, if he had, either wil to goodnes, or wit to learning, that could lacke being there, or should depart from thence for any need.*
        (E1: Ascham, *The Scholemaster*, 279)

(19)   *And however, I dare not suppress so strange an Observation, and therefore shall relate that which I had the luck to make of an odd sort of Electrical Attraction (as it seem'd,) not taken by* any *either Naturalist or other Writer, and it is this.*
        (E3: Boyle, *Electricity & Magnetism*, 26)

(20)   *That which is* every bodies *business, is* no bodies *business.*
        (E3: Walton, *The Compleat Angler*, 213)

While the forms under study do not take premodifiers, different kinds of post-head dependents occur in them, such as relative clauses (15), participle clauses (10), phrases introduced with the exclusive *but* (11), prepositional phrases with prepositions other than *of* (5 and 7), adjectives (18), appositive phrases (19) and the word *else* (14). Many of the postmodifers are relatively rare, and hence nothing can be said about their conditioning factors. Among the most frequent postmodifiers, the following differences have been observed: Relative clauses can modify all types of items, whereas the postmodifier *else* and the genitive suffix -*s* (example [20]) are only added to the compound forms.

While it is not difficult to find at least some dissimilarities in the syntactic behaviour of the pronouns, it is harder to get at semantic differences within the paradigms. As regards the pairs of the compound pronouns in Present-day English, both Quirk *et al.* (1985: 376 – 377) and Jespersen (1914: 444) consider them identical in meaning. On the other hand, Bolinger (1976) maintains that there is a semantic contrast, although it is too subtle to be readily noticed and hence normally dismissed as a case of free variation. He claims that the compounds in *-one* may still reflect both the numerical and pronominal values of *one*. He writes (1976: 230):

> It is natural for pronouns to embody references to distance from the speaker, to selfness and otherness. This is the prime characteristic of the personal pronouns and the demonstratives. If my hypothesis is correct, it also characterizes the indefinites: *one* and its compounds are marked for closeness to the speaker and for individualization (the pronominal and numerical values of *one* respectively), whereas *-body* is unmarked in these two senses. The *-body* compounds therefore are more like indefinite plurals, less concerned with the speaker-hearer's sense of the identity of the referent. As the unmarked term, *-body* can be used in most of the situations where *-one* can be used, but not vice versa.

According to Bolinger, the use of the *one* compounds in the partitive *of*-structures is an example of individualisation. It may not even be important whether there is a partitive *of*-phrase or not. In reference to an intimate or otherwise tightly knit group we tend to use the forms in *-one* and not the ones with *body*; Bolinger's examples are here *No one in the room spoke for some time* and *Nobody in the world is more patriotic than I am.* In fact my material includes some examples that can be compared with Bolinger's. My example (5) is comparable to Bolinger's first example, while my example (7) corresponds to his second. However, the pronoun in example (5) does not come from the *-one* series but is the simple pronoun *any*, which seems to share some characteristics with the Present-day English compound pronouns in *-one*. On the other hand, the *man* phrases appear to resemble the ones in *-body*, which have a very general indefinite reference.

It is important to notice that Bolinger only discusses tendencies and not rules. He performed a test with college students as subjects. The test comprised 38 sentences where either form had to be chosen. There was only one sentence where all the subjects chose the same variant, viz. the pronoun with *one* before a partitive *of*-phrase (*Anyone/*Anybody of my friends would be capable of that*, Bolinger 1976: 233).

Sahlin (1979: 17 – 18, 104 – 106) claims that the compound pronouns with personal reference *someone, somebody, anyone* and *anybody* always have the feature [-Selective], in other words, they cannot appear with a partitive *of*-phrase. According to her, only representatives of a separate numerical category of compound pronouns can appear with *of*-phrases. These numerical pronouns are characterised by being written as two words, *some one* and *any one*, and having a stress prominence on both elements. She claims that the head of these phrases is the numeral *one*, not the prop-word. The existence of this category is generally agreed upon (see e. g. Bolinger [1976: 231, 236] and Quirk *et al.* [1985: 378 − 379]), but the above discussion and Bolinger's examples show that nonnumerical pronouns occur in partitive structures.

It has been difficult to distinguish between numerical and nonnumerical senses in the few partitive phrases headed by forms in *-one* that are included in my data. It seems that especially in the early instances the numerical sense is relatively strong, but on the other hand, the cases included in the corpus are mixed and different emphatic readings are possible (examples [17] and [21]).

(21)   *And to the effect this yet more fully; acquaint them in all their Lectures and exercises,* some one *of them or other, who can tell first, to repeat where they have learned every hard word:* ...
(E2: Brinsley, *Ludus Literarius*, 47)

This examination shows that the units in the four paradigms are not interchangeable in all contexts. Here again we come across the problem variationists encounter in syntactic studies: although we aim at comparing different ways of saying the same thing, the expressions representing the same paradigm or variant field are not necessarily synonymous in all respects (for a survey, see e. g. Raumolin-Brunberg 1988: 140 − 141 and forthcoming), nor are their syntactic constraints the same. The paradigm-internal similarities and dissimilarities have to be kept in mind in the subsequent discussions in this paper.

4. Grammaticalisation

The main issue in the development of the compound forms under investigation is grammaticalisation. Grammaticalisation is a phenomenon that occurs when open-class lexical items develop into closed-class grammatical units. As Vincent (1980) claims, the change takes place from the iconic, rule-governed side of the language towards the symbolic. Traugott (1982) discusses grammaticalisation in the framework of Hallidayan systemic-functional grammar, and maintains that grammaticalisation generally proceeds unidirectionally from the propositional component of language (the main locus of the truth-conditional relations) towards the textual and expressive components.

As Nevalainen (1991: 12 — 16, 259 — 259) in her research on exclusive adverbs shows, there are different degrees of grammaticalisation. The lexical-semantic origin is among the key factors that influence the further development of grammaticalised items. This phenomenon is aptly called etymological conditioning. On this view, it is quite natural to expect the compound forms to exhibit at least some differences, since they originate from lexemes with different meanings: *man* and *body* have meant 'person', while *one* ultimately goes back to the numeral 'one'. However, as Mustanoja (1960: 301 — 305), among others, points out, *one* has also had the meaning 'person' in Middle English.

It is possible to posit a grammaticalisation continuum where the regular noun phrase is placed at one end and the pronoun at the other. The grammaticalisation of compound pronouns takes place along this continuum. One of the problems of this study is where to draw a borderline between the noun phrase and the pronoun. There are two questions of particular interest here: Were the forms with *man* ever grammaticalised as pronouns? When did the compounds in *-body* and *-one* become pronouns?

In order to answer these questions, we need criteria for the analysis of linguistic items as pronouns. Nouns and pronouns are not very different from each other. Pronouns form a varied set of closed-class items with nominal ("like a noun phrase") functions (Quirk *et al.* 1985: 335). The similarity of the syntactic functions of noun-headed and pronoun-headed noun phrases, and the characterisation of pronouns as noun "proforms" have led a scholar like Huddleston (1984: 231 — 232) to regard pronouns as a subclass of nouns. The resemblance between pronouns and noun phrases makes it more difficult to draw a borderline between them than for instance between noun phrases and adverbs in a grammaticalisation process (see Raumolin-Brunberg 1991: 96 — 97).

Quirk *et al.* (1985: 335 — 336) distinguish pronouns from nouns in the following ways: Semantically the meaning of pronouns is general and undetermined so that their interpretation depends to an unusual extent on what information is supplied by the context. Syntactically, most pronouns incorporate their own determiner. Morphologically, some pronouns have characteristics that noun phrases do not have: 1) contrast between subjective and objective cases, 2) contrast between first, second and third persons, 3) distinction between personal and nonpersonal as well as between masculine and feminine gender, 4) morphologically unrelated number forms. Some pronouns, for example personal pronouns, exhibit all these characteristics, and are hence regarded as the most central class of pronouns. Other pronouns may deviate from them in different respects, and are consequently characterised as less central.

An application of the above criteria to Present-day English compound pronouns with personal reference indicates that they are relatively peripheral among pronouns, because, as Quirk *et al.* (1985: 345) point out, they do not have the morphological characteristics of the central pronouns, such as case, person and gender distinctions. They are classified as pronouns, however, since they incorporate their own determiners, they are closed-class items and they have the kind of generalised meaning that we associate with pronouns. Their peripheral or NP-like character is, however, emphasised by the fact that they take the genitive suffix -*s*, which other pronouns do not.

The compound forms in my Early Modern English data are no different from the Present-day English ones analysed on the basis of the above features, except that we cannot use "closed class" as a criterion, because one of our goals here is precisely to find out whether they were grammaticalised closed-class items or not.

There is a further feature that can be made use of in Present-day English, viz. stress placement. If the main stress fell on the first morpheme in Early Modern English, as it does in Present-day English, we could be sure that the phrases represented compounds and not regular non phrases. However, there is no access to stress in written historical data. In Present-day English we could also test our phrases with an *else* test, in other words find out whether the postmodifier *else* could be added to the phrase, since it is almost exclusively used with pronouns and adverbs and not with noun phrases. It has already been shown that the Early Modern English compounds accepted this postmodifier (example [14]). The *OED* (s. v. *else*, 1.b) indicates, however, that the use of *else* in the meaning 'other' was common even in regular noun phrases during the Early Modern period. So unfortunately the *else* test is inoperative.

The above discussion shows how difficult it is to find formal criteria for deciding whether the compound forms in -*man*, -*body*, and -*one* were pronouns. Their characteristics, such as the use of the genitive -*s* and acceptance of various types of postmodification, indicate that their position on the noun phrase — pronoun continuum is much closer to the noun phrase end than that of the central pronouns. What we are left with is the semantic content, the question how much of the original lexical meaning has faded away to result in the very general meaning characteristic of pronouns.

I would like to suggest that the forms with *man* should be analysed as pronouns on these criteria, although they are not usually discussed among pronouns, except by Jespersen (1914: 445—446), who mentions them along with the compound pronouns in *-one* and *-body*. Their syntactic and morphological properties were similar to those of the Present-day English compound pronouns, and the meaning was very general and indeterminate. This analysis finds support from the earlier existence of the generic indefinite pronoun *man*, which disappeared during the Middle English era (Mustanoja 1960: 219—222).

It is more problematic to decide when the phrases with *body* and *one* became pronouns. The *OED* (s. v. *body* 13) gives the meaning 'a human being of either sex, an individual' from 1297 to 1833, and this lexeme is the original head morpheme of the compound pronoun. The *Helsinki Corpus* contains only one instance of *body* in this sense apart from the items with *some, any, no* and *every* included in the corpus. This fact would point to a relative infrequency of this word, for the synonym *person* appears far more often. It is most probable that the semantic content of the earliest instances of the phrases with *body* was still rather strong, but during the latter half of the seventeenth century, when the forms quickly became more frequent (see Figure 1), the forms were possibly felt to be pronouns rather than noun phrases.

The development of the compounds in *one* is different to the extent that the head morpheme was not an open-class lexical item but a grammatical one. The rise of the forms with *one* must be closely connected with the development of the substitute or propword *one* (see e. g. Rissanen 1967: 69—77; Mustanoja 1960: 301—305; Jespersen 1914: 245—271). It developed in Middle English, but its use apparently increased later on, when a change took place in the NP structure to the extent that practically all noun phrases came to have a separate head word (Görlach 1978: 97).

There are different views on the emergence of the propword (for overviews, see Mustanoja [1960: 301—305] and Rissanen [1967: 69—77]). According to Rissanen, the main sources were the pronoun *one*, meaning 'a person', and the anaphoric use of the pronominal *one*. The placement of *one* after some indefinite pronouns from Old English onwards, such as *æghwilc an*, later *euerichon, every one*, may have had an influence but could also be regarded as a parallel development.

The grammaticalisation of the oldest member of the *one* series, *every one*, available since the thirteenth century, probably took place during the Middle English period (for details on the earliest instances of *every one*, see Kahlas-Tarkka 1987: 155—156). The compounds *any one* and *some one* were introduced so late that they must have had both the general propword pattern and the compound pronoun *every one* as their models. If we attach more importance to the propword model, it is in fact possible to speak about repeated grammaticalisation, i. e. phrases headed by the substitute *one*, which developed via grammaticalisation from the numeral *one*, underwent a second stage of grammaticalisation and became indefinite pronouns.

As a general characterisation of the forms under study one can say that they represent a class that has undergone a relatively weak process of grammaticalisation. It is peculiar to them that many of the features of regular noun phrases are still observable in them.

5. Indefinite compound pronouns and their equivalents in Early Modern English

In order to increase the internal comparability of the data, a subcorpus was delimited from which all the forms with a partitive of-phrase were excluded.[5] Also, the occurrences in the Bible were omitted, since the third subperiod does not contain any Bible extracts. The resulting subcorpus contains 383 items.

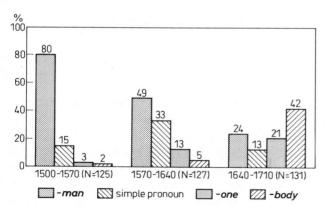

Figure 1. Indefinite compound pronouns and their equivalents in Early Modern English

Figure 1 describes the relative frequencies of the different types of items in the subcorpus during the three Early Modern English subperiods. The corresponding absolute figures for individual paradigms are given in Appendix 1. The total number of instances in the assertive 'someone' paradigm is too small for conclusions. On the whole, the following tendencies can be observed in the material.

In E1 (1500−1570) the variants with *man* form an overwhelming majority (80%), and simple pronouns are also relatively frequent (15%). A few instances of the phrases with *body* and *one* occur.

The second subperiod (1570−1640) exhibits a more even distribution of the items. The forms with *man* are still frequent (49%), but the relative proportion of the simple pronouns has increased to 33%. The growth of the share of the compounds in *-one* is mainly based on their high frequency in the universal 'everyone' paradigm.

E3 (1640−1710) witnesses a new distribution: The forms in *-body* are the most frequent type (42%), the share of *man* items has decreased to 24% and that of the simple pronouns to 13%. The relatively large proportion of the *one* forms (21%) is still due to their higher frequency in the universal paradigm.

Figure 1 discloses four interesting trends. First, the proportion of the forms with *man* decreases as time wears on. Second, the simple pronouns reach a "peak" during the second subperiod. Third, the increase in the forms with *body* in E3 is considerable. Fourth, there is a stable growth of the compounds in *-one*, led by *every one* in the universal paradigm.

The data also show that simple pronouns were used all through the Early Modern period, thus invalidating Görlach's argument (1978: 98, see the Introduction above) that *one* and *body* were obligatory elements after *some, any, no,* and *every* from the sixteenth century onwards.

6. Textual variation

The number of the occurrences in individual texts is mostly too small for statistical examination. More reliable results can be acquired by grouping texts together. I have used the rough division of the texts into oral and literate genres along the lines originally presented by Tannen (1982) and later used by Biber (1988: 104−108) and Biber−Finegan (1989), among others. "Oral" refers here to language produced in situations that are typical of speaking, "literate" in situations typical of writing. Conversation is a typically oral genre, academic prose a literate one. It is, of course, clear that a corpus of written texts can never represent spoken language, but some written texts have characteristics similar to those used in the spoken mode of expression. Here the oral genres include private letters, comedies, fiction, diaries, biographies, trial proceedings and travel books. The latter two constitute choices that are not self-evident. The trial depositions represent speech-based language, which makes them good candidates for analysis as oral, but the situations in which they have been expressed are very formal and official, far from a private chat, which is often the model for exchanges in comedies and jest books. I have given more emphasis to the spoken origin and included them among the oral. As regards most travel books, their main purpose seems to have been entertainment, and so they have also been included among the oral genres.

Table 3. Percentages of forms in oral genres

E1 (1500−1570)		E2 (1570−1640)		E3 (1640−1710)	
-*body*	100% (3/3)	-*body*	100% (6/6)	-*body*	75% (41/55)
-*one*	50% (3/6)	Simple	48% (30/63)	Simple	37% (13/(35)
Simple	39% (29/74)	-*man*	19% (20/106)	-*one*	34% (11/32)
-*man*	29% (42/146)	-*one*	15% (4/27)	-*man*	7% (2/30)

Table 3 shows the percentages and numbers of tokens of each type of item in the oral texts. The table is based on the original corpus presented in Table 2. The percentages have been calculated from the total of occurrences during each subperiod. So in E1 there were three instances of forms in -*body*, all of them in the oral texts, hence 100%. In E2 27 forms in -*one* occurred, but only 4 tokens in oral genres, hence 15%. The items have been placed in an order corresponding to the preference for the oral texts.

As a background for this analysis it is necessary to know that the share of the oral genres in the whole corpus is approximately 50% (E1 46%, E2 51% and E3 50%). So in an even or neutral distribution among the genres the percentages would be around 50.

There are three tendencies that can be observed here. First, the forms in -*body* are mainly used in the oral genres. In the first two periods, the few instances there are appear exclusively in these genres, while in the third period, when forms in -*body* are apparently better established in the language, they are also used in the literate genres but not very frequently. Second, the forms with *man* mostly behave in the opposite way, viz. are found relatively low down in the three lists and are thus found in the literate rather than the oral texts. This is especially true for E3. Third, the forms in -*one* do not seem to have strong preferences, except that in E2 there is some bias towards the literate.

An examination of individual genres yields an interesting observation. There is one text that especially favours *man*, viz. the Bible. In E1, 85% of all items in the Bible were compounds with *man*, in E2 80%. The role of the Bible as the preserver of the use of *man* becomes more evident when we examine how large a share the Bible takes up of the total number of the compounds with *man*. Tyndale's Bible accounts for 32% of all the instances with *man* in E1, while in the next period the share of the Authorised Version is 42%. The proportion of the Bible texts out of the whole corpus is much lower, however, about 12% in each subperiod. The role of the preserver of *man* is transferred to the sermons in the third subperiod, and they alone account for most of the forms with *man*, as the percentage is as high as 70.

7. Discussion and conclusion

The Early Modern English development of the compounds in -*body* seems to be a good specimen of natural change or change from below in Labovian terms (1972: 178 — 181). The first instances in the oral genres point to an origin in the spoken language, from which the pronouns only gradually spread into more literate genres. Even today the *body* compounds are regarded as less elegant or less literary than those in -*one* (Jespersen 1914: 444; Quirk *et al.* 1985: 376 — 378). In contrast with the E3 data, the pronouns in -*one* are more frequent than the ones in -*body* in Present-day English (Quirk *et al.* 1985: 378).

It is another matter to try to find motivations for a change like this. The most obvious solution would be to connect the developments of the compounds with *body* and *man*. Both words have meant 'person'. There is a syntactic and semantic resemblance between the two, as discussed in section 3 above. When the use of the *man* pronouns decreased, that of the *body* compounds increased. By now the *man* compounds have disappeared, except for some fixed phrases, such as *no-man's land* and *everyman's library*.

Why then should this have happened? Most probably it has connections with the semantic shift in the meaning of the word *man*. According to the *OED* (s. v. *man*, 1.) the prevailing use of the word in Old English was 'human being (irrespective of sex and age)'. Gradually it acquired other meanings, such as 'human being of male sex', and the development of unambiguous synonyms meaning 'person', such as *body* and *person*, narrowed the currency of *man* in this sense. The disappearance of the generic indefinite pronoun *man* during the Middle English period probably also belonged to this development and left the compounds in -*man* without its support. It is difficult to assess how important this type of support is. According to Bolinger (1976: 235—236), Scots and Scottish English, where *body* survives as an independent indefinite pronoun, have a pronounced preference for the *body* compounds, while British and American English both favour the pronouns in -*one*.

If lexical or grammatical support is important, it is easy to see that the compound pronouns with *one* have had a fair share of it. As mentioned above, their development must have been connected with the rise of the substitute or so-called propword *one*. Apart from the propword, the emergence of the indefinite generic personal pronoun *one*, which replaced *man*, gave its support to the development of the pronouns with *one*. (For the development of the indefinite personal pronoun *one* in Early Modern English, see Bald 1984.) The numeral or emphatic use in expressions like *any one person* also supported the development of the forms in -*one* (see footnote 2).

An easy explanation for the whole process under examination would be to say that *man* was replaced by *body* and that the propword *one* was attached to the simple pronouns to comply with the general pattern of noun phrases needing a separate headword. The early introduction of *every one* does not fit in this model, and textual variation provides evidence that this view cannot represent the whole truth. The pronouns with *body* did not replace the items with *man* in all genres. The *man* compounds had a bias towards the literate genres in all periods, while the forms with *body* were and still are more oral. What happened was rather that at the same time as the *man* compounds were becoming marked for the Bible and archaic at the literate end of the language, the forms in -*body* entered the language via the oral genres. In this context it is interesting to observe that present-day Bible translators (*The revised English Bible*) have not chosen forms in -*body* but those in -*one* in places where the Early Modern English translations have compounds with *man*.

Consequently, instead of the change from *man* to *body* there must have been other shifts in the paradigms. The E2 increase in the simple forms (see Figure 1) is interesting here. An explanation for it could be the need for an unmarked or neutral alternative at a time when the forms in -*man* were becoming marked, the compounds in -*one* were not yet fully established except for *every one*, and the forms with *body* were also rare and colloquial. In this situation the simple pronoun was a natural choice.

However, the simple pronouns had a heavy functional loading; they were both determiners and independent pronouns, they were both singular and plural, their reference was both human and nonhuman. Consequently, they did not really represent a good alternative. The compound forms were more suitable in that they distinguished independent pronouns from determiners and excluded the plural reference. They also followed the structural noun phrase pattern with a separate head word, which apparently was felt to be natural even within the pronoun category among its noncentral members.

In E3 the most frequent items, the *body* and *man* compounds, were more or less marked, the first colloquial, the second formal and religious. The remaining forms, the simple pronouns and the compounds in *-one* were the unmarked variants. Out of these two competing forms, it is natural that the compound gradually emerged as the winner, but this change was not completed during the Early Modern English period. In addition, the compounds with *body* also began to extend their territory towards the more formal genres.

In conclusion, it is important to point out that we are here dealing with changes that are far from abrupt. The establishment of new series of compound pronouns took centuries. When compared with some other changes within the pronoun category, such as the emergence of the possessive pronoun *its* within the lifespan of one generation in the seventeenth century, this represents a really slow process (see Nevalainen — Raumolin-Brunberg 1994). It at least shows that very different changes take place within the same grammatical category.

Appendix

Indefinite compound pronouns with personal reference and their equivalents in the Early Modern English section of the *Helsinki Corpus of English Texts* (partitive structures and the Bible texts excluded)

	E1 1500—1570		E2 1570—1640		E3 1640—1710	
	N	%	N	%	N	%
Assertive 'someone'						
Some	4	50	8	73	1	14
Some man	2	25	1	9	0	—
Some body	2	25	1	9	5	72
Some one	0	—	1	9	1	14
Total	8	100	11	100	7	100
Nonassertive 'anyone'						
Any	6	19	19	38	8	13
Any man	26	81	28	56	20	33
Any body	0	—	2	4	22	37
Any one	0	—	1	2	10	17
Total	32	100	50	100	60	100
Negative 'no one'						
None	9	17	15	42	7	19
No man	43	83	18	50	6	17
No body	0	—	3	8	23	64
Total	52	100	36	100	36	100
Universal 'everyone'						
Each	0	—	0	—	2	7
Every/each man	28	85	15	50	4	14
Every body	1	3	0	—	5	18
Every one	4	12	15	50	17	61
Total	33	100	30	100	28	100

Notes

* I would like to thank Dr. Leena Kahlas-Tarkka and Prof. Matti Rissanen for their valuable comments on this paper.
1. The example the *OED* gives for *anyone* from 1449 is in fact "any one person" (Pecock, *The Repressor of over much blaming of the clergy*), and the first quotation of *anyone* as an independent pronoun dates from as late as 1711.

2. In fact, picking up one referent is valid for the assertive and nonassertive paradigms. The universal forms refer to all individuals in the set singly (see e. g. Kahlas-Tarkka 1987: 89−90). The negative paradigm and modification by the exclusive *but* in general involve complex semantic issues, which I hope to be able to return to in a more detailed paper later on.

   In Present-day English there are separate pronouns for sets of two, viz. *either, both, neither* and *each*. According to Kahlas-Tarkka (1993), the distinction between *each* and *every* in this respect was not regularly followed in Early Modern English. The development of this reference among indefinite pronouns must also be left to another study.

3. There may be several factors affecting the late adoption of the form *no one*. The simple pronoun *none* may have been interpreted as a form containing the element *one* (I would like to thank Professor Matti Rissanen for pointing this out to me). The gradual loss of the *-n* element in the determiner *none* before vowels and the introduction of the prothetic [w] in the pronunciation of *one* may also have played a part.

   As regards Shakespeare's use of the compounds in *-one* and *-body*, Jespersen's comment (1914: 444) "Shakespeare evidently preferred *one*" is right to a certain extent, since Spevack (1969−1974) contains 70 forms with *one* and 36 with *body*. Out of the *one* compounds 49 represent *everyone*, 6 *someone*, 10 *anyone*, and 5 *no one*. It is, however, only in the universal and nonassertive paradigms where the forms in *one* are more frequent than the *body* compounds (0 tokens of *everybody* against 49 of *everyone* and 4 instances of *anybody* against 10 of *anyone*). In the negative set *nobody* is far more frequent than *no one* (24 against 5 occurrences) and in the assertive set the forms are almost as common (8 tokens of *somebody* against 6 of *someone*). This discussion does not account for the competing forms in *-man* and the simple pronouns.

4. After writing this passage it has come to my attention that at least in some parts of England only men took the oath (Cressy 1980: 64−65).

5. The internal comparability of the corpus is clearly enhanced by this procedure, but it does not lead to a total interchangeability of the items within the paradigms. For instance, only the compound pronouns can take the genitive *-s* suffix. The genitives were not excluded, however, because the simple pronouns have a semantically equivalent structure, the *of*-genitive.

Primary sources

Armin, Robert
    1842   *Fools and jesters: With a reprint of Robert Armin's Nest of Ninnies, 1608.*
            London: The Shakespeare Society.
Ascham, Roger
    1870   *The Scholemaster.* Written between 1563−1568. Posthumously published.
            (First edition 1570; Collated with the second edition 1571.) Ed. by E. Arber.
            English Reprints.
Boethius
    1899   *Queen Elizabeth's Englishings of Boethius, de Consolatione Philosophiae, A. D.*
            1593, Plutarch, de Curiositate, Horace, de Arte Poetica (Part) A. D. 1598.
            Ed. by C. Pemberton. (Early English Text Society, O. S. 113). London.

1695   *Ancius Manlius Severinus Boetius, of the Consolation of Philosophy, in Five*
            Books. Made English and Illustrated with Notes, by the Right Honourable
            Richard Lord Viscount Preston. London.
Boyle, Robert
1927   *Electricity and magnetism, 1675—1676.* (Old Ashmolean Reprints, 7.) Series
            ed. by R. W. T. Gunther. Oxford: University of Oxford. [Facsimile]
Brinsley, John
1917   *Ludus Literarius or the Grammar Schoole (1627).* Ed. by E. T. Campagnac.
            Liverpool: University Press and London: Constable & Co. Ltd.
Cecil, Robert
1913   *The Edmondes papers. A selection from the correspondence of Sir Thomas*
            Edmondes, Envoy from Queen Elizabeth at the French Court. Ed. by G. G.
            Butler. London: J. B. Nichols and Sons.
Haddock, Richard, Sr.
1965   *The Camden Miscellany, Volume the Eighth: Containing … Correspondence of*
[1883]   *the Family of Haddock, 1657—1719.* Ed. by E. M. Thompson. (Camden
            Society, N. S. XXXI.) London.
Locke, John
1933   *Directions concerning education.* Ed. by F. G. Kenyon. Oxford: Roxburghe
            Club.
More, Thomas
1947   *The correspondence of Sir Thomas More.* Ed. by E. F. Rogers. Princeton:
            Princeton University Press.
Mowntayne, Thomas
1859   *The autobiography of Thomas Mowntayne.* Narratives of the days of the
            Reformation, chiefly from the manuscrips of John Foxe the martyrologist.
            Ed. by J. G. Nichols. (Camden Society LXXVII.) London.
The New Testament
1911   *The Holy Bible.* An exact reprint in Roman type, page for page of the
            Authorized Version published in the year 1611. With an introduction by A. W.
            Pollard. London, Oxford, New York: Henry Frowde and Oxford University
            Press.
1938   Translated by William Tyndale, 1534. Ed. by N. H. Wallis, with an introduc-
            tion by I. Foot. Cambridge: Cambridge University Press.
Oxinden, Henry
1937   *The Oxinden and Peyton letters, 1642—1670. Being the correspondence of*
            Henry Oxinden of Barham, Sir Thomas Peyton of Knowlton and their circle.
            Ed. by D. Gardiner. London: The Sheldon Press and New York: The Mac-
            millan Company.
Taylor, Jeremy
1907   *The marriage ring* (1673). Ed. by F. Coutts. London and New York: John
            Lane.
The Trial of Lady Alice Lisle
1930   *A complete collection of state-trials and proceedings for high-treason, and other*
            crimes and misdemeanors; from the reign of King Richard II, to the end of the
            reign of King George I. (Second Edition). Vols. I and IV. Ed. by F. Hargrave.
            London: Printed for J. Walthoe Sen. Etc.

Walton, Izaak
1983　*The compleat angler, 1653—1676.* Ed. by J. Bevan. Oxford: Clarendon Press.

References

Bald, Wolf-Dietrich
1984　"Form and function of ONE: Diachronic aspects", in: Wolf-Dietrich Bald—Horst Weinstock (eds.), *Medieval studies conference Aachen 1983. Language and literature.* (Bamberger Beiträge zur Englischen Sprachwissenschaft 15.) Frankfurt am Main: Lang, 143—153.
Barber, Charles
1976　*Early Modern English.* London: Deutsch.
Biber, Douglas
1988　*Variation across speech and writing.* Cambridge: Cambridge University Press.
Biber, Douglas—Edward Finegan
1989　"Drift and the evolution of English style: a history of three genres", *Language* 65: 487—517.
Bolinger, Dwight
1976　"The in-group: *one* and its compounds", in: Peter A. Reich (ed.), *The second LACUS forum 1975.* Columbia, South Carolina: Hornbeam Press, 229—237.
Cressy, David
1980　*Literacy and social order. Reading and writing in Tudor and Stuart England.* Cambridge: Cambridge University Press.
Görlach, Manfred
1978　*Einführung ins Frühneuenglische.* (Uni-Taschenbücher 820.) Heidelberg: Quelle & Mayer.
Houlbrooke, Ralph A.
1984　*The English family 1450—1700.* London & New York: Longman.
Huddleston, Rodney
1984　*Introduction to the grammar of English.* Cambridge: Cambridge University Press.
Jespersen, Otto
1914　*A modern English grammar on historical principles*, Part II: *Syntax.* First volume. Heidelberg: Carl Winters Universitätsbuchhandlung.
Kahlas-Tarkka, Leena
1987　*The uses and shades of meaning for* every *and* each *in Old English.* (Mémoires de la Société Néophilologique de Helsinki 46.) Helsinki: Société Néophilologique.
1993　"Toward the Modern English dichotomy between *every* and *each*", in: Matti Rissanen—Merja Kytö—Minna Palander-Collin (eds), *Early English in the computer age: Explorations through the Helsinki Corpus.* Berlin: Mouton de Gruyter, 201—218.
Kytö, Merja (comp.)
1993　*Manual to the diachronic part of the Helsinki Corpus of English Texts: Coding conventions and lists of source texts.* (Second edition.) Helsinki: University of Helsinki, Department of English.

Labov, William
1972   *Sociolinguistic patterns.* Philadelphia: University of Pennsylvania Press.
Marius, Richard
1984   *Thomas More.* Glasgow: Collins.
Mustanoja, Tauno F.
1960   *A Middle English syntax,* part I. *Parts of speech.* (Mémoires de la Société
          Néophilologique de Helsinki 23.) Helsinki: Société Néophilologique.
Nevalainen, Terttu
1991   BUT, ONLY, JUST: *Focusing adverbial change in Modern English 1500—1900.*
          (Mémoires de la Société Néophilologique de Helsinki 51.) Helsinki: Société
          Néophilologique.
Nevalainen, Terttu — Helena Raumolin-Brunberg
1989   "A corpus of Early Modern Standard English in a socio-historical perspec-
          tive", *Neuphilologische Mitteilungen* 90: 67—111.
1993   "Early Modern English", in: Matti Rissanen — Merja Kytö — Minna Palander-
          Collin (eds.), *Early English in the computer age: Explorations through the
          Helsinki Corpus.* Berlin: Mouton de Gruyter, 53—75.
1994   "*Its* strength and the beauty *of it*: the standardisation of the third person
          neuter possessive in Early Modern English", in: Ingrid Tieken-Boon van
          Ostade — Dieter Stein (eds.), *Towards a Standard English 1600—1800.* Berlin:
          Mouton de Gruyter, 171—216.
The Oxford English Dictionary (OED)
1933   Edited by James A. H. Murray — Henry Bradley — William A. Craigie —
          Charles T. Onions. Vols 1—13. Oxford: Clarendon Press.
Quirk, Randolph — Sidney Greenbaum — Geoffrey Leech — Jan Svartvik
1985   *A comprehensive grammar of the English language.* London: Longman.
Raumolin-Brunberg, Helena
1988   "Variation and historical linguistics. A survey of methods and concepts".
          Neuphilologische Mitteilungen 89: 136—154.
1991   *The noun phrase in early sixteenth-century English: A study based on Sir
          Thomas More's writings.* (Mémoires de la Société Néophilologique de Helsinki
          50.) Helsinki: Société Néophilologique.
1994   "Prototype categories and variation studies", in: Francisco Fernán-
          dez — Miguel Fuster — Juan J. Calvo (eds.), *Proceedings of the 7th International
          Conference on English Historical Linguistics.*
The revised English Bible, with the apocrypha.
1989   Oxford University Press and Cambridge University Press.
Rissanen, Matti
1967   *The uses of* one *in Old and Early Middle English.* (Mémoires de la Société
          Néophilologique de Helsinki 31.) Helsinki: Société Néophilologique.
Rissanen, Matti — Merja Kytö — Minna Palander-Collin (eds).
1993   *Early English in the Computer age: Explorations through the Helsinki Corpus.*
          Berlin: Mouton de Gruyter.
Sahlin, Elisabeth
1979   Some *and* any *in spoken and written English.* (Acta Universitatis Upsaliensis.
          Studia Anglistica Upsaliensia 38.) Uppsala: Almqvist & Wiksell.
Spevack, Marvin
1969—74   *The Harvard concordance to Shakespeare.* Vols. IV—VI. Cambridge, Mass.:
          Belknap Press of Harvard University Press.

324   *Helena Raumolin-Brunberg*

Tannen, Deborah
    1982   "Oral and literate strategies in spoken and written narratives", *Language* 58:
                1—21.
Traugott, Elizabeth Closs
    1982   "From propositional to textual and expressive meanings: Some semantic-
                pragmatic aspects of grammaticalisation", in: Winfred P. Lehmann—Yakov
                Malkiel (eds.), *Perspectives on historical linguistics*. (Current Issues in Lin-
                guistic Theory 24.) Amsterdam & Philadelphia: Benjamins, 245—271.
Vincent, Nigel
    1980   "Iconic and symbolic aspects of syntax: Prospects of reconstruction", in:
                Ramat, Paolo (ed.), *Linguistic reconstruction and Indo-European syntax*. (Cur-
                rent Issues in Linguistic Theory 19.) Amsterdam: Benjamins, 47—65.

Social conditioning and diachronic language change

*Helena Raumolin-Brunberg — Terttu Nevalainen**

1. Introduction

The present paper can be taken as a tentative follow-up to the work we
carried out in the compilation of the Early Modern English section of
the *Helsinki Corpus of English Texts* (for a general presentation of the
corpus, see Rissanen *et al.*, 1993, and Kytö 1993). One of our main
guidelines was the use of extralinguistic criteria in the selection and
classification of texts. We have discussed the socio-historical aspects of
the Early Modern English period in Nevalainen — Raumolin-Brunberg
(1989).

It is not our purpose to devote much space to a detailed repetition of
our basic viewpoints. We would only like to clarify our background by
making some general statements. Although the focus of this paper is the
connection between social context and language change, this does not
mean that we would claim that social conditioning should be the one
and only or even a major factor in all language change. It is of course a
well-known fact that there are many other factors at play in change, both
language internal and external.

However, the sociolinguistic research that has been carried out in
recent decades has provided us with facts and hypotheses about the
connection between language change and social context. Here we only
need to refer to such names as William Labov, Peter Trudgill, Charles-
James Bailey, Lesley and James Milroy, and so on. And it is our belief
that their approaches should in principle also be applicable to diachronic
language studies. As a basis for the discussion that follows, we may quote
Suzanne Romaine's words in her *Socio-historical linguistics* (1982:
122 — 123): "... we accept that the linguistic forces which operate today
and are observable around us are not unlike those which have operated
in the past. Sociolinguistically speaking, this means that there is no reason
for claiming that language did not vary in the same patterned ways in
the past as it has been observed to do today."

This is based on the uniformitarian principle, which can be used as a
foundation for sociolinguistic reconstruction. The underlying idea is that

human beings are essentially the same, no matter whether they lived in the past or today. The basic biological and psychological properties of man have hardly changed during the millennia from which written records of human language are available. A word of caution is still appropriate here: although we believe that the basic characteristics of human beings have not changed, the societies human beings live in vary, and have changed in history. Just as we cannot directly apply the principles of a sociolinguistic study of a large city like New York to rural areas in Africa, we should be similarly cautious in our interpretations of historical research.

We would now like to turn to a more detailed discussion of Early Modern English, the period which is usually given the time boundaries 1500 and 1700. In the *Helsinki Corpus* we divided Early Modern English into three subperiods: Period I 1500 — 1570, Period II 1570 — 1640, and Period III 1640 — 1710. Within this framework, we concentrated on the first half of the sixteenth century, the turn of the century and the last few decades of the seventeenth century. This means, *inter alia*, that all the texts from the third subperiod come from the latter half of the seventeenth century.

2. Studies

Now that the corpus has been available for testing for some time, it has of course been of great interest for us to see the preliminary results. Several studies have shown that linguistic changes tend to culminate during the period from 1580 to 1660, that is, largely in our middle period. It would appear that this is a rather special period, and we have consequently collected Early Modern English changes from other sources in order to ensure that our impression is not based on some kind of latent bias in the corpus.

The following is a brief survey of studies concerned with Early Modern English grammar and lexis. We shall begin by looking at some peak phenomena.

One of the most conspicuous developments in our middle period is a sharp increase in vocabulary intake. The graph in Figure 1, from Nevalainen (1994), is based on the data in Finkenstaedt — Leisi — Wolff (1970). Despite some bias in the sampling of the *CED* data, the remarkable increase in the number of new words recorded cannot be contested.

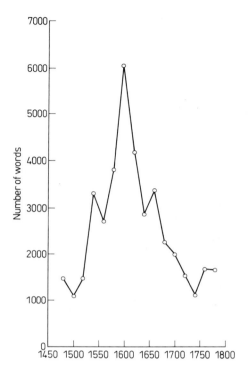

Figure 1. Vocabulary growth in Early Modern English (from Nevalainen forthcoming)

Proliferation of forms is also shown by Lass' (1994) study on the preterite (Pret) and past participle (PP) forms of the most frequent strong verbs in the *Helsinki Corpus*. The second major peak after the Middle English upheaval comes in our second period (Figure 2).

The use of periphrastic affirmative *do* also peaks in our second Early Modern English period. The data presented by Rissanen (1991) show a 1.6-fold increase in its frequency between Periods I and II in the *Helsinki Corpus*, and a 2.4-fold decrease between Periods II and III. A very similar frequency development is suggested by the quantitative data studied by Ellegård (1953: 162).

According to Kytö (1991), it is also within the second Early Modern English period that the auxiliary *will* is first generalised in the first person at the expense of *shall*. Kytö's results, shown in Figure 3, present the relative frequencies of first-person *shall* and *will* in the three Early Modern English periods of the *Helsinki Corpus*.

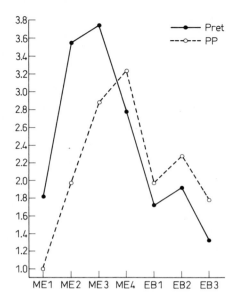

Figure 2. Preterite and past participle forms in Middle and Early Modern English (based on Lass 1994: 97)

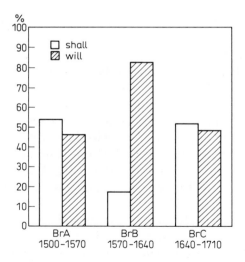

Figure 3. First person *shall* and *will* in Early Modern British English (based on Kytö 1991: 334)

The study of exclusive focusing adverbs in Nevalainen (1991) is based on a non-computerised 2.3 million-word corpus. It shows that the Early Modern English period from 1570 to 1630 is the only time when *but* clearly dominates over *only* in Modern English (e. g. *Mary is but/only a child*). It marks the peak in the two-prototype stage of this paradigm, which consists of altogether ten items that are partially synonymous with *only* (Figure 4).

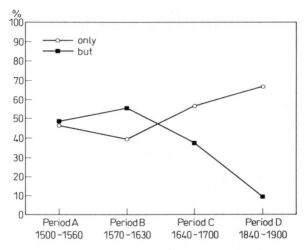

Figure 4. Frequency distributions of *but* and *only* in Modern English (from Nevalainen 1991: 166)

Rissanen (1989) demonstrates that the now obsolete subordinating conjunction *for that* enjoyed its peak frequency around our second period. Similarly, Dekeyser (1984) provides quantitative evidence of a sharp increase in the frequency of *that* as a nonrestrictive relative pronoun in the first half of the seventeenth century.

Concerning the expression of the possessive, Wales (1985) suggests that the use of generic-deictic *your* reached its climax in Jacobean drama in the first decade of the seventeenth century (e. g. *Your worm is your only emperor for diet*). Wales also observes that the usage only re-emerges in a modern TV-series in which the characters imitate an East London Cockney dialect.

Our Period II also appears to be the time when the use of the *of*-genitive reached its peak as opposed to the inflected *s*-genitive. Altenberg (1982) finds this to be particularly the case in formal prose from the period 1600 — 1635, and in the Rheims Bible (1582) and the Authorised Version (1611).

Besides these peak phenomena, we have recorded a number of other interesting developments which occur in Period II, including some troughs. We shall call them "paradigmatic restructurings". Kytö (1991), for example, provides evidence that Period II is the transition period in the rivalry between the auxiliaries *can* and *may*. The diagram in Figure 5 shows the rise of *can* in the 'root possibility' sense in the *Helsinki Corpus*.

Houston (1989) argues that the nominal gerund splits into a nominal and verbal gerund, and finds that important changes in the development took

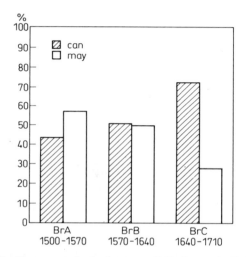

Figure 5. Can vs. *may* in the 'root possibility' sense in Early Modern British English (based on Kytö 1991: 243)

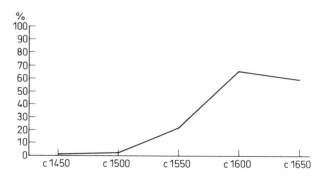

Figure 6. Verbal nouns with direct objects (based on Houston 1989: 178)

place around the end of the sixteenth century. The graph in Figure 6, based on Houston's figures collected from a variety of primary sources, depicts the increase in verbal nouns (nominal gerunds) with direct objects. Typical examples of this kind are *the bringing the army to London* and *the preferring some men* (both from the Verney Papers; Houston 1989: 189).

Stein (1987) provides evidence for the final stages in the rivalry between *-s* and *-th* as third person singular present tense suffixes. Around 1600, *-s* is also generalised in the printed materials, including drama. The development represents, according to Stein (1987: 412, 429), "a sharp turn towards *-s* forms that is quite unusual for linguistic change processes in its suddenness" — "an abrupt catching-up with the state of the spoken language".

The more formal registers also now accept the Northern plural form *are* of the verb *to be*. The systematic comparison of parallel passages in Nevalainen (1987) shows how *be* still predominates in the 1552 edition of the *Book of Common Prayer*, whereas the 1662 edition mainly uses *are*.

Using the *Helsinki Corpus*, Raumolin-Brunberg (this volume) shows how the indefinite prounoun system (*some-, any-, no-*) is diversified by the emergence of *body*-compounds at the expense of the old suffixless forms, and *one-* and *man-*compounds. Suffixless forms peak in Period II, and in most cases a crossing-over takes place between Periods II and III (Figure 7).

This change is much more gradual than the replacement of the third person neuter possessive pronoun *his* by the new form *its* (Nevalai-

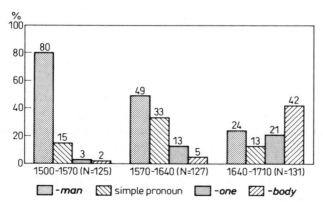

Figure 7. Compound forms of indefinite pronouns (from Raumolin-Brunberg, this volume)

nen — Raumolin-Brunberg 1994). The form *its* was first introduced around 1600. The *Helsinki Corpus* data show how it was generalised, as it were, at one fell swoop in most of the text types included in the *Corpus* in the latter half of the seventeenth century (Figure 8). This happened at the expense of the other possessive variants *his, thereof*, and *of the same*, but left the variant *of it* almost unchanged.

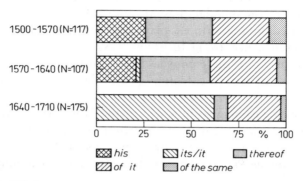

Figure 8. Third person neuter possessive pronouns (based on Nevalainen — Raumolin-Brunberg 1994: 189)

The relative pronoun paradigm also displays a number of important developments that alter its composition in the first half of the seventeenth century. They include, according to Dekeyser (1984), the following: *who* gets established in restrictive contexts; *which* is markedly dehumanised, and the Ø-relative becomes a significant alternative — partly at the expense of *that*. To this we could add the findings of Kemp (1979) pointing out the predominance of the headless relative *what* over *that which* in the writings of people who were born in the early sixteen-hundreds.

3. Discussion

The concentration of the peaks and crucial stages of paradigmatic restructuring in the middle period seems puzzling. Although we subscribe to the generally accepted view of the development of the English language, with Middle English as the era of thoroughgoing changes and Early Modern English as a period of minor polishings, why is there a time of instability around 1600? As far as Old and Middle English are concerned, nobody would deny the significance of such language-external factors as the Viking and Norman invasions. Possibly some explanations for Early

Modern changes could similarly be found in social factors, although no such upheavals took place then as they did in Mediaeval England.

Before going into these questions in depth, we should discuss certain counterarguments. Present-day sociolinguistic studies deal with spoken language and phonological details. We have no access to the spoken idiom of past times, and our field is concerned with changes in grammar and lexis. The corpora used are heterogeneous, there are always problems in timing first instances in dictionaries, and there is no detailed evidence on individual changes, such as is available in the sociolinguistic studies of Present-day English.

On the other hand, since it is difficult to find other reasons for the timing of these changes, one should at least consider social conditioning as a possible factor. Table 1 contains a presentation of Early Modern English society, which is a starting point for relating linguistic changes to social developments (Nevalainen — Raumolin-Brunberg 1989: 80 — 81).

Let us first discuss the changes in terms of the Milroyan network model. Lesley and James Milroy (1985 b) have hypothesised that linguistic changes spread via weak ties in social networks (see also J. Milroy 1992). A society with frequent loose and uniplex ties in social networks is more prone to rapid diffusion of linguistic changes than a society with close-knit networks.

The beginning of our period, early sixteenth century England, may be characterised as a strong-tie rather than a weak-tie society. Later in the century many changes begin to be seen. At least the following factors can be supposed to have caused an increase in the weak ties in social networks: population growth causing migration, urbanisation (under Demography in Table 1), commercial farming and economic diversification with more contacts between people of different trades, better communication networks (under Economy in Table 1), increased educational opportunities (under Culture in Table 1) and, last but not least, the Civil War (under Political Life in Table 1). During Restoration, English society gained new stability and conservatism, and strong network ties obviously increased.

Our question is: if the Milroyan model can be applied anywhere at all, would not Early Modern England be an appropriate case in point? It is then that a time of rapid change coincides with a period of weak ties in social networks.

The discussion has necessarily been somewhat abstract so far, and it is indeed very difficult to place it on a more concrete level. However, we

Table 1. Social and economic conditions in Early Modern England

16th Century: 'Age of Reformation'	17th Century: 'Age of Restoration'
1. Demography	
Rapid growth of population: 1500 over 2 million 1550 3.01 million 1600 4.11 million	Population growth slackens off: 1600 4.11 million 1650 5.23 million 1700 5.06 million
Internal migration common though regionally varied.	Apart from internal migration, substantial emigration to America and Ireland.
The vast majority of the population lives in the country-side. Urbanisation on the increase.	Continued urbanisation. The growth of London is remarkable.
Mortality crises especially common in towns (dearth and epidemic disease).	Mortality crises continue (disease, less dearth, at the end of the century). Periods
Periods of national crisis: 1555—59, 1594—98.	of national crisis: 1624—26, 1638—39, 1657—59, 1665—66, 1680—81.
Average expectation of life at birth about 37 years (1550—1600).	Average expectation of life falls to about 34 years (1650—1700).
2. Political Life	
Central government strengthened and occasional local uprisings curbed with a firm hand.	A series of disruptions: Civil War 1642—46 Execution of Charles I 1649 Interregnum 1649—60
Political influence of the clergy eliminated by the Reformation.	Restoration of the Stuarts 1660 Glorious Revolution 1688
Decline in the influence of the great lords.	Increase in the influence of the merchant
Popular Tudor monarchs.	community in English politics.
3. Economy	
Agricultural society: peasant farming.	Agricultural society: commercial farming with improved productivity.
Diversification of economic activity: in addition to traditional manufacturers, new industries and methods of production introduced.	Diversification continues both within the established industries and with the introduction of and increase in consumer goods industries.
High inflation favours the upper ranks and disfavours wage earners: polarisation of society.	Inflation and polarisation continue until the 1660s. General economic progress means welfare for all except the poor.
Dissolution of the monasteries means far-reaching changes in land-ownership.	
Preponderantly regional economies striving for self-sufficiency.	Integrated national economy emerging. Improved communication networks.
Peripheral country in international trade.	Central position in international trade. London's role crucial.

4. Social Order

Society highly stratified and hierarchical, with the main difference between gentleman and non-gentleman. Landownership forms the basis for the position and wealth of the gentry.

Social mobility: upwards via the professions, marriage or acquisition of land; downwards via general impoverishment or the position of a younger son.

Inflation of honours and multiplication of the gentry by 1640. Consolidation of the middle ranks. Upward social mobility declines from the 1640s onwards. Closing of the ranks.

5. Family and Kinship

Nuclear family with paternal authority.

Different marriage patterns in different social groups: the upper ranks marry younger and their marriages are often arranged, the lower ranks marry later and have a freer choice.

Marriages preferred between people of equal status.

More intermarriage between the gentry and professional people.

Upper ranks have larger families.

The importance of kinship ties outside the nuclear family varies: kinship often used as a basis for economic and other assistance, patronage etc. Kinship links break social boundaries.

6. Culture

Reformation and the establishment of the Church of England.

Catholic threat and Puritan opposition.

At first largely medieval cultural patterns. From court culture to a widening cultural market.

Dawning of the Augustan age of enlightenment. 'Popular' culture established.

Increase in educational opportunities on all levels. Enjoyed by higher ranks and upper levels of the middling sort.

Interest in higher education decreases from 1650 onwards.

Illiteracy a characteristic of the vast majority of the common people in England. An oral society.

Illiteracy slowly becomes a special characteristic of the poor. A semi-literate society.

English accepted as the national language suitable for most purposes.

English accepted even as the language of science.

Widening world views and heightened role of national identity towards the end of the century.

Continued widening of world views both by new explorations and scientific discoveries.

might ask for instance whether the extremely rapid diffusion of *its* between 1640 and 1660 (Nevalainen — Raumolin-Brunberg 1994) could be related to the unstable times of the Civil War and Interregnum. In addition, could we possibly connect the breakthrough of Northern forms, such as *are* or the third person suffix -*s*, to historically well-attested migration from north to south (Nevalainen — Raumolin-Brunberg 1989: 84)?

The second principle to be discussed is a more traditional one, viz. prestige. While Jespersen (e. g. 1922: 292) and other philologists spoke about imitation of the language of one's betters, modern sociolinguists have taught us that there is both overt and covert prestige (e. g. Trudgill 1983: 172 — 185). Both patterns can be characterised as adoption of linguistic forms from people with whom the language users wish to identify themselves.

One major development in England between 1540 and 1640 that can be related to questions of overt prestige was the extensive social mobility from the middle ranks to the gentry (see Social Order in Table 1). No doubt during a period like this, people can be expected to imitate the language of their betters. The illiteracy of the lower and even middle ranks makes it impossible to attest such linguistic stratification patterns as present-day sociolinguists have done, and it is not easy to relate our changes to prestige. It seems, however, that the *wh*-relatives could illustrate the development (Dekeyser 1984).

The patterns found in modern sociolinguistics come from spoken language, the mode which even today is the least standardised and standardisable of all (Milroy — Milroy 1985 a: 88 — 89). In our discussion based on written material, we cannot neglect the role of standardisation, a phenomenon that in fact operates against proliferation and natural changes. While its impact did not reach all private and nondocumentary writing in our first subperiod, during the Restoration it was more extensively implemented. The option-cutting among the strong verb forms in Lass' study (1994) serves as a good example of standardisation. Stein's argument (1987) that the adoption of third person -*s* in printed texts exhibited a rapid catching up with the spoken mode is a very interesting viewpoint, as it indirectly points to the openness of the emerging standard to spoken usage and different varieties. It seems that our material also contains linguistic phenomena that never found a place in standardised formal registers, namely the generic-deictic *your* (Wales 1985).

4. Conclusion

So far, Early Modern English, like most periods in language history, has either been studied as a whole or mainly from a language-internal point of view. The aim of the present article is to suggest, however, that social factors, indirect and complex though they are, should be taken into consideration, since they may provide important complementary evidence.

Note

* This paper was originally presented at the Inaugural Conference of the European Society for the Study of English (ESSE), Norwich 1991, in a section organised by the editor of this volume. Since the planned conference volume unfortunately did not materialise, I am very happy that the authors agreed to have their paper included in this volume, providing a useful summary of Early Modern English studies based on the *Helsinki Corpus* together with a lot of relevant background information taken for granted in most of the other contributions (D. K.).

References

Altenberg, Bengt
    1982   *The genitive versus the* of-*construction. A study of syntactic variation in the 17th century English.* Lund: Gleerup.
Dekeyser, Xavier
    1984   "Relativizers in Early Modern English: A dynamic quantitative study", in: Jacek Fisiak (ed.), *Historical syntax.* Berlin: Mouton de Gruyter, 61–87.
Ellegård, Alvar
    1953   *The auxiliary* do: *the establishment and regulation of its use in English.* Stockholm: Almqvist & Wiksell.
Finkenstaedt, Thomas – Ernst Leisi – Dieter Wolff (comps.)
    1970   *A chronological English dictionary.* Heidelberg: Winter.
Houston, Anne
    1989   "The English gerund: syntactic change and discourse function", in: Ralph Fasold – Deborah Schiffrin (eds.), *Language change and variation.* Amsterdam: Benjamins, 173–196.
Jespersen, Otto
    1922   *Language, its nature, development and origin.* London: Allen & Unwin.
Kemp, William
    1979   "On that that that *that* became which which became what", in: P. Clyne *et. al.* (eds.), *Papers from the Fifteenth Regional Meeting of the Chicago Linguistic Society.* Chicago: Chicago Linguistic Society, 185–196.
Kytö, Merja
    1991   *Variation and diachrony, with Early American English in focus: studies on* CAN/MAY *and* SHALL/WILL. Frankfurt/M.: Lang.
Kytö, Merja (comp.).
    1993   *Manual to the diachronic part of the Helsinki Corpus of English Texts. Coding conventions and list of source texts.* (Second edition.) Helsinki: Department of English.
Lass, Roger
    1994   "Proliferation and option cutting: the strong verb in the fifteenth to eighteenth centuries", in: Dieter Stein – Ingrid Tieken-Boon van Ostade (eds.), *Towards a Standard English 1600–1800.* Berlin: Mouton de Gruyter, 81–113.
Milroy, James
    1992   *Linguistic variation and change.* Oxford: Blackwell.

Milroy, James — Leslie Milroy
1985 a   *Authority in language.* London: Routledge & Kegan Paul.
1985 b   "Linguistic change, social network and speaker innovation", *Journal of Linguistics* 21: 339 — 384.
Nevalainen, Terttu
1987   "Change from above: a morphosyntactic comparison of two Early Modern English editions of *The Book of Common Prayer*", in: Leena Kahlas-Tarkka (ed.), *Neophilologica Fennica.* Helsinki: Société Néophilologique, 295 — 315.
1991   BUT, ONLY, JUST: *focusing adverbial change in Modern English 1500 — 1900.* (Mémoires de la Société Néophilologique de Helsinki 51.) Helsinki: Société Néophilologique.
forthcoming   "Early Modern English lexis and semantics", in: Roger Lass (ed.), *Cambridge history of the English language.* Vol. 3. *Early Modern English.* Cambridge: Cambridge University Press.
Nevalainen, Terttu — Helena Raumolin-Brunberg
1989   "A corpus of Early Modern Standard English in a socio-historical perspective", *Neuphilologische Mitteilungen* 90: 67 — 110.
1994   "*Its* strength and the beauty *of it*: The standardisation of the third person neuter possessive in Early Modern English", in: Dieter Stein — Ingrid Tieken-Boon von Ostade (eds.), *Towards a Standard English 1600 — 1800.* Berlin: Mouton de Gruyter, 171 — 216.
Raumolin-Brunberg, Helena
1993   "Development of the compound pronouns in *-body* and *-one*". This volume, 301 — 324.
Rissanen, Matti
1989   "The conjunction *for* in Early Modern English", *NOWELE* 14: 3 — 18.
1991   "Spoken language and the history of *do*-periphrasis", in: Dieter Kastovsky (ed.), *Historical English syntax.* Berlin: Mouton de Gruyter, 321 — 342.
Rissanen, Matti — Merja Kytö — Minna Palander-Collin (eds.)
1993   *Early English in the computer age: Explorations through the Helsinki Corpus.* Berlin: Mouton de Gruyter.
Romaine, Suzanne
1982   *Socio-historical linguistics: Its status and methodology.* Cambridge: Cambridge University Press.
Stein, Dieter
1987   "At the crossroads of philology, linguistics and semiotics: Notes on the replacement of *th* by *s* in the third person singular in English", *English Studies* 68: 406 — 431.
Trudgill, Peter
1983   *On dialect.* Oxford: Blackwell.
Wales, Katie
1985   "Generic 'your' and Jacobean drama: The rise and fall of a pronominal usage", *English Studies* 66: 7 — 24.

The position of *not* in Early Modern English questions

Matti Rissanen

1. Introduction

Late Middle and Early Modern English negative questions had the same alternatives for word-order as Present-day English. These alternatives are illustrated by (1 a) and (1 b), taken from Quirk *et al.* (1985: 11.7), and by (2 a) and (2 b) taken from a mid-sixteenth-century law court record:

(1)   a. Didn't they *warn you*?

       b. Did they not *warn you*?

(2)   a. *But because the wordes be not sore strayned against me, I praye you, Maister Atturney, why* might not I *haue tolde Maister Arnolde, that John Fitzwilliams was angrie with William Thomas, and yet knowe no cause of the Anger?* (*Trial of Throckmorton* 71 C 1)

       b. *Why* shulde hee not *bee suffered to tell Truthe?* (*Trial of Throckmorton* 70 C 2)

In (1 a) and (2 a), *not* is placed before the subject; in (1 b) and (2 b), after the subject pronoun.

In Present-day English questions, the verb preceding the negative particle is always an auxiliary or the copula *be*, or at least in theory, *have* indicating possession. As will be shown below, this is also the case in Early Modern English, with few exceptions. Furthermore, in Present-day English, the pre-subject *not* is almost always contracted and cliticised, as in (1 a). According to Quirk *et al.* (1985: 11.7), however, some speakers accept the construction, rather formal, in which the non-contracted *not* is placed between the verb and the subject:

(3)   Is not history *a social science*?

The cliticisation and the pre-subject position of the negative particle in questions seems to be characteristic of English alone amongst the Germanic languages.

In this paper I shall discuss the varying order of *not* and the personal pronoun subject in interrogative clauses in Early Modern English texts. I shall suggest, tentatively, that the gradual increase in the frequency of the order V/Aux + *not* + personal pronoun subject may be connected with the development of negative cliticisation, i. e. the forms *cannot, don't, shan't*, etc.

The study of the history of interrogative constructions, particularly the negative ones, is problematic because questions are more typical of spoken language than of (most types of) writing. For this reason, it is not easy to find sufficient evidence of negative questions in corpora of written texts. I have collected my Early Modern English examples from the *Helsinki Corpus of English Texts* by scanning all the occurrences of *not* and its enclitic forms.[1]

2. Word-order variants in negative questions in Early Modern English

Table 1 shows the number of occurrences of the word-order variants in the first Early Modern subperiod (1500 — 1570) in the *Helsinki Corpus.* The overwhelmingly dominant factor determining the order of the subject and *not* is the quality of the subject.

Table 1. The position of *not* in negative questions in the subperiod E 1 (1500 — 1570) in the *Helsinki Corpus* (N. b. 'Aux' also refers to the copula *be* and the possessive *have*.)

Subject	Aux + *not* + subj	Aux + subj + *not*	V + *not* + subj	V + subj + *not*
there	0	3	0	0
pers pr	18	42	1	16
Other pr	7	0	0	0
Noun	15	0	1	0

If the subject is a noun or a demonstrative or indefinite pronoun, *not* precedes the subject (examples [4]—[6]); if it is a personal pronoun, its position is variable.[2]

(4)   Dyd not christ *lykewyse ascend vnto his father vnto the grete mounte of heuen*? (Fisher 317)

(5)   *That is to saye: maye a man knowe a mans thought, as men may knowe the complexion or outward condicions of the bodye? Certes is not this lyke a myracle vnto a man that knowethe not, whye that swete thynges* ... (Boethius, Colville 109)

(6)   *... vseth hym sylfe verye honestlye: and* was not this *a good acte* (Harman 73)

There are no exceptions to the *not* + noun subject rule in the *Helsinki Corpus* material. The oldest instances of this order can be found in Chaucer and Wyclif, i. e. as soon as the unstressed particle *ne* could be deleted in negations (example [7]), and it predominates with the subject types mentioned above as early as the fifteenth century:

(7)   *Lord! why ordeyned* not God *suche ordre in þe olde lawe* (Wyclif, *Sermons* 32 358)

When the subject is a personal pronoun, it precedes *not* in the majority of the examples, both with auxiliary operators (42 instances as against 18 in Table 1), and, particularly, with finite full verbs (16 as against 1). In her study of the structures in Shakespeare's colloquial language Vivian Salmon (1966: 128 − 9) arrives at exactly the same results; it is of interest that this distribution is obvious even one or two generations before Shakespeare.

Why, then, does the noun subject regularly follow *not* in Early Modern English texts while the personal pronoun subject most often precedes it? The simplest and most obvious answer is that noun subjects are phonetically heavier than pronominal ones, and that the end weight principle determines the relative order of the negative particle and the subject. This may be one factor affecting the word-order but certainly not the whole truth. It seems that the information focus of the negation also plays an important role in the position of the subject in relation to the negative particle. The main semantic/referential difference between noun subjects and personal pronoun subjects is that while the latter generally have given referents, the former often, though of course not always, contain new information. Noun subjects are thus more likely to be included in the focus of the negation and/or interrogation than personal pronoun subjects. Even if a noun is used for a given referent, there is often a new angle or point of view in the referent to be emphasised, or some other reason to bring it into focus. This distinction gains in relevance in questions, where the position of the subject is post-verbal, i. e. typical of new information. Example (8) may illustrate my point:

(8)   *It is the power of God whereby the faithfull haue subdued kingdomes, wrought righteousnesse, obtained the promises, stopped the mouthes of Lions, quenched the violence of fire, escaped the edge of the sword: But take away their faith, and*

> *doth* not their strength *forsake them? are* they not *like vnto other men?* (Hooker 44)

Their strength indicates new information and is obviously part of the focus of the negation and interrogation. *They* in the next sentence represents a known discourse topic and is outside the focus. We could say that both clauses represent the natural order of a negative question. It is obvious that the order of the elements is also linked with stress and emphasis, but in a subtler way than simply through the phonetic length of the items.

This approach to the word-order would also explain why other pronouns than the personal ones share the order of noun subjects. The demonstrative pronoun *this*, for instance, puts the subject in focus, and thus it is easy to understand that it follows the same word-order pattern as noun subjects do (see examples [5] and [6] above). It is also understandable why existential *there* is always placed before the negative particle both in the *Helsinki Corpus* and in Salmon's corpus of colloquial Shakespearean English:

(9)   *The Kynge hath a greate meanye of wardes and I trowe there is a courte of wardes, why is there not a schole for the wardes as well as there is a courte for their landes?* (Latimer 28)

Existential *there* can hardly be part of the focus of the negation or the interrogation; therefore its natural position is before *not.*

3. The order V/Aux + *not* + personal pronoun subject as evidence of negative cliticisation

As mentioned above, and as shown by Table 1, there are many instances in the early sixteenth century subsection of the *Helsinki Corpus* with the personal pronoun following *not*, against the general rule. The most obvious reason for this is that the subject is part of the focus of the negative question, as in (10). This is also the natural order when the pronoun is followed by postmodifying elements (11):

(10)   *Iesus answered them: Have* not I *chosen you twelve, and yet one of you is the devyll?* (Tyndale, *Gosp. of John* 6 70)

(11)   *Why doe* not you of the Queenes learned Counsell *aunswere him?* (Trial of Throckmorton 72 C 2)

In (11) the postmodifying phrase does not only make the subject longer and more emphatic, it also places it in focus ('*You* should answer him because *you* are members of the Council').

In many of the nineteen instances in the 1500 — 1570 subsection of the *Helsinki Corpus*, the order *not* + personal pronoun subject can be explained by one or the other of these two factors. But there are instances in which it is difficult to see any particular reason for this order:

(12)   "*Mr. Holcroffet, howe have yow handlyd yourselfe yn your offyse? dyd* not I *send unto yow one Mowntayne that was both a traytor and a herytyke, to thys ende that he shulde have sufferyd deathe?* (Mowntayne 210)

(13)   Tib Talk. *And een as well knitte my nowne Annot Alyface.*
          R. Royster. *See what a sort she kepeth that must be my wife. Shall* not I *when I haue hir, leade a merrie life;* (Udall 263)

(14)   M. Mery. *Looke partly towarde hir, and drawe a little nere.*
          C. Custance. *Get ye home idle folkes.*
          M. M. *Why may* not we *be here; Nay and ye will haze, haze: otherwise I tell you plaine, And ye will not haze, then giue vs our geare againe.* (Udall 1043)

(15)   Diccon. *Yea mary sir, thus much I can say wel, the nedle is lost,*
          Bayly. *Nay canst* not thou *tel which way, that nedle may be found*
          Diccon. *No by my fay sir, though I might haue an hundred pound.* (Stevenson 66)

The central question asked in this paper is whether these examples and others like them might be taken as evidence of the early stages of the weakening and cliticisation of the negative particle. Jespersen (1917: 117) suggests that the contracted forms of *not* came into use in speech around 1600; not surprisingly, he bases his statement on evidence derived from Shakespeare. Later scholars have accepted Jespersen's dating without further discussion. In spellings (*-nt, -n't*), contraction and cliticisation can be seen in the second half of the seventeenth century, particularly in Restoration comedies.

If my assumption is correct, the beginnings of the development of negative cliticisation could be dated almost a century earlier, in the first half of the sixteenth century.[3] The evidence yielded by the *Helsinki Corpus* is, of course, far from conclusive and, at best, points to a trend which must be verified by a more extensive survey of available text material.[4]

It might be possible to try to determine the amount of stress and the degree of cliticisation of *not* through the stress patterns of early sixteenth-century comedies, such as *Gammer Gurton's Needle* or *Roister Doister.* Yet, as can be seen from examples (13)−(15), the metre of these plays, in their written form, is so irregular that no valid conclusions can be based on it. In these instances, scanning both with the full form of *not* and with the enclitic form would be possible.

Another way to form hypotheses on the possible cliticisation of *not* is to check spellings which combine the negative particle with the preceding operator. As mentioned above, the earliest recorded spellings of the reduced forms *-nt* or *-n't* appear in the second half of the seventeenth century. It is worth asking, however, whether the frequent spelling of *cannot* as one word in sixteenth-century texts might not be regarded as evidence of the weakening of *not.* This kind of evidence is of course shaky, but not altogether insignificant. There must be some explanation for the fact that, for instance, in a sample from Tyndale's *New Testament*[5] there are 22 instances of *cannot* spelt as one word and only four of *can not.* It is also worth pointing out that Tyndale (or his printer) is fond of compounding words spuriously, but this combining does seem to follow a certain logic: two stressed words are never coupled; the combination is always with at least one weakly stressed element. Combining *be* with the preceding *shall* to form *shalbe* is particularly common, and the indefinite article is often linked with the following noun.

If there is a connection between the contraction and cliticisation of *not* and the appearance of the order V/Aux. + *not* + personal pronoun subject, this word-order should show a clear increase in the course of the seventeenth century, with the growing popularity of negative cliticisation. Table 2 shows the frequencies of the two orders with pronominal subjects in the Early Modern English subsections in the *Helsinki Corpus* (E 1−3). Only instances with an auxiliary operator or *be/have* have been included.

Table 2. The position of *not* in negative questions in Early Modern English (Aux/*be*/*have* + *not* + pers. pron. subjects only)

	Aux/*be*/*have* + *not* + subj.	Aux/*be*/*have* + subj. + *not*
E 1 (1500−1570)	18	42
E 2 (1570−1640)	12[1]	44
E 3 (1640−1710)	34[2]	16

1. Including two instances of *cannot.*
2. Including two instances of *cannot* and four of *can't.*

As can be seen in Table 2, the order *not* + personal pronoun subject is rare in the first part of the seventeenth century; in fact, there are fewer instances than in E 1.[6] But in 1640 − 1700, in the period when contracted and enclitic forms can be seen even in print, the frequency of pre-subject *not* increases dramatically.

It is possible that the proportional increase of the order *not* + pronominal subject was supported by the analogy of *not* + noun subject. However, this can hardly be the main factor causing the development described above as noun subjects are much less frequent than personal pronoun subjects in negative questions (cf. the figures in Table 1).

Table 1 also shows that the order *not* + personal pronoun subject is tied up with an auxiliary or copula even in a period in which *not* could follow a full verb. There is only one exception to this rule in the *Helsinki Corpus*:

(16)   Saye not ye: *there are yet foure monethes, and then commeth harvest?* (Tyndale *Gosp. of John* 4 25)

This factor seems to support the hypothesis of the connection between word-order and early cliticisation: in general, clitics appear less naturally with full verbs than with auxiliaries or the copula.

4. Cliticisation and the development of *do*-periphrasis

What more general consequences, then, could the early dating of the weakening and cliticisation of *not* have for our views of the development of English in the Early Modern period? One possible suggestion is that we may here have one more factor relevant to the discussion of the many-faceted history of *do*-periphrasis. If, as Jespersen and the scholars following him suggest, negative cliticisation emerged in speech around 1600, this phenomenon would have been too late to have had much effect on the development of *do* in negative sentences. But the situation is different if we assume that the weakening trend of *not* was already well under way in the first half of the sixteenth century. As mentioned above, enclitic forms are typical of auxiliaries − the weakened forms of *not* were probably never appended to full verbs. Thus in the sixteenth century we may have had two alternatives for negative sentences with an auxiliary operator, one with an emphatic negative *not* and one with a reduced form, perhaps something like *canət, sha(l)nət, mus(t)nət, isnət,* etc. But if there was no auxiliary in the sentence, only the stressed negative was available: *think not, understand not.* The introduction of *do*-periphrasis would create the choice of two alternative expressions even in these cases. This line of reasoning would also offer an answer to the question of why *do*-periphrasis was not established with other negative particles, such as *never*: it was only *not* that tended to be cliticised. The weakening and cliticisation of *not* was certainly not the only factor contributing to the rise of periphrastic *do* in negative sentences, but it may have been one worth serious consideration.

5. Concluding remarks

Although the available evidence is much too scanty for reliable results, it is not unlikely that the contraction and cliticisation process of *not* began as early as the sixteenth century — or even earlier, soon after the loss of *ne*. As contraction is typically a spoken-language development, it is slow to make itself apparent in written language, but it leaves a decipherable imprint in the word-order of negative questions much earlier than can be seen in actual spellings, with the possible exception of the spelling *cannot*. If this is true, we might here have an example of the way in which tracing the development of spoken structures of the past is comparable to the work of an astronomer who tries to locate an invisible star on the basis of the irregularities its gravity field causes in the movements of surrounding visible stars.

Notes

1. The instances in which the inversion occurs in non-interrogative negative statements, e. g. in

    his reputation was at last run so low that he could not have held much longer,
    had not he *died in good time,*

    are not included in the present discussion. The number of these instances is low and does not affect the overall figures of distribution. For information on the *Helsinki Corpus,* see Kytö (1991); Kytö — Rissanen (1992); Rissanen *et al.* (1993). The Early Modern English part of the *Corpus* is introduced in Nevalainen — Raumolin-Brunberg (1989).
2. The type of the interrogative clause does not seem to affect the distribution of the two orders; cf. Salmon (1966: 129).
3. There are isolated instances of the order *not* + personal pronoun subject in the *Helsinki Corpus* texts dating from the second half of the fifteenth century. It seems, however, that in the few instances of this order there are always special reasons for the post-

ponement of the subject: mostly, it forms part of the focus of the negation or interrogation, as in

> *A, Lord, maydenys dawnsyn now meryly in Heuyn. Xal* not I *don so*? (Margery Kempe 50)

The small number of the late Middle English instances is mainly due to the low amount of dialogue in the genres represented by the Middle English samples of the corpus.
4. This will probably be the role played by the *Helsinki Corpus* in the diachronic study of many other structural features of English as well.
5. The Preface and the Gospels of St. Matthew and St. John, printed in 1534.
6. That the word order was in a state of flux in this period is further indicated by the fact that the quarto and folio editions of Shakespeare often give different readings (Jespersen 1917: 117).

Primary sources

Boethius, Colville = Colville, George
  1897   *Boethius' Consolation of Philosophy, translated from the Latin by George Colville, 1556.* (The Tudor Library 5.), edited by E. B. Bax. London: David Nutt.
Fisher = Fisher, John
  1935   *The English works of John Fisher, Bishop of Rochester.* Part I. (Early English
  [1876]   Text Society E. S. 27.), edited by John E. B. Mayor. London.
Harman = Harman, Thomas
  1937   *A caveat or warening for common cursetors vulgarely called vagabones.* [From
  [1869,   the 3rd edition of 1567 ... Collated with the 2nd edition of 1567 in the
  1898]   Bodleian Library, Oxford, and with the reprint of the 4th edition of 1573.]
            (Early English Text Society E. S. 9.), edited by Edward Viles — Frederick J. Furnivall. London.
Hooker = Hooker, Richard
  1969   *Two sermons upon part of S. Judes Epistle, 1614.* (The English Experience 195.) Amsterdam — New York: Theatrvm Orbis Terrarvm Ltd. — Da Capo Press. [Facsimile.]
Kempe, Margery
  1940   *The book of Margery Kempe.* Vol. I. (Early English Text Society 212.), edited by Sanford Brown Meech — Hope Emily Allen. London.
Latimer = Latimer, Hugh
  1868,   *Sermon on the ploughers, 18 January 1549; Seven sermons before Edward VI,*
  1869   *on each Friday in Lent, 1549.* (English Reprints.), edited by Edward Arber. London: Alex. Murray & Son.
Mowntayne = Mowntayne, Thomas
  1859   *Narratives of the days of the Reformation, chiefly from the manuscripts of John Foxe the martyrologist.* (Camden Society 77), edited by John Gough Nichols. London.
Trial of Throckmorton
  1730   *A complete collection of state-trials and proceedings for high-treason, and other crimes and misdemeanours; from the reign of King Richard II. To the end of the reign of King George I.* (Second edition.) Vol. I. Edited by Francis Hargrave. London: Printed for J. Walthoe Sen.

Tyndale, Gospel of St. John = Tyndale, William
  1938   *The New Testament. Translated by William Tyndale, 1534.* Edited by N. Hardy
            Wallis, with an introduction by Isaac Foot. Cambridge: Cambridge University
            Press.
Stevenson = Stevenson, William
  1920   *Gammar Gvrtons Nedle.* [By Mr. S. Mr. of Art.] (The Percy Reprints 2.),
            edited by H. F. B. Brett-Smith. Oxford: Basil Blackwell.
Udall = Udall, Nicholas
  1934   *Roister Doister.* (The Malone Society Reprints.) London: John John-
  [1935]   son – Oxford University Press. [Facsimile.]
Wyclif, Sermons = Wyclif, John
  1983   *English Wycliffite sermons.* Vol. I. Edited by Anne Hudson. Oxford: Claren-
            don Press.

References

Jespersen, Otto
  1917   *Negation in English and other languages.* (De Kgl. Danske Videnskabernes
            Selskab. Historisk-filologiske Meddelelser I 5). Copenhagen.
Kytö, Merja
  1991   *Manual to the diachronic part of the Helsinki Corpus of English Texts: Coding
            conventions and lists of source texts.* Helsinki: Department of English, Uni-
            versity of Helsinki.
Kytö, Merja – Matti Rissanen
  1992   "A language in transition: *The Helsinki Corpus of English Texts*", *ICAME
            Journal* 16: 7 – 27.
Nevalainen, Terttu – Helena Raumolin-Brunberg
  1989   "A corpus of Early Modern Standard English in a socio-historical perspec-
            tive", *Neuphilologische Mitteilungen* 90: 67 – 111.
Quirk, Randolph – Sidney Greenbaum – Geoffrey Leech – Jan Svartvik
  1985   *A comprehensive grammar of the English language.* London: Longman.
Rissanen, Matti – Merja Kytö – Minna Palander-Collin (eds.)
  1993   *Early English in the computer age: Explorations through the Helsinki Corpus.*
            Berlin: Mouton de Gruyter.
Salmon, Vivian
  1966   "Sentence structures in colloquial Shakespearean English". *Transactions of
            the Philological Society 1965.* Oxford: Basil Blackwell, 105 – 140.

William Turner and the English plant names

Mats Rydén

1. Introduction

Oscar Wilde once wrote: "The truth is rarely pure, and never simple."
This is, in the context of man as scholar and scientist, more true of the
sixteenth century than of most others. The sixteenth century is, by
definition, as part of the Renaissance, a pioneering period. It is the first
post-medieval century — a century of reconsiderations, revivals and new
vistas.

The sixteenth century was a time of fresh approaches and of fresh
systemic thinking. In terms of natural history, encyclopedias, which were
usually uncritical compilations, herbals, plant glossaries or vocabularies
and bestiaries were being replaced by descriptions based on first-hand
observation and on a critical attitude to authority, ancient and contemporary. It was a time when it was being realised, and made public in
print, that the concept of "scientific truth" is somewhat fuzzy or, to quote
Wilde again, that "The truth is rarely pure, and never simple."

The sixteenth century was also a time when language, as an overarching
literary national medium, was coming to the fore; it was a time of a
rising consciousness of the innate resources of the mother tongues and,
at the same time, of the necessity of an international outlook.

All this also applies to England as it developed in the sixteenth century
— in terms of humanistic as well as scientific scholarship, though a
separation of the two would have surprised the Tudor scholar. It was in
those days still possible for one man to master many disciplines. Specialisation was for the distant future.

In this England the true pioneer of natural history was William Turner
— theologian, physician, herbalist, botanist, ornithologist, philologist
and linguist. He was a man of national conscience and international
repute.

This paper, which is an interim report, will be devoted to William
Turner's achievements as linguist and naturalist.

---

2. Life and works

The intellectual England of William Turner was a land of revived humanism, i. e. of a revived interest in the classical texts as sources and resources, of religious turmoils and of an academic discussion of the English language as a scholarly medium, including the well-known controversy about "ink-horn terms".

The intellectual life of William Turner was characterised by a continuous search for scientific and linguistic accuracy, for the proper word in the proper context. His profession was that of a doctor, his religious belief was that of a resolute, not to say belligerent Protestant, but his passion was the discovery and the correct description and naming of the living particulars of Nature, the living world around us.

Turner was born at Morpeth, Northumberland, around 1510 and he died in London in 1568 (he is buried in St. Olave's Church, Hart Street, where there is a plaque commemorating him; the church is better known as the church of Samuel Pepys).

As appears from his books, even as a young boy he observed plants and birds in his native surroundings. Otherwise little is known about his early years. He came to Cambridge in the mid-1520s and at Pembroke Hall (College) he studied medicine, theology and Greek ("Physik and Philosophy" as he himself characterises his subjects in the terminology of the day). Among his teachers were Hugh Latimer and Nicholas Ridley (both were burnt at the stake at Oxford in 1555). The latter is also said to have taught Turner tennis and archery, a sport to be immortalised by Roger Ascham, another Cambridge man, in his *Toxophilus* of 1545.

Turner became an ardent and uncompromising Protestant and was forced into exile twice, in 1540 and in 1553. He spent twelve years in all on the Continent, years which were to be of crucial importance for his development as a naturalist. He travelled extensively — it is at least partially possible to follow his itineraries from references to places in his works (cf. Stearn 1965: 7–8). He met some of the most influential botanists and naturalists of the day, among others Luca Ghini, professor at Bologna, Leonhart Fuchs, the famous author of a herbal (*De historia stirpium* 1542) and, above all, Conrad Gessner, the Swiss scholar and scientist, the leading European naturalist of his day, with whom Turner formed a close friendship. Turner obtained an M. D. at either Bologna or Ferrara. The woodcuts from Fuchs's herbal were to be used by Turner in his herbal of 1551–1568 (cf. below).

As mentioned above, Turner travelled widely on the Continent, in Italy, Switzerland and Germany. He also visited Groningen, Louvain and Antwerp. He spent four years in "East Friesland", where he practised as a doctor at Emden (as physician to the Earl of Emden).

In 1544, in Cologne, he published his little book on birds, entitled *Avium praecipuarum ... brevis & succincta historia*. It is the first book written by an Englishman solely devoted to birds. It contains a list of birds as mentioned by Pliny and Aristotle, with commentaries on them and their names by Turner. It adds interestingly to the contemporary knowledge of British and European birds and to the names of birds of the time.[1]

In the preface, Turner says that "I will shortly, God willing, bring to the light of day a further edition of this little book with figures of the birds, their habits, and curative properties" (Evans 1903). In the *Peratio ad lectorem* he asks the reader for help with information for this new edition, which, however, was never published.

After returning to England, on the death of Henry VIII in 1547, Turner became physician to the Lord Protector, the Duke of Somerset, at Syon House, Isleworth. At Syon House he met William Cecil, later Lord Burghley, and the young Princess Elizabeth, with whom he conversed in Latin. While at Syon House Turner published, in 1548, his remarkable book *The Names of Herbes*, about which more will be said in this paper.

Between 1547 and 1552 Turner was a Member of Parliament and in 1551 he was appointed Dean of Wells in Somerset. In the same year he published the first part of his great herbal, which eleven and seventeen years later was to be followed by its second and third parts, including a book on "baths", i.e. spas in England and on the Continent, and a book on wines, in particular the medicinal properties of wines. Turner preferred "Rhennish and other small white wines". He was aware of the twofold effects of wine: "it maketh men merie, and to haue a good hope ... But wine if it be vsed out of measure, ouerthroweth and drowneth the liuely soundnesse and strength".

When Mary Tudor came to the throne in 1553 Turner again had to flee to the Continent. During this second exile, in 1557, he sent a letter to Conrad Gessner from Weissenburg on fishes and their names, which Gessner published in his *Historia animalium* the following year. It was edited and translated into English in *Archives of Natural History* of 1986.[2] As appears from the preface to the 1568 edition of his herbal, Turner considered a book on fishes: "I extend to set out a Booke of the names

and natures of fishes that are within youre Mayesties dominions." The
book was never completed.

Turner returned from his second exile in 1558, when Elizabeth became
Queen of England. He was reinstated as Dean of Wells, but he had to
relinquish that post in the mid-1560s due to controversies about clerical
clothing and ritual. He is said to have loathed even organ music.

His final years were spent in London. He had three children. His son,
Peter, was also a botanist (and a Puritan). His grandson rose to be
Professor of Geometry at Oxford. Turner's widow married Richard Cox,
later Bishop of Ely, and founded a scholarship at Cambridge in memory
of her first husband.

Throughout his life Turner wrote books and articles on religious
matters against the Catholic Church (his first book was published in
1534). He was a prolific writer, but his works were prohibited in 1547
and 1555 by "Royal Proclamation" and there are on the whole few
surviving copies. His principal adversary was Stephen Gardiner, Bishop
of Winchester and finally Lord Chancellor under Queen Mary (whom he
crowned).

3. Turner in his international and national context

As already implied, William Turner was a contemporary or near-contemporary of the renowned German fathers of botany: Bock, Brunfels, Fuchs
and Valerius Cordus. He was also a contemporary or near-contemporary
of leading naturalists like the Italians Luca Ghini (his teacher at Bologna
and one of the instigators of the herbarium or "hortus siccus"), Andrea
Cesalpino and Pier Andrea Mattioli, Jean Ruel, the Frenchman, Conrad
Gessner, the Swiss intellectual giant, and the Flemish botanists Rembert
Dodoens and Matthias de l'Obel (who spent many years in England,
where he became Botanist to James I). Most of these men were not only
naturalists in the traditional sense but also pioneers in the field of
systematic botany.

At the time when Turner came to Cambridge, in the mid-1520s, the
first two printed English herbals were published: Banckes's *Herbal* of
1525 (Banckes was the printer of the book) and *The Grete Herball* of
1526, the first English illustrated printed book on plants. Both are
medieval in character. *The Grete Herball* is essentially based on the French
work *Le grant herbier*, first printed around 1500.[3] The two herbals became

very popular, to judge from the many editions they went through in the course of the century.

As a student at Cambridge, Turner was not satisfied with the study of natural history in his day. In the preface to the 1568 edition of his herbal Turner states that at Cambridge he "could learne neuer one Greke/nether Latin/nor English name/euen amongest the Phisiciones of anye herbe or tre/suche was the ignorance in simples at that tyme/and as yet there was no Englishe Herbal but one [i. e. *The Grete Herball*]/ al full of vnlearned cacographees and falselye naming of herbes/and as then had nether Fuchsius/nether Matthiolus/nether Tragus written of herbes in Latin."

But, not doubt, there were many learned doctors of medicine at this time in England, which Turner also admits and gratefully acknowledges in his various prefaces. In his *Libellus de re herbaria novus* of 1538 he says that "I am unworthy to act as a bottle-washer to the most learned Doctor Clement. And I readily give place to many other most learned men." But he regrets that these men had not published anything in order to teach their fellow Englishmen.

Turner was however essentially right: natural history in early sixteenth century England was on the whole medieval. When Turner published his first book on natural history in 1538, the *Libellus de re herbaria novus*, this was really something new.

In the context of the second half of the sixteenth century in England, Turner was not a lone wolf of a naturalist. Names like John Gerard, Henry Lyte, Thomas Penny, John Caius and Edward Topsell come to mind, as do pharmacists and gardeners such as Hugh Morgan and John Rich. And in the Elizabethan era a number of minor herbals and garden books appeared. Today the best known of the men mentioned above is perhaps John Gerard, botanist and barber-surgeon, who published his famous — in certain respects also ill-reputed — herbal in 1597. Gerard had a garden in Holborn (between what is now Chancery Lane and Fetter Lane), where he grew some 1000 "species", native and foreign, of which he published a catalogue in 1596 and 1599, the first of its kind in England.[4] This garden was situated near St. Andrew's Church, where he was buried in 1612.

In the latter half of the sixteenth century and in the seventeenth century botany and zoology gradually emerged as separate sciences. This also included the rise of field botany and field zoology. The new interest in plants and animals for their own sake, not just as part of medicine and folklore, was crucially combined with a reawakened interest in the "correct" naming of plants and animals, which in turn necessitated a reassessment of the ancient authorities. In other words, the new situation required an amalgam of natural science and textual study. Sixteenth-century naturalists in Western Europe were not only naturalists — they were humanist-naturalists or, more precisely, naturalist-philologists. William Turner was one of them, one of the first and in his native England the very first.

4. Previous work on Turner

As a pioneering naturalist, Turner is well known in England in the circles which should know him. He is also familiar to theologians. The standard authority on Turner as naturalist is still Charles Raven's book of 1947, *English naturalists from Neckam to Ray* (where extensive sections are devoted to Turner). A recent, general biography is Whitney R. D. Jones's book of 1988, *William Turner. Tudor naturalist, physician and divine.*

Turner's names of plants, birds and fishes have also received attention, for instance in the various modern editions and reprints of his works (see, e. g., Stearn 1965). The comments we have usually derive from able naturalists. So far, however, Turner's names and his principles of naming have aroused little or no attention from linguists or philologists.

In histories of the English language, including those more especially devoted to the sixteenth century or to the early modern period as such, Turner is generally passed over in silence or relegated to footnotes (as in Jones 1953). Characteristically, Turner is not mentioned in Gabriele Stein's *The English dictionary before Cawdrey* (1985), in most respects an admirable and thorough work. As usual in such works, Sir Thomas Elyot is generously treated by Stein, but Elyot and Turner knew each other and used each other's books (see Raven 1947: 44 and 72 — 74). Elyot published his pioneering Latin-English dictionary in the same year, 1538, as Turner's *Libellus* was printed and the 1542 and 1545 editions of Elyot's dictionary were most likely made use of by Turner for his *Names of Herbes* of 1548.

Of course Turner's works have been consulted by the *OED*, but this dictionary is on the whole weak on early plant names. Turner's plant names are of course also considered, though rather haphazardly, in plant-name dictionaries like those by Britten — Holland (1878 — 1886) and Grigson (1974).

My study of plant names which occur in William Turner's works is part of my project "The English plant names in Early Modern English herbals and floras", a project which has to date produced a book on the English plant names in *The Grete Herball* (Rydén 1984a) and a few articles.

The present paper is essentially based on names found in the *Libellus* of 1538 and *The Names of Herbes* of 1548. I have so far been unable to find time for an analysis of his herbal. This work, which has a less markedly philological character than his earlier books, will certainly add a great many new data, but probably few crucial ones.

5. Turner as herbalist and botanist

An account of Turner's interest and achievements in the naming of plants must start with the herbalistic and floristic background, since Turner's stance towards naming was basically and ultimately a practical and didactic one. In other words, plant names were for Turner essentially tools for handling herbalistic and floristic detail and variation.

Turner was a professional doctor with a social conscience. In the preface to the 1551 edition of his herbal he maintains significantly that "so is Phisick more noble and more worthy to be set by, then all other sciences". As already mentioned, he obtained an M. D. in Italy in the early 1540s and throughout his life he practised as a physician both in England and on the Continent, for example during his four-year stay in Friesland (see above). Traditionally, botany was a handmaid to medicine. A herbal can be defined as a compendium of medicinal plants or as "a collection of descriptions of plants put together for medical purposes" (Brodin 1950: 11). It was the most popular of scientific publications in the Renaissance. The word *herbal* is first attested as part of the descriptive title of Banckes's *Herbal* of 1525.[5]

Although the *Libellus* and *The Names of Herbes* contain some herbalistic matter, Turner's chief herbalistic work is his herbal of 1551, 1562 and 1568, the first scholarly English herbal. It is the first English work in which plants, at least most of them, are recognisable from the illustrations given (some 400 are from Fuchs's herbal). The pictures in *The Grete Herball* (1526) are, on the other hand, so crude that only a handful of them are recognisable. In Turner's herbal, as in other similar works of the time, there are usually long sections devoted to the virtues and properties of the plants at issue, in addition to plant descriptions, information on habitats, plant localities and plant names, native and foreign.

As a herbalist, Turner wanted to be helpful to "al the sicke folke of thys Realme" (preface to *Names* 1548) and he wanted his works on plants to be aids to apothecaries and doctors. One of his ambitions here was to show these men where plants grow, "when as the ryghte herbes are required of thē" (ibid.).

As appears from the preface to *The Names of Herbes*, he had finished a herbal in Latin in 1546, but he had postponed the publication of the book until he had acquired a more thorough knowledge of English plants (it was never published). Or, as he puts it in this preface: "the aduise of Phisicianes in thys matter ... was that I shoulde cease from settynge out of this boke in latin tyll I had sene those places of Englande, wherein is moste plentie of herbes" including "the west cōntrey, which I never sawe yet in al my life" (he was to become Dean of Wells in Somerset three years later).

Both for herbalistic and floristic purposes Turner was eager to discover and describe as many plants as possible. His works are the earliest authority for some 300 species of British plants.

In the preface to the 1551 edition of his herbal he states that his ambitions were to show "in what place of England euery herbe may be had and found in". But Turner was also particular about noting differences between the continental flora and the flora of England; he wanted to know "what numbre of souereine & strang herbes were in Englande that were not in other nations" (preface to *Names* 1548). He was the first scholarly link between British and continental botany and botanical learning (see Stearn 1975).

As a floristic botanist, Turner was − apart from one or two stray indications in medieval manuscripts (see Harvey 1987) − the first to give localities, more or less precise, for English plants, most of which were in his native Northumberland and in the south-east of England. There are a considerable number of such references in *Names* (ca. 50) and in his herbal, including references to gardens and garden escapes. In the *Libellus* (sub "Mercurialis") there is only one such reference, viz. to the gardens of King's College in Cambridge. He also often gives references to localities on the Continent.

A few examples from *Names*:

It is much in Northumberland in a wodde besyde Morpeth called Cottingwod ("Aconitum", Paris quadrifolia, Herb Paris)
it is plentuous in Northumberlande by holy Ilande, and in Northfolke beside Lin, at Barrowe in Brabant, and at Norden in est freslande ("Absinthium", Artemisia absinthium, wormwood)

It groweth plentuously in Germany, but not in England that euer I coulde
see, sauynge in my Lordes gardine at Syon ("Ephemerum non lethale",
Convallaria majalis, lily of the valley)
Raspeses growe most plentuously in the woddes of east Freselande besyde
Aurik, and in the mountaynes besyde Bon, they growe also in certayne
gardines of Englande ("Rubus ideus", Rubus idæus, raspberries).
it groweth plentuously besyde Bonony in the mount Appenine, and in
swechyrlande beside Wallense, I heare saye that it groweth also in the west
countrey of Englande, but I haue not hearde yet the englishe name of it
("Cyclaminus", Cyclamen europaeum, sowbread)

On the other hand, he often states that a plant is very common and needs
no local specification, as with daisies and strawberries:

> *Dasies growe in al grene places in greate plentie*
> *Euery man knoweth wel inough where strawberies growe*

Given the detailed knowledge we have today of the flora of the British
Isles, Turner's knowledge was very restricted, but he was the first to have
a nation-wide perspective on the flora of England. He was also particular
about stating whether he had seen a plant in the wild or only in gardens;
he was also to some extent aware of the regional differences in English
flora.

However, Turner was not a taxonomist or systematic botanist in any
modern sense — he was plant-centred rather than system-centred — and
he had, to our knowledge, no thought of writing a Flora of England.
Such books were not to appear in England until the mid-seventeenth
century (see Rydén 1984 a: 24).

6. Turner and the English language

Turner was no doubt a learned man. Probably he had a fluent command
of Latin and he knew Greek (as a student of theology at Cambridge he
had studied the New Testament in its original language), though he seems
to have preferred reading Aristotle in the Latin translation of Theodore
Gaza.

Apart from his special interest in the naming of plants (and to some
extent of birds and fishes), Turner took, as so many other academics of
his day, an active interest in his native language. Except for his *Libellus*
and the book on birds, all Turner's publications are in English. The

language of his correspondence with foreign colleagues was of course Latin.

As naturalist, physician and theologian, Turner wanted to teach his fellow Englishmen in their own language. No doubt he would have fared better internationally if he had written in Latin. Linnaeus knew his herbal, however, but not, as far as we know, his other works.

Turner also cared linguistically for the doctors, apothecaries and herbalists of his time, whose knowledge of Latin was often poor or nil. In the preface to the 1551 edition of his herbal he says: "how many surgianes and apothecaries are there in England, which can vnderstande Plini in latin, or Galene and Dioscorides, where as they wryte ether in greke or translated into latin, of the names[,] descriptions and natures of herbes?" And, he adds, "whether were it better, that many men shuld be killed, or the herball shuld be set out in Englysh?"

7. Turner as plant-name scholar

The study of plant names and the naming of plants subsume a great many aspects — synchronic, diachronic, structural, semantic/associative, systemic/variational, etymological, geographical, social, etc. There is also the question of the emotive/situational value of plant names and the handling of plant names in literary contexts (see Rydén 1978 a and 1984 b). In addition there are normative aspects in terms of the diffusion and standardisation of plant names.

English plant-name study in a strictly scholarly sense started in the mid-nineteenth century in the wake of the rising concern for diachronic-comparative studies and for regional dialects. The interest in plant names is however very old due to the practical use of plants and the consequential crucial importance of their names as identifiers, i. e. the communicative significance of plant names in early societies. There are comments on plant names in medieval manuscripts, in particular in terms of supposed origin and motive of denomination (why is a plant X called Y?), occasionally in other respects (cf. Harvey 1987).

However, the first Englishman to evince a more systematic interest in plant names was William Turner. Turner's interest in plant names was basically linked with his obsession with identification and linguistic precision, i. e. it had a practical rather than a theoretical-systemic slant. On the other hand, his interest in plant names was not in any way restricted to the nomenclature of his own language.

William Turner had a passion for accuracy, scientifically and linguistically. He had a passion for correctness — in identification, in description (as based on first-hand, personal observation) and in naming.

As a plant-name scholar, he wanted to supply each plant he knew with a proper English name, or as he puts it in the preface to *The Names of Herbes*: "to set furth my iudgemēt of the names of so many herbes as I knew". He also had the ambition to "declare and teache the names" of the plants he had seen on the Continent and to give "the names of the moste parte of herbes, that all auncient authours write of both in Greke, Lattin, Englishe, Duche and Frenche" (preface to *Names* 1548). And finally he wanted to inform about "the commune names that Herbaries and Apotecaries vse" (title of *Names*). In other words, he intended to cover a wide spectrum of both national and international names.

The works by Turner that are the most significant here are *Libellus de re herbaria novus* of 1538 and *The Names of Herbes* of 1548. They are less known than his later herbal, but are paradoxically enough more original, at least in terms of onomastic commentary.

Libellus and *Names* can perhaps best be characterised as nomenclatural aids (cf. e. g. Franckenius 1638) as based on the Latin nomenclature of the day. But they can also be designated as the first attempts at a Latin—English plant-name dictionary, going far beyond the medieval plant vocabularies or plant-name lists, both as regards substance and critical attitudes to authority.

8. Turner's plant-name sources

What botanical, lexicographical and onomastic literature was available to Turner? I have already mentioned Turner's critical views of the state of botanical learning in England when he was a student at Cambridge (as expressed in the preface to the final edition of his herbal). But, of course, there were sources he knew and used, both literary and oral.

Of the contemporary written English sources, he certainly knew and made use of *The Grete Herball* of 1526 (see Rydén 1984 a: 56), as well as Elyot's dictionary of 1538 and its continuations. He must also have come across Elyot's *Castel of Helth* (ca. 1534 and later editions) and similar works of a herbalistic character. As regards Turner's acquaintance with earlier relevant English sources, we know practically nothing. In one place in *Names*, sub. "Thlaspi", he refers to an "olde saxon" name, which of course does not necessarily reveal any direct knowledge of Old English.

As for contemporary Continental sources, he was familiar with the works of the German and Italian botanists, the French botanist Jean Ruel and Conrad Gessner (cf. above). A direct onomastic source may have been Gessner's plant-name dictionary, published in 1542: *Catalogus plantarum latine, graece, germanice, & gallice,* or *Namenbuch aller Erd-gewächsen, Lat[e]inisch, Griechisch, Teütsch vnd Französisch* (Zürich). Further research will reveal relevant detail here.[6] To my knowledge, Gessner's plant-name dictionary has not been considered in detail and certainly not as a potential source of Turner's names.

The regional names and forms Turner cites in his works seem to stem essentially from his childhood and early youth in Northumberland and from his student days in Cambridge and its surroundings, eked out with some later information from other parts of England. His travels on the Continent during the years 1540—1547 and 1553—1558 supplied him with a considerable number of, especially, German names, both from oral and written sources.

9. Aspects of *Libellus* and *Names*

Let us now have a closer look at some of the features revealed in *Libellus* and *Names*.

9.1. Scope and organisation

Libellus is a booklet of only some 20 pages, *Names* one of some 60 pages. Both are unillustrated.

As a whole, *Names* is more comprehensive than *Libellus*, but some items occurring in *Libellus* are not included in *Names*. Both supply, in addition to plant names, some herbalistic matter and some information about habitats and about beliefs and customs associated with plants in Turner's England. The amount of information given under each entry varies considerably ranging from two to some 30 lines.

The organisation of the items is in the order of their Latin names, in roughly alphabetical order (cf. Illustrations 1 and 2). Following the me-dieval tradition, the headwords are usually one-word entries (90% in *Libellus*, 85% in *Names*).

The binomial Latin nomenclature, which is now standard, is often found in the traditional herbalistic-floristic literature, for instance in many cases in Gerard's herbal of 1597. It was suggested as "standard" by

ABSINTHIVM.

Bſinthium ab αψινθαι quod taƈtum ire ſignificat nomen haͤ bet, ex aduerſo nomen greci deflexerũt: quod nullũ aĩ al haͤc herbam ob inſignem amaritudinem attingat. Abſinthij tria ſunt genera, Ponticum: marinum & ſantonicum. Ponticum eſt uulgare hoc quod uocamus **woꝛmewod**. Marinum ſeriphiũ, uocatur, huius anglicum mihi nomen non occurrit. Santonicum quod a ſantonibus galliæ uomen traxit puto eſſe **Lauander cotton**.

ABROTONVM.

Abrotonũ latini, gecisꝗut inſiniatas alias uoces dcbent, hanc herbã galli euronum germani **Stubwurtz** angli **Sothernewod** nominant.

ACANTHVS.

Acanthi duo ſunt genera. Leue & aculeatum. Leuem acanthum pe derota, & melamphillon eruditi nominãt, offirine brancã urſinam, uulgus **Bꝛank vꝛſyne** appellat. Porro ſœde hallucinantur qui putant brancam urſinam eſſe **Beareſote** quum illud potius ſit helliborus niger. Aculeatum & criſpum dioſcorides ſylueſtrem acanthum uocat.

ACORVM.

Acorum aut xiphion, officinæ gladiolũ uocant. angli pro uarietate ſoli & regionis uarie nominãt Northumbrienſes **a ſeg** elienſes & in paluſtri bus locis, propter etiam habitantes **a lug**, tritiſſima noĩa ſunt **gladon & a flag, & a ꝑelowe ſloure** delyce.

ALISMA.

Aliſma dioſcoridæ, eſt recentioribus fiſtula paſtoralis, officinis & her barijs plantago aquatica aliquibus barba ſyluana noſtratibus **water plantane oꝛ water waybꝛede**.

ALTHEA.

Altheam aliqui ebiſcum, ſiue ibiſcum nominant. officinæ maluã biſmalˎ uam noſtrates, **Holp oke**.

ALLIARIA.

Alliaria eſt herba paſſim in ſepibus proueniens circinato ſolo allium odore mire referens. Hec eſt (ni conieƈtura fallor) **ſauce alone**, aut ut alij uocant **Iak of the hedge**.

ASINE,

A.ij

Illustration 1. A page from William Turner's *Libellus de re herbaria novus* (1538)

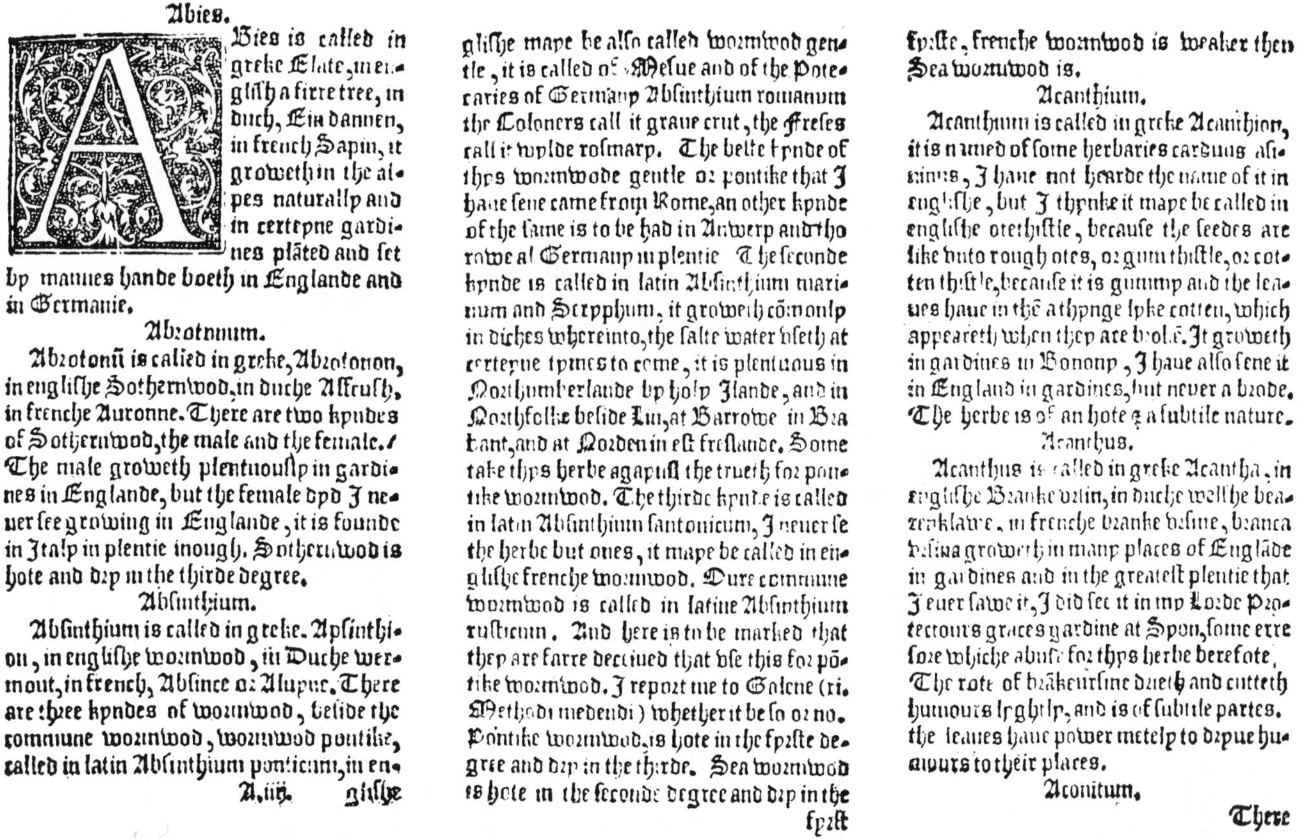

Abies.

Abies is called in greke Elate, in englysh a firre tree, in duch, Ein dannen, in french Sapin, it groweth in the alpes naturally and in certeyne gardines plāted and set by mannes hande boeth in Englande and in Germanie.

Abrotonum.

Abrotonū is called in greke, Abrotonon, in englishe Sothernwod, in duche Affrush, in frenche Auronne. There are two kyndes of Sothernwod, the male and the female. / The male groweth plentuously in gardines in Englande, but the female dyd I neuer see growing in Englande, it is founde in Italy in plentie inough. Sothernwod is hote and dry in the thirde degree.

Absinthium.

Absinthium is called in greke. Apsinthion, in englishe wormwod, in Duche wermout, in french, Absince or Aluyne. There are three kyndes of wormwod, beside the commune wormwod, wormwod pontike, called in latin Absinthium ponticum, in en-

A.iiij. glishe

glishe maye be also called wormwod gentle, it is called of Mesue and of the Potecaries of Germany Absinthium romanum the Coloners call it graue crut, the Freses call it wylde rosmary. The beste kynde of thys wormwode gentle or pontike that I haue sene came from Rome, an other kynde of the same is to be had in Antwerp and thorowe al Germany in plentie. The seconde kynde is called in latin Absinthium marinum and Seryphum, it groweth cōmonly in diches whereinto, the salte water vseth at certeyne tymes to come, it is plentuous in Northumberlande by holy Ilande, and in Northfolke beside Lin, at Barrowe in Brabant, and at Norden in est freslande. Some take thys herbe agaynst the trueth for pontike wormwod. The thirde kynde is called in latin Absinthium santonicum, I neuer se the herbe but ones, it maye be called in englishe frenche wormwod. Oure commune wormwod is called in latine Absinthium rusticum. And here is to be marked that they are farre deceiued that vse this for pōtike wormwod. I report me to Galene (ri. Methodi medendi) whether it be so or no. Pontike wormwod is hote in the fyrste degree and dry in the thirde. Sea wormwod is hote in the seconde degree and dry in the

fyrst

fyrste, frenche wormwod is weaker then Sea wormwod is.

Acanthium.

Acanthium is called in greke Acanthion, it is named of some herbaries carduus asininus, I haue not hearde the name of it in englishe, but I thynke it maye be called in englishe otethistle, because the seedes are like vnto rough otes, or gum thistle, or cotten thistle, because it is gummy and the leaues haue in thē a thynge lyke cotten, which appeareth when they are brokē. It groweth in gardines in Bonony, I haue also sene it in England in gardines, but never a brode. The herbe is of an hote & a subtile nature.

Acanthus.

Acanthus is called in greke Acantha, in englishe Branke vrsin, in duche wellthe bearenklawe, in frenche branke vrsine, branca vrsina groweth in many places of Englāde in gardines and in the greatest plentie that I euer sawe it, I did see it in my Lorde Protectours graces gardine at Syon, some erre sore whiche abuse for thys herbe berefote. The rote of brākeursine dryeth and cutteth humours lyghtly, and is of subtile partes. the leaues haue power metely to drybe humours to their places.

Aconitum.

There

Illustration 2. A page from William Turner's *The Names of Herbes* (1548)

Gaspard Bauhin in his famous *Pinax* of 1623 and was consistently applied by Linnaeus.

As appears from the titles of and the prefaces to his books, Turner's ambition was to supply not only English names but also Latin and Greek names, including the Latin names used by apothecaries and herbalists, and, in *Names*, also German and French names. In *Libellus*, which was written before Turner's periods of exile on the Continent, there is, as far as I have been able to detect, one German name, viz. *Stubwurtz* for "Abrotonum" (Artemisia abrotanum), a name probably taken from Brunfels's herbal, which he mentions in his preface. However, the submission of plant names is far from consistent and some entries are devoid of foreign names except for the Latin or Greek heading.

Names contains two interesting additions, indicative of Turner's originality, viz. (1) "Names of newe founde Herbes, wherof is no mention in any olde auncient wryter", and (2) "A table for the commune english names vsed nowe in al countreis [counties] of Englande", i. e. names Turner considered to be "standard" or more widespread than others.

9.2. Frequencies and synonyms

The total number of English plant names or forms in *Libellus* is some 250, referring to some 170 species of plants, native, naturalised and foreign. The corresponding figures in *Names* are 750 and 520, respectively. The sum total for the two books taken together is some 800 English names or forms as referring to some 540 plants.

In many cases synonyms or referential equivalents are provided. The equivalents given usually amount to two, to a maximum number of five (cf. Rydén 1978 b and 1984 a: 49 for corresponding figures in Gerard and *The Grete Herball*, respectively). It is obvious that, like the medieval herbalists, Turner was particular about giving as many names as he knew of, especially English names — for the sake of securing identification and for teaching purposes. If he did not know any name for a plant, he usually coined one (see 9.6.).

9.3. First records

Many of the English plant names found in Turner's works are — in addition to the names he obviously coined — first attested there, at least in the context of printed sources. But as Tony Hunt has shown in his recent book *Plant names of medieval England* (1989) — see here also Rydén (1984a) — we must be very careful, in view of our deficient

knowledge of medieval plant names, in our handling of early printed
names as "first records". The question of "first record" is, however,
subordinate to questions of derivation, diffusion and usage.

9.4. Dialectal names

There were of course in Turner's England both "standard" plant names
in the sense of traditional, often herbal names, national and international,
and "dialectal" names, i. e. names more or less restricted to certain regions
or areas.

One of the most interesting features of Turner's works is the information he gives about the local or regional use of plant names in England.
There are no such references in *The Grete Herball* (1526 and later editions)
or in other printed English works prior to Turner and only very rarely
so in medieval manuscripts (see Harvey 1987).

There are in *Libellus* and *Names* taken together some 25 explicit
references to local usage of plant names. Half of these references are to
Turner's native Northumberland, one to Yorkshire, one to Durham and
four to the "North". One example here is *Maydens heire* ("in the North
countrey") for *Galium verum*, 'lady's bedstraw'. The rest are to Cambrid-
geshire or generally to the "South".

Naturally, it is difficult to determine the regional or social status of
such names in Turner's day. No doubt, however, some of them had a
wider distribution than that indicated by Turner, for example *whin* (a
Scandinavian loanword) and *butterbur*. Today *whin* is the common name
for *Ulex europaeus* in the east and in the north and *butterbur* the standard
name (Flora name) for *Petasites*. In *Libellus* Turner notes two names for
Centaurea cyanus, the cornflower, viz. *blewblaw* and *blewbottell*, both
from Northumberland. In *Names* they are cited without regional provenance.

A number of the names or forms submitted by Turner were and are
regionally restricted, though not specified as such by Turner. Some such
examples are: *hauer* (for oats), *rountree* and *quicken tree* (for *Sorbus
aucuparia*), *birk* (for birch), *eke* (for oak), *sle* (for sloe) and *gyrs* (for
grass).

There are also many other variant forms of linguistic, though not
geographical significance like *celendine/celidony* (for *Chelidonium*) and
fænell/fyncle (for *Foeniculum*).[7]

Another interesting feature, not necessarily dialectal, is the use of two
or more words for one plant, one as a general term, the other(s) as

referring to a particular part of the plant, as in *Libellus* with *crowfoot/ kingcup/golland* ("eius flos uocatur Kyngcuppe, aut a Golland") for *Ranunculus* and as in *Names* with *strawberry leaf/strawberry* for *Fragaria vesca* ("Fragaria is called in english a strawbery leafe, whose fruite is called in englishe a strawbery").

9.5. Terms of usership

A remarkable feature of Turner's handling of plant names and plant-name contexts is the occurrence of terms of usership — apart from references to regional usage — especially in *Libellus*. In *Names* this nomenclature indicating general use or social stratification is usually reduced to "in English" or similar non-committal phrases. Specified layers of usage are however also occasionally referred to in *Names*, in terms of "gardeners", "schoolmasters", etc.

Terms indicating general use, though possibly with different connotations, in *Libellus* are:

angli, anglis, ab anglis, anglice
vulgus, vulgo, ab vulgo, vulgus nostrum, anglorum vulgus, vulgus hodie vocamus; nostrates, nostratibus, a nostris
omnes hodie
vernacula lingua vocamus, nostrati lingua, nostrata sermone
More restrictive terms are:
alii, aliqui, nonnulli; aliqui : alii (corresponding to *some : other(s)* in *Names*)
Specialised terms are for instance:
nostrates mulieres, a nostratibus mulieribus, nostratibus fœminis, rustici ('countryfolk')

The use of plant names by apothecaries or herbalists is referred to in terms such as:
officinæ, ab officinis, pharmacopolæ ('vendors of medicine')
herbarii, ab herbariis, herbariorum vulgus

Possibly, there is, for example, some difference implied in the use of *angli* vs. *vulgus*. The references to women here are in all probability to the herbwomen of the day, the chief collectors of simples (cf. Rydén 1978 b on Gerard).

9.6. Coinages and explanations

In his writings Turner wished to supply each plant adduced with an English name, in "common" or "dialectal" use. When no name was known or available to him, he coined one by way of translation of a foreign, usually Latin name or otherwise. Generally he uses here (in *Names*) the phrase "it may be called/named in English", which may, however, imply either that he is coining a name or that he just recommends a name already in use as appropriate.

In a great many cases, however, Turner implies or states explicitly that the name is new. Such a suggestion is often combined with an explanation of the name in terms of the underlying motive of denomination (cf. below). A few quotations from *Names*:

it hath no name in englishe that I knowe, it may be named Veruen mallowe, or cut malowe ("Alcea", Malva alcea).

It may be called in englishe Grapewurt, because it hath many blacke beries in the toppes lyke Grapes ("Christophoriana", Actaea spicata).

I haue not sene Medicā growe in Englād, wherefore I knowe no englishe name that it hath. It hath leaues like a clauer and horned cods wherein it hath sede somthynge facioned lyke Fenegreeke. Therefore it maye be called in englishe horned Clauer or snail Trifoly because the coddes are so wrythen in agayne as a water snayle or saynte corniliusses horne ("Medica", Medicago sativa, lucerne).

I neuer sawe it but in Italy. It maye be called in englishe Rose bay tree or rose Laurel ("Nerion", Nerium oleander).

I haue not sene it in Englande, sauyng in my Lordes gardine at Syon, but it may be called Panike ("Panicum", Setaria italica).

Papyrus groweth not in Englande ... It maye be called in englisshe water paper, or herbe paper ("Papyros", Cyperus papyrus).

I neuer sawe it in Englād, therfore I know no englishe name for it. Howe beit, if we had it here, it myghte be called in english sopewurt or skowrwurt ("Radicula", Saponaria officinalis)

it may be called spourge tyme in englishe, tyl we cā fynde a better name ("Peplum", Euphorbia peplus).

I haue hearde sume cal it in englishe a turnepe, and other some a naued or nauet, it maye be called also longe Rape or nauet gentle ("Napus", Brassica napus)

Ferula is called in greeke Narthex, but howe that it is named in englishe, as yet I can not tel, fot I neuer sawe it in Englande but in Germany in diuerse places. It maye be named in englishe herbe Sagapene or Fenel gyante ("Ferula", Ferula communis)

but I can not tel howe that it is called in englishe, for I neuer sawe it in Englande, sauying onely besyde Shene herde by the Temmes syde, howe be it after the followynge of the duche tonge it may be called dogleke or dogges onion ("Ornithigalum", Ornithogalum umbellatum).

Many of the names Turner coined or suggested for general use have passed into standard or Floranames, such as *bittersweet* (Solanum dulcamara), *hawkweed* (Hieracium), *loosestrife* (Lysimachia, Lythrum), *soapwort* (Saponaria) and *water plantain* (Alisma), others have not, as, e. g., *chokeweed* (Orobanche), *pond-plantain* (Potamogeton) and *water waybread* (Alisma).

A traditional herbal often included remarks on the meaning of plant names, in terms of the alleged motives of denomination, a feature revealing an innate interest in man in the "origin" of names and words.

Not unexpectedly, Turner perpetuates and extends this long tradition. A few quotations from *Names* (cf. also above):

It may be of his propertie called Chokeweede, because it destroyeth and choketh the herbes that it tyeth and claspeth wyth his roote ("Orobanche")
it maye be named in englishe Pondplantayne, or swymmynge plantayne, because it swymmeth aboue pondes and standyng waters ("Potamogeton")
It may be called in englishe sea wyllowe or prickwylowe because it hath the leaues of a wylowe and prickes lyke a thorne ("Halimus", Hippophaë).

9.7. Turner and authority

Turner was a man and a scholar of great integrity. True, he admired and praised some of his contemporary colleagues, in particular his friend Conrad Gessner, but at the same time he did not accept, or only reluctantly so, anything that did not tally with his own observations, experience and attitudes to linguistic detail and usage. In religious matters, his largely uncompromising views eventually led to his resignation as Dean of Wells.

Some quotations from *Names* are given below, revealing his critical mind in botanical and nomenclatural matters:

They are foully deceyued and shamefully deceyue other whiche holde in their wrytynges that our Marigold is Heliotropium Dioscoridis ("Heliotropium")
the Poticaries haue longe abused thys herbe for right Endyue, but they haue bene deceyued ("Lactuca")
Some take cockel for lolio, but thei are far deceyued as I shal declare at large if God wil, in my latin herbal ("Lolium")
Petroselinum … is not our cōmune persely, as many haue beleued ("Petroselinum")
Eryngium is named in englishe sea Hulver or sea Holly, it groweth plentuously in Englande by the sea syde. The herbes that Fuchsius and Riffius paint for Eryngium are not the true Eryngium ("Eryngium")

*The seconde is called Cromyon Schiston, in englishe in some place Hole
leke, it were better to call it Wynteronyon, because it hath blades as Onions
and not like leekes and endureth all the wynter ("Cepe")*

*Pityusa is called of some Herbaries Esula minor, and in englishe Spourge,
but it oughte to be called litle Spourge, or Lint spourge, for it hath smal
leaues like Flax, or an other herbe called Linaria ("Pityusa")*

*the scholemaisters in Englande haue of longe tyme called myricā heath, or
lyng, but so longe haue they bene deceyued al together ("Myrica")*

*Ligustrum is called in greke Cypros, in englishe Prim print or priuet, though
Eliote [Sir Thomas Elyot] more boldely then lernedly, defēded the contrary
as I shal prove in my latin herbal when it shal be set fourth ("Ligustrum")*

Anethum is wronge englished, of some, anise ("Anethum")

*Lithospermon is called of the Herbaries Milium solis, in englishe Grummel,
but it shoulde be called Gray myle ("Lithospermon")*

*Glastū is called in greke Isatis, in english wad, & not Ode as some corrupters
of the englishe tonge do nikename it ("Glastum", Isatis tinctoria)*

10. Conclusion

William Turner has been styled "The father of English botany". This is
correct, as long as we keep in mind that he was solely a descriptive and
floristic botanist. Taxonomy in any modern sense was not his field. In
this respect he differed from some of his continental colleagues. Turner
was an empiricist — although some medieval lore about plants and birds
still lurks in the pages of his works. His attitude to science and language
was basically a practical, though critical one. He had a passion for
accuracy and precision — in observation, identification, description and
naming. And he had a passion for his mother tongue as an informative
and didactic tool.

Turner has also been termed "The father of English ornithology". He
was on the whole the first influential English naturalist, with international
perspectives; he was the first Englishman to evince a systematic interest
in the discovery and description of the flora and fauna of the British
Isles.

Turner can also — given the philological and linguistic parameters of
his day — be characterised as "The father of English plant-name study".
As a plant-name scholar, he realised the variational, stratified and dynamic nature of linguistic usage and the need for a critical, comparative

approach to the formation and evaluation of plant names. He also displayed a genuine interest in the naming of birds and fishes.

When Turner came to Cambridge as a student in the mid-1520s, English botany was still largely medieval, as was the whole of English natural history, and no one had embarked on a scholarly study of English plant names. When he died some forty years later, he had put England on the international map both in the context of natural history and of the naming of plants.

William Turner is one of the outstanding English intellectuals of the first half of the sixteenth century. He was the true pioneer both of English natural history and of the study of English plant names, and, as a humanist-naturalist, a true representative of the Renaissance.

Notes

1. It was edited and translated into English by A. H. Evans in 1903 (see *References*).
2. See *References* sub Wheeler *et al*.
3. For detailed information on this herbal, see Rydén (1984 a).
4. The 1599 edition was reprinted in 1973 as nr. 598 in "The English Experience" series (Amsterdam – New York: Da Capo Press).
5. *Flora* was to be used much later, in England not until the second half of the eighteenth century, for books dealing − at first primarily , later solely − with plants in their own right, in terms of relationship, habitat, geographical distribution, etc.
6. Gessner's interest in local dialects and the modern vernaculars shows itself in his *Mithridates. De differentiis linguarum ... observationes* (1555). The book is on the origin and relationships of languages. It prints the Lord's Prayer in 22 languages. The work was praised by the famous nineteenth century philologist Jakob Grimm (1785 – 1863), who, like Gessner, combined a passion for philology with a taste for botany. Gessner was Professor of Greek at Lausanne before he turned botanist. He died of the plague in 1565 at the age of 49.
7. Cf. Rydén (1984 a: 42 – 43) for similar formal instability and variation in *The Grete Herball*.

References

Britten, James – Robert Holland
    1878 – 86   *A dictionary of English plant-names*. London: English Dialect Society.
Brodin, Gösta
    1950   *Agnus Castus. A Middle English herbal*. Uppsala: A – B. Lundequistska Bokhandeln.
Evans, A. H.
    1903   *Turner on birds*. Cambridge: Cambridge University Press.

Franckenius, Johannes
    1638   *Speculum botanicum.* Upsaliæ.
Grigson, Geoffrey
    1974   *A dictionary of English plant-names.* London: Lane.
Harvey, John
    1987   "Henry Daniel. A scientific gardener of the fourteenth century", *Garden History* 15: 81 — 93.
Hunt, Tony
    1989   *Plant names of medieval England.* Cambridge: Brewer.
Jones, R. F.
    1953   *The triumph of the English language.* London: Oxford University Press.
Jones, W. R. D.
    1988   *William Turner. Tudor naturalist, physician and divine.* London — New York: Routledge & Kegan Paul.
Raven, Charles
    1947   *English naturalists from Neckam to Ray.* Cambridge: Cambridge University Press.
Rydén, Mats
    1978 a   *Shakespearean plant names. Identifications and interpretations.* Stockholm: Almqvist & Wiksell.
    1978 b   "The English plant names in Gerard's *Herball* (1597)", in: Mats Rydén & Lennart Björk (eds), *Studies in English philology, linguistics and literature presented to Alarik Rynell 7 March 1978.* Stockholm: Almqvist & Wiksell, 142 — 150.
    1984 a   *The English plant names in The Grete Herball (1526).* Stockholm: Almqvist & Wiksell.
    1984 b   "The contextual significance of Shakespeare's plant names", *Studia Neophilologica* 56: 155 — 162.
    1991   "William Turner — en portalgestalt i engelsk naturalhistoria", *Svenska Linnésällskapets årsskrift* 1990 — 1991: 35 — 56.
Stearn, William, T. (ed.)
    1965   *William Turner,* Libellus *and* The Names of Herbes. Ray Society facsimiles. London: The Ray Society.
Stearn, William, T.
    1975   "History of the British contribution to the study of the European flora", in: S. M. Walters (ed.), *European floristic and taxonomic studies.* Cambridge: Botanical Society of the British Isles, 1 — 57.
Stein, Gabriele
    1985   *The English dictionary before Cawdrey.* Tübingen: Niemeyer.
Wheeler, Alwyne *et al.*
    1986   "William Turner's (c 1508 — 1568) notes on fishes in his letter to Conrad Gessner", *Archives of Natural History* 13: 291 — 305.

Full bibliographies (including original and facsimile eds. of Turner's works) are given in Jones (1988) and Rydén (1991).

The history of the English language and future English teachers

Viktor Schmetterer

In Austria every student of English who wants to become a secondary school teacher must enrol in at least one course in the history of English and is thus confronted with diachronic linguistics. Complaints are often made by both students and teachers that their academic studies do not (or did not) really meet the demands of their (future) profession.

Since I have been a "hybrid" for several years, both teaching English at a secondary school in Vienna and lecturing in the history of the English language at Vienna University, I would like to investigate what linguistic background teachers need and what university courses offer. In order to do this it seems advisable to describe the career of an average secondary school pupil in Austria, as far as foreign language training is concerned. At the age of ten, in the first year of an Austrian *Allgemeinbildende Höhere Schule*, pupils start with English, having five lessons a week, in the second year they have four lessons a week, in the third year and in all subsequent years up to the eighth and last there are three lessons of English a week. Depending on the type of school some pupils will start studying Latin in the third form. In the fifth form, when pupils are fourteen or fifteen years old, most of them start French, which they learn for four years.

It is my firm belief that all language teachers ought to have an idea of how language and communication work, even more so if they teach a foreign language. A few negative examples will illustrate my point. I have met teachers who set the following tasks as written tests: a verb form such as *he hunts* is to be changed to all English tenses, including the future perfect *he will have hunted*. Adding the progressive forms this will create monstrosities like *he will have been hunting*. The problem with such exercises or tests is not so much that the pupils are asked to produce some forms that are at best very unusual, but that they learn a set of verb forms they cannot make use of. To my mind, many Austrian teachers of English are overly concerned with the formal aspects of the language, perhaps to make up for the lack of inflectional endings in English as opposed to German or Latin. (It should be said, however, that this type of exercise is certainly more the exception than the rule.) Clearly, a more communicative approach towards language teaching will avoid any kind of exercise where pupils are left without a meaningful context.

Despite these critical remarks as to certain overly formal grammar exercises, this paper is intended as a plea for the value of linguistics, in particular historical linguistics, within the framework of teacher training. As Götz (1973: 7) puts it: "Linguistische Kenntnisse sind für den Sprachlehrenden unabdingbar, da er nur dann den Schüler in der Fremdsprache (und auch in der Muttersprache) unterrichten kann, wenn dieser Unterricht theoretisch durch die Linguistik fundiert ist." Similarly, Dirven (1985: 1) argues that "im Idealfalle sollte der Lehrer mit der wichtigsten neueren Sprachforschung vertraut sein, die sich gerade die Beschreibung und Erklärung des Sprachsystems zur Aufgabe gestellt hat." I intend to show in the following that English teachers clearly benefit from a basic knowledge of Middle English and Early Modern English and from a rough idea of the development of the English language from about 1500 onwards. (With German native speakers the case is slightly different as Old English, owing to its striking similarity to German, is usually an interesting experience for them.) Studying the history of a language will eventually make a student realise that language change is both inevitable and necessary in order to meet the requirements of the world around us. Even within the span of one teacher's professional life, we expect language to change to a degree that may make it necessary for the individual teacher to modify his own grammar of the language he teaches.

A second thing students should not only learn but actually experience when examining the development of a language is that "right" and "wrong" can be applied to language utterances only with the greatest possible caution. Too many teachers are too hasty in marking mistakes where they see offences against the rules of some prescriptive grammar. A pupil in his first or second year of English, who, when asked to write a dialogue between two friends who meet in the street, makes one of them say *How do you do?*, and receives the polite answer *How do you do?* to my mind makes a mistake at least as bad as if he had written *He don't know this*. Yet, there is no doubt that every English teacher in Austria would mark the *he don't* wrong, whereas they would probably not call the inappropriate dialogue a clear mistake.

I admit that a grammar written for school purposes will have to be prescriptive to some extent, especially if it is intended for beginners. There is no point in telling ten-year-old children in their first year of English that there are native speakers who will actually say *He don't smoke no more*, cf. Trudgill (1975: 31), who states that in Norwich 97% of the lower working class omit the *s* in third person singular present verbs. When, however, advanced pupils come across a phrase like that, say in a modern play, the teacher will have to offer some kind of explanation for what would clearly be a very bad mistake if the pupil produced it himself. At this stage it will be good for pupils to realise that a language consists of various levels, regional, social, and temporal. They can, however, only do this if their teacher has been trained to be sensitive to the various subsystems of a language.

When Early Modern English is discussed in connection with English teaching at secondary schools it is obvious to think of William Shakespeare. I do not think that future English teachers should study Early Modern English at university because they might later read a play by Shakespeare with advanced pupils. Time is very precious at school, with only three lessons of English a week in advanced classes, and teachers are busy enough trying to teach their pupils to express themselves adequately in spoken and written present-day language. It seems advisable to discuss the historical background of the late sixteenth and early seventeenth centuries with pupils, describe the Shakespearean stage, look at recorded performances or films available on video, and then read a few passages the teacher considers worthwhile. But, as the following will show, the attitude towards earlier forms of English within the framework of English teaching in Austria has changed. Three years ago a new syllabus was introduced in Austrian schools. The old one, which is now in its last year, and only in eighth forms, says about reading English texts in class that literary texts, in particular Shakespeare's plays, are to be read in annotated editions with English notes so that advanced pupils can practise Present-day English while discussing them. Today this sounds somewhat illogical to most English teachers. More than thirty years ago, however, editions of several of Shakespeare's plays were compiled that were especially designed to be read in Austrian secondary schools, clearly showing that a lot of time was devoted to reading Shakespeare in advanced classes. What strikes me as strange is that in those editions the peculiarities of Early Modern English are hardly pointed out to the pupils. In the introduction to *Macbeth* for example, the blank verse and the rich imagery of Shakespeare's language are discussed — in German (Hartmann 1948: 14—15). Then it says that the text — and the notes (!) — will show that in three centuries English has undergone certain changes: "Inwieweit aber der heutige Sprachgebrauch von dem Sprachgebrauch

Shakespeares und seiner Zeit abweicht — drei Jahrhunderte gehen an
einer Sprache nicht spurlos vorbei —, möge der Leser an Hand des
folgenden Textes und der dazugehörigen Fußnoten selbst beurteilen und
feststellen" (Hartmann 1948: 15). The text of the play appears in standardised modern spelling, and in the footnotes difficult words are explained, or more frequently, translated into German. Typical Early Modern English forms, however, such as *hath*, are not commented on because
the pupils are expected to understand them without any explanation.

Clearly, any Shakespearean text was (and still is) intended to be read
with advanced pupils, preferably in their last year at school. But in the
1950s Early Modern English and even Middle English texts were found
in textbooks for lower intermediate pupils as well. In an old Austrian
textbook for fourteen-year-old pupils, who by then had learned English
for merely three years, the opening scene of *King Lear* is to be found
after a lesson on road signs and a story about a family's first motor car
(Kögl 1955: 88—91). Some twenty-five pages earlier, thirty-six lines of
the *General Prologue* to the *Canterbury Tales*, where the Knight is introduced, are included. A note states: "This is a modern version of the old
epic. The original was a little different" (Kögl 1955: 62). The first four
lines are then quoted in Middle English. It is interesting, not to say
amusing, to read the follow-up exercises: "Ex. 1) Write a German version
of the poem as near [sic!] to the English text as possible . Find the places
and countries mentioned in the poem on a map. How can you get there
with modern means of transport? (Make conditional clauses: If I had to
go ... I should take ...)" (Kögl 1955: 63). Then there is a composition
exercise: "What is a perfect knight? (An old knight explains the ideals of
knighthood to a young shieldbearer)" (Kögl 1955: 63). Even if, in the
1950s, fourteen-year-old pupils were able to translate the poem or write
an essay on knighthood, which I doubt, they would not be able in most
cases to utter an English sentence or understand authentic English spoken
at normal speed. Modern textbooks for pupils of the same age offer a
lot of listening material on tapes plus exercises that encourage pupils to
speak and use their English actively in role play or questionnaires where
pupils have to interview each other and then report their answers to the
class. There is no trace of any earlier English but there are hints at stylistic
variants of the language. In an Austrian textbook pupils in their fourth
year of English are asked to produce four spoken or written invitations,
and they are reminded "not to make them too impolite or too polite"
(Heindler 1989: 44). They should realise that a girl who wants to invite

her boyfriend to go swimming and a headmaster inviting the mayor of the town to the school concert apply different styles in similar situations.

From what has been said so far it appears that thirty or forty years ago there was more justification for future English teachers to study earlier forms of English. The new Austrian syllabus of English does not even mention Shakespeare. It emphasises the importance of dealing with present-day literature and reading both literary and non-literary texts. Still, I am convinced that knowing something about the history of English is valuable for English teachers today, even though this is not the kind of knowledge they are likely to pass on to their pupils. As I have said before, I trust that students who have concerned themselves with Middle English or Early Modern English will accept the inevitability of language change. After all, their future pupils will often come across phrases and structures that are diametrically opposed to what their grammar-books teach them. Then it is important for their teachers to be familiar with the phenomenon of language change and not to comment, as I heard a colleague say, "The English are obviously losing the command of their own language." The following examples are taken from two contemporary novels, Patricia Highsmith's *Edith's diary* and John Wyndham's *The day of the Triffids*:

(1)   *Is Brett really liking his job in Trenton, liking the life there?*
         (Highsmith 1980: 32)

(2)   *She had known Elinor Hutchinson ... slightly since years.*
         (Highsmith 1980: 144)

(3)   *'What goes on here?' I asked him.* (Wyndham 1954: 128)

It is not for me to decide whether these sentences sound strange to native speakers; all I can say is that all of them contradict what pupils learn at Austrian schools, viz. that the "correct" version would be *Does Brett really like his job in Trenton, like life there?, She had known Elinor Hutchinson ... slightly for years,* and *'What is going on here?' I asked him.*

Since the majority of language teachers is convinced that language change is decay rather than progress and believes that the prime task of language teaching is to prevent further decay, occupation with older forms of English will at least show them that, owing to the mass media and also to school education, our age is probably affected by fewer changes in language than previous periods. I often ask my university students at the beginning of my course on the history of the English language what they consider to be signs of language decay with regard to their mother tongue. They usually object to too large a number of foreign elements in the lexicon, a lot of dialect forms intruding into the standard language, and a "sloppiness" with regard to case endings — and are invariably astonished to hear that they have just characterised Middle English.

It will perhaps help despairing teachers to cope with what they consider to be decay when they see that language change has always been rebuffed by contemporaries. Thus university teachers should not only teach their students that words like ME *half* and *calf* came to be pronounced as /haʊf/ and /kaʊf/ in Early Modern English, but should also quote Shakespeare's Holofernes in *Love's Labour's Lost* (V, 1), admittedly a caricature of a teacher, who complains about the new pronunciation.

Talking about interrogative and relative pronouns some teachers still insist on *whom*, as in *Whom did you see?*, saying (with disgust) that the *m* is occasionally dropped by careless speakers. Those teachers should have been told how old the forms without *m* are. "It is well worth noting that where such variations of reading are found [in Early Modern English texts] it is nearly always the earliest edition that has *who* and the later editions that find fault with this and replace it by *whom*. Most modern editors and reprinters add the *-m* everywhere in accordance with the rules of 'orthodox' grammar" (Jespersen 1949: VII, 242).

So what school teachers should know about Early Modern English are the most important sound changes, not only the Great Vowel Shift, but also lengthenings and shortenings that account for the discrepancy of spelling and pronunciation in Present-day English. After all, I have been asked by a thirteen-year-old pupil why words spelled with ⟨oo⟩ can have what she called "so many" different pronunciations. I am not suggesting that teachers ought to give pupils a detailed description of how ME /oː/ changed, but it seems a good idea for them to know the answer themselves and offer some kind of explanation. Besides, future teachers should learn that a fixed orthography is a fairly recent feature of the English language. Teachers who know that in thirteen manuscripts of Chaucer's works the word *through* appears in 28 spelling variants (cf. Markus 1990: 33) will stop grading their pupils' essays merely by the number of spelling mistakes. And, of course, English teachers must be familiar with the mixed vocabulary of the language. In Austria, pupils will see the similarities between English and German, and later on they will find Latin and French words in the English language when they start studying those languages.

So whatever we teach our students about Middle English or Early Modern English, we ought to bear in mind the requirements of their future profession. And this is why diachronic linguistics should have a firm place in the curriculum of future English teachers.

Texts and course books

Hartmann, Stephan (ed.)
   1948   *William Shakespeare: Macbeth.* Wien: Österreichischer Bundesverlag.
Heindler, Dagmar – Richard Huber – Gerhard Kuebel – David Newby – Alfred Scheuch –
         Karl Sornig – Helge Wohofsky
   1989   *Ticket to Britain 4. Coursebook.* Wien: Österreichischer Bundesverlag.
Highsmith, Patricia
   1980   *Edith's diary.* New York: Penguin.
Kögl, Richard – Ottokar Krasensky
   1955   *Looking beyond our own borders. Lehrgang der englischen Sprache.* Vol. 3.
         Wien: Franz Deuticke.
Kerrigan, John (ed.)
   1982   *William Shakespeare: Love's labour's lost.* Harmondsworth: Penguin.
Wyndham, John
   1954   *The day of the Triffids.* Harmondsworth: Penguin.

References

Dirven, René – Wolfgang Hünig – Wolfgang Kühlwein – Günter Radden – Jürgen Strauß
   1985   *Die Leistung der Linguistik für den Englischunterricht.* Tübingen: Niemeyer.
Faiß, Klaus
   1989   *Englische Sprachgeschichte.* Tübingen: Francke.
Görlach, Manfred
   1978   *Einführung in das Frühneuenglische.* Heidelberg: Quelle & Meyer.
Götz, Dieter – Ernst Burgschmidt
   1973   *Einführung in die Sprachwissenschaft für Anglisten.* (3. Auflage) München:
         Hueber.
Jespersen, Otto
   1949   *A Modern English grammar on historical principles.* Part. VII. *Syntax.* (Com-
         piled and published by Niels Haislund.) Copenhagen: Munksgaard.
Markus, Manfred
   1990   *Mittelenglisches Studienbuch.* Tübingen: Francke.
Pyles, Thomas – John Algeo
   1982   *The origins and development of the English language.* (3rd edition) New York:
         Harcourt – Brace – Jovanovich.
Trudgill, Peter
   1975   *Accent, dialect and the school.* London: Arnold.

You that be not able to consyder thys order of thinges:
Variability and change in the semantics and syntax of a mental verb in Early Modern English

Edgar W. Schneider

1. Introduction

The quotation in my title, taken from Colville's translation of Boethius' *De Consolatione Philosophiae* of 1556, is not meant as an allusion to the relationship between the reader and the structure of this paper; rather, it should serve to illustrate my topic, namely the evident structural and semantic change which the verb *consider* has undergone since the days of Early Modern English. Andreas Fischer recently proposed some fundamentals of "Historical lexicology", and hypothesised that this "Cinderella ... may turn out to be a princess after all" (1989: 89). I think he is perfectly right; accordingly, the present paper is intended as a modest contribution to this developing subfield and, in particular, to the study of lexical semantics of Early Modern English as compared to modern lexicosemantic structures.

There are two things in which I am specifically interested, both because I feel they are important to an understanding of the principles of lexical and semantic change and because I have worked on these problems in Modern English. One is the borderline area between lexical semantics and syntax, as reflected most conspicuously in verbal usage: the paradigmatic meaning relationships of verbs and syntagmatic verb complementation structures, and also the relationship between the two sides which has been a focus of recent research in modern linguistics. The other concerns the phenomenon of polysemy, the fact that a single form (*signifiant* in Saussure's terms) can express a whole set of context-bound meanings (sememes) which normally share some semantic common core. I have suggested a model of polysemy elsewhere (Schneider 1988 a, 1988 b); the line of inquiry in this paper should concern not only its synchronic structuring but also its role within semantic change. How do new meanings of a word develop, or old ones become obsolete?

A survey of the relevant literature indicates that these are questions to which but little attention has as yet been devoted, something also indicated by Fischer's account of historical lexicology. I have checked Fisiak's bibliography (1987) and found very little of even distant relevance — historical vocabulary studies are mostly descriptive accounts of a semantic field, in which several words are contrasted. There are some studies of verb complementation and verb valency in older stages of English, but nothing comparable with respect to Early Modern English, and Rohdenburg (1992) is the only study of which I know to address the semantics-syntax interface from a historical point of view. As to polysemy, we have above all Rudskoger's monumental study of four adjectives in Early Modern English (1952), while Aijmer (1986) examines questions related to the ones in which I am interested, but chooses modal verbs, i. e. function words, in their application. Barber (1976) has chapters on "changes of meaning" and "the expanding vocabulary", the former illustrating the familiar types suggested by Stern (1931), the latter describing the integration of loan words and word-formation processes. Görlach's book on Early Modern English (1978: 174—188) contains a very concise but also informative discussion of polysemy and semantic change which suggests necessary future developments in the field. On the whole, however, it can be safely stated that — apart from word-field studies — much work remains to be done in historical lexicology in general and the vocabulary of Early Modern English in particular.

In order to exemplify some of the above-mentioned points and as the material for inductive study, I have chosen a single highly polysemic verb on which I have worked extensively in Modern English, the word *consider*. This should give me the opportunity to relate the state of things in Early Modern English to the current situation and possibly detect any changes in between. Thus, the paper will attempt to give responses to the following questions:

a) What are the principal meanings of the verb *consider* in Early Modern English?

b) How is the verb used syntactically, and do the syntactic complementation structures correlate with its sememes?

c) Can we observe ongoing changes in the internal structure of *consider* within the Early Modern English period?

d) To what extent is the Early Modern English use of the verb different from its modern usage?

A study of this kind cannot operate in a theoretical vacuum, but this is not the place for a detailed discussion of lexicosemantic theory. I have done this elsewhere (Schneider 1988 a, 1988 b), and I am operating within the framework which I developed there; a very sketchy outline must suffice here. I believe that the meaning of words can be described as a combination of smaller semantic units, commonly called features, although I do not want to buy a variety of the proposed properties of such features, such as their atomic, metalinguistic, or notional status. The comprehensive semantic potential of polysemic lexemes is best seen as a conjunction of its individual context-bound meanings or sememes, which normally overlap to some extent, and have a common semantic core. I do believe there are prototypical meanings, which are more salient, more frequent, and possibly presupposed outside of disambiguating contexts, but I cannot see the advantage and the psycholinguistic reality of leaving these prototypes as holistic units defying further analysis. With Lipka (1990), I believe that the prototype theory and the feature theory can and must be reconciled, and that an important step toward that reconciliation is the acceptance of certain features as "inferential", with their status in the composition of the meaning of a word being not necessarily "defining" and "obligatory" but "typically associated". Finally, in an analysis of the linguistic properties of a lexical unit (in the sense of Cruse 1986: 76−77 and Lipka 1990: 131), it is important to describe not just its paradigmatic constituents but also its syntagmatic behaviour, to be grasped on four levels: the role frames which it implies (in the case of the verb *consider* this is a "thinker" and some mentally processed "information", typically realised as subject and object respectively); its syntactic complementation possibilities; the semantic specifications which it transfers onto its complements ("transfer features", following Weinreich 1966); and its habitual collocates on the lexical level.

2. Data and methodology

The following description is based on two sources of data. First, a corpus of Early Modern English texts was examined, and occurrences of the words sought for, with some appropriate context, were noted (see Schneider 1988c for an assessment of the problems and possibilities presented by a corpus-based lexical analysis). This corpus consists of letters and diaries only, because it was felt that these types of text represent natural linguistic usage more accurately than poetic writings. It includes the *Essex Papers* (Airy, ed. 1890), the *Hatton Family Correspondence* (2 vols; Thompson, ed. 1878), the *Hamilton Papers* (Gardiner, ed. 1880), two volumes (II, III,) of the *Diary of John Evelyn* (de Beer, ed. 1955), the first two volumes of the *Diary of Samuel Pepys* (Latham — Matthews, eds. 1970), and the *Letters of Dorothy Osborne* (Smith, ed. 1928). Second, thanks to the assistance of Matti Rissanen, Merja Kytö, and the Helsinki team, I was able to take into consideration the complete set of the occurrences of the word *consider* (including its spelling variants) in the Early Modern English section of the diachronic part of the *Helsinki Corpus of English Texts*.[1] The reading corpus provided 93 attestations of the verb *consider*, including all its inflectional forms, while the *Helsinki Corpus* contains 136 tokens of this verb, four of which overlap with my own corpus; thus, the following analysis is based on a total number of 225 occurrences of the verb *consider*.

The material was stored in a database management system, enabling me to assign to every word several semantic and syntactic qualifications and properties, and thus facilitating a comprehensive quantitative and qualitative analysis of this verb together with some of its properties in Early Modern English. A semantic paraphrase was assigned to each of these uses of the verb *consider*, and subsequently these were grouped according to common meanings and submeanings, and studied in connection with other properties such as their syntactic complementation, their semantic role partners in specific functions, possible collocates, and the years of origin of the respective attestations.

3. The sememes of the verb *consider*

The attestations of the verb *consider* in the corpus have been grouped into six different primary meanings, yet their distribution is fairly unequal in quantitative terms. There is an obvious core, or prototypical, meaning which accounts for almost 85% of all instances and can be further subdivided. Two further meanings may be observed to occur with a certain regularity; all the others are fairly rare and marginal, yet they are sufficiently distinct semantically to be dealt with in their own right.

The dominant meaning, which I call "integrative", or sememe A (SA), and which was counted 189 times, typically denotes a mental activity in which a thinking person intentionally and rationally processes some information in his or her mind. This information is in some way topical, i.e. the whole process has current relevance for the speaker, and he is interested in getting this thing mentally sorted out, integrating it into his sphere of knowledge. Typically, this process is done seriously, carefully, systematically, and with attention to some of the details in properties of the information thought about. The process is naturally durative, although extended duration is not implied. I distinguish between three major and two minor semantic subdivisions.

The most common subtype (131 instances) is A 1, to be labelled perhaps "integrative-revising", the case where this process is not specifically terminated or goal-oriented — the thinker is integrating the information in his system of mental beliefs, paying attention to some of its properties and features, and in this process perhaps revising slightly his mental model of the world. It is possible that the outcome of this mental process will be some decision or new stand on current issues, but this is not necessarily implied, and the thinking process as such is not immediately goal-oriented. For examples,[2] see (1) to (6).

(1)   *quhat more beis done be them your Grace sall best know be my self, but treulie I haue not muche reason to exspect muche qhen I consider in quhat disposicione this people continowes.*
        Hamilton Papers p. 94 (1639)

(2)   *('Throckmorton') sayde, I vnderstand you are appointed to conduct and carrie the Lord Priuie Seale into ('Spaine'); and considring the Daunger of the ('Frenchmen'), which you say arme them to the Sea apace, me thinke it well done, you put my sayde Lorde and his Traine on Lande in the West Country to avoyde all Daungers.*
        HC: THROCKM I, 65.C 2 (1554)

(3)   *and it is worth considering how unsafe it is to have children play up and down this lewd town, for these two boys, ..., were playing in Moore-Fields, and ...*
        HC: PEPYS VIII, 319 (1667)

(4)   *hee saw ... that Religion or honnour were things you did not consider att all, and that hee was confident you would take any Engagement, serve in any employment or doe any thing to advance yourself.*
        Osborne Letters p. 139 (1654)

(5)   *As to what is alledged on behalfe of y^e sd Kingdome of Ireland in relacon to y^e present warre, as an $argum^t$ for granting them y^e Liberty desired during y^e Warre, will easily be answered when it is considered that the whole burden of y^e warre lyes on y^e*

> *Kingdome of England, & that it partakes more of y^e effects of y^e warre by hindrance of trade than Ireland can doe.*
> *Essex Papers* p. 55 (1673)

(6) *a matter of so infinite concernment, as that of their eternal happiness. But then it is to be consider'd, that the proper remedy in this Case, is not to deprive men of this Priviledge, but to use the best means to prevent the abuse of it.*
  HC: TILLOTS II: ii, 451 (1679)

SA2 "integrative — authoritative" adds a further component to the previous sememe, namely authority and explicitness in making the decision. The thinker, typically a person of high social standing or a collective body of some public importance (*committee, parliament*, etc.), is entitled or even obliged to deliberate upon and decide a matter, and this decision will therefore typically have official status. Examples (7) to (11) illustrate this meaning.

Of these, however, (11) appears to be a special, slightly problematic case, as its interpretation is not perfectly clear. After some deliberation I have decided to leave it in this category, as it appears to be a closely related, possibly idiosyncratic variant of SA2. Syntactically, the structure can be understood in either of two ways. One might accept it as a lexicalised phrasal verb *consider off* in its own right, with a meaning something like "*not* to take into consideration, to take off the agenda"; but if this is the case, it is not in the *OED*, nor have I found any other evidence for it in Early Modern English or Present-day English. Alternatively, *off* can be interpreted as a quasi-adjectival predicate complement with a similar meaning, which would make the instance a case of the "qualifying" meaning SC,[3] or at least a hybrid between the two sememes. It is conceivable that the latter possibility could have formed a transitional (but ultimately unsuccessful) path toward the former.

(7) *But I desyred it might be rather refered to a Com^{tee}, wher it might be more fittly concider'd & digested.*
  Essex Papers p. 179 (1673)

(8) *It was last night resolved to stop the proclamation, and that the Councell shd. meete to day to consider if ye Parlimt. should sit ye 4th of Feb.;*
  Hatton Correspondence I p. 170 (1679)

(9)   *and so went up to the Committee of Parliament which are to*
           consider of the debts of the army and navy, and did give in our
           account of the 25 shipps.
           Diary of Pepys I p. 247 (1660)

(10)   *hence I went to sit in a Committè of which I was one, to consider*
           about the regulation of the Mint at the Tower,
           Diary of Evelyn III p. 361 (1663)

(11)   *none as yet ventured to move it in Councell … I have Interest*
           enough to prevent ye progress, & I hope even ye offering any
           such thing to be considered off at ye board,
           Essex Papers p. 146 (1673)

Two sub-variants can be distinguished. In the normal case (A2a, 32
occurrences, represented by the above examples), the object of the verb
is an abstract matter or a proposition. Occasionally, however (A2b, twice
in the corpus; see [12]), the object is a human noun or pronoun, and the
meaning to be inferred has to be complemented by something like "accept
this person to perform some function, fill a vacancy".

(12)   *The other day, talking wth King, I asked him about the sitting*
           of Parl: and whether he thought W. H. could be useful to him;
           he said yea, and that he would have me stay, and would consider
           me for it.
           Essex Papers p. 258 (1674)

Whereas A1 denoted a special type of mental process, and A2 con-
centrates upon a final stage of this process, A3 ("integrative — attentive",
9 examples; see [13]−[16]) emphasises its initial stage, the conscious,
typically instigated turning of one's attention to the matter to be thought
over.

(13)   *Consyder now how eche of these testymonyes conferme &*
           strengthe one another.
           HC: FISHER 1, 319 (1521)

(14)   *Having spoken thus farre of … It remaineth now, that wee*
           consider the thing prescribed, namely wherein we must bee built.
           HC: HOOKER 41 (1614)

(15)   *('Raleigh.') Methinks you fall out with your self; I say nothing.*
           ('Attorney.') By this Book you would persuade Men, that he is
           not the lawful King. Now let us consider some Circumstances:

> *My Lords, you know my Lord ('Cobham')*
> *HC:* RALEIGH I, 208.C 1 (1603)

(16)   I. *('First'), we will consider the nature of the sin here mentioned,*
which is ('scoffing') at Religion,
HC: TILLOTS II: ii, 418 (1671)

SA4 ("integrative — searching", 10 times) in a way goes one step further, in that the object of the verb is new not just in the sense that one turns one's attention to it but rather in the sense that it is actually being worked out, searched for, in the course of the ongoing mental process. As opposed to SA1, it does not relate to known information that is to be mentally integrated, but expresses the as yet unknown outcome, the information sought for or constructed in the process (see [17]–[19]).

(17)   *26. Haveing thus once got the opinion that it was possible to*
make it habituall, the next thing was to consider what way and
meanes was the likeliest to obteine it.
HC: LOCKE 46 (1693)

(18)   *Nor to consider what it is that causes so great a conflux of the*
atomical Particles of Fire, which are said to fly to a flaming
Body,
HC: HOOKE 13.5, 46 (1665)

(19)   *how he shou'd be confirm'd she was this wonder, before he us'd*
his power to call her to court, (where maidens never came,
unless for the king's private use) he was next to consider; and
while he was so doing, he had intelligence brought him, that
('Imoinda') was most certainly mistress to the Prince ('Oroon-
oko').
HC: BEHN 157 (1688)

Finally, the "integrative — processual" meaning A5 deviates from the prototypical common core of the sememe outlined above in that it lacks the components of complexity, purpose-orientation, and the mental integration of something new. Rather, what remains is a fairly neutral and general type of mental process, 'revolving something in one's mind, thinking of something'. This meaning is both atypical and relatively rare (5 cases). Examples:

(20)   *Let it suffice that I have hitherto described the Form of coun-*
terfeit Happiness: So that if thou considerest well, my Method
will lead me to give to thee a perfect Draught of the true.
HC: BOETHPR 124 (1695)

(21)   *('Bo.') Though I consider never so long, yet I can see no other thing.*
          HC: BOETHPR 143 (1695)

The second main sememe of *consider*, SB or "receptive" (10 instances), is a verb of mental reception, rather than one of integration or analysis. The information is new and previously unknown to the thinking person, and the verb denotes the moment when this information is received, realised by the thinker, who may or may not base a resulting decision and possible appropriate reaction upon this new knowledge. See (22) – (25).

(22)   *This we absolutely refuse'd: upon which they fell to attacque the house; but coming at last to consider that we might be persons of qualitie ... the company began to slink away, & our Enemie to grow so mild,*
          Diary of Evelyn III p. 5 (1650)

(23)   *seme confuse, darke, and troublesome to you that be not able to consyder thys order of thinges: the proper maner of gods prouidence directynge it selfe to good, disposeth and ordereth all thyngs.*
          HC: BOETHCO 108 (1556)

(24)   *Than it foloweth in the story of Kynge Henry / whan he had fermelye consyderyd the great conspyracy agayne hym by the forenamyd Lordys and other persones entendyd and Imagenyd to his dystruccyon /*
          HC: FABYAN 170R.C 1 (1516)

(25)   *Hence it is that although things may seem confused and disturbed to Men who cannot aright consider this Order, nevertheless the proper Manner and Course of every thing directs and disposeth to the true Good:*
          HC: BOETHPR 195 (1695)

In contrast to the previous two meanings, SC is static rather than dynamic, i. e. it denotes an opinion held by somebody, rather than a process in which such an opinion is formulated or modified. It is an opinion of a special kind, which I call "qualifying": the object is or represents a proposition in which a copula predicate connects a predicate complement with the clause subject, this complement semantically expressing a quality, a class membership or an adjectival property which the thinker believes the subject to hold. More explicitly, what is meant in an example such as *I consider them as children* (HC: LOCKE 53) is "I believe that they are children". This meaning is rare in Early Modern English (four examples; see (26)−(27).

(26)   *In the afternoon the [course] was chang'd; and the Bp. of Oxon*
         being consider'd as possess't of the Presidentship, a new question
         was putt to them, viz. whether they would obey him now he was
         in by the King's authority?
         Hatton Correspondence II p. 75 (1687)

(27)   *but generall talk againste the Mariage with ('Spaine'), and of*
         my departing Westwarde with the Earl of ('Devon'), which the
         sayde ('James') doth not auowe, and therefore I praye you
         consider it as not spoken.
         HC: THROCKM I, 71.C 2 (1554)

The fourth, "prospective" meaning, SD (also four instances), is likewise an opinion of a special type: the mental object is a possible future action or a state of affairs which the thinker will either carry out or cause to come into existence, yet at the moment of the *considering* in question this is no more than a mere future possibility, and there is no implication that it should be realised with some certainty. This implication of uncertainty is basically what distinguishes this sememe from other "prospective" verbs such as *intend* or *expect*. Note that in the case of *consider* it is necessary for the thinker to play an active role in the possible realisation of the dependent proposition: that is, what he is thinking about will concern him immediately and usually − if he realises it − should be to his advantage. (28) and (29) illustrate this meaning.

(28)   *I was told to day that it has bine considered ab^t bringing the*
         bill into ye Marshals court; but I beleeve there is nothing in it.
         Hatton Correspondence II p. 9 (1681)

(29)   *They have voted 1,600,000^{li} for ye navy ... They w^d not consider*
         of y^t for ye army, till they have more sattisfaction how ye K^g
         intends to dispose of the forces;
         Hatton Correspondence II p. 165 (1691)

In the case of sememe SE ("beneficial", 7 examples), the syntactic and semantic object of the verb is a person, and the predicate means that the thinker has this person's advantage in mind and also acts accordingly, i. e. some kind of taking care of or helping the person realised syntactically as object is implied. It is frequently the case that this person and the subject of the verb are coreferential, i. e. the object is a reflexive pronoun with -*self*, semantically supported in two out of the seven cases by the word *only* (see [30]−[32]).

(30)   *Blessed are they who consider the poore, ... shewing how we are oblig'd to relieve them not transitorily onely,*
        Diary of Evelyn III p. 517 (1668)

(31)   *Yet if it can bee any Ease to you to make mee more misserable then I am, never spare mee, consider your self only and not mee at all, tis noe more then I deserve for not accepting what you offer'd mee*
        Osborne Letters p. 120 (1653)

(32)   *however I am not displeased with it and if it may bee of any advantage to you, I shall not consider my self in it;*
        Osborne Letters p. 126 (1654)

There remains SF, the "visual" sense, which, while being less rare than some of the others (11 instances), is restricted nonetheless to three sources in the corpus (mainly Evelyn's diary), and which has "mental activity" only as an additional, secondary component. It expresses predominantly an intentional visual process, the action of looking at something, of watching something attentively. Evelyn typically uses this verb to denote his sightseeing activities as a gentleman tourist, with concrete physical things of some complexity and typically artistic or architectural value as its objects. Examples are (33)−(35).

(33)   *I went the next day to consider the Louvre more atentively, with all its severall Courts and Pavilions.*
        Diary of Evelyn II p. 103 (1644)

(34)   *Thence I pass'd through divers Galleries, Halls, & other Places filld with the rarest paintings; but had not time now to consider them.*
        Diary of Evelyn II p. 254−255 (1644)

(35)   *Next is the Brayne, of which it is marueylous to be considered and noted, how this (\Piamater\) deuideth the substaunce of the Brayne, and lappeth it into certen selles or diuisions, as thus: The substaunce of the braine is diuided into three partes or ventrikles,*
        HC: VICARY 30 (1548)

A word is appropriate with regard to the relationship between this classification and that provided by the *OED*, the source we would normally consult to find out about such matters. It is not at all my intention to downgrade the monumental task of compiling the *OED* or the value of the final product, but I may be permitted to state that I am not always satisfied with its meaning definitions and the internal structuring of polysemic items. One reason for this is the fact that in any specific case the structuring and ordering of senses follows heterogeneous criteria: the diachronic order of emergence of the principal senses, some internal semantic structuring, and also formal observations (such as transitive or intransitive uses, or uses with or without prepositions). Another, in my view, is that the definitions as such frequently lack clarity, in that they do not really define meaning components but rather employ other, semantically complex quasi-synonyms in explaining the senses of a word. Also, the *OED* does not tell us about token frequencies and the relative importance of the various sememes of a word, something which, given the quantitative proportions of the meanings of *consider*, is both important and of practical value.

The *OED* distinguishes between eleven senses of the verb *consider*, two of which are irrelevant here because they are not attested in my corpus and are hardly current in the period under investigation. Meaning 6. ("estimate, reckon, judge") becomes obsolete early in the study period (the last attestation is from 1539); 9. ("to hold in or treat with consideration and regard; ... esteem, respect") is cited as originating in 1692. Sememes 1. and 2. of the *OED* are the transitive and intransitive uses respectively of the verb in a visual sense, SF in my classification. Meanings 3. to 5. cover the main "integrative" sense SA (without making clear its dominant role) and also, as it were in passing and without distinguishing it clearly, the "receptive" SB (*OED*: "take note"); while the meaning paraphrases[4] are ample, I find them neither clear nor appropriately subdivided, and the division amongst the three sub-entries is based upon syntactic differences (3. is "trans.", 4. "with obj. clause", and 5. "intr."). Meaning 7. covers part of SA as well, I think, emphasising presumably what I have called the outcome of a mental integration process, an altered evaluation of disposition; note the circularity of the definition.[5] My SE, the "beneficial" meaning, roughly corresponds to or at least encompasses what the *OED* lists as its eighth meaning, "to recognise or take account of the services of a person in a practical way, to remunerate" — the plainly physical aspect of this semantic range, something like "give sth. to sb. in reward of ...", is not found in my corpus, whereas the more general or transferred aspect of "have somebody's well-being in mind and act accordingly" is not explicitly given in the *OED* (or is perhaps meant to be implied in the cryptic definition 7). The *OED*'s meaning 10., "to regard in a certain light or aspect", corresponds to the "qualifying" SC (but obscures most of its semantic complexity behind the unexplained quasi-synonym "regard") and will deserve closer attention when semantic change is discussed. Finally, 11., *consider of*, and 12., the participle *considered*, are distinguished on purely formal grounds; neither of the two can be accepted as themselves being or conveying semantic variants.

4. The syntax-semantics interface

To what extent do these semantic groupings correspond to syntactic complementation patterns? Tables 1 a and 1 b provide a crosstabulation of the two factors.

Table 1 a. Main sememes of *consider* by syntactic complementation types

Syntactic complementation	SA	SB	SC	SD	SE	SF	Total
intr, no complement	5	0	0	0	0	0	5
intr + *about*	1	0	0	1	0	0	2
intr + *of*	19	0	0	0	0	0	19
nominal direct object	89	7	0	2	7	9	114
obj − NP + *as* + NP/adj/pp	0	0	4	0	0	0	4
finite obj-clause + *that*	25	2	0	0	0	0	27
finite obj-clause − *that*	8	1	0	0	0	0	9
finite *wh*-object-clause	41	0	0	0	0	2	43
wh + *to*-inf object clause	1	0	0	0	0	0	1
NP + *to*-inf object clause	0	0	0	1	0	0	1
	189	10	4	4	7	11	225

Table 1 b. Submeanings of SA by syntactic complementation types

Syntactic complementation	SA 1	SA 2a	SA 2b	SA 3	SA 4	SA 5	Total
intr, no complement	1	2	0	0	0	2	5
intr + *about*	0	1	0	0	0	0	1
intr + *of*	8	9	0	0	0	2	19
nominal direct object	64	16	2	6	0	1	89
finite obj-clause + *that*	24	0	0	1	0	0	25
finite obj-clause − *that*	7	0	0	1	0	0	8
finite *wh*-object-clause	27	4	0	1	9	0	41
wh + *to*-inf object clause	0	0	0	0	1	0	1
	131	32	2	9	10	5	189

There is one clear case of a one-to-one relationship: SC, the "qualifying" meaning, is always expressed and also implied by a direct noun object followed by the word *as*, which represents an underlying copula, plus the respective predication complement (noun, adjective, or past participle). Otherwise, however, there are no clear correspondences between forms and meanings. Comparing the structures with modern English complementation patterns, one will note that although clauses frequently function as objects, the verb hardly ever accepts non-finite verb complements: my corpus contains not a single instance of a verbal *-ing* form as the object of *consider*, and only two instances of the predicate being realised as a *to-* infinitive. Finite object clauses with or without the complementiser *that* occur mostly with the "integrative" main meaning SA, in particular with SA1 ("integrative — revising") and occasionally with SA3 ("integrative — attentive"). SB ("receptive") is the only other sememe that was recorded with a finite *that*-object clause, yet the more common object type with this meaning is a plain noun phrase. Object clauses with a *wh*-element have been noted marginally with "visual" SF and, mainly, SA; this is the only complementation possibility with SA4 ("integrative — searching"), the *wh*-word representing the as yet unknown item.[6] Object phrases with a nominal head occur in all meanings. Human noun objects are indicative of SA2b ("integrative — authoritative", concerning a vacancy to be filled) or SE ("beneficial"), and physical objects as nouns frequently indicate a "visual" reading, SF; in all other cases, we find mostly grammatical pro-forms (*it, that*, etc.), or abstract nouns (*matter, case*, etc.). With one exception, intransitive usage of the verb signals mental integration, SA. In the majority of these instances, the semantically implied information thought about is explicitly expressed and represented syntactically as the complement of a preposition, mostly *of*, occasionally also *about*, a complementation type that has disappeared today.

   Certain tendencies can be observed with regard to semantic role partners and collocations. With SA1 ("integrative — revising"), the information that is mentally processed is typically either a proposition (which may be formally represented by an appropriate pro-form or empty noun such as *it, this*, or *things*) or an abstract noun, e. g. *reason* (three times), *(in)convenience, power* (two times both), *circumstances, suspicions*, etc. There are several deadjectival nominalisations in this position (*rareness, bigness, wysdome, equitie*), which is obvious, considering that the matter thought over is some abstract quality. With SA2a ("integrative — authoritative"), we find *matter, evidence* (twice) and *rules*. What is "considered" in the case of "integrative — attentive" SA3 is either a complex abstract property (*nature of, length of*) or a physical object (*creatures, herbs and trees*). SE, the "beneficial" sense, has human object nouns, typically personal pronouns, often reinforced by the -*self* form. Obviously, the "visual" sense SF requires physical objects, typically works of art. The subject of the verb is of course always human and in the majority of instances the personal pronoun *I* or *you*; only the "authoritative" SA2 has a marked set of distinctive "agents", bodies or persons with public authority including the collocates *Committee* (four times), *board, Councill, his/your grace, King*, and *Majesty* (twice each), or the *House, judges*, etc. Finally, as to adverbs, the "beneficial" SE collocates with *only* (twice out of seven instances), and "integrative" SA goes with modal adverbs that qualify the intensity of the mental process, including *well* (six times in the corpus), *thoroughly* (four times), *seriously* (three times), *deeply, substantially* (twice each), *intently, impartially*, etc.

5. Paths of semantic change and innovation

Table 2 investigates the temporal spread of the attestations of each sememe across the two centuries considered, in terms of their token frequencies per quarter-century.[7] The frequencies of the main sememe, SA, correlate well with the sum totals of the subperiods, a sign of its stable dominance throughout the period. Apparent concentrations in SE ("beneficial") and SF ("visual") are obviously due to idiolectal rather than period preferences, as four of the seven cases of SE are from Osborne's letters and eight of the eleven examples of SF from Evelyn's diary.

Table 2. Token frequencies of sememes per quarter-century 1500 – 1700

qu.c.	SA	SB	SC	SD	SE	SF	Tot.	SA1	SA2a	SA2b	SA3	SA4	SA5	Tot.
1500 –	5	1	0	0	0	0	6	4	0	0	1	0	0	5
1525 –	16	2	0	0	0	1	19	14	1	0	0	1	0	16
1550 –	27	1	1	0	1	0	30	20	4	0	2	1	0	27
1575 –	10	1	0	0	0	0	11	10	0	0	0	0	0	10
1600 –	13	1	0	0	0	0	14	9	1	0	2	1	0	13
1625 –	11	0	0	0	1	8	20	11	0	0	0	0	0	11
1650 –	63	2	1	0	5	2	73	35	21	2	1	3	1	63
1675 –	44	2	2	4	0	0	52	28	5	0	3	4	4	44
Total	189	10	4	4	7	11	225	131	32	2	9	10	5	189

A few details seem worth noting for the three other sememes, however, although in each case the number of occurrences is so low that the results may be chance products. Two meanings are obviously late innovations of this period. All four attestations of the "prospective" SD, by three different writers, are found in the final quarter of the seventeenth century, the earliest being from 1681. The production time of the cases of SC, the "qualifying" use, is similar, with three out of four instances being from 1673 and later, and the fourth one, an early occurrence in the Throckmorton trial of 1554, being slightly atypical in its semantic properties as well, as will be pointed out. One of the submeanings of SA, the "processual" SA5, also appears to be an innovation of the later part of our period: the earliest example, from Osborne in a letter of 1654, is the only transitive use, which is unusual in this sense and may be a sign of transition from the more central SA1, while the other four attestations are intransitive and later (from 1685 and 1695). On the other hand, the "receptive" reading SB is the only one which we find more strongly rooted in the fifteenth century and receding in the sixteenth. Five of the ten examples are from the earlier half of the period, the sixth in the sequence is from 1603, and after that only two further writers in the corpus use this meaning, twice each (Evelyn in his diary around mid-century and Richard Lord Viscount Preston in his translation of Boethius of 1695).

Now let me compare this documentation of the uses of the verb *consider* in Early Modern English with modern meanings. A detailed analysis and documentation of the latter, based mainly upon the *Brown* and *LOB* corpora, is given in Schneider (1988 a, 2: 59 – 70, 335 – 336, 347 – 348), with Schneider (1988 b: 161 – 166 and esp. 169) providing a shortcut survey of this. The raw data for comparison, both in terms of qualitative categories and for quantitative frequencies, is put together in Table 3.

The comparison shows continuity in the semantic core but change, both loss and expansion, at the periphery of the word's meaning. SA, the meaning of reflective integration, is still the most frequent one, although in terms of its token proportion it has lost ground substantially, more so in American English than in British English, having fallen from 84% of all tokens to 44 and 58% respectively. With respect to the subsememes of SA, the core meaning of mental revision has remained strongest overall, with American English but not British English still favouring this meaning over the others. SA2, the process leading to a formal decision, has remained fairly constant, especially in British English, and SA3, the guiding of somebody else's attention, has gained considerable ground.[8] The use of the verb in a neutral sense as just a general type of thinking process, SA5, which we found to emerge toward the end of the Early Modern English period, is still possible but has not gained ground. This is not surprising if we understand this sememe as the product of a semantic "bleaching" process entailing the loss of an earlier, semantically distinguishing force.

Table 3. Sememes and their frequencies of *consider* in Early Modern English and Present-day English

EModE				Present-day English			
				BrE		AmE	
Sememe	Freq	%	Sememe	Freq	%	Freq	%
SA	189	84	~ S2	223	58	153	44
SA1	(131	58)	~ S2.1	(64	17	96	28)
SA2	(34	15)	~ S2.2	(70	18	14	4)
SA3	(9	4)	~ S2.3	(79	21	33	10)
SA4	(10	4)	~ S2.1[9]	(4	1	5	1)
SA5	(5	2)	~ S2.4	(6	2	5	1)
SB	10	4	~ —				
SC	4	2	~ S3	104	27	135	39
SD	4	2	~ S1	23	6	39	11
SE	7	3	~ —				
SF	11	5	~ S6	4	1	2	1
			S4	27	7	10	3
			S5	3	1	8	2
Total	225	100		384	100	347	100

Freq: token frequencies; for Early Modern English in the present corpus, for BrE in the *LOB* corpus, for AmE in the *Brown* corpus.
Sememe designations for Modern English according to Schneider 1988a and 1988b.
"~"   = "corresponds with"
%   = relative proportion of sememe out of the total number of tokens in the corpus

A few of the Early Modern English meanings of the word have been lost or marginalised. SA4 may be a case in point — there is no objection against a construction like *he considered what the outcome would be* in Modern English, but such a use is exceptional and definitely rarer than in earlier days, and a modern speaker would probably prefer *wonder, ask oneself*, etc., as predicates. A meaning of Early Modern English that has been lost altogether is the "receptive" SB, which has been replaced by

realise or *recognise*. This loss may be in line with the weakening of the
"searching" sense SA4, in that the verb *consider* gradually loses the
property of binding semantically indeterminate objects: whatever is *considered* should normally be definite and known. Also, the semantic unity
of the word has been strengthened by the restriction of its meanings to
the purely mental sphere. SE ("beneficial"), which implies physical and
social activities such as remuneration, caring for a person, etc., has also
wholly disappeared. SF has not fully vanished but has lost its emphasis
on the visual side — we could no longer use it for the activities of a
tourist, we do not *consider sights, as Evelyn did. Rather, if there is still
a visual component in the meaning of the word, it is combined with and
mostly overridden by the corresponding mental activity; it means something like 'while watching something one broods, thinks deeply about it'.

On the other hand, there are two meanings of the verb *consider*, the
descendants of "qualifying" SC and "prospective" SD, that have become
essential sememes of the verb today and have greatly expanded with
respect to their token frequencies and their syntactic and semantic complexity. In Modern English, SD/S1, the thinking of a future action of
one's own as a possibility, is typically complemented by a verbal *ing*-
form, and often the verb itself is in the progressive form (*I am considering
doing something*). Alternative complementation possibilities also typically
reflect this critical activity component in the verb's argument, e. g. by
filling the object position with a deverbal nominalisation: a general may
consider attack or *withdrawal*. SC, the "qualifying" meaning closely related to *regard as*, is extremely common in Modern English and has
acquired three typical formal complementation possibilities, all of which
I understand as (more or less obvious) transforms of the underlying
copula predication: I can *consider someone a fool/foolish, consider someone
to be a fool/foolish*, or *consider someone as a fool/foolish*.

Finally, some isolated observations which will permit a number of
speculative statements on the nature of word-internal semantic change.
A closer look at the Early Modern English data reveals that a number
of the immanent changes can be detected in one way or another. These
points concern (a) the transitional semantic nature of some individual
attestations, (b) the relationship between the temporal spread of examples
in Early Modern English and the Modern English outcome, and (c) the
sequence of semantic and syntactic innovations, i. e. the nature of a
remodelling of the syntax-semantics interface.

The incipient loss of the "visual" meaning SF announces itself in a
sample distribution which vaguely reminds one of language death phe-

nomena: the purely visual uses are practically restricted to a single idiolect (John Evelyn's[10]) in the corpus. With the only other two instances in the corpus a strong mental component is already admixed (see [35]) and *since you are at Leasure to consider the moone, Osborne Letters*, p. 24, 1653). In fact, these "intermediate" instances presumably illustrate the verb's final stage of transition from its original visual sense, possibly derived from its literal etymological meaning, which is still found in Chaucer and given in the *Middle English Dictionary* as "watch (for a star)" (Kurath – Kuhn 1956 –: 536), to its more recent mental use. Similarly, some of the Early Modern English attestations appear to be intermediate cases which document the transition from the "integrative" mental process verb SA to the "qualifying" mental state meaning SC. While the latter is purely static in Modern English and indicates no more than a permanently stored subjective opinion and assessment, some of its earliest occurrences in the corpus vaccillate between a stative and a dynamic reading, expressing something like 'add and pay attention to a certain qualification when mentally processing sth., view sth. in a particular way'. The conscious attribution of a property as the "information" to be mentally integrated turns into a static belief, and it appears that in the long run the meaning of the verb changes appropriately. Cases in point are (26) and (27) or, more evidently, *desired ye Howse not to consider him as a Peere, but as a Gentleman* (*Essex Papers*, p. 163, 1673). It is probably a chance detail, but even among the few occurrences of the sememe the one with the purest static reading, that by Locke cited above in the discussion of SC, is the latest (of 1693).

It should be noted that the analysis of changes in the internal semantic structure during the Early Modern English period, as discussed on the basis of Table 2 above, would have perfectly predicted the present-day outcome pointed out in Table 3 — in other words, the processes that we found in the observation period must have continued and at least partly come to an end later. The future disappearance of "receptive" SB is foreshadowed in the temporal spread of its attestations, together with the gradual decline of its token frequencies; otherwise, I have found no indication of its weakness. Conversely, the "qualifying" and "prospective" meanings SC and SD are to be recognised as gaining ground by the fact that they appear either mostly or exclusively toward the end of the corpus period. Incidentally, these results might lend support to the assumption that the Civil War of the middle of the seventeenth century constituted a significant break in linguistic continuity, perhaps through a reevaluation of prestige patterns in society (Görlach 1978: 23; Nevalainen — Raumolin-Brunberg 1989: 79).

It is also noteworthy that we find these incipient modern meanings in the late seventeenth century, but not yet the complementation structures which we associate with these meanings in the present linguistic system. In other words, semantic change comes first, structural expansion comes later. The only complementation type of the "qualifying" use SC in the corpus is *NP as*; all the other structures which the verb has today are later by-products of its functional expansion. Similarly, the "intentional" meaning SD only has intransitive uses with *of* or *about* and also once a *to*-infinitive complement[11] (which would be impossible today; notably, this example is of 1699), but the characteristic modern complement type with a verbal *ing*-form has not yet emerged. Remarkably, the complement of *consider about* — see (28) — is in fact such a gerund; a construction of this type may be a formal source for the present structure. Be this as it may, the origin and establishment of a new meaning obviously precedes the development of an individual semantics-syntax interface.

6. Conclusion: A hypothesis regarding semantic change in polysemic words

The above discussion permits a few general statements with respect to the paths of semantic and syntactic change in a polysemic word, although I have to admit that at this point, given the restricted nature of my data, they are highly speculative. I would like to venture four generalisations.
1. It appears that new meanings develop along associative chains, through an extension of "prototypical" sememes to the extent that the old "identity" is no longer able to account systematically for the whole range of attestations/uses. Repeated use then establishes newly emergent semantic identities.
2. Alternatively, at the opposite end of the semantic range, meanings fall into disuse by becoming gradually restricted in their syntactic and stylistic ranges. During the final stages of their lifetimes they remain in active use with only a few individuals, until there is no one left to use them any longer.
3. New meanings can be either more specific than the old semantic prototype, thus meeting some linguistic demand, or more generic, being the product of a generally effective semantic bleaching process and thus

potentially resulting in the loss of a word's individuality. However, only the former type of innovation is likely to be successful and find dissemination in the language.

4. The more frequent a sememe is, the wider its range of possible syntactic complementation patterns will tend to be; on the other hand, individual meanings of a polysemic word will also tend to reserve certain structural patterns for themselves, occurring increasingly only in certain constructions and no longer in others. The ultimate principle appears to be that every meaning seeks to associate with a form (with this notion including a complementation structure type) of its own. This tendency comes later, however; it becomes effective only after the meaning itself has been firmly established. That is, new meanings begin in familiar syntactic patterns but tend to go their own formal ways once the sememe has achieved independent status.

Notes

1. See Kytö (1991) for a description of the Corpus and especially Nevalainen — Raumolin-Brunberg (1989) for the principles followed in the compilation of the Early Modern English section.
2. Quotations from the Reading Corpus are identified by a short name of the respective source text, the page reference, and the year of the example (in the case of letters and diaries, this is the actual year of writing). Examples from the *Helsinki Corpus* are followed by *HC:*, followed by the "abbreviated title" of the text extract (see Kytö 1991: 167 – 230), the page, and again the year of composition of the text sample.
3. I owe this suggestion to Lilo Moessner.
4. "3. To contemplate mentally, fix the mind upon; to think over, meditate or reflect on, bestow attentive thought upon, give heed to, take note of"; "4. To think, reflect, take note"; "5. To think deliberately, bethink oneself, reflect".
5. "7. To take into practical consideration or regard; to show consideration or regard for; to regard, make allowance for".
6. In this case, the difference between SA4 and SA1 or SA2 rests only upon the semantic interpretation of the *wh*-constituent. In SA1 a *wh*-form represents a focussed but known entity, whereas in the case of SA4 the identity of the *wh*-NP is unknown and wanted, possibly the outcome of the described process.
7. An interpretation of the absolute figures has to take into consideration the fact that the overall number of tokens is distributed quite unevenly over the two centuries, with noticeably higher numbers in the last half-century. To some extent, this effect mirrors the sample distribution in the corpus more strongly than a general increase of the frequency of the verb, in particular as my Reading Corpus contains substantially more material from the seventeenth than from the sixteenth century. To avoid such a possible bias, crosstabulations comparable to that in Table 3 have been carried out for the examples of the *Helsinki Corpus* only, using both the quarter-century periodisation and

that coded in the *Helsinki Corpus* (based on three Early Modern English subperiods E 1 to E 3). However, the resulting temporal distributions of the tokens of the individual meaning types are not much different, and the results reported in the text hold true in the same way.

8. It is tempting to suggest possible cultural correlates to explain such differences, although with the present evidence this is admittedly pure speculation. For example, can the reluctance of American English to use the word in the "authoritative" sense SA1 be taken to reflect the more egalitarian, democratic ethos of American society? Can the strong increase in associating the "attentive" meaning SA3 in the modern period, as opposed to Early Modern English, have to do with the division of labour, the upsurge of specialisation, and the growing importance of experts (who explain things to others, thus guiding their attention) in the modern world?

9. In the analysis of Present-day English, such instances were subsumed under S 2.1; I do not believe they should be credited independent sememic status today but were more common in Early Modern English. For the purpose of the quantitative comparison, the instances which correspond to SA4 were singled out in the *Brown* and *LOB* corpus data.

10. There even seems to be evidence of this development within Evelyn's *Diary*: his visual uses of the verb are all from the 1640s, whereas with one exception all attestations of the verb in the 1650s and 1660s are mental. However, this may be a chance result due to the contents of his diaries, with the earlier years being mostly about his travel experiences and the later entries being concerned more with sociopolitical activities.

11. It is interesting to assess this detail in the light of Rohdenburg's (1992) hypotheses concerning the historical "drift" of the English infinitive. It is in line with his observation that many English verbs have lost the property of binding *to*-infinitives in the course of the last few centuries but seems to contradict the postulated semantic specification of infinitives as expressing precisely prospective ("vorausschauend", "zukunftsorientiert") meanings in Modern English. However, his final thesis is that even with prospective verbs the infinitive expresses a strongly "positive" orientation while the verbal *-ing-* form typically has a "negative" polarisation, and this may correspond to the quality of expressing a low degree of likelihood and planning with the modern structure *to be considering doing sth.*

Reading Corpus

Airy, Osmund (ed.)
   1890   *Essex papers. Volume I. 1672—1679.* (Camden Society, New Series 47.) London: Camden Society.
   [1965]   [Reprinted New York: Johnson Reprint Corp.]
de Beer, E. S. (ed.)
   1955   *The diary of John Evelyn.* Vol. II: *Kalendarium, 1620—1649.* Vol. III: *Kalendarium, 1650—1672.* Oxford: Clarendon Press.
Gardiner, Samuel Rawson (ed.)
   1880   *The Hamilton papers: being selections from original letters in the possession of His Grace the Duke of Hamilton and Brandon, relating to the years 1638—1650.* (Camden Society, New Series 27.) London: Camden Society.

[1965]   [Reprinted New York: Johnson Reprint Corp.]
Latham, Robert—William Matthews (eds.)
1970   *The diary of Samuel Pepys. Volume I — 1660.* London: Bell & Sons.
Smith, G. C. Moore, (ed.)
1928   *The letters of Dorothy Osborne to William Temple.* Oxford: Clarendon Press.
Thompson, Edward Maundem (ed.)
1878   *Correspondence of the family of Hatton being chiefly letters addressed to Christopher First Viscount Hatton A. D. 1601—1704.* 2 vols. (Camden Society, New Series 22, 23.) London: Camden Society.
[1965]   [Reprinted New York: Johnson Reprint Corp.]

References

Aijmer, Karin
1986   "Polysemy, lexical variation and principles of semantic change — A study of the variation between *can* and *may* in Early Modern British English", in: Sven Jacobson (ed.), 143—170.
Barber, Charles
1976   *Early Modern English.* London: André Deutsch.
Cruse, David Allan
1986   *Lexical semantics.* Cambridge: Cambridge University Press.
Fischer, Andreas
1989   "Aspects of historical lexicology", in: Udo Fries—Martin Heusser (eds.), 71—91.
Fisiak, Jacek
1987   *A bibliography of writings for the history of the English language.* Berlin, New York, Amsterdam: Mouton de Gruyter.
Fries, Udo—Martin Heusser (eds.)
1989   *Meaning and beyond. Ernst Leisi zum 70. Geburtstag.* Tübingen: Narr.
Görlach, Manfred
1978   *Einführung ins Frühneuenglische.* Heidelberg: Quelle & Meyer.
Hüllen, Werner—Rainer Schulze (eds.)
1988   *Understanding the lexicon. Meaning, sense and world knowledge in lexical semantics.* Tübingen: Niemeyer.
Jacobson, Sven (ed.)
1986   *Papers from the third Scandinavian symposium on syntactic variation.* Stockholm: Almqvist & Wiksell.
Kurath, Hans—Sherman M. Kuhn (eds.)
1956—   *Middle English Dictionary.* Ann Arbor: University of Michigan Press.
Kytö, Merja
1991   *Manual of the diachronic part of the Helsinki Corpus of English texts: Coding conventions and lists of source texts.* Helsinki: Department of English, University of Helsinki.
Lipka, Leonhard
1990   *An outline of English lexicology.* Tübingen: Niemeyer.

402   *Edgar W. Schneider*

Ludwig, Hans-Werner (ed.)
  1988   *Anglistentag 1987 Tübingen. Vorträge.* Gießen: Hoffmann.
Mair, Christian — Manfred Markus (eds.)
  1992   *New departures in contrastive linguistics. Proceedings of the conference held at the Leopold-Franzens-University of Innsbruck, Austria, 10 — 12 May 1991.* 2. vols. (Innsbrucker Beiträge zur Kulturwissenschaft. Anglistische Reihe 4). Innsbruck: Amoe.
Nevalainen, Terttu — Helena Raumolin-Brunberg
  1989   "A corpus of Early Modern Standard English in a socio-historical perspective", *Neuphilologische Mitteilungen* 90: 67 — 110.
Rohdenburg, Günter
  1992   "Bemerkungen zu infiniten Konstruktionen im Englischen und Deutschen", in: Christian Mair — Manfred Markus (eds.), 187 — 207.
Rudskoger, Arne
  1952   *Fair, foul, nice, proper. A contribution to the study of polysemy.* Stockholm: Almqvist & Wiksell.
Schneider, Edgar W.
  1988 a   *Variabilität, Polysemie und Unschärfe der Wortbedeutung. Band 1: Theoretische und methodische Grundlagen. Band 2: Studien zur lexikalischen Semantik der mentalen Verben des Englischen.* (Linguistische Arbeiten 196, 197.) Tübingen: Niemeyer.
  1988 b   "On polysemy in English, considering *consider*", in: Werner Hüllen — Rainer Schulze (eds.), 157 — 169.
  1988 c   "Advantages and limitations of text corpora in the study of lexis", in: Hans-Werner Ludwig (ed.), 300 — 318.
Sebeok, Thomas A. (ed.)
  1966   *Current trends in linguistics. Vol. 3: Theoretical foundations.* The Hague, Paris: Mouton.
Stern, Gustaf
  1931   *Meaning and change of meaning: with special reference to the English language.* Bloomington;
  [1975]   [Repr. Westport, Conn.: Greenwood.]
Weinreich, Uriel
  1966   "Explorations in semantic theory", in: Thomas A. Sebeok (ed.), 395 — 477.

The expression of deontic and epistemic modality and the subjunctive

Dieter Stein

1. One of the hallmarks of Early Modern English is variability ("optionality") at all levels of language. At the morphosyntactic level one of the most notorious cases is the subjunctive, more precisely, the surface marking of modality. The present paper tries to establish whether or not there is any pattern in which forms segmentalise which modal meanings in which environment.

2. Most treatments of the subjunctive and modality have dealt with the history of one way or another of marking modality. A classic topic is the development of modals from (virtually) full verbs into auxiliaries with concomitant changes in their syntactic properties and semantic behaviour (e. g. Lightfoot 1979). Or attention has been paid to the history of inflectional marking in the use of the subjunctive, i. e. the history of genuine inflectional forms. For Early Modern English this inflectional marking was the absence of an inflection where there would have been one in the indicative (*if thou come, in order that he write a paper*). Inflectional marking in the subjunctive is very unevenly distributed over the person categories of the present: it exists only in person categories where the indicative would have a morph (third person and second person marked second singular, *thou comest*). There can be no inflectional marking in, i. e., the third person plural: *if they come*. Is there no subjunctive in these person categories?

The obvious approach is to start, not with the form, but with the function and then proceed to the kind of surface marking, or segmentalisation, of that content — in the present case a type of modal content. The content domain to be segmentalised is defined as the type of content that could theoretically be marked by an inflected subjunctive: this area of modal meaning is identified as potential semantic subjunctive space. We can then ask the following question: how is subjunctive content marked or segmentalised on the surface? In Early Modern English the candidates are: Ø, modal auxiliary, affixed form (third/second singular), and not marked at all. Note that this formulation presupposes a semantic equivalence of these forms, at least to the extent that there is considerable semantic overlap both between these individual possibilities of segmentalisation and between the individual modal auxiliaries. An attempt to identify patternings in "the subjunctive" has then to be rephrased as follows: how is the semantic subjunctive area segmentalised? Is there any recognisable pattern?

3. Trying to identify the semantic contexts which could be marked, in Early Modern English, by an inflected subjunctive is a highly complex task. The following paper will make the task more manageable by restricting it to a consideration of dependent sentences, the present tense, and deontic and epistemic contexts. *Irrealis* uses of the preterite are excluded, as well as main clause contexts and all other potential cases such as relative sentences, *-soever* etc. Typical epistemic contexts are dependent concessive, adversative and conditional sentences, normally introduced by a conjunction (*though, if, in case, despite*). Deontics typically contain a complementiser and/or a full lexical expression that contains a volitional or optative element (*to the intent that, I will that*). The texts/corpora analysed are listed in the appendix.

A look at the literature reveals three relevant points about the extent of our knowledge on the subject. First of all, there seems to be a presupposed *communis opinio* that within Early Modern English modal auxiliaries and inflectional marking are used indiscriminately: "By Early New English the original inflectional subjunctives had been largely taken over by phrases with auxiliaries like *should, would, might, may* — especially *should*", (Traugott 1972: 149).

Traugott (1972: 149) in particular notes "a recessiveness of subjunctive inflections". So we would expect to find less inflectional marking than auxiliaries. But there is an essential difference between earlier inflectional marking and that in Early Modern English: earlier: *-e*/plural *-en* were a positive morph, an addition to the stem. In Early Modern English ∅ was, negatively, a chance to drop an ending.

Harsh (1968), in a form-based approach, records the use of subjunctive forms (modal auxiliaries, inflectional subjunctives) and obtains a frequency measure by relating his absolute numbers to the number of finite verbs in order to establish comparability over different texts. He observes an overall decrease in the number of subjunctive markings (by either of these forms). In the Early Modern English period he notices some indeterminate movement in respect of the use of modal auxiliaries, and most interestingly, a renewed increase in inflectional subjunctive marking. This latter phenomenon is also pointed out by Brunner (1962) und Mustanoja (1960: 469), who note a renewed increase of inflectional marking in epistemic function, especially in the North of England, after a steady decrease of inflectional marking down to Late Middle English. In trying to explain this reversal of the diachronic trend, one has to bear in mind the nature of subjunctive marking in Early Modern English. Inflectional marking of the subjunctive in Early Modern English means leaving out an inflection: *-st, -eth*. Given the desire to avoid inflectional endings in morphological change processes, the presence of a semantic subjunctive context provides a good enough opportunity to leave out these dying endings.

4. Do our data from the segmentalisation of subjunctive space bear out these observations? A first analysis (Table 1) looks at the relative shares of modal auxiliaries and inflected subjunctive *(Ø)* in those person categories only where the indicative has an inflection (third person singular and person-marked second person singular).

Table 1. Numerical distribution of realisation forms

	Ø	MA (Modal auxiliary)
Deontics	102	92
Epistemics	208	49
Total	310	141

There is a clear overall predominance of subjunctive marking by Ø — a finding that does not bear out Traugott's statement (1972: 149) about the predominance of modal auxiliaries, at least not for the person categories marked with a morph in the indicative. This finding tallies with the idea that the renewed rise of the inflected subjunctive is due to the use of the Ø-subjunctive form as another evasion strategy to avoid endings.

As a next step, an analysis was carried out of the form of segmentalisation differentiated by person category. The analysis is based on a list of excerpts from texts listed in the appendix, (see Table 2).

To discuss deontics first, compared to Middle English, there is indeed an increase in the use of marking by modal auxiliaries. More unexpected, however, is the difference between the second and third person. In the third person modal auxiliaries predominate, in the second person Ø marking accounts for the majority of cases. No explanation can be offered at this point (but see Stein 1990). As to the category NM (i. e. person

Table 2. Subjunctive forms in deontics

The deontic area
The following data for subjunctive marking in the deontic area were obtained:
Absolute figures

	intent ∅	intent MA	totals	lest ∅	lest MA	lest do		vol ∅	vol MA	vol do		fin ∅	fin MA	fin do	
3S	—	21		19	23	—		25	50	1		22	49	3	
			21				42				76					74
2S	—	1		1	—	—		17	6	2		30	10	1	
			1				1				25					41
NM	6	27		4	15	1		35	34	3		22	14	2	
			33				20				72					38
	6	49		24	38	1		77	90	6		74	73	6	
Totals			55				63				173				153

Total of person category

	∅	MA	do/dost
3S	31	67	2
2S	71	25	4
NM	41	55	4

Table 3. Subjunctive markers with epistemics (the category "other" subsumes inflected *do* forms and preterite forms)

	except ∅	MA	do	aff	other	though ∅	MA	do	aff	other	if ∅	MA	do	aff	other
3S	10	1	2	—	—	6	4	3	2	—	104	33	24	2	2
2S	8	—	—	—	—	6	—	2	—	2	74	11	2	8	2
NM	17	1	1	—	—	7	1	3	—	—	44	7	11	—	—
	35	2	4	—	2	19	5	8	2	2	222	51	37	10	4

		∅	MA	do	aff	other	total
3S	abs. figs.	120	38	28	4	4	194
	%	62	20	14	2	2	
2S	abs. figs.	88	11	4	8	4	115
	%	77	10	3	7	3	
NM	abs. figs.	68	9	15	—	—	92
	%	74	10	16			

categories with no morph in the indicative), it should be noted that $\emptyset$ is not an inflection here.

The epistemics (see Table 3) show a much wider range and distribution of forms. For instance, the range of forms includes the normal indicative ending. There is no specialisation of forms for person categories as in the deontics area. Another significant difference lies in the much larger share of modal auxiliaries in deontics (50%), compared to epistemics (10%). This may reflect the fact (Traugott 1989) that epistemic meanings were late developers, and may have developed too late to be taken up for utilisation for the purposes under discussion. All in all, there are significant differences and different structurings of segmentalisation in the deontic and epistemic areas.

Table 4 gives the data for epistemics only from the analysis of another set of texts extending further backwards and forwards in time. It can be seen that the picture presented by the set of texts analysed for Table 3 is confirmed, and therefore seems to be stable from the inception of Early Modern English up to the latest Early Modern English.

Table 4. Modal forms in Late Middle English and Early Modern English texts

Singular	1 NM	aux	2 NM	aux	3 NM	aux	$\emptyset$
Paston Letters	2	3	2	1		7	5
Cely Letters	1					2	2
Hoby Castiglione	4	2	2	1		12	25
Stow Survey						2	3
Day Engl. Secr. 1586			1	1	1	1	1
Cavendish Sociable Letters 1664	5	2	3	1	11	6	12
Total Singular	12	7	8	4	12	30	48
Plural							
Hoby Cavendish	2	1	5		7	1	
Castiglione	1				18	10	
Total Plural	3	1	5		25	11	

In particular, inflectional marking by $\emptyset$ and modal auxiliaries share the segmentalisation burden in the normally morph-marked categories. With respect to the above (§ 2) speculation about the morphological motivation of the re-extension of the inflected subjunctive, this means that $\emptyset$ and modal auxiliaries do the same job — segmentalising modal content and in the process avoiding the use of undesired endings — a very elegant strategy.

5. In the person categories without a droppable morph (= NM), modal auxiliaries are the only formal means of segmentalising the subjunctive. Table 5 compares the degree of segmentalisation in deontics and epistemics.

Table 5. Degree of marking in NM

	actual total	potential total	% of actual occ.
Deontic	96 (66 MA 3 do 27 $\emptyset$)	143	67
Epistemic	24 (4 MA 10 do 10 $\emptyset$)	92	26
Temp.	3	22	14
-soever	2	7	29

It will be seen that deontics are much more strongly segmentalised than epistemics. Generally, epistemics are less segmentalised, and with a greater range of forms. Does this mean that the expression of modality is more important in deontics than in epistemics? It is redundant in both cases, since it is signalled by conjunctions or the semantics of lexemes. Again, the stronger affinity of modal auxiliaries with respect to deontic context is witnessed in Table 5.

6. The view that subjunctive area segmentalisation is exploited to solve morphological problems is supported by two further pieces of evidence. Around the middle of the 16th century the texts analysed for Tables 2 and 3 show a use of *do* as a segmentaliser of subjunctive context. This use is distributed as shown in Table 6.

This use of *do* seems to be a feature characteristic of the epistemic area. First of all, these data confirm the above result that the deontics show an affinity to modal auxiliaries, based on the basically deontic character of the modal auxiliaries. The same semantic point of view explains the preference of *do* for epistemics: after all, the grammaticalisation of *do* in questions, negations and as stressed *do* is an epistemisation of *do*.

Table 6. Realization of subjunctive contexts in the epistemic and deontic areas

	other forms (∅, MA)	do
epistemic	53	16
deontic	76	5

More important, as the data from the greatest supplier of subjunctive *do* occurrences, William Painter, *The Palace of Pleasure*, (1566 [1890]) show, there is an asymmetry in formal segmentalisation in that *do* tends to appear predominantly in the third singular, much less so in the person-marked second singular, and, most significantly, not at all in person categories where there is no morph in the indicative. The explanation can only be that subjunctive segmentalisation by an auxiliary (*do* or other modal auxiliary) is related to morph avoidance.

The second piece of evidence comes from Soederlind's (1951) analysis of Dryden (1631–1700). Of particular interest is the distribution of invariant *be* as a marker of subjunctive content, as in, e. g., *if they be in love with the subjunctive*. *Be* hardly ever occurs in the first person, with three exceptions, never at all in the second person, but regularly in the third person. In the plural a subjunctive *be* never occurs in the first person, never in the second person but — again — regularly in the third person. This uneven distribution over the person categories cannot possibly be a matter of the semantics of the third person, but is related to the fact that there used to be an inflectional ending that was undesirable. The use of subjunctive *be* is likely to have been an automatised habit that persisted long after the original cause had ceased to exist.

7. The evidence presented in this paper has shown that, in Early Modern English, the type of segmentalisation of the semantic subjunctive area is far from an unstructured chaos, but is structured along several dimensions. Apart from the semantic-based preferences for modal auxiliaries, the most suggestive result is that there seems to have been a structural tradition of using auxiliaries (on a par with ∅ — where eligible) to solve morphological problems, a tendency shown already extensively for *do* in Stein (1990: 233–250). More specifically, the distributional facts of the individual forms of segmentalisation over the person categories indicates that both the very extent of segmentalisation and the form of segmentalisation are likely to have been influenced by the desire to solve morphological problems. It is difficult to determine whether or not the wide use of modal auxiliaries and Ø in Early Modern English to segmentalise subjunctive modal content was solely due to this factor, and whether it started to decrease the moment the morphological problems were solved.

More research on this topic must include the question to what extent the data are skewed by stylistic factors: are there texts/authors with a tendency to use certain forms? Is it possible that uses in later Early Modern English are politeness-induced?

Primary Sources

Caxton: *Blanchardin and Eglantine* (1489)
Atkynson: *De Imitatione Christi* (1502)
Fisher: *Works* (1525—1530)
Tyndale: *Answer to Thomas More* (1531)
Bourchier: *Huon of Burdeux*, Vol. II (1534)
Palsgrave: *Acolastus* (1540)
Bale: *Works* (1540—1550)
Latimer: *Seven Sermons before Edward VI* (1549)
Painter: *Palace of Pleasure* (1566)
Stubbes: *Anatomy of Absurdity* (1583)
Deloney: *Novels* (1596—1600)

References

Brunner, Karl
    1962   *Die englische Sprache*, Vol. 2. Tübingen: Niemeyer.
Harsh, Wayne
    1968   *The subjunctive in English*. Alabama: University of Alabama Press.
Lightfoot, David W.
    1979   *Principles of diachronic syntax*. Austin: University of Texas Press.
Mustanoja, Tauno
    1960   *A Middle English syntax. Parts of speech*. Helsinki: Société Néophilologique.
Soederlind, Johannes
    1951   *Verb syntax in John Dryden's prose*. Cambridge, Mass.: Harvard University Press.

Stein, Dieter
   1990   *The semantics of syntactic change. Aspects of the evolution of* do *in English.*
               Berlin, New York: Mouton de Gruyter.
Traugott, Elizabeth Closs
   1972   *The history of English syntax.* New York: Holt, Reinhart & Winston.
Visser, Frederikus Theodorus
   1963—73   *An historical syntax of the English language.* 3 vols. Leiden: Brill.

Any as an indefinite determiner in non-assertive clauses: evidence from Present-day and Early Modern English*

Gunnel Tottie

1. Introduction

The present article is an exploratory foray into the use of *any* as an indefinite determiner in Present-day and Early Modern English. It is intended to form part of a diachronic study of indefinite determiners in English, especially the use of *any* (Tottie, forthcoming). Here I will focus on the use of *any* with singular count nouns in Present-day English and Early Modern English, and especially on the use of unstressed *any* as an indefinite article.

My point of departure is the observation that although much has been written about the use of and variation between *some* and *any* in assertive and non-assertive contexts in Present-day English (see, e. g., Lakoff 1969 and Sahlin 1979), comparatively little has been said about the variation between *any* and the indefinite article or zero determiner in non-assertive contexts. Several handbooks intended either for non-native learners (e. g. Svartvik — Sager 1977: 273 A or Johansson — Lysvåg 1986: 9.27) or for the English-speaking world in general make incorrect claims concerning the use, or rather non-use, of *any* with singular count nouns in non-assertive contexts. Thus Quirk *et al.* (1985: 5.14) list only the indefinite article *a/an* as a possible determiner of singular count nouns in sentences like (1 a), thus excluding the possibility of (1 b). *Any* is exemplified only with plural or non-count forms, as in (2):

(1)   a. *Have you got* a pen?
       b. *Have you got* any pen?

(2)   *Have we got* any rolls/bread *for tomorrow?*[1]

However, in a different section, 6.61, where they discuss the difference between *any* and *either*, Quirk *et al.* (1985) use *any* with a singular count noun in (3):

(3)   *Can you see* $\left\{ \begin{array}{l} \text{any part } of\ the\ roof? \\ \text{either end } of\ the\ tunnel? \end{array} \right.$

The authors further remark (ibid.) that *any* "is also (sic!) used for plural and noncount phrases".

Pronouncements by authors of specialised studies on determiners or definiteness are also often incomplete at best, or confused, or wrong. Chesterman (1991) pays no attention to determiners in non-assertive contexts, and neither does Yotsokura (1970: 50). Hogg, in his study of English quantifiers (1977: 142), discusses the acceptability of *any* as a determiner with singular count nouns in negative sentences, using (4) and (5) as examples. (The author's original numbers are given after the sentences, a practice I will follow whenever possible.)

(4)   *At the party I didn't see* any boy. (Hogg 6.2)

(5)   a. *At the party I didn't see* any boys. (Hogg 6.3 a)
       b. *At the party I didn't drink* any milk. (Hogg 6.3 b)

According to Hogg, (5 a) and (5 b) are "more acceptable" than (4), but he asserts that "the effect is marginal", and that (4) "is grammatical".

In his study of definiteness and indefiniteness, Hawkins (1978: 188) asserts categorically that there is only one negation possible of (6), viz. (7 a):

(6)   *Fred saw a cyclist.* (Hawkins 4.57)

(7)   a. *Fred didn't see* a cyclist. (Hawkins 4.58)

However, many interviewed native speakers find (7 b) with *any* perfectly acceptable. It is conceivable that there is a difference between British speakers, like Hawkins and Hogg, and Americans here, but that is a matter which is not a major concern in the present study.

(7)   b. *Fred didn't see* any cyclist.

Furthermore, it is difficult to contextualise (7 a) as it stands; one would need some extension to find it acceptable, as in (8) or (9):

(8)   *Fred didn't see a cyclist who was coming down the hill and hit him.*

(9)   *Fred didn't see a cyclist but a man on horseback.*

Notice that (10) is not as good as (8), and that (11) is completely impossible:

(10)   *?Fred didn't see a cyclist and hit him,*

(11)   **Fred did not see any cyclist and hit him.*

The reason for the impossibility of (11) is obvious: *any* is non-specific, whereas (8) is acceptable because it refers to a specified cyclist, i. e. the one that was coming down the hill. The reason for the lower acceptability of (10) is most likely the absence of contextual features which make it clear that the cyclist is specific. Compare (12), taken from the *Lancaster-Oslo/Bergen Corpus of written British English (LOB)*, with the indefinite article functioning as determiner, and the constructed variant with *any* in (13), which is also acceptable but which clearly has a very different meaning from (12). This is demonstrated by the fact that it cannot be followed by the same sentence in (13 b), but that (13 c) is OK:

(12)   a. *I didn't like the look of* a patient *who came to see me a few evenings ago.*

        b. *He rushed for the surgery and was breathing heavily.* (F 33 100)

(13)   a. *I didn't like the look of* any patient *who came to see me last week.*

        b. **He rushed for the surgery and was breathing heavily.*

        c. *Everybody looked pale and emaciated ...*

The most detailed modern treatment of *any* that I have found is that in Sahlin (1979). She does compare the use of *any* with the use of the indefinite article or zero in non-assertive clauses (1979: 91 ff.) and she provides a useful classification into three categories which she calls *Any I, Any II,* and *Any III* (1979: 88 ff.), which I will summarise below. The quoted examples are taken from the *London-Lund Corpus of English Conversation (LLC*; cf. Svartvik — Quirk 1980. I have followed the notational conventions of Svartvik — Quirk but give page references to Sahlin's quotations).[2]

Any I is an indefinite non-assertive article, lacking in stress, as in (14) and (15).

(14)   *have you made any 'serious at'tempt to* *PREPARE your'self 'for it*

                               (S. 3.1.635, Sahlin p. 89)

(15)   *there was never any* ⟋*NEED for a re'public of* ⟋*IRELAND*
                                              (S. 2.8.265, Sahlin p. 89)

Any II is a stressed indefinite non-assertive unlimited quantifier, as in
(16) and (17):

(16)   *... I don't have 'any* \\⟋*ANSWER to 'that*
                                              (S. 3.6.659, Sahlin p. 89)

(17)   *... did you read 'any of the* ⟋*TALES*
                                              (S. 3.1.734, Sahlin p. 97)

Finally, *Any III* is the stress-prominent determiner found in assertive
clauses, meaning 'no matter what or which'. An example is given in (18):

(18)   *...* *ANY old drain # was* *GOOD e'nough for* ⟋*PEEL*
                                              (S. 1.6.1222, Sahlin p. 113)

Sahlin's major interest is not quantification, but she does provide some
statistics concerning the use of *any* in general in the *London-Lund Corpus*,
showing that 310/415 (75%) countable nouns with *any* were in the
singular, thus a majority, but that only 49/105 (47%) of the countable
nouns with *Any I* occurred in the singular. She concludes that this may
account for the fact that this use has not been observed by other grammarians, e. g. Quirk *et al.* (1972), or is pronounced less acceptable (Hogg
1977; cf. above).[3]

2. *Any* in Present-day spoken and written English

In order to get an overall view of the use of *any* in relation to other
determiners in non-assertive Present-day English sentences, I made a
comparative study of the use of indefinite determiners in negative sentences in speech and writing. I used material from Tottie (1991 a), viz. a
subset of the *London-Lund Corpus* (the texts published in Svartvik – Quirk
1980) and a subset of the *Lancaster-Oslo/Bergen Corpus of written British
English, LOB*, comprising expository prose only. Only sentences where
any, the indefinite article, or zero determiner occurred after a finite verb
form were included. The data include both *Any I* and *Any II*; *Any III* was
by definition excluded. Both count and non-count singular nouns as well
as plural nouns were included, and in addition, a residual category labelled
$+/-$ Count had to be introduced to accommodate a small number of
uncertain cases.

The results are given in Table 1, which shows that *any* is indeed unusual in both spoken and written Present-day English, but that it occurs more frequently in spoken English, i. e. in 29/163 cases (18%), compared with 9/139 cases (6%) in written English. This overall difference between speech and writing is statistically significant at p < .005 (chi-square 8.735, 1 d.f.). However, if we look only at the use of *any* with countable nouns in the singular, the material is not large enough to show a significant difference, although the proportions differ (3/55 — 5% — in *LOB* and 12/72 — 17% — in *LLC*).

Table 1. Indefinite determiners after the finite verb in negative sentences in *LOB* and *LLC*

Noun type		*LOB* zero	*a(n)*	*any*	All	*LLC* zero	*a(n)*	*any*	All
SG	+ Count	—	52	3	55	5	55	12	72
	— Count	44	1	3	48	45	1	10	56
	+/− Count	3	—	—	3	1	4	—	5
PL		30	—	3	33	23	—	7	30
		77	53	9(6%)	139	74	60	29(18%)	163

The fact that *any* occurs more frequently in the spoken language tallies well with the observations of the *Advanced Learner's Dictionary*, quoted and endorsed by Sahlin (1979: 92), that *any* is "more 'concrete' or 'familiar', less 'formal, impersonal, objective or detached' than the generic use of *a* (and the zero form)" but should probably also be related to a need for emphasis and explicitness; see further the discussion below.[4]

It is worth noticing, however, that *any* does occur, and does occur as a determiner of count nouns in the singular, also in the written sample, and that at least in two cases it must be the unstressed article, *Any I*, that is used, viz. in (19) from a science text and (20) from a newspaper:

(19)   *... relative movements within the assembly should not provide* any *serious problem ...*

(J 07 189)

(20)   *... these exchanges have not been seen on* any *wider basis ...*

(A 03 27)

The third example, (21) from the genre *belles-lettres*, seems to have *Any II*:

(21)   *Further, I would not willingly charge with falsehood* any *searcher after truth ...*

(G 02 114)

As Sahlin's examples of *any* from written English are all instances of American English taken from the *Brown Corpus*, it is interesting to have these examples of *any* from written varieties of British English as well.

3. *Any* in Early Modern English

It then seemed interesting to try to ascertain whether the difference in the frequency and use of *any* in spoken and written English is a recent development, with spoken English paving the way for a more widespread use of *any* as a determiner. As shown in Tottie (1991 a: 319 ff.), negation by means of *not* and an indefinite noun phrase, as in *He did not see any lion(s)*, is more frequent in speech than in writing, which prefers negation that is "incorporated" into the noun phrase, *no*-negation in the terminology of Tottie (1991 a), as in *He saw no lion(s)*. *No*-negation is the older form, dating back to Old English, whereas *not*-negation only developed in Middle English. *Not*-negation has clearly spread faster in the spoken language, whereas *no*-negation is being retained to a greater extent in the more conservative written medium (cf. Tottie 1991 b.). It seemed to me not unlikely that a differentiation between different types of determiners in sentences with *not*-negation would also have first occurred in more recent times, and could also have first gained ground in the spoken language.

There are obviously no spoken records for the older periods of the English language, but there are records of genres which come close to the spoken medium, such as drama, letters, and trials. I decided to use a sample from the *Helsinki Corpus of English Texts*, viz. the section covering Early Modern English 1500 – 1710.[5] This corpus includes subsamples of several different text types, viz. secular instruction, religious instruction, chronicles, travel writing, fiction, drama, trials, and private correspondence. In order to arrive at a sample matching my Present-day English material, I extracted all negative sentences with indefinite noun phrases following a finite verb except those where the indefinite noun phrase was *any thing* or *any body*, still often written as two words in Early Modern English and therefore not comparable with Present-day usage. I also excluded cases where the indefinite noun phrase occurred in sentences containing *not without* or *not only*, as they are not semantically negative; cf. (22) and (23). (MOD 1 in the references indicates Early Modern English, sub-period 1, MOD 2 subperiod 2, etc.)

(22)   *I speake* not without *certaine knowledge*
                    (MOD 1 TR TRL THRC SAMPLE: 6)

(23)   ... *for hir Hyghnesse hath* not onely *Power over hys Bodye,*
            Lands, and Goodes, but ouer his Lyfe also.
                    (MOD 1 TR TRL THRC SAMPLE: 3)

Furthermore, I excluded instances where there did not seem to exist any possibility of variation with *any*. Admittedly, this is a somewhat dangerous procedure, as one does not have access to the intuition of native speakers for the older periods of the language. These cases were few, however, and seemed to me clear-cut, witness (24):

(24)   *I am afraid I shal not have* money *to serve mee to Easter.*
                    (MOD 1 PC PRIL PLUM)

Clear candidates for inclusion were sentences like, e. g., (25) and (26):

(25)   *it apperteneth not to us to prouide* Bookes *for you*
                    (MOD 1 TR TRL THRC SAMPLE: 2)

(26)   ... *they woulde not confounde the true Vnderstanding of* Wordes
            and Deedes ...
                    (MOD 1 TR TRL THRC SAMPLE: 9)

The overall distribution of indefinite determiners, including zero, in the entire Early Modern English sample is shown in Table 2.

Table 2. Indefinite determiners after the finite verb in negative sentences in the *Helsinki Corpus* sample of Early Modern English (1500−1740) (Sentences with *any thing, any body* excluded)

Noun type		zero	a(n)	any	All	% any
	+ Count	7	135	31	173	18%
SG	− Count	163	−	23	186	12%
	+/− Count	16	3	1	20	5%
PL		67	−	15	82	18%
		253	138	70	461	15%

We see again that although *any* is the only determiner that can occur with all three types of noun phrases, it is the least frequent one, with only 70/461 instances, or an overall frequency of 15%. Its frequency of occurrence with singular count nouns is even somewhat higher: 31/173 or 18%. The distribution remains remarkably stable over time in the

Early Modern English period, with very small fluctuations between the three sub-periods spanning 70 years each, 1500—1570, 1570—1640, and 1640—1710, as can be seen from the breakdown in Table 3.

Table 3. Indefinite determiners after the finite verb in negative sentences in the *Helsinki Corpus* sample of Early Modern English, by subperiods

1500—1570 Noun type		zero	a(n)	any	All	% any
SG	+ Count	–	30	6	36	17%
	– Count	44	–	6	50	12%
	+/– Count	7	–	–	7	
PL		25	–	7	32	22%
		76	30	19	125	15%

1570—1640 Noun type		zero	a(n)	any	All	% any
SG	+ Count	3	60	14	77	18%
	– Count	64	–	11	75	15%
	+/– Count	1	–	–	1	
PL		21	–	4	25	16%
		89	60	29	178	16%

1640—1710 Noun type		zero	a(n)	any	All	% any
SG	+ Count	4	45	11	60	18%
	– Count	55	–	6	61	10%
	+/– Count	8	3	1	12	
PL		21	–	4	25	16%
		88	48	22	158	14%

The figures for the Early Modern English sample are thus closer to those for the spoken sample of Present-day English, but precisely because of the varied composition of the *Helsinki Corpus*, these overall figures do not permit us to draw any conclusions about developments over time in spoken and written genres.[6]

It is possible to glean more interesting information concerning the use of *any* by looking more closely at its use in specific text types. First, it is striking that *any* is much more frequent in law texts than in other text types. A typical example is (27), which, besides the instances of *any* after a finite verb form, *any other p˜sone* and *for any Cappe* contains one instance of *any* before the verb, coordinated with *no Capper Hatter*, viz. *any other p˜sone.*

(27)   *And that no Capper Hatter nor* any *other p˜sone shall not take by hymself or* any *other p˜sone to his use for* any *Cappe made of the fynest ...*

(MOD 1 LA LAW STAT UnKnown: 9)

Table 4 shows that there were 28 instances of *any* in Law texts alone, and 42 instances in all other text types taken together. The total number of indefinite determiners, including zero, in law texts was 60, and the total number of indefinite determiners in all other text types was 401 (cf. Table 2, which shows that the total number of determiners in the Early Modern English sample was 461). The proportion of *any* in legal texts is thus 28/60, or 47%, to be compared with 42/401, or a mere 10% in other text types. This difference is significant at $p < .001$ (chi-square 53.084, 1 d. f.).

Table 4. *Any* in legal and non-legal texts in the Helsinki Corpus Early Modern English sample

Noun type		+L	−L	All
SG	+ Count	13	18	31
	− Count	6	17	23
	+/− Count	0	1	1
PL		9	6	15
		28	42	70

The obvious question is then: Why are there so many more instances of *any* in legal texts than in the rest of the Early Modern English sample? I think example (27) above gives a very good clue: in legal texts there is a necessity to stress the universal applicability of the law, statute, or rule that is being set down, or in other words, the total non-specificity of *person* or *cap*. What we have in (27) is typical: the regulation it expresses clearly applies to all hatters, all other people, and to all possible types of headgear. As this is a written text, we have no prosodic indications, but it seems obvious to me that if this text were to be read aloud, all three instances of *any* would bear heavy stress. They would thus be instances of *Any II* in Sahlin's terminology.

We may compare (27) with (28), taken from a trial, where the use of the indefinite article as a determiner clearly shows that a specific "unknown Man" is intended:

(28)   *And thogh I be no wise Man, I am not so rash to utter to* an
            unknowen Man (for so may I call him *in comparison) a matter*
            so dangerous for me to speake, and him to heare ...
                            (MOD 1 TR TRL THRC SAMPLE)

It is also enlightening to look at a breakdown of the incidence of *any* in
the other text types in the Early Modern English sample, as in Table 5.
Here we see that two text types, viz. trials and private correspondence,
have a higher incidence of *any* than the other ones, viz. 12 and 10,
respectively, compared with four in secular instruction, five in religious
instruction, six in chronicles, none in travel books, four in fiction and
only one in drama. We thus have a total of 22 instances of *any* in two
text types, out of a total of 115 determiners, and 20 in all others (except
law texts), out of a total of 286. This is a significant difference (p < .001,
chi square 12.886, 1 d. f.), and again, we must ask ourselves why such a
difference should exist.

Table 5. *Any* in different text types in Early Modern English (*Helsinki Corpus*, 1988 version)

Noun type		Law	SI	RI	Chr	Trav	Fic	Dr	Tri	PrC	Totals
	+ C	13	1	2	1	—	2	—	6	6	31
SG	− C	6	1	1	5	—	2	1	3	4	23
	+/− C	—	—	1	—	—	—	—	—	—	1
PL		9	2	1	—	—	—	—	3	—	15
		28	4	5	6	—	4	1	12	10	70

Key: SI = secular instruction, RI = religious instruction, Chr = chronicles, Trav = travel,
Fic = fiction, Dr = drama, Tri = trials, PrC = private correspondence

In the case of trials, we can probably expect some spill-over from legal
style, but there must certainly also be the same pragmatic need for
explicitness, emphasis and exhaustiveness as in the legal texts. (29) − (31)
are cases in point:

(29)   *And notwithstanding the old Error amongst you, whiche did not*
            admit any *Witnesse to speake, or* any *other matter to be hearde*
            in the favor of the Aduersarie ...
                            (MOD 1 TR TRL THRC SAMPLE: 2)

(30)   *You ought not to haue* any *Bookes red here at your Appoint-*
            ment ...
                            (MOD 1 TR TRL THRC SAMPLE: 2)

(31)   *('Raleigh') I protest before God, I meant it not by* any *Privy-*
           Counsellor: but because Money is scant, he will juggle on both
           sides.
                                        (MOD 2 TR TRL RAL UnKnown: 8)

It is more difficult to explain the high incidence of *any* in private letters;
here, a more detailed study of a larger material would be necessary, as
we would certainly have to account for a large number of individual
styles. The extract from a letter in (32) also refers to some legal procedure,
but it is likely that personal involvement and emphasis are the chief
reasons for introducing *any* here (on involvement, cf. Chafe 1972). That
could be a characteristic of private correspondence, a text type we know
is often close to spoken language.

(32)   *... sith I refused to swere, I wolde not declare* any *speciall parte*
           of that othe that grudged my conscience ...
                                        (MOD 1 PRIL MORE UnKnown: 6)

That *any* is used as an indicator of emphatic non-specificity and hence,
any as an indicator of universality, can be clearly seen from (33), taken
from a text of religious instruction, where the word *bywalkes* is used first
with zero determiner, and then, emphatically, with *any*.

(33)   *He wolde not walke in* bywalkes, *where are many balkes.*
           Amongest many balkinges, is much stumbling and by stombling
           it chaunceth many tymes to fal downe to the ground. And
           therfore, let vs not take any *biwalkes, but let gods word directe*
           vs ...
                                        (MOD 1 RI SERM LATM SAMPLE: 5)

It is indeed the case that in the whole Early Modern English sample, *any*
does tend to be used for explicitness and emphasis, as examples (34)−(37),
taken from different text types, show:

(34)   *therefore I would not wish* any *('Horse-man') of vertue at* any
           time to be without it ...
                                        (MOD 2 SI HAND MARK UnKnown: 7)

(35)   *The strength of every building, which is of God, standeth not in*
           any *mans armes or legs: it is in our faith ...*
                                        (MOD 2 RI SERM HOOK UnKnown: 15)

(36)   *Neuerthelesse, i haue made a vowe not to loue* any *man for this*
          tweluemoneths space.
                    (MOD 2 FN FICT NEWB UnKnown: 17)

(37)   *... you to trouble your selfe no further in this matter till that*
          time be expired: and then if I finde you be not intangled to any
          other, and that by triall I finde out the truth of your loue ...
                    (MOD 2 FN FICT NEWB UnKnown: 17)

Given the tendency to use *any* as an emphatic marker of non-specificity
and universality, and furthermore its extensive use in genres close to
speech, such as trials and private correspondence, it is somewhat surprising that there was only one instance of *any* in the drama subsample.
An explanation of this finding would require a detailed study of the
included drama texts, which may be more literary than mimetic of spoken
language. On the other hand, it is definitely not surprising that *any* does
not occur at all in travel texts, which tend to be factual and to have few
instances of negation.

4. Summary and discussion

Sahlin (1979) showed that *any* does occur with singular count nouns in
non-assertive contexts in Present-day spoken British English as well as
in written American English, in both uses as *Any I* and *Any II*. My
investigation of negative sentences shows that *any* also occurs in both
uses with singular count nouns in Present-day written British English,
and that there is a significant difference between the two varieties in that
any occurs more frequently with all types of nouns in the spoken language.
On the whole, however, *any* is the least frequent of the indefinite determiners.

   In the Early Modern English sample, *any* was also the determiner with
the lowest frequency of all, only 18%. Although there is only written
evidence and native speaker intuitions cannot be appealed to, it appears
that *any* is used exclusively in its function as "stressed unlimited quantifier", i.e. as *Any II*. The fact that *any* is most frequent in law texts is
likely to be due to the need to express universally applicable rules in such
texts. However, the extensive use of *any* in private letters and trials
probably reflects a characteristic of speech: emotionality and involvement.
This use could then have led to an extended use of *any* as an unstressed
article in these genres, spreading to other text types. We thus seem to

have some support for the hypothesis that the use of the unstressed article *Any I* has emerged in the spoken language and spread from there in the period between Early Modern English and Present-day English.

It is obvious that the *some/any* problem has preempted the attention of scholars and made many grammarians overlook the weakened use of *any* as an article with singular count nouns, and that it has also made them regard the use of *any* in assertive contexts, *Any III*, as a curiosity somehow separated from the other uses. A unitary analysis of the different uses of *any* has been proposed by Labov (1972: 794 f) and is tentatively supported by Sahlin (1979: 137), who regards *Any III* as well as *Any I* as "secondary to" *Any II*.[7] It is not entirely clear whether Sahlin intends this statement to have a diachronic import, but it seems entirely likely that the historical facts would bear out such an interpretation. I hope to return to the problem in future work.

Notes

* I thank Valerie Adams for discussing an earlier version of this paper with me. She bears no responsibility for any remaining mistakes or inadvertencies.
1. 5.14, note [b] also mentions the use of *any* with singular count nouns in assertive clauses in the sense 'it doesn't matter which/who/what' as in *I will consider any offer.*
2. References are to texts and tone units as given in Svartvik–Quirk (1980), with minor deviations from Sahlin, whose references are sometimes inaccurate. Upper-case lettering denotes the nucleus of the tone unit, \ indicates a falling tone, / a rising tone, \/ a fall-rise, /\ a rise-fall, ' stress, and # a tone unit boundary. Other symbols have been omitted.
3. Sahlin gives no comparable statistics for her (American) written material, the *Brown Corpus*, but does mention that there could be some variety-specific usages with regard to the pro-forms *one* and *any* (1979: 93).
4. I shall ignore here other factors, especially discourse factors, which clearly have an influence on the choice of determiner, as indicated by Sahlin (1979: 98 ff.) and also demonstrated for the *LOB Corpus* by Persson (1990).
5. I am grateful to Matti Rissanen for giving me access *in situ* to a pre-publication version of the *Helsinki Corpus* and to Merja Kytö for helping me to use Word-Cruncher to extract relevant examples.
6. For a discussion of the comparability of existing computer corpora, see Tottie (1992).
7. Sahlin (1979: 135 ff.) also gives a useful summary of different authors' views. For an overview of treatments by philosophers and theoretical linguists, see Taglicht (1984: 191–205).

Primary sources

The Helsinki Corpus of English texts: diachronic and dialectal.
The Lancaster-Oslo/Bergen Corpus of British English, for use with digital computers (LOB).
Bergen: The Norwegian Computing Centre for the Humanities.
The London-Lund Corpus of Spoken English. See Svartvik—Quirk 1980.

References

Chafe, Wallace
　　1982　　"Integration and involvement in speaking, writing, and oral literature", in:
　　　　　　Deborah Tannen (ed.), *Spoken and written language.* Norwood, N. J.: Ablex,
　　　　　　35—53.
Chesterman, Andrew
　　1991　　*On definiteness.* Cambridge: Cambridge University Press.
Hawkins, John A.
　　1978　　*Definiteness and indefiniteness.* London: Croom Helm.
Hogg, Richard
　　1977　　*English quantifier systems.* Amsterdam: North Holland.
Johansson, Stig—Per Lysvåg
　　1986　　*Understanding English grammar. A handbook for Norwegian university stu-*
　　　　　　dents. Oslo: Universitetsforlaget.
Labov, William
　　1972　　"Negative attraction and negative concord", *Language* 48: 773—818.
Lakoff, Robin
　　1969　　"Some reasons why there can't be any *some-any* rule", *Language* 45: 608—615.
Persson, Ann-Marie
　　1990　　"*Any* with singular count nouns in British English." [Unpublished term paper,
　　　　　　Uppsala University.]
Quirk, Randolph—Sidney Greenbaum—Geoffrey Leech—Jan Svartvik
　　1972　　*A grammar of contemporary English.* London: Longman.
　　1985　　*A comprehensive grammar of the English language.* London: Longman.
Sahlin, Elisabeth
　　1979　　*Some and any in spoken and written English.* (Studia Anglistica Upsaliensia
　　　　　　38.) Uppsala University.
Svartvik, Jan—Olof Sager
　　1977　　*Engelsk universitetsgrammatik.* Stockholm: Esselte Studium.
Svartvik, Jan—Randolph Quirk (eds.)
　　1980　　*A corpus of English conversation.* Lund: Gleerup.
Taglicht, Josef
　　1984　　*Message and emphasis. On focus and scope in English.* London: Longman.
Tottie, Gunnel
　　1991 a　*Negation in English speech and writing. A study in variation.* New York:
　　　　　　Academic Press.

1991 b   "Lexical diffusion in syntactic change: Frequency as a determinant of linguistic conservatism in the development of negation in English", in: Dieter Kastovsky (ed.), *Historical English syntax*. Berlin: Mouton de Gruyter, 439 – 464.

1992   "Comments on Rissanen, 'The diachronic corpus as a window to the history of English'", in: Jan Svartvik (ed.), *Directions in Corpus Linguistics. Proceedings from the Nobel Symposium 82 on corpus linguistics*. Berlin: Mouton de Gruyter, 206 – 209.

fortcoming   Indefinite determiners in English.

Yotsukura, Sayo

1970   *The articles in English. A structural analysis of usage*. The Hague: Mouton.

Loss of postvocalic *r*: Were the orthoepists really tone-deaf?

Michael Windross

1. Introduction

The evolution of the standard language has been one of the main threads in the historiography of the Early Modern Period. In the case of the *spoken* standard before the advent of sound-recording, this is a matter of reconstruction from written forms, using the statements and descriptions of orthoepists, spelling-reformers, etc. We know from the testimony of observers like Puttenham (1589) that the accent of the wealthy and educated classes in and around London was beginning to serve as a model — for one level of society at least — in the country at large, although he states that its adoption was slower than that of the written standard (Puttenham 1589: 257). How is this early standard speech related to present-day Received Pronunciation (RP), or to put it more bluntly, how close was it to our speech? The prevailing view seems to be that it was the "direct ancestor" of RP:

> A survey of grammarians and lexicographers on the pronunciation of English over the last four hundred years reveals, in the majority of cases, *a single phonological system*, which has been evolving in time.
> Present-day RP represents [the latest] stage in the evolution of a long-standing system. (Gimson 1984: 46, 48) [Emphasis mine, M. W.].

One school of thought also maintains that the emerging standard was fairly "advanced" and progressed rapidly: by Shakespeare's day it would already have had a familiar ring to it, and the changes over the next two hundred years were relatively slight — the only major change being the loss of *r* in the 18th century — so that by 1800, the standard accent had settled down very much into its present RP form (cf. Honey 1989: 18 – 20).

Roger Lass has already questioned the supposed "modernity" of the early standard. He finds that a number of vowel changes which are meant to have happened in the late 16th century are quite unsupported by the orthoepical evidence. This seems to indicate a much slower progress than has been made out; for Lass, 17th century phonology remains "archaic" and closer to Middle English (Lass 1989: 109).

In the present paper I want to turn to the tail-end of the story.[1] I shall argue that postvocalic *r* could not have been lost in standard 18th century speech, as is generally claimed. My case rests not only on the direct statements of the orthoepists about *r*, but also on their vowel values before *r*. We shall find that the 18th century vowel-system retains a number of important Early Modern features which distinguish it from RP;[2] in other words, the pace of change is again slower than has hitherto been supposed. But there is more at stake than chronology; I shall also be asking whether the sound change we call the "general loss of *r*" happened at all — at least in the way it is meant to have happened — and if my argument holds up, then it calls into question the whole idea of a gradually evolving single phonological system.[3]

2. The general loss in the literature

The loss of postvocalic *r* has been seen as the final stage in a gradual and long-term weakening process.[4] For Luick, this weakening process began in the 17th century and *r* disappeared from Southern speech in the course of the 18th century ([1964]: pp. 728 and 1120). Jespersen proposes a similar time-scale ([1954]: 11.61 and 13.24); indeed a long list could be drawn up of standard works claiming an 18th century loss (e. g. Strang 1970: 112; Prins 1974: 154; Barber 1976: 306).[5] We can represent the historical process in a number of stages:

	(i)		(ii)		(iii)		(iv)
(1)	Vr(C)	>	V ɹ(C)	>	Vv(C)	>	V:(C)

where we see a typical "lenition process", with a decrease in the consonantal strength of postvocalic *r* as it becomes more vowel-like and finally vocalises. Stages (iii) and (iv) claim that *r* first reduced to a vowel glide which subsequently undergoes monophthongisation with the original V, thus producing a long vowel. Lenition processes are well-attested in the historical record (cf. Lass 1984: 177−183; Hock 1986 a: 80−85). Some have also seen this as a case of "compensatory lengthening" (CL) (e. g. Strang 1970: 13; Newton 1972: 568). One of the traditional categories of historical sound change, CL is supposed to preserve the quantitative integrity of the syllable (cf. Jeffers−Lehiste 1979: 12). De Chene and Anderson question the status of CL as an explanatory mechanism. Schemata such as Vr(C) > V:(C), which give the appearance that consonant loss is being compensated by vowel length, represent, they say, the phonologisation of phonetic change, the way such a change is "digested" by the system (1979: 505). Their claim is that such apparent cases of CL can always be analysed into two distinct phonetic processes: consonantal weakening to a vowel glide and subsequent monophthongisation, as in (1). Besides these theoretical objections to CL *per se* (see Hock 1986 b for a partial reply) it will become clear in section 2 below that even (1) is an oversimplification, and the data do not support CL.

While there is general agreement that the general loss was the result of a weakening process, the 18th century dating is not accepted by all. Dobson (who believes weakening began already in the late 15th century) thinks that *r* was maintained in good speech throughout the 18th century − "not until Batchelor (1809) is there clear evidence of its loss from good StE." (1968: ii, 744). Ekwall too suggests that the present-day distribution of *r* dates from the early 19th rather than 18th century (1975: 65−66). Indeed, it is worth noting Sweet (1891: 868): "in the present century *r* has been dropped everywhere except before a vowel". Others see an earlier loss. Kökeritz (1944: 154) claims that Mather Flint (1740) shows "unequivocal evidence of the reduction or elimination of preconsonantal *r* ... which means that present StE. usage may safely be dated as far back as the very beginning of the 18th C.".[6] J. Milroy (1984: 20−21) says "general loss of post-vocalic /r/ was probably in progress in the sixteenth century (see e. g. the spellings of Henry Machyn c. 1550) but could hardly have been complete in 'polite' London English until around 1700." Proponents of the earlier dating have tended to go by the spellings found in diaries and correspondence of the period (rather than the orthoepical evidence) where there are frequent *r*-less spellings like *passel* 'parcel', *mossel* 'morsel', *fust* 'first', alongside spellings like *marster* 'master', *carssel* 'castle', with excrescent *r*. On the basis of such evidence Wyld (1936: 298−299) concluded that the pronunciation of the upper classes in the 17th century must have been much as in his own day. On closer examination, Wyld's case proves to be flawed. In the first place, reverse spellings like *carssel* are at best ambiguous; if modelled on, e. g., *cart*, with silent *r*, they would indicate that *r* was vocalised, but equally well they could be a phonetic spelling for someone with an *r* in *castle, answer*, etc. − such pronunciations are still heard today in the rhotic West-Midland accents (see *LAE* Ph 194 *daughter*). As has widely been pointed out in the literature (e. g. Dobson 1968: ii, 992), the *r*-less spellings, while indicating loss of *r*, are quite distinct from the later general loss; "early loss" is sporadic, occurs in specific environments (before dental clusters) and leaves the preceding vowel short, contrary to the general loss, which is across the board and leaves all vowels long. Jespersen (1954: 7.79) says it has nothing to do with the general loss, but could it, as Wełna (1978: 163) claims, indicate that *r* has weakened?

As is well known, *r* displays a wide variation of phonetic types, not only between languages, but within the dialects of a single language, between different speakers, and even for an individual speaker according to its position in the word. In spite of the tendency to treat apical trilled *r* as the prototype *r*, it is hard to imagine a uniform *r* in the past when communities were so much more isolated. I shall assume, then, that there has always been this variety. Apart from its influence on preceding vowels (which can tell us something about the nature of *r*) *r* has also been involved in a number of distinct historical processes, e. g. rhotacism, breaking, metathesis. One can try and reconstruct *r* using the Phonetic Effect Argument, by arguing from "known" effect to likely cause, i. e. a sort of matching-up of process with a particular *r*-type (see Lass 1977: 6). One of the pitfalls in this approach, it seems to me, is that one is likely to get into circular arguments. A case in point is Old English *r*-metathesis, where *r* appears to move towards dentals (e. g. *hros* > *hors*), and the process is interpreted as "dental attraction". To the question what sort of *r* is most likely to have taken part in such a process, the answer is, predictably, dental (apical) *r* (cf. Alexander 1985; Howell 1987). But what if the dental attraction premise is false — if, for instance, the process were triggered by the onset cluster? Early loss has been seen as the assimilation of *r* to the following dental cluster. In a detailed examination of this sound change, Hill (1940: 313—314) supposes, naturally, that the most likely *r*-type to undergo this change is the one most like a dental, i. e. tongue-point *r*. He does not, however, think it had to be a weakened *r* because *r* is also lost in those dialects today with a strongly articulated *r* (fn. 11). Anyone familiar with, say, the Glasgow accent, e. g. [wʌst in ðə wʌrəld], will take his point; here, we see loss of the *r* before the dental cluster in *worst* contrasting with vowel epenthesis in *world* due to a strong trilled *r*. It is to be noted that in his study of the "vulgar" speech of London in the Early Modern period, Matthews (1937: 218) found not only frequent loss of *r* before dentals, and even before nondentals, e. g. *Baber* 'Barber', *clake* 'clerk', but also 17th century spellings such as *paraliment* 'parliament', *Charelles* 'Charles', *gerrelds* 'girls', which seem to indicate a strong *r*. There is certainly evidence in support of Hill's claim that assimilatory loss of *r* does not assume a reduced *r*, so that early loss of *r* cannot, apparently, be linked to the long-term weakening which resulted in the general loss.

I said above that arguments from *r*-processes to the nature of *r* tend to be circular. It seems to me that the treatment of early loss in the literature is in danger of becoming so. What grounds are there for claiming that *r*-loss is due to dental assimilation? Only that *r* (assumed to be dental) is lost before dentals, which amounts to nothing more than stating the context in which it happens, explains little, and leaves us with a lot of evidence which is hard to reconcile or understand. In section 4.1., I shall put forward an alternative view of early *r*-loss.

2. The impact of *r*-loss on the phonological system

The general loss of *r* is not simply the loss of a segment; it is responsible for some major restructuring in the phonological system, coming at the end of a long process of phonetic change due to the influence of *r* on the preceding vowels. The main lines of change are given in (2).

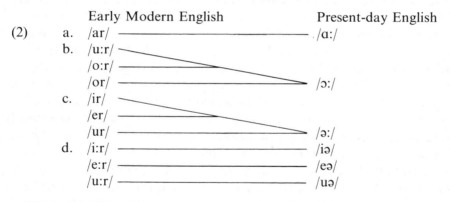

— Early Modern English /ar/ is from Middle English ăr (*barge, carp*) and sometimes from Middle English ĕr (*clerk, sergeant*). The following *r* prevented fronting to [æ] which occurred when *a* was in free position, but caused lengthening to [a:r] for which there is evidence from the late 16th century onwards. Present-day English /ɑ:/ shows a more retracted vowel.

— Early Modern English /u:r/ is from Middle English ūr (*court, source*) and from Middle English ōr (*sword, whore*). From the late 17th century there is a lowering process which first causes a merger with Middle English ǭ (*boar, glory*), then with the lengthened reflexes of Middle English ŏr (*corn, horse*).

— Early Modern English /ir/, /er/, /ur/, are from Middle English ĭr, ĕr, ŭr (*birth, herb, curse*). In Present-day English these are /ə:/. The evidence regarding this coalescence is confusing — probably because of actual differences among speakers. Jespersen ([1954]: 11.12) claims that it occurred in two stages: first /ir/ and /ur/ merged, to be joined later by /er/. Dobson (1968: ii, 258–259) seems to suggest that the earlier stage was the merger of /ir/ and /er/, while /ur/ first had to be opened to [ʌr] before it could become [ər].

— Early Modern English /i:r/ is from Middle English ēr (*clear, peer*); Early Modern English /e:r/ is from Middle English ę̄, ār, air (*beat, hare, hair*); Early Modern English /u:r/ is from Middle English ǭr (*moor, poor*) in so far as these escaped lowering. The present-day dipthongs could have developed in two ways: either a vowel-glide developed between the original vowel and the r or the glide is a residue from the r.

The main effect of r has been to lengthen and lower the preceding vowel (Dobson 1968: ii, 517–525, 724–762). At first sight, it might seem that the system is impoverished by the mergers in (b) and (c). It should be borne in mind, however, that the Early Modern vowels before r were simply allophonic variants of the vowels in free position; thus for Cooper (1685) the vowels in *cap* and *carp* would have had the same quality, differing only in length (Dobson 1968: ii, 517). Likewise, the vowels in e. g. *source, fear, hair, moor* were identified with those in *so, fee, hay, mood*. Some of these identifications would have become strained or even lost as a result of phonetic change; thus, in the 18th century the vowel in *carp* becomes associated with the (new) lengthened sound in *path, past*, [ɑ:] which is qualitatively different from *cap* [æ] or [a]; *source* (Early Modern English [u:r]) lowers (with most speakers) to [o:r] falling together with *sword*, but not yet with *horse* [ɔ:r]. The major phonological realignments, however, come with the loss of r; before then, the long central phoneme [ə:] did not exist, nor did the centring diphthongs; [ɔ:] was represented by the lengthened reflex of Middle English ŏr, e. g., *horse* and a class of *a*-words like *ball, war, haunt*, (cf. Walker 1791 on the latter), but the loss of r swelled its number (with *source, court*, etc.). Meanwhile, the vowels in free position continue to develop in their own way: [o:] in *so* becomes [ou] and [e:] in *hay* becomes [ei].

The traditional account so far offers a plausible description: the gradual vocalisation of r causes a phonetic change in the vowels, and with the loss of the conditioning factor we get phonological restructuring. The general loss of r is, thus, a watershed in the development of the system, hence it is important to know when it happened. From our brief survey, we have seen that scholarly opinion — discounting the "early loss" — tends to go for the 18th century, which still leaves a margin of error of a hundred years.

3. The orthoepical evidence

The broad agreement on the 18th century loss has been reached in spite of the orthoepical evidence. There is a long tradition of mistrust of the orthoepists — a belief that they did not record what they actually heard around them, but what they considered to be correct, which was a refined, affected, type of speech dominated by spelling (cf. Horn — Lehnert 1954: 920 — 921).

3.1. John Walker (1791)

John Walker's *Critical pronunciation dictionary* (1791) was probably the most popular and certainly the most influential of a spate of pronouncing dictionaries published in the last quarter of the 18th century. In the introduction to the stereotyped edition, which appeared in 1809, two years after Walker's death, the editor makes the remarkable claim that Walker has "fixed" English pronunciation, thus giving "stability and permanence to the pronunciation of a language now spoken in most parts of the known world". While she acknowledges Walker's immense influence on pronunciation, Sheldon (1947: 130 — 131) finds him "a much less honest recorder, a much more prescriptive reformer" than Thomas Sheridan (1780).

Walker seems to have anticipated some of his later critics. In the preface to his dictionary, he takes issue with Dr. Johnson's dictum that "those are to be considered as the most elegant speakers who deviate least from the written word". This is clearly impossible in the case of English, says Walker, where orthography and pronunciation differ so greatly. He further points out that Johnson failed to see the essential difference between accented and unaccented vowels, so characteristic of English. Johnson thought this a matter of *solemn* versus *familiar* speech; Walker comments:

> the *a* in *able* has its definite and distinct sound; but the same letter in *tolerable* goes into an obscure and indefinite sound approaching short *u*;

nor can any solemnity or deliberation give it the long open sound it has in the first word. (vi, references to 1818 edition)

He clearly had grasped the principle of vowel reduction, and the distinction between letters and sounds. As far as his prescriptiveness is concerned, the following is noteworthy:

> nor have I the least idea of deciding as a judge, in a matter of such much delicacy and importance as the pronunciation of a whole people ... my design is principally to give a kind of history of pronunciation, and a register of its present state. (ix)

Walker uses a system of diacritic numerals in his entries. The key to the pronunciation of the vowels is as follows:

A	E	I	O	U
f$\overset{1}{\text{a}}$te	m$\overset{1}{\text{e}}$	p$\overset{2}{\text{i}}$ne	n$\overset{1}{\text{o}}$	t$\overset{1}{\text{u}}$be
f$\overset{2}{\text{a}}$r	m$\overset{2}{\text{e}}$t	p$\overset{2}{\text{i}}$n	m$\overset{2}{\text{o}}$ve	t$\overset{2}{\text{u}}$b
f$\overset{3}{\text{a}}$ll			n$\overset{3}{\text{o}}$r	b$\overset{3}{\text{u}}$ll
f$\overset{4}{\text{a}}$t			n$\overset{4}{\text{o}}$t	

In the introductory *principles* to the dictionary, he distinguishes only three qualities of A-sound, which can be long or short. Thus, the sound in *father* is the long "middle sound" of A, while that in *fat* is the short "middle sound". In designating *far* $\overset{2}{\text{a}}$, he recognises lengthening, and most likely also the phonemic status of $\overset{2}{\text{a}}$ i.e. the sound in *far* is not just an allophonic variant of the sound in *fat*.

Walker does not keep strictly to the principle of one symbol one sound: $\overset{2}{\text{o}}$, it turns out, is the same as $\overset{1}{\text{u}}$ (the glide is not important and it is simply a matter of spelling); further, as he points out (*principles*, 167, p. 39), the sounds referred to by $\overset{3}{\text{a}}$ and $\overset{3}{\text{o}}$ are exactly the same. He is again making a concession to spelling, and uses $\overset{3}{\text{a}}$ on *a -/au-/aw-* spellings and $\overset{3}{\text{o}}$r on *or* -spellings e. g. b$\overset{3}{\text{a}}$wl 'ball', sh$\overset{3}{\text{o}}$rt. It is clear that *au* and *aw* are Walker's way of representing /ɔ:/, but while $\overset{3}{\text{o}}$ = $\overset{3}{\text{a}}$, it is not the case that $\overset{3}{\text{o}}$r = $\overset{3}{\text{a}}$ (or $\overset{3}{\text{a}}$u or $\overset{3}{\text{a}}$w); as Walker says in *principle* 167, *former* could have been written *faurmer* (not **faumer*!) Nowhere do we find reverse entries of the type **b$\overset{3}{\text{o}}$rl* 'ball'.

Walker's entries for *or*-words fall into two distinct groups:
$\overset{1}{\text{o}}$r   *court, force, hoard, source*, etc.
$\overset{3}{\text{o}}$r   *corn, horn, horse, short*, etc.

This tells us that the final levelling (cf. [2 b]) had not yet taken place and that a distinction was still made between the reflexes of ME ūr, ọ̄r, ǭr, which are designated $\overset{1}{\text{o}}$r, i. e. /o:/, and those of lengthened ME ŏr, which have $\overset{3}{\text{o}}$r, i. e. /ɔ:/. As Dobson points out, the correct etymological distinctions could still be recognised in the late 18th century, and only disappeared with the loss of *r* (ii, 743 – 744).

With regard to the development of Early Modern English /ir/ /er/ /ur/, Walker has:

$\overset{2}{\text{e}}$r *fir, firm, fern, virgin*, etc.
$\overset{2}{\text{u}}$r *fur, burn, dirt, shirt*, etc.

Evidently the first stage of the levelling has occurred, but Walker observes a distinction between /er/ and /ʌr/. Even so, his discussion of the difference between the *virgin* group and the *shirt* group (*principles* 108 – 110) sounds contrived, and his statement that more attention ought to be paid to the distinction suggests that for most speakers the levelling on /ər/ had taken place. It was, however, only with the loss of *r* that the new central sound /ə:/ came into being.

Turning to the evolution of the centring diphthongs (cf. fig. 2 d), Walker has:

$\overset{1}{\text{e}}$r *beer, cheer, fear*, etc.
$\overset{1}{\text{a}}$r *bare, chair, fair, there, where*, etc.
$\overset{1}{\text{o}}$r *poor, moor, whore*,[7] etc.
$\overset{1}{\text{u}}$r *cure, lure, sure*, etc.

where the long vowels before *r* are identified with their counterparts in free position. The most striking here is the identification of *fair, where*, etc. with $\overset{1}{\text{a}}$ – a characteristic feature of rhotic accents. However, Nares (1784) had remarked that *r* does not unite perfectly with preceding long vowels (p. 130) and for him the sounds in *fare* and *fate* are not exactly alike (p. 80). Nares' remark would lose all point if the *r* were not sounded in *fare*.

Walker's entries in the body of the work give no evidence at all of the general loss of *r*. We could perhaps accuse him of inflexibility, of a failure to register phonetic variants, but in fairness to him, his system, being roughly phonemic, was not equipped to handle such distinctions.

In contrast to the dictionary entries, the introductory principles do contain a number of references to an *r*-less type of pronunciation, which leaves no doubt that *r* was vocalised in less correct forms of speech:

> *r* is often too feebly sounded in England, and particularly in London where it is sometimes completely sunk ... the *r* in *lard, bard, card, regard*, is

pronounced so much in the throat as to be little more than the middle or Italian *a*, lengthened into *laad, baad, caad, regaad* (419, p. 63)

Under "rules to be observed by the natives of Ireland";

Thus *storm* and *farm* seem sounded by them as if written *staw-rum, fa-rum*, while the English sound the *r* so soft and so close to the *m*, that it seems pronounced as if written *stawm, faam*. (p. 14)

Some of his statements need a careful reading. He says, for instance, that the letter *r* is never silent, but its sound is sometimes transposed, so that the *r* is pronounced after *e* in final *re*, e. g. *centre, sceptre*. Looking at this through RP spectacles, one might suppose that Walker has been misled by a silent *r*. This is not the case; in the following paragraph, he tells us that the same transposition occurs in *apron, citron, saffron*, which are pronounced *apurn, citurn, saffurn*, which must at least indicate *r*-coloured vowels (416, 417, p. 62 − 63). It is sometimes claimed that Walker catches himself out in statements like the following:

There is a corrupt pronunciation ... among the vulgar, which is giving the *au* in *daughter, sauce, saucer*, the sound of Italian *a*, and nearly as if written *darter, sarce, sarcer*, (217, p. 44).

This does not, however, mean /ɑ:/ but /a:r/, and once again I refer to *LAB* Ph 194 *daughter*, where his statement is corroborated. Similarly, with regard to the final sound in *window, fellow*:

the vulgar shorten this sound, and pronounce the *o* obscurely and sometimes as if followed by *r*, as *winder, feller* (327, p. 52)

Pace Ellis (1869: i, 201) this must be taken literally;[8] Walker had a good enough ear to hear the difference between [ə] and [ər].

3.2. Thomas Batchelor (1809)

It might be argued that Walker, born in 1732, was describing the pronunciation of his generation rather than general usage. It is useful, therefore, to check his statements with those of Thomas Batchelor, born in 1775. In the introduction to his critical facsimile edition of Batchelor (1809), Arne Zettersten says Thomas Batchelor "occupies a distinguished place in the history of English phonology", he is described as a "keen observer, who does not silently accept the evidence of other orthoepists" (p. vii − ix). In particular, Batchelor is regarded as providing the crucial evidence on the diphthongisation of Middle English ę̄ > [ei], and Middle English ǭ > [ou]. As already mentioned, Dobson regards Batchelor as the first observer to clearly show the general loss of *r*:

The *u*, as in *but*, has always been supposed to maintain one uniform length; but this also appears to be something longer when preceding *r*, as in *burn*, than in other cases. It is difficult, however, to ascertain what portion of the sound belongs to *r*, as both this letter and *l* [as in *balm*] seem to be but slight alterations or additions to the unaccented *u* in *nostrum* (p. 19)

The comparison between *balm* and *burn* is certainly persuasive, but the point Batchelor is making, viz. that post-vocalic *r* and [ə] are very similar, renders his description ambiguous. A speaker with retroflex *r*-coloured vowels would likewise not be able to differentiate between the vowel and the *r* in *burn*. Elsewhere, his description is built on the fact that postvocalic *r* is indeed pronounced:

Mr. Sheridan and his successors appear to think, that the long vowels are pronounced in the same manner before *r*, as before other consonants; yet due consideration ... will prove that this is not the case (p. 99). The long vowels which precede *r*, in *near* (niyr), *pear* (peyr), *fire* (fuyr), *power* (powr), *tour* (tuwr), ... are imperfectly pronounced even by the best speakers. (p. 59) (cf. Nares above)

He gives *before, floor, course, force*, the value (owr), which is the same as for *moan, groan, throat*, and therefore agrees with Walker's ȯ̇; whereas *horse, border, order, organ*, are (or), which is also the vowel for *saw, draw, claw*, thus, Walker's ȯ̈.

Person, circle, virgin, virtue, are (er) − (ur) in provincial speech − while *first, durst, worst*, are (ur) (109 − 110). In his rules for the dialect of Bedfordshire, he notes that when *r* precedes *s* it is frequently not pronounced, so that *horse* becomes *hos* (105) and he further gives the well-known *fust, dust, wust*, etc. forms. Interestingly, he repeats Walker's claim that words terminating in *ow* are often mispronounced with (ur) and he gives *elbur, puteatur, windur*, 'elbow, potato, window' (110).

3.3. Benjamin Smart (1836)

A. J. Ellis (1869) has little good to say of Walker:

Walker has undoubtedly materially influenced thousands of people, who, more ignorant than himself, looked upon him as an authority. But his book has passed away, and his pronunciations are no longer accepted ... Smart's *Walker Remodelled*, 1836 and Worcester's *Critical Pronouncing Dictionary*, 1847, are those now most in vogue ... in Smart we have great consideration bestowed upon final *r* and its diphthongal action on the preceding vowel. (Vol. 2, 625)

Benjamin Smart was born in 1786. He had already published a *Grammar of English sounds* in 1812, where he distinguishes two articulations of *r*:

440 Michael Windross

R is an utterance of the voice either while the tongue is made to jar against the upper gum, as in *ray*, or while it is curled back so as to give the voice a hollow sound as in the throat, as in *mar*. (10)

He adds later:

Both these sounds are liable to frequent misuse. The latter, or smooth R, is often pronounced with so little force, as to be nothing more than the vowel AH. Thus *bar, nor, far*, are pronounced bah, naw, fa-ah.

The similarity to Walker's observations is obvious. The later pronouncing dictionary (1836) bore the title *Walker remodelled*. Intended as a update of Walker, the preface says "Mr. Smart has really produced a new work".[9] The work follows a similar pattern to Walker's. After introducing his rather cumbersome sound-scheme, Smart expands on each sound in a long set of *principles*, divided into paragraphs to which reference is made by number in the entries themselves. Here, he more or less repeats his earlier descriptions of *r* as pronounced "in well-bred London society":

with us, the letter *r* is sometimes a consonant, as in *ray, tray, stray*, ... and sometimes a guttural vowel sound. In the former capacity, it is formed by a strong trill of the tongue against the upper gum; in the latter case there is no trill, but the tongue *being curled back during the progress of the vowel preceding it*, the sound becomes guttural [emphasis mine, M. W.]

It is, he says, always possible to use the trill, but this will sound foreign, provincial, or overdone:

The extreme amongst the vulgar in London doubtlessly is, to omit the *r* altogether − to convert *far* into fàh, *hard* into hằhd, *cord* into cằwd ... (p. vii).

He adds (p. 33) "among mere cocknies this substitution of ằ for *ar* is a prevailing characteristic". Smart's "guttural vowel sound" is plainly a retroflex *r* which produces strongly *r*-coloured vowels.

Whereas Walker advocated a clear distinction between *virtue* with [er] and *shirt* with [ʌr], Smart seems to suggest that a levelling has taken place:

virtue (vertue), *irksome* (erksome), and *mirth* (merth) are delicacies of pronunciation which prevail only in the more refined classes of society. Even in these classes, sur, durt, and burd, ... are the current pronunciation of *sir, dirt*, and *bird*.

as indeed they were for Walker! Levelling is on [ʌr], i. e. there is still no [ə].

Smart maintains the distinction in or-words between ằwr and ōre, so *form* meaning 'figure' is (fằwrm) while *form* meaning 'a bench' is (fōurm).

The following are pronounced (åwr), å being the sound heard in *all:*
corn, fork, horse, perform, important, etc. The following are (ōre) or (ōur),
ō being the sound in *no: more, sword, sworn, court, borne, divorce,* etc.;
cf. *source* (sōurce), *sauce* (såwce).

He gives clear evidence (p. iv) for the diphthongisation of ā as in *pay:*
"in the mouth of a well-educated Londoner ... it is not quite simple, but
finishes more slenderly than it begins, tapering, so to speak, towards the
sound e̍", i. e. towards [i:]. It is therefore somewhat surprising to find
that *there, where, fair,* etc. are still identified with ā.

3.4. Summary

There is nothing in the orthoepical evidence 1791 — 1836 to indicate the
general loss of postvocalic *r* in standard speech. In this position *r* is
described as having a retroflex articulation, and the vowels acquire an *r*-
colouring. Most of the rhotic vowel-system of Walker (1791) remains
intact in Smart (1836) and even at this later date the *r*-less pronunciation
(incipient RP) is regarded as "vulgar". I conclude, then, that the conventional chronology for the general loss of postvocalic *r* is wrong; there
was no 18th century loss in standard speech. Furthermore, there seems
to have been no smooth transition within the phonological system from
the one type of speech to the other, as the gradual version has it.

Not wanting to finish on this negative note, I shall briefly put forward
an alternative view of *r*-loss.

4.   An alternative view
4.1. Early r-processes

r is involved in three processes in the Early Modern period:
(i) early loss, e. g. *worst* > *wost*, (ii) epenthesis, e. g. *girl* > *gerrel*, (iii)
metathesis, e. g. *forst* > *frost.* In the literature the first two have been
"explained" in articulatory terms, thus (i) is due to the assimilation of a
(weak) dental assimilation to a following dental consonant, (ii) on the
other hand, is due to a strongly articulated *r*. (iii) has been largely ignored;
Dobson (1968: ii, 1005) has a short paragraph on metathesis, but the
cases he mentions are in the other direction, e. g. *brid, drit* > *bird, dirt,*
(as in Old English *r*-metathesis). The ones I am concerned with show a
shift of *r* away from the syllable coda back to the onset, thus reversing
(in many cases) the effects of early Old English *r*-metathesis (cf. Epinal
frost, Corpus *forst*). Old English *r*-metathesis has also been seen in terms

of articulation, i. e. as "dental attraction" (Alexander 1985; Howell 1987); how, then, are we to explain this later metathesis, where *r* moves away from dentals?

At present, these three are seen as disparate processes, and early loss, certainly, as a dialectal feature (Dobson 1968: ii, 965). I would like to find a more unified account, especially because they are not confined to the dialects of English, but occur on wide-scale in the Flemish dialects and in Frisian. A vast amount of data has been collected on Flemish *r*-loss, which is still there in words where *r* appears before *-s(t)*, e. g. West Flemish *dorst* [dʌst] 'thirst'. Flemish *r*-loss has generally been seen in articulatory terms, as involving dental assimilation. The process is no longer productive, so these forms are relics left over from the period when *r*-loss was active, i. e. from roughly the 15th century down to the end of the 18th century.[10] Vowel epenthesis, however, is still active in Dutch between *r* and a following non-homorganic consonant, so *kerk* 'church', *kern* 'core', *korf* 'basket', *vork* 'fork', are regularly [kerək, kerən, korəf, vorək]. There is also evidence of epenthesis from late Middle Dutch and the early modern period, e. g. *berrent* from *bernen* 'burn', *heerefst* from *herfst* 'harvest'. Recent treatments of epenthesis in Dutch, while noting that its occurrence is subject to articulatory conditions, have not regarded this as the causal factor; Kooij (1981 − 2: 316) and Hickey (1985: 229) both suggest that epenthesis has to do with syllable quantity. It is well known that a vowel is lengthened when followed by a sonorant + C; epenthesis has the effect of breaking up overlong syllables. Interestingly, Hickey links epenthesis and (vowel) syncope: "with both processes phonetic substance is added or deleted in order to arrive at structures which are acceptable in terms of syllable structure".

This offers a fresh approach to the early *r*-processes. Given that *r* causes lengthening of vowels, and, as a sonorant in the coda, adds to the overall syllable weight, I claim that early *r*-loss (syncope) and epenthesis each served to break up overlong syllables;[11] they are in complementary distribution, i. e. there is syncope of *r* when it occurs before dentals, and epenthesis when it occurs before non-dentals. In this way we can bring in process (iii): *r*-metathesis can be seen (a) as a strategy to prevent the loss of phonetic material, a sort of rescue operation, or (b), as yet another way of lessening syllable weight by shifting *r* from the coda to the onset (indeed, both (a) and (b) could work together).[12] Though the evidence for loss of *r* before non-dentals is sparse (see Matthews 1937 above), it could also be accommodated within this framework.

4.2. The general loss of postvocalic r

The conventional view puts forward a plausible scenario for the general loss of *r*, as the final stage in a long-term weakening process. Having argued that it did not happen in this way, I must explain how it comes that standard pronunciation is an *r*-less accent.

Since the work of Labov in the 1960s, it has become established practice to link the pronunciation of *r* to social factors, such as age, sex, and class differentiation. For instance, in her study of postvocalic *r* in Edinburgh speech, Romaine (1978) finds an increase of *r*-lessness among boys of primary school age, and the substitution of frictionless continuant [ɹ] for the traditional flapped or trilled *r*, among girls of the same age. The latter was also observed as a marker of "polite" speech among middle-class teenage girls. Wells (1984: 59) finds that the prestige norm (RP) is exerting an influence in urban areas like Southampton and Bristol which traditionally have rhotic accents; he finds that *r*-lessness increases as one moves up the social scale.

In the evidence we have been looking at, it is striking how the loss of *r* is always described as "vulgar", and characteristic of the London accent (which links up nicely with occasional loss of *r* before non-dentals found in Matthews (1937)). Very little has been made of this social dimension in the treatment of the general loss.

Honey (1989: 20−22) mentions the enormous growth in the population of London in the period 1500−1800 from 50,000 to nearly a million; he also emphasises the social aspirations of this expanding population, and their desire to emulate correct speech:

> one aspect of its pronunciation was constant: its educated speakers were aware that there was a standard form of accent that anyone aspiring to high social position ought to copy (Honey 1989: 22).

Once again we are back to the idea of a "single system", where the standard accent is, as it were, passed on by its privileged guardians to the rest of society. But this view largely ignores one of the most important shifts in the social structure of industrialised England: the rise of the new middle class. The historian Phyllis Deane points to their enormous influence on the shaping of the country both materially and intellectually in the post-1830 period (1979: 284). We should expect this shift to be reflected at the level of language. As Weinstock observes (*DEMEP* 1976: 23−24) the social classes differed not only in their speech habits, but also in their evaluation of language. In the latter, the opposite ends of the scale, the upper and lower classes (however their actual speech habits differed) resembled each other in their conservatism, in their sticking to traditional pronunciation; it was the upsurging middle classes, uncertain in their speech habits, who provided the impetus for rapid sound change. It is my view that the rising middle class brought their *r*-less accent with them, and this ousted the older type of pronunciation descibed by Walker and his fellow orthoepists. The prestige norm had changed.

Notes

1. The papers presented at this conference have nearly all focused on the 16th and 17th centuries. One of the ways of dividing the Modern period is Early Modern (1450 – 1700) and Late Modern (1700 – 1900) (cf. Rydén – Brorström (1987; 9)). In contrast, the proposed *Dictionary of Early Modern English pronunciation* will cover the period 1500 – 1800; the arguments for including the 18th century (and works like Batchelor 1809) are cogently set out in Weinstock's contribution (*DEMEP*, 9 – 39).
2. Much has been made of the vagaries of 18th century pronunciation, especially those which lived on into the 19th century with some speakers, giving them an "old-world charm"; such pronunciations as *obleege* 'oblige', *'ospital* and *'umble* 'hospital, humble', *gyuard* and *gyarden* 'guard, garden', *goold* 'gold', *yaller* 'yellow', etc. (not forgetting their lower-class counterparts, e.g. *scholard* 'scholar', *wunst* 'once' (see Honey 1985: 249; Phillipps 1984: 128 – 142).
   The features I want to draw attention to are of a more systematic, if less anecdotal, nature.
3. Perhaps this is not so iconoclastic – cf. Dobson in the preface to the first edition of his book; "many elements went to make up the developing standard spoken language of the Early Modern English period; ... the accepted norms of pronunciation of one generation were not merely apt to differ from, but were sometimes not even directly developed from, those of a previous generation" (p. vii)
4. King (1969: 109 – 110) argued that loss of segments is always abrupt; indeed he took the case of postvocalic *r* as an example. Whatever logical reasons there are to support this view, it has proved useful to distinguish between loss resulting from a long-term weakening and abrupt loss (syncope). Loss of *r* can occur in either way. For a restatement of King's position cf. Toon (1983: 63).
5. With this difference, Strang says *r* was reduced to a vocalic element *early* in the century, while Barber says it was a *late* 18th century loss.
6. Reduction and elimination are not the same thing, and Flint's evidence only supports the former: *r* is "fort adouci, presque muet" (p. 41).
7. Walker gives two pronunciations: hôòr [u:] and hóre [o:]. He comments: "if there can be a polite pronunciation of this vulgar word, it is the first of these."
8. Cf. Ellis (1869: 1, 201) "illiterate speakers ... usually interpose an (r) between any back vowel ... and a subsequent vowel (e.g. in *drawing, law of the land, window of the house*). From this habit, a very singular conclusion has been commonly drawn by a great many people, namely, that such persons habitually say (drAAr, lAAr, windər) when *not* before a vowel – a feat which they are mostly incapable of performing. They will indeed rhyme *window, cinder*, not because they say (windər, sindər) as generally assumed, ...

but because they say (wində, sində) or (windɹ, sindɹ) omitting to trill the *r* in both cases."

Ellis' argument is muddled. The point is not whether they insert a trilled *r*, but whether they insert *any* sort of *r*, that is to say, there is a contrast between [wində] and [windɹ]. Probably the source of the confusion is Ellis' inability to distinguish between plain schwa and *r*-coloured schwa. Cf. vol. 5, p. 830: "the Southern *r* ... often becomes lost after (a:) (o:), or considered as a mere symbol of the change of *a, o* into these sounds, and is identified in other cases with a vowel somewhat like (ə, ə:) but probably different from them, as the tip of the tongue is certainly a little too raised for any real vowel to be uttered." Comparing this description with my own pronunciation of [ə:], where the tip of the tongue is lowered, I would have to conclude that Ellis had *r*-coloured vowels.

9. The preface also claims as one of its chief features "a method of indicating the pronunciation of words, which by renouncing altogether the pretence of exhibiting no more letters than sounds, is less barbarous to the eye, and at once intelligible." In fact, Smart's sound scheme abounds in redundancies, is difficult to use, and is in this respect inferior to Walker's, even if it does try to give more detail.

10. Two pieces of evidence can be put forward to show that *r*-less forms are relics: (i) on the assumption that *r*-loss is due to dental assimilation, the appearence of *r*-less forms in the dialect of Ghent, which today has uvular *R*, shows that they must date to a period before the change to unvular *R*, (ii) in West Flemish, *gras* regularly becomes *gas*, which is from metathetic *gars*; the latter, however, has not survived, therefore *gas* is a relic.

11. This claim is further supported by the Frisian evidence, where there is *r*-loss before dentals. Traditionally regarded as a dental assimilation (Cohen *et al.* 1972: 130), syllable-quantity seems to play an important role. Tiersma (1979: 142): "*r* seems to delete more easily after *any* long vowel or falling diphthong (both of which may be considered long vocalic nuclei) than when preceded by a short vowel".

12. A more fully worked out version of these ideas is presented in Windross (1988: 188−200). Charles Jones makes a similar link between *r*-metathesis and syllable quantity (Jones 1989: 190−195).

References

Alexander, James D.
  1985   "R-metathesis in English: A diachronic account", *Journal of English Linguistic* 18: 33−40.
Barber, Charles L.
  1976   *Early Modern English*. London: André Deutsch.
Batchelor, Thomas
  1809   See Zettersten 1974
Cohen, A.−C. L. Ebeling−K. Fokkema−A. F. G. Van Holk
  1972   *Fonologie van het Nederlands en het Fries.* 'S Gravenhage: Martinus Nijhoff.
Cooper, Christopher
  1685   *Grammatica linguae Anglicanae.* Scolar Press Facsimiles (EL 86).
Deane, Phyllis
  1979   *The first Industrial Revolution.* (2nd edition). Cambridge: Cambridge University Press.

De Chene, Brent—Stephen R. Anderson
  1979   "Compensatory lengthening", *Language* 55: 505—535.
DEMEP
  1976   *Dictionary of Early Modern English pronunciation 1500—1800*. Report based
            on the *DEMEP* symposium and editorial meeting at Edinburgh 23—26
            October 1974. Stockholm: Almqvist & Wiksell.
Dobson, E. J.
  1968   *English pronunciation 1500—1700*. 2 vols. (2nd edition). Oxford: Clarendon
            Press.
Ekwall, Eilert
  1975   *A history of Modern English sounds*. (trans. Alan Ward) Oxford: Blackwell.
Ellis, Alexander J.
  1869   *On Early English pronunciation*. (5 parts) (EETS.) London: Oxford University
            Press.
Flint, Mather
  1740   See Kökeritz 1944
Gimson, Alfred Charles
  1984   "The RP accent", in: Peter Trudgill (ed.), 45—54.
Hickey, Raymond
  1985   "The interrelationship of epenthesis and syncope: Evidence from Dutch and
            Irish", *Lingua* 65: 229—249.
Hill, Archbald A.
  1940   "Early loss of *r* before dentals", *PMLA* 55: 308—357.
Hock, Hans Henrich
  1986 a   *Principles of historical linguistics*. Berlin—New York—Amsterdam: Mouton
            de Gruyter.
  1986 b   "Compensatory lengthening: In defence of the concept 'mora' ", *Folia Lin-
            guistica* 20: 431—460.
Honey, John
  1985   "Acrolect and hyperlect, the redefinition of English RP", *English Studies* 66:
            241—257.
  1989   *Does accent matter?* London: Faber and Faber.
Horn, Wilhelm—Martin Lehnert
  1954   *Laut und Leben. Englische Lautgeschichte in der neueren Zeit (1400—1950)*.
            2 vols. Berlin: Deutscher Verlag der Wissenschaften.
Jeffers, Robert—Ilse Lehiste
  1979   *Principles and methods for historical linguistics*. Cambridge, Mass.: MIT Press.
Jespersen, Otto
  1909   *A Modern English grammar on historical principles*. Part I, *Sounds and spell-*
  [1954]   *ings*. Reprinted London: Allen and Unwin.
Jones, Charles
  1989   *A history of English phonology*. London and New York: Longman.
King, Robert D.
  1969   *Historical linguistics and generative grammar*. New Jersey: Prentice Hall.
Kökeritz, Helge
  1944   *Mather Flint on early eighteenth-century pronunciation*. Uppsala: Almqvist &
            Wiksell.

Kooij, J. G.
1981   "Epenthetische schwa: processen, regels en domeinen", *Spektator* 11 — 4: 315 — 325.
LAE
1978   *The linguistic atlas of England*, ed. Harold Orton — Stewart Sanderson — and John Widdowson. London: Croom Helm.
Lass, Roger
1977   "On the specification of Old English /r/", *Studia Anglica Posnaniensia* 9: 3 — 16.
1984   *Phonology. An introduction to basic concepts.* Cambridge: Cambridge University Press.
1989   "How early does English get 'Modern'? or what happens when you listen to orthoepists and not to historians", *Diachronica* 6: 75 — 110.
Luick, Karl
[1964]   *Historische Grammatik der englischen Sprache.* [Reprinted.] Stuttgart: Tauchitz.
Matthews, William
1937   "The vulgar speech of London in the XV — XVII centuries", *Notes and Queries*, Jan — Apr. 1937.
Milroy, James
1984   "The history of English in the British Isles" in: Peter Trudgill (ed.), 5 — 31.
Nares, Robert
1784   *Elements of orthoepy.* London: printed for T. Payne and son.
Newton, Brian E.
1972   "Loss of /r/ in a modern Greek dialect", *Language* 48: 566 — 572.
[1972]   [The Kent State University Press, facsimile reproduction of 1906 reprint].
Philipps, K. C.
1984   *Language and class in Victorian England.* Basil Blackwell in association with André Deutsch.
Prins, A. A.
1974   *A history of English phonemes from Indo-European to present-day English.* Leiden: University Press.
Puttenham, George
1589   *The art of English poesie.*
Romaine, Suzanne
1978   "Postvocalic /r/ in Scottish English: sound change in progress?", in: Peter Trudgill (ed.), 144 — 157.
Rydén, Mats — Sverker Brorström
1987   *The be/have variation with intransitives in English with special reference to the late modern period.* Stockholm: Almqvist & Wiksell.
Sheldon, Esther
1947   "Walker's influence on the pronunciation of English", *PMLA* 67: 130 — 146.
Sheridan, Thomas
1780   *A general dictionary of the English language.* Scolar Press facsimiles (EL 50).
Smart, Benjamin
1812   *A grammar of English sounds or the first steps in English elocution.* London.
1836   *Walker Remodelled. A new critical pronouncing dictionary of the English language.* London, printed for T. Cadell.
Strang, Barbara M. H.
1970   *A history of English.* London: Methuen.

Tiersma, Pieter M.
1979   *Aspects of the phonology of Frisian.* (Fryske Akademy nr. 573.) Amsterdam:
          Vrije Universiteit Amsterdam.
Toon, Thomas E.
1983   *The politics of early Old English sound change.* New York — London: Academic
          Press.
Trudgill, Peter (ed.)
1978   *Sociolinguistic patterns in British English.* London: Edward Arnold.
1984   *Language in the British Isles.* Cambridge: Cambridge University Press.
Walker, John
1791   *A critical pronouncing dictionary and expositor of the English language.* [18th
[1818]   edition, London: stereotyped and printed by A. Wilson]
Wells, J. C.
1984   "English accents in England" in, Peter Trudgill (ed.), 55 — 69.
Wełna, Jerzy
1978   "On the rise of the New English central phoneme /ə:/", *Leuvense Bijdragen*
          67: 163 — 167.
Windross, Michael
1988   *R-metathesis and early r-loss in English and Dutch: a diachronic account.*
          [Unpublished doctoral diss. Katholiek Universiteit Leuven.]
Wyld, Henry C.
1936   *A history of modern colloquial English.* Oxford: Basil Blackwell.
Zettersten, Arne
1974   *A critical facsimile edition of Thomas Batchelor: 'An orthoepical analysis of*
          the English language' and 'An orthoepical analysis of the dialect of Bedfordshire'
          (1809). (Lund Studies in English 45.) Lund: Gleerup.

Early Modern London business English

Laura Wright

1. Introduction

This paper will be concerned with accounts, written primarily in London, during the early part of the Early Modern period. They are interesting linguistically for numerous reasons, but here I shall concentrate on form and function. This is because the form of accounts-keeping became divergent in the Early Modern period, and this divergence seems to be innovative.

London accounts of the Middle English period were kept not in English, but in a deliberate, rule-governed mixture of Latin and English, or Anglo-Norman and English.[1] Most modern London business accounts are kept in English, with a small amount of residual Latin formulae. This changeover occurred in the main during the Early Modern period, but it did not happen overnight. For at least a century the two conventions continued side by side, until eventually the Latin and Anglo-Norman content dropped out of use and English predominated.

1.1. Data

The paper will focus largely on the archive of London Bridge, but there is a large body of London business accounts extant from the Early Modern period. Many churches and livery companies kept series of accounts during this period, as did official civic bodies such as the Customs Office, and some private individuals kept personal records.[2]

2.1. Convention # 1: macaronic structure

The earlier form of accounts-keeping was the form inherited from the late Middle English period. This is the practice of constructing accounts from a mixture of two languages, usually either Latin and English, or Anglo-Norman and English. At first sight this seems rather a perverse convention, but it has a redoubtable history, and examples exist from at least the eleventh century to the sixteenth century.[3]

The mixed or "macaronic" style of accounts-keeping was still productive in the Early Modern period in London. I use the term "macaronic" here to mean that two languages were deliberately mixed in a rule-governed, but not word-predictable, fashion. From the fourteenth century the rule was, very broadly speaking, that only NPs, including verbal nouns, could surface in L 2. All other parts of speech were written in L 1. That it was not word-predictable means that although any NP could surface in L 2, it was not compulsory that it should do so:

(1) 1464 × 1465[4]

... Ꝉt pro vj payles emptꝰꝑ oꝑibz Cementarī xv d . Ꝉt pro iij baskettₑ emptꝰ iiij d . Ꝉt pro iiij shevers emptꝰ iiij d . Ꝉtꝑ j poley (ij d) & ij barelł (viij d) emptꝰ & positꝰ in ten̄ suꝑ pontemꝑ . traxione aque x d . Ꝉt Nich̄o Walterꝑ . viij remisꝰ ab ipō emptꝰ v sꝰ . Ꝉtꝑ . iij . scopisꝰ (vj d) & bromes (j d) emptꝰꝑ vsū pontisꝰ vij d . Ꝉtꝑ . vno parī sufflomī emptꝰꝑ Cementarī iij d . Ꝉtꝑ . iiij^{or} parꝰ nouaꝝ ocreaꝝ emptꝰ de Nich̄o Walter vocatꝰ Tydebotesꝑ stauro pontꝰ xiiij s̑ . Ꝉtꝑ . vj . bȝ testaꝝ ostreoꝝ emptꝰ & expn̄ in posic̄oe noui oꝑis lapidei pontis hoc anno p^{c}cꝰ cȝ . bȝ iij d xviij d . Ꝉtꝑ . iij lb̄ de tough̄ emptꝰ & expn̄ in calkyng batelł iij d . Ꝉt [ ] Brice Mercerꝑ xvj vlnisꝰ pannī linei ab ipō emptꝰ & expn̄ in facturꝰ iij . mappaꝝ . & j Cuppeborde clothe & iij napkyns remān viij s̑ viij d . Ꝉt Joh̄i Garetꝑ . j rolle & xiij pelł pgamenī ab ipō emptꝰꝑ . librꝰ huiꝰ Compī Indenturꝰ obligac̄onib̄z ac alijs evidencꝰ & remoꝝ & pontis concernencꝰ . suꝑscribend xj s̑ Ꝉt Wilło Westram pro encausto expn̄ in vsu pontis hoc anno v d ob̄ Ꝉt pro j Reme papirī iij s̑ iiij d Ꝉtꝑ . bromes emptꝰ & expn̄ in oꝑibz Cementarī iiij d . Ꝉt ꝑ . j shodeshouelł emptꝰ iiij d . Ꝉt [ ] Wantyngfeld .ꝑ iiij virgꝰ & dī & dī quarter pannī nigrī vocatꝰ blak of lire engreyn̄ delibatꝰ Thome Vrsewyk recordatorī Joh̄i Baldewyn̄ c̄oi seruientī Thome Rygby subvicꝰ & M Will̄o Dunthorn̄ c̄oi Cl̄ico Ciuitatis london̄ pro eoꝝ attendencꝰ & labore diu^{e}cꝰ vicibzꝑ c̄oi vtilitate Ciuitatꝰ p^{d}d̄ce in discussione Jurī̄s & titl̄i iij acraꝝ pratī nuꝑ in̄ demand intꝰ Coītatem d̄ce Ciuitatis & Ab̄btem de Stratford p^{c}cꝰ cȝ virgꝰ vij s̑ vj d — xxxiiij s̑ viij d .

'And for 6 pails bought for the mason's work 15 d. And for 3 baskets bought 4 d. And for 4 shevers bought 4 d. And for 1 pulley 2 d, and 2 barrels 8 d, bought and placed in a tenement on the bridge for the drawing of water 10 d. And to Nicholas Walter for 8 oars bought from him 5 s. And for 3 shovels 6 d, and brooms 1 d, bought for the use of the bridge 7 d. And for 1 pair of bellows bought for the masons 3 d. And for 4 pairs of new boots bought from Nicholas Walter, called tideboots, for the bridge store 14 s. And for 6 bushels of oyster shells bought and used in setting the new stone work of the bridge this year, price 3 d a bushel, 18 d. And for 3 lbs of tow bought and used for caulking the boat 3 d. And to [ ] Brice mercer for 16 ells of linen cloth bought from him and used to make 3 cloths, one cupboard cloth and 3 napkins remaining, 8 s 8 d. And to John Garet for 1 roll and 13 skins of parchment bought from him for writing out the book of this account, indentures, bonds and other evidences and remembrances concerning the bridge work, 11 s. And to William Westram for ink bought and spent in bridge use this year 5½ d. And for 1 ream of paper 3 s 4 d. And for brooms bought and used in the mason's work 4 d. And for 1 shodshovel bought 4 d. And to [ ] Wantyngfeld for 4 and a half yards and half a quarter of black cloth called grained black of lire, delivered to Thomas Ursewyk recorder, John Baldewyn common sergeant, Thomas Rygby undersheriff and Master William Dunthorn common clerk of the City of London; for their attention and labour on diverse occasions for the common benefit of the aforesaid city, in discussion of the right and title of 3 acres of meadow lately in a claim between the commonalty of the said city and the Abbot of Stratford, price of each yard 7 s 6 d. 34 s 8 d.'

Example (1) was taken from the archive of London Bridge, which mixes Latin (L 1) and English (L 2). I have retained the abbreviation and suspension system used by contemporary scribes because it forms an integral part of the text, as I shall discuss below. The next example, number (2), shows how the structure of a macaronic text developed over the century:

(2)   1553[5]

... vnū le sowyng presse 13 les bordes voc shelfes quatuor les pryntyng presses duo par de cases wythe letters to prynte cū pyctures & historijs quatuordecem par del wood [ ] decem les bordes to layvppon paper duo leʒ deles formes one longe & nother shorte tres leʒ pottes for pryntynge Ink duo Ink blak boxes wythe a redde boxe duos boxes of canon of grete Roman duo le Forme of Inglysshe letter sett in a chase one forme of the grete primer letter sett in a chase one forme of pica bownde vp in pagies duo forme of the longe primer letter in pages vnū le shelffe vnū le baskett vnū le baskett (sic) vnū le boxe full of stykes for the presses cum diuᵖsis alijs rebʒ circa le pryntynge howse vnū parr del empty caseʒ vnū lapidem cū vno le muller to grynde colours wytheall vnū le box cum grete wooddeñ letters duo parr of Cases wythe letters septem bakettₑ wythe letters vnū le forme and d̄ of a new pye letter duo les shelfes cum picturis quatuor par del Ireñ Chases vnū le baskett full of old letters cum diuᵖsis alijs rebʒ circa

eandem domū vnū librum voca Grayle in ꝑchement vnū le stole cū diu̇sis Chaseis
del wooḑ vnū par del trestles dicers Instrument cum Tolis to bynde wythe ...

> 'one sewing press; 13 boards called shelves; four printing
> presses; two pairs of cases with letters to print with pictures
> and histories; fourteen pairs of wood [ ]; ten boards to lay
> upon paper; two deal forms, one long, another short; three
> pots for printing ink; two ink black boxes with a red box; two
> boxes of canon of great roman; two forms of English letter
> set in a chase; one form of the great primer letter set in a
> chase; one form of pica bound up in pages; two forms of the
> long primer letter in pages; one shelf; one basket; one basket
> (sic); one box full of sticks for the presses with various other
> things around the printing house; one pair of empty cases;
> one stone with one miller to grind colours with; one box with
> great wooden letters; two pairs of cases with letters; seven
> baskets with letters; one and a half forms of a new pye letter;
> two shelves with pictures; four pairs of iron chases; one basket
> full of old letters with various other things around the same
> house; one book called Grayle in parchment; one stole with
> various wooden chases; one pair of trestles; a lot[6] of instru-
> ments with tools to bind with ...'

This inventory exemplifies the tradition of macaronic Latin accounts-
keeping as it had evolved by the middle of the sixteenth century. Whereas
in macaronic Latin of the Middle English period only NPs appeared in
L 2, this example shows that by the middle of the sixteenth century it is
only articles, numbers, prepositions and conjunctions which regularly
appear in L 1, along with catch-all formulae like *diversis aliis rebus*. Notice
also the rather odd inclusion of the definite article in the NP, after the
numbers and before the nouns.[7]

   Scribes sometimes emphasised the macaronic nature of the style by
representing the same word in both Latin and English in a single entry.
Example (3), also taken from the archive of London Bridge, shows a
single scribe representing the technical term *bricktile* three different ways,
both in Latin and in English, thereby demonstrating competence in both
languages:

(3)   1417 × 18[8]

Itᵖ r̃ᵖ manⁿ Simonis sergeauntᵖ vj Ml viij C tegul vocᵖ Brike venditᵖ ...
Itm̃ r̃ᵖ xxiiijᵒʳ Ml iiij C & dj̃ de Briktill venḑ ...
Itm̃ recᵖᵖ Ml vij C tegul de Bryke venḑ ...

'And received by the hands of Simon Sergeaunt for selling
6,800 tiles called brick ... And received for selling 24,450
bricktiles ... And received for selling 1,700 tiles of brick'

The main point I want to make about the written macaronic form is that
it was a contemporary functional norm for accountants, with a history
stretching back over many centuries, and which had evolved and changed
over time, as one expects a living linguistic form to do.

2.2. Convention #2: English

The second, subsequent form for keeping accounts was to use monolingual English. English accounts appear from the financial year 1479/1480
in the archive of London Bridge. Individual monolingual English accounts
certainly appear earlier than this, but it is safe to say that this style
overtakes the macaronic style in volume in the Early Modern period. Cf.
example (4):

(4)   1530 × 1531[9]

pd to the Coke Thom^{as} pker for his labo^r x s
pd to mynyon washedyshe for iij dayes ix d ...
pd to the skolyon for swepyng the Chȳney ij d

The English accounts of the period are set out on the page in the same
way as the macaronic accounts, they follow the same stylistic contraints,
and they also make use of the Latin abbreviation and suspension system.

   This kind of document has not been targeted by linguists before,
despite being source material for an investigation of Early Modern
London English. This is presumably because the stylistic constraints of
accounts-keeping have been thought to be too limiting to provide any
kind of sustained evidence. Nevertheless such accounts do provide linguistic evidence, and I give here two brief examples to illustrate the
potential scope of study.

2.2.1. Syntactic evidence
Business accounts provide evidence, of a limited kind, of synchronic
English syntax. Example (5) shows how costs related to the same expense
are often entered contiguously, and so pronouns can refer back to a head
noun mentioned in a previous entry:

(5)   1520[10]

Itm paid to the men that clensed the drawght[11] *in the howse off willm Alderston*
for vij ton the ton͛ ijˢ ijᵈ Smᵃ xv s ij ᵭ
Itm for a Reward for them to Drynke ij ᵭ
Itm paid to a Man͞ to owˢe the͞m ᵽᵗ nyght iiij ᵭ
Itm paid for spredyng a brode of that that Restid in the vowte and for makyng
clene of the Towell of the same sege xx ᵭ
Itm paid for a bourde to cow͛ ᵽᵗ place that they brake in to ᵽᵉ vowte iiij ᵭ
Itm paid for a Illi candyll for them that nyght i ᵭ

Despite the stylistic conventions of accounts-keeping, entries can consist
of more than one clause. Example (5) shows some relative clauses, which
exploit the multiple functions of the word *that* in Early Modern English
(cf. Modern London English *the men* who *cleansed the toilet; for spreading
abroad of that* which *rested in the vault; to cover that place* where *they
broke into the vault*). There is some difficulty about how to view this
term; whether to regard it as a connective particle which merely links the
clause to its antecedent without having any syntactic function, or whether
to regard it as a relative pronoun (for a summary of the discussion about
the status of the relative *that* see van der Auwera (1985: 149−179) and
also Seppänen (1990, 1991)).

2.2.2. Semantic evidence
Accounts tend to contain vocabulary which is not listed in dictionaries,
and whose meaning or etymology can often be obscure:

(6)   1503 × 1504[12]

*... to williā Ayleworth bogeman for Cariage of x pypes of water to the besines
of the fire on͞ the bridge xij ᵭ ... To walter Duffe bogeman for Cariage of grete
nombre of boges wᵗ water to the same besines v s̄ . to Robert Clement Bogeman
for cariage of grete nombre of boges to the sayd besynes of the fire by all the hole
nyght vj s̄ viij ᵭ to his ᵝuᵃnte of rewarde for his deligence and suche harmes as
he saith͞ he susteyned at the besines of the same fire by the co͞maundement of
my lord maisʳ iij s̄ iiij ᵭ*

The term *bogeman* is not recorded in dictionaries, and in this extract
seems to mean 'one who carries buggies of water'; that is, a prototype
fireman. The term *boge* may be derived from Old French *bouge* 'leather
bag' (*MED* bouge n. (1)). The modern term *buggy* 'cart' is not attested
before 1773 (*OED* buggy sb.). Its etymology is unknown. This example
may be showing the missing link between 'leather water bag' and the
extended meaning, 'cart which ferries leather water bags'.

2.3. The overlap between #1 and #2

The linguistic structure of business accounts can be thus summarised:

Table 1. Structure of Early Modern Business accounts

Early Modern Business accounts =	(1) macaronic	[L 1 + L 2]
	(2) non-macaronic	[L 2]
		+ L 1
and language choice of (1) =	(1) + NP =	+ L 2
	(2) − NP =	+ L 1
where L 1 = Latin or Anglo Norman, L 2 = English		

There is a certain overlap between these two styles, however. It is not possible to keep them entirely apart, because some forms are ambiguous, and could belong to both Latin and English:

(7)   1462 × 1463[13]

Et eidm̄ Patricio pro car̄ xxxiij lodes robissh̄ a diu̇s̄ tenement̄ pontis infra Ciuitatem hoc anno capient̄p q̄ lode iij d̦

> 'And to the same Patrick for carriage of 33 loads of rubbish from diverse bridge tenements within the City this year taking for each load 3 d'

In this macaronic Latin extract the loans <*diu̇s̄ tenement̄*> are well-formed English lexemes ('diverse tenements') as well as wellformed Latin lexemes ('diversis tementis'), and follow English word-order. Macaronic writing thus exploits the overlap, where L 1 maps onto L 2. It is true that the abbreviation marks used to indicate case endings or internal suspension of letters sometimes clarifiy Latin loans in context as being specifically English or Latin representations, but they do not always do so. In 1479/1480 the macaronic Latin accounts of London Bridge switched into English:

(8)   1481 × 1482[14]

Therof spent for the floure of a sege in the teñt atte signe of the Cornysshe Choughꝫ vp̄on the Brigge

In example (8) the precise form <*teñt*> can be regarded as specifically English, because this particular configuration rarely occurs in macaronic Latin entries; but in the English section-heading for accounts for the year 1516/1517:

(9)   a. 1516 × 1517[15]

vacacions of teñtis

the precise form <*teñtis*> has to be regarded as both Latin and English,
as it is commonly found in the earlier Latin entries, cf. examples (9 b)
and (9 c):

　　　　b. 1473 × 1474[16]

*Ɪt p iiijᵒʳ lodes de hertlatthe hoc anno emptᵖ & expenditᵖ tam in tegulacȯe tene-
mentoꝝ ponti ᵖdc̄ ppt̄m qᵃm in factura muroꝝ diuisibil in teñtis euisdem̄ pontis*
...

　　　　　　　　'And for 4 loads of heartlath bought and spent this year both
　　　　　　　　in tiling tenements of the aforesaid bridge property and in
　　　　　　　　making partition walls in the same bridge tenements'

　　　　c. 1473 × 1474[17]

*... & sup videnꝗ &p uidensᵖp emendacᵖ stagni & lez flodegates molendini & alioꝝ
defectᵖ tenementoꝝ pontis ꝭm & usqȝ depford vs zd & Grenewich̄ pro terrᵖ &
teñtis ꝭm sup uidenꝗ ad diꝰsas vices hoc anno — zsᵖ izꝗ*

　　　　　　　　'and overseeing and supervising mending the pond and mill
　　　　　　　　floodgates and other defects in the bridge tenements there and
　　　　　　　　at Deptford, 5 s 10 d; and at Greenwich for looking over
　　　　　　　　tenants and tenements there at various times this year, 10 s
　　　　　　　　9 d'

The three features which made this kind of overlap possible are:
a) borrowing of Latin roots into English
b) shared orthographical representation of certain morphemes, both free
　 and bound[18]
c) borrowing of the Latin abbreviation and suspension system into
　 English texts
In short, early Early Modern macaronic business Latin consists of NPs
in L 2, other parts of speech in L 1, and certain morphemes, both free
and bound, which are identical in L 1 and L 2. It forms a visual fusion
between the two languages.[19] We are, perhaps, familiar with the notion
of registers enlarging or restricting their scope to become multifunctional
(e. g. one of the criteria of a standard dialect is that it should be multifunctional); here we are dealing with a function (business writing) becoming multistructural.

3. The convergence model

Some time has been spent detailing this because Early Modern business English is a rather unfamiliar form. But it is of linguistic interest because it exemplifies from (Early Modern) English a model of linguistic change that has been identified in several other languages.

Mühlhäusler (1982) found that lexical items in Tok Pisin frequently had their source in not one but two languages, and were the result of lexical conflation. An example is the Tok Pisin word *antap* meaning 'on top, roof', which has sources in both English *on top* and Tolai *antip* 'thatched roof' (Mühlhäusler 1982: 103). Mühlhäusler cites Le Page (1974: 49) (Mühlhäusler 1982: 102, whence quoted) in connection with the origin of West African Pidgin English: "Coincidence of form with some similarity of meaning between items from two codes will mean that such items will have a high probability of survival in the emergent pidgin code." Mühlhäusler concludes (1982: 116): "It appears that, at some point of development, a large proportion of pidgin and creole lexical items can be assigned jointly to more than one source language." This then begs the question, how do speakers of the pidgin interpret the conflated form? Does it mean one thing to speakers of L 1, and another to speakers of L 2? Mühlhäusler suggests that this might be the case: (1982: 106) "Tok Pisin *salat* is related to both German *salat* 'lettuce' and Melanesian *salat* 'stinging nettle'. For a German missionary, to use this word to mean 'stinging nettle' would be a metaphor. For a Papua New Guinean the situation would be exactly the reverse."

Aitchison (1991), working with Indian English, found that the most common form of negation in Indian English followed the same paradigm as negation in Hindi. When negating in Hindi, the negative is, for the most part, placed in front of the verb. Aitchison found that in Indian English, there is also a preference for placing a negative before the verb, whereas speakers of British English do not favour this construction. She concludes: "a 'multiple birth' model is the most revealing for an understanding of language change, in which the language sprouts out various options ... In short, the notions of 'profligacy' followed by 'selection', especially selection via convergence, are key factors in understanding language change" (Aitchison 1991: 7).

The model of convergence then becomes a motivating force, leading to various outputs. In the Tok Pisin examples, two phonetically similar but etymologically unrelated lexical items conflate, facilitated by the coincidence of a semantic overlap. This leads to the survival of this hybrid form in the emergent pidgin. In the Indian English example, pressure from the Hindi negating paradigm lead to a preference for that model in spoken and written Indian English. Paradigmatic convergence lead to one surface form being prioritised above other alternatives. The common factor between these outcomes is one of enhanced resilience and durability.

It is possible to apply this model to Early Modern business English. Consider, for example, the point where macaronic Latin stops and English takes over in the London Bridge archive. This happens on folio 308 of MS Bridge House Rental 3, which is the entry detailing rents taken from tenants of Bridge property for the year 1479 to 1480. The recto is written in macaronic Latin, and the verso in English:

(10)   1479 × 1480[20]
        fo 308 r

D Joħe Stevyns viij ꝫ D Ricõ kirkeby peyntour ᴢl ꝫ D Clemente Richard peynto^r *ᴢᴢᴢ ꝫ D Joħe Godfrey ᴢᴢvj ꝫ viij � d D Joħe hande fabro ᴢl ꝫ D Nicħo violet* *weᴢchaundeler iiij ło ᴢ ꝫ viij d D laurencio Stokhale saidiller ᴢᴢ ꝫ D Bernardo* *andrew duchemañ ᴢ ꝫ ...*
fo 308v
The Rentall of the foreȳn Rente renewid atte Mighelmesse anno ᴢiᴢ^{uo} of kyngℯ *Edward the fourtħ / leuesham / Of Will^am Bouchier for the ferme of the Brigge-* *hous in lĕuesham w^t the app^rten^ance ovir ᴢiiij ꝫ iᴢ d oꝟ paid to the Priour of* *Shene & iij ꝫ to the lord Revers of quyte Rente goyngℯ of the same yerely . ᴢlvj* *ꝫ viij d*

This is a change from macaronic Latin (consider the prepositions and Christian-name suffixes) to a vestigially macaronic English. The English passage contains Latin lexemes (*annus*), and abbreviation marks indicating Latin lexemes (*obolus, novendecim, denarius*), much as some people today still render the date in Roman numerals, or head their notes with the word *memorandum*, or use the *libra* sign to indicate pounds sterling. It is still greatly facilitated by the use of abbreviation and suspension marks, which are an integral and essential feature of macaronic accounts-keeping. For example, the abbreviation *ꝫ̃* above could be interpreted as representing both *solidus* and *shilling*; and the abbreviations *r̃* , *rec̃* in example (3), or *Rℯ* in example (11):

(11)   1479 × 1481[21]

Dona & legat̃ Yiftis and bequestis for the sayd ij yere In p^rimis Rℯ of Joħn *Crosby Carpynter for a trespase done a yenste þ^e ᴩesshe ᴢij d*

could be interpreted as representing both *receptum* and *received.*

It seems that a principle of convergence, similar to those discussed by Aitchison and Mühlhäusler, partly underlies the evolution and survival of macaronic business writing, and in particular, the heavy reliance on abbreviated and suspended forms. Early Modern business English demonstrates that the convergence model applies to the written domain as well as the spoken. The studies outlined above were concerned primarily with synchronic speech, although Aitchison's work was in fact based on written data.

There is no difficulty in stating that the principle of convergence giving rise to multiple interpretation has been identified as a model of linguistic change in synchronic speech. Consider the case of the model of convergence giving the output of reinterpretation. An example from Modern English might be the spoken form *shouldn't've*. In speech, *shouldn't've* is commonly synchronically reinterpreted and expanded as *shouldn't of*, rather than *shouldn't have*, which is the historical underlying form. This reinterpretation depends upon the surface conflation of both *have* and *of* to /v/ in a low-stress context.

It is of value, therefore, to notice that the same paradigm is identifiable in written language, reinforcing the argument that written language is a legitimate domain of enquiry in its own right. The occasional visual convergence of written Latin and English words, and the more frequent visual convergence of abbreviated or suspended written Latin and English words, gave rise to a plurality of potential interpretation.[22] The next question to be considered is who was doing this interpretation.

4. Readers and writers

Who wrote this kind of text, who read it, and how did it come about?[23] Following Biber's (1988: 29) terminology, the *addressor* is the person who produces the text, in this case the accounts-clerk, the *addressee* is the intended recipient, in this case the auditor, and the *audience* are the other readers, in this case, people who were either officially required to be able to read accounts, such as other customs officers or other bridge wardens, or private individuals who read them, for whatever reason. We must bear in mind that the skills of reading and writing were not reciprocal, and that there may well have been many more people able to read than write. We have to further bear in mind that with macaronic accounts, we are dealing with addressors who could write in at least two languages (to

some extent at least), and addressees and audiences who could read both
of these (though again, full competence was not requisite for comprehen-
sion). Clearly, in the context of the Middle Ages this is not as remarkable
as it would be today — fewer could write, but more of those who could
were trained in Latin and Anglo-Norman.

From the writer's viewpoint, one of the most salient characteristics of
this text type is its rapidity and concision. Practically any word over
three graphs long could be abbreviated, as could many common grapheme
clusters, thus providing a minimum of "work" for the writer, and producing a minimum of visual matter for the reader. It is possible, therefore,
that certain physical constraints may have influenced this development.
For example, most texts as they have survived are what we would think
of as "fair copy", for which there is often internal evidence such as when
clerks are paid for "doubling" the accounts. We could posit a hypothesis
that originally clerks were writing from dictation, and copied up later.
How could this be tested? One suggestion might be to look at "mistakes".
Certain mistakes could, perhaps, only be aural, and others, only visual:

(12)   a. King's Lynn, Norfolk 1503 × 1504[24]

E Naŭ voc² Publicañ de Dordright vnde Adrianus Jansoñ est m̃ int² eodm̃ die

'And a ship called Publican of Dordrecht whereof Adrian
Janson is master entered the same day'

In Naŭ voc² le Pelycañ de Dordright vnde Adrianus Johnsoñ est m̃ ex² eodm̃ die

b. 'In a ship called the Pelican of Dordrecht whereof Adrian
Johnson is master departed the same day'

Given the dates and position of entry in the account, it is almost certain
that these entries refer to the same ship. It is interesting that it first
appears as the *Publican*. Other ships of the vicinity and date are normally
named after people, either real or biblical, and the only other ships with
non-personal names are the *Dragon* and the *Unicorn*, also from Dordrecht
(Gras 1918: 672). In the 1549/1550 account from the same port, King's
Lynn, there are ships named *Pelican* listed from Dordrecht (626), Rot-
terdam (627) and Dunkirk (632); and also ships named after other
animals: the *Olyphaunt* of Arnemuiden (630), the *Antheloppe* of Lynn,
and the *Phenyx* of Lynn (631). By contrast, there are no ships, at this or
any other port that I have seen, that were named after trade occupations.
Synchronically a *publican* meant a tax-gatherer; the meaning 'a licenced
victualler' is not attested until the eighteenth century. So it is reasonable

to assume that *Publican* is a mistake for *Pelican*. It is possible to make a case for this being an aural mistake: the clerk misheard the name (especially if the speaker were Dutch). But equally, it could simply be a slip of the pen, if the clerk were used to writing the word *publican* in another context. Although the posited scenario of the fruit of original dictation copied up at a later date seems very attractive, I am not sure that proof is to be found through scribal mistakes.

Leaving aside the question of dictation as unresolved, let us turn to the question of how the addressees and the audience read macaronic business texts. Were they functionally bilingual? To answer this question some consideration of the processes of reading is required. We cannot assume a left-to-right, top-to-bottom approach as with prose, and the material is not set out on the page in the same way as prose. I have already referred to the paucity of visual information presented in accounts (as compared to other text types), which is due in part to heavy use of the abbreviation and suspension system. The reader had a compressed block of text to deal with. Much of it would have been transparent to a monolingual reader, however. A large amount of the lexical items were presented in English, or were loans into English from Middle Dutch or Old Norse as well as from Anglo-Norman and Latin itself; and hence can be counted as synchronic English lexemes. The comprehensibility of the text increased for a monolingual English reader the greater the amount of L2 it contained, and as we have seen, this development took place. Nevertheless to grasp the finer details the reader did at least need to know the L1 directional prepositions, to know whether a ship were entering or leaving, or whether an entry is referring to money in or money out. So there was a minimum of L1 that needed to be learnt. Morphologically, however, most of the information was presented in abbreviated form; so the readers could interpret either by expanding as they went along, or simply by ignoring it and depending on word order alone. This suggests that the addressees and audience could have had a wide range of reading capability, varying from total to minimal competence in L1, and yet still be able to use business accounts for extracting information. With this kind of text we have to confront the possibility and likelihood of a continuum of reading skill, with full competence at one end of the scale and only partial competence at the other. Usually, it is taken for granted that literacy means being able to recognise and interpret all the words in a text. With macaronic accounts this no longer holds good, and the degree of functional literacy could well correlate with a fairly low rate of actual identification and interpretation of forms, that is, well under one hundred per cent.

Is there any evidence in business accounts of synchronic London speech? On the one hand, such a formal, bureaucratic convention as accounts-keeping could be thought of as bearing least resemblance to speech of all the text types. It could even be held to fall into that category where writing is the primary medium, and speech the secondary, as identified by Vachek (1973: 14) with regard to readers reading a foreign language which they can read but not speak. Yet an English NP embedded in a Latin string would appear to have considerable claim to spoken currency, or why is it there at all? Biber (1988: 199) has said "there is no single, absolute difference between speech and writing in English; rather there are several dimensions of variation", and on the whole these dimensions seem to require a constituent larger than the NP for identification. The signal *voc^{o}* 'called' would seem to indicate that the following NP had spoken currency, but the syntactic domain is too small to make this of much interest. Even if we were to discover some diagnostic that would identify larger oral constituents, we still would not know how far they were diffused throughout the speech community, that is, outside the professional discourse of the trade. On the other hand, monolingual accounts may prove to be a source of evidence of London English, because they are not transmitted through the filter of literary stylistic endeavour.[25]

5. Conclusion

To sum up, I have attempted to present the functional variety of business accounts, and to note that they diverge structurally in the Early Modern period. The received tradition in London was to use a macaronic structure, but by the end of the Early Modern period, this was superseded and the monolingual convention predominated.

I have also speculated on the rôle of accounts-clerks and auditors with regard to the macaronic type. Pragmatically, a macaronic structure gave multiple options to both writer and reader. It could be written abbreviated or expanded, and read fully or partially. It required little L1 knowledge to read, but this was not due to L1 ignorance on the part of the writer. The multiple options favoured the writer as well as the reader. Abbreviations and suspensions were functionally favourable in a dictation situation, but expanded forms also occur, keeping the formal register of accounting to the fore. Nevertheless, despite such fluidity and resilience, the genre had, by the end of the Early Modern period, finally outworn its usefulness; and the practice of keeping accounts in English is to be included as one of the innovations of that very innovatory era.

Notes

1. For a discussion of the structure of macaronic business texts see Wright (1992).
2. E. g. Guildhall Library MS 11571/4 Grocer's Company Warden's Accounts 1521 – 1533; Guildhall Library MS 2596/1 Clothworker's Company Warden's Accounts 1520 – 1558; Guildhall Library MS 1239/1 St Mary at Hill Churchwarden's Accounts 1420 – 1559; Guildhall Library MS 4570/1 St Margaret Pattens Churchwarden's Accounts 1506 – 1557; Guildhall Library MS 593/1 St Stephan Wallbrook Churchwarden's Accounts 1474 – 1553; Petty Customs Accounts 1480 – 1481 Public Record Office MS E 122/194/25; Philip Henslowe's personal accounts, published in Foakes (1977).
3. For the eleventh century see, for example, the Billingsgate tolls of London, transcribed (in expanded form) in Gras (1918: 154 – 155). For the sixteenth century see example (2).
4. This example of the macaronic Latin style of business accounts is taken from the annual account of the expenses and income of the estate of London Bridge: London, Corporation of London Records Office, MS Bridge House Rental 3 fo 76 v. The x notation denotes manuscript-internal dating.
5. London, Public Record Office, Common Plea Roll 1156, Michaelmas Term, 1st Mary (PRO CP 40 1156), published in (inaccurate) transcript (Moran 1976: 45). This document is now deemed unfit for public viewing due to deterioration, so I have been unable to check it. There is, however, a partial facsimile on page 21.
6. See *OED* Dicker *sb.*[1] b. "A considerable number; a 'lot', a 'heap'"; first attestation 1580.
7. There is no need to invoke the notion of foreign workmen in the shop to account for the language mix, as Moran (1976: 45) attempted: "The inventory was written partly in Latin, partly in French and partly in English. This was not the work of a clerk ... but possible of foreign workmen working at the house at the time." On the contrary, it is a perfectly regular development of the domestic usage of macaronic Latin.
8. CLRO MS Bridge House Rental 1 fo 70 v.
9. Grocer's Company Warden's Accounts, Guildhall Library MS 11571/4 fo 417 v.
10. Accounts of St Mary at Hill, Guildhall Library MS 1239/1 fo 441 v.
11. *Drawg͞ht* = 'toilet'.
12. CLRO MS Bridge House Rental 4 fo 244, 244 v.
13. CLRO MS Bridge House Rental 3 fo 59.
14. CLRO MS Bridge House Rental 3 fo 350 v. *Sege* = 'toilet'.
15. CLRO MS Bridge House Rental 5 fo 141 v.
16. CLRO MS Bridge House Rental 3 fo 210 v.
17. CLRO MS Bridge House Rental 3 fo 212.
18. For example, the suffix ⟨-is⟩ represented, among other things, the dative and ablative plural of some Latin nouns and adjectives, the genitive singular of some Latin nouns, and the plural form of most English nouns. The preposition *in* could mean the same thing in both languages.

19. See Wright (forthcoming a) for further examples of visual fusion between Medieval Latin and Middle English.
20. CLRO MS Bridge House Rental 3 fo 308.
21. Accounts of St Mary at Hill, Guildhall Library MS 1239/1 fo 29; published in Littlehales (1904: 94).
22. Further, there is also, of course, visual conflation with French words. Cf. example (6), where the form written *app^{r}ten^{a}nce* could appear identically in an Anglo-Norman text.
23. For another hypothesis on the origins of macaronic business writing see Wright (forthcoming b).
24. London, Public Record Office MS E 122/98/16, published in Gras (1918: 664, 667).
25. The extract given under example (5) seems to my ear to be a perfectly acceptable present-day construction in London English, if the relative marker is changed to its modern variant (*paid for a board to cover that place where they broke into the vault*), although I suspect it would be deemed imperfect or somewhat clumsy Standard English.

References

Aitchison, Jean
　　1991　　"Tadpoles, cuckoos and multiple births: language contact and models of change". [Paper presented to the International Conference on Language Contact and Linguistic Change, Rydzyna, Poland, June 1991.]
Biber, Douglas
　　1988　　*Variation across speech and writing.* Cambridge: Cambridge University Press.
Fasold, Ralph W. — Deborah Schiffrin (eds.)
　　1989　　*Language change and variation.* Amsterdam — Philadelphia: Benjamins.
Fisiak, Jacek
　　forthc. a　*Language contact and linguistic change.* Berlin: Mouton de Gruyter.
　　forthc. b　*Medieval dialectology.* Berlin: Mouton de Gruyter.
Foakes, Reginald Anthony (ed.)
　　1977　　*The Henslowe papers.* London: Scolar.
Görlach, Manfred
　　1990　　*Studies in the history of the English language.* Heidelberg: Winter.
Gras, Norman Scott Brien
　　1918　　*The Early English customs system.* Cambridge, Mass.: Harvard University Press.
Kurath, Hans — Kuhn, Sherman McAllister — Lewis, Robert E. (eds.)
　　1953 —　*Middle English Dictionary.* Ann Arbor: University of Michigan Press.
Lass, Roger
　　1987　　*The shape of English.* London — Melbourne: Dent.
Le Page, Robert Brock
　　1974　　"Processes of pidginization and creolization", *York Papers in Linguistics* 4: 41 — 69.
Littlehales, Henry (ed.)
　　1904 — 05　*The medieval records of a London city church (St. Mary at Hill) A. D. 1420 — 1559*, (Early English Text Society: Original Series 125, 128). London: Oxford University Press.

Moran, James
1976   *Wynkyn de Worde, father of Fleet Street*. London: Wynkyn de Worde Society.
Mühlhäusler, Peter
1982   "Etymology and pidgin and creole languages", *Transactions of the Philological Society*, 80: 99—118.
Rissanen, Matti—Ihalainen, Ossi—Nevalainen, Terttu—Taavitsainen, Irma (eds.)
1992   *History of Englishes*. Berlin: Mouton de Gruyter.
Seppänen, Aimo
1990   "On analysing the relative *that*". [Paper presented to the Sixth International Conference on English Historical Linguistics, Helsinki, May 1990.]
1991   "The typology of relativisation strategies and Early Modern English relative clauses". [Paper presented to the Early Modern English Conference, Tulln bei Wien, Austria, July 1991.]
Shaklee, Margaret
1980   "The rise of Standard English", in: Timothy Shopen—Joseph M. Williams (eds.), 33—62.
Shopen, Timothy—Williams, Joseph M. (eds.)
1980   *Standards and dialects in English*. Cambridge, Mass.: Winthrop.
Simpson, John Andrew—Weiner, Edmund Simon C. (eds.)
1989   *The Oxford English Dictionary*. (2nd edition.) Oxford: Clarendon.
Vachek, Josef
1973   *Written language: central problems and problems of English*. The Hague—Paris: Mouton.
van der Auwera, Johan
1985   "Relative *that* — a centennial dispute", *Journal of Linguistics* 21: 149—179.
Wright, Laura Charlotte
1992   "Macaronic writing in a London archive; 1380—1480" in: Matti Rissanen *et al.* (eds.), 762—770.
forthc. a   "Middle English *-end(e)* and *-ing*: a possible route to grammaticalisation", in: Jacek Fisiak (ed.), forthcoming a.
forthc. b   "A hypothesis on the origins of macaronic business writing", in: Jacek Fisiak (ed.), forthcoming b.

The mystery of the modal progressive

Susan Wright

1. Introduction

The development of the verb phrase (notably the modal verbs and dummy auxiliary *do*) in Early Modern English (1500 to 1700) is marked by a gradual semantic-pragmatic process of subjectivisation. The modals become increasingly intimately tied up with epistemic modality; dummy *do* in declarative sentences ceases to be "superfluous" (in Samuel Johnson's terms), and acquires first the gloss of affirmation (Traugott 1972), and then its modern, regular function of emphasis. These semantic-pragmatic developments accompany the syntactic maturation of the verbs in their syntactic functions as auxiliary verbs. It is striking that despite details of chronology and the patterns of variation which appear to characterise each construction's history in Early Modern English, there does seem to be a diachronic movement towards subjectivity (*pace* Traugott 1982). However, it is increasingly possible that this interpretation is at least partially encouraged by the material that we have to work with — written, often literary, and as the centuries wear on, Standard English texts. Now the problem of Standard English texts as a basis for examining how subjectivity is encoded linguistically in earlier stages of the language is a sticky as well as productive area of debate.[1] This paper is intended to be a contribution to an issue which has some bearing on the conduct of this debate. It seems to me that we have to be wary of asserting generalisations about the increasing subjectivity of language in time, since it may well be that this trend merely manifests a growing tendency for writers to put into written form things that they have always and easily said. And with this trend, it is easy to see how standard varieties gradually mature for the job of expressing speaker subjectivity, within the medium of written, often literary texts.

In this paper, I examine the question of subjectivity in relation to aspects of the history of another auxiliary construction: the progressive (*be* + *ing*) construction (Wright 1986, etc.). The Present-day English construction is the subject of continual study; its meaning (e. g. the semantic difference between simple and progressive "tenses"); what enables it to collocate with some verbs (*walk, talk, go*) but not others (*own*); its apparent inability to pattern with stative or existential predicates. Its origins, as Strang (1982) comments, are a matter of controversy, and its subsequent history, though syntactically relatively straightforward, is still gappy.

In recent historical linguistics, one of the main trends in the study of the construction has been to examine what I call the maturation of the progressive, within the frame of another history — the history of prose narrative — the novel. Here I refer particularly to Strang (1982), Arnaud (1982) and their antecedents (cf. Hatcher 1951, Bodelsen 1936/37, Dennis 1940). In this context, a diachronic line is traced from the use of the construction as a framing device (in Jespersen's terms), often in subordinate clauses introduced by adverbs such as *while, as*; in the prose narratives of the early eighteenth century, to its foregrounding function in main clauses in the nineteenth century novel. The focus in these studies is on the progressive's role as an important ingredient in the literary technique of free indirect style.

What I am interested in is this *foregrounding* function of the progressive, where it is used to focus on an experience from the point of view of the subject (or narrator). This use is extremely common in Present-day English, although it is still treated as "special", that is to say, "aberrant", relative to what might be termed its aspectual use.[2] The "modal", "experiential" use of the progressive has been described by Zandvoort (1941) as "emotive", by Jespersen (1949) as "vivid", by Ljung (1977) as "interpretative", by Goldsmith and Woisetschlaeger (1982) as "phenomenal". Leech (1971: 21) treats this use of the construction as applying to a special subset of collocations — verbs generally held to imply passive or inert perception or cognition are usually "inimical to the Progressive Aspect". Yet, he goes on, they can be (and indeed are) collocated with the construction when "they are intended to describe active perception or cognition, so that the speaker goes out of his/her way to focus attention on some object" (Leech 1971: 23). In other words, for Leech, these uses of the progressive focus on the consciousness of the speaker in the act of sensation, perception or cognition. According to Leech, verbs like *think, consider, imagine* and *feel, smell, listen, hear* can be made to position the cognitive or emotional experience of the speaker at the centre of what's being said at the moment of utterance. Ljung (1977) argues that it is not the case that this applies solely to those verbs which apparently normally resist collocation in the progressive. Indeed, taking Bolinger's (1972) analysis of the slippage between "close" and "loose-fit" predicates, he argues that the modal use of the progressive ought properly to be described as "interpretative". His analysis draws upon the link between the description of an event or action (what is true) and its construal or interpretation in terms of its implications for the context in which it occurs. For example, faced with the clearly speaker-centred utterances in (1), we could identify the source of their modal force as the interpretative (rather than truth-conditional or aspectual) function they serve in particular given contexts:

(1)   a. *I'm warning you.*
        b. *You're imagining things.*
        c. *I'm not talking to you.*
        d. *I'm not drinking, I'm driving.*

None of these utterances can be judged in terms of general aspectual criteria like duration, temporariness, iteration or framing. Instead, each functions as a kind of construal of the situation in which the speaker finds herself. For example, since (1 c) is said, uttered, it is blatantly a contradiction. Yet it effectively captures the speaker's own assessment of a particular situation, for which we might assemble any number of components. For example, in the following text:

(1)   e. *Alan sat down again, knotting his legs around one another so that he made a dangerously tight parcel. 'All right', he said quietly, 'I'm selfish. I go out all day to college having a lovely time while you stay at home making yourself ill. I don't have to go. I don't have to pass exams or get a job, we don't need the money — oh no, I do all this purely for my own amusement.' 'I'm not talking to you.' She stood by the oven, rubbing one bare foot against the other, glaring at the toast which was already burnt.*
                    (Jane Rogers, Her living image [Faber 1984: 126])

Forced by circumstance to answer her addressee, but against her inclination, the speaker in (1 e) leaves him in no doubt that this is the case. She has to speak, on this occasion, but indicates in her utterance that she will not engage in relevant talk. Similarly, (1 d) is the usual, very effective explanation for refusing the offer of a beer. Instead of going through the process of first refusing and then explaining the reason for the refusal, the speaker simply says (1 d). The point, however, is that, strictly speaking, it is not true at the moment of utterance that the speaker is driving, and it is not necessarily true that she is not drinking. So the utterance is interpretative rather than aspectual in truth-conditional terms. None of these utterances is odd or peculiar in ordinary usage; they simply do not serve a primarily aspectual function. It is this use of the construction which I shall call "modal", as it effectively provides an interpretation of the speaker's attitude and perspective of the situation; and in so doing, conveys the epistemic stance of the speaker at a particular moment in the context of utterance.

Perhaps one of the most vivid ways of illustrating the extent of the subjectivity of this use of the progressive is by examining its occurrence in a text like the following (2):

(2)   *It's night, I find myself in a dark wood, and suddenly there's a man coming towards me. He's calling my name and moving closer. But I don't recognise the voice ...*

I'm waking up. I'm in an enormous, very light room. A voice I remember is repeating my name over and over. But it's very far away.

... Then I woke up. And all I could remember was the quality of the voice.

This text could be a sample of psycho-narration in a modern novel, or the recounting of the experience of a dream in the historic present. What it does is present an experience from the perspective of the experiencer. It is not so much affective as interpretative, yet the sense of the proximity between experience and speaker makes the speaker's modal stance dominate the episode entirely.

2. The modal progressive in Modern and Early Modern English

The modal uses of the progressive provide, then, yet another example of the way subjectivity may be encoded in the grammar of a language. Most of the relevant accounts are contemporary semantic-pragmatic studies of the construction, as the modal progressive is almost exclusively associated with Modern English. But, bearing in mind the dangers posed by assuming a unidirectional trend in the development of subjectivity, and the often unacknowledged inference that this trend is a diachronic one (since that is all the material we have to go on), it seems that the lack of any treatment of the modal semantics of the progressive in earlier stages of the language is a yawning gap in the history of the construction's semantics. It is not clear, for instance, what the historical status of this modal, interpretative use of the progressive is. Modal (experiential) uses occur, for example, in the language of intimate, private letters as early as the seventeenth century (see Wright 1986, 1989 a for discussion). Examples are:

(3)   a. I am disputeing *againe though you tolde mee my fault soe Plainly, ile give it over and tell you that Parthenessia is now my company, my Brother sent it downe and I have almost read it.*
(Dorothy Osborne [1652 — 1654])

    b. I am combing *and* curling *and* kissing *this Lock all day, and* dreaming *ont all night*
(Dorothy Osborne [1662 — 1654]

    c. *'Tis so long since I had a letter from dear Mrs. Hewet I should think her no longer in the land of the living if Mr. Rasigade did not assure me he was happier than I, and had heard of your health from your own hand, which makes me fancy that my last miscarried, and parhaps you* are blaming *me at the same time that you* are thinking *me neglectful of you.*
(Lady M. W. Montagu to Mrs. Hewet, 27 March 1710;
Lady Mary Wortley Montagu [1713 — 1776])

    d. *Daughter, daughter, don't call names. You* are always abusing *my pleasures, which is what no mortal will bear. Trash, lumber, sad stuff, are the titles you give to my favourite amusements.*
(Lady M. W. Montagu to Lady Bute, 30 September, 1757;
Lady Mary Wortley Montagu [1713 — 1776])

In each of these quotations, the writer conveys a very clear impression of her own attitude to what she's talking about, and to her correspondent. The modernity of these expressions is striking, not strangely, because these are precisely the kinds of usage that Leech, Ljung and others examine as characteristic of the progressive's use in Present-day English. A cursory survey of seventeenth and eighteenth century grammar (contemporary with these texts) reveals that the progressive construction, even in formal syntactic terms, was very poorly understood. Apart from Pickbourn (1789) and Christopher Cooper (1653) (see Michael 1970), John Fell (1784: 121 — 123) attempts briefly to give a sense of the usage of the present progressive: "The participle of the present tense denotes the continuance of the action, passion, energy, or state, expressed by the verb". Although we might speculate that the terms *passion* and *energy* are intended to describe the modal effect of the progressive, this interpretation would be more hopeful than sensible.[3]

In the absence of any truly informative and unambiguous treatment of these early modal progressives, it is necessary to construct some basic formal diagnostics for identifying potential modal uses of the progressive. Biber (1988) and Biber and Finegan (1989, 1990) have developed a model for characterising text-types in terms of their most salient situational features.[4] By measuring the proportions of selected linguistic features, they argue that a text may be characterised as more or less informational, elaborate or involved. On extra-linguistic grounds, we would expect Restoration prose comedies for example, to incline more to the involved dimension than to the elaborate or the informational. Now we could take some of their features in order to confirm this impression of the overall situational status of the texts, but this supra-textual characterisation could not be a solid guarantee of the modal use of the progressive construction itself. To test this, we need to have more narrow collocational features, that is, features which directly frame the construction. The bare sequence in (4) is a first step in what is essentially an exercise in historical pragmatics:

(4)   Diagnostics for the modal progressive (non-aspectual, non-truth conditional);
   a. syntactic environment: main vs. subordinate clause;
   b. tense: present vs. past;
   c. lexical support: adverbial modification;
   d. verb type: private (cognitive) vs. activity;
   e. identity of subject: first, second, third person;

These are ranked for convenience rather than on any strictly principled basis. The earlier the text, the more important these features become in identifying a modal use of the progressive. Each of these features is partly instrumental in conveying the modal force of the progressive in the letter extracts in (3). The progressive occurs in main clauses, combined with present tense and first person subject pronoun in Dorothy Osborne's letter extracts. She also uses private verbs, such as *dispute* and *kiss*. Lady Mary Wortley Montagu adopts the progressive in subordinate clauses as well as main clauses, with the accusing second person, and adverbial support (*always*), which appears to reinforce the modal strength of interpretative verbs like *abuse, blame* and *think*.

If these features support a modal reading of the progressive in texts as early as the letters of Dorothy Osborne, where else do these kinds of uses occur — in what kinds of texts? Strang (1982) argues that extended prose narrative is the medium most conducive to analysing and clarifying the growth of the construction in the late eighteenth century onward. However, this choice of medium, because it is itself developing as a genre in her chosen period, partially obscures the issue. In particular, it is easy to either confuse or merge the history of the modal construction with that of the (literary) genre itself. So it is possible to infer a diachronic line between subordinate, backgrounding, aspectual use of the progressive, and its main clause, foregrounding, modal use. This gives the impression that the progressive acquires modality (subjectivity) as a parallel development to the diachronic relation between historical narrative and psychological narrative styles, in the context of the history of the novel.

It is useful to examine a text type in which the distribution of main and subordinate clauses is not aligned with a distinction of styles, but can be assessed within the same medium. Unlike extended prose narrative, prose comedy does not separate narrative and dialogue, and furthermore, the genre itself has a degree of stability. In addition, this medium is a performative one, and thus affords some degree of comparability with the kinds of example and illustration dealt with by linguists examining the present-day construction.

I looked at prose comedy from 1670 to 1710. The basis for the selection of dramatic texts is the observation that in a range of texts published in 1711, the prose drama of Susannah Centlivre contained the highest proportion (though not the greatest number) of main clause progressives.[5] I reproduce these figures for information below. Note that the overall frequencies of the progressive construction are very low, despite the sample size per author.

(5)   Distribution of main clause progressives in eight 1711 texts:
(Corpus of 41,000 words each)

Centlivre	76.4%	=	26 main clause	Total:	34
Shaftesbury	35%	=	7 main clause	Total:	20
Swift	35%	=	7 main clause	Total:	20
Steele	35%	=	17 main clause	Total:	48
Addison	32%	=	21 main clause	Total:	66
Whiston	25%	=	4 main clause	Total:	16
Boyer	10%	=	2 main clause	Total:	21

The new corpus for analysis contains sixteen prose comedies written by four playwrights, including Susannah Centlivre, between 1670 and 1710. Verse drama, despite the most famous occurrence of the modal progressive in Cleopatra's *I am dying, Egypt, dying* is not included in the corpus. In the confines of a form dominated by and crafted in terms of metre, the progressive is potentially an extremely marked construction (and may be construed as aberrant). The sample for each playwright is around 90,000 words, large enough to find out firstly, whether there is any exponential increase over time in the overall frequency of the construction, and secondly, whether there is a notable change in the proportion of main clause to subordinate clause occurrence. The motivation behind examining frequency first was to gain a diachronic picture of distribution within the medium.

Now remembering the incidence of modal progressives in Dorothy Osborne's letters (1653), I decided to track back from 1710 to 1670 to find out whether there is any overall increase in the sheer frequency of the construction, and whether there is a notable change over time in the proportion of main clause to subordinate clause occurrence. Further, I wanted to see whether the situation of the progressive in prose drama is comparable with that noted by Strang for extended prose narrative. In fact there was no significant change in the drama over time.

(6)   Restoration and Augustan prose drama: Percentage distribution of progressive:

[16 plays]	Wycherley	Behn	Congreve	Centlivre
Main clause	78	70	68	67
Subordinate	22	30	32	31
100% (N) =	101	74	106	67
Mean per play:	26	21	36	12
Mean % main:	78%	67%	55,5%	67%

Interestingly, the percentage of main clause progressive occurrences across all plays for each playwright does not vary very dramatically, except perhaps for the earliest, Wycherley. (These figures exclude the construction *be going to*.)

These figures afford a brief diagnosis of the extent to which the progressive is used in main clauses in what is evidently a performative context. A quick comparison of this profile with the cross-genre profile for 1711 is instructive. There is a remarkable degree of consistency in the use to which the progressive is put in the plays, whereas it varies in the

1711 texts. It is also worth noting that despite the range over four decades, the relative proportions of main to subordinate clause use do not increase dramatically (contrary to Strang's findings for extended prose narrative in the second half of the eighteenth compared with the beginning of the nineteenth century). The diagnostic figures presented, let's have a look at what, precisely, the progressive is employed to do.

Clearly, not all main clause uses, though arguably foregrounding rather than backgrounding in terms of syntactic environment, will be experiential. There are the predictable aspectual and intentional uses. *Be going to*, used to convey intention, for instance, occurs 25 times in the corpus as a whole (I have excluded these from the figures given). Collocations with *come* and *go* have variable frequencies for each playwright:

(7)　　　　Percentage frequency of *come* and *go*:

	Wycherley	Behn	Congreve	Centlivre
come	12%	16%	7%	9%
go	3%	5%	10%	16%
Others	85%	79%	83%	75%

These proportions are not surprising, given historical and contextual factors. On the historical side, it is evident that the progressive, since Old English (cf. Anglo-Saxon Chronicles, for example), has collocated with verbs of motion. On the contextual side, it is somewhat predictable that these verbs should figure prominently in a setting in which characters are constantly coming and going. They are particularly likely to do so in these Restoration and early Augustan dramas, in which the elements of sex comedy, political farce and intrigue are dependent on the momentum created by unplanned meetings, departures, clashes and misses. The warning comes at opportune moments in order to get the heroine or hero out of a sticky (compromising) situation: Examples:

(8)　　　a. ⟨*Florinda*⟩ *Belvile! Heavens! My Brother too is coming, and 'twill be impossible to escape.*

　　　　　　　　　　　　　　　　　　　　(Behn, *The Rover* III.iii)

　　　　　b. ⟨*Hippolita*⟩ *Peace, peace, my father's coming this way.*
　　　　　　　　　(Wycherley, *The Gentleman Dancing-Master* III.i.145)

　　　　　c. ⟨*Servant*⟩ *Mr Ranger, sir, is coming up.*
　　　　　　　　　　　　　　(Wycherley, *Love in a Wood* II.iv.55)

d. ⟨*Gripe*⟩ *Softly, softly — they are coming in.*
(Wycherley, *Love in a Wood* II.iv.36)

The next prominent group of verbs in collocation with the progressive concerns verbs of saying. *Say* (as in the very common *as I was saying*) and *speak* (as in the equally common *this fellow I am speaking of*) occur most often in subordinate clauses, and as verbs of report. But verbs like *talk, tell* and certainly more private or expressive verbs, like *consider, rave, ruminate, debate, praise, brag, cry, presume, reckon, whisper,* tend to occur in main clauses, often not simply to describe an act or event, but to construe them, to interpret them. So Congreve's Maskwell (*Double Dealer*) raves on:

(9)   a.   ⟨*Maskwell*⟩ *Let me perish first, and from this hour avoid all sight and speech, and, if I can, all thought of that pernicious Beauty. Ha! but what is my distraction doing? I* am wildly talking *to myself, and some ill chance might have directed malicious Ears this way.*
(Congreve, *The Double Dealer* V.i.43−47)

Here, *talk* occurs in collocation with lexical support provided by the adverb *wildly*. Following a self-directed question, itself modal in its function, Maskwell quite obviously provides some interpretation, some gloss of what he is doing. Verbs of saying occur as explanation for other peoples' actions, as in Wycherley's *The Gentleman Dancing-Master*. Here, the salient verb (*whisper*) serves first in the simple present as an accurate description, and then, in Don Diego's words, in the progressive as a conclusion, as affirmation:

(9)   b.   ⟨*Caution*⟩ *See, see, they whisper, brother, to steal a kiss under a Whisper! O the harlotry!*
⟨*Don Diego*⟩ *What's the matter, friend?*
⟨*Hippolita, to Gerrard*⟩ *I say, for my sake, be in humour and do not discover yourself but be as partial as a dancing-master still.*
⟨*Don Diego*⟩ *What, she* is whispering *to him indeed!*
(Wycherley, *The Gentleman Dancing-Master* IV.i.670−76)

Another particularly prominent verb is *think*, again occurring as a strongly modal instrument for conveying characters' attitudes to themselves and to one another. Quite often, these uses strike me as particularly modern. For example, in Congreve's *The Way of the World*:

(9)   c. ⟨*Fainall*⟩ *No, I'll give you your Revenge another time, when*
       you are not so indifferent; you are thinking *of something else*
       now, and play too negligently.
                        (Congreve, *The Way of the World* I.i.5 — 7)

How far do the contextual and syntactic props (listed in [4]) aid the
identification of the progressive as a syntactic resource for expressing a
speaker's or character's attitude to what is being said or done? The focus
is on the main clause uses exclusively (assuming that subordinate clauses
often, but not invariably, suggest backgrounding or modification). Interestingly, the corpus contains no instances of the progressive with predicates, as in the common Present-day English:

(10)   *Josh is being boring /crazy/ difficult/* etc.

Instead, the construction occurs exclusively with verbs, mostly with
"loose-fit" verbs, in Bolinger's terms. These verbs do not describe an
activity so much as comment upon it. Thus we find in Wycherley's *Plain
Dealer*:

(11)   a. ⟨*Manly*⟩ *Damn all these impertinent, vexatious people of busi-
          ness, of all sexes. They* are still troubling *the world with the
          tedious recitals of their lawsuits, and one can no more stop their
          mouths than a wit's when he talks of himself, or an intelligencer's
          when he talks of other people.*
          ⟨*Widow*⟩ *And a pox of all vexatious, impertinent lovers. They*
          are still perplexing *the world with their tedious narrations of
          their love-suits and discourses of their mistress.*
                        (Wycherley, *The Plain Dealer* I.i.505 — 18)

The progressive clearly plays an important role in the verbal jousting
between the Plain Dealer Manly and the litigious Widow. It is lexically
supported, but here with the temporal/durational *still*. What is most
interesting, however, is the occurrence of abstract, even psychological
verbs — *trouble, perplex*. The subject in each case is the anonymous or
at least general third person plural *they*, rather than first or second
person. Yet the situation itself (as Ljung would argue) signposts the
significance of the progressive.

Lexical support in the form of adverbs is useful in pointing to modal
uses of the progressive in these plays. As mentioned before, the earlier
the text, the more useful these essentially formal features become in

identifying and analysing modal uses of the construction. Here are some instances of lexically supported progressives:

(12)   a. ⟨*Don Diego*⟩ *Besides, if you remember*, they were perpetually putting *me out of the room — that was, sister, because they had a mind to be alone.*

   (Wycherley, *The Gentleman Dancing-Master* I.ii.77 – 79)

   b. ⟨*Chrisante*⟩ *I confess, Sir, we women do not love these rough fighting Fellows,* they're always scaring us *with one Broil or another.*

   (Behn, *The Widow Ranter* IV.iii)

   c. ⟨*Daring*⟩ *Ranter — Gad, I'd sooner marry a She-bear, unless for a Penance for some horrid Sin*; we should be eternally challenging *one another to the Field, and ten to one she beats me there, or if I should escape there, she wou'd kill me with drinking.*

   (Behn, *The Widow Ranter* IV. iii)

   d. ⟨*Brisk*⟩ *Careless, this is your trick*; you're always spoiling *Company by leaving it.*
   ⟨*Careless*⟩ *And* thou art always spoiling *Company by coming into't.*

   (Congreve, *The Double Dealer* I.i.25)

   e. ⟨*Brisk*⟩ *Who, my Lady Toothless! O, she's a mortifying Spectacle;* she's always chewing *the Cud like an old Yew.*

   (Congreve, *The Double Dealer* III.i.616 – 8)

   f. ⟨*Charles*⟩ *And who knows what that unlucky Dog, Marplot, told him; nor can I imagine what brought him thither; that Fellow* is ever doing *Mischief; and yet, to give him his due, he never designs it.*

   (Centlivre, *The Busie Body* III)

Indeed, as the context or situation in which the construction occurs itself influences the reading of any function the progressive may have, it is reasonable to suggest that in many early cases, the choice of adverb will take on the bulk of the modal burden. In other words, the adverb itself signposts the construction as operating modally; it is explicitly, lexically subjective. As the combination becomes more and more usual, the adverb begins to bear less responsibility for the subjective reading, which may then be increasingly associated with the progressive itself (whether adverbially modified or bare). Some early examples of adverbially-modified (and apparently modal) progressives (cited by Visser 1973):

(13)   a. *Sir Jamys* is evyr choppyng *at me when my modyr is present,*
              with syche wordys as he thynkys wrathe me.

(Paston Letters 1422 — 1509)

        b. *Thou* art alwayes talking *of Love*

(Lyly, *Euphues* 1580)

        c. *Thou* art alwayes figuring *diseases in me*

(Shakespeare, *Measure for Measure* 1603)

        d. *They* are continually buffeting *one another with the Scripture.*

(R. Barclay, *Apol. Quakers* 1678)

        e. *She* is always seeing *Apparitions, and* hearing *Death-Watches.*

(Addison, *Spectator* no 7, 1711)

Now sceptics might object that it is the adverbial itself which supplies
the modal reading in each of these cases, and that by extension, it is the
combination of progressive with the adverb which ensures the subjectivity.
If the adverb were omitted, it would follow then that the modal force of
the remaining bare construction would be much weakened. The problem
with this argument is that we would still be left with a range of cases in
which the bare progressive evidently has modal meaning. Consequently,
while certainly helpful in diagnosis, the adverbial is not necessarily the
primary element in ensuring modal force.

While the examples discussed so far are interpretative (in Ljung's
sense), and though they evidently mark the speaker's attitude more
powerfully than they do any special aspectual meaning, it is possible that
they might not show sufficiently the weight of the subjectivity that I am
arguing is already an important and well-utilised resource in the language
at this time. It is notable that many of the verbs in the following examples
are predicated of the first person, and they are often used metaphorically
(*dying, fainting*); and most persuasively of all for an experiential perspective, they occur in the present tense. Interpretative readings are quite
clearly not precluded from use in the past tense, but for the intensity of
the psychological picture, the present tense is evidently salient.

Aphra Behn's *Widow Ranter*, perhaps because it is not a straightforward situation comedy or intrigue in the same way that many of the
plays in my sample are, provides the clearest examples of this modal
progressive (coming closest to the psycho-narration in [2]). Hume (1976:
211) comments that the "drastically mixed plot [is] used to brilliant effect",
so,

General Bacon's heroical love for the Indian Princess Semerina, his accidental killing of her, and his suicide form a moving tragic action perfectly

set off by two comic elements: satire on the corrupt and cowardly members of the governing council, and a contrasting series of 'love' affairs: Hazard and Madame Surelove, Chrisante and Friendly, Mrs Flirt and Parson Dunce, virtuous General Daring and the buxom Widow Ranter. As a mixture, the plot is a remarkably well-integrated three-level hierarchy touching equally on government and love. (Hume 1976: 211)

And it is indeed in the heroic part of the play that the progressive is most effectively used as a modal resource. The progressive could be said to capture a moment in the experience of a speaker, and in so doing, present that experience in a subjective or modal way. The effect then is to provide a verbal window on the soul of a speaker. In this extract, the Indian king is dying (IV.ii):

(14)   ⟨*Bacon*⟩ *You've only breath'd a Vein, and given me new Health and Vigour by it.* [They fight again, wounds on both sides, the King staggers; Bacon takes him in his Arms; the King drops his Sword.] *How do you, Sir?*
⟨*King*⟩ *Like one* — *that's* hovering *between Heaven and Earth; I'm* — mounting — *somewhere* — *upwards* — *but giddy with my flight,* — *I know not where.*

These instances of the modal construction are the more remarkable, since the progressive has a low overall frequency relative to the other plays in this corpus. *The Widow Ranter* has the greatest frequency of progressive constructions of the four Behn plays. The same experiential perspective provides the impulse behind Bacon's description of Love (II. i):

(15)   ⟨*Queen*⟩ *Alas for me if this should be Love* [Aside]
⟨*Bacon*⟩ *It makes us tremble when we touch the fair one; and all the Blood runs shivering through the Veins, the Heart's surrounded with a feeble Languishment, the Eyes* are dying, *and the Cheeks are pale, the Tongue* is faltring, *and the Body* fainting.

The progressive is used by Behn's speakers to express momentary but intense experiences; experiences which are, moreover, cognitive or emotional, rather than physical. So the King's last moments are turned into a spiritual journey; Love turns the experiencer into a languishing, afflicted body. These are the most affecting instances of the modal progressive in my sample; and it is very likely that they are thus because we are not dealing here with comedy pure and simple.

It is perhaps time to consider the relation between these modal, experiential uses of the progressive and the nature of the medium. The Restoration and post-Restoration plays flourish in a period which celebrates conversation (but not necessarily colloquialism). Conversation is the domain par excellence for the practice of wit. This is most frequently noted in the plays of Congreve and Wycherley. Yet Behn and Centlivre were both considered accomplished and effective dramatists in their day, even if their work has been neglected in comparison. The rhetorical flourishes which frame the conversational jousting in almost all of these plays work on the levels of word association and pragmatic implication to portray characters as prototypes or stereotypes. It is very seldom that a character's verbal tic makes itself felt at the level of grammar. For example, although Monsieur and Don Diego (Wycherley's *The Gentleman Dancing-Master*) make much of their French and Spanish inclinations respectively, this is done very obviously, through manner and deportment (high camp and machismo) and dress. On the linguistic level, the odd lexical borrowing, idiom and outrageous approximation to a foreign (French) accent give these characters their place. But the manipulation of auxiliary syntax, for instance, remains unaffected. Except, that is, for the conversational manipulation of existing resources.

3. Concluding remarks: Subjectivity and conversation

Strang suggests that the progressive in the eighteenth century is conversational, noting that it occurs consistently and frequently in dialogue (and not only that dialogue which is marked as nonstandard or regional). I would go further than this, as regards the modal, experiential progressive. It is a use that is instantly available as a "foregrounding" device, an instrument for registering a speaker's interpretation of an event or situation. It is, moreover, aided by performance — by intonation and register. It is available to other media — to the writing of private letters, and much later, to the narrative techniques used in the novel. But because it is emphatically conversational, it is at least unlikely that it can seamlessly cross the barriers erected by the conventions which go with much letter-writing, and certainly by those guiding the development of written narrative literary genres. The grammatical basis for expressing subjectivity exists in constructions like the progressive (and in dummy auxiliary *do*, and nascently in the modal verbs) from before the end of the sixteenth century. However, this fact has been obscured by studies of the subjectivity of syntax in media such as extended prose narrative, which are themselves undergoing considerable changes between 1600 and 1800. The subjectivity which surrounds the pragmatics of such constructions becomes manifest in this kind of written, literary text long after its exploitation in texts informed by the practice of conversation.

Appendix

Frequencies of progressive in 16 plays

	Main	Sub.	Present	Past	Total
Willian Wycherley:					
Mean per play:	25				
Love in a Wood (1671)	19	4	18	3	23
The Gentleman Dancing-Master (1672)	19	5	13	8	24
The Country Wife (1675)	18	4	18	3	22
The Plain Dealer (1676)	23	9	18	9	32
Total	79	22	67	23	101
Aphra Behn:					
Mean per play:	19				
The Rover (1677)	10	6	10	5	16
The False Count (1681)	6	3	7	2	9
The Lucky Chance (1686)	17	6	20	1	23
The Widow Ranter (1689)	19	7	19	7	26
Total	52	22	56	15	74
William Congreve					
Mean per play:	27				
The Old Batchelor (1693)	15	11	15	11	26
The Double Dealer (1694)	21	9	23	6	30
Love for Love (1695)	20	7	17	7	27
Way of the World (1700)	16	7	18	4	23
Total	72	34	73	28	106
Susannah Centlivre					
Mean per play:	17				
The Gamester (1705)	12	8	13	5	20
Love at a Venture (1706)	9	8	12	4	17
The Busie Body (1709)	11	3	12	2	14
The Man's Bewitch'd (1709)	14	2	14	2	16
Total	46	21	51	13	67

Notes

1. See recent work on *do* by Rissanen (1990) and by Stein (1990), the Helsinki standardisation workshop, Tannen's work on tense and narration in Romance, for example. These deal both with the issues of standardisation and with the roles of oral and written language in the investigation of speaker subjectivity.

2. I have serious qualms about reducing and relegating the semantics of the progressive to main aspectual and special modal uses, but this is not the paper in which to explore them.

3. Our speculation is aided here by the possibility that these terms may have their etymological senses; more or less: 'experience', 'participation in action'. I am grateful to Roger Lass for pointing this out.

4. This model is not without its problems for sociohistorical linguistic research. Firstly, it was developed for use in the analysis of Modern English spoken and written texts, and so the selected linguistic features making up the three dimensions mentioned here are not discriminated on historical grounds. For example, while Biber and Finegan (1989) assign constant situational values to the linguistic features, it is evident that particular features have situational values which are contingent on historical context. For example, the distribution and manner of the use of dummy auxiliary *do* in early eighteenth century prose suggests that it is an index of modernity (most advanced in prose comedy and the periodical essay), while at the same time, the choice of *wh-* as opposed to zero or *that* as a relative clause marker is considered more "correct" in formal "literary" modes of discourse. See Wright (1994) for discussion of the latter two features.

5. This was in work done for a paper on Joseph Addison. See Wright (1994).

Primary Sources:

Aphra Behn
  The Rover. London, 1677.
  The False Count. London, 1681.
  The Luckey Chance. London, 1686.
  The Widow Ranter. London, 1689.
Susannah Centlivre
  The Gamester. London, 1705.
  Love at a Venture. London, 1706.
  The Busie Body. London, 1709.
  The Man's Bewitch'd. London, 1709.
William Congreve
  The Old Batchelor. London, 1693.
  The Double Dealer. London, 1694.
  Love for Love. London, 1695.
  The Way of the World. London, 1700.
William Wycherley
  Love in a Wood. London, 1671.
  The Gentleman Dancing-Master. London, 1672.
  The Country Wife. London, 1675.
  The Plain Dealer. London, 1676.

References

Arnaud, René
1982   "On the progress of the progressive in the private correspondence of famous British people (1800—80)", in Sven Jacobson (ed.), *Papers from the Second Scandinavian Symposium on Syntactic Variation.* Stockholm: Almqvist & Wiksell, 83—94.
Biber, Douglas—Finegan, Edward
1989   "Drift and the evolution of English style: A history of three genres", *Language* 65: 487—517.
Bodelsen, C. A.
1936/37   "The expanded tenses in Modern English", *Englische Studien* 71: 220—238.
Bolinger, Dwight
1972   *Degree words.* (Janua Linguarum Series Maior 53.) The Hague: Mouton.
Dennis, Leah
1940   "The progressive tense. Frequency of its use in English", *PMLA* 55: 855—865.
Fell, John
1784   *An essay towards an English grammar.* London.
Goldsmith, John—Woisetschlaeger, Eric
1982   "The logic of the English progressive", *Linguistic Inquiry* 13: 79—89.
Hatcher, Anna Granville
1951   "The use of the progressive form in English", *Language* 27: 254—280.
Hume, Robert D.
1976   *The development of English drama in the late seventeenth century.* Oxford: Clarendon.
Jespersen, Otto
1949   *A Modern English grammar on historical principles.* 7 vols. (completed and published by Niels Haislund.) Copenhagen: Ejnar Munksgaard.
Leech, Geoffrey
1971   *Meaning and the English verb.* London: Longman.
Ljung, Magnus
1977   *Reflections on the English progressive.* (Gothenburg Studies in English 46.) Göteborg: Acta Universitatis Gothoburgensis.
Markley, Robert
1988   *Two edg'd weapons: Style and ideology in the comedies of Etherege, Wycherley and Congreve.* Oxford: Oxford University Press.
Michael, Ian
1970   *English grammatical categories and the tradition to 1800.* Cambridge: Cambridge University Press.
Nehls, Dietrich
1988   "On the development of the grammatical category of verbal aspect in English", in: Jürgen Klegraf and Dietrich Nehls (eds.), *Essays on the English language and applied linguistics on the occasion of Gerhard Nickel's 60th birthday.* (Studies in Descriptive Linguistics Volume 18.) Heidelberg: Groos.
Pearson, Jacqueline
1988   *The prostituted muse: Images of women and women dramatists 1642—1737.* London: Harvester Wheatsheaf.
Stein, Dieter
1990   *The semantics of syntactic change. Aspects of the evolution of* do *in English.* Berlin: Mouton de Gruyter.

Strang, Barbara M. H.
1982   "Some aspects of the history of the *be* + *ing* construction", in John Anderson (ed.), *Language form and linguistic variation*. Amsterdam: Benjamins, 427–474.
Traugott, Elizabeth Closs
1972   *The history of English syntax*. New York: Holt, Rinehart and Winston.
1982   "From propositional to textual to expressive meanings: some semantic-pragmatic aspects of grammaticalisation", in: William P. Lehmann – Yakov Malkiel (eds.), *Perspectives on historical linguistics*. Amsterdam: Benjamins, 245–271.
Thompson, John
1984   *Language in Wycherley's plays*. Alabama: University of Alabama Press.
Vissen, Frederikus Theodorus
1973   *An historical syntax of English*. II. 2. Leiden: Brill.
Wright, Susan
1986   *Tense, aspect and text: Processes of grammaticalisation in the history of the English auxiliary*. [Unpublished Ph. D. dissertation, Cambridge University.]
1989 a   "Stylistic change, syntactic change and the progressive construction". (Paper presented in Helsinki, September 1989.)
1989 b   "Private letters made public: the language of letters as literature", *Poetics* 18: 549–578.
1994   "The critic and the grammarians: Joseph Addison and the Prescriptivists", in: Dieter Stein – Ingrid Tieken-Boon van Ostade (eds.), *Towards a Standard English 1600–1800*. Berlin: Mouton de Gruyter, 243–284.
Zandvoort, R. W.
1941   A concise English grammar.

Index of subjects and languages

abbreviation and suspension 451, 453, 456, 458, 459, 461

above 111, 123, 124

abstract meaning 48

accent 165, 194, 196–200

accent, foreign 481

accent, Glasgow 432

accounts 449, 450, 452–455, 459–463

active construction 217, 220, 221, 226

additive adverb 254, 256

address 275

adjective, elementary 246–252, 257

adjuncts 12

adverb 129, 130, 133

adverb, evaluative 253

adverb, exclusive 254, 256

adverb, focusing 329

adverb, intensifying, see: intensifier; booster

adverb, modal 253, 257

adverb, of degree 5, 269–287

adverb, of manner, see: manner adverb

adverb, qualitative 271

adverb, quantitative 269

adverb, speech act 253

adverb formation 243, 246, 257; see also: pleonastic –

adverbial 3, 5, 11–38

adverbial, epistemic 14, 19

adverbial, epithetical 14

adverbial, evaluative 14, 19

adverbial, focusing 5, 243, 244, 252, 254–257

adverbial, non-sentence 11, 12, 17, 21, 35, 36, 37

adverbial, sentence 5, 11–14, 20, 21, 24, 26, 36, 37

adverbial particle 129

adversative sentence 40

affirmation 467

African 70

age-related variation 273, 275

agent 48–54, 56, 221–223; see also: *by*-agent; quasi-agent

agent noun 45–57

agreement 233, 235

agreement phrase 234

Alfredian 79

Alliterative Revival 195

allophonic variant 434

alternating stress, see: stress, alternating

American English 71, 200, 394, 400, 418, 424, 425; see also: General American

analogy 86

andative 4, 59

andative future 71

Anglian 177–179

Anglicisation 295

Anglicism 290

Anglo-Frisian 262

Anglo-Norman 153, 187, 199, 449, 455, 460, 461, 464

Anglo-Saxon 93, 292

Anglo-Saxon Chronicle 24, 475

animate 49, 51, 54

antonymy 205, 213

any, unitary analysis of the different uses of 425

any as an indicator for emphatic non-specificity 423, 424

any as an indicator of universality 423

any det. with sg. count nouns in neg. sentences 414

any in assertive contexts 425

any in legal texts 421, 422, 424

any in non-assertive clauses 413, 415, 416, 424

any in private letters 423, 424

any in spoken and written language 417, 418, 420, 424

any in text types in Early Modern English 422, 424,

any in trials 424

any indefinite article 413

Index of names